A SHARED FUTURE

Fostering Communities of Inclusion in an Era of Inequality

EDITED BY

Christopher Herbert
Jonathan Spader
Jennifer Molinsky
Shannon Rieger

The Harvard Joint Center for Housing Studies advances understanding of housing issues and informs policy. Through its research, education, and public outreach programs, the center helps leaders in government, business, and the civic sectors make decisions that effectively address the needs of cities and communities. Through graduate and executive courses, as well as fellowships and internship opportunities, the Joint Center also trains and inspires the next generation of housing leaders.

The views expressed in A Shared Future: Fostering Communities of Inclusion in an Era of Inequality do not necessarily represent the views of Harvard University, the Policy Advisory Board of the Joint Center for Housing Studies, or other sponsoring organizations.

Principal funding for the symposium and this book was provided by the Ford Foundation with additional support from JPMorgan Chase, the Kresge Foundation, the Melville Charitable Trust, and NeighborWorks® America.

ISBN-13:978-1727435559
ISBN-10:1727435559

Library of Congress Control Number: 2018912029

Table of Contents

Acknowledgments

The papers in this volume were initially developed for a symposium organized by the Joint Center for Housing Studies in April 2017. The symposium brought together leading academics, practitioners, and policymakers to take stock of recent patterns of residential segregation and to propose and discuss concrete steps that might achieve meaningful improvements. Given the multi-faceted nature of this topic, the symposium and the resulting book benefited at all stages of its development from the input of funders, advisors and participants who collectively brought diverse perspectives and expertise to this enterprise.

We are deeply grateful to the symposium's funders, the Ford Foundation, JPMorgan Chase, the Kresge Foundation, the Melville Charitable Trust, and NeighborWorks America, for providing the support that allowed us to convene the symposium and develop this set of papers. We are also grateful for the project's advisory group members, who were instrumental in conceptualizing and framing the symposium — and who challenged us to design a gathering that would encourage authors and participants to look at key issues with fresh eyes and to be ambitious in proposing changes needed to address them. We offer our thanks to Dolores Acevedo-Garcia, Janis Bowdler, Alan Branson, Don Chen, Ingrid Ellen, Fred Karnas, Terri Ludwig, Jerry Maldonado, Kalima Rose, Jonathan Rose, Susan Thomas, Margery Turner, and Paul Weech for their insights and input at all stages of the project.

In addition, we thank the authors and moderators for their willingness to take time away from their other obligations to engage with important questions that are broader than traditional research or policy analyses. We also thank all of the symposium participants for their engagement and energy in grappling with the questions posed by the speakers and their thoughtful discussion and analyses, which improved the discussion papers during the revision process. We also give special thanks to Tiffany Manuel and Solly Granatstein for keynote talks, which generated vigorous discussion on the importance and role of public perceptions and political will in carrying out the changes envisioned in these papers.

Finally, we owe a debt of gratitude to our colleagues at the Joint Center, as well as to the team of editors and designers who helped us produce this volume. Many thanks go to James Chaknis, Kerry Donahue, Angela Flynn, Mary Lancaster, David Luberoff, Eiji Miura, and other people at the Joint Center who worked to make the symposium a reality and to disseminate the ideas in this volume. We also thank Eric Idsvoog for his expeditious and thorough work to copyedit text and clarify the ideas in this volume, and C&G Partners for their creativity and vision in turning these ideas into a book volume.

Fostering Inclusion: Whose Problem? Which Problem?

XAVIER DE SOUZA BRIGGS
Ford Foundation

Asking "what would it take"—about transforming housing segregation or any other challenge—assumes some level of agreement that a given social condition is, in fact, a problem that needs to be solved.[1] But in America, we have never been able to take that for granted, not about most of our big challenges, not even about the things that seem profoundly inconsistent with core American values of fairness and equal opportunity. The persistence of stark race and class segregation in housing is one of those great inconsistencies and one of the nation's most stubborn problems. It is also one of the central mechanisms reproducing inequality, over years and even generations. But attention to growing inequality in America has not—yet—mobilized significant new attention or commitment to addressing segregation. Why is that?

As a country, we have shown a very particular indecision and impasse when it comes to treating housing segregation as a problem and acting on it in a meaningful way. Put plainly, changing segregation is a cause with few champions.

The political Left remains ambivalent about it: it wonders, first, whether it is urgent to address segregation *per se* as part of tackling crime, school failure, job and health disparities, and other problems that segregation contributes to; second, whether such effort comes at an unacceptable cost to other efforts that make demands on precious and scarce public attention, political capital, and funding; third, whether segregation can be tackled in ways that do not stigmatize those most affected (poor people of color in particular); and, finally, even whether hoped-for reforms can shift big, entrenched patterns affecting millions of people. As such, on the Left, the seemingly natural allies for an agenda to tackle inequality by addressing segregation have mixed feelings about both the problem and at least some of the solutions: Are the solutions legitimate—consistent with our values, laws, and political traditions—and if so, could they actually work?

The political Right, on the other hand, has been generally hostile to the idea that segregation is a problem, even if most Americans, on both Left and Right, agree

10

that discrimination in the housing market is not only illegal but morally wrong.[2] Of those on the Right who do agree that segregation itself is a problem, many are unconvinced that it warrants government intervention — let alone that such intervention could succeed. Yet Richard Rothstein's encyclopedic new book, *The Color of Law: A Forgotten History of How Our Government Segregated America*, shows how early and how effectively the government built segregation into the fabric of urban and suburban development, virtually ensuring America's gaping and growing racial wealth gap.[3] Libertarian and other conservative commentators are suggesting that Rothstein's analysis is one more reminder that government cannot be trusted with even the most well-intended "social engineering" to undo wrongs. The Right generally recommends that change agents focus on two things. The first is empowering individuals to make different choices. This, however, is a challenging prescription when so many in the housing market have such limited choices available to them. Second, the Right advocates freeing individuals from excessive government regulation. Yet it seems naïve to argue that merely lifting regulations will allow the free market to somehow correct housing segregation when that market has itself been shaped, as Rothstein and others have shown exhaustively, by decades of regulations that have exacerbated segregation; when it comes to regulatory reform, in other words, the devil is in the details.

These are some of the reasons that we, as a country, "rediscover" segregation and its enormous human costs every decade or so, only to conclude that it is too intractable or questionable to tackle with serious resolve. This rediscovering happened after the civil unrest in Los Angeles in 1992, again after Hurricane Katrina put geographically concentrated black poverty and public outrage squarely on TV screens nationwide in 2005, and again as political and media attention to extreme inequality has grown in recent years.

Among scholars and opinion leaders, the influential work of economist Raj Chetty and colleagues at the Equality of Opportunity Project points to segregation as a key barrier to economic mobility in America — with effects that vary sharply between more and less segregated regions of the country.[4] This latest-generation work, which has garnered bipartisan interest in multiple regions of the country, supports earlier conclusions, by sociologists Douglas S. Massey and Nancy A. Denton in *American Apartheid: Segregation and the Making of the Underclass* and by others, that housing segregation by race and income is, in fact, one of the lynchpins of American inequality.[5] Along with mass incarceration, extreme and persistent segregation in housing and communities is one of the structural patterns that differentiates America from other wealthy nations (though Europe faces serious and growing segregation of immigrant ethnic minorities).

Segregated housing patterns are durable and enduring in part because they are sustained by forces that many view as legitimate and even unavoidable, if unfortunate. These patterns have been called out explicitly at least since lawyer and planning professor Charles Abrams's 1955 book, *Forbidden Neighbors: A Study of Prejudice in Housing*, and by national policymakers since the landmark Kerner Commission report on the riots that tore apart American cities fifty years ago.[6] For now, there are no signs that we as a people are serious about changing segregation.

In this brief foreword, I'd like to offer a specific reading of the editors' very thoughtful essay, "Fostering Inclusion in American Neighborhoods," which introduces this volume, and the larger project of which it is a part. I work at a philanthropic foundation long committed to expanding knowledge about, and promoting solutions to, inequality, including solutions that center on housing and specifically housing segregation. I have also pursued these aims over several stints in federal government service and tackled them as a community planner at the local level. Finally, some seventeen years ago, when I was a researcher and educator, I organized a symposium and collection of papers — led by the Harvard Civil Rights Project and cosponsored by the Joint Center for Housing Studies and the Brookings Institution's Metropolitan Policy Program — focused on segregation, its causes and consequences, and "what it would take" to effect real change at scale. That symposium produced an edited volume, *The Geography of Opportunity: Race and Housing Choice in Metropolitan America.*[7] With this background, I want to briefly look back — asking what has or has not changed in our understanding of the problems and potential solutions over the past two decades — and also look forward.

STARTING POINTS

The 2001 symposium had several points of departure, and revisiting them now offers some perspective on how our national mood, key attention-getting trends, political leadership, housing markets and perceived housing problems, and more have evolved since then. One starting point was the sharply increased attention, in the late 1990s, to America's dominant pattern of urban sprawl and the idea of pursuing more sustainable or "smart growth" alternatives. The interest in this issue sparked healthy debate, though mainly among scholars, planners and allied professionals, about the tradeoffs between environmental aims and values of equity, including housing affordability. On the issue of sprawl, just like segregation, there was and still is a big gap between the scholarly focus on defining the problem and its consequences — with great care and exhaustive data — and the wider public conversation, in which the issue may or may not be considered a significant problem that needs to be solved. On a related point, in the 1990s, the environmental justice movement began to draw attention to spatial inequality, focusing on the highly disproportionate exposure of poor communities of color to toxins and other environmental risks. Segregated and limited housing choices are directly implicated in that persistent, costly, and unjust exposure. Should the country view reducing segregation as part of a vital environmental health agenda? Or should we focus entirely on reducing disparities in exposure without changing the housing choices available to everyone?

Advancing that debate, and similar debates about education and crime risks, seemed especially important in light of evidence that economic inequality was increasing sharply in America, whether measured in terms of wealth, income, or other dimensions. We wondered about more environmentally sustainable but increasingly unaffordable communities pulling away from distressed, built-up and — in some cases — highly polluted places.

Other starting points arose from even more tectonic, large-scale demographic changes. A national Initiative on Race, launched by President Clinton in 1997, produced the landmark National Research Council volume, *America Becoming: Racial Trends and Their Consequences*, with empirical analysis and discussion of these tectonic changes and of the history of the "color line" in America's culture, politics, and economy.[8] The headlines are as important now as they were two decades ago. For example, much of the wealthy world has modest to zero population growth, largely because of falling birth rates, but America is different. We are a large and still-growing nation, thanks mainly to immigration, which is, in turn, driving greater racial and ethnic diversity. In the 1990s, for example, the populations of most American cities would have shrunk if not for immigration.[9] Urban vitality is bound up with growing diversity, so understanding that diversity and "getting it right" is crucial for all of us.

What is more, we saw that as of the 2000 census, an estimated one-third of the built environment needed to accommodate population growth in America over the subsequent generation did not yet exist and would therefore need to be built in the years to come. This finding underscored the huge stakes associated with *how* we grow, particularly the prospects for more inclusionary, less segregated and unequal growth. It also underlined the fact that our debates about persistent segregation cannot be limited to public housing in inner cities or to other long-established fixtures of our current spatial footprint. We always need to be asking about what's next, too — about the course of new development, both infill and at the edges of urban regions. And of course, we need to pay attention to how these development trends influence each other and influence our politics and sense of what's possible.

To sum up, in 2001, for the intersecting reasons outlined above, we asked: Can an increasingly diverse nation hope to deal with growing economic inequality if the dominant growth model "on the ground" is one of persistent segregation by race and income? Do the parts of that equation add up?

By comparison, the introductory chapter for this volume centers more squarely on the growth of inequality per se and the much greater political and cultural salience of the issue now versus 15 to 20 years ago. That salience is encouraging. And so is the recognition that we have generally used the racial and economic make-up of neighborhoods and localities as a proxy, sometimes a weak one, for access to opportunity. Years on from the extensively researched Moving to Opportunity (MTO) experiment, which showed neighborhood poverty rates to be a limited proxy for access to opportunity, and based on significant work over the last two decades to map "opportunity" much more meaningfully for many types of families, the editors of this volume rightly emphasize, in their introduction, that the real goal should not be a particular race or class make-up in every community but "universal access to high-opportunity neighborhoods." Our concern about segregation — in simple terms, our wish for a more balanced make-up than that of the status quo — follows logically from that need to expand access.

In terms of local trends, as the chapters in this volume reflect, researchers, the media and the public are even more aware now than after the economic boom of the late 1990s that "cities are back." Major cities that still showed substantial decline a decade or more ago — New Orleans and large sections of Detroit, for example — have since then seen their population trends reverse and have attracted enormous investment, especially over the course of recovery from the Great Recession. Housing prices are up along with the job economy in those and other revitalizing cities. So, a debate about the drivers of segregation and responses to it today appropriately gives greater weight than did earlier discussions to the power of urban redevelopment to either exacerbate or alleviate segregation — and hence to the need for "development without displacement," as advocates in revitalizing cities frame the need. Increasingly, major media coverage and not just scholarly work recognizes that these pressures are structural, large in scale, and stubbornly reinforced by local land-use and tax policy and other institutional forces — not by a single business cycle or isolated local market boom.[10]

The sense of displacement, of being pushed out, is much sharper now than in 2001. But in point of fact, the pattern is nothing new, and some observers forecasted this predicament long ago, linking it to the forces driving a new urban vitality after decades of decline. For example, in *Dual City: Restructuring New York*, John H. Mollenkopf and Manuel Castells showed that New York's comeback from the low point of the bankruptcy crisis of the 1970s had made the city a global magnet for investment capital and high-income occupations, sharply inflating land values and housing prices.[11] Over the 1980s, they reported, poverty had been pushed outward, "like a ring donut," from neighborhoods in the city's core to its outer boroughs as well as its more racially diverse, fiscally vulnerable inner suburbs. The subsequent decades have sustained and accelerated those trends, with New York City and surrounding cities and suburbs showing the region to be one of the proverbial canaries in the coal mine. What Detroit and other cities are seeing and debating now, New York, Boston and other "comeback cities" experienced a couple of decades earlier. And again, the pressures driving both prosperity and inequality are structural, not artifacts of one business cycle. In fact, these trends were barely interrupted by the Great Recession.

On a final comparative note, having thus far emphasized those durable, long-run structural trends, I want to highlight more recent developments as well. In addition to the growth of inequality, the introductory essay and the other chapters in this volume reflect the enormous impacts of the foreclosure crisis, which we had only dimly foreshadowed in the 2005 book's chapter on "The Dual Mortgage Market: The Persistence of Discrimination in Mortgage Lending," by William C. Apgar and Allegra Calder.[12] Beyond a huge loss of housing wealth and greater regulation in the mortgage market, there is another important legacy of the crisis, and it is a healthy one. We are much more conscious now than in the real estate boom of the early 2000s of how profoundly the workings of the real estate industry, and its rapid evolution thanks to information technology, can hurt us. In that vein, one of the most ground-breaking sections in this book focuses on the present and future of housing searches in an era of online platform apps, algorithms, and technology-mediated screening of many kinds. These essays — and the symposium session where they were first presented — put housing scholars in direct exchange with senior analysts and strategists from the online real estate search companies that now dominate the housing marketplace. Moreover, with microtargeted advertising, Facebook and other major social media companies, not Zillow or others in real estate, play an increasingly important but still poorly understood role in shaping the marketplace and how the demographic make-up of communities evolves over time. Housing searches were different and our understanding of them much more limited fifteen years ago, prior to the foreclosure crisis and the rapid rise of social media and mobile apps in many industries.

THE SOLUTION SET AND THE MISSING STORY

If the unequal housing marketplace has evolved — dramatically in some ways — over the past fifteen-plus years, our sense of the best available levers for changing segregation has not. Nor has our story about why acting on segregation is both legitimate and urgent, big and structural but also doable and achievable. To be fair, by some measures, our prescriptions today are not all that different from those championed by the open housing movement — the inheritors of the civil rights movement and the Kerner Commission's warnings — in the early 1970s. This suggests at least three lessons over the long run.

The first is that we, as a country, lack will more than we lack imagination — let alone sophisticated analysis. I introduced this essay with some of the reasons that we, as a nation, appear to lack that will. Building it depends on generating enough agreement that some condition is, in fact, a problem that needs to be solved *and* that the means of doing so are broadly supportable. When it comes to tackling housing segregation, we are not there yet on either count.

The second lesson is that we need new stories and ways to tell them. In recent memory, the very best case against segregation was made by a comedian, John Oliver, who in 2016 used his satirical cable news program Last Week Tonight to explain three extremely important things about how America works: first, how school and housing segregation directly enable each other; second, why they guarantee that America will reproduce stark inequalities from one generation to the next; and third, why these closely linked forms of segregation so effectively resist change.[13] In effect, in the context of such high, persistent, and stubbornly defended segregation, a popular comic ridiculed our claim that America *can* offer equal opportunity for all — and our resignation to the country never quite making good on the offer.

The third lesson over the long run is that beyond lacking a compelling story to motivate change, we sometimes lack perspective as well on where the leverage for change lies, on what exactly we need to solve for. Take the persistent tendency to conflate discrimination, which the framing chapter emphasizes, with segregation.

People in America continue to experience housing discrimination, which is illegal, and continue to under-report it. As we analyzed in detail in the 2005 book, such discrimination, while inconsistent with public opinion in America, is challenging to detect and enforce against. But the larger and less acknowledged point was and is the following: discrimination, whether conscious or unconscious, against particular kinds of consumers is less important as a driver of segregation than is the avoidance of certain neighborhoods or localities by those with the best housing options, especially whites and higher-skill, higher-income people of color.[14] This "self-steering" behavior has big social and fiscal costs, as scholars of segregation have pointed out for decades now. But it is not illegal. Moreover, as sociologist Camille Charles argued in her 2005 chapter on attitudes toward the racial make-up of neighborhoods, many of us balance what we think we owe our families with what we think might contribute, however modestly, to a fairer and more just society.[15] And many of us experience these values as frequently in conflict, especially when faced with the decision to move somewhere.

What does this mean? It means that laws against housing discrimination by realtors, lenders or others in the marketplace are important and should be enforced vigorously and fairly. But because of white avoidance and self-steering in particular, doing so would have limited effects on racial segregation. Because of growing income segregation, it would also have limited effects on the tendency of upper-income and wealthy people to live apart from everyone else. At the risk of belaboring the point, though fighting illegal housing discrimination is important, as the contributors to this volume show, it is at least as important to directly expand housing options, especially for lower-income people of color, and to understand how people choose among the options available to them. The body of research in this volume represents a very healthy step in that direction.

THE FOUR SEGREGATION DEBATES — AND WHAT COMES NEXT

Finally, and most broadly, this important volume encompasses an extraordinarily rich and in-depth update of what I think of as the four enduring debates about segregation: the "what" (the descriptive patterns or shape of the problem), the "why" (causes), the "so what" (consequences), and the "now what" (solutions). And thanks to big data, mobile broadband, a more visible inequality debate, and other developments, the volume offers a very contemporary and vital rethink of what's possible, at least in concept, when it comes to change. In the language of our 2005 redux, the "now-what" solutions boil down to "curing" segregation (changing stubborn housing patterns) or "mitigating" it (making the patterns less socially costly, by shifting the relationship between where people live and the risks and resources they encounter).[16] Curing centers on household relocation and inclusionary housing development strate-gies. Mitigating centers on community reinvestment, connectivity, and expanding disadvantaged people's access to what economist Frank Levy calls "equalizing institu-tions"— sometimes life-changing ones — beyond one's segregated neighborhood.[17] Both kinds of solution, cure and mitigate, are legitimate and consistent with our values, laws, and best political traditions of working together to create a more level playing field in America — and both are also vital for practical reasons. No one approach will move the needle enough.

This new body of research and those solutions deserve an equally serious and committed story — a resonant narrative — joined to an advocacy and constituency-building effort that's relevant in a changing, polarized, deeply unsettled American body politic. Without that narrative and that effort, we seem consigned, in practice, to continue rediscovering segregation and also to continue lamenting that it is just too hard — or worse yet, un-American — to undo.

Bibliography

Abrams, Charles. 1955. *Forbidden Neighbors: A Study of Prejudice in Housing*. New York: Harper.

Apgar, William, and Allegra Calder. 2005. "The Dual Mortgage Market: The Persistence of Discrimination in Mortgage Lending." In T*he Geography of Opportunity: Race* *and Housing Choice in Metropolitan America*, edited by Xavier de Souza Briggs, 45-80. Washington, DC: Brookings.

Badger, Emily. 2017. "What Happened to the American Boomtown?" *New York Times*, December 6.

Baumgartner, Frank, and Bryan Jones. 1993. *Agendas and Instability in American Politics*. Chicago: University of Chicago Press.

Briggs, Xavier de Souza, ed. 2005a. The Geography of Opportunity: Race and Housing Choice in Metropolitan America. Washington, DC: Brookings.

———. 2005b. "More *Pluribus*, Less *Unum*? The Changing Geography of Race and Opportunity." In *The Geography of Opportunity: Race and Housing Choice in Metropolitan America*, edited by Xavier de Souza Briggs, 17-41. Washington, DC: Brookings.

———. 2005c. "Politics and Policy: Changing the Geography of Opportunity." In *The Geography of Opportunity: Race and Housing Choice in Metropolitan America*, edited by Xavier de Souza Briggs, 310-41. Washington, DC: Brookings.

Charles, Camille Zubrinsky. "Can We Live Together? Racial Preferences and Neighborhood Outcomes." In *The Geography of Opportunity: Race and Housing Choice in Metropolitan America*, edited by Xavier de Souza Briggs, 45-80. Washington, DC: Brookings.

Chetty, Raj, John Friedman, and Nathaniel Hendren. 2018. The Equality of Opportunity Project. http://www.equality-of-opportunity.org/.

Ellen, Ingrid Gould. 2000. *Sharing America's Neighborhoods: The Prospects for Stable Racial Integration*. Cambridge, MA: Harvard University Press.

Kingdon, John. 1984. *Agendas, Alternatives, and Public Policies*. Boston: Little, Brown.

Last Week Tonight. 2016. "School Segregation: *Last Week Tonight* with John Oliver (HBO)." YouTube video, 17:58. October 30. https://www.youtube.com/watch?v=o8yiYCHMAlM.

Levy, Frank. 1999. *The New Dollars and Dreams: American Incomes in the Late 1990s*. New York: Russell Sage Foundation.

Massey, Douglas S., and Nancy A. Denton. 1993. *American Apartheid: Segregation and the Making of the Underclass*. Cambridge, MA: Harvard University Press.

Mollenkopf, John, and Manuel Castells. 1991. *Dual City: Restructuring New York*. New York: Russell Sage Foundation.

National Advisory Commission on Civil Disorders. 1968. *Report of the National Advisory Commission on Civil Disorders*. March 1. Washington, DC: US Government Printing Office.

Pastor, Manuel, Jr. 2001. "Geography and Opportunity." In *America Becoming: Racial Trends and Their Consequences,* vol. 1, edited by Neil Smelser, William Julius Wilson, and Faith Mitchell, 435-68. Washington, DC: National Academies Press.

Rothstein, Richard. 2017. *The Color of Law: A Forgotten History of How Our Government Segregated America*. New York: W.W. Norton.

Sampson, Robert J. 2011. *Great American City.* Chicago: University of Chicago Press.

Schelling, Thomas C. 1971. "Dynamic Models of Segregation." *Journal of Mathematical Sociology* 1(2):143-186.

Smelser, Neil, William Julius Wilson, and Faith Mitchell, eds. 2001. *America Becoming: Racial Trends and Their Consequences.* 2 vols. Washington, DC: National Academies Press.

Endnotes

1   On the important distinction between a social condition, even a serious and persistent one, and a "problem" that needs to be solved, and on how some conditions become problems, see political scientist John Kingdon's (1984) seminal analysis of what lands—or does not—on the agenda for policy makers' attention. Or, as Kingdon put it, "How does an idea's time come?" See also Baumgartner and Jones (1993).

2   See Briggs (2005c).

3   Rothstein (2017).

4   Chetty, Friedman, and Hendren (2018).

5   Massey and Denton (1993).

6   Abrams (1955); National Advisory Commission (1968).

7   Briggs (2005a).

8   Smelser, Wilson, and Mitchell (2001).

9   For review and discussion of these trends as we made sense of them at the turn of the millennium, see Briggs (2005b) and Pastor (2001).

10 See, for example, Badger (2017).

11 Mollenkopf and Castells (1991).

12 Apgar and Calder (2005).

13 Last Week Tonight (2016).

14 See, for example, Schelling (1971), Ellen (2000), and Sampson (2011).

15 Charles (2005).

16 Briggs (2005c).

17 Levy (1999).

1

Defining Objectives and the Rationale for Action

Fostering Inclusion in American Neighborhoods

JONATHAN SPADER, SHANNON RIEGER,
CHRISTOPHER HERBERT, AND JENNIFER MOLINSKY
Joint Center for Housing Studies of Harvard University

While residential segregation and concentrated disadvantage are not new challenges in the United States, the evolving demography, income distribution, and geography of American communities are changing the nature of these problems and the solutions needed to foster more inclusive communities. The bursting of the housing bubble and the Great Recession greatly exacerbated distress among poor communities — in particular, poor communities of color — leading to an enormous increase in the concentration of poverty in recent years. In cities throughout the country, job growth in central cities, improved neighborhood amenities, and increased demand for urban living have simultaneously fostered rapid increases in housing costs in longstanding low-income and minority communities in urban cores. While gentrification has been one of the most visible signs of these changes, the suburbanization of lower-income households and the growing self-segregation of high-income households into wealthy enclaves are equally consequential.

At the same time, the racial and economic geographies of many communities remain deeply shaped by the legacies of historical segregation and exclusion. A long history of discrimination by both government and private institutions and individuals has produced stark patterns of racial segregation in US cities. In the decades since the Fair Housing Act of 1968, the extent and nature of discrimination have changed, but its imprint remains visible in many cities; it continues to influence choices about where people of different races, ethnicities, and income live. In recent years, evidence suggests that these patterns have been sustained by white households' acceptance of only modest levels of racial integration in their neighborhoods, regulatory constraints on affordable housing development, and lingering discrimination in housing markets.

A longstanding body of research documents the severe costs of this separation for all members of society, as well as the disproportionate burdens imposed on residents of neighborhoods with concentrated disadvantage. Residents of such neighborhoods — who are most often members of minority racial and ethnic groups — face risks to their health, safety, and economic mobility. At a national scale, these individual costs constrain the economy from reaching its full potential while also increasing levels of prejudice and mistrust within the populace and impairing the functioning of our democracy.

While these challenges are complex, a robust set of tools exists for taking positive steps, creating opportunities for progress if only the political will can be found to do so. The Harvard Joint Center for Housing Studies — with support from the Ford Foundation, NeighborWorks America, the JPMorgan Chase Foundation, the Melville Trust, and the Kresge Foundation — therefore convened a symposium that takes stock of the current patterns of residential segregation and integration in the United States and examines the concrete steps that can be taken to foster a more inclusive future. The symposium is organized around a series of discussion papers in which leading academics, practitioners, and policymakers engage with the following question: what it would it take to achieve meaningful progress in reducing and/or mitigating the consequences of residential segregation? At the symposium conference, discussion papers were enriched by the responses of participants from academia, philanthropy, industry, journalism, government, and nonprofits. The result, we hope, is a series of proposals that offer a way forward, describing concrete steps that can be taken over the next five to ten years to achieve meaningful change.

In this framing paper, we offer a brief summary of existing evidence and introduce the rationale and structure for the symposium. The initial sections present an overview of the extent of current residential segregation by race/ethnicity and income, the causes of residential segregation in the United States, and the consequences for individuals and society. The paper then draws upon this evidence to examine the rationale for government action and the painful public costs of continuing the status quo. Lastly, the final section identifies key levers for action going forward, and introduces the organiza-tion of the symposium and the book chapters that will follow.

CURRENT PATTERNS OF RESIDENTIAL SEGREGATION AND INTEGRATION

The symposium is concerned with two dimensions of integration, racial/ethnic and socioeconomic. Given that racial and ethnic minorities are disproportionately repre-sented among those with lower income, wealth, and education, these two dimensions are highly intertwined. Yet the factors contributing to each pattern segregation are also in part distinct, and therefore so are the potential responses to them. In this section, we examine trends in segregation first by race and ethnicity and then by income, and finally assess segregation along both dimensions together.

Residential Segregation by Race and Ethnicity

For much of US history, discussions of racial segregation have focused on blacks and whites. But with a sharp rise in immigration beginning in the 1970s, rapid growth in the Hispanic and Asian populations has broadened discussions beyond the historical black-white dichotomy. Between 1970 and 2015, the non-Hispanic white share of US households decreased from 83 to 62 percent, and the black share of households increased slightly from 11 to 12 percent. Meanwhile, the Hispanic share of households increased from 4 to 17 percent, and the Asian share of households increased from 1 to 5 percent.[1]

Measuring changes in the extent of residential segregation over time requires choosing among several existing measures.[2] One common measure of residential segregation is the "dissimilarity" index, which measures the extent of segregation between two groups — defined as the percent of households in each group that would have to move in order to achieve an even distribution across neighborhoods. Exhibit 1 displays the dissimilarity index values for black-white, Hispanic-white, and Asian-white segregation for each Decennial Census from 1940 to 2010.

Tracking the dissimilarity index over time suggests that the residential segregation of black households has declined from Civil-Rights-era highs, but remains considerable. Glaeser and Vigdor calculate the dissimilarity index for black versus non-black segregation for every Decennial Census of the twentieth century, showing that residential segregation of black households increased steadily during the first half of the century to a peak in 1970.[3] In the years since, the residential segregation of black households has declined slowly and consistently, but remained in 2010 at levels above those observed at the start of the twentieth century. The trendlines in Exhibit 1 also indicate that black-white segregation remains well above the levels of observed Hispanic-white and Asian-white segregation. In 2010, the value of the dissimilarity index implies that 59 percent of black households or of white households would have to move to achieve an even distribution of the two groups across neighborhoods, compared to 49 percent for Hispanic-white segregation and 41 percent for Asian-white segregation.[4]

The trendlines in Exhibit 1 for Hispanic-white and Asian-white segregation do not show declines in recent decades. Instead, these measures suggest that Hispanic-white and Asian-white segregation remained relatively constant between 1980 and 2010, even as the population of these groups increased. For both groups, the lack of change in the dissimilarity index belies two offsetting trends: increasing segregation of Hispanic and Asian households in metro areas with large populations, and population flows of Hispanic and Asian households to less segregated areas of the United States.[5]

Exhibit 1: Changes in Residential Segregation by Race/Ethnicity, 1940–2010 (Dissimilarity Index).

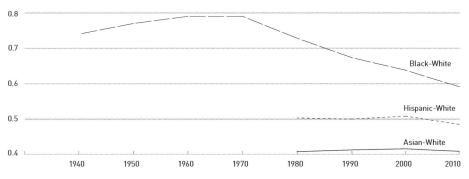

Note: The national average values of the dissimilarity index are the weighted average of all metropolitan areas with weights defined to reflect the number of minority group members in the metro.

Source: Logan and Stults (2011).

Exhibit 2 presents an alternative measure of residential segregation that describes the average neighborhood composition of individuals of each race and ethnicity using the most recent Census data available, the 2011–2015 American Community Survey 5-year estimates. This measure, frequently called the "exposure" index, provides insight into the extent to which individuals of each race and ethnicity live in neighborhoods where individuals of different races and ethnicities account for a large or small share of neighborhood residents. This measure is also referred to as the "isolation" index when describing the share of neighborhood residents of the same racial or ethnic group.

The results offer a snapshot of current differences in the neighborhoods occupied by white and minority households. The average white individual currently lives in a neighborhood that is 76 percent white, 10 percent Hispanic, 7 percent black, 4 percent Asian, and 3 percent multiracial or some other race or ethnicity. By contrast, the average black individual lives in a neighborhood that is 44 percent black, 35 percent white, 14 percent Hispanic, 4 percent Asian, and 3 percent other/multiracial. Similarly, the average Hispanic individual lives in a neighborhood that is 45 percent Hispanic, 36 percent white, 10 percent black, 6 percent Asian, and 3 percent other/multiracial. Only Asian and other/multiracial individuals have average neighborhood compositions where individuals of the same race/ethnicity are not a plurality. For each of these two groups, whites account for the largest share of neighborhood residents.

These patterns vary systematically across cities of different sizes, with whites accounting for larger population shares in smaller metros and non-metropolitan areas. For example, in the 10 largest metropolitan areas, the average black individual lives in a neighborhood that is 49 percent black and 23 percent white, compared to 40 percent black and 52 percent white in non-metropolitan areas. Similarly, the average

Exhibit 2: Average Neighborhood Composition by Race and Ethnicity across All US Census Tracts.

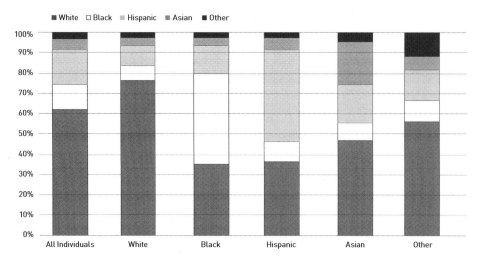

Notes: Neighborhoods are defined as census tracts. Metropolitan areas are defined by CBSA boundaries. White, black, Asian, and other/multiracial individuals are non-Hispanic.

Source: JCHS tabulations of American Community Survey 5-year estimates 2011–2015.

Hispanic individual in the 10 largest cities lives in a neighborhood that is 51 percent Hispanic and 27 percent white, compared to 28 percent Hispanic and 61 percent white in non-metropolitan areas. Appendix Table 1 provides the full set of exposure indices for each group, which show that patterns of residential segregation by race/ethnicity are evident in all areas but that the extent of segregation is most severe in large cities.

Nonetheless, the extent of residential segregation by race and ethnicity also varies substantially between large metropolitan areas, with higher levels of black-white segregation in older Northeastern cities and lower levels in Western cities that have experienced recent growth. For example, among the 50 largest metropolitan areas in the United States, the Detroit, Milwaukee, and Chicago metropolitan areas rank among the top five metros with the highest levels of black-white segregation according to both the dissimilarity index and the isolation index. In contrast, Las Vegas, Riverside, and Phoenix rank among the five metros with the lowest levels of black-white segregation with respect to each index. This pattern is also apparent for Hispanic-white and Asian-white segregation measures, although the patterns of segregation among Hispanics and Asians are also greater in metros with larger populations of each group.[6]

Residential Integration by Race and Ethnicity

While the presence of racially *integrated* neighborhoods is related to the trends in residential segregation described in the previous section, it is a distinct phenomenon that merits separate attention. In particular, the trends in residential segregation and desegregation reflect residential outcomes in communities throughout the United States regardless of their overall level of diversity. To supplement these measures, a growing literature describes the incidence and characteristics of neighborhoods with substantial levels of racial and ethnic integration. While such neighborhoods remain a minority of all US neighborhoods, their presence, stability, location, and racial composition are each relevant to understanding the prospects for future declines in the extent of residential segregation.

Ellen, Horn, and O'Regan provide the most recent analysis of trends in integration at the national level, describing trends from 1990 to 2010 for four types of integrated neighborhoods — white-black, white-Hispanic, white-Asian/other, and white-mixed minority — which they define as census tracts in which at least 20 percent of neighborhood residents are white and at least 20 percent are in the identified minority group.[7] Conversely, racially segregated neighborhoods by this definition are those where no group other than the dominant one accounts for more than 20 percent of the population. The results show substantial and consistent growth in the presence of integrated neighborhoods from 20 percent of all metropolitan census tracts in 1990 to 30 percent in 2010. White-Hispanic neighborhoods account for nearly half of the overall increase in the presence of integrated neighborhoods, with each of the other types of integrated neighborhoods also showing growth from 1990 to 2010.

A small portion of this growth is consistent with patterns of gentrification. Specifically, 5.5 percent of non-integrated black-majority neighborhoods in 2000 became integrated neighborhoods by 2010, and these transitions were associated with central city location, lower homeownership rates, fewer families with children, and increases in median income and the share of residents with college degrees. However, the vast majority (93 percent) of neighborhoods that transitioned from nonintegrated to integrated between 2000 and 2010 were initially predominantly white neighborhoods, and these neighborhoods do not show similar signs of gentrification. Equally important, the likelihood of integrated neighborhoods remaining integrated 10 years later increased from the 1990s to the 2000s, offering some hope that these neighborhoods will become stably integrated and are not simply transitory phases between nonintegrated categories.[8]

The primary caveat to these findings is that no consensus definition exists regarding what constitutes an integrated neighborhood. Ellen, Horn, and O'Regan acknowledge that their choice of 20 percent as the cutoff is somewhat arbitrary, noting that their key findings are robust to alternative thresholds and definitions. Alternatively, Lee, Iceland, and Farrell advocate using a measure in which a neighborhood is considered integrated only if no group accounts for 50 percent or more of the neighborhood population (i.e., no group is a majority in the neighborhood) — but also conclude that racial/ethnic integration has increased consistently in recent decades using this measure.[9] Other studies vary widely in the group shares by which they define integration, the size of defined neighborhoods, and the extent to which they rely solely on neighborhood composition or also incorporate measures of social interaction.[10]

Studies raise questions about whether the benefits of integration are realized if different blocks within the tract remain segregated or if little social interaction occurs across residents. For example, in case studies of the South End in Boston and Shaw/U Street in Washington, DC, Tach and Hyra find limited social interaction between residents of mixed-income, mixed-race neighborhoods.[11] Hyra argues that such limited interaction between races limits the potential to realize the benefits that might flow from integration and equal access to neighborhood amenities.[12] Yet, some benefits of integration, such as access to schools, police protection, or environmental assets, are likely to occur at the neighborhood level or higher.[13] While neighborhood integration has received increased attention from researchers in recent years, more research is necessary to shed light on these questions and to evaluate alternative methods for measuring changes across time in the extent of integration.

Residential Segregation by Income

Current patterns of residential segregation by income are relevant to discussions of neighborhood inclusion both because of the growing segregation of low- and high-income households and because of the correlation between race, ethnicity, and income in the United States. According to JCHS analysis of the 2015 American Community Survey 1-year estimates, the median household income among non-Hispanic white households is $61,000, compared to $36,000 among black households and $44,800 among Hispanic households. The upshot of these differences is that changes in income segregation are likely to translate into changes in the observed patterns of residential segregation and integration described in the previous sections. At the same time, the growing residential segregation of low- and high-income households creates obstacles to the economic inclusion of low-income households and contributes to pockets of concentrated disadvantage.

Residential segregation by income has grown in recent decades at all levels of the income distribution.[14] When measured among families in metropolitan areas with population of at least 500,000 people, income segregation shows substantial increases from 1970 to 2009.[15] Exhibit 3 displays the trends in income segregation during this period, showing increases at the 10th, 50th, and 90th percentiles of the income

Exhibit 3: Residential Segregation by Income, 1970–2009.

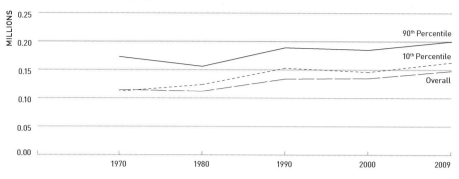

Note: Values reflect the rank-order information theory index for families in metropolitan areas with populations of at least 500,000 people.[16]
Source: Bischoff and Reardon (2014).

distribution — with the fastest increases occurring during the 1980s and the 2000s. The 10th percentile index measures the extent to which families with incomes at or below the 10th percentile of the income distribution live in different neighborhoods than families in the remainder of the income distribution. This measure captures the *segregation of poverty*, showing that income segregation is more severe among families with very low incomes than among the overall population.

The 90th percentile measure reflects the *segregation of affluence*, and shows that the most extreme levels of residential segregation by income exist among families in the highest income decile. The segregation of affluence has been referred to as "opportunity hoarding" because these most affluent neighborhoods provide residents with access to higher-quality public services, environmental quality, and access to man-made and natural amenities, leaving fewer, worse-quality resources for all other communities. The growing residential segregation of affluent households over time primarily reflects the increasing concentration of high-income households in specific cities and in wealthy enclaves within these cities. In contrast, the increases in income segregation among both low- and middle-income households have occurred at a smaller geographic scale, with households sorting across neighborhoods and munici-palities within rather than across metropolitan areas.[17]

Rising income inequality is a primary contributor to the growth in income segre-gation.[18] Reardon and Bischoff estimate that increases in income inequality explain between 40 and 80 percent of the rise in income segregation between 1970 and 2000.[19] However, while income inequality best explains the rise in income segregation among high-income households, increasing inequality is less able to explain changes in income segregation at lower income levels.[20] Instead, the remaining changes likely reflect a multitude of other factors such as the deindustrialization of American cities and changing patterns of racial/ethnic segregation.[21]

Exhibit 4: Average Neighborhood Composition by Income across All U.S. Census Tracts.

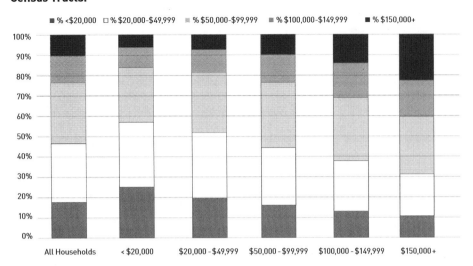

Notes: Neighborhoods are defined as census tracts.
Source: JCHS tabulations of American Community Survey 5-year estimates 2011–2015.

Exhibit 4 describes the current levels of segregation by income, presenting exposure index values using the 2011–2015 American Community Survey 5-year estimates. While these figures suggest that income segregation may not be as stark as segregation by race/ethnicity, they nonetheless reveal considerable segregation between low- and high-income households. The average household with income below $20,000 lives in a neighborhood where 25 percent of neighborhood households have income below $20,000, 32 percent have household income between $20,000 and $50,000, and only 16 percent have household income above $100,000. By contrast, the average household with income above $150,000 lives in a neighborhood where 11 percent of neighborhood households have incomes below $20,000, 21 percent have incomes between $20,000 and $50,000, and more than 40 percent have incomes above $100,000.

These national figures again mask systematic variation across metropolitan areas. Appendix Table 2 replicates the information in Exhibit 4 for metropolitan areas of different sizes, showing that the extent of income segregation increases consistently with the size of the metropolitan area. For example, in non-metropolitan areas, the average neighborhood compositions of households with incomes below $20,000 and above $150,000 differ by less than 6 percentage points for each of the categories shown in Exhibit 4. By contrast, in the 10 largest metropolitan areas, the average household with income below $20,000 lives in a neighborhood in which only 21 percent of residents have household incomes above $100,000 and 53 percent have household income below $50,000. Meanwhile, the typical household in these metros with income above $150,000 lives in a neighborhood in which 47 percent of households have incomes above $100,000 and only 27 percent of households have incomes below $50,000. These results reflect both the clustering of high-income households in large metropolitan areas and increased residential segregation of households by income within these areas.

Residential Segregation by Income and Race/Ethnicity

In considering the interaction between segregation by income and by race/ethnicity, there are two questions of interest: whether there are differences in the extent of income segregation by race/ethnicity, and the extent to which differences in income levels by race/ethnicity contribute to segregation by race/ethnicity.

On the first question, Bischoff and Reardon describe changes in the extent of income segregation among racial and ethnic groups, showing considerable change across time.[22] In particular, income segregation among black families was lower than that among white families in 1970 but has grown quickly in subsequent years. By 2009, income segregation among black families exceeded income segregation among white families by 65 percent.[23] While the initial growth in income segregation among black families likely reflects the movement of middle- and high-income black families into white suburbs and wealthy black enclaves in response to reduced housing discrimination, the drivers of continued growth in the 2000s are less clear. Less evidence exists regarding the long-term trends among Hispanics and Asians; however, in recent decades Hispanic families show a similar trend to that of black families, with Hispanics exhibiting both higher levels of income segregation and faster increases in the 2000s than whites.[24]

Other studies examine the extent to which differences in income by race/ethnicity explain observed patterns of residential segregation by race/ethnicity. Such studies consistently find that controlling for household income is not sufficient to explain observed patterns of racial/ethnic segregation.[25] Moreover, black and Hispanic households are more likely than white households with similar incomes to live in neighborhoods with lower median incomes and higher poverty rates. For example, Logan and Stults show that even affluent black and Hispanic households — defined as having income greater than $75,000 per year — live in neighborhoods with lower incomes, on average, than equally affluent white households.[26] While a portion of these differences is likely to reflect racial/ethnic differences in wealth and other socioeconomic characteristics, they also reflect the patterns of racial/ethnic segregation in US communities.[27]

Taken together, these patterns highlight the complex interrelationships between patterns of residential segregation by race/ethnicity and income. An initial upshot is that clarity in distinguishing between income and race/ethnicity is necessary in considering residential segregation patterns and potential response options. At the same time, such discussions must also recognize the close relationship between income and race/ethnicity in interpreting changes in residential segregation patterns and anticipating the consequences of any action.

Neighborhoods with Concentrated Poverty

While income segregation is highest among high-income households, the concentration of poverty has particular importance for policy and efforts to foster greater economic and racial/ethnic inclusion. In particular, one of the rationales for studying broader patterns of segregation by income and race/ethnicity is that increases in residential segregation among more advantaged households may limit the resources and opportunities available in less advantaged areas.[28]

The prevalence of neighborhoods with concentrated poverty has increased substantially since 2000.[29] Between 2000 and the 2009–2013 ACS 5-year estimates, the number of census tracts with concentrated poverty — defined as a poverty rate above 40 percent — increased from 2,510 to 4,412, an increase of 76 percent. This increase more than offset the reduction in concentrated poverty observed between 1990 and 2000, a decade of broadly-shared income growth.[30]

Minorities are disproportionately represented within neighborhoods with concentrated poverty. Across all concentrated poverty tracts in the US, 36 percent of residents are black, 31 percent are Hispanic, 25 percent are white, and 7 percent are Asian, multiracial, or some other race or ethnicity. These outcomes reflect the overlap between concentrated poverty and the patterns of residential segregation by race/ethnicity. According to the 2009–2013 ACS, 7.5 percent of poor whites lived in neighborhoods with concentrated poverty, compared to 25.2 percent of poor blacks and 17.4 percent of poor Hispanics.[31]

The post-2000 growth in neighborhoods with concentrated poverty includes several trends that run counter to these historical patterns. First, while the majority of neighborhoods with concentrated poverty are located in large metropolitan areas, small and mid-sized metros show the fastest rates of recent growth, particularly in the Midwest.[32] Since 2000, this growth has increased the share of poor white households that live in concentrated poverty neighborhoods. Additionally, concentrated poverty neighborhoods in large metropolitan areas have become slightly less clustered, producing a larger number of small pockets of poverty in place of the larger clusters of concentrated poverty tracts that existed in 1990. Lastly, while suburbs continue to account for only a small number of neighborhoods with concentrated poverty, the suburbanization of poverty has increased the share of poor households living in suburban areas, as well as the number of suburban neighborhoods exceeding 10 percent or 20 percent poverty rates.[33]

Looking forward, it is not yet clear whether the recent increases in the number of tracts with concentrated poverty will persist as the economy recovers. Trends since the 1990s suggest that the concentration of poverty is quite sensitive to the rise and fall in the distribution of household incomes. Thus, if recent gains in household incomes continue, some improvement may be evident at the neighborhood level. But given the enormous increases in the number of these distressed neighborhoods since 2000, it would take a prolonged period of income growth to register significant recovery. Moreover, recent rises in household income have primarily benefited those at the top of the socioeconomic ladder; unless this trend is mitigated, it is unlikely that further overall income increases will much improve the fortunes of high-poverty communities.

CONTRIBUTORS TO RESIDENTIAL SEGREGATION AND INTEGRATION

In order to identify the levers that may be employed to promote greater degrees of integration by race/ethnicity and income, it is important to understand the forces that have produced these patterns. The segregated communities that exist today are the result of numerous factors, including the legacy of a long history of discriminatory practices and the multitude of influences that have shaped households' choices about where to live in recent decades.[34] As a means of both motivating and framing policy responses, this section reviews the primary contributing factors to segregation today.

Historical Government Actions

First and foremost, many of the cities with the highest levels of racial/ethnic segregation continue to reflect the residential patterns that emerged during the Great Migration of black households from the rural South to Northern cities between 1910 and 1970. During this period, racially discriminatory public policies and the collective actions of whites limited the neighborhoods available to black households. While many of these policies are no longer in place, current patterns of residential segregation in many cities still follow the historical lines of separation that these policies and practices generated.

The process of redlining is the most notable, although far from the only, government action that contributed to historical patterns of residential segregation. This process was formally initiated by the Homeowners Loan Corporation (HOLC) in the 1930s with the establishment of a neighborhood quality index.[35] Under this rating system, black neighborhoods were universally given the poorest quality rating and declared unfit for investment from banks and other lenders. The result in these neighborhoods was to cut off demand for owner-occupied housing by both blacks and whites and to encourage a downward spiral of investment. As a result, the broad adoption of the

HOLC system and other redlining practices by private banks, the Federal Housing Administration (FHA), and the Veterans Administration (VA) institutionalized redlining broadly throughout the housing market.

Both prior to and during this period, racially restrictive covenants — provisions written into property deeds that prohibited black occupancy of a property — were legal and widespread, further limiting black households' access to white neighborhoods. While neighborhood associations and realtors were instrumental in encouraging white homeowners to adopt such covenants, they were also encouraged by the FHA and VA until the US Supreme Court declared them unconstitutional in 1948.[36] The impacts of these covenants were reinforced by other forms of discrimination in housing markets and by the expansion of mortgage financing through the FHA and VA, which further contributed to the outmigration to the suburbs of white households with preferences for new construction over rehab, greenfield over city, and other incentives that made it cheaper for them to buy suburban homes than to stay in the city.[37]

The Federal Highway Act of 1956 and concurrent urban renewal policies further segregated many cities, subsidizing the development of white suburbs and erecting highway infrastructure that displaced black households and separated white and black neighborhoods. The construction of segregated public housing developments accompanied this process under policies that reserved specific public housing developments for white households and others for black households. The cumulative result of this history is the nearly complete residential segregation of black and white households by 1970 (shown in Exhibit 1).

Discrimination in Housing Markets

The residential segregation of black and white households during the twentieth century was reinforced by the collective actions of whites, in both professional roles and as private citizens. In particular, realtors and other housing market professionals played central roles in facilitating residential segregation by race. The code of the National Association of Real Estate Brokers instructed members that "a Realtor should never be instrumental in introducing into a neighborhood members of any race or nationality whose presence will clearly be detrimental to property values in the neighborhood" — a provision that remained until 1950.

Neighborhood associations and loosely organized mobs further used intimidation and violence to prevent blacks from moving into white neighborhoods, often aided by the inaction of police.[38] Such actions appeared frequently during the early decades of the twentieth century and continued into later periods, including the decades following the Supreme Court's ban on racially restrictive covenants.

The Fair Housing Act of 1968 eventually prohibited discrimination on the basis of race, color, religion, and national origin at any stage of the process for renting or buying a home. However, absent effective enforcement mechanisms, the law did not have a significant impact on the prevalence of discriminatory treatment in the market.[39] As a result, studies employing paired-testing methodologies continued to find clear signs of discrimination against minority homeseekers in the decades following the passage of the Fair Housing Act. HUD's initial housing discrimination study in 1977 found that black renters and homebuyers were commonly told that advertised units were not available or were shown fewer units than equally qualified whites.[40] A similar 1989 audit study also found significant levels of discrimination on these measures against both black and Hispanic homeseekers.[41]

The extent of such discrimination has declined in more recent decades, but has not disappeared. HUD's most recent housing discrimination study in 2012 finds no significant differences between whites and blacks, Hispanics, or Asians in the likelihood of being told that an advertised unit is available or of being told about at least one available unit. However, the 2012 study continues to find significant differences in the number of units about which minority homeseekers are told, as well as the number of units that these homeseekers are shown.[42]

Evidence on the presence of discrimination in mortgage lending similarly suggests that the nature of discrimination has evolved but not disappeared in the decades following passage of the Fair Housing Act of 1968 and the Equal Credit Opportunity Act of 1974, which outlaws discrimination in any step of the mortgage lending process.[43] The Federal Reserve Bank of Boston in 1992 concluded that black and Hispanic mortgage loan applicants in Boston were 60 percent more likely to be denied credit than equally qualified whites.[44]

More recently, Wells Fargo's settlement for discriminatory lending practices during the 2000s subprime lending boom is the most high-profile example of the lending practices that led subprime loans to be disproportionately concentrated in minority communities.[45] In describing the practices used to steer minority customers into subprime mortgage products, the Wells Fargo case also highlights the potential for aggressive marketing practices to produce disparities in the cost and terms of credit.

In a similar way, it is possible that less discriminatory forms of advertising and marketing may contribute to residential segregation patterns by altering the nature of information to which different homeseekers are exposed as they evaluate their ability to afford a home in various neighborhoods.[46] However, little research examines whether disparities exist in the information available to homeseekers prior to inquiring about a unit.[47] While the advent of the internet and online information sources have dramatically increased the amount of information broadly available to the public, disparities in the use of online information or in the types of online tools consulted may allow search processes to vary widely across racial/ethnic groups.

Neighborhood Preferences of Homeseekers

Research on the neighborhood preferences of white and minority homeseekers suggests that households' voluntary sorting processes further contribute to residential segregation patterns. In particular, white survey respondents on average rank communities with higher shares of white residents as the most desirable and show the greatest aversion to living in neighborhoods with more than a small percentage of black residents.[48] For example, using a representative telephone-based survey that presented alternative neighborhood options, Emerson, Chai, and Yancey found that white respondents reported on average that they preferred neighborhoods where fewer than 10 percent of residents were black, were "neutral" toward neighborhoods that were 10–15 percent black, and would be unlikely to purchase a home in neighborhoods where more than 15 percent of residents are black.[49]

By contrast, multiple studies over time have suggested that the preferred neighborhood for the average black household is one with approximately 50 percent black residents and 50 percent residents of other races.[50] These studies further suggest that many black households are willing to consider neighborhoods with lower shares of black households, but that few black households prefer to live in predominantly white or predominantly black neighborhoods. In particular, many black households prefer not to be one of the first black households to move into predominantly white neighborhoods due to concerns about white hostility.[51] Recent evidence further suggests that neighborhood preferences are particularly pronounced among parents with children, with white parents disproportionately sorting into neighborhoods with segregated white public schools and black parents showing fewer differences from non-parents in their neighborhood choices.[52]

Taken together, these neighborhood preferences are consistent with racial 'tipping' models in which the differences between the neighborhood preferences of whites and blacks over time lead whites to avoid mixed neighborhoods, resulting in increasing shares of black residents in these neighborhoods.[53] Discussions of these tipping models highlight that this outcome can be self-reinforcing to the extent that white avoidance of integrated neighborhoods is due to expectations of future neighborhood change and its implications for property values. Ellen calls the use of a neighborhood's racial composition to form perceptions about neighborhood amenities or future neighborhood outcomes "race-based neighborhood stereotyping," and shows that it may be a primary contributor to white avoidance of integrated neighborhoods.[54]

While the literature on neighborhood preferences predominantly focuses on white-black dynamics, recent studies suggest that white avoidance of Hispanic and Asian neighbors exists, though to a lesser degree than white avoidance of black neighbors.[55] Preferences for in-group clustering may also play a larger role in explaining patterns of residential segregation among Hispanic and Asian households, particularly among recent immigrants who may seek out neighbors who emigrated from the same birth country or who speak shared languages.

Affordability Barriers

Differences in purchasing power contribute directly to the segmentation of housing markets as households sort across neighborhoods in response to differences in neighborhood amenities and the associated costs of housing. Local public finance theory implies that differences in neighborhood amenities, such as school quality and safety, will be capitalized into the costs of housing as households bid up home prices based on these amenities.[56] Residential segregation by income is a direct result of this process if affordable units are not set aside in higher-income neighborhoods. Moreover, because income and wealth disparities correlate with race/ethnicity, affordability barriers also contribute to residential segregation by race/ethnicity.

Land use and zoning restrictions have exacerbated the extent of affordability barriers in many high-cost areas by artificially limiting the number and types of units available, particularly the development of new multifamily and affordable units. In a study of communities in the nation's 25 largest metropolitan areas, Pendall found that low-density zoning — which he defines as fewer than eight dwelling units per acre — reduced local shares of both multifamily and rental housing over the period studied.[57] At the same time, a study of 187 Massachusetts cities and towns suggests that municipalities with less restrictive multifamily zoning issued more multifamily housing permits.[58] In this way, local decisions to institute minimum lot sizes or otherwise limit the land available for multifamily development reduce the supply of multifamily units and are associated with higher levels of income segregation, particularly the segregation of affluent households.[59]

Conversely, inclusionary zoning, subsidies for the development of affordable housing, and lower barriers to the development of lower-cost units can serve as counter-weights to income segregation. While such measures increase lower-income households' access to higher-cost neighborhoods, they do not fully resolve the differences in affordability across neighborhoods. Additionally, because economic differences explain only a small share of observed residential segregation by race/ethnicity, such measures may do more to reduce segregation by income than by race/ethnicity, particularly between black and white households.

Geographic Population Flows

Lastly, longer-term shifts in the regional distribution of the US population and in economic activity also contribute to the observed levels of residential segregation by income and race/ethnicity. Since 1970, the geographic distribution of the population has shifted considerably, with the fastest rates of growth appearing in Sunbelt cities and much slower rates of growth in Northern cities. To the extent that high-growth and low-growth cities have varying levels of residential segregation, these population flows carry implications for national-level figures. For example, Glaeser and Vigdor argue that population loss from majority-black neighborhoods in Northern cities and the corresponding flows to both suburbs and Sunbelt cities contributed to reductions in black-white segregation between 1970 and 2010.[60]

Recent changes in the intracity geography of jobs and population carry further implications for residential outcomes. In particular, recent decades have witnessed increasing flows of high-income jobs and residents to central-city neighborhoods.[61] While the gentrification of central-city neighborhoods is one of the most visible outcomes, the increasing presence of low-income and minority households in suburban neighborhoods is equally consequential.[62] More research is needed to understand how these changes will contribute to increased or decreased residential segregation by both income and race/ethnicity.

THE CONSEQUENCES OF SEGREGATION FOR INDIVIDUALS AND SOCIETY

An enormous empirical literature documents the wide range of costs associated with racial and economic residential segregation, particularly for minorities living in racially segregated areas of concentrated poverty. Residents of such communities tend to have poor outcomes in a number of areas — including educational attainment, employment and socioeconomic mobility, and health.[63] Additionally, segregation has been shown to carry substantial costs for society and the economy overall, by undermining social cohesion, perpetuating racial stereotyping and prejudice, eroding democracy, fomenting social instability, and dragging down long-term economic growth.

Given the amount of research on the effects of residential segregation and concentrated disadvantage on residents' outcomes, this section provides only a brief overview of the costs of segregation for both individuals and society. In particular, this review pays attention to the disproportionate costs imposed on residents of racially segregated areas of concentrated poverty, which we refer to hereafter as neighborhoods with *concentrated disadvantage*.

Costs of Segregation to Individuals

Segregation creates vastly different environmental and social conditions that tend to constrain access to quality education, housing, and job opportunities for residents of communities with concentrated disadvantage. As a result, the residents of such neighborhoods have been shown to have worse life outcomes on a number of measures, including educational attainment and achievement, economic mobility, and health.

Educational Outcomes

Segregation has been described as a "stubborn, multidimensional, and deeply important cause of educational inequality."[64] Racial segregation is shown to be a significant contributor to racial disparities in educational performance, with one study finding that fully one-quarter of the black-white SAT score gap can be attributed to racial residential segregation.[65] Segregation by socioeconomic status also has damaging educational outcomes for children who live in neighborhoods with concentrated disadvantage. Youth who grow up in high-poverty neighborhoods perform worse in school, are more likely to drop out of high school, and are less likely to go to college than their peers in more affluent communities.[66] The amount of time children spend in neighborhoods with concentrated disadvantage while growing up has also been found to be important. Children who spend longer living in high-poverty neighborhoods have worse educational outcomes,[67] while those who move from high- to low-poverty areas experience better outcomes in income and college attendance; the younger children are when they move away from disadvantaged neighborhoods, the better their outcomes.[68]

Importantly, because school enrollment areas are often tied to residential location, neighborhood and school diversity (and segregation) are highly interconnected; indeed, as Rusk and Schwartz have both noted, "housing policy is school policy."[69] Research has thoroughly documented that schools in high-poverty neighborhoods tend to have high dropout rates and poor academic achievement overall.[70]

Economic Opportunity

As Massey and Denton argue in their seminal *American Apartheid*, "Barriers to spatial mobility are barriers to social mobility, and by confining blacks to a small set of relatively disadvantaged neighborhoods, segregation constitutes a very powerful impediment to black socioeconomic progress."[71] Evidence conclusively shows that segregation is negatively correlated with upward economic mobility.[72] Chetty and colleagues demonstrate that segregation's negative effect on upward mobility is strongest for the residents of high-poverty areas and areas with large African American populations, leaving them least likely to move up in income distribution.[73]

Employment outcomes are demonstrably worse for minorities living in highly segregated metro areas, contributing to their limited upward mobility. Dickerson studied employment rates for residents of the 95 largest US cities between 1980 and 2000, and found that for both blacks and Latinos, employment rates were lower in cities where racial segregation was worse and decreased further as segregation increased over time.[74]

Health and Well-being

Decades of research convincingly illustrate that segregation has contributed to worse health and safety outcomes for residents of high-poverty and racially isolated minority communities. Studies show that after taking individual-level factors into account, neighborhoods with concentrated disadvantage have a detrimental influence on adult and infant mortality, physical and mental health of children and adults, and health behaviors.[75] For example, Aneshensel and Sucoff found that youth living in neighborhoods of low socioeconomic status are more likely than their peers living in more affluent neighborhoods to perceive their neighborhoods as dangerous and consequently to suffer from anxiety, depression, and other mental health disorders.[76] Similarly, Ellen finds that studies agree that in the long-term, the accumulated stress of living in a disadvantaged community erodes the overall health of residents in ways that make them more vulnerable to disease and other negative health outcomes.[77]

Given the close connection between racial and economic segregation in the US, poor minorities are far more likely to live in in conditions of concentrated poverty compared with poor whites, putting minorities in "double jeopardy" of negative health consequences associated not only with individual but also with neighborhood poverty.[78] In an extensive review of the scale and breadth of black-white health disparities, Williams and Collins conclude that racial residential segregation "creates conditions inimical to health in the physical and social environment" by constraining socioeconomic mobility and limiting minorities' residential options to areas with lower-quality housing and urban infrastructure, higher homicide rates, and less access to nutritious and affordable food and to medical care.[79] The environmental justice literature further chronicles how poor minority communities are not only disproportionately likely to host various environmental hazards including poor air quality and high levels of toxins,[80] but also have less access to urban green space, which is related to promoting physical activity, psychological well-being, and general public health.[81]

Social and Economic Costs of Segregation

As the above sections describe, substantial empirical evidence indicates that living in a racially segregated, high-poverty neighborhood is detrimental to resident outcomes in a number of arenas. Turner and Rawlings note that these disparities "ultimately hurt everyone" by depressing residential property values and property tax revenues and reducing the competitiveness of the nation's workforce.[82] Evidence also indicates that segregation has detrimental consequences for society at large by reducing social cohesion and fueling prejudice, hindering democracy, and dampening long-term economic growth.

Prejudice and Trust

In a review of over 500 studies, Pettigrew and Tropp found that intergroup contact significantly reduces intergroup prejudice by increasing knowledge about the out-group, reducing anxiety about intergroup contact, and increasing empathy and perspective-taking.[83] By limiting intergroup contact, segregation hinders the development of social cohesion and trust while perpetuating social fragmentation and instability — both of which have costs for economic performance and for the effectiveness of democracy at the national level.[84]

Putnam's research on "generalized trust" (where one believes that people in general can be trusted) further elucidates how segregation reduces overall social cohesion.[85] Putnam finds that while segregation may actually result in higher levels of in-group trust, it significantly reduces inter-group trust by limiting social interactions across racial and ethnic lines. Because the condition of "generalized trust" is dependent on both forms of trust, it is undermined by segregation. Although evidence suggests that transitional periods of increasing diversity can be characterized by lower levels of social cohesion and trust as people temporarily "hunker down" in response to long-term change, researchers find that simply increasing opportunities for meaningful social interactions across ethnic lines allows for diversity and trust to complement one another.[86]

Democracy

Segregation has a negative effect on democracy by decreasing the political influence and participation of residents of low-income minority neighborhoods. Massey and Denton argue that persistent residential segregation has resulted in the political disenfranchisement of African Americans, in particular, by undermining their ability to build coalitions with other groups and accumulate political power.[87] Since segregated black ghettos typically contain few residents from other racial/ethnic groups, resources allocated to black neighborhoods have few, if any, benefits for other groups, leaving little incentive for interracial coalitions to form.[88] Racial residential segregation has therefore decreased blacks' capacity to participate in the democratic process by limiting their political influence and marginalizing them within the American polity.[89]

Oliver presents complementary evidence of the negative impact of socioeconomic segregation on democratic processes.[90] Oliver finds that socioeconomic segregation has a dampening effect on public participation for those at both the upper and lower ends of the economic spectrum, and consequently that civic participation is highest in diverse, middle-income cities. Poor urban residents may find themselves "unable to exit from their circumstances or to shape city policies from fiscal constraints" and decide to disengage from political life, while the residents of homogeneous, affluent suburbs have fewer social "needs" and are distanced from the social issues of the larger metropolitan economy on which they depend, lowering their incentive for civic involvement.[91] Oliver concludes that metropolitan fragmentation is therefore a "cause for alarm" that "may be undermining the health of American democracy."[92]

Economic Growth

In addition to threatening democracy, research also demonstrates that segregation may have damaging consequences for long-term economic growth. As the sections above describe, segregation constrains opportunity and exacerbates negative educational and economic outcomes for poor minorities living in disadvantaged areas while accentuating the advantages of white residents of wealthy enclaves, thus perpetuating socioeconomic inequality. Importantly, research suggests that income inequality has negative outcomes not just for poor individuals but also for economic growth and social stability overall, implying that persistent residential segregation plays an important role in producing worse outcomes for the nation as a whole.

Benner and Pastor note that traditional economic theory posits there is a "tradeoff between equity and efficiency, between fairness and economic growth."[93] However, in the 1990s, a wave of new studies arose that challenged the notion that equity and economic growth are at odds. In a review of this literature, Aghion, Caroli, and Garcia-Penalosa note that these studies all drew the "impressively unambiguous" picture that "greater inequality reduces the rate of growth."[94] Bénabou specifically connected segregation to weak economic growth, finding that the racial and economic segregation responsible for the "typical pattern of city-suburb polarization" in the US reduces the productivity of regional economies by constraining skill development and workforce participation of those in segregated areas.[95]

More recently, international studies conducted by researchers at the IMF and the OECD to measure the effects of increasing income inequality have reaffirmed that in the long term, a trade-off between efficiency and equality does not exist. Berg, Ostry, and Zettelmeyer reviewed economic growth in 140 countries between 1950 and 2000, and found that "duration of growth spells is strongly related to income distribution: more equal societies tend to sustain growth longer."[96] Similarly, a 2015 OECD report analyzed how inequality affected growth in OECD countries and found that "when income inequality rises, economic growth falls." The report ties income inequality to a reduced capacity of the poorer segments of the population to invest in their own skills and education, which in turn "drags down economic growth" overall.[97]

Scholars have produced similar results at the metropolitan level for these United States. Benner and Pastor apply the methodology used by Berg, Ostry, and Zettelmeyer to study international economic growth trends to US metros.[98] In line with Berg, Ostry, and Zettelmeyer's results, they found that the "most significant and important predictor" of sustained growth was the metropolitan area having a lower Gini coefficient, indicating a lower level of income inequality.[99] Earlier studies substantiate these findings, indicating that economic growth in US metros is negatively associated not only with income inequality, but also more specifically with city-suburb disparities, the re-production of concentrated poverty, and racial residential segregation.[100]

THE CASE FOR CHANGE

The previous section highlights the extent to which the substantial costs of residential segregation and concentrated disadvantage extend across multiple outcomes and ultimately affect all members of society. These costs, along with the potential benefits of greater integration for both individuals and the nation as a whole, provide a compelling and central justification for public action.[101] Still, several arguments are commonly used to question whether integration, particularly racial and ethnic integration, is necessary to realize these benefits. Since the symposium is based on the premise that racial, ethnic, and socioeconomic integration should be an important policy goal, these alternative points of view need to be considered.

Argument #1: To the extent that the costs of segregation flow from the fact that segregation has produced communities lacking adequate public and private amenities, redistribution of public investment and incentives for private investment could address these shortfalls without the need to integrate these communities. Put another way, this argument suggests that there is no reason why predominantly African American, Latino, or Asian communities cannot be vibrant, healthy communities of opportunity, with racial and ethnic enclaves having the potential to provide greater social cohesion and to shield residents from the effects of prejudice and discrimination.

While there is validity to the view that predominantly minority communities can be communities of opportunity, several counterpoints should be considered before this view is allowed to guide broader policy decisions. First, given that wealth and political power are concentrated among the white majority population, it has historically been challenging to generate support for the public and private investment needed in predominantly minority communities. Relatedly, in many areas the minority population may not be large enough to create a broad range of predominantly minority neighborhoods. Finally, given that a large share of the existing neighborhoods that offer high levels of opportunity for well-being and advancement are majority-white and relatively affluent, efforts to expand access to these neighborhoods for a broader range of households by race/ethnicity and socioeconomic status must be a part of any strategy to expand access to opportunity.

In short, while supporting and expanding the set of predominantly minority neighborhoods that are strong, vibrant communities remains a desirable objective, there is still a strong justification for expanding the range of integrated neighborhoods in which people can choose to live. Nor are these objectives mutually exclusive in practice. Instead, fostering more inclusive communities in the United States requires simultaneous efforts both to foster greater integration and to attract public and private investments to neighborhoods with concentrated disadvantage.

Argument #2: A related argument in support of fostering stronger predominantly minority communities is that a racially and ethnically integrated community is not the same as one that is inclusive, and that inclusion is necessary to truly reap the benefits of integration.

An inclusive community is one in which all community members have equal voice in collective decisions about the use of public resources and the rules and norms that affect residents' quality of life. This argument therefore asserts that racial and ethnic integration by itself does not ensure that communities are inclusive of all residents and so may not deliver the hoped-for benefits from integration. Mayorga-Gallo's *Behind the White Picket Fence* paints a portrait of how simply having a racially and ethnically diverse community does not necessarily produce a situation where all groups have equal voice. In her study, she finds that longstanding white homeowners still make most decisions about the use of resources and community norms, with minorities, renters, and more recent arrivals largely excluded from the neighborhood power structure. Similarly, Hyra illustrates that simply creating mixed-income, mixed-race neighborhoods may not result in inclusive, cohesive communities if people do not also develop meaningful social interactions across race and class groups.[102] Hyra notes that in some HOPE VI developments, for example, higher-income residents have dominated resident boards, leaving low-income residents with limited influence over their neighborhoods. Mary Pattillo's *Black on the Block* documents a similar power dynamic in a predominantly African-American neighborhood in Chicago where higher-socioeconomic status homeowners wield more power and influence than lower-status renters.[103]

To be clear, the issue of whether integration without inclusion is likely to produce the same level of benefits is an important one. However, the challenge of achieving meaningful inclusion does not detract from the value of integration itself. Even if the goal of inclusion is not fully realized, increased integration may still provide access to better-quality schools, safer and healthier communities, and regional employment opportunities. Ultimately, integration and inclusion should be kept in mind as distinct goals: inclusion brings valuable additional benefits to integration, and spatial integration by race/ethnicity and socioeconomic status is an important and necessary step on the path to inclusion. For example, Rob Breymaier's discussion paper for this symposium describes the Oak Park Regional Housing Center's "Pyramid of Progress," which defines diversity as a foundation for integration, followed by inclusion, and ultimately by equity.

Argument #3: While segregation clearly imposes costs, the appropriate response is to remove barriers to unfettered choice about where to live rather than pursue explicit efforts to foster integration. On this argument, efforts should concentrate on removing discrimination and allowing market forces to determine where individuals live, with efforts that go beyond removing obstacles to affirmatively support integration amounting to "social engineering."

This argument presumes that market forces alone are likely to increase neighborhood choice. To what extent will they in fact do so? Even if it were possible to remove all explicit and implicit traces of discrimination, people would be choosing where to live in an environment that has been shaped by the long historical legacy of discrimination. The highly segregated patterns of living that exist today did not arise through simple market forces; on the contrary, they reflect the accumulation of efforts to keep certain racial/ethnic groups and the poor in segregated communities. Given that the existing locations of both people and the housing stock will influence people's future choices about where to live, there is a good argument that conscious action is needed to remedy this past legacy and to create a broader range of choices as to both the degree of integration and the types of housing available in different communities. Additionally, white households' preferences for majority-white communities are undoubtedly shaped by a history that suggests any other population mix is inherently unstable. These views will change only to the extent that integrated neighborhoods exist to show that such areas can be stable, healthy, vibrant communities.

Finally, the view that free market forces alone should be allowed to determine residential choices ignores social benefits from integration that go beyond the benefits individuals derive from where they live. In the language of economics, these externalities, which include a more productive economy and the diminishment of misperceptions and prejudice that sustain segregation, warrant public action to bring about a greater degree of integration than markets by themselves would provide.

It is for all these reasons that the symposium is focused on what can be done to promote greater racial/ethnic and socioeconomic integration.

A PATH FORWARD

The role of housing in determining the well-being of individuals is central to the discussions planned for the symposium. As the previous sections make clear, housing and residential segregation play critical roles in determining the schools and jobs available to individuals, as well as the water they drink, the air quality that surrounds them, and all of the other features of the environment that shape how we interact with the world. Put simply, place matters to individuals' life chances and overall well-being. While other individual-level factors also contribute importantly to these outcomes, this symposium focuses on the role of housing and residential segregation.

Given the complexity of these challenges, the symposium is also designed with the understanding that the path forward is really multiple paths: just as segregation has many causes, fighting it will require many solutions. There is no silver bullet. The responses below, as well as those proposed in the symposium papers, should therefore be understood not as mutually exclusive, but rather as complementary and mutually reinforcing.

Enforce Anti-Discrimination Laws

A foundational step in responding to the causes of residential segregation by race/ethnicity is to ensure that existing anti-discrimination laws are enforced broadly and effectively. The groundbreaking Civil Rights Act of 1964 banned racial discrimination and segregation in schools, in the workplace, and in public facilities. A few years later, the Fair Housing Act of 1968 prohibited discrimination specifically in housing sales, rentals, and financing, banning the type of explicit racism inherent in redlining and other housing policies of the early twentieth century. Enforcement of these provisions and of their subsequent amendments and other related legislation is a critical and necessary step in ensuring equal treatment in housing markets.

While much progress has been made since the passage of the Fair Housing Act in 1968, the findings of HUD's 2012 housing discrimination study highlight the need for enforcement of anti-discrimination law to remain a foundational component of any effort to reduce residential segregation. Important questions exist about whether to expand the set of groups defined as protected classes, about which methods are most effective in implementing fair housing enforcement, and about how to best allocate limited resources.[104]

In addition to addressing ongoing discrimination in the housing market, the Fair Housing Act's affirmatively-furthering fair housing (AFFH) mandate acknowledges the need for anti-discrimination measures to take affirmative steps to remedy the consequences of past discrimination. HUD strengthened the rules associated with this AFFH mandate in 2016, issuing a Final Rule that encourages local recipients of HUD funds to meet their longstanding obligations to affirmatively further fair housing in their use of those funds. However, the introduction of this rule also illustrated the uneven compliance with fair housing law since the passage of the Fair Housing Act.[105]

Support Efforts to Improve Understanding and Reduce Prejudice

Fostering racially integrated neighborhoods depends not only on legal prohibitions against discrimination, but also on changes in the beliefs and perceptions of home-seekers. As research on the neighborhood preferences of homeseekers makes clear, differences in preferences across racial and ethnic groups — particularly white house-holds' lower tolerance for racially and ethnically integrated neighborhoods — contribute to racial/ethnic segregation and to the instability of racially integrated neighborhoods. As a result, efforts to foster intergroup contact and otherwise reduce prejudice are likely necessary if integrated neighborhoods are to become commonplace.

While such efforts have been relatively infrequent, several localities have pioneered them. For example, in the 1970s, the township of Oak Park, Illinois instituted some of the first local-level policies designed to promote racial diversity. More recently, a handful of cities and counties across the country, including Seattle (Washington); St. Paul (Minnesota); Madison, Wisconsin; Portland, Oregon; and King County, Washington, have sought to complement local policies that promote socioeconomic inclusion by establishing racial equity initiatives intended to foster racial inclusion and achieve equitable outcomes.

Fostering integration within schools may also be a particularly effective channel for increasing intergroup contact and reducing prejudice. Studies of the long-term effects of school desegregation suggest that attending a diverse high school leaves students better prepared for life in a racially diverse society and better able to understand people from backgrounds different than their own than they otherwise would have been.[106] Recent school-based efforts to support integration have further developed intentional strategies for designing curriculum and other tools to foster intergroup contact and understanding within diverse student bodies.

Remove Exclusionary Barriers

While the preceding actions focus on eliminating racial prejudice and discrimination, further steps are needed in response to growing income segregation. Beyond their direct effects on income segregation, such actions are likely to produce gains in racial integration due to the close relationship between income and race/ethnicity. A foundational step in responding to growing income segregation is to address exclu-sionary barriers to the development of multi-family buildings, affordable housing, and other units accessible to lower-income households. However, because such efforts involve reviewing and revising local zoning and land use requirements, they have been hampered by local politics.

Instead, several of the most promising approaches involve state- and regional-level efforts to facilitate development. For example, the state of Oregon established a comprehensive approach for managing urban sprawl that includes prohibitions against exclusionary zoning and that has effectively reduced the extent of income segregation in its cities.[107] State-level programs in Massachusetts and New Jersey offer alternative approaches to reducing the influence of exclusionary actions at the local level.

Preserve and Increase the Stock of Affordable Units

While taking steps to remove exclusionary barriers to development is critically necessary, it will reduce income segregation only to the extent that the market can support the introduction of new supply in high-opportunity neighborhoods. As a result, increasing neighborhood choice and opportunity for low-income residents requires that such efforts be coupled with increases in support for the development and preservation of affordable housing units. State and local inclusionary zoning programs offer one promising tool for ensuring that affordable units are developed in higher-cost areas experiencing substantial development. State and local housing trust funds, community land trusts, tax-increment financing programs, and other approaches offer additional options for supporting the provision of affordable housing. However, these models operate at relatively small scales compared with the level of assistance delivered through federal housing programs.

As a result, federally assisted housing programs are likely to be a central component of any effort to increase the stock of affordable units in higher-income neighborhoods. The scoring systems used to award low-income housing tax credits (LIHTCs) shape the location of new construction of assisted units.[108] Management and preservation of the existing stock of federally assisted units will require critical decisions at the federal level about the incentives and resources that determine whether (and if so, which) units are lost from the stock of affordable units. Lastly, the small-area fair market rent demonstration program has illustrated the extent to which the incentives built into the Housing Choice Voucher program can alter the residential locations of voucher recipients.[109]

Federal support has further increased the availability of income-restricted homeownership units, as well as down payment assistance and housing counseling programs that support homeownership attainment. In all cases, increased support for federal assistance is a critical determinant of the extent to which lower-income households are able to find and retain housing units in socioeconomically integrated neighborhoods.

Invest in Neighborhoods with Concentrated Disadvantage

Lastly, a comprehensive solution to the challenges of residential segregation by race/ethnicity and income requires investment in neighborhoods of concentrated disadvantage. While a more detailed consideration of the most effective programs and strategies for investments in these neighborhoods is beyond the scope of this symposium,[110] it is nonetheless a necessary component of a comprehensive approach to the challenges of residential segregation and concentrated disadvantage. As we describe above, the path forward is in fact multiple paths, and the proposals outlined in this symposium should be pursued concurrently with a strategy of investment in neighborhoods with concentrated disadvantage.

The Symposium: Identifying A Path Forward

Tremendous work remains to be done in achieving universal access to inclusive, high-opportunity neighborhoods. Taken together, the current patterns and causes of racial and socioeconomic segregation point to a multitude of potential levers for action in public policy, in local land use planning, in private-sector real estate practices, and in households' decision-making processes. The goal of this symposium is to identify and explore forward-thinking strategies capable of achieving meaningful improvements in racial and socioeconomic inclusion in neighborhoods throughout the country. Each of the symposium's seven panels therefore explores a different facet of this challenge.

The first panel motivates the symposium by examining the definition of inclusion and the central goals for efforts to support it. In this introductory discussion, panelists examine the rationales and objectives for public actions to reduce residential segregation by race/ethnicity and income, as well as the costs of segregation for children, adults, and society at large. By tracing the roots, evolution, and outcomes of the deep racial and socioeconomic divides that characterize our nation's communities, and examining what the alternative scenario of inclusion could look like, this first panel sets the stage for those that follow.

The second panel turns to the role of individual agency in driving patterns of residential sorting, asking the question, "What would it take to promote residential choices that result in greater integration and more equitable neighborhood outcomes?" Recognizing the interaction of individual preferences and housing search processes in households' decisions about where to live, this panel examines how shifting racial attitudes and the advent of new technologies, data, and search processes might improve (or exacerbate) patterns of residential segregation, as well as how these new phenomena might open new avenues of policy response to segregation.

The third panel takes a regional view of both residential patterns and potential responses, asking the question, "What would it take to make new neighborhoods and remake old ones so that regions move decisively toward integration?" This panel turns to case studies of three very different metropolitan areas — Houston, Chicago, and Washington, DC — to examine this question within different regional contexts. In each area, the discussion will shed light on both the changing nature of residential settlement patterns and the steps that might be taken to foster greater inclusion.

Federal housing policy represents another key lever for change. The fourth panel focuses on the Department of Housing and Urban Development's (HUD's) recent and important new federal commitment to fair housing, its Affirmatively Furthering Fair Housing (AFFH) rule. This panel is dedicated to the question, "What would it take for the HUD AFFH rule to meaningfully increase inclusion?" Panelists assess the rule's potential and the roles of HUD, localities, civil rights lawyers, and community groups in its implementation in coming years.

The fifth panel examines a broad and complex topic that has been the focus of considerable research and debate: housing subsidies. Its motivating question is, "What would it take for housing subsidies to overcome affordability barriers to inclusion in all neighborhoods?" Panelists were asked to identify promising approaches and priorities for action. In particular, this panel delves into the questions of how to balance the development of assisted housing in higher-income neighborhoods with investments in low-income communities; how to increase the neighborhood options available to subsidized housing recipients; and how to better structure financial incentives and subsidies for homeownership to promote inclusion rather than exclusion.

The sixth panel returns the focus to cities, exploring potential responses to the growth in gentrification and displacement pressures in many urban communities across the county. This panel asks, "What would it take for cities experiencing gentrification pressures to foster inclusion rather than replacement?" It acknowledges that while gentrification has historically often lead to the disenfranchisement or displacement of legacy residents, there may be potential to instead leverage it to foster stable mixed-income neighborhoods. In addition to asking if and how we can re-imagine gentrification as a possible force for increasing neighborhood integration, this panel seeks to promote fruitful discussion around how to ensure that existing residents' voices are represented in local decision-making processes.

The final panel examines the complex interdependencies between housing and school outcomes, asking the question, "What would it take to foster residential outcomes that support school integration, and vice versa?" While many facets of residential segregation — specifically housing policy, housing search processes, and housing affordability — are specific to housing markets, this section acknowledges and examines the interaction between residential segregation and school segregation. The discussion unpacks the role of school quality in creating residential segregation, identifies effective strategies for reducing school segregation, and discusses proven ways to create and sustain neighborhood and school integration.

Taken together, these topics are not intended to be an exhaustive review of potential strategies for responding to residential segregation. Instead, they represent a selection of topics offering opportunities for progress. Solving the multifaceted challenges of residential segregation in the context of evolving American cities will ultimately require a combination of these and other proposals.

Bibliography

Acevedo-Garcia, Dolores, Theresa L. Osypuk, Nancy McArdle, and David R. Williams. 2008. "Toward a Policy-Relevant Analysis of Geographic and Racial/Ethnic Disparities in Child Health." *Health Affairs* 27, no. 2: 321–33.

Aghion, Philippe, Eve Caroli, and Cecilia Garcia-Penalosa. 1999. "Inequality and Economic Growth: The Perspective of the New Growth Theories." *Journal of Economic Literature* 37, no. 4: 1615–60.

Andrews, Nancy O., David J. Erickson, I. J. Galloway, and E. S. Seidman. 2012. "Investing in What Works for America's Communities." San Francisco: Federal Reserve Bank of San Francisco and Low Income Investment Fund.

Aneshensel, Carol S., and Clea A. Sucoff. 1996. "The Neighborhood Context of Adolescent Mental Health." *Journal of Health and Social Behavior* 37, no. 4: 293–310.

Apgar, William C., and Allegra Calder. 2005. "The Dual Mortgage Market: The Persistence of Discrimination in Mortgage Lending." Working Paper W05-11. Cambridge, MA: Joint Center for Housing Studies of Harvard University.

Bayer, Patrick, Robert McMillen, and Kim Rueben. 2004. "What Drives Racial Segregation? New Evidence Using Census Microdata." *Journal of Urban Economics* 56, no. 3: 514–35.

Bénabou, Roland. 1996. "Equity and Efficiency in Human Capital Investment: The Local Connection." *The Review of Economic Studies* 63, no. 2: 237–64.

Benner, Chris, and Manuel Pastor. 2015a. "Brother, Can You Spare Some Time? Sustaining Prosperity and Social Inclusion in America's Metropolitan Regions." *Urban Studies* 52, no. 7: 1339–56.

— — —. 2015b. *Equity, Growth, and Community: What the Nation Can Learn from America's Metro Areas.* Oakland, CA: University of California Press.

— — —. 2016. "Whither Resilient Regions? Equity, Growth and Community." *Journal of Urban Affairs* 38, no. 1: 5–24.

Berg, Andrew, Jonathan D. Ostry, and Jeromin Zettelmeyer. 2012. "What Makes Growth Sustained?" *Journal of Development Economics* 98, no. 2: 149–66.

Bischoff, Kendra, and Sean Reardon. 2014. "Residential Segregation by Income, 1970-2009." In *Diversity and Disparities: America Enters a New Century*, edited by John R. Logan, 208–33. New York: Russell Sage Foundation.

Brooks-Gunn, Jeanne, Greg J. Duncan, and J. Lawrence Aber. 1997. *Neighborhood Poverty, Volume 1: Context and Consequences for Children*. New York: Russell Sage Foundation.

Brooks-Gunn, Jeanne, Greg J. Duncan, Pamela Kato Klebanov, and Naomi Sealand. 1993. "Do Neighborhoods Influence Child and Adolescent Development?" *American Journal of Sociology* 99, no. 2: 353-95.

Burdick-Will, Julia, Jens Ludwig, Stephen W. Raudenbush, Robert J. Sampson, Lisa Sanbonmatsu, and Patrick Sharkey. 2011. "Converging Evidence for Neighborhood Effects on Children's Test Scores: An Experimental, Quasi-Experimental, and Observational Comparison." In *Whither Opportunity? Rising Inequality, Schools, and Children's Life Chances*, edited by Greg J. Duncan and Richard J. Murnane, 255-76. New York: Russell Sage Foundation.

Calem, Paul, Kevin Gillen, and Susan Wachter. 2004. "The Neighborhood Distribution of Subprime Lending." *Journal of Real Estate Finance and Economics* 29, no. 4: 393-410.

Card, David, and Jesse Rothstein. 2007. "Racial Segregation and the Black–White Test Score Gap." *Journal of Public Economics* 91, no. 11: 2158-84.

Carr, James, and Nandinee Kutty. 2008. "The New Imperative for Equality." In *Segregation: The Rising Costs for America*, edited by James Carr and Nandinee Kutty, 1-37. New York: Routledge.

Chetty, Raj, and Nathaniel Hendren. 2015. "The Impacts of Neighborhoods on Intergenerational Mobility: Childhood Exposure Effects and County-Level Estimates." Cambridge, MA: Harvard University and National Bureau of Economic Research.

Chetty, Raj, Nathaniel Hendren, Patrick Kline, and Emmanuel Saez. 2014. "Where Is the Land of Opportunity? The Geography of Intergenerational Mobility in the United States." *The Quarterly Journal of Economics* 129, no. 4: 1553-1623.

Clark, Rebecca L. 1992. "Neighborhood Effects on Dropping Out of School Among Teenage Boys." Washington, DC: Urban Institute.

Clark, W. A. V. 1991. "Residential Preferences and Neighborhood Racial Segregation: A Test of the Schelling Segregation Model." *Demography* 28, no. 1: 1-19.

Clement, Scott. 2015. "Millennials Are Just as Racist as Their Parents." *Washington Post,* June 23.

Collinson, Robert, and Peter Ganong. 2016. "The Incidence of Housing Voucher Generosity." Working Paper. June. https://ssrn.com/abstract=2255799.

Couture, Victor, and Jesse Handbury. 2015. "Urban Revival in America, 2000 to 2010." Working Paper. http://faculty.haas.berkeley.edu/couture/download/Couture_Handbury_Revival.pdf.

Crowder, Kyle, and Maria Krysan. 2016. "Moving Beyond the Big Three: A Call for New Approaches to Studying Racial Residential Segregation." *City and Community* 15, no. 1: 18-22.

Crowder, Kyle, and Scott J. South. 2011. "Spatial and Temporal Dimensions of Neighborhood Effects on High School Graduation." *Social Science Research* 40, no. 1: 87-106.

Cutler, David M., and Edward L. Glaeser. 1997. "Are Ghettos Good or Bad?" *The Quarterly Journal of Economics* 112, no. 3: 827-72.

Cutler, David M., Edward L. Glaeser, and Jacob L. Vigdor. 1999. "The Rise and Decline of the American Ghetto." *Journal of Political Economy* 107, no. 3: 455-506.

De la Roca, Jorge, Ingrid Gould Ellen, and Katherine M. O'Regan. 2014. "Race and Neighborhoods in the 21st Century: What Does Segregation Mean Today?" *Regional Science and Urban Economics* 47: 138-51.

Dickerson, Niki T. 2007. "Black Employment, Segregation, and the Social Organization of Metropolitan Labor Markets." *Economic Geography* 83, no. 3: 283-307.

Dickerson vonLockette, Niki T., and Jacqueline Johnson. 2010. "Latino Employment and Residential Segregation in Metropolitan Labor Markets." *Du Bois Review: Social Science Research on Race* 7, no. 1: 151-84.

Diez-Roux, Ana V., Sharon Stein Merkin, Donna Arnett, Lloyd Chambless, Mark Massing, F. Javier Nieto, Paul Sorlie, Moyses Szklo, Herman A. Tyroler, and Robert L. Watson. 2001. "Neighborhood of Residence and Incidence of Coronary Heart Disease." *New England Journal of Medicine* 345, no. 2: 99-106.

Dornbusch, Sanford M., Philip L. Ritter, and Laurence Steinberg. 1991. "Community Influences on the Relation of Family Statuses to Adolescent School Performance: Differences between African Americans and non-Hispanic Whites." *American Journal of Education* 99, no. 4: 543-67.

Duncan, Greg J. 1994. "Families and Neighbors as Sources of Disadvantage in the Schooling Decisions of White and Black Adolescents." *American Journal of Education* 103, no. 1: 20-53.

Duncan, Greg J., and Richard J. Murnane, eds. 2011. *Whither Opportunity?: Rising Inequality, Schools, and Children's Life Chances.* New York: Russell Sage Foundation.

Ellen, Ingrid. 2000. *Sharing America's Neighborhoods: The Prospects for Stable Neighborhood Integration.* Cambridge, MA: Harvard University Press.

Ellen, Ingrid, Keren Horn, Yiwen Kuai, Roman Pazuniak, and Michael David Williams. 2015. "Effect of QAP Incentives on the Location of LIHTC Properties." Washington, DC: US Department of Housing and Urban Development Office of Policy Development and Research.

Ellen, Ingrid, Keren Horn, and Katherine O'Regan. 2012. "Pathways to Integration: Examining Changes in the Prevalence of Racially Integrated Neighborhoods." *Cityscape* 14, no. 3 (2012): 33-53.

Emerson, Michael, Karen Chai, and George Yancey. 2001. "Does Race Matter in Residential Segregation? Exploring the Preferences of White Americans." *American Sociological Review* 66, no. 6: 922-35.

Engel, Kathleen, and Patricia McCoy. 2008. "From Credit Denial to Predatory Lending: The Challenge of Sustaining Minority Homeownership." In *Segregation: The Rising Costs for America*, edited by James Carr and Nandinee Kutty, 81–124. New York: Routledge.

Essene, Ren and William Apgar. 2007. "Understanding Mortgage Market Behavior: Creating Good Mortgage Options for All Americans." Working Paper. Cambridge, MA: Joint Center for Housing Studies of Harvard University.

Farley, Reynolds, Elaine Fielding, and Maria Krysan. 1997. "The Residential Preferences of Blacks and Whites: A Four Metropolis Analysis." *Housing Policy Debate* 8, no. 4: 763–800.

Farley, Reynolds, Howard Schuman, Suzanne Bianchi, Diane Coasanto, and Shirley Hatchett. 1978. "Chocolate Cities, Vanilla Suburbs: Will the Trend toward Racially Separate Communities Continue?" *Social Science Research* 7, no. 4: 319–44.

Farley, Reynolds, Charlotte Steeh, Maria Krysan, Tara Jackson, and Keith Reeves. 1994. "Stereotypes and Segregation: Neighborhoods in the Detroit Area." *American Journal of Sociology* 100, no. 3: 750–80.

Fischer, Claude, Gretchen Stockmayer, Jon Stiles, and Michael Hout. 2004. "Distinguishing the Geographic Levels and Social Dimensions of US Metropolitan Segregation, 1960–2000." *Demography* 41, no. 1: 37–59.

Fossett, Mark. 2006. "Ethnic Preferences, Social Distance Dynamics, and Residential Segregation: Theoretical Explorations Using Simulation Analysis." *Journal of Mathematical Sociology* 30, no. 3–4: 185–273.

Fukuyama, Francis. 1995. *Trust: The Social Virtues and the Creation of Prosperity.* New York: Free Press Paperbacks.

Galster, George. 2002. "An Economic Efficiency Analysis of Deconcentrating Poverty Populations." *Journal of Housing Economics* 11, no. 4: 303–29.

— — —. 2012. *Driving Detroit: The Quest for Respect in the Motor City.* Philadelphia, PA: University of Pennsylvania Press.

— — —. 2013. "Neighborhood Social Mix: Theory, Evidence, and Implications for Policy and Planning." In *Policy, Planning, and People: Promoting Justice in Urban Development*, edited by Naomi Carmon and Susan Fainstein, 307–36. Philadelphia: University of Pennsylvania Press.

GAO (Government Accountability Office). 2010. "Report to Congressional Requesters: HUD Needs to Enhance Its Requirements and Oversight of Jurisdictions' Fair Housing Plans." Washington, DC..

Garner, Catherine L., and Stephen W. Raudenbush. 1991. "Neighborhood Effects on Educational Attainment: A Multilevel Analysis." *Sociology of Education* 64, no. 4: 251–62.

Glaeser, Edward L. 2011. "Rethinking the Federal Bias toward Homeownership." *Cityscape* 13, no. 2: 5–37.

Glaeser, Edward L., and Jacob Vigdor. 2012. *The End of the Segregated Century: Racial Separation in America's Neighborhoods, 1890–2010*. New York: Manhattan Institute for Policy Research.

Graham, Bryan, and Patrick Sharkey. 2013. "Mobility and the Metropolis: How Communities Factor into Economic Mobility." Washington, DC: The Pew Charitable Trusts Economic Mobility Project.

Harris, David R. 1999. "'Property Values Drop When Blacks Move In, Because...': Racial and Socioeconomic Determinants of Neighborhood Desirability." *American Sociological Review* 64, no. 3: 461–79.

Holme, Jennifer Jellison, Amy Stuart Wells, and Anita Tijerina Revilla. 2005. "Learning through Experience: What Graduates Gained by Attending Desegregated High Schools." *Equity & Excellence in Education* 38, no. 1: 14–24.

Hyra, Derek. 2015. "Greasing the Wheels of Social Integration: Housing and Beyond in Mixed-Income, Mixed-Race Neighborhoods." *Housing Policy Debate* 25, no. 4: 785–88.

— — —. 2017. *Race, Class, and Politics in the Cappuccino City.* Chicago: University of Chicago Press.

Iceland, John, Daniel H. Weinberg, and Erika Steinmetz. 2002. "Racial and Ethnic Residential Segregation in the United States: 1980–2000." Report of the US Census Bureau.

Jackson, Kenneth T. 1995. *Crabgrass Frontier: The Suburbanization of the United States.* New York: Oxford University Press.

Jargowsky, Paul. 2013. "Concentration of Poverty in the New Millennium: Changes in the Prevalence, Composition, and Location of High-Poverty Neighborhoods." New York: The Century Foundation.

— — —. 2014. "Segregation, Neighborhoods, and Schools." In *Choosing Homes, Choosing Schools: Residential Segregation and the Search for a Good School*, edited by Annette Lareau and Kimberly Goyette, 97–136. New York: Russell Sage Foundation.

— — —. 2015. "Architecture of Segregation: Civil Unrest, the Concentration of Poverty, and Public Policy." New York: The Century Foundation.

Jencks, Christopher, and Susan E. Mayer. 1990. "The Social Consequences of Growing Up in a Poor Neighborhood." In *Inner-City Poverty in the United States*, edited by Laurence E. Lynn, Jr., and Michael G.H. McGeary, 111–86. Washington, DC: National Academy Press.

Kaldor, Nicholas. 1977. "Capitalism and Industrial Development: Some Lessons from Britain's Experience." *Cambridge Journal of Economics* 1, no. 2: 193–204.

Kawachi, Ichiro, and Lisa F. Berkman, eds. 2003. *Neighborhoods and Health.* New York: Oxford University Press.

Knaap, Gerrit, Stuart Meck, Terry Moore, and Robert Parker. 2007. "Zoning as a Barrier to Multifamily Housing Development." The Planning Advisory Service, Report Number 548. Washington, DC: American Planning Association.

Kneebone, Elizabeth, and Alan Berube. 2014. "Confronting Suburban Poverty in America." Washington, DC: Brookings Institution Press.

Kneebone, Elizabeth, and Natalie Holmes. 2016. "US Concentrated Poverty in the Wake of the Great Recession." Washington, DC: Brookings Institution Press.

Krysan, Maria, and Reynolds Farley. 2002. "The Residential Preferences of Blacks: Do They Explain Persistent Segregation?" *Social Forces* 80, no. 3: 937-80.

Kuznets, Simon. 1955. "Economic Growth and Income Inequality." *The American Economic Review* 45, no. 1: 1-28.

LaVeist, Thomas A. 1993. "Segregation, Poverty, and Empowerment: Health Consequences for African Americans." *The Milbank Quarterly* 71, no. 1: 41-64.

Lee, Barrett, John Iceland, and Chad Farrell. 2013. "Is Ethnoracial Residential Segregation on the Rise? Evidence from Metropolitan and Micropolitan America Since 1980." Report of Project US 2010.

Lens, Michael, and Paavo Monkkonen. 2016. "Do Strict Land Use Regulations Make Metropolitan Areas More Segregated by Income?" *Journal of the American Planning Association* 81, no. 1: 6-21.

Leventhal, Tama, and Jeanne Brooks-Gunn. 2000. "The Neighborhoods They Live In: The Effects of Neighborhood Residence on Child and Adolescent Outcomes." *Psychological Bulletin* 126, no. 2: 309-37.

Logan, John R., and Brian J. Stults. 2011. "The Persistence of Segregation in the Metropolis: New Findings from the 2010 Census." Census Brief prepared for Project US 2010.

Massey, Douglas S. 2008. "Origins of Economic Disparities: The Historical Role of Housing Segregation." In *Segregation: The Rising Costs for America*, edited by James Carr and Nandinee Kutty, 39-80. New York: Routledge.

Massey, Douglas S. and Nancy A. Denton. 1988. "The Dimensions of Residential Segregation." *Social Forces* 67, no. 2: 281-315.

— — — . 1993. *American Apartheid: Segregation and the Making of the Underclass.* Cambridge, MA: Harvard University Press.

Mayorga-Gallo, Sarah. 2014. *Behind the White Picket Fence: Power and Privilege in a Multiethnic Neighborhood.* Chapel Hill, NC: University of North Carolina Press.

McKenzie, Evan, and Jay Ruby. 2002. "Reconsidering the Oak Park Strategy: The Conundrums of Integration." Working Paper. https://astro.temple.edu/~ruby/opp/3qrpt02/finalversion.pdf.

McLoyd, Vonnie C. "Socioeconomic disadvantage and child development." *American Psychologist* 53, no. 2 (1998): 185-204.

Munnell, Alicia H., Geoffrey MB Tootell, Lynn E. Browne, and James McEneaney. 1996. "Mortgage Lending in Boston: Interpreting HMDA Data." *The American Economic Review* 86, no. 1: 25-53.

OECD (Organization for Economic Co-operation and Development). 2015. In *It Together: Why Less Inequality Benefits All.* Paris: OECD Publishing. http://dx.doi.org/10.1787/9789264235120-en.

Oliver, J. Eric. 1999. "The Effects of Metropolitan Economic Segregation on Local Civic Participation." *American Journal of Political Science* 43, no. 1: 186-212.

Oliver, Melvin L., and Thomas M. Shapiro. 2006. *Black Wealth/White Wealth: A New Perspective on Racial Inequality, 10th Anniversary Edition.* New York: Routledge.

Orfield, Gary, and Chungmei Lee. 2005. "Why Segregation Matters: Poverty and Educational Inequality." Cambridge, MA: The Civili Rights Project, Harvard University.

Orfield, Myron. 1997. "Metropolitics: A Regional Agenda for Community and Stability." Washington, DC: Brookings Institution, 1997.

Pastor, Manuel. 2006. "Cohesion and Competitiveness: Business Leadership for Regional Growth and Social Equity." Prepared for the OECD International Conference on Sustainable Cities: Linking Competitiveness with Social Cohesion.

Pastor, Manuel, and Chris Benner. 2008. "Been Down So Long: Weak Market Cities and Regional Equity." In *Retooling for Growth: Building a 21st Century Economy in America's Older Industrial Areas,* edited by Jennifer S. Vey, 89-118. Washington, DC: Brookings Institution Press.

Pastor, Manuel, Jim Sadd, and John Hipp. 2001. "Which Came First? Toxic Facilities, Minority Move-in, and Environmental Justice." *Journal of Urban Affairs* 23, no. 1: 1-21.

Pattillo, Mary. 2008. *Black on the Block: The Politics of Race and Class in the City.* Chicago: University of Chicago Press.

Pendall, Rolf. 2007. "Local Land Use Regulation and the Chain of Exclusion." *Journal of the American Planning Association* 66, no. 2: 125-42.

Pettigrew, Thomas F., and Linda R. Tropp. 2008. "How Does Intergroup Contact Reduce Prejudice? Meta analytic Tests of Three Mediators." *European Journal of Social Psychology* 38, no. 6: 922-34.

Pickett, Kate E., and Michelle Pearl. 2001. "Multilevel Analyses of Neighbourhood Socioeconomic Context and Health Outcomes: A Critical Review." *Journal of Epidemiology and Community Health* 55, no. 2: 111-22.

powell, john a., and Kaloma Cardwell. 2014. "Homeownership, Wealth, and the Production of Racialized Space." In *Homeownership Built to Last: Balancing Access, Affordability, and Risk after the Housing Crisis,* edited by Eric Belsky, Christopher Herbert, and Jennifer Molinsky, 31-49. Washington, DC: Brookings Institution Press.

Putnam, Robert D. 2001. *Bowling Alone.* New York: Simon and Schuster.

— — —. 2007. "E pluribus unum: Diversity and Community in the Twenty First Century." *Scandinavian Political Studies* 30, no. 2: 137-74.

Reardon, Sean. 2011. "Measures of Income Segregation." Working Paper. Stanford University Center on Poverty and Inequality.

Reardon, Sean, and Kendra Bischoff. 2011a. "Growth in the Residential Segregation of Families by Income, 1970-2009." Report prepared for Project US2010.

— — —. 2011b. "Income Inequality and Income Segregation." *American Journal of Sociology* 116, no. 4: 1092-1153.

Reardon, Sean, Lindsay Fox, and Joseph Townsend. 2015. "Neighborhood Income Composition by Household Race and Income, 1990-2009." *Annals of the American Academy of Political and Social Science* 660, no. 1: 78-97.

Rich, Peter. 2017. "Choosing Segregation: The Importance of School Racial Composition in the Housing Choices of White Parents." Working Paper.

Ross, Stephen, and John Yinger. 1999. "Sorting and Voting: A Review of the Literature on Urban Public Finance." In *Handbook of Regional and Urban Economics. Volume 3: Applied Urban Economics*, edited by Edwin S. Mills and Paul Cheshire, 2001-60. Amsterdam: Elsevier Science BV.

Rusk, David. 1993. *Cities Without Suburbs*. Washington, DC: Woodrow Wilson Center Press.

— — —. 2002. "Trends in School Segregation." In *Divided We Fail: Coming Together through School Choice. The Report of The Century Foundation Task Force on the Common School,* edited by Richard Kahlenberg, 61-85. New York: The Century Foundation.

Sampson, Robert J., Jeffrey D. Morenoff, and Thomas Gannon-Rowley. 2002. "Assessing 'Neighborhood Effects': Social Processes and New Directions in Research." *Annual Review of Sociology* 28, no. 1: 443-78.

Schelling, Thomas C. 1971. "Dynamic Models of Segregation." *Journal of Mathematical Sociology* 1, no. 2: 143-86.

Schuman, Howard, Charlotte Steeh, Lawrence Bobo, and Maria Krysan. 1997. *Racial Attitudes in America: Trends and Interpretations.* Rev. ed. Cambridge, MA: Harvard University Press.

Schwartz, Heather. 2010. "Housing Policy is School Policy: Economically Integrative Housing Promotes Academic Success in Montgomery County, Maryland." New York: The Century Foundation.

Schuetz, Jenny. 2006. "Guarding the Town Walls: Mechanisms and Motives for Restricting Multifamily Housing in Massachusetts." Working Paper W06-3. Cambridge, MA: Joint Center for Housing Studies of Harvard University.

Sharkey, Patrick, and Jacob W. Faber. 2014. "Where, When, Why, and for Whom Do Residential Contexts Matter? Moving Away from the Dichotomous Understanding of Neighborhood Effects." *Annual Review of Sociology* 40: 559-79.

Sin, Ray, and Maria Krysan. 2015. "What is Racial Residential Integration? A Research Synthesis, 1950-2013." *Sociology of Race and Ethnicity* 1, no. 4: 467-74.

Squires, Gregory. 2008. "Prospects and Pitfalls of Fair Housing Enforcement Efforts." In *Segregation: The Rising Costs for America*, edited by James Carr and Nandinee Kutty, 307-23. New York: Routledge.

Stolle, Dietlind, Stuart Soroka, and Richard Johnston. 2008. "When Does Diversity Erode Trust? Neighborhood Diversity, Interpersonal Trust and the Mediating Effect of Social Interactions." *Political Studies* 56, no. 1: 57-75.

Tach, Laura. 2009. "More than Bricks and Mortar: Neighborhood Frames, Social Processes, and the Mixed-Income Redevelopment of a Public Housing Project." *City & Community* 8, no. 3: 269-99.

Tach, Laura, Rolf Pendall, and Alexandra Derian. 2004. "Income Mixing Across Scales: Rationale, Trends, Policies, Practice, and Research for More Inclusive Neighborhoods and Metropolitan Areas." Washington, DC: The Urban Institute.

Turner, Margery Austin, and Lynette Rawlings. 2009. "Promoting Neighborhood Diversity: Benefits, Barriers, and Strategies." Washington, DC: The Urban Institute.

Turner, Margery Austin, Rob Santos, Diane K. Levy, Doug Wissoker, Claudia Aranda, and Rob Pitingolo. 2013. "Housing Discrimination against Racial and Ethnic Minorities, 2012." Washington, DC: US Department of Housing and Urban Development.

Turner, Margery, Raymond Struyk, and John Yinger. 1991. "Housing Discrimination Study Synthesis." Washington, DC: US Department of Housing and Urban Development.

Voith, Richard. 1998. "Do Suburbs Need Cities?" *Journal of Regional Science* 38, no. 3: 445-64.

Watson, Tara. 2009. "Inequality and the Measurement of Residential Segregation by Income in American Neighborhoods." *Review of Income and Wealth* 55, no. 3: 820-44.

Wienk, Ronald E., Clifford E. Reid, John C. Simonson, and Frederick J. Eggers. 1979. "Measuring Discrimination in American Housing Markets: The Housing Market Practices Survey." Washington, DC: US Department of Housing and Urban Development.

Williams, David R., and Chiquita Collins. 2001. "Racial Residential Segregation: A Fundamental Cause of Racial Disparities in Health." *Public Health Reports* 116, no. 5.

Wodtke, Geoffrey T., David J. Harding, and Felix Elwert. 2011. "Neighborhood Effects in Temporal Perspective: The Impact of Long-Term Exposure to Concentrated Disadvantage on High School Graduation." *American Sociological Review* 76, no. 5: 713-36.

Wolch, Jennifer R., Jason Byrne, and Joshua P. Newell. 2014. "Urban Green Space, Public Health, and Environmental Justice: The Challenge of Making Cities 'Just Green Enough.'" *Landscape and Urban Planning* 125: 234-44.

Zubrinsky, Camille L., and Lawrence Bobo. 1996. "Prismatic Metropolis: Race and Residential Segregation in the City of the Angels." *Social Science Research* 25, no. 4: 335–74.

Endnotes

1   These figures slightly understate the extent of change over time, as the black and Asian population totals for the 1970 Census include individuals who also identify as Hispanic. The Asian population for the 1970 estimate also includes Pacific Islander individuals, who have been excluded from the 2015 figure.

2   See Appendix B of Iceland, Weinberg, and Steinmetz (2002) or Massey and Denton (1988) for more complete discussions of alternative measures. The concept of "neighborhood" is commonly defined to be the census tract, although studies of segregation may also use the more fine-grained geography of either blocks or block groups.

3   Glaeser and Vigdor (2012).

4   Logan and Stults (2011).

5   Logan and Stults (2011); De la Roca, Ellen, and O'Regan (2014).

6   Logan and Stults (2011).

7   Ellen, Horn, and O'Regan (2012). Tracts are defined to be white-mixed minority if at least 20 percent of neighborhood residents are white and the minority shares for at least two of the other groups exceed 20 percent.

8   Ellen, Horn, and O'Regan (2012).

9   Lee, Iceland, and Farrell (2014).

10   Sin and Krysan (2015); Ellen (2000).

11   Tach (2009); Hyra (2017).

12   Hyra (2015)

13   Tach, Pendall, and Derian (2014).

14   Reardon, Fox, and Townsend (2015).

15   Bischoff and Reardon (2014).

16   See Reardon (2011) for a more detailed discussion of the rank-order information theory index and alternative measures of income segregation.

17   Reardon and Bischoff (2011b); Fischer et al. (2004).

18   Watson (2009).

19   Reardon and Bischoff (2011b).

20   This pattern is mirrored in findings about the effects of land use controls, which are associated with higher levels of residential segregation among high-income households but not to segregation of the poor. See Lens and Monkkonen (2016).

21   Bischoff and Reardon (2014).

22   Bischoff and Reardon (2014).

23   This statistic is based on the rank-order index (H) using the 1970–2000 Decennial Censuses and the 2005–2009 American Community Survey for metropolitan areas with at least 500,000 residents. See Bischoff and Reardon (2014).

24   Reardon and Bischoff (2011a); Bischoff and Reardon (2014).

25   Jargowsky (2014); Sharkey and Faber (2014); Logan and Stults (2011); Bayer, McMillan, and Rueben (2004).

26   Logan and Stults (2011).

27   Reardon, Fox, and Townsend (2015).

28   Carr and Kutty (2008).

29   Kneebone and Holmes (2016); Jargowsky (2015).

30   Jargowsky (2015).

31   Ibid.

32   Jargowsky (2013).

33   Kneebone and Holmes (2016); Kneebone and Berube (2014).

34   For a more exhaustive review of the history and causes of residential segregation in the United States, see Massey and Denton (1988).

35   Jackson (1985).

36   powell and Cardwell (2015); Jackson (1985).

37   Massey (2008).

38   In one instance in 1963, a mob of 600 whites descended on a Detroit-area home rumored to have been purchased by a black man and his pregnant wife, throwing stones and bottles. The terrified owner could not persuade the local police chief and deputy to act until his lawyer produced documents to show that he had merely rented the home to a white man who had hired two black men as movers, one of whom had brought along his pregnant wife. See Galster (2012).

39   Massey and Denton (1993).

40   Wienk et al. (1979).

41   Turner, Struyk, and Yinger (1991).

42   Significant disparities appear for black, Hispanic, and Asian rental inquiries and for black and Asian home purchase inquiries. See Turner et al. (2013).

43   Engel and McCoy (2008).

44   Munnell et al. (1996).

45   Calem, Gillen, and Wachter (2004).

46   Essene and Apgar (2007); Apgar and Calder (2005).

47   Turner and Rawlings (2009); Crowder and Krysan (2016).

48   Ellen (2000); Zubrinsky and Bobo (1996).

49   Emerson, Chai, and Yancey (2001). While it is tempting to think that such attitudes might be less prevalent among the diverse Millennial generation, recent survey evidence suggests that white Millennials' racial attitudes are at best only slightly more tolerant than those of white Baby Boomers. Citing the General Social Survey, the *Washington Post* reports that 15 percent of white Millennials oppose living in majority-black neighborhoods, compared to 20 percent of white Baby Boomers. See Clement (2015).

50   Krysan and Farley (2002); Farley et al. (1978); Farley et al. (1994); Schuman et al. (1997); Farley, Fielding, and Krysan (1997).

51   Krysan and Farley (2002).

52   Rich (2017).

53   Fossett (2006); W. Clark, (1991); Schelling (1971).

54   Ellen (2000).

55   Zubrinsky and Bobo (1996); Ellen (2000).

56   Ross and Yinger (1999).

57   Pendall (2000).

58   Schuetz (2006).

59   Lens and Monkonnen (2016); Glaeser (2011); Knaap et al. (2007).

60   Glaeser and Vigdor (2012).

61   Couture and Handbury (2015).

62   Kneebone and Berube (2014).

63 Jencks and Mayer (1990); Cutler and Glaeser (1997); Brooks-Gunn (1997); Leventhal and Brooks-Gunn (2000); and Sampson, Morenoff, and Gannon-Rowley (2002).

64 G. Orfield and Lee (2005), 5.

65 Card and Rothstein (2007).

66 Brooks-Gunn et al. (1993); R. Clark (1992); Dornbusch, Ritter, and Steinberg (1991); Duncan (1994); Garner and Raudenbush (1991).

67 Crowder and South (2011); Wodtke, Harding, and Elwert (2011).

68 Chetty and Hendren (2015).

69 Rusk (2002); Schwartz (2010).

70 Leventhal and Brooks-Gunn (2000); Burdick-Will et al. (2011); Duncan and Murnane (2011).

71 Massey and Denton (1993), 14.

72 Chetty et al. (2014), Massey and Denton (1993); Cutler, Glaeser, and Vigdor (1999); Graham and Sharkey (2013).

73 Chetty et al. (2014)'s geographical unit of analysis is the "commuting zone," defined as "geographical aggregations of counties that are similar to metro areas but cover the entire US, including rural areas."

74 Dickerson vonLockette and Johnson (2010); Dickerson (2007).

75 LaVeist (1993); Aneshensel and Sucoff (1996); Diez-Roux et al. (2001); Pickett and Pearl (2001); Kawachi and Berkman (2003).

76 Aneshensel and Sucoff (1996).

77 Ellen (2000).

78 Acevedo-Garcia et al. (2008).

79 Williams and Collins (2001), 116.

80 Pastor, Sadd, and Hipp (2001).

81 Wolch, Byrne, and Newell (2014).

82 Turner and Rawlings (2009), 3. See also Harris (2009); M. Orfield (1997); Rusk (1993); Carr and Kutty (2008).

83 Pettigrew and Tropp (2008).

84 For a discussion of costs for economic performance, see Fukuyama (1995). For costs to democracy, see Uslaner (2002).

85 Putnam (2000); Putnam (2007).

86 Stolle, Soroka, and Johnston (2008); Putnam (2007).

87 Massey and Denton (1993)

88 Ibid.

89 Massey and Denton (1993), 14.

90 J. Oliver (1999).

91 Ibid., 206.

92 Ibid., 206.

93 Benner and Pastor (2015a), 25. See also Kaldor (1977); Kuznets (1955).

94 Aghion, Caroli, and Garcia-Penalosa (1998), 1617.

95 Bénabou (1996), 249.

96 Berg, Ostry, and Zettelmeyer (2012), 150.

97 OECD (2015), 15.

98 Benner and Pastor (2015b); Berg, Ostry, and Zettelmeyer (2012).

99 Benner and Pastor (2016), 7.

100 Rusk (1993); Pastor (2006); Pastor and Benner (2008); Voith (1998).

101 See Galster (2002) and Galster (2013) for more detailed discussions of the rationales for public action to foster greater integration.

102 Mayorga-Gallo (2014); Hyra (2015).

103 Pattillo (2008).

104 Squires (2008); Turner and Rawlings (2009).

105 GAO (2010).

106 Holme, Wells, and Revilla (2005).

107 M. Oliver and Shapiro (2006).

108 Ellen et al. (2015).

109 Collinson and Ganong (2016).

110 For such a discussion, see Andrews et al. (2012).

Appendix Table 1: Average Neighborhood Composition by Race and Ethnicity across All US Census Tracts and by Metropolitan Area Population.

	Metropolitan Areas by CBSA Population Rank					
	All Tracts	10 Largest	11-50	51-150	150+	Non-CBSA
All Individuals						
% White	62%	53%	62%	64%	72%	76%
% Black	12%	14%	13%	11%	10%	10%
% Hispanic	17%	22%	16%	17%	13%	9%
% Asian	5%	8%	6%	4%	2%	1%
% Other/multiethnic	3%	2%	3%	3%	4%	4%
White Individuals						
% White	76%	67%	74%	77%	83%	86%
% Black	7%	8%	8%	7%	6%	6%
% Hispanic	10%	15%	11%	10%	7%	5%
% Asian	4%	8%	5%	3%	2%	0%
% Other/multiethnic	3%	2%	3%	3%	3%	3%
Black Individuals						
% White	35%	23%	36%	44%	51%	52%
% Black	44%	49%	45%	39%	37%	40%
% Hispanic	14%	21%	12%	11%	8%	5%
% Asian	4%	5%	4%	3%	1%	0%
% Other/multiethnic	3%	2%	3%	3%	3%	2%
Hispanic Individuals						
% White	36%	27%	40%	37%	51%	61%
% Black	10%	13%	10%	7%	6%	7%
% Hispanic	45%	51%	40%	49%	38%	28%
% Asian	6%	7%	7%	4%	2%	1%
% Other/multiethnic	3%	2%	3%	3%	3%	3%
Asian Individuals						
% White	47%	42%	48%	49%	66%	74%
% Black	9%	9%	8%	8%	7%	7%
% Hispanic	19%	22%	17%	17%	12%	8%
% Asian	22%	24%	22%	18%	10%	5%
% Other/multiethnic	4%	3%	4%	8%	6%	6%
Other/Multiracial Individuals						
% White	56%	47%	57%	56%	63%	56%
% Black	11%	16%	12%	10%	7%	4%
% Hispanic	15%	22%	16%	15%	10%	5%
% Asian	7%	10%	8%	8%	3%	1%
% Other/multiethnic	12%	5%	6%	11%	18%	34%
Population	316515020	83924977	89221741	58392185	66479066	18497052
% of Population	100%	27%	28%	18%	21%	6%

Source: JCHS tabulations of ACS 5-year estimates 2011-2015. N=72,424 census tracts.

Appendix Table 2: Average Neighborhood Composition by Household Income across All US Census Tracts and by Metropolitan Area Population.

	Metropolitan Areas by CBSA Population Rank					
	All Tracts	10 Largest	11-50	51-150	150+	Non-CBSA
All Households						
% <$20,000	18%	16%	16%	18%	20%	23%
% $20,000-$49,999	29%	26%	28%	30%	32%	35%
% $50,000-$99,999	30%	29%	30%	31%	31%	29%
% $100,000-$149,999	13%	15%	14%	13%	11%	9%
% $150,000+	10%	15%	11%	9%	6%	4%
Households with Income <$20,000						
% <$20,000	25%	24%	24%	26%	26%	27%
% $20,000-$49,999	32%	29%	31%	33%	33%	35%
% $50,000-$99,999	27%	26%	27%	27%	27%	27%
% $100,000-$149,999	10%	11%	10%	9%	9%	8%
% $150,000+	6%	10%	7%	5%	4%	3%
Households with Income $20,000-$49,999						
% <$20,000	20%	18%	18%	20%	21%	24%
% $20,000-$49,999	32%	29%	31%	33%	34%	36%
% $50,000-$99,999	29%	29%	30%	30%	30%	29%
% $100,000-$149,999	11%	13%	12%	11%	10%	8%
% $150,000+	7%	11%	8%	6%	5%	4%
Households with Income <$50,000-$99,999						
% <$20,000	16%	14%	14%	16%	18%	22%
% $20,000-$49,999	28%	25%	27%	30%	32%	34%
% $50,000-$99,999	32%	31%	33%	33%	32%	30%
% $100,000-$149,999	14%	16%	15%	13%	11%	9%
% $150,000+	10%	14%	11%	8%	6%	4%
Households with Income <$100,000-$149,999						
% <$20,000	13%	11%	12%	13%	16%	21%
% $20,000-$49,999	25%	21%	23%	26%	30%	34%
% $50,000-$99,999	31%	29%	32%	32%	32%	30%
% $100,000-$149,999	17%	19%	18%	17%	14%	11%
% $150,000+	14%	19%	15%	12%	8%	5%
Households with Income $150,000 or more						
% <$20,000	11%	9%	10%	11%	15%	21%
% $20,000-$49,999	21%	17%	20%	23%	28%	33%
% $50,000-$99,999	28%	26%	29%	30%	32%	30%
% $100,000-$149,999	18%	19%	19%	17%	14%	10%
% $150,000+	23%	28%	23%	18%	11%	6%
Households	116926311	29572546	33193208	21663498	25302450	7194610
% of All Households	100%	25%	28%	19%	22%	6%

Source: JCHS tabulations of ACS 5-year estimates 2011-2015. N=72,247 census tracts.

Integration as a Means of Restoring Democracy and Opportunity

SHERYLL CASHIN

Georgetown University

> "This innocent country set you down in a ghetto in which in fact it intended that you should perish... the heart of the matter is here, and the root of my dispute with my country."
>
> — James Baldwin, *The Fire Next Time*

I am a law professor, not a social scientist. In my academic discipline, I am allowed to have intuitions or theories for why things are, even if I do not have empirical proof. In that spirit, this essay presents my intuitions and some social science research about the damage that segregation does to individuals and the nation. Explaining the role of physical separation in undermining race relations, democracy, and opportunity also makes the case *for* integration.

Intentional effort at integration and inclusion is necessary for fixing what is broken in this country. I begin by explaining the role of racist ideology and propaganda about black and brown bodies in institutionalizing segregation. I then turn to the consequences of segregation for politics, opportunity, and human relations, exploring the very difficult challenges to creating public support for integration. People of all colors often desire racial comfort and maximum opportunity. This and fear, particularly of poor black people, are at the heart of the matter. In the final section of this essay I speculate about the possibilities for transcending fear and explain the emergence of "culturally dexterous" whites that have less need for the racial comfort of a predominantly white neighborhood. In my dreams, I imagine a future in which coalitions of progressive people of color and culturally dexterous whites fight together for the public policies that promote and sustain integrated neighborhoods and schools. At bottom, I hope to show in this essay why such integration is necessary to restoring both democracy and opportunity in America.

WHAT IS BROKEN: THE ROLE OF RACIST IDEOLOGY AND PROPAGANDA

Donald Trump began his campaign for the presidency with a speech that cast Mexicans as rapists, part of his bid to ingratiate himself with voters who dislike or fear undocumented immigration. During a debate, he associated "the blacks" with "inner cities," which he described as "a disaster education-wise, job-wise, safety-wise, in every way possible."[1] Both of these stereotypes, of Mexicans and African-Americans, are premised, in differing ways, on divergence of these groups from a presumed norm of dominant American whiteness.

That norm, sometimes unspoken or dog-whistled, sometimes stated plainly by avowed white supremacists or nationalists, was constructed and reified for centuries. It predates the old Jim Crow. The ideology of white supremacy — created and propagated by patriarchs — required separation in all forms of social relations. The ideology told whites in particular that they could not marry, sleep with, live near, play checkers with, much less ally in politics with a black person. It built a wall that supremacists believed was necessary to elevate whiteness above all else. A dominant whiteness constructed by law and often backed by racial terror was embedded in people's habits.

This ideology was the organizing plank for regimes of oppression that were essential to American capitalism and expansion — from slavery, to indigenous and Mexican conquest, to exclusion of Asian and other immigrants, and later to Jim Crow. Lawgivers constructed whiteness as the preferred identity for citizen and country and then set about protecting this fictional white purity from mixture. Segregation law began with penalizing interracial sex in the seventeenth century. Over the next three centuries, our nation was caught in a seemingly endless cycle of political and economic elites using law to separate light and dark people who might love one another, or revolt together against supremacist regimes created by the economic elite.[2]

As Gunnar Myrdal would write in his classic treatise on America race relations, *An American Dilemma*, the central animating rationale for the regime of Jim Crow segregation was fear of black men having sex with white women.[3] It was easy to use this ruse to garner widespread support for segregation, and false accusations against black men would regularly incite lynching. The ideology of supremacy animated not only Jim Crow but also eugenics laws authorizing state-enforced sterilization of undesired populations, as well as a 1924 federal law that banned or severely restricted immigration for all nationalities except people from northern Europe. Limiting immigration of colored and olive people, forcing sterilization, and forcing separation by Jim Crow laws and private practices would continue for much of the twentieth century, and all of it redounded to the benefit of white upper classes.[4]

The Supreme Court's landmark case of *Village of Euclid v. Ambler Realty* was decided in 1926. In it the court condoned what is now referred to as "Euclidian zoning," endorsing the idea that certain uses of land, like duplexes, were "parasitic" on single-family homes and the people who lived there and therefore should be separated from these idealized neighborhoods. The court had banned racial zoning in *Buchanan v. Warley* in 1917, but Euclidian zoning and other practices like racially restrictive covenants and unregulated racial discrimination would accomplish the widely held goal of residential racial segregation. Physical segregation, like the vanquished regime of anti-miscegenation, is also a legacy of our nation's multi-century effort to construct and insulate whiteness. The history of orchestration and intention behind physical segregation is beyond the scope of this essay but has been told by many.[5] Suffice it to say that the ideology of supremacy animated this orchestration, and the architecture of separation endures. As Maria Krysan and co-authors argue in their paper for this symposium, both discrimination against renters and buyers and racially biased preferences by those seeking housing contribute to segregation. Race continues to shape housing markets, as do weak antidiscrimination enforcement and exclusionary zoning in which affluent towns intentionally prevent affordable housing, even market-rate apartments, from invading their turf. These practices and zip code profiling, which steers commercial and retail investment toward overwhelmingly white, poverty-free areas, enable current masters of the universe, and others with choices, to insulate themselves from populations they do not want to deal with.[6]

Racial polarization and contestation remain. Gerrymandering segregates politics. The average Republican congressperson represents a district that mirrors the overwhelmingly white America of 1972, while the average Democrat represents a district that looks like the projected diversity of America in 2030.[7] The end result is a clash of distinctly different worldviews — the difference, say, between those who resented and those who loved a Super Bowl commercial featuring "America the Beautiful" sung in seven different languages. In a segregated nation where many people and the leaders who represent them get little practice at pluralism, democracy is broken.

THE CONSEQUENCES FOR OPPORTUNITY

Segregation not only damages democracy, it undermines opportunity. The American dream is also broken for many in the United States. As underscored in the framing paper for this symposium and the recent work of economists and others, place, where one lives, greatly affects opportunity. Only about 30 percent of black and Latino families reside in middle-class neighborhoods where less than half of the people are poor. Meanwhile, more than 60 percent of white and Asian families live in environs where most of their neighbors are not poor. The majority of whites and Asians live in neighborhoods with a poverty rate below 14 percent. As urban sociologist John Logan put it, "It is especially true for African Americans and Hispanics that their neighborhoods are often served by the worst-performing schools, suffer the highest crime rates, and have the least valuable housing stock in the metropolis."[8]

Five decades of social science research demonstrate what common sense tells us. Neighborhoods with high poverty, limited employment, underperforming schools, distressed housing, and violent crime depress life outcomes. They create a closed loop of systemic disadvantage such that failure is common and success aberrational. Even the most motivated child may not be able to overcome unsafe streets, family dysfunction, a lack of mentors and networks that lead to jobs and internships, or the general miasma of depression that can pervade high-poverty places. One study found that a high-poverty neighborhood virtually guarantees downward mobility.[9] Living in a severely disadvantaged neighborhood impedes the development of verbal cognitive ability in children, correlates to a loss of a year of learning for black students, and lowers high school graduation rates by as much as 20 percent.[10] Most of the families living in urban, high-poverty neighborhoods have been stuck there for generations.[11]

At the other extreme, those privileged to live in high-opportunity neighborhoods rise easily on the benefits of exceptional schools and social networks. Anyone who has spent time in high-opportunity quarters knows intuitively what this means — the habits you observe, the people and ideas you are exposed to, the books you are motivated to read. Segregation of the highly educated has increased even faster than that of the affluent. As of 2009, according to census data, only seventeen counties in America had a population in which more than half are college educated. College graduates living in America's most highly educated metro areas are more residentially isolated than African Americans.[12]

The same forces that create geographic disadvantage for many blacks and Latinos also disadvantage struggling white people. In an American metropolis stratified into areas of low, medium, and high opportunity, place is a disadvantage for anyone who cannot afford to buy a home in a premium neighborhood.[13] One study found that only 42 percent of American families now live in middle-income neighborhoods, down from 65 percent in 1970.[14] This is due to the rising segregation of the affluent and the poor from everyone else. As the framing paper discusses, income segregation has grown fastest among black and Hispanic families, and high- income families of all races are now much less likely to have middle- or low-income neighbors. Concentrated poverty neighborhoods and the number of people living in them have risen dramatically since 1970. And concentrated poverty is growing fastest in the suburbs.[15]

What happens in a society in which income and wealth are increasingly concentrated in certain neighborhoods? Bastions of affluence tend to create disadvantage elsewhere. Douglas Massey invokes Charles Tilley's phraseology and calls it "opportunity hoarding." Massey argues that where social boundaries conform to geographic ones, the processes of social stratification that come naturally to human beings become much more efficient and effective. In his words: "If out-group members are spatially segregated from in-group members, then the latter are put in good position to use their social power to create institutions and practices that channel resources away from the places where out-group members live." The same power can be used to "direct resources systemically toward in-group areas."[16] Segregation puts affluent, high-opportunity places in direct competition with lower-opportunity communities for finite public and private resources. And affluent jurisdictions are winning, sometimes because they are subsidized by everyone else.[17]

Rising geographic separation of the affluent, then, appears to contribute to rising inequality.[18] It is not surprising that both income inequality and income segregation rose at the same time. As those with power to set wages for others became ever more residentially isolated from people who really need their paychecks, CEO-to-worker pay rose precipitously, increasing 875 percent between 1978 and 2012.[19]

Meanwhile, places with a sizeable middle class that enable poor families to live among them have higher rates of upward mobility for poor children.[20] And yet segregation, and the parochial benefits that come with it for those living in poverty-free havens, undermine the willingness of many to try integration. As one town councilman in a distressed older suburb bemoaned, "We've lost that sense as Americans that we can all live together and that's part of what's made the inequality in this country so crass and gross. People don't want to be around each other anymore."[21]

As the framing paper sets out, integration produces ample social and economic benefits, including reducing racism. While there are many fairness arguments for increasing equity or reducing inequality of opportunity between advantaged and disadvantaged places and people, advocates of equity must acknowledge that segregation is an underlying cause of the political constraints to procuring more equity. Affluent people concentrated in advantaged enclaves don't volunteer to pay more taxes to invest in other people's children or other jurisdictions' needs. At minimum, integration and equity advocates should acknowledge that the ends of equity and integration are not mutually exclusive. Coalitions to support integration are likely to have many natural reasons for supporting more equitable investments in disadvantaged places.

Integration weariness is common among black folk, perhaps as much as integration wariness or avoidance is common among non-dexterous whites (as I describe in the next section). Integration weariness on the part of African Americans may stem from being tired of being disappointed by an America that has not lived up to the ideals of *Brown v. Board of Education*. It may also stem from exhaustion with anti-black micro- and macro-aggressions. Whatever the source of integration weariness, by whoever harbors it, here is a hard truth: we can't fix what is broken in politics, in human relations, in disparate opportunity, without addressing a fundamental underlying cause: segregation. There are many public policies that help promote integration and have been shown to produce successes, including inclusionary zoning (Montgomery County, MD) and magnet schools (The Sheff Movement, Hartford metropolitan area). What is missing is more political will, and there are pointed reasons for this lack of support.

THE CHALLENGES TO CREATING PUBLIC SUPPORT FOR INTEGRATION

Dr. Robin DiAngelo, an anti-racism scholar and educator, coined the term "white fragility" to describe "a state in which even a minimum amount of racial stress becomes intolerable, triggering a range of defensive moves." Segregation fuels it. Most whites in America live in majority-white settings. As the framing paper points out, the average white person lives in a neighborhood that is 76 percent white. For segregated whites, their social environment "protects and insulates them from race-based stress," DiAngelo writes. Such insulation "builds white expectations for racial comfort while at the same time lowering the ability to tolerate racial stress." "Racial stress," she continues, "results from an interruption to what is racially familiar."[22]

We don't like to admit that the ideology of white supremacy is still with us in the expectations that many whites have. Expectation of racial comfort, of white dominance, may explain why most whites still state preferences for majority-white neighborhoods. As the framing paper points out, in 2001, the threshold at which whites would likely avoid purchasing a home in a neighborhood was 15 percent blackness. Hopefully, whites' current capacity for neighborhood exposure to black people has risen. But whatever the threshold for avoidance is today, it is important to consider the *reasons* for such avoidance. Black people remain the group all non-blacks are least interested in integrating with. Why? Allow me to speculate.

Social psychologists have documented implicit associations of blackness with criminality.[23] While the stereotype of the black male sexual predator helped justify the old Jim Crow, I believe a modern stereotype of the "ghetto" dweller or "ghetto thug" is part of the spoken and unspoken subtext of fair housing debates. There is a spatial dimension to anti-black stereotyping that goes beyond class. Residents of hyper-segregated neighborhoods are more likely than other groups to be black.[24] Hyper-segregation facilitates a unique form of othering. To be "ghetto" has a widespread negative connotation in America, one that many if not most people of all colors disassociate from.

There are codes of the street, incubated in concentrated black poverty, that some black males feel pressured to adopt as a mode of personal survival.[25] Such codes, participated in by a small subset of black urban residents, glorified in gangsta' rap, propagated in near-constant news stories about urban crime, may explain widespread fear of black males. My mild-mannered, slight, conventionally-dressed, Harvard-educated husband watches women cross the street when he encounters them on the sidewalk. An African-American man who lives in a tony suburb speaks of the dramatic difference in how he is treated when he walks the neighborhood with and without his family, even among neighbors who know him. When he walks solo, he says, he becomes a "thug."[26] Only a relatively small number of census tracts might be called a "ghetto," whether by folk who live elsewhere who are casting aspersions or by residents themselves who may use the term to describe their reality. (I have heard both).

Despite its European origins, in the United States the word is associated not just with concentrated poverty but also with blackness. Demographers use a threshold of 40 percent poverty to define concentrated poverty and, as the framing paper points out, the number of these census tracts has risen from about 2500 in the year 2000 to 4400 in 2009–2013. Below is a table of extreme poverty census tracts with some of the features associated with ghettoes — very high levels of household and child poverty, violence, single motherhood, boarded or vacant properties, to name some of the potential indicia. The table underscores that not all of the most distressed, concentrated poverty census tracts are predominantly black, though many of them are. Such places, small in number, loom large in the American psyche and in American race relations. They contribute to a continued fear and loathing about black bodies, and sometimes middle- and upper-class black people are participating in the othering. Even in Washington, DC, where Democrats outnumber Republicans by about 12 to 1, and where African Americans for many years controlled government, political leaders pursued punitive laws that fueled mass incarceration and filled DC prisons with young black men.[27] The same black political leadership was also slow to adopt an inclusionary zoning ordinance and pursued policies that displaced many poor residents from the city.[28]

Concentrated poverty, particularly of the black kind, contributes to the flight of others with choices to perceived higher ground.[29] Families with children are especially motivated to avoid high-poverty schools or neighborhoods, such is the fear that a child will be caught in the undertow of downward mobility associated with concentrated poverty and described above in the section on disparate opportunity.[30] Elsewhere I have described the intentional public policies that created concentrated black poverty.[31] Had governments not intentionally created black ghettoes, I suspect we would be much further along in the project of dismantling Jim Crow. If you, the reader, can indulge yourself in the thought experiment of a nation without ghettoes, perhaps you can also imagine the wider range of choices people of all classes and races might have for schools and neighborhoods in a ghetto-free nation. Blackness would be less likely to be associated, consciously or unconsciously, with hysterical negatives. Policies and preferences of avoidance might be less common and individuals and institutions less risk averse, more willing to try to enter or invite robust diversity. Above all, poor

Table 1. Sample US neighborhoods with high levels of poverty, violence, and other features possibly associated with "ghetto."

Census Tract Number	Neighborhood	Percentage Poor (Source: 2014 American Community Survey, Census Bureau)	Violent Crime Rate Per 1000 people (Source: Uniformed Crime Report/ local precinct reports)	Ethnic Makeup (2010 Census)	Percentage of Households run by Single Mothers (Source: 2010 Census)	Kids in Poverty (ACS)	Vacant Houses (American Housing Survey)	Percentage of Workers in Service Sector (American Community Survey)
540101	Altgeld Gardens, Chicago, Ill	60.80%	99.02	94% African American	62.20%	76%	37.40%	54.70%
170200	Baltimore, MD (State Center Metro Around N MLK Blvd)	54.60%	91.03	91% African-American	3.9%	7.40%	17.20%	61.7
357300	Indianapolis, (In South of Fountain Square)	40.80%	84.30	29.8 % African-American 12% Hispanic 58% white	22%	67.5%	15.30%	47.20%
0029000	Toledo, OH (LaGrange St./ Water St.)	82.70%	77.30	24% white 55% black 26% Hispanic	26.6%	89.20%	17.30%	26.10%
001000	Rockford, Ill (Kishwaukee St.)	62.70%	75.80	44% African-American, 22% white, 17% hispanic	55.8%	78%	42.20%	38.50%
114300	Cleveland, OH, (Kinsman Rd)	87.10%	70.30	98% African-American	66.50%	88.10%	27.10%	38.60%
026900	Toledo, OH (LaGrange St./ Water St.)	82.70%	77.30	24% white 55% black 26% Hispanic	26.6%	89.20%	17.30%	26.10%
009801	Rockford, Ill (Kishwaukee St.)	62.70%	75.80	44% African-american 22% White 17% Hispanic	55.8%	78%	42.20%	38.50%
500400	E. St. Louis (Caseyville Ave)	48.40%	66.27	97.7% African-American	55.6%	97.50%	22.90%	34.60%
000500	Anniston, Alabama	58.50%	62.57	91.7% African American	31.6%	80.90%	38.9	37.70%

black people might be more apt to be seen as three-dimensional human beings, worthy of the moniker "citizen."

Of course, poor black people are not the only subgroup subject to stereotyping and exclusion. A small minority of poor whites, 7.5 percent according to the framing paper, live in concentrated poverty, compared to a quarter of all poor blacks and 17.4 percent of poor Hispanics. With some suburbanization of concentrated poverty, and the winnowing out of working- and middle-class jobs in many places, there is an emerging conception of poor white dysfunction, of a white underclass that is also defined by geography. They live apart from and are not well understood by coastal elites.[32] This is part of the distinct cultural binary that animated the 2016 election.

Those who live far away from distressed communities — whether rural, suburban, or inner-city — can develop a lack of empathy for struggling people, a sense that they are "deplorable" and undeserving of policy interventions or real inclusion. Segregation, then, is both a symptom and a cause of race and class tensions in America.

TRANSCENDING FEAR: THE RISE OF THE "CULTURALLY DEXTEROUS"

Given the enduring effectiveness of divide-and-conquer, dog-whistling politics, I have little hope of a class-consciousness arising to unify struggling people of all colors. I am, however, optimistic about the possibilities for creating ascending coalitions of culturally dexterous whites and progressive people of color that could fight together for integration and equity in the regions where they live.

Elsewhere I have defined "cultural dexterity" as the quality of being able to enter very diverse settings and feel comfortable, even when outnumbered by people of a different race or ethnicity. It requires effort, a willingness to work at learning about and being immersed in someone else's culture. And for those who undertake the effort, the process of honing cultural dexterity is never-ending. Rising interracial intimacy, immigration, demographic change, generational replacement, and increasing geographic diversity — all of these forces will have a powerful *cumulative* impact on our future. Because of these forces, the ranks of those who live with diversity and are forced to acquire dexterity will continue to expand, perhaps exponentially, in coming decades.[33]

The cultural dominance of integrators will be most palpable in dense metropolitan areas, where intense diversity will be inescapable. Emerging global neighborhoods, places where no particular group or culture dominates, will contribute to the rise of the culturally dexterous. An influx of global aspirants changes the complexion of a former white-flight suburb, and many whites decide to stay rather than escape to whiter exurbs. In the 50 largest US metro areas, 44 percent of suburban residents currently live in multiracial, multiethnic suburbs.[34] And younger whites are moving to cities that their parents and grandparents fled decades before. With proximity comes more opportunity for practicing pluralism and creating new norms of inclusion. In these spaces, the culturally dexterous could invest in public institutions that foster inclusive opportunity because they value diverse peoples and must make diversity work. This vision is distinct from mere gentrification borne of population movement and displacement. It is premised on the hope that those who value diversity will intentionally create programs, especially housing policies, and new civic institutions that actively promote robust inclusion of the poor, middle class, and affluent of all colors. Segregation and supremacy were pursued with aggressive intention for three centuries in this country. Persistent structures and practices of exclusion and non-dexterous mindsets will not be overcome without conscious effort to dismantle and replace them and to instill a new culture of inclusion.

Integration, pursued with care and intention, enables the willing, privileged integrationist to live in a diverse society without fear and enables poor and struggling people to access opportunity rather than be excluded from it. As an affluent citizen who lives within walking distance of subsidized housing and sends my children to a diverse public charter school where a quarter of the children are poor, I can attest to the benefits of such robust inclusion for my family and other families. At our school and in our mixed-income residential environs, people of all races and classes get practice dealing with each other, build trust and advocate together for policies and investments that will improve our schools and neighborhood. Poor black people inhabit both the school and the neighborhood, and no one thinks of them as scary aliens to be avoided.

Some communities already approximate the saner, inclusive spaces of the future. More than 400 counties, cities, or towns require or strongly incentivize new housing development to be mixed-income and 5 to 10 percent of the US population currently lives in these communities.[35] Integrated places typically result from permissive zoning laws that allow more density in residential development, including apartments and town houses, and they exhibit lower levels of racial prejudice. Integrated jurisdictions like Montgomery County, Maryland; West Hartford, Connecticut; and Portland, Oregon also tend to invest more in education and offer more social mobility for poor children. In contrast, segregated communities tend to have highly restrictive zoning that limits density and elevated levels of racial prejudice.[36]

Rising cultural dexterity may not end the exclusion and marginalization of the black and Latino poor. Accepting a majority-minority nation is one thing, ending plutocracy and ghettoes is quite another. While half of whites may be culturally dexterous by 2040, some unknowable portion will not. Some political liberalization will happen as a result of demographic changes and rising dexterity. However, concerted effort to mobilize multiracial constituencies will be necessary. No jurisdiction will enact an inclusionary zoning ordinance, welcome public transportation from less advantaged places, invest more in the disadvantaged side of town, without a loud insistent chorus of voices, an organized coalition like chapters of the Industrial Areas Foundation, demanding such policies of government!

As more of us acquire dexterity and habits of inclusion, it will become much easier to create winning coalitions and communities of civility, where a debate about school funding is more a spirited exchange about what actually works than a zero-sum fight. Many communities of decency do exist today. They support inclusionary zoning laws that allow struggling people to live near great schools and employers that might hire them. Imagining the third Reconstruction in dexterous places of the future brings a smile to my face. Research by Robert Putnam suggests that non-dexterous people burrow in and avoid civic engagement when they enter diverse settings.[37] But, this avoidance trend is less likely in the future, when more people will have acquired comfort with out-groups. Such communities will multiply as the culturally dexterous multiply. There are places today that declare they are welcoming to immigrants because they want to bring vitality to their struggling communities. They work at helping new residents and existing ones to get to know and understand each other. They are building new human bridges and yes, sometimes are whipsawed by the tensions.

Bibliography

Andersen, Mark. 2014. "How D.C.'s Plan to Save Low-Income Housing Went Wrong." *Washington City Paper*. October 29. http://www. washingtoncitypaper.com/news/city-desk/blog/13069268/ how-d-c-s-plan-to-save-low-income-housing-went-wrong

Cashin, Sheryll. 2004. *The Failures of Integration: How Race and Class Are Undermining the American Dream*. New York: PublicAffairs.

— — —. 2014. *Place Not Race: A New Vision of Opportunity*. Boston: Beacon Press.

— — —. 2017. *Loving: Interracial Intimacy in America and the Threat to White Supremacy*. Boston: Beacon Press.

Chetty, Raj, Nathaniel Henderson, Patrick Kline, and Emmanuel Saez. 2013. "Summary of Project Findings: Executive Summary." Equality of Opportunity Project. https:// www.scribd.com/document/157408091/Harvard-Berkeley-study

Coates, Ta-Nahisi. 2013. "Beyond the Code of the Streets." *New York Times,* May 4.

DiAngelo, Robin. 2011. "White Fragility." *International Journal of Critical Pedagogy* 3, no. 3: 54–70.

Domina, Thurston. 2006. "Brain Drain and Brain Gain: Rising Educational Segregation in the United States, 1940–2000." *City and Community* 5, no. 4: 387–407.

Forman, James, Jr. 2017. *Locking Up Our Own: Crime and Punishment in Black America*. New York: Farrar, Straus & Giroux.

Jackson, Kenneth T. *Crabgrass Frontier: The Suburbanization of the United States*. New York: Oxford University Press, 1985.

Kang, Jerry. 2005. "Trojan Horses of Race." *Harvard Law Review* 118, no. 5: 1489–1593.

Kneebone, Elizabeth, and Alan Berube. 2013. "Confronting Suburban Poverty in America." Washington: Brookings Institution Press.

Kneebone, Elizabeth, Carrie Nadeau, and Alan Berube. 2011. "The Re-Emergence of Concentrated Poverty: Metropolitan Trends in the 2000s." Washington, DC: Brookings Institution. https://www.brookings.edu/wp-content/ uploads/2016/06/1103_poverty_kneebone_nadeau_berube.pdf.

Logan, John R., and Brian J. Stults. "The Persistence of Segregation in the Metropolis: New Findings from the 2010 Census." Census Brief prepared for Project US2010. https://s4.ad.brown.edu/Projects/Diversity/Data/Report/report2.pdf.

Massey, Douglas S. 2007. *Categorically Unequal: The American Stratifcation System.* New York: Russell Sage Foundation.

Massey, Douglas S., and Nancy A. Denton. 1993. *American Apartheid: Segregation and the Making of the Underclass.* Cambridge, MA: Harvard University Press.

Massey, Douglas S, and Jacob S. Rugh. 2014. "Segregation in Post-Civil Rights America: Stalled Integration or End of the Segregated Century?" *Du Bois Review* 11, no. 2: 205–32.

Mock, Brentin. 2016. "Donald Trump's Blaxploitation of 'Inner Cities.'" *Citylab*, October 11. http://www.citylab.com/crime/2016/10/donald-trumps-blaxploitation-of-inner-cities/503714/.

Murray, Charles. 2012. *Coming Apart: The State of White America, 1960–2010.* New York: Crown.

Myrdal, Gunnar. 1944. *An American Dilemma: The Negro Problem and Modern Democracy.* New York: Harper & Row.

NPR Staff. 2014. "Six Words: 'With Kids, I'm Dad. Alone, Thug.'" November 17. http://www.npr.org/2014/11/17/361804353/six-words-with-kids-im-dad-alone-thug.

Nevins, Sean. 2015. "Beyond Gentrification: Hundreds of DC Residents Being Forced From Their Homes." *MPN News.* April 20. http://www.mintpressnews.com/beyond-gentrification-hundreds-of-dc-residents-being-forced-from-their-homes/204543/

Orfield, Myron, and Thomas Luce. 2013. "America's Racially Diverse Suburbs: Opportunities and Challenges." *Housing Policy Debate* 23, no. 2: 395–430.

powell, john a. 2002. "Opportunity-Based Housing," *Journal of Affordable Housing & Community Development Law* 12, no.2: 188–228

Putnam, Robert D. 2007. "E pluribus unum: Diversity and Community in the Twenty First Century. The 2006 Johan Skytte Prize Lecture." *Scandinavian Political Studies* 30 no. 2: 137–74.

Reardon, Sean F., and Kendra Bischoff. 2011. "Income Inequality and Income Segregation." *American Journal of Sociology*, 116 no. 4: 1092–1155.

Rothstein, Richard. 2017. *The Color of Law: A Forgotten History of How Our Government Segregated America.* New York: Liveright.

Rotondaro, Vinnie. 2015. "Once-Aspirational Philadelphia Suburbs Struggle with Poverty." *National Catholic Reporter,* March 25. https://www.ncronline.org/news/faith-parish/once-aspirational-philadelphia-suburbs-struggle-poverty.

Sabadish, Natalie, and Lawrence Mishel. 2013. "CEO Pay in 2012 Was Extraordinarily High Relative to Typical Workers and Other High Earners." Issue Brief #367. Washington, DC: Economic Policy Institute. http://www.epi.org/files/2013/ceo-pay-2012-extraordinarily-high.pdf.

Sampson, Robert J. 2008. "Durable Effects of Concentrated Disadvantage on Verbal Ability among African American Children." *Proceedings of the National Academy of Sciences of the United States of America* 105, no. 3: 845–52.

Samuels, Robert. 2013. "In District, affordable-housing plan hasn't delivered." *The Washington Post*. July 7. https://www.washingtonpost.com/local/in-district-affordable-housing-plan-hasnt-delivered/2013/07/07/789f1070-bc03-11e2-97d4-a479289a31f9_story.html?utm_term=.b5081a7587d7

Sharkey, Patrick. 2009. "Neighborhoods and the Black-White Mobility Gap." Economic Mobility Project, Pew Charitable Trust. http://www.pewtrusts.org/~/media/legacy/uploadedfiles/wwwpewtrustsorg/reports/economic_mobility/pewshar-keyv12pdf.pdf.

— — —. 2013. *Stuck in Place: Urban Neighborhoods and the End of Progress Toward Racial Equality.* Chicago: University of Chicago Press.

Wodtke, Geoffrey T., David J. Harding, and Felix Elwert. 2011. "Neighborhood Effects in Temporal Perspective: The Impact of Long-Term Exposure to Concentrated Disadvantage on High School Graduation." *American Sociological Review* 76, no. 5: 713–36.

Endnotes

1   Mock (2016).

2   Cashin (2017).

3   Myrdal (1944).

4   Cashin (2017).

5   Rothstein (2017); Cashin (2004); Massey and Denton (1993); Jackson (1985).

6   Cashin (2004), ch. 3.

7   Cashin (2014), ch. Beacon Press, 2014, Chapter 1.

8   Logan and Stults (2011), 21.

9   Sharkey (2009).

10   Sampson (2008); Wodtke, Harding, and Elwert (2011).

11   Sharkey (2013).

12   Domina (2006), 394.

13   powell (2002).

14   Reardon and Bischoff (2011).

15   Kneebone and Berube (2013), 18; Elizabeth Kneebone, Nadeau, and Berube (2011).

16   Massey (2007), 19.

17   Cashin (2004).

18   Reardon and Bischoff (2011).

19   Sabadish and Mishel (2013).

20   Chetty et al. (2013).

21   Rotondaro (2015).

22   DiAngelo (2011), 54, 57–65.

23   Kang (2005).

24 Massey and Denton (1993).

25 Coates (2013).

26 NPR Staff (2014).

27 See, for example, Forman (2017).

28 See, for example, Nevins (2015); Samuels (2013); Andersen (2014).

29 Massey & Denton (1993).

30 Cashin (2014), ch. 2.

31 Cashin (2014), ch. 7.

32 See, for example, Murray (2012).

33 Cashin (2017), ch. 8.

34 Orfield and Luce (2012).

35 Ibid.

36 Orfield and Luce (2012); Chetty et al. (2013); Massey and Rugh (2014).

37 Putnam (2007).

Consequences of Segregation for Children's Opportunity and Wellbeing

NANCY MCARDLE
diversitydatakids.org

DOLORES ACEVEDO-GARCIA
Brandeis University

"Men and women of all races are born with the same range of abilities. But ability is not just the product of birth. Ability is stretched or stunted by the family that you live with, and the neighborhood you live in — by the school you go to and the poverty or the richness of your surroundings. It is the product of a hundred unseen forces playing upon the little infant, the child, and finally the man."

— President Lyndon B. Johnson, Commencement Address at Howard University, June 4, 1965[1]

As the child population becomes "majority-minority," racial segregation remains high, income segregation among families with children increases, and the political and policy landscape undergoes momentous change, it is a particularly crucial time to consider the consequences of segregation for children's opportunity and wellbeing. Not only is residential segregation more extreme for children than for adults, but the close links between residential and school segregation mean that children are often isolated from opportunity across multiple environments during the developmental period when neighborhood and school resources critically impact their wellbeing, opportunities, and life chances.

Beyond this reality of segmented opportunities lies a greater question — whether such separation and difference in the quality of children's environments by race/income is morally or socially right. Segregation spatially isolates groups and limits social interaction, and, for children, this isolation occurs during the crucial period when racial attitudes are being formed. The degree of this separation challenges the values of unity and equal opportunity that we as a nation espouse, especially to the extent that purposefully exclusionary policies contribute to high levels of residential segregation. Further, segregation reifies notions of difference and supremacy by making separation into a physical reality. As illustrated by the account of a young, black student in a wealthy Boston suburb who was bused into the inner-city after school because of the mistaken assumption that he must be a desegregation program participant rather than a resident of that suburb[2], segregation fosters powerful perceptions of who belongs where, who deserves "access."

As the US becomes increasingly racially and ethnically diverse, particularly among the young, the harms of segregation will affect a growing share of the population. While children of color currently comprise about half of the child population, this share is projected to rise to over 60 percent by 2050, with particularly strong growth of the Hispanic child population.

Suburban/urban demographic shifts present both new challenges and opportunities as families of color continue to move to the suburbs. Further, a changed political land- scape arguably favors a host of policy changes that could exacerbate segregation. New policy directions regarding taxes and entitlements, fair housing, and school choice, to name a few, all have great potential to exacerbate economic and racial/ethnic segrega- tion, making this an especially significant moment to understand the extent and costs of segregation for children.

CHILDREN MORE SEGREGATED THAN ADULTS; INCOME SEGREGATION RISING FOR FAMILIES WITH CHILDREN

For every major racial/ethnic group, levels of residential segregation from whites are higher for children than they are for adults.[3] Children are also more economically segregated than adults, but income alone does not explain their high levels of racial/ ethnic segregation. Even among poor children (those below the federal poverty line), segregation indices for all major racial/ethnic groups, relative to poor white children, are extremely high — in fact, substantially higher than the rates for children of all incomes.

Over the past few decades, increases in household income segregation have occurred predominantly among families with children, whose segregation levels are about twice as high as those of childless families. Owens finds that rising residential income segre- gation for families with children is largely related to increases in income inequality and the structure of school options, as characterized by school district boundaries and fragmentation. Upper-income families with children, benefiting from rising incomes, have been able to buy into more exclusive neighborhoods, further separating them- selves from lower-income households.[4]

This segregative behavior is a main mechanism by which higher-income families with children are actively separating themselves. Many privileged families choose to live in exclusionary communities by race, income, or both, largely by seeking high-performing school districts, sometimes using test scores or school racial composition as a proxy for school quality. This separation is facilitated by zoning that excludes housing types affordable to lower-income families, who are disproportionately black and Hispanic. Upper-income families who choose to live in cities often sequester themselves in exclusive neighborhoods where schools reflect neighborhood demographics, or they send children to private or exam schools, leaving lower-income black and Hispanic children in less advantaged neighborhoods and schools.

SEGREGATION IS ASSOCIATED WITH VASTLY DIFFERENT CHILD ENVIRONMENTS

Segregation is not benign. The neighborhoods where children live and grow are both separate and also greatly unequal along racial/ethnic lines in ways that have profound impacts on opportunities for healthy child development and wellbeing. The differences in neighborhood characteristics and opportunities between racial/ethnic groups are dramatic not just on average, but for large majorities of their populations.

For example, using neighborhood poverty rate as a proxy for neighborhood quality, we found that large shares of all black and Hispanic children live in higher-poverty neighborhoods than do the worst-off white children. We defined "worst-off white children" as the 25 percent who live in the highest-poverty neighborhoods for white children in each of the 100 largest US metropolitan areas.[5] On average, about 76 percent of black children and 69 percent of Hispanic children live in neighborhoods with poverty rates higher than those found in the neighborhoods of the worst-off white children. These differences remain even after taking children's own poverty status into account. About 74 percent of poor black children and 60 percent of poor Hispanic children live in neighborhoods with higher poverty rates than those of the worst-off poor white children.[6]

Furthermore, we find that *metropolitan areas with the highest segregation levels have the most unequal geographies of neighborhood poverty.* In the five metro areas (of the largest 100) where black children experience the highest levels of residential segregation, 86 percent of black children live in higher-poverty neighborhoods than the worst-off white children. But in the five least segregated metros, 57 percent of black children live in higher-poverty neighborhoods than the worst-off white children. The corresponding figures for Hispanic children in high- and low-segregation areas are 74 percent and 44 percent.[7]

CHILDREN'S NEIGHBORHOOD DIFFERENCES EXTEND BEYOND POVERTY

Research on neighborhoods has more recently advanced beyond use of single indicators, such as poverty, to more complex aggregate indices that capture a range of neighborhood assets and stressors. These measures incorporate an understanding that the effects of neighborhood stressors on child wellbeing can be cumulative, as when high poverty neighborhoods also have high levels of violent crime, but can also be offset by positive neighborhood factors.[8]

One such aggregate measure of neighborhood factors is the Child Opportunity Index (COI), developed by diversitydatakids.org and the Kirwan Institute for the Study of Race and Ethnicity. For the 100 largest metropolitan areas, the COI combines 19 separate component indicators in three overall domains — Education, Health and Environment, and Social and Economic — into a composite opportunity index score, which positions/ranks each neighborhood (census tract) relative to all other neighborhoods in its metro area. Each of the individual indicators was vetted for relevance to child development based on empirical literature on neighborhood effects and/or conceptual frameworks of neighborhood influences on children. In addition to relevance, data availability guided indicator selection for each domain.[9]

For each metro area, neighborhoods were assigned one of five Child Opportunity Index categories — Very Low, Low, Moderate, High, Very High — based on the quintile rank of their opportunity index scores. Thus, the census tracts identified as "very high" opportunity represent the top 20 percent of scores among census tracts within a metro area. Conversely, census tracts identified as "very low" opportunity represent the lowest scoring 20 percent of tracts within a metro area.

Combining these COI opportunity categories with the residence patterns of children by race/ethnicity shows that minority children, particularly black and Hispanic children, are dramatically more likely to live in lower-opportunity neighborhoods. While only 9 percent of white children live in the 20 percent of neighborhoods ranked as lowest in opportunity, 32 percent of Hispanic and 40 percent of black children live in such neighborhoods. These disparities remain after controlling for children's own poverty status. Looking just at poor children, 22 percent of white children live in the 20 percent of neighborhoods ranked as lowest in opportunity, but 45 percent of Hispanic and 57 percent of black children live in such neighborhoods (Figure 1). As in our analysis of neighborhoods by poverty status, we find that racial/ethnic inequities in neighborhood opportunities for children are larger in metro areas with higher levels of segregation.[10]

Figure 1: Percent of Poor Children, by Race/Ethnicity, Living in Each Neighborhood Opportunity Category

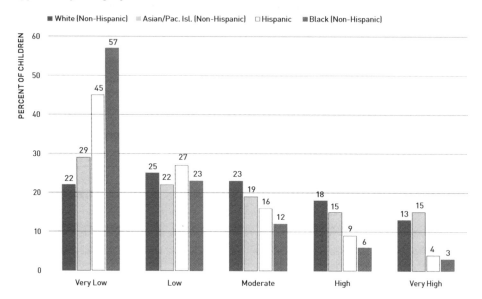

Note: Data are for 100 largest metropolitan areas combined. Racial groups exclude Hispanic members. Hispanics may be of any race.

Source: diversitydatakids.org/Kirwan Institute Child Opportunity Index and U.S. Census Bureau, American Community Survey, 2011, 5-year estimates.

EFFECTS OF RESIDENTIAL SEGREGATION ON CHILDREN

The separate and unequal neighborhoods where children of different backgrounds reside have strong associations with child outcomes. While much of the pertinent research on this topic focuses on a single measure of neighborhood environment, commonly poverty, and does not draw causal conclusions, several rigorous, causal studies substantiate the detrimental effects that neighborhood socioeconomic disadvantage has on children.[11]

The connections between neighborhood socioeconomic status and a host of child and adolescent outcomes have been well documented, including links to behavior problems, juvenile delinquency, academic achievement, and health. Additional studies find that other neighborhood factors, such as public safety, levels of trust among neighbors, availability of safe recreational spaces, and access to affordable, healthy food also influence children. Differential exposure to neighborhood violent crime is one important stressor which arguably differs by race/ethnicity and has important implications for child development. While national data on exposure to crime is not available, several studies utilizing Chicago data cast important light. Timberlake and Kirk find that, by either a subjective measure (e.g., seeing someone attacked by a knife, saw someone get shot, or heard a gunshot within previous year) or an objective measure based on neighborhood crime statistics, white children are much more likely than blacks to live the vast majority of their childhood years in virtually violence-free neighborhoods. Also focusing on Chicago, Sharkey finds that exposure to homicide impairs children's cognitive functioning and self-regulatory behavior through the mechanism of generating acute psychological distress among their caregivers. It is perhaps unsurprising, given the sharp differences in segregated neighborhoods and the choices and life trajectories that youth in disadvantaged neighborhoods foresee, that segregation has also been associated with altering youth decision-making processes. Although most of these studies do not establish causality between neighborhood conditions and child outcomes, they strongly suggest that, beyond neighborhood poverty, a wide range of neighborhood characteristics may influence children.[12]

Isolating the precise effects of neighborhood conditions on child outcomes is challenging because the same factors that lead people to choose certain types of neighborhoods may also impact their children's outcomes. Nevertheless, a few rigorous studies do separate family from neighborhood influences and find independent neighborhood effects. Sampson, Sharkey, and Raudenbush found that the verbal abilities of black children residing in severely disadvantaged neighborhood were reduced by a magnitude equivalent to a year or more of schooling, on average. An analysis of Moving to Opportunity program data showed greater earnings and higher-quality college education as adults for children who moved from a high-poverty to a low-poverty neighborhood before the age of 13, as compared to children remaining in high-poverty areas. Further, Santiago and colleagues found that several neighborhood characteristics predict outcomes for low-income Latino and African-American children across multiple dimensions, even after controlling for many household, child, and caregiver traits. Among the impacted domains are exposure to violence, risky behaviors, physical and behavioral health, education, marriage and childbearing, and youth labor market outcomes. For example, in neighborhoods where greater shares of residents work in high-prestige occupations, children had better educational outcomes and engaged in fewer risky behaviors. Also, children living in areas with lower property crime rates had better health outcomes with regard to conditions such as anxiety, depression, obesity, asthma, and neurodevelopmental disorders. While these studies find that neighborhoods themselves matter for child development, the precise mechanisms through which these effects occur is an important area of further exploration.[13]

SEGREGATED NEIGHBORHOODS/SEGREGATED SCHOOLS
Highest Levels of Segregation Occur at Critical Preschool Age
Segregated schools are perhaps the most powerful pathways through which segregated neighborhoods affect children. Seventy-eight percent of all students attend public schools to which they have been assigned, usually based on neighborhood of residence, and 84 percent of public school students attend assigned schools. Charter schools,

which have more flexibility to draw students from wider and potentially more diverse areas, are even more racially segregated than traditional public schools, while private schools draw a disproportionately large share of white students. A new study of private school vouchers finds that, on net, they also are likely to exacerbate segregation.[14]

Ironically, children are most separate at the very ages when they are developing racial attitudes. Preschool children are segregated by the types of programs they attend and also within such programs. Those children from higher socioeconomic status families more commonly attend center-based preschools, while Hispanic families are disproportionately less likely to attend such programs. Further, the development of certain programs, such as Head Start, specifically as avenues to provide opportunities for low-income children, has led to disproportionate enrollment of low-income and black students.[15]

While it is difficult to examine the extent of segregation across all preschool settings, in a study of almost 28,000 public school preschools, Frankenberg found that over half of Hispanic and black students attend schools that are at least 90 percent children of color. This degree of isolation exceeds that experienced by students in grades K-12. Still, white students experience the highest levels of racial isolation relative to their own specific racial/ethnic group. Comprising 41 percent of enrollment, white students attend preschools that are, on average, almost 70 percent white.[16]

As in segregated K-12 schools, black and Hispanic children attending racially isolated preschools suffer from less adequate resources, including less qualified teachers. Preschool segregation also squanders a particularly fruitful time during child development and an environment that could be potentially ideal for fostering intergroup contact necessary for developing healthy racial attitudes. Research has found that the most positive effects of integration occur when inter-racial experiences are earliest, and that cross-racial friendships are most common among younger children. Not only can these relationships and friendships help to counter prejudice, but even being exposed to diverse faces at young ages can reduce people's implicit bias towards blacks when they become adults.[17]

Rising Income Segregation Isolates Poor and Minority Students in Disadvantaged Schools

Increasing income segregation, parental choices, governmental and school policies, and, in some areas, fragmentation of geography into many, individual school districts, leave large numbers of lower-income, black and Latino students in isolated and disadvantaged schools. These inequities are increasingly consequential as students of color comprise larger shares of school enrollment. In 2014, white students made up less than half of public school enrollment, down from 79 percent in 1970, and

Hispanic students now comprise over a quarter of enrollment. It is primarily this changing racial composition, rather than increasingly uneven distributions of different races/ethnicities across schools, that has led to white students experiencing greater exposure to non-white classmates at the same time that black and Hispanic students are increasingly isolated, often to an extreme degree.[18]

At the same time, income segregation has been rising, driven in part by growth in income inequality. Between 1990 and 2010, between-*district* income segregation increased by more than 15 percent for families with children in public schools. Over roughly the same period, between-*school* segregation of students who were eligible and those who were ineligible for free lunch increased by more than 40 percent in large school districts.[19]

The interaction between race/ethnicity and income means that black and Hispanic students are often segregated into both racially isolated and high-poverty schools. While public school students of all races/ethnicities are increasingly in schools with larger shares of low-income students, there are clear inequities by race/ethnicity.[20] By 2013, when low-income students made up 52 percent of enrollment, the average black or Hispanic student attended schools that were 68 percent low-income, while the average white or Asian students attended schools that were 40 percent and 42 percent low-income, respectively.[21]

Effects of Segregation/Integration on Academic Achievement

The disadvantages of attending a concentrated poverty school have been well documented, most prominently in the influential Coleman report as well as in a more recent analysis of the same data showing that the socioeconomic status of a student's school was even more important in predicting achievement than a student's own status. Numerous studies have shown the detriments of attending segregated, high-poverty schools on math and reading scores as well as on drop-out rates, while others have shown that black and Hispanic students exhibit improved achievement in integrated settings, while white students are not harmed. More recently, Schwartz's study of low-income children living in public housing in Montgomery County, Maryland whose families were randomly assigned to housing in neighborhoods with different poverty rates (with corresponding differences in school poverty) found that, in both math and reading, elementary school students who had been assigned to low-poverty schools significantly outscored their peers in moderate-poverty schools after five to seven years. By the end of elementary school, the substantial achievement gap between public housing children in the district's most advantaged schools and non-poor students was cut in half for math and by one-third for reading.[22]

The relationships between racial/ethnic segregation and achievement gaps are complex. However, in a comprehensive study, Reardon concluded that all of the association between segregation and achievement gaps could be explained by differential exposure to school poverty alone and that black/Hispanic achievement gaps with whites are much higher when they attend schools with higher poverty concentrations. The mechanisms through which schools with less concentrated poverty improve achievement include "more equitable access to important resources such as structural facilities, highly qualified teachers, challenging courses, private and public funding, social and cultural capital," significantly higher educational expectations from school staff and students, and lower levels of violence and social disorder than segregated schools. Higher per-pupil spending and lower student-teacher ratios are also mechanisms by which integrated schools lead to an increased likelihood of graduation among black students, according to a recent study on exposure of black students to court-ordered desegregation which found a 2-percentage-point increase in the probability of graduating high school for every year spent in an integrated school under court oversight.[23]

School Integration Brings Benefits Beyond Achievement Gains

Education policy has focused intensely on achievement over the past several years. However, the growing diversity of the nation and globalization of economies suggest that other educational goals are worth pursuing. Integrated, diverse education has been shown to improve critical thinking and problem solving skills, the development of cross-racial trust, and the ability to navigate cultural differences. Integrated schooling holds promise even for helping to break the vicious cycle of segregated housing and education, as students who attend integrated schools have been shown to more commonly seek out integrated settings in later life, including being more likely to live in diverse neighborhoods following graduation.[24]

These benefits accrue not only to individuals, but arguably to the economy and civic society as well. Cross-cultural navigational skills are valued in the marketplace, as shown by the overwhelming response of major employers that it is "important" that employees be "comfortable working with colleagues, customers, and/or clients from diverse cultural backgrounds." The reduction in bias and stereotypes, along with increased empathy and understanding of other races fostered by integrated education, all prepare students to be better citizens in our increasingly diverse democracy.[25]

DISCUSSION

As the child population becomes increasingly racially/ethnically diverse and income segregation among families with children grows, the consequences of segregation become even more far-reaching. At the same time, the new and still developing federal political and policy landscape appears challenging. Both the 2016 Republican Party platform and the Secretary of Housing and Urban Development have fiercely criticized important advances in Fair Housing, such as the Affirmatively Furthering Fair Housing rule.[26] The extent of the new administration's tax and entitlement/benefits policies is still unknown. But if these policies serve to further increase income inequality, they are likely to also further fuel segregation and its costs.

The Department of Education has signaled support for school choice policies, although with a strong emphasis on privatization and certain mechanisms, such as private school vouchers, which would arguably increase rather than reduce segregation. In some cases, such as interdistrict choice, magnet schools, intentionally diverse charter schools, and controlled choice when accompanied by parent information and transportation programs, choice policies can reduce segregation. The interdistrict magnet school program which draws from the City of Hartford, Connecticut and surrounding communities, while not without its challenges, is one example of providing high-quality, diverse education. Even charter schools, which have typically been highly segregated, can foster integration when intentionally designed, as with the dozens of schools participating in the National Coalition of Diverse Charter Schools. Any type of school choice program must work to inform and empower those parents who face special barriers to participation, so that choice does not just benefit children of the already advantaged. And, of course, the mere desegregation of schools is only the necessary first step in achieving integration — further intentional measures must be taken both within schools and within classrooms to foster the environment and processes critical to reaping the rewards of diversity.

At the local level, the combination of exclusionary zoning, which keeps affordable, rental, and multi-family housing (especially larger units suitable for families with children) out of higher opportunity areas; fragmented municipal and school boundaries; growing income inequality; and school districts largely funded through property taxes all conspire to exacerbate segregation of children. While it is now almost a cliché that "housing policy is school policy," it is undeniably true. Given the close connection between residential patterns and school assignment, the policies that encourage neighborhood integration, including affirmatively furthering fair housing, enforcing anti-discrimination laws, providing incentives for affordable housing construction in higher opportunity areas, and inclusionary zoning, would likely also reduce segregation in schools.

Mounting research evidence increasingly reveals the cost of such segregation in terms of children's health, education, and long-term economic success. Beyond its impact on access to important neighborhood and school resources, the separation of children during childhood perpetuates the development of racial prejudices and stereotypes, or, in the words of Dr. Martin Luther King, Jr. "the false sense of superiority of the segregators and the false sense of inferiority of the segregated."[27] Optimistic claims that we had moved into a "post-racial" era following the Obama election have been sadly refuted by police shootings of unarmed blacks, the subsequent rise of the Black Lives Matter movement and its backlash, and the racially/ethnically charged anti-immigrant rhetoric of the 2016 presidential campaign. In that integration can promote cross-racial understanding and empathy, it is a valuable tool to enhance not only the wellbeing of individuals, but of our society as a whole.

Segregation is a demographic and spatial reality, as described above, but, more critically, it is also a device used by a dominant group for maintaining their higher status vis-à-vis others through limiting social interaction.[28] It is natural for families to desire the best for their children, but to the extent that those with power and advantage are able to influence and perpetuate policies in order to hoard benefits and opportunity, leaving disadvantaged children in circumstances which may dramatically influence their life courses for the worse, we must question whether we are and will be "one nation, indivisible."

Bibliography

Aboud, Frances E., Morton J. Mendelson, and Kelly T. Purdy. 2003. "Cross-Race Peer Relations and Friendship Quality." *International Journal of Behavioral Development* 27, no. 2: 165–73.

Acevedo-Garcia, Dolores, Erin F. Hardy, Nancy McArdle, Unda Ioana Crisan, Bethany Romano, David Norris, Mikyung Baek, and David Reece. 2016. "The Child Opportunity Index: Measuring and Mapping Neighborhood-based Opportunities for U.S. Children." diversitydatakids.org and Kirwan Institute for the Study of Race and Ethnicity. http://www.diversitydatakids.org/files/Library/Child%20 Opportunity/COI%20Report%20Final%207_29_16.pdf.

Acevedo-Garcia, Dolores, Theresa L. Osypuk, Nancy McArdle, and David R. Williams. 2008. "Toward A Policy-Relevant Analysis Of Geographic And Racial/Ethnic Disparities In Child Health." *Health Affairs* 27, no. 2: 321–33.

Borman, Geoffrey D, and Maritza Dowling. 2010. "Schools and Inequality: A Multilevel Analysis of Coleman's Equality of Educational Opportunity Data." *Teachers College Record* 112: 1201–46.

Brief of 553 Social Scientists. 2006. "Brief of 553 Social Scientists as Amici Curiae in Support of Respondents." *Parents Involved in Community Schools v. Seattle School District* No. 1. 551 U.S. 701.

Carson, Ben S. 2015. "Experimenting with Failed Socialism Again." *The Washington Times*, July 23. http://m.washingtontimes.com/news/2015/jul/23/ ben-carson-obamas-housing-rules-try-to-accomplish-/.

Chetty, Raj, Nathaniel Hendren, and Lawrence F. Katz. 2016. "The Effects of Exposure to Better Neighborhoods on Children: New Evidence from the Moving to Opportunity Experiment." *American Economic Review* 106, no. 4: 855–902. doi: doi: 10.1257/aer.20150572.

Cloutier, Jasmin, Tianyi Li, and Joshua Correll. 2014. "The Impact of Childhood Experience on Amygdala Response to Perceptually Familiar Black and White Faces." *Journal of Cognitive Neuroscience* 26, no. 9: 1992–2004. doi: 10.1162/jocn_a_00605.

Diez-Roux, Ana V. 2003. "The Examination of Neighborhood Effects on Health: Conceptual and Methodological Issues Related to the Presence of Multiple Levels of Organization." In N*eighborhoods and Health,* edited by Ichiro Kawachi and Lisa F. Berkman, 45–64. New York: Oxford University Press.

diversitydatakids.org and Kirwan Institute for the Study of Race and Ethnicity. 2014. Child Opportunity Index Mapping. Waltham, MA: Brandeis University.

Ellen, Ingrid Gould , and Sherry Glied. 2015. "Housing, Neighborhoods, and Children's Health." *The Future of Children* 25, no. 1: 135–53.

Fiel, Jeremy E. 2013. "Decomposing School Resegregation: Social Closure, Racial Imbalance, and Racial Isolation." *American Sociological Review* 78, no. 5: 828–48.

Frankenberg, Erica. 2016. "Segregation at an Early Age." Center for Education and Civil Rights, Penn State University.

Frankenberg, Erica, Genevieve Siegel Hawley, Jia Wang. 2010. *Choice Without Equity: Charter School Segregation and the Need for Civil Rights Standards.* Los Angeles: The Civil Rights Project/Proyecto Derechos Civiles at UCLA.

Freeman, Linton C. 1978. "Segregation in Social Networks." *Sociological Methods & Research* 6, no. 4: 411–29.

Galster, George C., and Sean P. Killen. 1995. "The Geography of Metropolitan Opportunity: A Reconnaissance and Conceptual Framework." *Housing Policy Debate* 6, no. 1: 7–43.

Hart Research Associates. 2013. "It Takes More Than a Major: Employer Priorities for College Learning and Student Success." Washington, D.C.: Hart Research Associates.

Howes, Carollee, and Fang Wu. 1990. "Peer Interactions and Friendships in an Ethnically Diverse School Setting." *Child Development* 61, no. 2: 537–41. doi: 10.2307/1131113.

Iceland, John, Kimberly A. Goyette, Kyle Anne Nelson, and Chaowen Chan. 2010. "Racial and Ethnic Residential Segregation and Household Structure: A Research Note." *Social Science Research* 39, no. 1: 39–47.

Jargowsky, Paul A. 2014. "Segregation, Neighborhoods, and Schools." *In Choosing Homes, Choosing Schools: Residential Segregation and the Search for a Good School*, edited by Annette Lareau and Kimberly Goyette. New York: Russell Sage Foundation.

Johnson, Lyndon B. 1965. "To Fulfill These Rights" (Commencement Address at Howard University). The American Presidency Project.

Johnson, Rucker C. 2015 (Revised). "Long-run Impacts of School Desegregation & School Quality on Adult Attainments." Working Paper. Cambridge, MA: National Bureau of Economic Research.

Joshi, Pamela, Kimberly Geronimo, and Dolores Acevedo-Garcia. 2016. "Head Start since the War on Poverty: Taking on New Challenges to Address Persistent School Readiness Gaps." *Journal of Applied Research on Children: Informing Policy for Children at Risk* 7, no. 1: article 11.

Kawachi, Ichiro, and Lisa F. Berkman, eds. 2003. *Neighborhoods and Health*. New York: Oxford University Press.

King, Martin Luther, Jr. 1963. "Letter from a Birmingham Jail." April 16.

Leventhal, Tama, Véronique Dupéré, and Jeanne Brooks-Gunn. 2009. "Neighborhood Influences on Adolescent Development." In *Handbook of Adolescent Psychology*, edited by Richard M. Lerner and Laurence Steinberg, 411–443. Hoboken, NJ: Wiley.

Mickelson, Roslyn Arlin. 2008. "Twenty-First Century Social Science on School Racial Diversity and Educational Outcomes." *Ohio State Law Journal* 69: 1173–1228.

— — — . 2016. "School Integration and K-12 Educational Outcomes: A Quick Synthesis of Social Science Evidence." Washington, DC: The National Coalition on School Diversity.

Newburger, Harriet, Eugenie L Birch, and Susan M Wachter. 2011. *Neighborhood and Life chances: How Place Matters in Modern America.* Philadelphia: University of Pennsylvania Press.

Noel, Amber, Patrick Stark, and Jeremy Redford. 2016. Parent and Family Involvement in Education, from the National Household Education Surveys Program of 2012: First Look." Washington, DC: Institute of Education Sciences, National Center for Education Statistics, U.S. Department of Education.

Orfield, Gary, Jongyeon Ee, Erica Frankenberg, and Genevieve Siegel Hawley. 2016. "*Brown* At 62: School Segregation By Race, Poverty And State." Los Angeles: Civil Rights Project/Proyecto Derechos Civiles at UCLA.

Owens, Ann. 2016. "Inequality in Children's Contexts." *American Sociological Review* 81, no. 3: 549–74. doi: doi:10.1177/0003122416642430.

Owens, Ann, Sean F. Reardon, and Christopher Jencks. 2016. "Income Segregation between Schools and School Districts." Working Paper. Stanford Center for Education Policy Analysis.

Phillips, Kristie J. R., Robert J. Rodosky, Marco A. Muñoz, and Elisabeth S. Larsen. 2009. "Integrated Schools, Integrated Futures?" In *From the Courtroom to the Classroom: The Shifting Landscape of School Desegregation*, edited by Claire E. Smrekar and Ellen B. Goldring, 239–270. Cambridge, MA: Harvard Education Press.

Potter, Haley. 2017. "Do Private School Vouchers Pose a Threat to Integration?" New York: The Century Foundation.

Reardon, Sean F. 2015. "School Segregation and Racial Academic Achievement Gaps." Working Paper No. 15-12. Stanford Center for Education Policy Analysis.

Reid, Jeanne L. 2016. "Racial/ethnic Diversity and Language Development in the Preschool Classroom." In *School Integration Matters: Research-based Strategies to Advance Equity*, edited by E. Frankenberg, L.M. Garces, and M. Hopkins, 39-55. New York: Teachers College Press.

Reid, Jeanne L, and Sharon Lynn Kagan. 2015. "A Better Start: Why Classroom Diversity Matters in Early Education." The Century Foundation, Poverty & Race Research Action Council.

Republican Party Platform Committee. 2016. Republican Party Platform 2016.

Russell, Jenna. 2004. "Report on METCO Bus Mix-up Faults 'Assumptions' on Race." *Boston Globe*, February 1.

Sampson, Robert J., Patrick Sharkey, and Stephen W. Raudenbush. 2008. "Durable Effects of Concentrated Disadvantage on Verbal Ability among African-American Children." *Proceedings of the National Academy of Sciences* 105, no. 3: 845-52. doi: 10.1073/pnas.0710189104.

Santiago, Anna Maria, George C Galster, Jessica L. Lucero, Karen J. Ishler, Eun Lye Lee, Georgios Kypriotakis, and Lisa Stack. 2014. "Opportunity Neighborhoods for Latino and African-American Children: Final Report." Washington, DC: U.S. Department of Housing and Urban Development, Office of Policy Development and Research.

Schwartz, Heather. 2010. "Housing Policy is School Policy: Economically Integrative Housing Promotes Academic Success in Montgomery County, Maryland." New York: The Century Foundation.

Sharkey, Patrick. 2013. *Stuck in Place: Urban Neighborhoods and the End of Progress toward Racial Equality*. Chicago: University of Chicago Press.

Sharkey, Patrick T., Nicole Tirado-Strayer, Andrew V. Papachristos, and C. Cybele Raver. 2012. "The Effect of Local Violence on Children's Attention and Impulse Control." *American Journal of Public Health* 102, no. 12: 2287-93. doi: 10.2105/AJPH.2012.300789.

Suitts, Steve. 2016. "Race And Ethnicity In A New Era Of Public Funding Of Private Schools: Private School Enrollment In The South And The Nation." Atlanta: Southern Education Foundation, Inc.

Tench, Meghan. 2003. "Questions Follow Lapse on Wellesley Metco Bus." *Boston Globe*, September 6.

Theall, Katherine P., Stacy S. Drury, and Elizabeth A. Shirtcliff. 2012. "Cumulative Neighborhood Risk of Psychosocial Stress and Allostatic Load in Adolescents." *American Journal of Epidemiology* 176, suppl. 7: S164-74. doi: 10.1093/aje/kws185.

Timberlake, Jeffrey M, and David S Kirk. 2011. "A Spatio-Temporal Assessment of Exposure to Neighborhood Violence." Washington, DC: Population Association of America.

Wells, Amy Stuart, and Robert L. Crain. 1994. "Perpetuation Theory and the Long-Term Effects of School Desegregation." *Review of Educational Research* 64, no. 4: 531–55. doi: 10.2307/1170586.

Wells, Amy Stuart, Lauren Fox, and Diana Cordova-Cobo. 2016. "How Racially Diverse Schools and Classrooms Can Benefit All Students." New York: The Century Foundation.

Wells, Amy Stuart, Jennifer Jellison Holme, Anita Tijerina Revilla, and Awo Korantemaa Atanda. 2009. *Both Sides Now: The Story of School Desegregation's Graduates.* Berkeley: University of California Press.

Endnotes

1   Johnson (1965).

2   Tench (2003); Russell (2004).

3   Iceland et al. (2010); Jargowsky (2014).

4   Owens (2016).

5   Upper quartile poverty rates for white children ranged from a low of 4 percent to a high of 20 percent across these markets, excluding outlier metro McAllen, TX with an upper quartile rate for white children of 37 percent.

6   Acevedo-Garcia et al. (2008).

7   For each racial/ethnic group, differences are highly significant by segregation level (p < 0.005); ibid.

8   Theall, Drury, and Shirtcliff (2012).

9   diversitydatakids.org and Kirwan Institute for the Study of Race and Ethnicity (2014).

10 Acevedo-Garcia et al. (2016).

11 Ibid.

12 Leventhal, Dupéré, and Brooks-Gunn (2009); Kawachi and Berkman (2003); Ellen and Glied (2015); Sharkey (2013); Newburger, Birch, and Wachter (2011); Timberlake and Kirk (2011); Sharkey et al. (2012); Galster and Killen (1995).

13 Diez-Roux (2003); Sampson, Sharkey, and Raudenbush (2008); Chetty, Hendren, and Katz (2016); Santiago et al. (2014).

14 Noel, Stark, and Redford (2016); Frankenberg, Siegel, Hawley, and Wang (2010); Suitts (2016); Potter (2017).

15 Frankenberg (2016); Joshi, Geronimo, and Acevedo-Garcia (2016).

16 Frankenberg (2016).

17 Reid and Kagan (2015); Reid (2016); Brief of 553 Social Scientists (2006); Aboud, Mendelson, and Purdy (2003); Howes and Wu (1990); Cloutier, Li, and Correll (2014).

18 Wells, Fox, and Cordova-Cobo (2016); Orfield et al. (2016); Fiel (2013).

19 Owens, Reardon, and Jencks (2016).

20 Defined as those eligible for free- or reduced-price school lunch.

21 Orfield et al. (2016).

22 Borman and Dowling (2010); Wells et al. (2009); Mickelson (2008); Schwartz (2010).

23 Reardon (2015); Wells, Fox, and Cordova-Cobo (2016); R. Johnson (2015).

24   Wells, Fox, and Cordova-Cobo (2016); Mickelson (2016); Phillips et al. (2009).

25   Hart Research Associates (2013); Wells, Fox, and Cordova-Cobo (2016); Wells and Crain (1994).

26   Republican Party Platform Committee (2016); Carson (2015).

27   King (1963).

28   Freeman (1978).

Challenging Group-Based Segregation and Isolation: Whether and Why

JENNIFER HOCHSCHILD AND SHANNA WEITZ
Harvard University

Liberal[1] polities are as committed to ending segregation and isolation in principle as they are engaged in maintaining them in practice. That contradiction is partly explained by the perennial gap between ideals and practices; this volume focuses on strategies for closing that gap. But the contradiction between ideal and practice also rests on a deeper base. Understood through a particular lens, liberal ideals permit, and in some circumstances encourage, group isolation and separation. Some public policies reflect that understanding of liberalism, and need to be taken into account as we seek to end impermissible segregation and isolation.

Another contradiction complicates the first. Segregation among racial or ethnic groups is, overall, declining in the United States from a high starting point; segregation among economic classes is rising from a low starting point. Policymakers and analysts can turn to well-established norms, laws, practices, and advocacy organizations in seeking to lessen racial and ethnic isolation. But the United States lacks a parallel set of norms, laws, practices, and advocates for lessening class isolation — in fact, the societal infrastructure does more to reinforce than to eliminate it. From the vantage point of liberal ideals, should we consider group and class segregation independently from one another? If so, how do we evaluate their frequent intersection, even as one is rising and the other declining?

Without resolving them, this chapter explores these two fundamental contradictions, between ideals and practice and between race and class, in light of liberal norms. That is, the rest of this symposium focuses on *how* Americans can effectively intervene to reduce the disadvantages of isolated or segregated communities; here we explore *whether* and *why* to do so.

PATTERNS OF RACIAL, CLASS, AND RELIGIOUS SEPARATION

We begin by documenting changing patterns of racial/ethnic and class segregation in American cities. The former was ubiquitous and deep for most of the twentieth century.[2] By most measures, it is now declining.[3] The latter, however, is increasing[4]; the combination is creating a new spatial dynamic in much of America.

We measure racial or ethnic segregation through the Dissimilarity Index (DI) measures provided by Brown University's American Communities Project for census years 1980 through 2010. We calculate it for 2015 with the 2011–2015 American Community Survey (ACS). The DI ranges from 0 to 100, with 0 representing no segregation and 100 representing perfect segregation between two racial or ethnic groups. The DI uses census tracts to measure the segregation level between groups within a given geographic location; here we analyze non-Hispanic Whites, non-Hispanic Blacks, and Hispanics of any race. We have complete DI measures for 1,498 cities and towns[5] for 1980 through 2015.

We measure income segregation in American cities via the rank-order information theory index.[6] Using census reports of income distribution, this measure ranges from 0 to 1, where 0 represents perfect integration and 1 represents perfect segregation. We use family (rather than individual) income due to its availability over time. We have complete income segregation measures for 3,055 cities and towns for the census years 1980, 1990, and 2000, and for 2010 and 2015 from the 2006–2010 and 2011–2015 ACS's, respectively. (For many of these locations we also have racial segregation measures, as described above.)

Racial or ethnic and economic segregation have, of course, been intertwined throughout American history. Among the 284 cities with 2015 populations of 100,000 or greater for which we have complete data, the correlation between White-Black and economic segregation was 0.31 in 1980 (0.34 for the South), and 0.24 (0.32 for the South) in 2015. In addition to region, the proportion of Black residents matters to the amount of overlap between race and class in a given location. Among cities with more than 100,000 people in 1980, we identified 151 with more than 10 percent Black residents, and 133 with fewer than 10 percent. The correlation between income segregation and racial segregation was 0.33 in the former, and only 0.20 in the latter. The difference in this association was even greater in 2015 — 0.30 for the cities with many Black residents and 0.06 for cities with few.

As the declining correlations from 1980 to 2015 indicate, group and class segregation are slowly diverging. Of the 1,542 cities with relevant data, 46 percent experienced *increasing* economic segregation and *decreasing* White-Black segregation between 1980 and 2015.[7] Figure 1 shows these trends clearly:

However, just as the association between economic and racial segregation varies across place and time, so do the trends shown in Figure 1. White-Black segregation has declined

Figure 1: Family income segregation rose, and White–Black segregation declined, in U.S. cities, 1980 – 2015*

A. Family Income Segregation

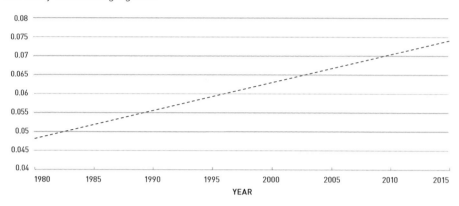

B. White-Black Segregation

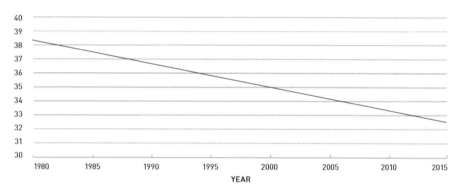

Source: Authors' analyses; see text for data sources. These are fitted values; note that scales on the Y-axes differ.

the most over the past 35 years in absolute terms; Black-Hispanic segregation decreased by just 2 points, while White-Hispanic segregation increased by over 7 points.[8] As a result, 40 percent of the 1,498 cities with data on Latinos in 1980 have seen a simultaneous rise in economic segregation and decline in Black-Hispanic segregation since 1980; the corresponding figure is only 19 percent for White-Hispanic segregation.

Large cities were more likely than smaller ones to experience the trends shown in Figure 1. Fully 94 percent of cities with 2015 populations over 500,000 experienced growing divergence between racial and class segregation over the thirty-five year span, compared with only 44 percent of cities with populations under 100,000.

Finally, the trends shown in Figure 1 differ geographically. Economic segregation has risen similarly across all four regions since 1980, while White-Black segregation rose slightly in the West but nowhere else, White-Hispanic segregation rose slightly in the South and substantially in the Midwest, and Black-Hispanic segregation rose in the West.

The growth of economic segregation has been exacerbated by a simultaneous increase in income inequality within as well as across racial or ethnic groups. The Gini index[9] for the whole American population rose from 0.4 in 1972 to 0.46 in 2015; it also rose within each racial or ethnic group. As in the United States as a whole, in our sample of 326 cities,[10] urban African Americans have higher levels of internal income segregation in 2015 than do Whites or Latinos; Latinos are close behind. From its high starting point, intra-Black income segregation also increased the most over this period. These 326 cities represent 26 percent of the total US population in 2015; intra-Black income segregation increased in them by 53 percent, intra-White income segregation by 23 percent, and intra-Hispanic income segregation by 30 percent.

Segregation and isolation persist, in short, but the kind of separation is changing and it differs across space and group. Racial or ethnic segregation remains high but is declining especially between Whites and Blacks; class segregation is growing in general and within racial or ethnic groups. American cities, whose politics have been oriented along a racial/ethnic axis for a century, are confronting a new situation of increasingly affluent and increasingly poor neighborhoods; racial isolation is no longer the only axis of isolation with which to contend.

THE MANY COSTS AND OCCASIONAL BENEFITS OF GROUP SEPARATION

Both racial/ethnic and economic segregation have many well-documented harms, particularly for disadvantaged groups and the poor. Given the excellent and detailed reviews in the Joint Center's framing paper and McArdle and Acevedo-Garcia's paper in this symposium, we need do no more than stipulate their findings. Nonetheless, as political scientists, we cannot resist adding a few comments on the political costs of group isolation.

Although concerted political effort might be able to change entrenched structural disadvantages, low-income communities have little political power. Black residents in poor neighborhoods participate in politics at lower rates than do Black residents of less poor neighborhoods.[11] The poor vote at lower rates, are less likely to attend community meetings, and participate less in civic or church organizations, which can be springboards for political participation.[12]

Lack of political participation in poor communities has a range of causes, from mistrust of elites, authorities, and fellow residents[13]; to a high proportion of non-citizens or disfranchised ex-felons[14]; to the failure of political parties and candidates to engage in outreach and mobilization.[15] Compared with better-off neighborhoods, poor communities are subject to higher rates of crime, more intense police oversight, and concentrations of residents involved in the criminal justice system — all of which further erode civic ties and trust in one another and political institutions, not to speak of physical access to meetings and voting booths.[16] Thus the public benefits of social bonds among neighbors who trust one another, and the consequent "shared willing-ness to intervene for the public good" through community mobilization and political participation,[17] is hard to come by.[18]

To our knowledge, no public actor in the United States any longer endorses *de jure* racial or ethnic segregation of neighborhoods, schools, jobs, or any other public association. Similarly, whereas 40 percent of Americans agreed strongly or slightly in 1972 that "white people have a right to keep Negroes out of their neighborhoods if they want to, and Negroes should respect that right," by 1996, only 12 percent did so (most respondents disagreed "strongly").[19] Mandatory segregation so obviously violates laws and liberal norms, and causes such harm to individuals, communities, and the society at large, that we need not rehearse why most Americans (at least in public) and all laws reject it. However, this judgment rests on the term "mandatory" — voluntary group separation is more complicated. Americans sometimes endorse group members' choice to live among people like themselves, and voluntary isolation can benefit as well as harm. Put more formally, in addition to its many harmful effects, group or class isolation may have some positive externalities.

For example, a robust scholarly literature explores the benefits of ethnic enclaves for immigrants and their descendants. Communities with high proportions of co-national migrants offer connections to housing, employment, and legal services, as well as to valued cultural practices, normative interactions, and family dynamics.[20] Religious organizations in immigrant enclaves help newcomers find employment and gain higher wages.[21] As one authoritative review puts it, "the enclave is more than just a shelter for the disadvantaged who are forced to take on either self-employment or marginal work in small businesses. Rather, the ethnic enclave possesses the potential to develop a distinct structure of economic opportunities as an effective alternative path to social mobility."[22] Even when children of low-status immigrants are upwardly mobile, marry outside their group, and move away from ethnic enclaves,[23] they value persistent ties with concentrated communities of co-ethnics.[24] So one cannot assume that group separation is always coerced or that its costs always outweigh its benefits to members of the group.

A parallel literature endorses self-chosen isolation among African Americans. Analysts and activists have insisted for decades that racial solidarity and even group separation are necessary to advance economically, enhance political power, reinforce cultural values, and enjoy social interactions.[25] The philosopher Tommie Shelby, for example, denies that justice always requires racial residential integration: "some blacks avoid residing in white neighborhoods to limit unpleasant experiences with whites ... [or] to avoid interracial conflict....There is also ... the positive preference for a black neighborhood.... Black self-segregation is still a choice.... [T]he problem is not closing ranks per se."[26]

Ordinary Americans sometimes concur. In 1982 (the only year that the General Social Survey (GSS) asked this question), a third of black respondents wanted to live in an all or mostly black neighborhood (N=172); 15 percent made a similar choice in June 1995, according to an NBC News poll. A fifth of Hispanics preferred a "mostly Hispanic" neighborhood in a 2003 survey.[27] In a survey that one of us conducted in 2014, more than half of the respondents preferred to be among many members of their own group rather than in more integrated environments if they could be assured of equally good schools, high salaries, or responsive political representatives.[28]

Even the isolated poor can benefit in some ways from remaining in their neighborhood. Moving to a less poor neighborhood risks the loss of social connections, with their associated emotional and material benefits. Residents of a mixed-income Hope VI community in Seattle, for example, lack common experiences and physical proximity to other residents, so they find social interaction difficult.[29] Poor families who have moved to dispersed public housing in mixed-income neighborhoods use neighborhood ties in job searches less frequently than do residents of clustered public housing.[30] Further, moving from public housing to integrated neighborhoods decreases voter turnout, probably due to a loss of social ties.[31] A significant body of work documents the difficulties poor residents have in building interpersonal networks when moving from low- to mixed-income neighborhoods.[32]

Like scholars, activists, and members of the public, laws and judicial decisions sometimes endorse certain forms of or reasons for group separation. Again, the distinction between mandatory and voluntary is crucial here. Exclusionary racial zoning was ruled unconstitutional in 1917,[33] and the ruling was reinforced in 1948.[34] The 1968 Fair Housing Act prohibited housing discrimination, and it was strengthened in a "momentous" though little-noticed Supreme Court decision in 2015.[35] However, zoning laws and ordinances, gated communities, and condo associations continue to sustain some forms of separation and isolation.

Zoning laws are not facially discriminatory; their purpose is "to divide a municipality into residential, commercial, and industrial districts (or zones) ... with the use of property within each district being reasonably uniform."[36] But given "additional restrictions that can be quite detailed,"[37] zoning laws can and easily do separate people by class.[38] The Wharton Residential Land Use Regulation Index (WRLURI) shows that across the

United States, "community wealth is strongly positively correlated with the degree of local land use regulation. … Researchers and policy-makers should seriously consider exclusionary desires as a motivation in many instances."[39] With most Americans supporting zoning laws,[40] class segregation remains difficult to address without infringing on individual choice.

Americans are even more likely to accept, or endorse, religious groups' desire to live separately from other Americans. In *Wisconsin v. Yoder*[41] the Supreme Court held that Amish families could ignore a state's compulsory schooling law after the eighth grade precisely because they lived in an isolated, self-segregated community: "This concept of life aloof from the world and its values is central to their faith. … [T]he Amish have demonstrated the … interrelationship of belief with their mode of life … and the hazards presented by the State's enforcement of a statute generally valid as to others." The Court did not claim that the Amish are unique. And in fact, state and local governments have accommodated Jewish communities through charter schools "with a mission to teach Hebrew,"[42] and other communities through Afrocentric[43] and creationist[44] schools.

These cases are rare, and far from the core concerns of this symposium. But they underline the fact that group isolation may not always be wrong; one must specify criteria for whether and why it is appropriate to "propose strategies for reducing the extent of residential segregation and/or mitigating its consequences." We turn now to that question.

WHETHER AND WHY TO REDUCE RESIDENTIAL SEGREGATION

The difficulty here is that liberal norms mandate several, perhaps contradictory, responses to group-based segregation and isolation, depending on how one understands liberal norms, groups and class, and segregation. So even if liberalism — rather than democracy, liberty, community, faith, or some other powerful set of norms — ought to determine the polity's response to isolation and segregation, there is no clear path forward. Instead, there are several.

Tommie Shelby articulates the liberal response to segregation that mostly drives this symposium's goal of promoting more inclusive communities. In his terms, the commitment to abolish poor black ghettos (which is not the same as ending black communities) is not merely a matter of overcoming prejudice or poverty. Rather, it is "an aggressive attempt at fundamental reform of the basic structure of our society." Ghetto abolitionism attacks racism and class-based stratification in the name of "equal and extensive liberty for all, from freedom of expression and association to the right to an unconditional social minimum and to participate as equals in collective self-governance."[45] Constitutional rights, democratic governance, equal opportunity, liberty — all are fostered by policies to overcome isolation and unchosen segregation among subordinated groups.

Justice William O. Douglas's partial dissent from the *Yoder* decision articulates another liberal view, compatible with Shelby's but with a different emphasis. He focuses on children's right to escape isolation through school and other non-group interactions in order to be able to choose their own future: "It is the student's judgment, not his parents', that is essential if we are to give full meaning to what we have said about the Bill of Rights and of the right of students to be masters of their own destiny." A generalized version of Douglas's focus on the Amish case is the classic liberal claim that a decent polity owes children the resources, skills, and opportunities to choose their futures. Children have a much more difficult time attaining those resources, skills, and opportunities in isolated, segregated, poor communities than in broadly inclusive and diverse communities.

Another way of looking at liberal norms, however, loosens the links between them and the urgency of abolishing isolated, segregated communities. There are two sub-arguments here. The first we have already discussed: liberalism might entail that minority communities have the right of self-determination. If African Americans, Latinos, recent immigrants, the Amish, Muslims, and so on find value in living with people like themselves, even at the cost of greater poverty and isolation than might otherwise be the case, a liberal might argue that group members should have the right to make that choice. The second sub-argument is, for us at any rate, more difficult: do the wealthy, or non-Hispanic whites, racists, or xenophobes have the same liberal right to choose to live among people like themselves so long as others are not legally excluded? Gated communities and zoning laws imply that Americans' answer is "yes." So, is isolation and separation of Whites or the well-off unjust, and to be fought by public policies?[46] By one understanding of liberal norms, the answer must be "no."

Someone espousing liberal norms as the touchstone for public policies must also consider three final complexities. First, what would people choose if they had experienced and understood the implications of *both* voluntary group separation *and* extensive integration and inclusion? That is, how can a polity enable people to determine what is in their own best interests and accords with their deepest values, given that they are necessarily choosing from within a partial, one-sided vantage point? One answer focuses on schooling, roughly in accord with Douglas's partial dissent in *Yoder*: regardless of where and how they live, the state should ensure that children receive an education that allows them to learn about and experience diversity of classmates, ideas, forms of knowledge, and adult role models so that they have more material from which to choose the type of community they want to live in as adults. This argument holds equally for disadvantaged minorities, religiously-based groups, and affluent or dominant groups. We share that view — but it does violate many people's religious, ethnic, or cultural commitments. The point of the *Yoder* plaintiffs was precisely that they did not want their children to experience other ways of life, and then choose between those alternatives and the Amish "mode of life."

Second, do race or ethnicity and class present the same sort of criteria for intervention on the grounds of liberal principles? As we noted above, the United States has a robust set of norms and institutions designed to reduce racial/ethnic separation, but it has no such norms and institutions designed to reduce class separation — in fact, the reverse is true. Zoning laws, geographically districted schools, many legislative districts, 401Ks, and mortgage subsidies in tax law all have the effect, if not the intent, of reinforcing class separation. But liberal activists challenge them much less frequently than they challenge racially discriminatory practices. Given that class separation is rapidly increasing, while group separation is moderating or even slowly declining, the Joint Center's attention to segregation and isolation may reveal a deep contradiction within liberal individualist norms.

Finally, what is the most important public interest in this arena? Perhaps, even if minority groups choose separation, the powerful research evidence showing inequality and failure in outcomes such as education, health, political impact, and economic mobility for the isolated poor requires that policymakers pursue integration in order for the United States as a whole to move forward. But is the public interest best served by promoting policies that run counter to the expressed interests and lived choices of many Americans? In particular, if desegregation requires, as it often does, that the disadvantaged group bear much of the burden of incorporation and diversity,[47] how should we decide what is in the public interest?

We are left with the contradiction with which this paper started. Liberal polities are and should be committed to policies that eliminate isolation and segregation of identifiable groups — except when they should not. Though this contradiction probably cannot be resolved, it can be eased. On the one hand, as Shelby suggests, public policy should increase investment in low-income communities so that poor people of any race or ethnicity have genuine options about whether to move or stay in pursuit of opportunities. Such investment could include protection of affordable housing and local institutions in gentrifying neighborhoods as well as construction of more housing and important amenities for low- and middle-income urban residents. It could also include public sector jobs, subsidies for private sector jobs, robust community colleges and job training facilities, and child support. On the other hand, as Justice Douglas suggests, public schools should be provided with the resources and structures to be able to introduce children to a variety of potential future selves. That could imply desegregation by class as well as by race, a range of types of classrooms or schools with distinctive profiles so students can try out different contexts, incentives to lure suburban children into urban schools and vice versa, and a more robust and explicit commitment to treating public schooling as a public good.[48] Perhaps Americans should directly challenge zoning laws, or pass laws that encourage density and discourage suburban sprawl, or otherwise use choice architecture to promote one type of liberalism without violating the rights and commitments implied by the other type.[49] Liberal polities have never sorted out the tension between individual rights and group autonomy and probably never will — but that is no excuse for failing to take the steps toward freedom of choice and exciting opportunities to flourish that any liberal should embrace.

Bibliography

Alba, Richard, and Steven Romalewski. 2012. "The End of Segregation? Hardly." New York, City University of New York Graduate Center, Center for Urban Research.

Alex-Assensoh, Yvette. 1997. "Race, Concentrated Poverty, Social Isolation and Political Behavior." *Urban Affairs Review* 33, no. 2: 209–27.

Alex-Assensoh, Yvette, and A.B. Assensoh. 2001. "Inner-City Contexts, Church Attendance and African-American Electoral Participation." *Journal of Politics* 63, no. 3: 886–901.

Bell, Derrick. 1976. "Serving Two Masters: Integration Ideals and Client Interests in School Desegregation Litigation." *Yale Law Journal* 85, no. 4: 470–516.

Binder, Amy. 2002. *Contentious Curricula : Afrocentrism and Creationism in American Public Schools.* Princeton: Princeton University Press.

Bischoff, Kendra, and Sean Reardon. 2014. "Residential Segregation by Income, 1970–2009." In *Diversity and Disparities: America Enters a New Century*, edited by John Logan, 208–33. New York: Russell Sage Foundation.

Branch, Glenn. 2016. "Creationism in a Lawsuit against Charter Schools." National Center for Science Education. https://ncse.com/news/2016/09/creationism-lawsuit-against-charter-schools-0018369.

Burch, Traci. 2013. *Trading Democracy for Justice: Criminal Convictions and the Decline of Neighborhood Political Participation.* Chicago: University of Chicago Press.

Case, Anne, and Angus Deaton. 2017. "Mortality and Morbidity in the 21st Century." *Brookings Papers on Economic Activity.* Spring.

Chetty, Raj, Nathaniel Hendren, Patrick Kline, and Emmanuel Saez.. 2014. "Where Is the Land of Opportunity? The Geography of Intergenerational Mobility in the United States." *Quarterly Journal of Economics* 129, no. 4: 1553–1623.

Clampet-Lundquist, Susan. 2004. "Hope VI Relocation: Moving to New Neighborhoods and Building New Ties." *Housing Policy Debate* 15, no. 2: 415–47.

— — —. 2010. "'Everyone Had Your Back': Social Ties, Perceived Safety, and Public Housing Relocation." *City and Community* 9, no. 1: 87–108.

Cohen, Cathy, and Michael Dawson. 1993. "Neighborhood Poverty and African American Politics." *American Political Science Review* 87, no. 2: 286–302.

Connor, Phillip. 2011. "Religion as Resource: Religion and Immigrant Economic Incorporation." *Social Science Research* 40, no. 5: 1350–61.

Crowder, Kyle, Jeremy Pais, and Scott J. South. 2012. "Neighborhood Diversity, Metropolitan Constraints, and Household Migration." *American Sociological Review* 77, no. 3: 325–53.

Curley, Alexandra. 2009. "Draining or Gaining? The Social Networks of Public Housing Movers in Boston." *Journal of Social and Personal Relationships* 26, nos. 2–3: 227–47.

Dawson, Michael. 2001. *Black Visions: The Roots of Contemporary African-American Political Ideologies.* Chicago: University of Chicago Press.

FindLaw. "Land Use and Zoning Basics." http://realestate.findlaw.com/land-use-laws/land-use-and-zoning-basics.html (accessed April 1, 2017).

Frey, William. 2010. "Census Data: Blacks and Hispanics Take Different Segregation Paths." *State of Metropolitan America.* Washington, D.C.: Brookings Institution. https://www.brookings.edu/opinions/census-data-blacks-and-hispanics-take-different-segregation-paths/.

— — —. 2014. *Diversity Explosion: How New Racial Demographics Are Remaking America.* Washington, D.C.: Brookings Institution Press.

Fry, Richard, and Paul Taylor. 2012. "The Rise of Residential Segregation by Income." Washington, D.C.: Pew Research Center.

Gay, Claudine. 2012. "Moving to Opportunity: The Political Effects of a Housing Mobility Experiment." *Urban Affairs Review* 48, no. 2: 147–79.

Gest, Justin. 2016. *The New Minority: White Working Class Politics in an Age of Immigration and Inequality.* New York: Oxford University Press.

Glaeser, Edward, and Jacob Vigdor. 2012. *The End of the Segregated Century: Racial Separation in America's Neighborhoods, 1890–2010.* New York: Manhattan Institute. No. 66.

Goffman, Alice. 2014. *On the Run: Fugitive Life in an American City.* Chicago: University of Chicago Press.

Gyourko, Joseph, Albert Saiz, and Anita Summers. 2008. "A New Measure of the Local Regulatory Environment for Housing Markets: The Wharton Residential Land Use Regulatory Index." *Urban Studies* 45, no. 3: 693–729.

Heilman, Uriel. 2013. "Jewish Public Schools? Hebrew Charter Franchises Offer Radically Different Models." *Jewish Telegraphic Agency*, July 1.

Hochschild, Jennifer. 2012. "Race and Cities: New Circumstances Imply New Ideas." *Perspectives on Politics* 10, no. 3: 647–58.

Hochschild, Jennifer, and Nathan Scovronick. 2004. *The American Dream and the Public Schools*. New York: Oxford University Press.

Hochschild, Jennifer, and Vesla Weaver. 2016. "'Birds of a Feather,' 'Diverse Groups,' 'Go for the Money!' or 'Race Has Nothing to Do with That Choice': A Survey Experiment on Group- and Class-Based Decisions About Schools, Jobs, and Candidates." Chicago: annual meeting of the Midwest Political Science Association. April.

Iceland, John. 2009. *Where We Live Now: Immigration and Race in the United States*. Berkeley: University of California Press.

Kasinitz, Philip, John H. Mollenkopf, Mary C. Waters, and Jennifer Holdaway. 2008. *Inheriting the City: The Children of Immigrants Come of Age*. New York and Cambridge, MA: Russell Sage Foundation and Harvard University Press.

Kleit, Rachel. 2001. "The Role of Neighborhood Social Networks in Scattered Site Public Housing Residents' Search for Jobs." *Housing Policy Debate* 12, no. 3: 541-73.

— — —. 2005. "HOPE VI New Communities: Neighborhood Relationsips in Mixed-Income Housing." *Environment and Planning A* 37, no. 8: 1413-41.

Leiserowitz, Anthony, Edward Maibach, Connie Roser-Renouf, and Nicholas Smith. 2011. "Climate Change in the American Mind: Americans' Global Warming Beliefs and Attitudes in May 2011." Yale Project on Climate Change Communication and George Mason Unviersity Center for Climate Change Communication.

Lerman, Amy, and Vesla Weaver. 2014. *Arresting Citizenship: The Democratic Consequences of American Crime Control*. Chicago: University of Chicago Press.

Logan, John, Wenquan Zhang, and Richard D. Alba. 2002. "Immigrant Enclaves and Ethnic Communities in New York and Los Angeles." *American Sociological Review* 67, no. 2: 299-322.

Massey, Douglas. 1985. "Ethnic Residential Segregation: A Theoretical Synthesis and Empirical Review." *Sociology and Social Research* 69: 315-50.

Massey, Douglas and Nancy Denton. 1993. *American Apartheid: Segregation and the Making of the Underclass*. Cambridge: Harvard University Press.

Massey, Douglas, Jonathan Rothwell, and Thurston Domina. 2009. "The Changing Bases of Segregation in the United States." *Annals of the American Academy of Political and Social Science* 626: 74-90.

Popkin, Susan. 2008. *New Findings on the Benefits and Limitations of Assisted Housing Mobility*. Washington, D.C.: Urban Institute.

Putnam, Robert. 2000. *Bowling Alone: The Collapse and Revival of American Community*. New York: Simon & Schuster.

Rosenblum, Nancy. 2000. *Membership and Morals: The Personal Uses of Pluralism in America*. Princeton: Princeton University Press.

Rothstein, Richard. 2015. "The Supreme Court's Challenge to Housing Segregation." *The American Prospect,* July 5.

Rothwell, Jonathan, and Douglas Massey. 2010. "Density Zoning and Class Segregation in U.S. Metropolitan Areas." *Social Science Quarterly* 91, no. 5: 1123–41.

Sampson, Robert, Jeffrey Morenoff, and Felton Earls. 1999. "Beyond Social Capital: Spatial Dynamics of Collective Efficacy for Children." *American Sociological Review* 64, no. 5: 633–60.

Sampson, Robert, Jeffrey Morenoff, and Thomas Gannon-Rowley. 2002. "Assessing 'Neighborhood Effects': Social Processes and New Directions in Research." *Annual Review of Sociology* 28: 443–78.

Shelby, Tommie. 2016. *Dark Ghettos: Injustice, Dissent, and Reform*. Cambridge: Harvard University Press.

Shihadeh, Edward, and Nicole Flynn. 1996. "Segregation and Crime: The Effect of Black Social Isolation on the Rates of Black Urban Violence." *Social Forces* 74, no. 4: 1325–52.

Singer, Audrey. 2006. *The New Metropolitan Geography of Immigration*. Washington, D.C.: Brookings Institution.

Teasley, Martell, Jandel Crutchfield, Sheara A. Williams Jennings, M. Annette Clayton, and Nathern S. A. Okilwa. 2016. "School Choice and Afrocentric Charter Schools: A Review and Critique of Evaluation Outcomes." *Journal of African American Studies* 20, no. 1: 99–119.

Thaler, Richard, and Cass Sunstein. 2009. *Nudge: Improving Decisions About Health, Wealth, and Happiness*. New York: Penguin Books.

Verba, Sidney, Kay Lehman Schlozman, and Henry Brady. 1995. *Voice and Equality: Civic Voluntarism in American Politics*. Cambridge: Harvard University Press.

Washington, Booker T. 1901, rpt. 2015. *Up from Slavery*. Skyhorse Publishing.

Widestrom, Amy. 2015. *Displacing Democracy: Economic Segregation in America*. Philadelphia: University of Pennsylvania Press.

Zhou, Min. 2004. "Revisiting Ethnic Entrepreneurship: Convergencies, Controversies, and Conceptual Advancements." *International Migration Review* 38, no. 3: 1040–74.

Zine, Jasmin. 2007. "Safe Havens or Religious Ghettos: Narratives of Islamic Schooling in Canada." *Race, Ethnicity, and Education* 10, no. 1: 71–92.

Endnotes

1   "Liberal" refers to the ideology that calls on governments both to foster individual rights and dignity and also to promote equality of opportunity through active intervention in political, economic, or social realms.

2   Massey and Denton (1993); Iceland (2009); Frey (2010).

3   Glaeser and Vigdor (2012); Frey (2014); Hochschild (2012). But see also Alba and Romalewski (2012); Crowder, Pais, and South (2012).

4   Bischoff and Reardon (2014); Massey, Rothwell, and Domina (2009); Fry and Taylor (2012).

5   We measure segregation in cities and towns, rather than across metropolitan areas, to enable one to connect trends in segregation to the characteristics of particular local governments. In general, trends at the city and town level resemble trends measured at the metropolitan level.

6   From Bischoff and Reardon (2014). Like them, we use the Geolytics Neighborhood Change Database (NCDB) as the source of family income data, in order to keep the geography of census tracts constant over time.

7   Conversely, only 470 (15 percent) of the 3,055 cities for which we have relevant data saw a decline in income segregation from 1980 to 2015.

8   That rise is largely explained by demographic change. The share of Latinos in the American population rose from about 6.5 percent in 1980 to almost 18 percent in 2015 — a three-fold increase. For most of that period, migrants moved to a few "gateway" cities and states (Singer 2006), making ethnic segregation very hard to avoid.

9   The Gini index measures economic inequality within a population. It ranges from 0 to 1, with 0 representing perfect income equality across all individuals and 1 representing complete inequality (for example, one person has all of the income and the others have none).

10 The sample of cities in this analysis is much smaller than in the previous analyses, since we use only cities with at least 1,000 families of a given racial or ethnic group. In addition, due to data limitations we also restrict this analysis to the years 2000 and 2015. This constraint allows for a more reliable measure of group income segregation than if we used all cities, but also greatly limits the analysis. Our sample includes 326 cities with complete data from 2000 and 2015 for all racial and ethnic groups.

11 Alex-Assensoh (1997); Cohen and Dawson (1993); Widestrom (2015).

12 Cohen and Dawson (1993); Verba, Brady, and Schlozman (1995).

13 Sampson, Morenoff, and Earls (1999); Goffman (2014).

14 Burch (2013).

15 Gest (2016); Widestrom (2015).

16 Burch (2013); Lerman and Weaver (2014); Shihadeh and Flynn (1996).

17 Sampson, Morenoff, and Gannon-Rowley (2002), 457; Putnam (2000).

18 Research on isolated, low-income Whites is mostly recent and is much less well developed than parallel research on non-Whites. However, a dismal portrayal of economically depressed and geographically isolated White communities is emerging. Case and Deaton (2017); Chetty et al. (2014).

19 General Social Survey (GSS). The question referred to Blacks in 1996. 1972 was the first year for the GSS, and 1996 was the last year in which it included this item.

20 Logan, Zhang, and Alba (2002); Massey (1985).

21 Connor (2011).

22 Zhou (2004), 224.

23 Kasinitz et al. (2008).

24 Logan, Zhang, and Alba (2002).

25 Dawson (2001); Washington (1901).

26 Shelby (2016), 59.

27 Hispanic N=551. About 15 percent of non-Hispanic blacks (N=446) chose "mostly black" for the corresponding question asked of them (Civil Rights and Race Relations Survey 2004, Nov. 2003). See also Gallup Organization, *Race Relations Poll*, Jan. 4-Feb. 28, 1997.

28 A majority of White and Latino respondents preferred the own-group option in all three conditions (school, job, political representation). A majority of Black respondents chose the own-group option only for schools. Hochschild and Weaver (2016).

29 Kleit (2005).

30 Kleit (2001).

31 Gay (2012).

32 Clampet-Lundquist (2004); Clampet-Lundquist (2010); Curley (2009); Popkin (2008).

33 *Buchanan v. Warley*, 245 U.S. 60.

34 *Shelley v. Kraemer*, 334 U.S. 1.

35 *TDHCA v. ICP,* 576 U.S.; Rothstein (2015).

36 FindLaw.

37 Ibid.

38 Rothwell and Massey (2010).

39 Gyourko, Saiz, and Summers (2008), 695, 710.

40 Leiserowitz et al. (2011).

41 406 U.S. 205, 1972.

42 Heilman (2013).

43 Binder (2002); Teasley et al. (2016).

44 Branch (2016).

45 Shelby (2016), 275, 278.

46 Nancy Rosenblum (2000) offers the best analysis of how hard a liberal polity should strive to promote liberal norms within voluntary groups or associations. Her answer is, roughly, "not very hard"; freedom of association is a normative and constitutional right, as well as an essential element of civil society.

47 Shelby (2016); Bell (1976).

48 Hochschild and Scovronick (2004).

49 Thaler and Sunstein (2009).

What Would It Take to Promote Residential Choices that Result in Greater Integration?

Household Neighborhood Decisionmaking and Segregation

JUSTIN STEIL AND REED JORDAN
Massachusetts Institute of Technology

How households make decisions about where to live has obvious implications for residential segregation by both race and class. Technological developments, such as the availability of online search engines, have the potential to change aspects of households' neighborhood decisionmaking process. What do we know about households' decisionmaking processes about neighborhoods, and what are the potential leverage points in those processes where intervention can contribute to the creation of more integrated places?

HOUSEHOLD- AND NEIGHBORHOOD-LEVEL CHARACTERISTICS

Neighborhoods play a particularly focal role in the housing search process in the United States in part because they significantly shape access to opportunity. They do so largely because the decentralized structure of government in the United States leaves the provision of many goods and services, and the raising of a substantial share of government revenue, to municipal governments.[1] Over fifty years ago, the economist Charles Tiebout proposed a "consumer-voter" model of municipal selection in metropolitan areas with high numbers of distinct localities. In Tiebout's model, residents sort into municipalities by selecting the one that best meets their preferred set of amenities and their desire (or ability) to pay for those amenities through taxes. A substantial literature has extended and critiqued Tiebout's consumer-voter thesis, exploring the interaction of income, race, and socioeconomic status in shaping neighborhood choices.[2] According to Tiebout's model, the proliferation of smaller municipalities should best meet the needs of consumer-voters by providing a range of taxation levels and public services suited to their varying preferences. In reality, municipal fragmentation has also facilitated exclusionary zoning policies, racial and economic segregation, and opportunity hoarding by wealthier households. The general principle, however, that both household-level characteristics, such as income and race, and municipal or neighborhood-level characteristics, such as school performance or tax rates, affect the decisionmaking process in the choice among neighborhoods is widely accepted.

The extensive range of amenities associated with a neighborhood in the United States extends from shared community resources (e.g., parks), to infrastructure (e.g., public transportation networks), services (e.g., schools), regulatory structures (e.g., zoning), demographic characteristics (e.g., income distribution), social characteristics (e.g., crime rates), environmental factors (e.g., sources of air and water pollution), physical factors (e.g., structure type and age), and tax rates.[3] Housing prices then represent not only the value of the structure of the home itself but also the quality of local services and neighborhood conditions that are capitalized into home values.[4]

Neighborhood-level factors have been found to be the strongest determinants of household location choice.[5] Among the neighborhood-level factors studied, (e.g., crime, property tax, median housing value), school quality exerted the largest influence on household location decisions.[6] Research using restricted US Census data to examine housing prices along school attendance zone boundaries has similarly found that school performance, as well as neighborhood educational levels and neighborhood racial composition, all exert significant influence on household locational decisions.[7] As one might expect, higher levels of school district fragmentation within a metropolitan area are therefore associated with higher levels of between-district racial residential segregation.[8]

Given the capitalization of neighborhood attributes, such as school performance, into housing prices, the ability to move into a neighborhood of one's choice depends, of course, on household wealth and income. Over the past four decades, neighborhoods have become more segregated by income. Two-thirds of families in 1970 lived in neighborhoods with a median income similar to that of the region overall — essentially middle-class, mixed income communities.[9] But today, less than half of households live in mixed-income neighborhoods as more and more live instead in either very poor or very wealthy ones.[10] Part of the reason for this increase in residential segregation by income is the hollowing out of the middle class in general. But local-level factors, such as municipal and school district boundaries and zoning and housing policies, play a significant role in either exacerbating or ameliorating the sorting of households by income.[11] Nationwide, the poor, and especially the rich, are increasingly isolated from each other and from the middle class. By concentrating the advantages of wealthy households and the disadvantages of low-income households, income segregation accentuates the differences in neighborhood conditions that households face.

Nevertheless, differences in income by race cannot explain the persistently high levels of residential segregation by race. For instance, the average black household with an income greater than $75,000 lives in a neighborhood with a higher poverty rate than the average white household with an income *below* $40,000.[12] Research has consistently found that income differences alone cannot explain either residential segregation by race or the disparities in neighborhood resources that are correlated with racial segregation.[13] Analysis of restricted US Census data with precise location information has found that for black-white segregation, observable sociodemographic characteristics, including education, income, language, and immigration status, can explain less than one-third of contemporary levels of residential segregation.[14]

THE CONTINUING SIGNIFICANCE OF NEIGHBORHOOD RACIAL COMPOSITION

Notwithstanding the significance of schools and other local amenities, the racial composition of a neighborhood remains a significant determinant in the residential decisionmaking process. As Krysan and Crowder write in this volume, residential segregation is reinforced through a housing search process shaped by neighborhood perceptions and homophilous social networks that are themselves already shaped by segregated residential patterns. Krysan and Crowder emphasize that the housing search process cannot be understood through a neat rational decisionmaking model because 1) housing searchers have significant blind spots created by incomplete, and sometimes inaccurate, information about the range of neighborhoods in a metropolitan area; 2) the gaps in housing searchers' knowledge are shaped by their lived experiences and social networks and may therefore be colored by existing segregated living patterns; and 3) the search process is multi-staged, and a large set of housing options are eliminated in preliminary stages using heuristics rather than a careful rational-choice model and cost-benefit analysis of all possible options. Neighborhood racial composition becomes a common, explicit or implicit, heuristic through which neighborhood choice sets are narrowed throughout the search process.

Not only does neighborhood racial composition matter to homeseekers, it matters differently depending on who the homeseeker is. Whites tend to favor predominately white neighborhoods (estimated at less than 20 percent non-white) and are often reluctant to move into neighborhoods with more than a few non-white households.[15] Black homeseekers prefer significantly more integrated neighborhoods, on average ones that are about 50 percent black.[16] According to black homeseekers, their preference for at least some black presence in their neighborhoods is driven by fear of experiencing white hostility.[17]

Research on preferences for neighborhood racial composition has found the existence of a racial hierarchy in preferred neighborhood racial composition. Whites are the most-preferred "out-group"—a race different from the homeseeker—and blacks are consistently the least preferred out-group neighbors. Asians and Latinos are usually located in the center of the hierarchy, with Asians generally more preferred than Latinos.[18]

While early studies established that neighborhood racial composition affects home-seeking behavior, more recent work has analyzed whether the observed neighborhood racial preferences are driven by race itself or whether race serves as a convenient proxy for other socioeconomic factors. Existing research has consistently identified independent effects of neighborhood racial composition beyond socioeconomic factors.[19]

For example, after controlling for crime rates, school quality, and housing values — commonly cited neighborhood characteristics for which homeseekers may see race as a proxy — the percentage of black and Latino residents continues to have a significant independent impact on whites' likelihood of purchasing a house, while the proportion of Asian households has no effect on white home purchases.[20] These findings suggest that race plays an independent role in neighborhood preferences, and, further, that the neighborhood compositions preferred by whites are primarily driven by resistance to living in neighborhoods with substantial shares of black and, to a lesser extent, Latino residents, rather than by a preference for living in white neighborhoods.[21] Turning to measures of neighborhood satisfaction, subjective neighborhood condition (such as property upkeep) and objective neighborhood conditions (such as poverty rates) have been found to explain little of white residents' self-reported neighborhood satisfaction when compared with neighborhood racial composition.[22] In other words, "after accounting for community social characteristics, distinct effects of racial/ethnic composition persist, supporting the idea that there is something about race, above and beyond social class, that propels neighborhood satisfaction."[23]

Perhaps the strongest evidence that racial composition matters independently of class or other neighborhood characteristics when whites make housing decisions comes from studies employing experimental methods to directly test the racial proxy hypothesis.[24] In one experimental study, researchers showed respondents videos of neighborhoods in which the researchers manipulated the racial and class characteristics of the neighborhood in order to test the independent effects of race and class characteristics on neighborhood preference. For example, researchers would show a video of the exact same neighborhood scene but change the race of visible neighborhood residents or the class valence of their activities. White homeseekers consistently rated all-white neighborhoods as the most desirable. The effect of race was smaller for blacks, who identified racially mixed neighborhoods as the most desirable.[25]

In addition to differences by race in preferred neighborhood racial composition and neighborhood perception, segregation is exacerbated by the "mismatch" between whites' desired neighborhood racial composition and the composition of neighborhoods in which they perform their housing search. Whites search in neighborhoods with even higher percentages of whites than they say they would prefer. In contrast, black and

Latino homeseekers conduct their search in neighborhoods that correspond to their stated preferences.[26] While whites mainly search in overwhelmingly white communities, black homeseekers search in communities with a variety of racial compositions.[27]

Less examined are specific differences in how these racialized patterns of neighborhood-seeking behavior unfold between households seeking to purchase homes versus rent, and how access to mortgage capital may shape housing searches. Moreover, little is known about the experience of recent immigrants, especially those with limited English proficiency, in the neighborhood search process. Hum's research in this volume examines the role of minority-owned community banks in providing credit for foreign-born residents who may not qualify for conventional loans. Hum also identifies the role of those same banks in facilitating property purchases by international investors that may drive up housing costs for other buyers and for renters and contribute to neighborhood change through gentrification.

SOURCES OF INFORMATION IN THE HOUSING SEARCH PROCESS

Given what we know about how neighborhood preferences contribute to residential segregation, it is helpful to look in more detail at the processes through which these preferences are transformed into actual neighborhood search decisions and home purchases. In particular, the sources and information that homeseekers use to support and guide their search have implications for segregation and may suggest points of leverage for pro-integration interventions.

A range of types and sources of information are available to homeseekers when searching for homes and neighborhoods. Formal sources of information include real estate agents, newspaper advertisements, and internet-based real estate services. Informal sources include homeseekers' own experiences with particular neighborhoods as well as information passed by word of mouth through friends, family, coworkers, or other social networks. Research on the differential use by race of sources of information in the home search process has found that, after controlling for relevant demographic factors, including income, education, and type of search (buyer versus renter), blacks and whites generally use the same types of search strategies (e.g., networks, realtors, newspapers). However, some differences in the housing search process do exist. Early studies found that black homeseekers are more likely to rely on networks, such as friends and family, and slightly less likely to use the internet in their search than whites, even after controlling for demographic factors and type of search.[28] Much of this research, however, was conducted before use of the internet had become as widespread as it is today. As a result, more research is needed to understand the role of information sources in different types of search processes, with particular emphasis on how the greater availability of data through the internet is changing search processes.[29]

Such further research on housing searches is particularly important given that years of carefully conducted experimental evidence has shown that black and Latino home-seekers continue to be shown fewer units than similarly situated whites, significantly raising the cost of housing searches for black and Latino buyers and limiting their housing options.[30] Previous research has also demonstrated that black renters are often provided less information about units, shown fewer units, and quoted higher rental prices, and that black homebuyers receive less assistance with financing and are steered into lower-income neighborhoods and communities with higher proportions of racial and ethnic minorities.[31]

NEW TECHNOLOGY AND UNANSWERED QUESTIONS IN THE SEARCH PROCESS

In general, homeseekers, regardless of race, increasingly rely on the internet for infor-mation about housing decisions. The vast majority of homebuyers in 2015 (87 percent) still turned to real estate agents at some point in the search, but 42 percent of buyers used the web as the first step of their search, and 89 percent used online sources at least once.[32] The effect of the increased availability of online real estate information on segregation is not yet clear. Easy access to online listings and neighborhood informa-tion may allow consumers to expand the set of neighborhoods considered and avoid segregative steering by informal or formal sources, but formal sources, such as brokers, are governed by the Fair Housing Act and may have the potential to play an integrative role by pointing out neighborhoods that homeseekers might otherwise have ignored.

As McLaughlin and Young write in this volume, greater access to real estate data comes in three general forms: property-specific data, neighborhood-specific data, and "user-customized" data (such as estimates of mortgage borrowing capacity based on information provided by the user, such as household income). Although the increased availability of real estate data will improve the efficiency of the home search process, it could affect residential sorting (and therefore segregation) in two countervailing ways. On the one hand, greater access to data could contribute to larger choice sets of neighborhood options than would have otherwise been considered and ultimately to greater residential integration by race and class. On the other hand, greater access to data, especially regarding neighborhood characteristics such as school performance and public safety, could increase the demand for and price of housing in areas with high levels of access to opportunity. Without a corresponding expansion in supply, price stratification across neighborhoods could increase, contributing to increased segregation by class and also potentially by race.[33]

Further, through the provision of different search results tailored to users' IP address location or shaped by users' prior searches and social networks, online searches have the potential to introduce even less visible segregative effects. And in other ways, online services in the housing market have shown evidence of how new technology can exacerbate, instead of ameliorate, discriminatory effects. For instance, evidence from the short-term rental platform Airbnb is illustrative. Airbnb hosts are less likely to accept guests with distinctively African American names, and black hosts earn less for renting similar apartments than white hosts after controlling for quality, location, and other relevant factors.[34]

As the examples from Airbnb demonstrate, a primary concern about new technological platforms, algorithmic matching services, and the increased availability of information about consumers is that new forms of discrimination may emerge that have wide-spread impacts but that are hard for individual users to identify. How can new search tools and data sources contribute to residential integration instead of to perpetuating segregation? Municipalities such as Oak Park, Illinois and Shaker Heights, Ohio undertook concerted efforts to encourage the creation and maintenance of racially integrated communities at a time when white flight and blockbusting by realtors was the primary concern. Are there ways to modernize those efforts to encompass the growing use of new, wide-reaching online platforms? Discrimination can at least be partially addressed through the design of online markets — by, for example, limiting the availability of information based on which people discriminate and instituting incentives for users to reduce discrimination. While much recent attention has focused on bias in machine learning and search engines, little has been done to understand how search engines can prevent segregation or even encourage integration.

The literature on neighborhood search processes highlights the fact that whites' general reluctance to move into predominantly minority neighborhoods perpetuates segregation. This fear and stigmatization of black spaces can be cyclical — integration has historically focused on opening up white spaces to black people, which can simultaneously valorize white spaces and stigmatize the black spaces left behind.[35] But the experience of high-cost cities also raises the question of what happens when whites move into predominantly black and Latino neighborhoods, initially fostering integration, but, in the long term, contributing to gentrification, displacement, and new forms of segregation. How can we revise integration efforts, often created in response to fears of white flight, for a context where the primary concerns vary from white avoidance of neighborhoods with predominantly black and Latino residents all the way to white displacement of low-income black and Latino residents in gentrifying neighborhoods? The chapters in this section provide a helpful starting point.

Bibliography

Bayer, Patrick, Fernando Ferreira, and Robert McMillan. 2007. "A Unified Framework for Measuring Preferences for Schools and Neighborhoods." *Journal of Political Economy* 115, no. 4: 588–638.

Bayer, Patrick, Robert McMillan, and Kim Reuben. 2004. "The Causes and Consequences of Residential Segregation: An Equilibrium Analysis of Neighborhood Sorting." Working Paper. https://pdfs.semanticscholar.org/9332/32 35844af1ff6649dd2f755c091cd646388f.pdf.

Bayoh, Isaac, Elena G. Irwin, and Timothy Haab. 2006. "Determinants of Residential Location Choice: How Important are Local Public Goods in Attracting Homeowners to Central City Locations?" *Journal of Regional Science* 46, no. 1: 97–120.

Bischoff, Kendra, and Sean F. Reardon. 2013. "Residential Segregation by Income, 1970–2009 | Center for Education Policy Analysis." US2010 Project. http://cepa.stanford. edu/content/residential-segregation-income-1970-2009 (accessed March 16).

Briffault, Richard. 1990. "Our Localism: Part I —The Structure of Local Government Law." *Columbia Law Review* 90, no. 1: 1–115.

Charles, Camille Zubrinsky. 2000. "Neighborhood Racial-composition Preferences: Evidence from a Multiethnic Metropolis." *Social Problems* 47, no. 3: 379–407.

— — — . 2008. "Who Will Live Near Whom?" *Poverty & Race Research Action Council* 17, no. 5.

Dunning, Richard, and Andrew Grayson. 2014. "Homebuyers and the Representation of Spatial Markets by Information Providers." *International Journal of Housing Markets and Analysis* 7, no. 3: 292–306.

Edelman, Benjamin G., and Michael Luca. 2014. "Digital Discrimination: The Case of AirBnB.com." Working Paper 14–054. Cambridge, MA: Harvard Business School.

Edelman, Benjamin G., Michael Luca, and Dan Svirsky. 2016. "Racial Discrimination in the Sharing Economy: Evidence from a Field Experiment." Working Paper 16–069. Cambridge, MA: Harvard Business School.

Ellen, Ingrid G. 2008. "Continuing Isolation: Segregation in America Today." In *Segregation: The Rising Cost for America*, edited by James H. Carr and Nandinee K. Kutty, 261–78. New York: Routledge.

Ellen, Ingrid Gould, Justin Steil, and Jorge De la Roca. 2016. "The Significance of Segregation in the 21st Century," *City and Community* 15(3): 8–13.

Farley, Reynolds, Elaine Fielding, and Maria Krysan. 1997. "The Residential Preferences of Blacks and Whites: A Four Metropolis Analysis." *Housing Policy Debate* 8, no. 4: 763–800.

Fennell, Lee Anne. 2001. "Beyond Exit and Voice: User Participation in the Production of Local Public Goods." *Texas Law Review* 80, no. 1: 1–87.

Fischel, William A. 2009. *The Homevoter Hypothesis*. Cambridge, MA: Harvard University Press.

Fischel, William A., and Wallace E. Oates. 2006. *The Tiebout Model at Fifty: Essays in Public Economics in Honor of Wallace Oates*. Lincoln Institute of Land Policy.

Frug, Gerald E. 2001. *City Making: Building Communities without Building Walls*. Princeton: Princeton University Press.

Galster, George. 2001. "On the Nature of Neighbourhood." *Urban Studies* 38, no. 12: 2111-24.

Ge, Yanbo, Christopher R. Knittel, Don MacKenzie, and Stephen Zoepf. 2016. "Racial and Gender Discrimination in Transportation Network Companies." Working Paper no. 22776. Cambridge, MA: National Bureau of Economic Research.

Havekes, Esther, Michael Bader, and Maria Krysan. 2016. "Realizing Racial and Ethnic Neighborhood Preferences? Exploring the Mismatches Between What People Want, Where They Search, and Where They Live." *Population Research and Policy Review* 35, no. 1: 101-26.

Krysan, Maria. 2008. "Does Race Matter in the Search for Housing? An Exploratory Study of Search Strategies, Experiences, and Locations." *Social Science Research* 37: 581-603.

Krysan, Maria, and Michael Bader. 2007. "Perceiving the Metropolis: Seeing the City Through a Prism of Race." *Social Forces* 86, no. 2: 699-733.

Krysan, Maria, Mick P. Couper, Reynolds Farley, and Tyrone A. Forman. 2009. "Does Race Matter in Neighborhood Preferences? Results from a Video Experiment." *American Journal of Sociology* 115, no. 2: 527-59.

Krysan, Maria, and Reynolds Farley. 2002. "The Residential Preferences of Blacks: Do They Explain Persistent Segregation?" *Social Forces* 80, no. 3: 937-80.

Krysan, Maria, Reynolds Farley, and Mick P. Couper. 2008. "In the Eye of the Beholder." *Du Bois Review: Social Science Research on Race* 5, no. 1: 5-26.

Lewis, Valerie A., Michael O. Emerson, and Stephen L. Klineberg. 2011. "Who We'll Live with: Neighborhood Racial Composition Preferences of Whites, Blacks and Latinos." *Social Forces* 89, no. 4: 1385-1407.

Logan, John R., and Brian J. Stults. 2011. "The Persistence of Segregation in the Metropolis: New Findings from the 2010 Census." Census Brief Prepared for Project US2010.

McLaughlin, Ralph, and Cheryl Young. 2017. "Data Democratization and Spatial Heterogeneity in the Housing Market." This volume.

National Association of Realtors. 2015. "2015 Profile of Home Buyers and Sellers."

Owens, Ann. 2016. "Inequality in Children's Contexts: Income Segregation of Households With and Without Children." *American Sociological Review* 81 (3):549-574.

Owens, Ann. 2017. "Racial Residential Segregation of School-Age Children and Adults and the Role of Schooling as a Segregating Force." *Russell Sage Foundation Journal of the Social Sciences* 3 (2):63–80.

Pattillo, Mary. 2014. "The Problem of Integration." In *The Dream Revisited*, edited by Ingrid Ellen Gould and Justin Steil. January. http://furmancenter.org/research/iri/essay/the-problem-of-integration.

Reardon, Sean F., and Kendra Bischoff. 2011. "Income Inequality and Income Segregation." *American Journal of Sociology* 116, no. 4: 1092–1153. doi:10.1086/657114.

Rhode, Paul, and Koleman Strumpf. 2003. "Assessing the Importance of Tiebout Sorting: Local Heterogeneity from 1850 to 1990." *The American Economic Review* 93, no. 5: 1648–77. doi:10.1257/000282803322655482.

Rothwell, Jonathan T., and Douglas S. Massey. 2010. "Density Zoning and Class Segregation in US Metropolitan Areas." *Social Science Quarterly* 91, no. 5: 1123–43.

Sampson, Robert J., and Stephen W. Raudenbush. 2004. "Seeing Disorder: Neighborhood Stigma and the Social Construction of "Broken Windows." *Social Psychology Quarterly* 67, no. 4: 319–42.

Steil, Justin, Jorge De la Roca, and Ingrid Gould Ellen. 2015. "Desvinculado y Desigual: Is Segregation Harmful to Latinos?" *The ANNALS of the American Academy of Political and Social Science* 660, no. 1: 57–76. doi:10.1177/0002716215576092.

Swaroop, Sapna, and Maria Krysan. 2011. "The Determinants of Neighborhood Satisfaction: Racial Proxy Revisited." *Demography* 48, no. 3: 1203–29.

Tiebout, Charles M. 1956. "A Pure Theory of Local Expenditures." *Journal of Political Economy* 64, no. 5: 416–24.

Turner, Margery Austin, and Stephen L. Ross. 2005. "How Racial Discrimination Affects the Search for Housing." In *The Geography of Opportunity: Race and Housing Choice in Metropolitan America*, edited by Xavier de Sousa Briggs, 81–100. Washington, D. C.: Brookings Institution Press.

Turner, Margery Austin, Robert Santos, Diane K. Levy, and Douglas A. Wissoker. 2013. "Housing Discrimination against Racial and Ethnic Minorities 2012: Full Report." The Urban Institute.

Watson, Tara. 2009. "Inequality and the Measurement of Residential Segregation by Income in American Neighborhoods." *Review of Income and Wealth* 55, no. 3: 820–44.

Yang, Rebecca, and Paul A. Jargowsky. 2006. "Suburban Development and Economic Segregation in the 1990s." *Journal of Urban Affairs* 28, no. 3: 253–73.

Endnotes

1   See Briffault (1990); Frug (2001).

2   See, for example, Fennell (2001); Rhode and Strumpf (2003); Fischel and Oates (2006); Fischel (2009).

3   Galster (2001).

4   Dunning and Grayson (2014).

5   Bayoh, Irwin, and Haab (2006).

6   Ibid.

7   Bayer, Ferreira, and McMillan (2007).

8   Owens (2017).

9   Bischoff and Reardon (2013).

10   Ibid.

11   Owens (2017); Rothwell and Massey (2010); Watson (2009); Yang and Jargowsky (2006).

12   Logan and Stults (2011).

13   Ibid.

14   Bayer, McMillan, and Reuben (2004).

15   Charles, "Who Will Live Near Whom?"; Ellen.

16   Krysan and Farley (2002).

17   Krysan and Farley (2002); Farley, Fielding, and Krysan (1997).

18   Charles (2008); Charles (2000).

19   For a summary, see Krysan (2008).

20   Lewis, Emerson, and Klineberg (2011).

21   Ibid.

22   Sampson and Raudenbush (2004); Krysan et al. (2009); Krysan, Farley, and Couper (2008).

23   Swaroop and Krysan (2011), 1215.

24   Krysan et al. (2009); Krysan, Farley, and Couper (2008).

25   Krysan et al. (2009).

26   Havekes, Bader, and Krysan (2016).

27   Krysan (2008); Krysan and Bader (2007).

28   Krysan (2008).

29   Ellen (2008).

30   Turner et al. (2013).

31   Turner and Ross (2005); Turner et al. (2013).

32   National Association of Realtors (2015).

33   McLaughlin and Young (2017); see also Ellen, Steil, and De la Roca (2016) regarding changes over time in the significance of segregation.

34   Edelman, Luca, and Svirsky (2016); Edelman and Luca (2014). See also Ge et al. (2016) on discrimination in Uber.

35   Pattillo (2014).

Data Democratization and Spatial Heterogeneity in the Housing Market

RALPH MCLAUGHLIN
Veritas Urbis Economics

CHERYL YOUNG
Trulia

T he internet has democratized data, improving access to information for millions of households worldwide and, in the process, making them better informed. The residential real estate industry is no exception, as the democratization of data has empowered the public with a wealth of information previously available only to real estate agents and other industry professionals. Left unexplored is how improved access to residential real estate data might affect spatial patterns of residential choice. In this paper, we posit that the democratization of real estate data ultimately makes the home search process more efficient. In turn, we argue, increased efficiency in the home search process has two potentially countervailing effects on the spatial heterogeneity of residential settlement patterns: (1) housing search choice sets expand to include properties in neighborhoods that are more diverse than choice sets developed by consumers in a less efficient environment, and (2) demand to live near amenities increases without an appropriate increase in housing supply, and thus "prices out" existing and future residents. However, we argue that the extent to which households might be priced out of a neighborhood is directly influenced not by data availability per se, but by the ease to which housing supply can be increased to meet demand in such locations. We therefore divide our policy recommendations into three specific efforts: (a) helping the market increase housing choice by reducing exclusionary and restrictive zoning policies in our nation's most expensive, amenity-laden markets, (b) giving housing choice voucher (HCV) recipients the option to hide their voucher status from landlords during the application process, and (c) requiring a portion of the two-dollar per capita LIHTC funding to be used in Census tracts that qualify as high value.

This paper is structured as follows: in the next section, we present descriptive analysis of how consumers use online real estate data in the homebuying and rental search process. Next, we review existing literature and develop a conceptual model of the effects of home search efficiency on spatial heterogeneity. In the penultimate section, we analyze measures of home value heterogeneity and racial diversity across the 100 largest housing markets in the United States. Last, we conclude with policy recommendations based on our findings in the previous section.

DEMOCRATIZATION OF DATA AND CONSUMER SEARCH BEHAVIOR IN REAL ESTATE

The internet has created, delivered, and disrupted the traditional process of finding, evaluating, and purchasing goods and services. The residential real estate industry is no exception, as both real estate and non-real estate-specific online purveyors of data have allowed homebuyers and renters to make more informed decisions.[1] Prior to the digital age, most real estate information was effectively proprietary: homebuyers and renters would have to contact real estate agents, landlords, and mortgage brokers to obtain the information needed for decision making. Sharing this information was a core service added to the traditional value chain by real estate professionals, and consumers would often start the homebuying process by gathering information with their help. Post-internet, the ubiquity of accessible data on homes, neighborhoods, and financial products has empowered consumers to gather these data on their own, by using either online real estate marketplaces (Redfin, Trulia, Zillow, etc.) or other internet services providing neighborhood-level information (Google Maps, Yelp, GreatSchools, etc.). Consumers today often gather much of this information before employing an agent, thereby altering the traditional real estate agent-consumer interaction.

While consumers now have access to an abundance of housing market data online, many continue to use real estate agents. For example, in a broad survey of 13,249 consumers by Zillow Group conducted in 2016, 87 percent of buyers use online resources and 75 percent select a real estate agent or broker to work with, suggesting that most buyers combine these two resources. In fact, buyers who utilize online resources are significantly more likely to also use an agent (77 percent versus 59 percent who do not use online resources).

Consumers are also initiating the home search process on their own. Only about half (51 percent) of buyers using an agent employ one at the beginning of their home search. Forty-one percent start the search process on their own, but ultimately use an agent before making an offer. This includes 27 percent who employ an agent after searching for a while but before touring homes, and an additional 14 percent who use an agent after visiting open houses but before submitting offers. Just 7 percent of all buyers who use an agent wait until they are ready to make an offer before enlisting the agent's services.[2] Below, we identify the types of online information that homebuyers and renters are likely using during their home search process.

Figure 1: Top Resources Used to Search, Shop, or Purchase a Home

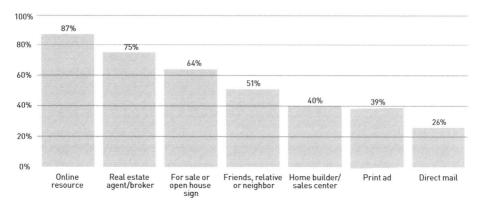

Online resource: 87%
Real estate agent/broker: 75%
For sale or open house sign: 64%
Friends, relative or neighbor: 51%
Home builder/sales center: 40%
Print ad: 39%
Direct mail: 26%

Figure 2: Property-Specific Information on Trulia

Map View Street View Crime Schools Shop & E

FOR SALE OPEN HOUSE

$320,000

222 Maple St
North Austin, Austin TX 78758

3 Beds — Single Family
2 Baths — 6,300 sqft Lot Size
2,200 sqft — Built in 1964
$382 sqft — 5 Days on Trulia

Home Details

A house this size is a rare find in North Austin. Great layout for entertaining. Extended driveway provides room for boat, RV, etc. It is tucked away in a quiet cul-de-sac that is easily accessible from 183 and North Lamar: 15 minutes from UT, downtown, ACC Highland & Northridge campuses, The Domain and

Types of Data Available to Modern Homebuyers and Renters

In general, there are three primary types of online data available to homebuyers and renters. These are: (1) property-specific data, (2) neighborhood-specific data, and (3) user-specific data. We briefly describe and provide examples of each below.

Property-Specific Data. Detailed information about residential properties form the backbone of the most popular online real estate marketplaces, including consumer brands within Zillow Group (Zillow, Trulia, Hotpads, Streeteasy, NakedApartments), the Move brands (Realtor.com, Move.com, Doorsteps.com, SeniorHousingNet. com), Homes.com, and Redfin.com. These property-specific data include two subtypes: (a) public records data, which constitute the official record of home type, square footage, lot size, number of bedrooms and bathrooms, legal lot description, property taxes paid, year built, and sales history of a given property, and (b) property listings data, which typically include listing price, pictures, seller/leasing description, agent contact information, and property details not available from public records. Public records originate from county assessor and recorder offices, while listing data can originate from a variety of sources, including real estate agents, multiple listing services (MLS), property owners (for-sale and for-rent), property managers, and third party aggregators. Three marketplaces — Zillow, Trulia and Redfin — also use these data to provide home value estimates.

Figure 3: Neighborhood-Specific Data on Trulia

Neighborhood-Specific Data. Homebuyers and renters can also find a wealth of easily accessible information on neighborhoods surrounding properties of interest. Examples include local information on crime, school location and quality, business location and quality, natural hazards, and commute times. These data are available on many online real estate marketplaces, but often originate from third-party providers who also provide the information on their own websites. For example, Zillow, Trulia, Redfin, and Realtor.com all provide school rating information originating from GreatSchools.org, but the latter has its own site dedicated to providing the public with the same data. Other examples of neighborhood-specific data provided by online real estate marketplaces, but derived from third-party providers, include: the location and quality of local businesses provided by Yelp.com, crime data provided by SpotCrime.com and CrimeReports. com, and walking and transit scores provided by WalkScore.com.

Figure 4: Amenities of a Home - What Drives Home Selection

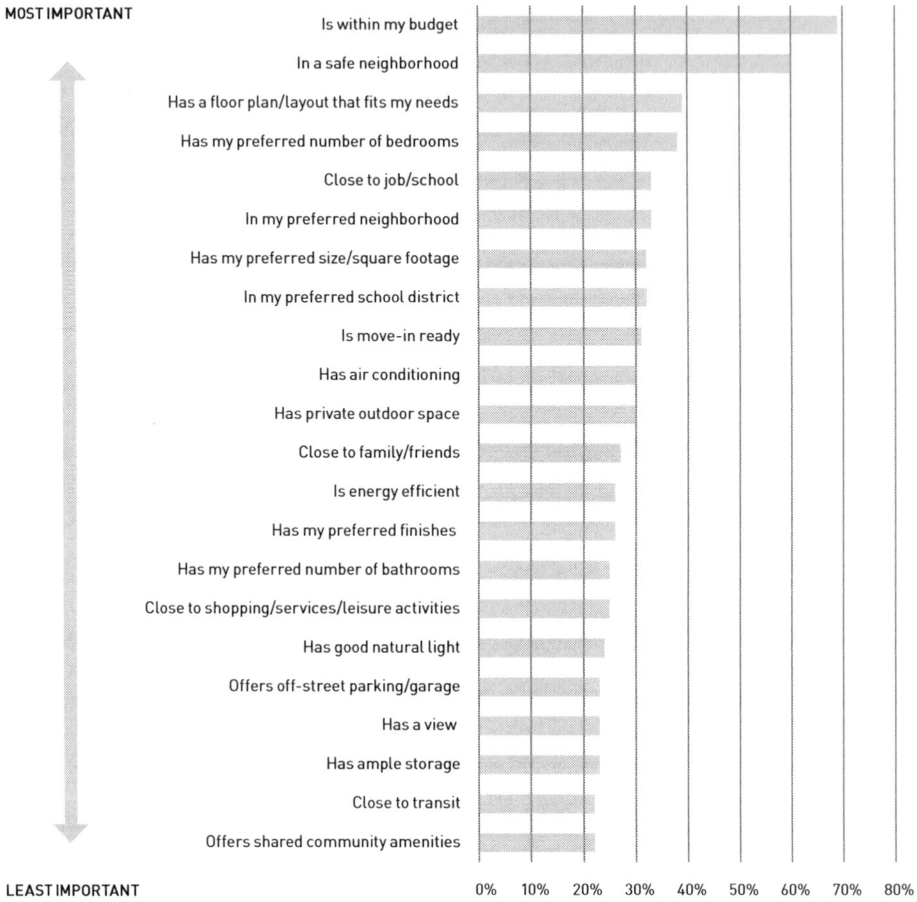

User-Customized Data. In addition to property- and neighborhood-specific information, online real estate marketplaces also provide customized information for homebuyers and renters. Such information includes customized estimates of borrowing power, housing affordability, whether it is better to rent or buy a home, commute times, and mortgage quotes. This information is delivered primarily through standalone calculators on these websites, or in the case of commute time and affordability estimates, through individual property display pages. Similar to neighborhood-specific information, user-customized information can also be found on non-real estate websites. For example, commute times between two locations can be calculated using Google Maps, mortgage quotes can be obtained on Bankrate.com, and affordability estimates can be found on Nerdwallet.com.

Amenity Preferences

Using a survey of homebuyers conducted by Zillow Group, we find that consumers indeed value amenities that can be found using the three types of data discussed above. Figure 4 shows the share of households who value a specific amenity when selecting a home for more than 20 different amenity types. Online marketplaces offer data on most of these amenities. For example, nearly 70 percent of homebuyers say a home "within my budget" is important, which can be generated using online afford-ability calculators (user-customized data); 60 percent say a home in a "safe neighbor-hood" is important, and visualized crime data and other user-generated content offer a starting point (neighborhood-specific data); and nearly 40 percent say a home with "a floorplan/layout that fits my needs" is important, which can be found using online listings (property-specific data). Clearly, the democratization of real estate data online can help consumers more efficiently search for a home that meets their preferences.

However, the impacts of this democratization of data on household sorting and spatial heterogeneity are less clear. In the following section, we present two conceptual mechanisms by which increased search efficiency might affect household sorting.

NEIGHBORHOOD AMENITY PREFERENCES AND RESIDENTIAL CHOICE

In the home search process, traditional methods of information gathering — through word of mouth, scouring newspaper ads, or directly from a real estate agent — can result in information asymmetries and/or cost considerable time. Online real estate marketplaces complement these methods and introduce efficiency, particularly at the beginning of the process when homeseekers develop a choice set of properties. Theoretically, a more efficient search process should expand this choice set because it will allow more properties to be filtered in a given time period. Below, we discuss how spatial heterogeneity might be affected by a more efficient housing search process.

Household preferences have long played a role in spatial heterogeneity, as households tend to geographically sort themselves into communities with the bundle of goods and services best matching their preferences. This process of "voting with one's feet" is often based on local amenities, public goods, and tax rates.[3] This encourages people with like preferences to coalesce in groups that are able to take advantage of local collective benefits produced only through economies of scale.[4] Online search resources may enhance this self-sorting process.

Despite what is known about the role of preferences in housing choice, very little research has been done on the effects of online real estate marketplaces on traditional search methods. These methods have certainly changed in recent decades. In 1981, home searches were primarily initiated by consulting newspaper ads (22 percent) and relying on word of mouth (8 percent).[5] By 2016, online searches were the most common method (44 percent), word of mouth dropped to fifth, and printed news-paper ads no longer registered. Online resources clearly provide more information at lower search costs; however, only emerging empirical evidence exists about how they have materially affected search patterns.

One of the few studies on the topic — a survey of house hunters in Wake County, North Carolina in the early 2000s — found that the use of the internet increased the number of homes visited by respondents in their search.[6] A more recent study shows that "search pressure," a measure of the online popularity of search locations, high-lights where demand for housing is high.[7] In these examples, online searches unveil the ability of consumers to conduct low-cost, extensive searches across geographies and property parameters to expand their housing choice sets.

Theoretically, democratization of real estate data could change neighborhood composi-tion in two countervailing ways. First, it may lead to more spatial heterogenity through the expansion of consumer housing choice sets. More competitive online shopping for mortgates, for example, could have such an effect: when households receive the lowest possible mortgage rate for their credit profile, their qualifying loan amount is maximized and thus so is their housing choice set. And improved search efficiency for properties could lead homeseekers to discover neighborhoods that they would not find through traditional methods, such as word of mouth or newspaper listings. As consumers filter a large volume of disparate information, biases towards certain neighborhoods might be lifted as they encounter homes that fit their preferences. The question in both cases is whether a larger choice set will also be qualitatively more diverse: if so, the expanded choice set would lead to greater diversity within cities, and vice versa.

Second, however, data democratization could lead to increased housing costs where certain amenities are in high demand, which, in turn, could exacerbate existing patterns of spatial homogeneity by pricing out lower-income households. Competition for amenities such as safe neighborhoods or good school districts could create an "amenity effect," raising the demand for a neighborhood to a level at which higher-income individuals could outbid others. Unless these neighborhoods had perfectly elastic supply, those that are outbid would be priced out. Exclusionary zoning is an existing practice that has created such amenity effects; it influences who settles in an area by increasing housing prices through either density restrictions or impact fees to cover public services.[8]

THE RELATIONSHIP BETWEEN RESIDENTIAL SEGREGATION AND HOUSING CHOICE

Both the passage of the Fair Housing Act in 1968 and the ability of online real estate marketplaces to reduce information asymmetries leading to discriminatory action has largely protected homebuyers and renters from explicit forms of discrimination. This section explores how historic processes of segregation led to path-dependent inertia in housing availability, particularly for those at the lower end of the housing market. Housing choice sets are constrained not just by the information available to housing consumers, but also by the diversity of housing supply across geographies.

The relative concentration of home values may help to explain persistent racial and income segregation in urban housing markets as homeseekers face expanding or contracting housing choices as they search across their neighborhoods of interest. These characteristics in the housing stock reflect ingrained effects of discrimination that continue to impact where and what type of housing is available. For example, the effects of redlining, which began in the late 1930s, can still be read in the socioeconomic outcomes of neighborhoods in cities today,[9] despite the fact that redlining is currently unlawful under the Fair Housing Act. More recently, in the wake of the Great Recession, researchers found that the incidence of foreclosures resulting from predatory lending of subprime mortgages was highly correlated with racial segregation.[10] The uneven impact of the foreclosure crisis on neighborhoods demonstrates that segregation can entrench inequalities of opportunity for years to come.

In order to examine whether racial segregation may be related to limited choice sets across metropolitan areas, we develop an index of home value segregation and compare it to measures of racial segregation. Racial segregation in this paper is measured by calculating the index of dissimilarity between white and nonwhite residents, or how unevenly distributed distinct groups are across Census tracts in a given metropolitan area.[11] Data on race are from the US Census's 2015 5-Year American Community Survey. Home value segregation is measured by calculating the ratio of the median value of homes in a given Census tract to the median value of all homes in the metropolitan area. These ratios are placed into one of six buckets, and the very low value and very high value Census tracts are added together to obtain the share of tracts in the most extreme value buckets and expressed through the home value segregation index.[12] This measure captures the share of Census tracts in a metropolitan area that contain the most extreme home values, and like measures of racial segregation, provides a snapshot of how unevenly distributed home values are across the metropolitan area. Home value data are provided by the online real estate marketplace Trulia. Racial segregation and home value segregation indices are calculated for the 100 metros[13] with the highest number of occupied housing units.

The link between measures of home value segregation and racial and income segregation is particularly revealing, and may help to explain persistent residential segregation. The relationship between the segregation of housing values and white-nonwhite segregation is positive and statistically significant, producing a Pearson's correlation

Figure 5: Home Value Segregation versus White-Nonwhite Segregation Across 100 Largest Metros

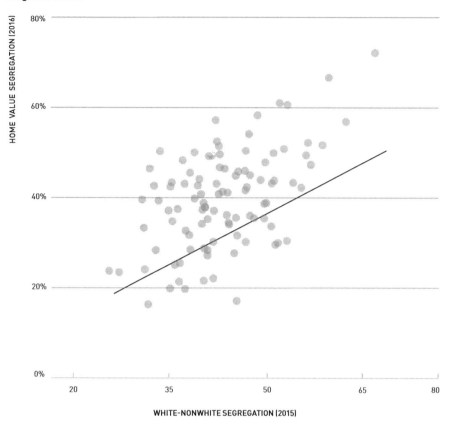

Source: US Census 2015 5-Year ACS and Trulia data.

coefficient of 0.53. Figure 5 shows that white-nonwhite segregation tends to rise as home value segregation rises across the most populated 100 metropolitan areas. In fact, variation in metropolitan segregation patterns can be at least partially explained by within-metro variation in how segregated housing choice sets are based on the polarization of home values neighborhood by neighborhood.

This relationship suggests that efforts to decrease racial and income segregation could be addressed by expanding choices in the housing market. The lack of housing diversity by price constrains homeseekers, particularly those that are lower-income. As a result, they are relegated to find homes where they are available, further entrenching racial and income segregation. Expanding housing choices entails providing equal access for households by reducing disparities in housing affordability. The next section concludes this paper and explores policy recommendations that expand housing choice despite the path-dependent inertia of housing supply.

SUMMARY AND POLICY RECOMMENDATIONS

In this paper, we have examined the various mechanisms by which the democratization of real estate data might affect spatial heterogeneity in the housing market. Specifically, we argue that democratization of real estate data improves home search efficiency. In turn, this improved efficiency can affect residential settlement patterns if (1) it encourages consumers to settle in neighborhoods that are systematically different than ones they would otherwise have settled in, and (2) demand to live near amenities increases without a proportionate increase in housing supply. Our findings also show that racial segregation is tied very closely to home value segregation in the largest US metropolitan areas, suggesting that increasing housing choice in the most expensive metropolitan submarkets might help reduce spatial patterns of racial homogeneity. Given the empirical evidence presented in the previous sections show that supply-side, rather than demand-side, factors are more to blame for patterns of residentia segregation in the U.s., we focus our policy recommendations on reform of existing housing choice policies rather than on household preferences.

Reform of Existing Housing Choice Policies

Our policy recommendations are subdivided into three specific efforts: (a) helping the market increase housing choice by reducing exclusionary and restrictive zoning policies in our nation's most expensive, amenity-laden markets; (b) giving housing choice voucher (HCV) recipients the option to hide their voucher status from landlords during the application process; and (c) requiring a portion of the two-dollar per capita LIHTC funding to be used in Census tracts that qualify as high value. We discuss these three in turn below.

Restrictive Zoning Policies. A large and growing body of scholarly work suggests that restrictive zoning laws make housing more expensive not only through supply restrictions but also because they reduce affordable housing choices.[14] While land use authority in the US is primarily in the hands of states and municipalities, the federal government can provide incentives for local and state governments to zone for more affordable housing types. Such incentives might include allocation of Department of Housing and Urban Development Community Development Block Grants, Department of Transportation Safety Grants, or Department of Education Local Education Agencies Grants that would be tied to increases in housing choice in areas with high demand and few affordable homes.

Since land use authority constitutionally rests with states, there is also room for addressing exlusionary policy reform at the state level. Such reforms would likely need to allocate both market-rate and below-market-rate housing unit targets for local governments. Enforcement measures are key to efficacy, and would need to take a balanced approach using both incentives and penalities, such as tying infrastructure and school funding as well as local land use powers to these housing targets. Maryland's Priority Funding Areas and Florida's now defunct Growth Management Act provide relevant examples for how states might address the housing provision problems arising from exclusionary zoning.

Housing Choice Voucher Reform. Housing choice vouchers theoretically allow families to make geographically flexible housing decisions because the subsidy is attached to the person(s) rather than to a housing unit fixed in space. However, there have been obstacles to this flexibility in practice. Up until last year, fair market rent (FMR), which are used to determine the amount of voucher subsidies, was set at the metropolitan level. Given that rents are typically non-uniform across a housing market, the metropolitan-wide FMR would essentially limit HCV recipients to poorer neighborhoods. The Obama administration helped remedy this problem last year by introducing a limited roll-out of FMR at the zip code level, but implementation has since been postponed. Still, two challenges remain. First, landlords are not required to accept Section 8 tenants, and second, applicants are required to disclose their intent to use an HCV to landlords. Both requirements introduce avenues for discrimination based on landlords' willingness to accept HCVs. This could be remedied by making the Section 8 Housing Choice Voucher Program a single-blind process, where landlords are not allowed to ask about the voucher status of their applicants but voucher holders are free to use them for any property. Foe example, Seattle's fair housing laws provide a model for preventing landlords from discriminating against tenants based on their source of income and use of a Section 8 certificate or other subsidy programs.

Low-Income Housing Tax Credit Reform. Finally, place-based housing choice programs, such as Low-Income Housing Tax Credits (LIHTC), provide market-based subsidies to developers of affordable housing through issuing of resalable tax credits. Developers of affordable housing typically sell the credits they receive from the LIHTC program and use the proceeds to grow their equity stake in the project, which in turn improves their chances of attracting debt or equity financing to complete the project. To further increase the efficacy of the LIHTC program in expanding housing choice where choice is needed most, we propose requiring a proportion of the existing two-dollar per capita LIHTC funding to be used in the most income-segregated Census tracts. That proportion might be directly tied to current levels of spatial homogeneity in the housing market. For example, if the share of very high value Census tracts in an area were 20 percent, then 20 percent — or 40 cents — of the two-dollar per capita LIHTC allocation would need to be used in such Census tracts. In effect, this would allow municipalities with very high value tracts a choice in how to increase more affordable housing opportunities in their community: they could either amend their zoning laws to encourage lower-cost, market-rate housing that would remove classification of the Census tract(s) as very high value, or allow LIHTC projects to be built using the spatial inequality-related LIHTCs.

Bibliography

Bayer, Patrick, Hanming Fang, and Robert McMillan. 2014. "Separate when Equal? Racial Inequality and Residential Segregation." *Journal of Urban Economics* 82: 32-48.

Boustan, Leah Platt. "Racial Residential Segregation in American Cities." 2012. In *The Oxford Handbook of Urban Economics and Planning*, edited by Nancy Brooks, Kieran Donaghy, and Gerrit-Jan Knaap, 318-39. Oxford: Oxford University Press.

Bratt, Rachel G., and Abigail Vladeck. 2014. "Addressing Restrictive Zoning for Affordable Housing: Experiences in Four States." *Housing Policy Debate* 24, no. 3: 594-636.

Card, David, Alexandre Mas, and Jesse Rothstein. 2008. "Tipping and the Dynamics of Segregation." *The Quarterly Journal of Economics* 123, no. 1: 177-218.

Cherif, Emna, and Delvin Grant. 2014. "Analysis of e-Business Models in Real Estate." *Electronic Commerce Research* 14, no. 1: 25-50.

Emerson, Michael O., Karen J. Chai, and George Yancey. 2001. "Does Race Matter in Residential Segregation? Exploring the Preferences of White Americans." *American Sociological Review* 66, no. 6: 922-35.

Havekes, Esther, Michael Bader, and Maria Krysan. 2016. "Realizing Racial and Ethnic Neighborhood Preferences? Exploring the Mismatches Between What People Want, Where They Search, and Where They Live." *Population Research and Policy Review* 35, no. 1 (2016): 101-26.

Huffman, Forrest E., Arthur C. Nelson, Marc T. Smith, and Michael A. Stegman. 1988. "Who Bears the Burden of Development Impact Fees?" *Journal of the American Planning Association* 54, no. 1: 49-55.

Ihlanfeldt, Keith R., and Timothy M. Shaughnessy. 2004. "An Empirical Investigation of the Effects of Impact Fees on Housing and Land Markets." *Regional Science and Urban Economics* 34, no. 6: 639-61.

Kucuk, Umit S., and Sandeep Krishnamurthy. 2006. "An Analysis of Consumer Power on the Internet." *Technovation*, 27, no. 1-2: 47-56.

Levitt, Steven D., and Chad Syverson. 2008. "Market Distortions when Agents Are Better Informed: The Value of Information in Real Estate Transactions." *Review of Economics and Statistics* 90, no. 4: 599-611.

Madrigal, Alexis C. 2014. "The Racist Housing Policy that Made Your Neighborhood." *The Atlantic*, May 22.

Massey, Douglas S., and Jonathan Rothwell. 2009. "The Effect of Density Zoning on Racial Segregation in US Urban Areas." *Urban Affairs Review* 44, no. 6: 779-806.

McGuire, Martin. 1974. "Group Segregation and Optimal Jurisdictions." *Journal of Political Economy* 82, no. 1: 112-132.

National Association of Realtors. 2016. "Home Buyer and Seller Generational Trends Report 2016." Washington, D.C.: National Association of Realtors.

— — —. 2017. "Real Estate in a Digital Age 2017 Report." Washington, D.C.: National Association of Realtors.

Nelson, Robert K., LaDale Winling, Richard Marciano, Nathan Connolly, et al. 2015. "Mapping Inequality: Redlining in New Deal America." In *American Panorama: An Atlas of United States History*, edited by Robert K. Nelson and Edward L. Ayers. Web. https://dsl.richmond.edu/panorama/redlining (accessed December 15, 2016).

Palm, Risa, and Michelle A. Danis. 2001. "Residential Mobility: The Impacts of Web-based Information on the Search Process and Spatial Housing Choice Patterns." *Urban Geography* 22, no. 7: 641-55.

Piazzesi, Monika, Martin Schneider, and Johannes Stroebel. 2015. "Segmented Housing Search." Working Paper No. 20823. Cambridge, MA: National Bureau of Economic Research.

Rae, Alasdair. 2015. "Online Housing Search and the Geography of Submarkets." *Housing Studies* 30, no. 3: 453-72.

Rugh, Jacob S., and Douglas S. Massey. 2010. "Racial Segregation and the American Foreclosure Crisis." *American Sociological Review* 75, no. 5: 629-51.

Schelling, Thomas C. 1978. *Micromotives and Macrobehavior.* New York: Norton.

Tiebout, Charles M. 1956. "A Pure Theory of Local Expenditures." *Journal of Political Economy* 64, no. 5: 416-24.

Waldfogel, Joel. 2008. "The Median Voter and the Median Consumer: Local Private Goods and Population Composition." *Journal of Urban Economics* 63, no. 3: 567-82.

Zillow Group. 2016. "Consumer Housing Trends Report 2016."

Endnotes

1 Levitt and Syverson (2008).

2 Zillow Group (2016).

3 Tiebout (1956).

4 McGuire (1974).

5 National Association of Realtors (2017).

6 Palm and Danis (2001).

7 Rae (2015).

8 On density restrictions and racial segregation, see Massey and Rothwell (2009). On impact fees, see Huffman et al. (1988) and Ihlanfeldt and Shaughnessy (2004).

9 Madrigal (2014).

10 Rugh and Massey (2010).

11 White residents are those that report their race to be white alone and non-Hispanic. Nonwhite persons include people of all nonwhite races, plus people of Hispanic origin regardless of race.

12 The six value buckets, as defined by the ratio of median value in a Census tract to median value of the metro, are: 1) very low value — less than 0.67; 2) low value — 0.67 to 0.8; 3) low-middle value — 0.8 to 1.0; 4) high-middle value — 1.0 to 1.25; 5) high value — 1.25 to 1.5, and 6) very high value — greater than 1.5.

13 Metropolitan regions include Census Metropolitan Statistical Areas, or metropolitan divisions, where available.

14 Bratt and Vladeck (2014).

Minority Banks, Homeownership, and Prospects for New York City's Multi-Racial Immigrant Neighborhoods

TARRY HUM
City University of New York

New York City's global city status is, in part, attributable to its diverse immigrant neighborhoods. Fueled by post-1965 immigration from Asia, Latin America, and the Caribbean, a full 38 percent of New Yorkers were born outside of the United States. The immigrant presence is even greater in the borough of Queens, where nearly half of all residents are foreign-born and neighborhood streetscapes reflect a "hyperdiversity" of ethnicities, languages, and cultures.[1] Asian and Latino residential choices have been a driving force of neighborhood racial change; however, immigrant settlement has not tempered anti-Black segregation, which remains a durable feature of the spatial ecology of the city's neighborhoods.[2] My paper investigates the neighborhood locations and mortgage financing for Asian home purchasers for two years, 2010 and 2015 (the most recent year the data is available). As the primary strategy for individual asset building, homeownership contributes to neighborhood stability and higher levels of civic engagement, and home purchasers may be indicative of neighborhood demographic trends with respect to race and class.[3]

Asian Americans are the fastest growing racial group in the United States. Since Asian Americans are also highly diverse, an aggregated socioeconomic profile that claims parity with non-Hispanic whites is misleading. As a majority immigrant population, many Asians continue to face multiple incorporation challenges due to limited English language ability, low levels of educational attainment, and concentration in informal economies. Recent studies find deepening economic disparities (including high rates of poverty) among Asian Americans based on ethnicity and class.[4] My paper focuses on the role of Asian minority banks, formed to serve the underbanked population, in facilitating home mortgage lending.[5] The nearly exclusive lending to Asian borrowers by Asian minority

Thanks to Michela Zonta, Center for American Progress and Francesc Ortega, Queens College Department of Economics, for data assistance and helpful comments.

banks expands the sources of credit for this population group. However, between 2010 and 2015, the share of mortgage loans originated by Asian minority banks for property purchases by Asian investors, as opposed to owner-occupants, increased significantly. This finding raises concerns about the impact of investment real estate capital on neighborhood stability, affordability, and demographic composition.

I utilize several public databases to locate New York City's multi-racial immigrant neighborhoods and examine home mortgage lending patterns and property sales prices. I focus on the role of minority financial institutions, including community banks, in originating home mortgages to Asian borrowers, both owner-occupants and investors, for residential property purchases in Queens and Brooklyn. I conclude with a discussion of the potential impacts of Asian investment capital in the city's multi-racial immigrant neighborhoods.

DATA AND METHODS

The 1975 Home Mortgage Disclosure Act (HMDA) requires mortgage companies and depository institutions, such as commercial banks and credit unions, to collect and make public home mortgage loan data including applicant race and ethnicity, income level, census tract of property, lender, loan amount, and application decision. HMDA also includes an occupancy variable that differentiates between individuals buying homes for their primary residence (owner-occupied purchasers) and individuals buying homes as investments or as second or vacation homes (non-owner occupied purchasers). Although the HMDA data does not indicate whether a non-owner-occupant purchase is intended as a vacation or second home or as an investment, New York City outer borough neighborhoods are not prime locations for pieds-à-terre, so it is highly probable that most of the non-owner-occupant home purchases are for investment purposes rather than for a vacation or second home.[6]

I utilize the occupancy variable in HMDA to study the trends and impact of minority banks and investor property purchases on the prospects for neighborhood diversity and stability. New York City is a high-priced housing market, and the outer boroughs such as Brooklyn and Queens have experienced recent spikes in residential property values.[7] The share of home mortgage lending to non-owner-occupants may be an indication of rising property values and rents. Investments in residential properties may price out renters who seek to become homeowners and may also result in direct displacement of those who can no longer afford market rents.[8] For this study, I focus on first-lien home purchase mortgages for one- to four-family properties including individual condominium or cooperative units in buildings with more than four units. Finally, my paper examines trends in the average sales prices for these property types in neighborhoods with significant numbers of investor purchases. Neighborhoods with such purchases experience increased real estate speculation and prospects for socio-demographic change.

My research draws from several public databases, including the 2011–2015 American Community Survey 5-year estimates and 2010 and 2015 HMDA. On the municipal level, I utilize the New York City Department of City Planning (DCP) Neighborhood Tabulation Area (NTA) definitions and the Department of Finance sales data for 2010 and 2015 to develop a two-year profile of purchasers of one-to-four family properties by race and occupancy status (owner-occupied and investor), lending institutions, and neighborhood location. Studies on neighborhood diversity employ a typology based on the racial composition of census tracts.[9] While I similarly identify majority race and diverse or integrated tracts, I then locate these census tracts in neighborhoods based on the NYC DCP NTA definitions because neighborhoods encompass the local geography of everyday life, civic engagement, and social identity. Based on aggregating census tracts into neighborhoods, I focus on those with significant clusters of integrated and majority-minority census tracts for a deeper look at minority banks, mortgage lending and homeownership, and neighborhood diversity.

LOCATING NYC'S DIVERSE NEIGHBORHOODS

I modified the census definitions in a NYU Furman Center 2012 report to categorize New York City's census tracts into three broad types — majority race (at least 70 percent of tract population is comprised of one racial group); integrated white (with at least 30 percent non-Hispanic whites and at least 20 percent of another racial group); and integrated nonwhite where non-Hispanic whites are less than 10 percent and a combination of minority groups (each at least 20 percent) comprise the largest share of the tract's population (see Table 1). Integrated (white and nonwhite) tract typologies were further categorized according to the two largest racial groups that make up the tract population.[10] While the census tract typologies are mutually exclusive, neighborhoods are typically larger spatial geographies and are defined by aggregating a number of census tracts. Therefore, the neighborhood composition may include multiple census tract typologies, and this is often the case for New York City's immigrant neighborhoods.

The majority of New York City's multi-racial neighborhoods inclusive of Asians are located in Brooklyn and Queens. These are also the neighborhoods where Asian homeownership is concentrated and where new homebuyers, especially Asians, are purchasing one- to four-family properties. Asian-white, white-Asian, and White mixed census tracts are concentrated in Brooklyn's Bensonhurst, Dyker Heights, Bay Ridge, Gravesend, Sheepshead Bay, and Bath Beach, which are largely clustered in south Brooklyn.[11] In 2013, the NYU Furman Center found that nearly all Bensonhurst's residents lived in a racially integrated census tract.[12] In Queens, Asian-white and

Table 1: New York City Population by Census Tract Typology and Borough

Census Typology	Num. of Census Tracts	Total Population	Racial Composition					Distribution of Census Tracts by Borough				
			Non Hispanic White	NH Black	NH Asian	Hispanic Latino	Other Race	Manhattan	Brooklyn	Queens	Bronx	Staten Island
Majority Race Tracts												
Majority White	464	1,887,647	77%	3%	8%	10%	2%	120	200	63	16	65
Majority Black	333	1,082,809	5%	79%	3%	11%	3%	12	193	105	23	0
Majority Latino	175	830,411	8%	10%	7%	74%	2%	19	36	54	65	1
Majority Asian	46	196,793	9%	3%	72%	12%	3%	5	7	34	0	0
Integrated White Tracts												
White-Asian	172	627,801	55%	3%	28%	11%	3%	32	71	65	1	3
White-Latino	146	516,661	56%	5%	9%	28%	2%	18	36	55	25	12
White Mixed	132	510,358	33%	13%	22%	29%	3%	12	32	74	3	11
Latino-White	66	277,315	30%	7%	8%	53%	2%	11	10	20	21	4
Asian-White	60	215,704	33%	2%	52%	11%	2%	3	27	30	0	0
White-Black	55	184,956	36%	44%	5%	12%	3%	5	44	4	2	0
Integrated Nonwhite Tracts												
Latino-Black	192	892,240	5%	30%	3%	61%	2%	23	25	12	129	3
Black-Latino	142	613,562	6%	57%	3%	32%	2%	17	57	6	43	9
Asian-Latino	62	248,902	9%	6%	48%	31%	6%	3	6	53	0	0
Latino-Asian	44	199,715	9%	5%	31%	50%	4%	3	4	32	5	0
Mixed Nonwhite	33	124,928	6%	26%	25%	24%	20%	0	3	27	3	0
Asian-Black	4	13,130	7%	26%	41%	14%	12%	4	0	0	0	0
Black-Asian	2	3,811	5%	32%	22%	18%	23%	0	0	2	0	0

Source: American Community Survey 2011–2015 5-year estimates.

white-Asian census tracts are concentrated in affluent and once-exclusive neighborhoods such as Auburndale, Douglaston, Forest Hills, and Oakland Gardens. Forest Hills' fierce resistance to the city's scattered-site housing program that sought to integrate white middle-class neighborhoods received extensive media coverage during the 1970s. Mediation by then-Mayoral appointed attorney, Mario Cuomo, resulted in a compromise that reduced the number of proposed housing units by half, with 40 percent set aside for seniors.[13]

Majority Asian tracts anchor several Asian-Latino neighborhoods including Sunset Park in Brooklyn and Elmhurst in Queens. Roger Sanjek's *The Future of Us All* chronicled the public spaces, namely the community board, where Elmhurst-Corona's majority-minority transition was negotiated during the 1980s.[14] "Quality-of-life" issues such as illegal conversions, overcrowded and strained infrastructure (including public schools, subways, and sanitation services), and the lack of youth recreational facilities continue to be sources of tension in Elmhurst, Corona, and Sunset Park. Most recently, a long-time Community Board 4 member was removed for her comment that bicycle lanes would no longer be necessary once President Trump deports the neighborhood's "illegals."[15]

Asian-Latino and Latino-Asian tracts are also concentrated in majority Latino neighborhoods such as Woodhaven and Jackson Heights in Queens. Jackson Heights is widely recognized as one of the world's most diverse neighborhoods.[16] The neighborhood's largely South Asian population is reflected in Indian, Bangladeshi, and Pakistani small businesses clustered around Diversity Plaza. Jackson Heights also anchors northwest Queens' small but visible Himalayan population, including Nepalis and Tibetans. The pan-Latino population includes Columbians, Ecuadorians, and Mexicans, all similarly reflected in the commercial streetscape.[17] Even though community activists thwarted a proposal to expand a Business Improvement District along Roosevelt Avenue, a major commercial corridor linking Queens' dense, multi-racial immigrant neighborhoods, real estate market pressures and rising commercial rents threatening small businesses have not abated.[18]

South Asian New Yorkers are also concentrated in the southern Queens neighborhoods of South Ozone Park and Richmond Hill, with sizable numbers of mixed nonwhite, Asian-Latino, Latino-Asian, and black-Asian census tracts. These neighborhoods make up "Little Guyana," representing the heart of New York City's Indo-Caribbean community as well as the epicenter of the 2008 foreclosure crisis for Asian New Yorkers.[19] In addition to providing assistance in multiple South Asian languages, Chhaya CDC's studies documented the prevalence of illegal conversions.

While two black-Asian census tracts are located in South Ozone Park, three of the four Asian-Black census tracts are part of Queens' concentrated African American and Afro-Caribbean middle-class neighborhoods of Jamaica Estates-Holliswood, Hollis, and Queens Village. Along with Richmond Hill, Ozone Park, and South Ozone Park, these neighborhoods are concentrated across southeast Queens with relatively high levels of Black and Asian homeownership.[20] One Asian-black census tract is part of downtown Flushing, Queens, and this tract is mostly occupied by Bland Houses, one of Flushing's two New York City Housing Authority complexes. Like many urban neighborhoods during the 1950s, Flushing's working-class African American community was destroyed by "slum clearance," a section of it razed for the city's first municipal parking lot.[21] Some residents were relocated to newly constructed public housing along the industrial waterfront.

MINORITY BANKS

The United States has a long history of minority banks that formed to meet the credit needs of populations excluded from mainstream financial institutions. The Federal

Deposit Insurance Corporation (FDIC) defines a minority bank as a federally insured depository institution with 51 percent or more of the voting stock owned by minority individuals who are Black American, Asian American, Hispanic American, or Native American. Historically, minority banks were primarily Black-owned institutions, but at present Black-owned banks represent a mere 15 percent of all minority banks while nearly one in two (48 percent) are owned by Asian Americans. The statutory framework for minority banks was established by the Financial Institutions Reform, Recovery, and Enforcement Act (FIRREA) of 1989, which included a section outlining the federal government's support to preserve and promote minority ownership of insured financial institutions through its Minority Depository Institutions Program, provision of training, technical assistance, and educational programs, and efforts to preserve the minority character in the event of failing institutions.[22]

Most minority banks are community banks that make credit decisions with nonstandard data garnered through their community insider positions, local knowledge, and long-term relationships. This "special skill set" provides a competitive advantage to financial institutions that "play a crucial role to many minority communities and small businesses, *often serving as the only option for their customers.*"[23] Much of the literature on Asian minority banks emphasizes the social and cultural nature of institutional practices such as relationship banking.[24] Established to counter financial exclusion due to discrimination and linguistic and cultural barriers, minority banks serve as a "key facilitator for capital circulation" by establishing ethnic businesses, expanding the spatial boundaries of residential communities, and promoting opportunities for immigrant homeownership.[25] As a Chinese immigrant homeowner in Forest Hills explained, "major banks have trouble evaluating our credit history and sources of money."[26]

The FDIC defines community banks based not on an asset size threshold, but rather on standard lending and deposits gathering activities as well as geographic scope of operations.[27] Noncommunity banks are institutions with more than 10 percent of total assets in foreign holdings or more than 50 percent of total assets in specialty banking companies.[28] Based on this definition of a community bank, the FDIC reported at the end of 2013 that 93 percent of all FDIC-insured institutions, approximately 6,313 institutions, are community banks, with the remaining 499 institutions as noncommunity banks.[29] While all black, Native American, and multi-race banks are community banks, this is not the case for Asian and Latino minority banks, whose shares of community banks, at 88 percent and 83 percent respectively, fall below the national share (90 percent) of minority banks that qualify as community banks (see Table 2). There is only one Latino minority bank based in New York that is also a community bank– Ponce De Leon Federal Bank — and in 2015 this bank originated only two mortgages to Latino purchasers of a one- to four- family property. Transnational banks such as Banco Popular are also on the FDIC list of minority banks. Even though Banco Popular was rebranded

Table 2: Minority Banks by Racial Group, Total Assets, and Community Banks

Minority Banks	Number	Percent	Total Assets July 13, 2016 (000s)	Average Assets (000s)	Community Banks	% Community Banks	NY-NJ HQs
Total	162	100%	$199,837,714	$1,233,566	146	90%	13
Asian	78	48%	$95,742,702	$1,227,471	69	88%	11
Latino	41	25%	$95,352,089	$2,325,661	34	83%	1
Black	24	15%	$5,997,961	$249,915	24	100%	1
Native American	18	11%	$2,674,390	$148,577	18	100%	0
Multi-Race	1	1%	$70,572	$70,572	1	100%	0

Source: FDIC Minority Depository Institutions Program.

Popular Community Bank in 2012 and has numerous branches in majority Latino neighborhoods, this bank originated no home mortgages in New York City in 2015.

While Asian minority banks include transnational banks (i.e., noncommunity banks with foreign holdings), there are eleven Asian community banks established in the New York metropolitan area, including Abacus Federal Savings Bank and First American International Bank. Asian-owned banks now make up the largest segment of minority banks; however, the scope and mission of a significant number of Asian banks is to serve a transnational rather than a community-oriented market. In addition to minority banks, there are financial institutions such as mortgage companies that also originate residential mortgages. Self-described as a "full service mortgage banking entity," Summit Mortgage Bankers, Inc., serves a largely Asian American market through its main office in Flushing, Queens.[30] With a focus on the majority immigrant population, these minority banks and lending institutions offer an additional option for Asian Americans not typically available to other borrowers.

PROFILE OF NEW YORK CITY HOME PURCHASERS BY RACE AND OCCUPANCY STATUS

In 2010, lenders originated about 29,000 first-lien home mortgages to purchasers of one- to four-family properties including condominiums and cooperative apartments in New York City. Although far below the loan volumes in the years preceding the 2008 foreclosure crisis, the number of home purchase mortgages did increase by 10 percent to about 32,000 mortgages in 2015. The pre-2008 foreclosure crisis peak year for New York City home mortgage lending was 2004, when nearly 60,000 mortgage loans were originated for a one- to four-family property purchase. The volume of residential mortgage originations in 2015 represents only 54 percent of this peak year loan volume (see Table 3). There are notable racial differences in mortgage lending in the post-crisis period, particularly for Asians, who have rebounded most strongly with a 2015 loan volume at 80 percent of the 2004 peak year. We will see that the rebound for Asian borrowers is driven by loan originations to finance investor property purchases.

Table 3: Mortgage Originations for 1- to 4-Family Property Purchase in 2004 and 2015

	Peak Year 2004	% Loans by Race Group 2004	2015	% Loans by Race Group 2015	Difference in Loan Volume	% Peak Year Loans
Total	59,659	100%	32,127	100%	-27,532	54%
Non Hispanic White	26,105	44%	14,812	46%	-11,293	57%
Asian	9,862	17%	7,880	25%	-1,982	80%
Black	8,801	15%	2,545	8%	-6,256	29%
Latino	6,886	12%	2,375	7%	-4,511	34%
Other	290	0.5%	176	1%	-114	61%
No Information	7,715	13%	4,339	14%	-3,376	56%

Source: NYU Furman Center 2011b and 2015 Home Mortgage Disclosure Act Data.

In contrast, 2015 residential mortgage lending to blacks and Latinos is well below the peak year levels: black and Latino borrowers received only 8 percent and 7 percent, respectively, of the mortgage loans originated in 2015.

If borrowers are differentiated based on occupancy status, it is evident that the recent increase in home mortgage loans between 2010 and 2015 is due to the growth of lending to investor borrowers. While the overwhelming majority of home mortgages in 2010 and 2015 were for owner-occupants, in 2015, the number of loans to investors more than doubled to 4,775 mortgage loans (see Table 4). Moreover, the local geography of investor purchases expanded. In 2010, nearly one in two investor mortgages was for a property in Manhattan. This was not the case for 2015, as the volume of mortgages for investor purchases in the outer boroughs of Brooklyn and Queens increased dramatically, with the largest number in Queens. Even though owner-occupants remain the dominant type of borrower, the number of mortgage loans to owner-occupants declined slightly in Brooklyn and Queens in 2015.

While the total volume of home mortgage loans to New Yorkers increased from 2010 to 2015, this was not the case for black borrowers, whose numbers of home mortgage loans declined by 15 percent (see Table 5). Among the racial groups that experienced an increase in home mortgage loans, the increases were uneven, with Latinos at a nominal 5 percent while loans to Asian borrowers increased by 21 percent. The racial profile of borrowers who financed the purchase of a one- to four-family property with a mortgage in New York City remained consistent in 2010 and 2015: about 45 percent were non-Hispanic white, 25 percent were Asian, and Latinos and Blacks comprised 10 percent or less.

Asian borrowers drove the dramatic increase in investor mortgage loans for purchasing one- to four-family properties in 2015. In 2010, investor borrowing accounted for

Table 4: Mortgage Originations for 1- to 4-Family Property Purchase Secured by 1st Lien

	2010			2015			Change 2010-2015		
	Owner-Occupied	Investor	Total	Owner-Occupied	Investor	Total	Owner-Occupied	Investor	Total
New York City	27,036	2,195	29,266	27,328	4,775	32,127	1%	118%	10%
Manhattan	6,285	1,013	7,316	6,794	1,376	8,177	8%	36%	12%
Brooklyn	7,449	500	7,956	6,780	1,319	8,105	-9%	164%	2%
Queens	8,861	518	9,387	8,565	1,567	10,139	-3%	203%	8%
Bronx	2,025	71	2,096	2,103	215	2,321	4%	203%	11%
Staten Island	2,416	93	2,511	3,086	298	3,385	28%	220%	35%

Source: 2010 and 2015 Home Mortgage Disclosure Act Data

less than 10 percent of total originated home mortgages, of which the majority were secured by non-Hispanic white investors. This profile changed in 2015, when the number of investor loans more than doubled and loans to Asian borrowers exceeded the number of loans to non-Hispanic white borrowers. In fact, among Asian borrowers in 2015, loans to investors represent more than one-fifth (22 percent) of total home mortgage loans for one- to four-family properties, which is the highest share of loans to non-owner-occupants for all racial groups. The spike in investor purchases results from several trends related both to the migration of a sizable middle and upper middle class Asian population and to an influx of Chinese real estate investment capital, from sources ranging from transnational corporations to individuals.[31]

In 2015, a comparable number of mortgages for one- to four-family properties were made to Asian investors (1,760 loans) and non-Hispanic white investors (1,682), but there is a significant geographic difference in that 56 percent of the properties mortgaged by Asian investors were in Queens, compared to only 14 percent for non-Hispanic white investors. The concentration of Asian investor purchases in Queens portends continued Asian population growth, but increased investments raise property values and rents and may therefore have consequences for neighborhood integration and stability.

The median income for non-Hispanic white home purchasers exceeds the median incomes of Asian, Latino, and black home purchasers in 2010 and 2015. Generally, the median income of investor borrowers is greater than that of owner-occupant borrowers, with the exception of Asian investors in 2015 (see Table 6). In addition to banks, credit unions, and nonbank mortgage companies, minority banks present another source of capital for Asian borrowers. The median income of Asian investors in 2015 is $87,000, which is significantly lower than the median income of non-Asian investors as well as co-ethnic borrowers purchasing a one- to four-family property for a primary residence.

Table 5: First-Lien Mortgage Originations for 1- to 4-Family Property Purchase by Race Group

	2010			2015			Change 2010-2015		
	Owner-Occupied	Investor	Total	Owner-Occupied	Investor	Total	Owner-Occupied	Investor	Total
Total	27,036	2,195	29,266	27,328	4,775	32,127	1%	118%	10%
Non Hispanic White	12,018	1,046	13,068	13,128	1,682	14,812	9%	61%	13%
Asian	5,989	539	6,531	6,120	1,760	7,880	2%	227%	21%
Black	2,950	59	3,010	2,457	87	2,545	-17%	47%	-15%
Latino	2,190	75	2,266	2,239	134	2,375	2%	79%	5%

Source: 2010 and 2015 Home Mortgage Disclosure Act Data.

There are several reasons why Asian investor borrowers with exceptionally modest incomes are able to secure mortgages to finance investment property purchases. One reason is that Asian minority banks offer niche products such as the post-2008 reduced-documentation loans also called "portfolio loans." While portfolio loans do not require tax returns, they may require as much as a 50 percent down payment as well as proof that a borrower can cover closing costs and has reserves in the bank.[32] Lenders typically keep portfolio loans on their books rather than securitizing and selling them in the secondary mortgage market. Established in 1999 in Sunset Park, a majority Latino-Asian neighborhood in southwest Brooklyn, First American International Bank (FAIB) is a Chinese community bank also designated as a Community Development Financial Institution (CDFI); it offers reduced document portfolio loans with different down payment thresholds by borrower type.[33] For an owner-occupant borrower, FAIB requires a down payment of 35–40 percent; for an investor borrower, the minimum is 45 percent. FAIB services these reduced document portfolio loans in-house.

The 2014 Manhattan District Attorney's indictment of Abacus Federal Savings Bank for mortgage fraud provides further insight on the practices that may account for the modest median income of Asian investors.[34] The indictment listed numerous counts of falsifying business records in the form of gift letters toward the purchase of residential properties. In two cases involving properties in Flushing, Queens, gift letters exceeded $300,000. An explanation for the modest median income of Asian investors is that these practices enable borrowers to provide sizable down payments in cash, which reduces the loan-to-value ratio.

In 2010, Asian financial institutions made about 1,600 loans to Asian borrowers for the purchase of a one- to four-family home as a primary residence in New York City. These loans represent 27 percent of all mortgages originated for Asian owner-occupant borrowers. Notably, the sources of these mortgages are largely from a handful of Asian

Table 6: Median Applicant Income and Loan Amount by Race and Occupancy Status

| | 2010 | | | | | | 2015 | | | | | |
| | Investors | | | Owner-Occupied | | | Investors | | | Owner-Occupied | | |
App. Race	Num. Loans	App. Inc. (000)s	Loan Amt. (000)s	Num. Loans	App. Inc. (000)s	Loan Amt. (000)s	Num. Loans	App. Inc. (000)s	Loan Amt. (000)s	Num. Loans	App. Inc. (000)s	Loan Amt. (000)s
Non Hispanic White	1,046	$238	$368	12,018	$114	$364	1,682	$251	$463.5	13,128	$136	$432
Asian	539	$131	$353	5,891	$85	$319	1,760	$87	$420	6,120	$96	$378
Latino	75	$158	$330	2,190	$81	$332	134	$131	$407.5	2,239	$92	$373
Black	59	$118	$282	2,950	$80	$342	87	$111	$315	2,457	$91	$396

Source: 2010 and 2015 Home Mortgage Disclosure Act Data.

financial institutions, including Summit Mortgage Bankers, Inc. In 2015, the relatively modest share of home mortgages made by Asian financial institutions declined to only 15 percent of all mortgages secured by Asian owner-occupant borrowers. Notably, the drop in mortgage originations by Abacus Federal Savings Bank is quite steep (from 330 plus loans to only 3) and may be explained by the highly publicized Manhattan District Attorney's indictment and subsequent criminal trial in 2015 charging the bank of fraudulent practices such as falsification of loan documents including employment verification and income.[35]

While the volume of home mortgage lending by Asian financial institutions to Asian owner-occupant borrowers declined by 43 percent between 2010 and 2015, this was not the case for loans to Asian investors. As in 2010, Asian financial institutions continued to be a key source of financing for investors purchasing one- to four-family properties and originated 26 percent of all mortgages to investors in 2015. This represents a notably greater share than their lending to Asian owner-occupant borrowers at 15 percent. Minority community banks such as First American International Bank (FAIB) were top lenders to Asian investors in both 2010 and 2015. In fact, FAIB made more loans to Asian investor borrowers for one- to four-family residential properties than CTBC BK Corp. and East West Bank, two transnational banks with local branches in New York City neighborhoods with large Chinese immigrant populations.

A final observation is that nearly a third of all investor loans originated by Asian lenders were to borrowers who did not provide information about their race and ethnicity. For a significant number of Asian lenders, including Cathay Bank, BCB Community Bank, United Orient Bank, and local community banks such as Abacus Federal Savings Bank and Amerasia Bank, the number of loans originated to investor borrowers who did not provide information about their race and ethnicity exceeds the number of loans originated to Asian investors. Lenders are required to record the race and ethnicity of

Table 7: Investor Loans and Average Sales Prices in Select Neighborhoods

Neighborhood	2015 Asian 1-4 Family Purchase			1 Family House		2 Family House		3 Family House	
	Asian Investor Loans	Total Mortgage Loans	% Investor Loans	10-15 Differential (000)s	Avg. Sales Price 2015 (000)s	10-15 Differential (000)s	Avg. Sales Price 2015 (000)s	10-15 Differential (000)s	Avg. Sales Price 2015 (000)s
Integrated White-Asian									
College Point, Queens	64	116	55%	$159	$621	$166	$724	$86	$725
Dyker Heights, Brooklyn	44	97	45%	$224	$831	$420	$1,094	$404	$1,119
Bayside, Queens	54	173	31%	$137	$761	$266	$1,012	$288	$1,050
Bensonhurst, Brooklyn	82	304	27%	$201	$817	$222	$886	$226	$982
Integrated Asian-White									
Flushing, Queens	94	227	41%	$170	$760	$214	$922	$207	$982
Integrated Latino-Asian									
Sunset Park, Brooklyn	62	82	76%	$561	$1,099	$330	$1,016	$471	$1,080
Corona, Queens*	75	136	55%	$151	$557	$195	$667	$118	$792
Elmhurst, Queens	66	184	36%	$151	$634	$201	$785	$90	$924
Woodhaven, Queens	44	140	31%	$86	$408	$123	$516	$157	$580

*Includes North Corona
Source: 2015 Home Mortgage Disclosure Act Data and NYC Department of Finance Data 2010 and 2015.

loan applicants, but when an application is made via mail, telephone, or the Internet and the applicant fails to provide this information, the lender indicates the information was not provided. It is highly likely these borrowers are Asian because Asian financial institutions lend almost exclusively to co-ethnics, and this would mean that Asian lenders provided the financing for 39 percent of the mortgages for Asian investors compared to 15 percent for Asian owner-occupant borrowers in 2015.

NEIGHBORHOOD PROPERTY SALES AND ASIAN INVESTOR PURCHASES

Real estate investments in New York City's multi-racial neighborhoods increase the value of homeowner equity and contribute to rising property values and residential rents. While property owners benefit, rising market prices make the cost of homeownership prohibitive for many, including immigrants whose initial settlement catalyzed the neighborhood's revitalization. In 2015, the number of neighborhoods with significant Asian investments in residential properties includes majority white-Asian neighborhoods in Queens such as Bayside and College Point, and Bensonhurst and Dyker Heights in Brooklyn. Notably, Asian investor purchases were also significant in Latino-Asian neighborhoods including Elmhurst, Queens, and Sunset Park, Brooklyn as well as in the majority Latino neighborhoods of Corona, North Corona, and Woodhaven, Queens. Flushing continues to serve as an epicenter of Asian capital, with a high number of property purchases particularly among investors. For a number of neighborhoods including Sunset Park, Corona, and Dyker Heights, investors represent the majority of Asian home purchasers.

CONCLUSION

Minority banks provide a key source of credit, especially for Asians who may not qualify for conventional loans. However, minority banks also play a significant role in financing mortgages for investor purchases. In multi-racial immigrant neighborhoods, particularly in Brooklyn and Queens, the growing presence of Asian investment capital contributes to two trends: rising property prices that are prohibitive for prospective low- and moderate-income purchasers and which place renters at risk of displacement; and illegal conversions as homeowners (both owner-occupants and investors) are incentivized to subdivide their property to make mortgage payments or exploit the outstanding demand for affordable housing. In New York City's tight housing market, these trends may destabilize neighborhoods and facilitate transformative change in a neighborhood's race and class composition.

Bibliography

Barbanel, Josh. 2016. "New York City Property Values Surge." *Wall Street Journal,* January 15.

Board of Governors of the Federal Reserve System. 2011. "The Mortgage Market in 2010: Highlights from the Data Reported under the Home Mortgage Disclosure Act." *Federal Reserve Bulletin* 97, no. 6: 1–60. https://www.federalreserve.gov/pubs/bulletin/2011/pdf/2010_HMDA_final.pdf (accessed March 8, 2017).

Chamoff, Lisa. 2013. "Reduced Documentation and Other Mortgage Loans." *Newsday,* January 3.

Chhaya Community Development Corporation. 2009. "Fifty Percent of Homes in Pre-Foreclosure Are Owned by South Asian Immigrants in Sections of New York City." Press Release. www.guidestar.org/ViewEdoc.aspx?eDocId=2029242&approved=True (accessed March 8, 2017).

Chu, Peter. 2017. "'The Best Coffee in Flushing' Shuts Down." *World Journal,* March 1.

Colon, David. 2017. "Queens Community Board Member Promises Bike Lanes Won't Be Needed Once Trump Gets Rid of Immigrants." *Gothamist,* March 1. http://gothamist.com/2017/03/01/queens_bike_lane_trump.php (accessed March 8, 2017).

Dymski, Gary, and L. Mohanty. 1999. "Credit and Banking Structure: Insights from Asian and African-American Experience in Los Angeles." *American Economic Review Papers and Proceedings* 89, no. 2: 362–66.

FDIC (Federal Deposit Insurance Corporation). 2002. "Policy Statement Regarding Minority Depository Institutions." 67 Fed. Reg. 18620. https://www.fdic.gov/regu-lations/laws/rules/5000-2600.html#fdic5000policyso (accessed March 8, 2017).

— — —. 2012. "Community Banking Study 2012." https://www.fdic.gov/regulations/resources/cbi/report/cbi-full.pdf (accessed March 8, 2017).

— — —. 2014. "Minority Depository Institutions: Structure, Performance, and Social Impact." *FDIC Quarterly* 8, no. 3: 33–63.

— — —. "FDIC Definition of Minority Depository Institution Program." https://www.fdic.gov/regulations/resources/minority/MDI_Definition.html (accessed March 8, 2017).

Feng, Stevenson E. 2016. "Small Investors Join China's Tycoons." *New York Times,* December 11.

Flores, Ronald J.O., and Arun Peter Lobo. 2013. "The Reassertion of a Black/Non-Black Color Line: The Rise in Integrated Neighborhoods Without Blacks in New York City, 1970–2010." *Journal of Urban Affairs*, 35, no. 3: 255–392.

Guo, Jeff. 2016. "The Staggering Difference Between Rich Asian Americans and Poor Asian Americans." *The Washington Post,* December 20.

Immergluck, Dan, and Geoff Smith. 2003. "Measuring Neighborhood Diversity and Stability in Home-Buying: Examining Patterns by Race and Income in a Robust Housing Market." *Journal of Urban Affairs* 25, no. 4: 473–91.

Independent Community Bankers of America. 2012. "A Guide to Minority Banks." http://docplayer.net/14147314-A-guide-to-minority-banks.html (accessed March 8, 2017).

Kasinitz, Philip, Mohamad Bazzi, and Randal Doane. 1998. "Jackson Heights, New York." *Cityscape* 4, no. 2: 161–77.

Li, Wei, Gary Dymski, Yu Zhou, Maria Chee, and Carolyn Aldana. 2002. "Chinese-American Banking and Community Development in Los Angeles County." *Annals of the Association of American Geographers,* 92, no. 4: 777–796

Miyares, Ines M. 2004. "From Exclusionary Covenant to Ethnic Hyperdiversity in Jackson Heights, Queens." *The Geographical Review* 94, no. 4: 462–83.

Morgenson, Gretchen. 2015. "A Tiny Bank's Surreal Trip Through a Fraud Prosecution." *New York Times,* July 17.

New York Times. 1953. "City Parking Lots Move Step Nearer; Bids Opened for Constructing Flushing 'Pilot Project' on a Slum-Cleared Site." *New York Times,* April 30.

New York University Furman Center. 2009. "Mortgage Lending During the Great Recession: HMDA 2009." http://furmancenter.org/files/publications/HMDA_2009_databrief_FINAL.pdf (accessed April 13, 2017).

— — —. 2011a. "The Changing Racial and Ethnic Makeup of NYC Neighborhoods." http://furmancenter.org/files/sotc/The_Changing_Racial_and_Ethnic_Makeup_of_New_York_City_Neighborhoods_11.pdf (accessed March 8, 2017).

— — —. 2011b. "The State of Mortgage Lending in New York City." http://furman-center.org/files/publications/The_State_of_Mortgage_Lending_in_New_York_City_11.pdf (accessed March 8, 2017).

O'Reilly, Anthony. 2017. "Fearing the ICEman in Little Guyana." *Queens Chronicle*, March 2.

People of the State of New York v. Abacus Federal Savings Bank. Indictment no. 2480 (NY Supreme Court, 2012). http://nylawyer.nylj.com/adgifs/decisions/060112abacus.pdf (accessed March 8, 2017).

Pettit, Kathryn L.S., and Audrey E. Droesch. 2003. "A Guide to Home Mortgage Disclosure Act Data." Washington, D.C.: The Urban Institute.

Putzier, Konrad, and Cathaleen Chen. 2016. "NYC's Multibillion-dollar Enigma: A Deep Dive into the Inner Workings of the City's Chinese Immigrant Real Estate Market." *The Real Deal*, October 3.

Roberts, Sam. 2006. "Black Incomes Surpass Whites in Queens." *New York Times,* October 1.

Roberts, Sam. 2017. "Jerry Birbach, Leader of Fight to Block Poor Tenants in Queens, Dies at 87." *New York Times,* March 1.

Russonello, Giovanni. 2017. "The Life and Imminent Death of a Latin Jazz Club in Queens." *New York Times,* January 27.

Sanjek, Roger. 1998. *The Future of Us All: Race and Neighborhood Politics in New York City.* Ithaca, NY: Cornell University Press.

Tonnelat, Stephane and William Kornblum. 2017. *International Express: New Yorkers on the 7 Train.* New York: Columbia University Press.

Weller, Christian E., and Jeffrey Thompson. 2016. "Wealth Inequality Among Asian Americans Greater Than Among Whites." Washington, D.C.: Center for American Progress.

Yee, Vivian. 2017. "Immigrants Hide, Fearing Capture on 'Any Corner.'" *New York Times*, February 22.

Zonta, Michela. 2012. "Applying for Home Mortgages in Immigrant Communities: The Case of Asian Applicants in Los Angeles." *Environment and Planning A* 44: 89–110.

Endnotes

1 Miyares (2004).

2 Flores and Lobo (2013).

3 Immergluck and Smith (2003).

4 Weller and Thompson (2016); Guo (2016).

5 A major deficiency in HMDA data is the inability to disaggregate racial categories by ethnic groups. In October 2015, the Consumer Financial Protection Bureau announced improvements in HMDA data collection and reporting to include disaggregated data on ethnicity for Asian Americans starting in 2018.

6   Board of Governors of the Federal Reserve System (2011), 8–9.

7   Barbanel (2016).

8   Pettit and Droesch (2003), 16.

9   Flores and Lobo (2013); Immergluck and Smith (2003); NYU Furman Center (2011a).

10 Majority race tracts are those where at least 70 percent of the census tract population is comprised of one racial group. Integrated white tracts are those where at least 30 percent of the population is non-Hispanic white, and the sequence of the hyphenated typology indicates the first and second largest racial groups that add up to a majority 80 percent or more of the tract population. Integrated White mixed tracts are those tracts with at least 30 percent non-Hispanic white and a significant presence (20 percent or greater) of two other racial groups. Integrated nonwhite tracts are those where non-Hispanic whites are less than 10 percent of the tract population, and the sequence of the hyphenated typology similarly indicates the first and second largest racial groups. Integrated nonwhite mixed tracts are those where non-Hispanic whites are less than 10 percent and more than two nonwhite racial groups have a significant presence (20 percent or greater).

11 Neighborhood maps of Brooklyn and Queens showing the boundaries of community board districts are included in the Appendix.

12 NYU Furman Center 2013 defines a racially integrated tract as one with 20 percent or greater white population and 20 percent or greater of at least one other racial category.

13 The neighborhood's lead protestor of racial integration died in early March 2017. See Roberts (2017).

14 Sanjek (1998)'s ethnographic research site was defined by the boundaries of Queens Community Board 4 that primarily encompasses two neighborhoods, Elmhurst and Corona.

15 Colon (2017). Since Trump's election, the climate of fear is palpable in New York City's immigrant neighborhoods. See for example O'Reilly (2017) and Yee (2017).

16 Miyares (2004); Kasinitz, Bazzi, and Doane (1998). See also Frederick Wiseman's 2015 documentary, *In Jackson Heights*.

17 Tonnelat and Kornblum (2017) is an example of recent scholarship on the hyperdiversity of Queens neighborhoods and public spaces.

18 Russonello (2017). The Chinese language newspaper, *World Journal*, published an article about a popular café in Flushing, Queens that closed in early March because the owners could no longer pay the $30,000 monthly rent; Chu (2017).

19 Chhaya Community Development Corporation (2009).

20 Roberts (2006).

21 New York Times (1953).

22 FDIC (2002).

23 Independent Community Bankers of America (2012), 1 (emphasis added).

24 Li et al. (2002); Dymski and Mohanty (1999); Zonta (2012).

25 Li et al. (2002), 779.

26 Jing Wang, interviewed by the author, February 8, 2017.

27 FDIC (2012).

28 Specialty banking companies are credit card specialists, consumer nonbank banks, industrial loan companies, trust companies, and bankers' banks; FDIC (2012), 1–2.

29 FDIC (2014), 33.

30 See http://www.smb-mortgage.com (accessed April 13, 2017).

31 Feng (2016); Putzier and Chen (2016).

32 Chamoff (2013).

33 Phone conversation with FAIB mortgage specialist, April 13, 2017.

34 *People of the State of New York v. Abacus Federal Savings Bank.*

35 Morgenson (2015).

Promoting Integrative Residential Choices: What Would It Take?

MARIA KRYSAN
University of Illinois at Chicago

KYLE CROWDER
University of Washington

To promote residential choices that result in more integration and more equitable communities would take a more realistic perspective of how people end up living where they do. Specifically, the traditional model of understanding the neighborhood processes that translate into segregation runs something like this: people hold preferences about the racial composition of their community (and other things, of course, but in the case of our understanding of segregation, it is often framed in terms of racial composition), and in the absence of discrimination, and assuming an ability to pay, they move to a place where their preferences are met. And this process, repeated thousands and thousands of times by homeseekers all over a metropolitan area, translates into segregation.

In a recent book, *Cycle of Segregation: Social Processes and Residential Stratification* (2017), we advance a new theoretical framework — the social structural sorting perspective — that attempts to break out of these traditional understandings of the causes of segregation. In it, we draw attention to a range of social factors — social networks, lived experiences, and the media — that are crucial to consider if we are to understand how segregation is perpetuated, and what it would take to break the cycle. Specifically, we argue that social networks (family, friends, co-workers, neighbors, people at church, etc.), lived experiences (where a person has lived, tried to live, worked, shopped, goes to have fun, and even places they have accidentally stumbled upon), and the media (from local news shows to settings of movies to the jobs advertised in a community) are crucial factors that shape the information, perceptions, and experiences that people have about the neighborhoods and communities in their metropolitan area — those places that could become targets of a housing search. In short, because of the way that our social networks and lived experiences tend to be racially segregated — a segregation that is in part a function of residential segregation itself — the information we acquire from them is also racially circumscribed.[1]

In our book, we use the lens of how people actually end up living where they do, to highlight the ways that economics, discrimination, and preferences work independently and in conjunction with these social processes to create a cycle of segregation. To disrupt that cycle, we suggest, requires interventions that extend beyond simply improving racial attitudes, increasing economic resources, and eliminating housing discrimination. To be sure, all of these things must happen, given the way in which decades of baked-in segregation has set in motion a self-perpetuating system of segregation; but because of the underappreciated role of more complex social factors, these efforts to address discrimination, economic disparities, and racial bias are necessary, but not sufficient.

The social structural sorting perspective draws attention to how social factors like social networks, lived experiences, and the media operate both independently and in conjunction with discrimination, economics, and racial residential preferences to create a system of self-perpetuating segregation in our nation's cities.[2] In this chapter, due to space constraints, we focus only on the example of racial residential preferences to illustrate how these factors can shape residential choices, often in a way that perpetuates segregation. After reviewing what we know from surveys about racial residential preferences, we apply our social structural sorting perspective to highlight a puzzle about those preferences, and in so doing, draw attention to specific features of the residential choice process that often results in segregation. We then turn the question on its head and ask specifically: what kinds of policies and programs could be undertaken to shape these processes in a way that promotes integration instead?

WHAT PUZZLES EMERGE WHEN WE ASK PEOPLE WHAT THEY WANT IN TERMS OF A NEIGHBORHOOD'S RACIAL COMPOSITION?

If one were to take seriously and at face value what survey data tell us about people's racial residential preferences, we face some puzzles. For example, the city of Detroit has been — and remains — one of the most segregated metropolitan areas in the nation. And in the past forty years, it has barely moved the needle in terms of reducing this segregation. But data from surveys of Detroit area residents' racial residential preferences conducted in 1976, 1992, and 2004, show substantial changes in those attitudes.[3] Specifically, these surveys included an innovative (at the time) way to gauge how people felt about living with people of a different racial background.[4] Survey respondents were presented with cards portraying 15 homes, which were shaded to indicate different percentages of black and white residents. Respondents were asked to indicate which neighborhoods they found most attractive, which ones they would consider moving into, and which they would contemplate moving out of. Based on these data, for white respondents, there has been a very clear trend towards reporting increasing openness to living with African American neighbors. Between 1976 and

2004, the percentage of white Detroiters who reported being comfortable living in a neighborhood that was 20 percent black grew from 58 percent to 83 percent.

For their part, African American Detroiters have always been far more open to living with whites in their neighborhood than whites have been to living with African Americans.[5] Although there is evidence of a slight shift over time towards preferences for neighborhoods with somewhat higher percentages of African Americans, the vast majority of Detroit-area African Americans have consistently been open to living in neighborhoods with a wide range of racial compositions: only all-white and all-black neighborhoods have faced much objection.[6]

Social psychologists and survey methodologists, including ourselves, would be quick to point out that we ought not to take literally the preferences reported by survey respondents in the context of hypothetical decisions about hypothetical neighborhoods. For example, although the trend data point in the direction of whites being increasingly open to living in neighborhoods with higher percentages of African Americans, we should not assume this openness will translate into residential choices that exactly match those preferences.

Indeed, a study in Chicago — also a heavily segregated metropolitan area — calls into question the idea that hypothetical preferences will directly translate into housing choices that match them. In this 2004 study, Chicago-area residents were asked to create their ideal (hypothetical) neighborhood racial composition. Whites, blacks, and Latinos all drew very diverse neighborhoods and their ideal neighborhoods were far more racially diverse than the neighborhoods in which they actually lived.[7] What was innovative in this study is that the researchers *also* asked respondents to identify areas where they had searched for housing in the past ten years. The researchers could then compare the racial composition of the areas that were 'searched' to the 'ideal' neighborhood racial composition and, also, to the racial composition of the neighborhood in which the respondent currently lived. These comparisons revealed a mismatch for whites: in comparison to their hypothetically ideal neighborhood, the communities in which whites actually searched for housing had substantially higher percentages of white residents. For their part, African American and Latino residents searched in places that matched fairly well their ideal hypothetical neighborhood, but when it came to where they actually lived, there was also a mismatch: African Americans and Latinos lived in neighborhoods with substantially greater percentages of their own racial group compared to where they wanted *and* where they actually searched. In other words, at two quite different stages in the housing search process for whites as compared to African Americans and Latinos, the translation of preferences into outcomes falls apart.[8]

These puzzles — substantially greater reported openness among whites for living with African Americans; the mismatches between those attitudes and actual search behaviors; and an inability among Latinos and African Americans to translate searching in diverse neighborhoods into moving into those same neighborhoods — raise important questions about how racial composition preferences actually play out in real housing searches and how, ultimately, they shape residential outcomes.

The social structural sorting perspective can be used to begin to solve these puzzles, because it draws attention to features of housing searches and insights into how racial residential preferences operate.[9] Consequently, it sheds light on how these searches ultimately perpetuate segregation. Using this framework as a tool for unpacking residential mobility processes points out ways to intervene in housing search processes that will help searchers translate their hypothetical preferences for diversity into moves that foster integration rather than perpetuate segregation. We explore this idea in the rest of the chapter, focusing on how racial residential preferences are intertwined with, and shaped by, social networks, lived experiences, and the media.[10] We suggest that efforts that break people out of the racialized nature of the housing information process — to move beyond their customary social networks, lived experiences, and what are often heavily racialized media portrayals of communities — can ultimately disrupt the residential processes that currently perpetuate racial residential segregation.

WHAT WOULD IT TAKE TO ENCOURAGE MOVES THAT PROMOTE INTEGRATION?

The following sections describe three ways in which we might alter the perceptions and realities governing housing searches so as to promote integrative moves: we must erase people's racial blind spots, interrupt the perception that racial composition is correlated with other desirable or undesirable neighborhood characteristics (e.g., school quality, crime rate), and interrupt the reality of such correlations where they in fact exist.

Erase People's Racial Blind Spots

To achieve one's preferences with regard to housing options, one must know about places that will fit those preferences. Traditional models of segregation are built on the assumption — implicit if not always explicit — that all homeseekers have full and complete information about all possible options and thus are aware of all of the communities that would match their preferences. On the face of it, this assumption is unlikely to be accurate. Research shows that not only do people lack complete knowledge, but also that the knowledge people have is racially circumscribed.[11] People, in general, are more aware of communities in which their own group predominates. Interestingly, whites also seem to know less than other racial/ethnic groups about racially diverse communities — even those where whites are the majority.[12]

Given these racial blind spots, segregation may be driven, to an under-appreciated extent, by differences in familiarity with particular neighborhoods. Thus, one way to promote integrative residential choices is to recognize these racial blind spots and make efforts to erase them. Because perceptions of communities and the preferences they shape are influenced to an important extent by the information available through media (broadly construed), community leaders interested in supporting integration should consider education, public relations, and media campaigns that push back against the images people have or are receiving through other sources about either the existence, or features, of diverse communities. Communities that are diverse, or diversifying, either by design or by circumstance,[13] provide some good ideas for how to do this. One example is Oak Park, Illinois, which has been intentional about promoting integration for decades.[14] Oak Park, particularly in its earlier efforts, advertised its community's charms outside of its borders with the goal of putting Oak Park on the radar screen of potential residents. These ads were placed both in metro-wide (*Chicago Magazine*) and national (*New Yorker*) outlets. Michael Maly describes how three communities (Uptown in Chicago; Jackson Heights, New York; and San Antonio-Fruitvale in Oakland, California) engaged in similar activities to affirmatively market their integrated communities by embracing diversity as an asset and "attempt[ing] to brand the area as diverse" with the goal "to sell the diversity and integration as community strengths rather than as risks."[15] These concerted marketing and media campaigns can be used to raise awareness — and erase blind spots — about certain communities so that searchers will include them in their househunting.

Communities that are predominantly white need to engage in a different sort of effort. Given that such communities can suffer among people of color from a reputation of being unwelcoming, there are two kinds of needs. First, the community must be put on the radar screens of people of all races/ethnicities. Second, the communities must create outreach efforts that overcome perceptions of anticipated discrimination. Since integration can be stable only if there is demand from all races and ethnicities, efforts to influence the kind of information available about communities, and to add to (and perhaps counter) what is learned through lived experiences and social networks, would put and keep these places in the set of communities or neighborhoods in which people will consider living.

Intervene in How People Develop Perceptions of Places

One of the core tenets of the social structural sorting perspective is that we need to understand that people's perceptions and knowledge of communities and neighborhoods are socially constructed.[16] These perceptions are the outcome of social processes that impact whom we talk to, whom we get information from, and what places we have exposure to because of how our social lives are structured. The core point is that not only are there differences in the places we know about, but what (we think) we know about those places is also the outcome of a social process that is structured importantly by race.

One of the people we interviewed for our book, Aaron, was a young white man who owned a home in the Chicago suburbs.[17] We spent a lot of time in our interview asking him to describe the characteristics of places throughout the metropolitan area. After finding out what places were part of his 'routine' (where he has lived, gone to school, worked, played, etc.), we also branched out into conversations about places that he may not have actually been to. Sometimes we asked him to 'just guess' about the features of those places — what kind of schools were there? What kind of shopping? What kind of people lived there? How safe was it? How much did homes probably cost? Towards the end of this free-flowing conversation, we asked him where he gets his information about communities. His pithy response captures the essence of our argument about how social factors shape community perceptions — and these community perceptions, of course, factor heavily into whether people will consider living in them. Aaron explained,

> From what I see. Mostly the news. My friends. I don't know. I don't write it down, where I get it from. It just kind of compiles in this big ol' noggin right here [*pointing to his head*].

In other words, lived experiences, social networks, and the media shape his perceptions and they do so in an amorphous, subconscious manner. The information is absorbed and acquired through daily living.

Take the case of social networks. We can imagine a number of ways that social networks shape our perceptions of neighborhoods and communities. When we visit friends and family, we are exposed to the places they live. When people are talking around the "water cooler" at work, we learn about the places they live or where they went over the weekend. But there are also indirect ways that people develop perceptions of places through assumptions they make: if my friend lives there, and that friend is white and middle class, then the neighborhood is probably mostly white and middle class. Since our social networks are generally racially homogeneous,[18] the information that flows from those networks is likely racialized.

Similarly, we also know that our lived experiences — how and where we move about the city — differ based on our race/ethnicity.[19] And these experiences can shape our perceptions and eventually influence what areas we are willing to consider. One of our respondents was quite reflective about how, over the course of her life, these lived experiences came to be more expansive, and how this fundamentally changed how she viewed her residential options:

I'm a Northsider. I was born and raised on the North Side. Generally south of the 00 line wasn't really a consideration.[20] Not so much because I would absolutely not live there, just because that's what I was familiar with. Once I started working father south and started exploring more neighborhoods south, that's when I started opening up my search south.

If we reflect on how both social networks and lived experiences often feed us information about certain places — and fail to feed us information about certain other places — then we can think about ways to bolster, complement, or in some cases override that information.[21] This can be done through programs that expose people to places that are not on their radar screen, or are off their radar screen because of inaccurate assumptions. For example, in some racially integrated suburbs, organizations provide guided tours to people who otherwise would be either unfamiliar or misinformed about the features of their community. South Orange/Maplewood, New Jersey and Shaker Heights, Ohio both offer such tours to prospective homebuyers (in the former through the South Orange/Maplewood Community Coalition on Race, and in the latter through their village website).[22] The challenge for this sort of program is figuring out how to attract people who are not already aware of and interested enough in the community to sign up for a tour. It is people who are unfamiliar with communities or who have misperceptions that are most in need of these information interventions, yet they may be least likely to stumble across such tours. Active outreach could overcome this problem.

General online housing/rental search engines could be used to reach prospective renters and buyers in a more proactive manner. In theory, these tools could be designed in a way that provides searchers with information about places that fit their search criteria, but might otherwise have been eliminated due to inaccurate or non-existent knowledge or perceptions. Mobility Programs, designed to assist Housing Choice Voucher (HCV) holders in making moves to opportunity areas, are one arena in which this style of intervention has been implemented.[23] The strategies used by these programs reflect an understanding that what is greatly needed is an expansion of information sources and content used by a searcher during a housing search. The purpose of the information is to influence which communities a person targets for further research. Mobility Programs do this by providing information about neighborhoods or communities with high opportunity through online search tools (Inclusive Communities Project) or brochures and colorful maps (Housing Choice Partners). This information is disseminated online, in group presentations (some of which are required of new voucher recipients), or in one-on-one counseling. The program organizers clearly recognize the importance of supplementing existing and traditional influences (e.g., social networks and personal experiences) to ensure that the communities and neighborhoods in which people are searching are not racially circumscribed and will not therefore result in a segregative move. As the Baltimore Mobility program explains:

> For many inner city families, the suburban counties and towns exist beyond the realm of consciousness. There is a good chance they've never visited suburban neighborhoods and don't know firsthand that these areas have plenty of shops and other amenities. When applicants entering the program come to MBQ's office in downtown Baltimore for their orientation, one of the first things they do is board a charter bus for a tour of some of these communities. On these tours, MBQ housing counselors ask riders to notice how the streets with closely packed homes and small yards and corner grocers and liquor stores give way to strip malls with an array of stores and townhouses with bigger yards and driveways not alleys. Guides also point out schools, doctor's offices, businesses, bus and metro stops, and other notable amenities. [24]

These programs work, therefore, to supplement the information provided by social networks and lived experiences in a way that encourages moves that are integrative rather than segregative. As research by Jennifer Darrah and Stefanie DeLuca has shown, these programs can have long-term impact on people's preferences. [25] Communities and municipalities would do well to learn from the lessons of these successful mobility programs and adapt and apply them to people outside of the HCV population. Such programs could identify creative ways to encourage people to consider places they would not otherwise learn about or consider if they relied on the traditional sources to inform their perceptions of places.

Interrupt the Assumption of Correlated Characteristics

Part of the challenge of intervening in housing searches is that rather than conducting thorough research about each and every possible opportunity, people often rely on shortcuts — or heuristics — to guide the complex decision that is a housing search. [26] Because of a reliance on heuristics, (1) people perceive various features of neighborhoods as correlated; therefore, (2) they can use a single cue to 'stand in' for a range of other features; and, of particular relevance to our goals, (3) neighborhood racial composition is an important feature of the process. [27] So, for example, people assume that if they know a neighborhood's racial composition, they also know things like how much its housing costs, its crime level, how welcoming it is to people of color, and so on. And too often, the application of these shortcuts, which vary to some extent based on a person's racial background, results in perceptions that lead whites away from black or integrated neighborhoods, and which also lead African American homeseekers away from predominantly white communities.

For example, when we asked Russell, an African American man living in the city of Chicago, to talk to us about his perceptions of several predominantly white outlying suburbs, he said:

> I think that some of the areas like New Lenox, Mokena, Frankport — it seems like a community that was built for a specific type of family. A specific type of people. I don't foresee many African Americans living [there]. I don't — I think that it's going to cater towards wealthier white families in this area.

When we asked him why he thought these things, he gave the following reply:

> Yeah, that's a good question. I never really thought about why I feel like that. I just got the impression like, "Ugh, that's not a neighborhood that would welcome me," kind of thing. Not saying that they would do anything to dissuade me or redline me or anything, but I don't see that being — it's nowhere I ever considered living.

From talking to residents in the Chicago area, it became clear that African Americans and Latinos had impressions and stories to tell about family or friends who experienced discrimination, or about specific communities that had histories of racial animus towards people of color.[28] But what is striking in Russell's example is that these are relatively new communities, and he has no particular knowledge of them as being welcoming or unwelcoming. He nevertheless perceives them as places not "built for" him. For this reason, he rules them out as options.

JoAnn, a middle-aged white woman living on the North Side of Chicago, demonstrates the power of correlated characteristics — in her case, it is the exception that proves the rule. She describes something surprising she realized about a neighborhood on the South Side of Chicago:

> I know about Beverly because I know there's a Montessori School down there. I was surprised to find out that it's a pretty wealthy white community, 'cause it's on the South Side of Chicago and when you don't grow up here and you don't know these things, you just make assumptions about neighborhoods, 'cause it's just easier to make decisions that way.

JoAnn exemplifies the power of correlated characteristics: she reveals that she had always assumed that a place on the South Side of Chicago could not be middle class, and that it would not have white people. And she was surprised to discover a place that was all three of these things. Moreover, we also see from her discussion the reason why these correlated characteristics can figure importantly in a housing search: "it's just easier to make decisions that way." That is, it's easier to make assumptions and not bother to do research into specific communities.

The point is that people rely on shortcuts to quickly narrow their search down to a handful of communities or neighborhoods.[29] And to the extent that the one good reason people use to eliminate a place from consideration is its racial composition, the implications for segregation are clear. For whites, the negative qualities (e.g., crime, school quality, property values) they perceive as correlated with the percentage of African Americans in a community's population means that they may eliminate diverse or predominantly black communities from the very start. They never do the further research that would be required to find the instances where this correlation does not hold. Similarly, African Americans may presume that a predominantly white community will be hostile to African Americans, and for this reason they eliminated it from consideration.

The challenge we face if we are interested in encouraging integrative moves by people of all races is to disrupt these bundled perceptions. The bus tours for prospective buyers in South Orange/Maplewood and Shaker Heights described above are one example; the Oak Park Regional Housing Center (OPRHC) is another, though its focus is the rental market. The OPRHC offers a free apartment referral service, providing listings of available units to potential renters. The staff finds that clients routinely arrive in OPRHC's offices with preconceptions about where *within* Oak Park they want to move: white apartment-seekers have been advised by friends, family, and sometimes personal observation that they should avoid the east side of Oak Park (where a higher percentage of African Americans live). Black apartment seekers have been told they should avoid the west and north sides of Oak Park (where a higher percentage of white residents live). These clients are using "correlated characteristics" and making assumptions about other features of the area based on its racial composition. Areas with a larger African American population are ruled out by whites because they perceive them as having bad schools and high crime rates; the whiter parts of Oak Park are eliminated by African Americans because they are perceived as not welcoming to African Americans. Through the use of one-on-one counseling, the staff works to disrupt the operation of this heuristic — a heuristic that would otherwise funnel clients into making segregative moves. This intensive counseling effort is quite successful: analysis of these data from recent years show that of the OPRHC's approximately 3,500 clients each year, about 1,000 end up moving to Oak Park. Of those, about 70 percent move into an area or apartment building where their own racial group does not predominate.[30]

We have focused here on what diverse communities can and have done, but it is important to also note that predominantly white communities need to consider proactive efforts to dispel the impression that they are unwelcoming to people of color. In addition to the obvious need to ensure the enforcement of fair housing, publicizing a commitment and openness to people of all races and ethnicities could be done through public statements, public relations campaigns, and/or visual images conveying a diverse community. In addition, mobility counseling and other efforts to disrupt the use of racial composition as the 'best cue' of whether a place is welcoming to people of color need to pay explicit attention to this issue.

Interrupt the Reality of Correlated Characteristics

Thus far we have focused our discussion of possible interventions on what might be understood as marketing: counselors and communities attempt to impact the kind of information circulating about their community, and communities attempt to overcome the assumption of "correlated characteristics" that people rely upon in their heuristic-driven housing search process. But all of the marketing in the world cannot be effective if the underlying premise is false: if a community is said to be welcoming to people of all races when it is not; if a neighborhood is said to be safe when it is not; if property values are said to be rising when they are not.[31]

The challenge we face is that in all of these assumptions, there is a kernel of truth: there *are* profound inequalities across neighborhoods based on their racial composition. Some neighborhoods *are* unwelcoming to people of color. Past and persistent institutional racism have created the conditions that regularly breathe life into these correlations. Despite evidence to the contrary that any particular community can provide, so long as our nation is dominated by deeply divided neighborhoods, there will continue to be fuel for these heuristics.

To be sure, upending the severe racial inequalities across space is a daunting task and requires substantial resources and commitment at all levels. But as this discussion focusing on the specific role of preferences and perceptions has highlighted, there are also efforts that can be undertaken at the local level. Oak Park is again instructive. When housing counselors drive their white clients to apartments in neighborhoods with a higher percentage of African Americans, the units are as nice — if not nicer — than those on the "whiter" side of town. When clients ask about school quality, the counselors can show data that all of the elementary schools in Oak Park are both diverse and high-performing. And they can show crime statistics to assure potential residents that they are as safe on one side of town as another. It took intentional efforts by the community that were both symbolic and concrete to ensure that in Oak Park, race and class characteristics did not become correlated. To take a few examples, Oak Park passed a local fair housing ordinance before the national one; school zoning boundaries are drawn to maintain racial balance across all of the elementary schools; ordinances were passed to stave off blockblusting.[32] One concrete program that works synergistically with their housing counseling program is a "Multifamily Housing Incentive Grant," which provides grants of up to $10,000 to apartment building owners to improve their building's marketability.[33] In exchange, the grantee must affirmatively market their units through the OPRHC. The South Orange/Maplewood Community Coalition on Race has also worked to ensure that characteristics are not correlated. Homeowner loans are available to improve the external attractiveness of homes so as to ensure that no single section of their community looks better maintained than another.[34]

Through these efforts and others, communities invest in programs that attempt to shape the behaviors of individual potential residents, but also consciously distribute resources throughout a community or neighborhood in a manner that provides new information, defies the stereotypes, and decouples the characteristics that outsiders or potential new residents might assume to be correlated. The socially structured processes through which people search for housing, left unattended to, will perpetuate segregation. However, if these processes are supplemented, supplanted, and interrupted, it will become possible to encourage integrative moves.

Bibliography

Bruch, Elizabeth, and Fred Feinberg. 2017. "Decision Making Processes in Social Contexts." *Annual Review of Sociology* 43: 207–27.

Bruch, Elizabeth, and Joffre Swait. 2014. "All Things Considered? Cognitively Plausible Models of Neighborhood Choice." Paper presented to the annual meetings of the Population Association of America, Boston, May 1–3.

Darrah, Jennifer, and Stefanie DeLuca. 2014. "'Living Here Has Changed My Whole Perspective': How Escaping Inner-City Poverty Shapes Neighborhood and Housing Choice." *Journal of Policy Analysis and Management* 33, no. 2: 350–84.

Engdahl, Lora. 2009. "New Homes, New Neighborhoods, New Schools: A Progress Report on the Baltimore Housing Mobility Program." Washington, D.C.: Poverty & Race Research Action Council; Baltimore: Baltimore Regional Housing Campaign. Available at http://www.prrac.org/pdf/BaltimoreMobilityReport.pdf.

Farley, Reynolds. 2011. "The Waning of American Apartheid?" *Contexts* 10, no. 3: 36–43.

Farley, Reynolds, Howard Schuman, Suzanne Bianchi, Diane Colasanto, and Shirley Hatchett. 1978. "Chocolate City, Vanilla Suburbs: Will the Trend toward Racially Separate Communities Continue?" *Social Science Research* 7, no. 4: 319–44.

Farley, Reynolds, Charlotte Steeh, Maria Krysan, Tara Jackson, and Keith Reeves. 1994. "Stereotypes and Segregation: Neighborhoods in the Detroit Area." *American Journal of Sociology* 100, no. 3: 750–80.

Goodwin, Carole. 1979. The Oak Park Strategy: Community Control of Racial Change. Chicago: University of Chicago Press.

Havekes, Esther, Michael Bader, and Maria Krysan. 2016. "Realizing Racial and Ethnic Neighborhood Preferences? Exploring the Mismatches Between What People Want, Where They Search, and Where They Live." *Population Research and Policy Review* 35, no. 1: 101-26.

Jones, Malia, and Anne R. Pebley. 2014. "Redefining Neighborhoods Using Common Destinations: Social Characteristics of Activity Spaces and Home Census Tracts Compared." *Demography* 51, no. 3: 727-52.

Krysan, Maria, and Michael Bader. 2007. "Perceiving the Metropolis: Seeing the City through a Prism of Race." *Social Forces* 86, no. 2: 699-73.

— — —. 2009. "Racial Blind Spots: Black-White-Latino Differences in Community Knowledge." *Social Problems* 56, no. 4: 677-70.

Krysan, Maria, and Kyle Crowder. 2017. *Cycle of Segregation: Social Processes and Residential Stratification.* New York: Russell Sage Foundation.

Maly, Michael. 2008. *Beyond Segregation: Multiracial and Multiethnic Neighborhoods. Philadelphia:* Temple University Press.

McPherson, Miller, Lynn Smith-Lovin, and James M. Cook. 2001. "Birds of a Feather: Homophily in Social Networks." *Annual Review of Sociology* 27: 415-44.

Palmer, John R.B. 2013. "Activity-Space Segregation: Understanding Social Divisions in Space and Time." PhD diss., Princeton University.

Silm, Siiri, and Rein Ahas. 2014. "Ethnic Differences in Activity Spaces: A Study of Out-of-Home Nonemployment Activities with Mobile Phone Data." *Annals of the Association of American Geographers* 104, no. 3: 542-59.

Wong, David W.S., and Shih-Lung Shaw. 2011. "Measuring Segregation: An Activity Space Approach." *Journal of Geographical Systems* 13, no. 2: 127-45.

Endnotes

1   Silm and Ahas (2014); Palmer (2013); McPherson, Smith-Lovin, and Cook (2001).

2   This chapter draws heavily on Krysan and Crowder (2017).

3   Farley (2011).

4   Farley et al. (1978).

5   Farley et al. (1978); Farley et al. (1994); Farley (2011).

6   Krysan and Bader (2007); Farley et al. (1994).

7   Havekes, Bader, and Krysan (2016).

8   Ibid.

9   Krysan and Crowder (2017).

10   As noted above, we are focusing on racial residential preferences in this chapter. An equally robust discussion is possible — with attendant policy implications — if we focus on discrimination, economics, and each of the social

factors independently (social networks, media, and lived experiences). For an elaboration of the complete argument, and exploration of these additional areas, please see Krysan and Crowder (2017).

11 Krysan and Bader (2009); Krysan and Crowder (2017).

12 Krysan and Bader (2009).

13 Maly (2008).

14 In the 1960s, Oak Park was facing the prospect of white flight and racial turnover, which had begun to occur in the bordering Chicago neighborhood of Austin. Today, Oak Park is racially integrated (22 percent African American, 7 percent Latino, and 68 percent white) while neighboring Austin is 85 percent black. Staving off racial turnover was the outcome of a series of deliberate actions by advocates and local officials which are chronicled in Carole Goodwin's (1979) excellent analysis and description.

15 Maly (2008), 222.

16 Krysan and Crowder (2017).

17 For a description of the methods used, see Krysan and Crowder (2017).

18 McPherson, Smith-Lovin, and Cook (2001).

19 Jones and Pebley (2014); Palmer (2013); Silm and Ahas (2014); Wong and Shaw (2011).

20 This is a reference to Chicago's street numbering system: "00" is the beginning point — the corner of Madison and State Streets in downtown Chicago.

21 Krysan and Crowder (2017).

22 For South Orange/Maplewood, see www.twotowns.org; for Shaker Heights, see www.shakeronline.com/city-services/moving-to-shaker.

23 See http://www.housingmobility.org.

24 Engdahl (2009), 22.

25 Darrah and DeLuca (2014).

26 Bruch and Feinberg (2017); Bruch and Swait (2014).

27 Krysan and Crowder (2017).

28 Krysan and Crowder (2017).

29 Bruch and Swait (2014).

30 Krysan and Crowder (2017).

31 Ibid.

32 Goodwin (1979).

33 See www.oak-park.us/village-services/housing-programs.

34 See http://twotowns.org/neighborhoods/home-maintenance-loan-program.

What Would It Take to Make New and Remake Old Neighborhoods so that Regions Move Decisively Toward Integration?

Pathways to Inclusion: Contexts for Neighborhood Integration in Chicago, Houston, and Washington

ROLF PENDALL
Urban Institute

What would it take to make new and remake old neighborhoods so that a large, complex, metropolitan area moved decisively toward integration by race and income in the next 15 years? This paper provides background for the following case studies in this volume that try to answer this question in three regions: Chicago, Houston, and Washington, DC. The paper begins with a broad-brush overview of the major demographic changes that are expected to continue transforming housing markets in the US: population growth, aging, racial and ethnic diversity, and shifting household composition. It then describes the two principal patterns of political geography in metropolitan areas that affect decisionmaking about neighborhood inclusion: fragmentation and polycentricity. In the final two sections, the paper shows how national population growth trends could play out in each of the three commuting zones (CZs, analogous to metropolitan areas).[1] It then closes with a discussion of the political geography of each region, offering thoughts about how fragmentation and polycentricity influence how the authors of the three case-study papers answer the question for the panel.

POPULATION GROWTH AND CHANGE, 2015–2040

The United States is becoming more diverse by age, race and ethnicity, household composition, and income even as its population continues to grow. Major metropolitan areas are the crucible of these changes. They account for most of the nation's population growth and a disproportionate share of its non-white population, have a greater diversity of household types and sizes, and feature much sharper income inequality than the rest of the US. Their responses to aging, diversification, and growth will likely have an outsized impact on the future of the entire nation.

Growth

The US has faster population growth than many other large, high-income countries. A mid-range projection by the US Census Bureau suggests that the nation is on track to add over 70 million people between 2010 and 2040. The 20 most populous commuting zones in 2010, where almost 125 million of the 309 million US residents lived, could grow by nearly 28 million people, or 11 million additional households. Five of these commuting zones—Los Angeles, Houston, Washington, Atlanta, and Phoenix—would add over 1 million households each. (Dallas-Fort Worth, if considered as a single region instead of two commuting zones, would also rank among the areas adding over 1 million households from 2010 to 2040.) Among all 741 commuting zones, however, around 300 could lose population over these three decades if recent trends persist, the largest of which are in the Great Lakes states.

Older Adults

Across the nation, local decisionmakers face unprecedented growth in the number of older adults. Baby boomers are aging into their late 60s and 70s, following a much smaller generation. They also are expected to live longer than previous generations, magnifying the impact of their large numbers. Already, thanks to the growth in lifetime income and wealth that boomers have enjoyed, these older adults remain living by themselves in their own homes in much greater proportion than older adults of just two decades ago. At the same time, however, boomers are more racially diverse and more unequal by income and wealth than was the preceding generation. This diversity will therefore translate into increasing numbers not just of affluent homeowners in their 70s and 80s, but also of poor elderly renters, many of whom may not live as long as their more privileged contemporaries.

We still can only guess at the impacts of growing numbers of older adults on local housing markets. It may be that, like previous generations, baby boomers will have a low propensity to move; even so, the purchasing power even of a small proportion of this much larger population of older adults could encourage unforeseen innovations in housing that profoundly change many US metropolitan areas. These innovations could reduce relocation costs, resulting in greater propensity to relocate to a different housing unit, either within the same metropolitan area or elsewhere. Innovations and changes in demand could also shift property owners' calculus about how to use their homes, apartments, and parcels, and their perspective on what counts as adequate local infrastructure.

Racial and Ethnic Diversity and Immigration

At the same time, the nation is becoming more diverse, especially at younger ages, across numerous dimensions. Nationally, Hispanics, African Americans, Asians, and multiracial people are expected to account for nearly 90 percent of the net growth in households between now and 2030, as the rate of mortality among older white non-Hispanics approaches the rate of household formation by young white non-Hispanics. Many of these new households will remain renters for more of their life courses, since

Hispanic and African American homeownership rates still lag behind those of white non-Hispanics by between 25 and 30 percentage points, with Asians trending about 10 percentage points below whites. If housing prices fall, incomes rise, and access to homeownership become easier to obtain via policy and market innovation, then many young adults of color with parents who have little wealth could become homeowners, resulting in stable or rising homeownership rates overall and a smoother handoff from baby boomer homeowners to their heirs. If the stars do not align well enough, however, then some metropolitan areas could face long-term turbulence in both their rental and their homeownership markets.

Household Composition

Household compositions have also become steadily more diverse, a trend that shows no sign of abating. Single-person households have become much more common, in part because some people live by themselves for decades but also because people's adult household status will differ across their life course to a greater extent than was the case for people born in the first half of the 20th century. People already spend a longer period in their 20s and 30s unmarried and/or without children, sometimes living with parents and sometimes alone. The decisions to have children and to marry have become less closely linked. With higher divorce rates among baby boomers compared with previous generations, the large growth in older households will also mean large growth in in single-person households. Along with this diversification by both race and composition, households have also become more diverse by wealth and income, a trend that shows no signs of abating anytime soon.

POLITICAL GEOGRAPHY: LANDSCAPES OF INCLUSION AND EXCLUSION

As the US grows, ages, and diversifies in the next 25 years, what are the chances that the nation will see a growth in inclusive neighborhoods? The answer to this question depends in large part on the geography of the municipalities, townships, and counties in which these neighborhoods are located, because in every state—even those with growth management systems[2]—local governments set rules and manage approval processes for residential growth: where, how much, and what types of housing can be built, as well as what community services must be provided to accompany it. Cities and counties also conduct an array of other activities that shape neighborhood change: programs for redevelopment of blighted areas, housing rehabilitation, affordable housing, and many others.

Fragmentation: The Tiebout Landscape of the Northeast and Midwest

In commuting zones dominated by small municipalities and townships, a small number of jurisdictions—usually medium-sized to large cities—accounts for a disproportionate share of the less expensive rental stock, including subsidized housing. Such commuting zones predominate in the Northeast and Midwest,[3] in part because of the longstanding tradition of local land-use control and infrastructure governance at the town (New England) or township (mid-Atlantic and Midwest) level.

The small municipalities in these CZs have political and fiscal incentives that push them toward internal homogeneity. According to some theories, notably Charles Tiebout's, people choose to live in these communities based on their preferences for public services and their willingness to pay for them.[4] These preferences also extend to their willingness to share facilities and neighborhoods with people of other races and income levels.[5] Because people and businesses can "vote with their feet," local decisionmakers must follow their taxpaying, voting, and campaign-contributing constituents' preferences or face either electoral defeat or exit. Zoning is a necessary element for controlling the amount and character of development, according to these theories, because zoning imposes barriers to entry on people who might consume more public services than they are able to pay for. Zoning limits housing density and otherwise makes rental housing hard to build and expensive to occupy, reducing the number of people of color and low-income households who can live there.[6]

CZs in New England, the mid-Atlantic states, and the Midwest also have a number of characteristics that have allowed housing construction to outpace housing demand at the regional scale. Small, pro-growth jurisdictions at the urban fringe accommodate builders' and landowners' development applications, often on large lots with on-site septic systems and wells rather than public sewers and water systems, both of which are preconditions for dense development. As new supply comes on-line for the most affluent households at the regional fringe, older housing close to the urban core loses its value and becomes subject to absentee ownership, vacancy, and abandonment. Galster calls this "the regional housing disassembly line."[7]

The pathways to inclusion in these fragmented CZs almost certainly have to involve at least some action by either state legislatures or federal and state courts. Massachusetts' "anti-snob zoning" law, Chapter 40B, is a long-standing example of a mandate for inclusion that came about because of Boston's political strength in the state legislature in the late 1960s; the law allows developers to appeal local denials of affordable housing proposals to a state override board and has been responsible for the production of tens of thousands of housing units since its enactment. Recent changes to state law have complemented it with fiscal incentives to suburban towns that agree to zone for denser housing development. Another route has been through legal challenges, exemplified by the *Mount Laurel* and *Westchester* cases.[8] In all these cases, more exclusive communities are being forced to reduce their barriers to affordable housing construction.

Segregation among cities and townships (whose boundaries often coincide with school-district boundaries) has eroded in some of these CZs in recent years as inner suburban housing has aged and become more affordable to low-income households and people of color, with immigrants playing an important role in the diversification of some suburbs.[9] This growth in suburban diversity can be one route to the erosion of exclusionary practices in more affluent and whiter communities; Orfield describes a process in Minnesota in which state legislators from Minneapolis and St. Paul aligned with suburban representatives in a legislative coalition that improved regional planning for growth management and inclusion.[10] Coalitions of inner suburbs have also emerged in Cleveland and St. Louis, spurred in part by organizing by the faith-based Gamaliel organization.[11]

Polycentricity: Urban Politics in Suburban Metropolitan Areas of the South and West

The local political geographies in the South and West differ fundamentally from those in the Midwest and Northeast. Counties make decisions about land development in unincorporated areas, and townships do not exist as independent decisionmaking entities. These CZs tend, therefore, to be less jurisdictionally fragmented than those in the Midwest and Northeast, though the precise degree depends in part on state laws and constitutional provisions on annexation and incorporation. Where incorporation is relatively challenging and annexation easy, as was the case in Texas for most of its history, large cities dominate the landscape. Where incorporation is easy and annexation challenging, by contrast, CZs can become quite fragmented. Because medium-sized to large jurisdictions cover so much territory in these CZs, the politics of suburban development can be much less predictable than in the fragmented "Tiebout landscape" of the Northeast and Midwest. Elected officials need to respond to electoral pressure not only from the "median voter," but also from small interest groups with intense interests, including landowners, builders, business leaders, civil rights organizations, community organizers, and others. That is, the politics can resemble urban politics. And with a smaller number of neighboring jurisdictions, elected and appointed officials understand more clearly that they cannot rely entirely on other cities or counties to accommodate all the low-cost housing.

While local decisionmakers in these less fragmented CZs may not be able or want to exclude low-income people and renters entirely from their borders, they often face intense pressure to keep people separated into homogeneous neighborhoods or districts. In these cases, the politics around housing development and subsidy often reflect the boundaries of school districts. Some western CZs also have a high degree of school-district fragmentation. Where a county has a single school district (as in most of the South), the politics of exclusion revolve around school attendance zones, with homeowners in public-school attendance areas where school test scores are high and students are predominantly white and Asian rallying to limit incursions by developers of low-cost and rental housing.

HOUSTON, CHICAGO, AND WASHINGTON, DC: THREE METROPOLITAN SETTINGS FOR WORKING TOWARD INCLUSION

Houston, Chicago, and Washington are three of the largest metropolitan areas in the US, with 3.4 million households in the Chicago commuting zone and about 2.4 million each in Houston and Washington in 2010. They also have substantial political complexity, with dozens of cities, multiple counties, and myriad special districts and school districts making decisions that affect housing supply and demand. The relationship between the central cities and other jurisdictions, too, varies: Chicago and Houston are both the largest jurisdictions in their commuting zones, whereas Washington, DC has a smaller residential population than three large suburban counties in Maryland and Virginia.

Segregation

All three regions are known for their racial and economic segregation, but here, too, there are differences (Figures 1a-1c). Of the top 100 commuting zones in the US, Chicago ranked 20th in the nation in 2010 for economic segregation, 10th

Figure 1a. Combined Economic and Racial Segregation, 100 Most Populous Commuting Zones, 2010.

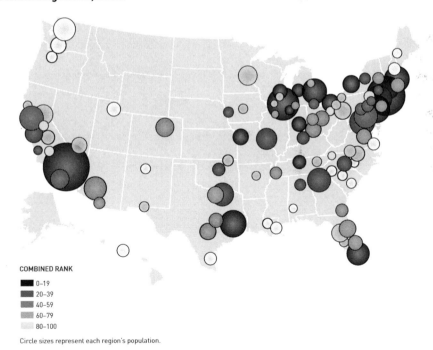

COMBINED RANK
- ■ 0–19
- ■ 20–39
- ▨ 40–59
- ▨ 60–79
- □ 80–100

Circle sizes represent each region's population.

Source: Urban Institute, "The Cost of Segregation," http://www.urban.org/policy-centers/metropolitan-housing-and-communities-policy-center/projects/cost-segregation.

Note: Darker shades indicate lower combined ranks and thus more segregated CZs. The combined rank is the unweighted average of black-white, Hispanic-white, and income-based segregation as measured by the spatial proximity index (a measure of racial clustering) and the generalized neighborhood sorting index (a measure of income clustering).

Figure 1b. Economic Segregation: Most Advantaged and Most Disadvantaged 10 Percent of Census Tracts in Chicago, Houston, and Washington Commuting Zones, 2006–10.

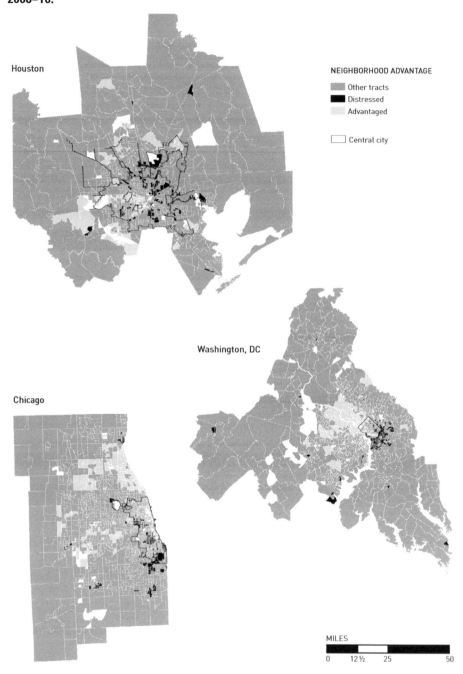

Source: Pendall and Hedman (2015). Base data: American Community Survey 2006–10.

Note: Index based on a composite score of average household income, percent of adults with college degrees, percent homeownership, and median housing value. Blue areas are the highest 10 percent of tracts; orange areas are the lowest 10 percent of tracts, 2006–10.

Figure 1c. Racial Segregation: Percent White Non-Hispanic, Chicago, Houston, and Washington Commuting Zones, 2011–15.

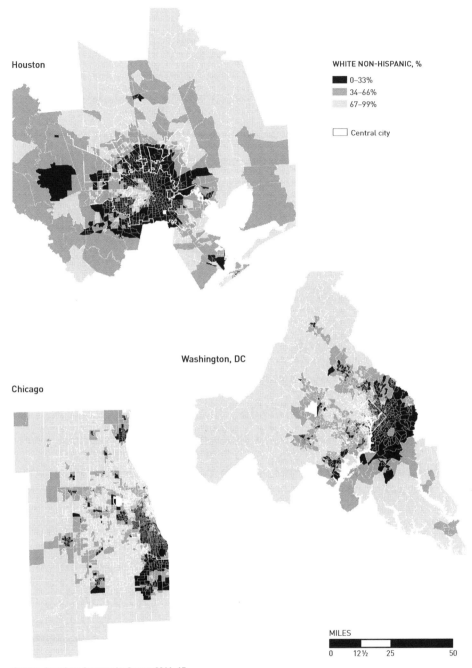

Source: American Community Survey 2011–15.

Figure 2. Households, 1990–2010 Observed and 2010–2040 Projected, Chicago, Houston, and Washington Commuting Zones.

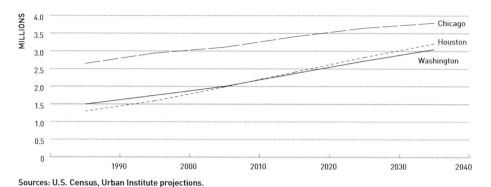

Sources: U.S. Census, Urban Institute projections.

for black-white segregation, and 9th for Hispanic-white segregation. Washington's economic segregation level is higher—17th in the nation—but its black-white and Hispanic-white segregation levels are notably lower (34th and 49th). Houston, finally, has the lowest economic and black-white segregation of the three areas (28th and 45th, respectively), but higher Hispanic-white segregation than Washington (20th).

Growth

Recent and projected future growth trends for these three commuting zones range from very rapid in Houston to moderate in Chicago (Figure 2). From 1990 to 2010, the Houston CZ experienced 52 percent growth in households; Washington households grew by 33 percent, and households in Chicago grew 18 percent. The magnitude of household growth from 1990 to 2010 is impressive: Houston added 681,000, Washington 502,000, and Chicago 460,000. If future growth trends resemble those of the recent past, each region, because of its youth, diversity, and attractiveness for economic activity, would add even more new households in this decade and the 2020s. Between 2010 and 2030, Houston could add another 850,000 households or more, Washington over 725,000, and Chicago another half million households.[12] Like the rest of the nation, all three of these CZs will add a substantial number of older adult households over the next two decades (Figure 3). By 2030, over 1.1 million Chicago households are likely to be headed by someone aged 65 or older, compared with only 610,000 in 2010. Both Houston and Washington are likely to grow to over 700,000 older adult households in 2030 and over 800,000 in 2040, up from between 300,000 and 350,000 in 2010. The regions differ, however, in the growth prospects for households headed by people under 65 years old. If recent demographic trends hold in the next 25 years, then Chicago has apparently peaked at about 2.5 million households with a householder under 65 years old, whereas both Washington and Houston are on track to add between 600,000 and 700,000 households with householders under 65 years old from 2010 to 2040.

Figure 3. Households Headed by Older Adults and People Under Age 65, Chicago, Houston, and Washington Commuting Zones, 1990–2040.

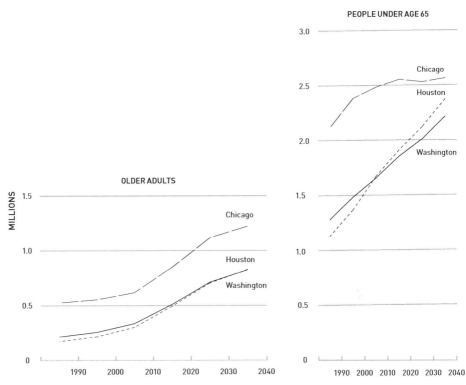

Sources: U.S. Census, Urban Institute projections.

Figure 4. Households by Race of Householder, Chicago, Houston, and Washington Commuting Zones, 1990–2040.

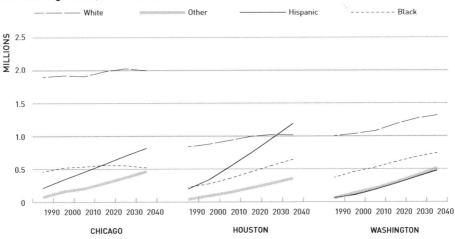

Sources: U.S. Census, Urban Institute projections.

Figure 5. Households by Tenure, Chicago, Houston, and Washington Commuting Zones, 1990–2040.

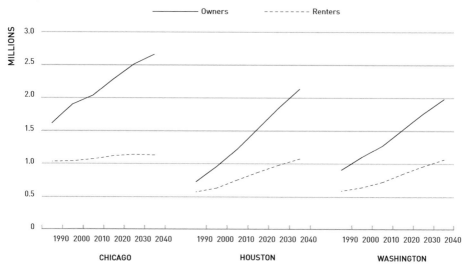

Sources: U.S. Census, Urban Institute projections.

In all three CZs, the bulk of the household growth is likely to be produced by increasing numbers of people of color (Figure 4). Already by 2010, no racial or ethnic group accounted for the majority of Houston's householders; white non-Hispanic householders in Houston will peak at about 1.0 million in the 2020s, and sometime in the 2030s Hispanics will surpass whites as the group with the largest number of householders. Washington is about to surpass Chicago among these three CZs with the largest number of black householders and will also experience robust growth in Hispanic and other-race householders. Chicago, finally, will continue to experience household growth almost entirely on the basis of growth in its Hispanic, Asian, and multiracial households. Black household growth has slowed significantly in Chicago and would turn negative in the 2020s if recent trends continue.

Notwithstanding the national trend of fast-growing demand for rental housing, all three of these CZs have homeownership attainment trends that tilt toward homeownership (Figure 5). They all had higher homeownership rates in 2010 than they did in 2000. Hispanics and other-race non-Hispanics account for bigger shares of their population and households than the national average, and both groups have in recent years exhibited stronger growth (or less decline) in homeownership than white and black non-Hispanics. Black non-Hispanics in Washington outnumber Hispanics and others, but their homeownership exceeds the national average and fell less in the recent crisis than did black homeownership in other parts of the US.

Local Political Landscapes as Fields of Play for Inclusive Growth

The three CZs discussed in this paper also have different geographies of land-use and housing decisionmaking that shape the locus of action for efforts to boost inclusion in different kinds of neighborhoods. The papers by Novara and Khare (Chicago) and Fulton and Shelton (Houston) both focus mainly or exclusively on the central city as the main actor in pursuing inclusive policies; Lung-Amam (Washington), by contrast, goes decisively to the regional level with her paper. While this may seem inconsistent, the underlying principle is quite consistent: focus energy for political change where the payoff is greatest.

Chicago's political geography exemplifies fragmented land-use and housing decision-making. It has 302 villages, cities, and counties that exercise control over planning, zoning, and subdivision regulations within a state legislative framework that allows much and demands little in the way of economic and racial inclusion or exclusion (Table 1). The city of Chicago accounts for 34 percent of the CZ population, but over 40 percent of the population lives in municipalities and unincorporated county areas with fewer than 50,000 residents. Apart from Chicago, only six jurisdictions have more than 100,000 residents, and none of these has more than 250,000. That is, the Chicago CZ conspicuously lacks a tier of medium-sized jurisdictions. Given the disappointing results of the Affordable Housing Planning and Appeals Act of 2004, an "anti-snob zoning" law modeled on Massachusetts's Chapter 40B, action to reduce exclusion in the more affluent suburbs looks from ground level like more effort than it may be worth, while efforts to boost the predominantly low-income African American suburbs south and west of Chicago could be at least as challenging, considering their very low level of municipal capacity.

Logically, then, Novara and Khare spend most of their time on tactics to integrate higher-opportunity and distressed neighborhoods in Chicago itself. They point out that the political energy and policy innovation have centered mainly on sustaining affordability in gentrification-prone neighborhoods and to an extent on creating more opportunity in safe, high-opportunity neighborhoods with dense and diverse housing, decent elementary schools, and good access to transit. But many other Chicago neighborhoods have suffered disinvestment and population loss for so long that they face dim prospects for near-term redevelopment. Reducing the concentration of new affordable housing in these neighborhoods seems like a logical necessity, but what resources does the city have to stimulate economic development and attract middle-class households to these neighborhoods?

Like Novara and Khare, Fulton and Shelton place most of their emphasis on the largest city in their CZ, but for another reason: it's practically the only jurisdiction with enough population to make a difference. The city of Houston accounts for 37 percent

Table 1. Land-Use Decisionmaking Jurisdictions, Chicago, Houston, and Washington, 2010.

Population of jurisdiction (thousands)	Chicago		Houston		Washington	
	Jurisdictions	Population	Jurisdictions	Population	Jurisdictions	Population
<10	139	553,003	77	172,175	70	185,228
10-25	91	1,545,338	21	322,410	11	195,199
25-50	44	1,476,391	8	304,797	4	135,965
50-100	21	1,405,431	5	357,744	6	376,891
100-250	6	805,688	1	149,043	5	719,458
250-500	0	0	2	700,269	2	652,402
500-1M	0	0	0	0	3	2,043,910
1M+	1	2,695,598	2	3,660,914	1	1,042,465
Total	302	8,481,449	116	5,667,352	102	5,351,518

percent of total

	Jurisdictions	Population	Jurisdictions	Population	Jurisdictions	Population
<10	46%	7%	66%	3%	69%	3%
10-25	30%	18%	18%	6%	11%	4%
25-50	15%	17%	7%	5%	4%	3%
50-100	7%	17%	4%	6%	6%	7%
100-250	2%	9%	1%	3%	5%	13%
250-500	0%	0%	2%	12%	2%	12%
500-1M	0%	0%	0%	0%	3%	38%
1M+	0%	32%	2%	65%	1%	19%

Source: U.S. Census 2010.

of the CZ's population, but another 28 percent of the CZ's population (1.6 million) lives in unincorporated areas within Harris County, mostly in the extraterritorial jurisdictions of Houston (which extend up to five miles beyond its city limits) or smaller municipalities. (Texas cities' authority to regulate subdivisions, issue building permits, and enforce building codes—but not to zone—extends into extraterritorial jurisdictions (ETJs), unincorporated areas whose boundaries range from one-half mile to five miles beyond city limits.) Texas grants broad land-use planning, zoning, and subdivision regulation to its home-rule cities (including most of the cities in the CZ), but does not require any of these controls; as Fulton and Shelton note, Houston does not have zoning but instead uses other regulations to accomplish many of the purposes of zoning. Counties in Texas do not have power to zone unincorporated areas beyond ETJs, having been extended only the prerogative of subdivision regulation and building permit approval.[13] Only one other city, Pasadena, has more than 100,000 people. But the dominance of Houston and Harris County means that only 14 percent of the CZ's residents live in jurisdictions under 50,000 residents.

Initiatives within the city of Houston itself therefore have the potential to make a significant difference in access to opportunity. The city still has large amounts of vacant land and many thousands of acres in locations where it would be profitable to increase development density. Low-income residents currently live in many of these areas and are actively being displaced, but state law provides few mechanisms that allow cities to negotiate with developers to preserve affordability in gentrifying areas. Fewer tools yet are available to make inroads on inclusion in the unincorporated county areas where much new development occurs. No unit of local government can exercise much influence there on new development, especially beyond the ETJ, where developers can bypass city approvals for sewer and water connections by creating their own municipal utility districts (MUDs), special-purpose governments that finance infrastructure development on bonds that are repaid through property taxes on new residents.[14]

With 602,000 residents in 2010, Washington, DC, is only the fourth-largest jurisdiction in its CZ; Fairfax (VA), Montgomery (MD), and Prince George's (MD) counties each have more residents. Six other counties and one city have over 100,000 residents. Only 9 percent of the CZ population lives in jurisdictions under 50,000 residents. Counties are strong units of government in both Maryland and Virginia for planning and zoning; in Maryland, they sometimes control zoning and building permits even within incorporated cities. Virginia's incorporated cities (e.g., Alexandria) are not sub-units of its counties, and they generally cannot annex outlying territory. Maryland is well-known as a "smart growth" state, requiring its jurisdictions to adopt comprehensive plans that designate areas for development and for preservation consistent with state law; state funds for significant infrastructure development are channeled to the "priority funding areas" developed as part of the planning process. Montgomery County in particular has led the nation in its adoption of a transfer of development rights program to preserve rural land by allowing development credit transfers from rural to urban areas, and also in its long-standing Moderately Priced Dwelling Unit ordinance, a productive local source of affordable housing that has resulted in substantial income mixing within developments throughout the county. Virginia's cities and counties do not face such state-level requirements; on the contrary, the prevailing "Dillon's rule" character of the state leads to the interpretation that local authority to do anything rests on explicit state grants of power.[15] The District of Columbia, finally, has controlled its own land use since the 1970s Home Rule Act was passed. Development on non-federal land (about 75 percent of the city) is governed by the District's comprehensive plan and zoning ordinance, the main federal constraint to which is a maximum building height limit of 130 feet.

As Lung-Amam's paper shows, the Washington region's more affluent jurisdictions and the District itself have innovated for decades to build and preserve affordable housing. Yet the intensity of housing demand, especially given the region's rising income inequality, can make local advocates feel that it is already too late to turn back the tides of gentrification that are undermining affordability, transforming neighborhoods beyond recognition, and leading increasing numbers of lower-income young people (especially African Americans and Latinos) to live in suburban areas rather than in the District. To keep up with these changes in the region's housing market, Lung-Amam argues, the big jurisdictions that have until recently sought solutions by themselves would do better to join forces and take on the opportunities and challenges of growth together.

CONCLUDING THOUGHTS: REGIONAL CHALLENGES, REGIONAL APPROACHES?

Advocates, scholars, and planners have long advocated regional solutions to the challenge of inclusion. In some states and regions, this advocacy has borne fruit with fair-share systems that legislate the allocation of housing demand among jurisdictions (e.g., New Jersey, California, and Minneapolis-St. Paul). One of the most promising inventions of recent years in this regard, however, is the regional Assessment of Fair Housing (AFH), a voluntary approach to the requirement for planning and analysis that advances the Fair Housing Act's affirmatively furthering fair housing (AFFH) requirement.[16] As a precursor to the regional AFH, HUD required metropolitan planning organizations and their partners to prepare Fair Housing and Equity Assessments (FHEAs) as a condition of receiving Sustainable Communities Planning Grants (SCPGs) awarded between 2010 and 2014.[17]

While regional AFHs are not required and HUD's commitment to the AFFH rule under the current administration remains unknown, Chicago's metropolitan planning organization (CMAP) is already using its FHEA as the basis for a regional AFFH.[18] The Houston-Galveston Area Council (HGAC) also received a Sustainable Communities Planning Grant and prepared its own FHEA.[19] The Metropolitan Washington Council of Governments (MWCOG) was unsuccessful in its SCPG applications, but recent work by Urban Institute researchers as well as planners from MWCOG could form the basis of a regional AFH. The requirement for the FHEA, its evolution into the regional AFH, and the relationships built during the SCPG process among housing agencies, transit providers, regional transportation planners, and local land-use planners, may together be shifting the politics of regional planning for inclusion. The authors of these three papers have provided a good basis for future research that would explore how AFFH changes the calculus and political tactics of local stakeholders in their approaches to building more inclusive neighborhoods.

Bibliography

Breymaier, Rob, Morgan Davis, and Patricia Fron. 2013. "Fair Housing and Equity Assessment: Metropolitan Chicago." Chicago Metropolitan Agency for Planning and Chicago Area Fair Housing Alliance. Available at http://www.cmap.illinois. gov/livability/housing/fair-housing.

Butler, Kent S., and Dowell Myers. 1984. "Boomtime in Austin, Texas: Negotiated Growth Management." *Journal of the American Planning Association* 50, no. 4: 447-58.

Danielson, Michael N. 1976. *The Politics of Exclusion.* New York: Columbia University Press.

DeGrove, John Melvin. 1992. *The New Frontier for Land Policy: Planning & Growth Management in the States.* Cambridge, MA: Lincoln Institue of Land Policy.

Galster, George. 2012. *Driving Detroit: The Quest for Respect in the Motor City.* Philadelphia: University of Pennsylvania Press.

Henneberger, John, Kristin Carlisle, and Karen Paup. 2010. "Housing in Texas Colonias." In *The Colonias Reader: Economy, Housing, and Public Health in US-Mexico Border Colonias,* edited by Angela J. Donelson and Adrian X. Esparza, 101-114. Tucson: University of Arizona Press.

Houston-Galveston Area Council. 2013. "Fair Housing Equity Assessment." Available at http://www.ourregion.org/FHEA/FHEA-FINAL.pdf.

Keating, W. Dennis, and Thomas Bier. 2008. "Greater Cleveland's First Suburbs Consortium: Fighting Sprawl and Suburban Decline." *Housing Policy Debate* 19, no. 3: 457-77.

Orfield, Myron. 1997. *Metropolitics: A Regional Agenda for Community and Stability.* Washington, DC: Brookings Institution Press.

———. 1998. *American Metropolitics: The New Suburban Reality.* Washington, DC: Brookings Institution Press.

Pendall, Rolf. 2000. "Local Land Use Regulation and the Chain of Exclusion." *Journal of the American Planning Association* 66, no. 2: 125-42.

Pendall, Rolf, and Carl Hedman. 2015. *Worlds Apart.* Washington, DC: Urban Institute.

Pendall, Rolf, Robert Puentes, and Jonathan Martin. 2006. "From Traditional to Reformed: A Review of the Land Use Regulations in the Nation's 50 Largest Metropolitan Areas." Brookings Institution Metropolitan Policy Program.

Pendall, Rolf, Sandra Rosenbloom, Diane K. Levy, Elizabeth Oo, Gerrit Knaap, Arnab Chakraborty, and Jason Sartori. 2013. "Can Federal Efforts Advance Federal and Local De-Siloing? Lessons from the HUD-EPA-DOT Partnership for Sustainable Communities." Washington, DC: Urban Institute. http://www.urban.org/ publications/412820.

Richardson, Jesse J., Jr. 2011. "Dillon's Rule Is from Mars, Home Rule Is from Venus: Local Government Autonomy and the Rules of Statutory Construction." *Publius: The Journal of Federalism* 41, no. 4: 662-85.

Singer, Audrey. 2004. *The Rise of New Immigrant Gateways.* Washington, DC: Center on Urban and Metropolitan Policy, the Brookings Institution.

Swanstrom, Todd. 2006. "Regionalism, Equality, and Democracy." *Urban Affairs Review* 42, no. 2: 249–57.

Tiebout, Charles M. 1956. "A Pure Theory of Local Expenditures." *Journal of Political Economy* 64, no. 5: 416–24.

Endnotes

1   I use commuting zones (CZs) rather than metropolitan statistical areas (MSAs) because the Urban Institute develops CZ-based population projections by age and race. One advantage of CZs over MSAs is that they take in both urban and rural areas; the entire territory of the US is in a CZ. The three CZs this paper explores overlap substantially with year-2013 MSAs defined by the Office of Management and Budget. Some outlying counties in each case do not overlap.

2   DeGrove (1992).

3   Pendall, Puentes, and Martin (2006).

4   Tiebout (1956).

5   Danielson (1976).

6   Pendall (2000).

7   Galster (2012).

8   *U.S. ex rel. Anti-Discrimination Center v. Westchester County,* 668 F. Supp. 2d 548, 563 (SDNY 2009); *Southern Burlington County NAACP v. Township of Mount Laurel,* 67 NJ 151, 336 A.2d 713 (1975).

9   Orfield (1997).

10   Orfield (1997); Orfield (1998).

11   Swanstrom (2006); Keating and Bier (2008).

12   These projections use the Urban Institute's Mapping America's Futures local population projections, August 2015 vintage, and assume trends in household formation and homeownership attainment that will be documented in a forthcoming appendix.

13   Henneberger, Carlisle, and Paup (2010).

14   Butler and Myers (1984).

15   Richardson (2011).

16   See 78 FR 43716, https://www.federalregister.gov/d/2013-16751/page-43716.

17   Pendall et al. (2013). See also https://portal.hud.gov/hudportal/HUD?src=/program_offices/economic_development/place_based/fhea.

18   See Breymaier, Davis, and Fron (2013).

19   Houston-Galveston Area Council (2013).

An Equitable Future for the Washington, DC Region?: A "Regionalism Light" Approach to Building Inclusive Neighborhoods

WILLOW LUNG-AMAM
University of Maryland

The Washington, DC metropolitan area is a large, economically robust region. It contains roughly 5.5 million people spread out over three states, the District of Columbia, 23 counties and independent cities, and 90 municipalities. The region's economy is heavily dependent upon public sector employment, especially the federal government and private companies that contract with the government. Roughly 38 percent of the region's economic output is related to government spending.[1] The region also has a relatively well-paid and well-educated workforce. In fact, it is among the most educated metropolitan areas in the country, with nearly half of residents 25 or older holding a bachelor's degree in 2010.[2] Poverty rates are only about half the national average.[3]

The region is racially and economically diverse, but is also among the most segregated metropolitan areas in the country.[4] The region is majority-minority, with non-Hispanic Whites making up 47 percent of the population. More than one in five residents in the region are foreign-born. The eastern half of the region, including the neighborhoods east of the Anacostia River in the District and large parts of Prince George's County, carry the region's burden of poverty and distress. This includes neighborhoods with the majority of the region's minority populations, poor residents, subsidized housing, its lowest home values, and its highest crime rates. In contrast, the District's western neighborhoods and suburbs enjoy the bulk of the region's prosperity, jobs, amenities, and high-valued neighborhoods.[5] Various state laws and the lack of a regional government with land use authority give local governments, particularly counties, a lot of discretion in adopting housing policy, and contribute to uneven patterns of development.

The Washington, DC region is also one of the most expensive places in the country to live. In 2013, the median house price was over double that of the nation and median rents were over 60 percent higher.[6] While the region is among the wealthiest in the nation, more than a third of households spend more than 30 percent of their income on housing. Not surprisingly, those at the bottom are the most cost-burdened. In the District, 64 percent of the lowest-income residents devote half or more of their income to housing.[7] Tens of thousands remain on the waiting list for public housing and rental vouchers. As of December 2016, both lists were closed. Scores of homeless families fill the region's shelters, which lack thousands of beds.[8]

In recent years, the housing crisis has been exacerbated by sharp demand for new housing combined with a constrained supply, particularly after the Great Recession. Young, educated professionals have moved into the region's most popular neighborhoods, largely inside the District. Between 1990 and 2010, the region grew by 37 percent, outpacing all other northeast metro areas. In the District, new residents have reversed decades of population loss while also pushing up property values and rents. Between 2000 and 2015, the average year-end sale price of a home in the region increased by 118 percent and as much as 275 percent in the District, compared to only 53 percent nationwide.[9] The vast majority of new units catered to higher-income renters and homeowners. These trends have led to the direct and indirect displacement of many long-term residents and have helped to push poverty into the most disadvantaged neighborhoods in the District and its inner and outer suburbs.[10]

What would it take to remake neighborhoods to move the region toward integration by race and income in the next few decades? In this paper, I propose strategies that build towards regional housing policies and plans, but also recognize the tough political realities of making regionalism work. This "regionalism light" approach stresses the need for broader adoption of and coordination across policies that are currently working at the local level while also building upon promising regional inroads. While regional cooperation on housing policies and planning has been by far the exception rather than the rule in the US, the Washington, DC metropolitan area has already made progress where many have failed. Given the strength of the region's economy and its progressive municipalities, who are already national leaders on affordable housing issues, it is well-poised to continue to do so.

INCLUSIVE HOUSING GROWTH AND PRESERVATION STRATEGIES

While many different tools could be used to build more inclusive neighborhoods in the Washington, DC region, the protection and the production of affordable housing is key given the region's current affordability crises. I focus on four strategies that can break down barriers to housing inclusion in existing neighborhoods as well as build a strong platform for current and future residents to be a part of the region's continued growth and prosperity. These are to preserve existing affordable units through aggressive anti-displacement strategies; capture land value to produce new affordable housing, especially near transit; increase the density and diversity of suburban housing; and tackle the region's stark east-west divide with fair-share policies.

Preserving What We Have through Aggressive Anti-Displacement Strategies

One of the most significant challenges that the DC region faces is preserving its existing stock of affordable housing in the midst of intense market pressures. The District, for example, had about half as many low-cost rental units in 2013 as it did in 2002.[11] To combat these trends, the region needs a more strategic approach to preserving existing subsidized and "naturally occurring" affordable units, and more aggressive anti-displacement measures that will keep existing low-income renters and homeowners in place.

The District has a good system to monitor and preserve existing subsidized units that can be strengthened and adopted more widely across the region. The DC Preservation Network is comprised of representatives from city housing agencies, the US Department of Housing and Urban Development (HUD), community-based organizations, and affordable housing developers. It maintains a database of assisted multifamily properties, organizes tenants, and reaches out to owners and managers to preserve affordable units in properties at risk of losing their subsidies. The city should redouble their efforts and coordinate their actions to prioritize those properties that receive federal subsidies, serve vulnerable populations, and maintain economic diversity in neighborhoods.[12] The Metropolitan Washington Council of Governments (MWCOG), the region's metropolitan planning organization, should organize a regional network to play a similar function and act as a central repository for monitoring and prioritizing affordable housing preservation strategies.

Preservation strategies are also needed for "naturally occurring" or market-rate affordable housing units. Municipalities that have been successful preserving the affordability of these units, such as Cook County, Illinois, have done so by incentivizing landlords to retain below-market-rate units with tax abatements and exemptions. To ensure that market-rate units are kept not only affordable, but also in good repair, such efforts should be combined with programs that focus on code enforcement and assistance for housing repairs. Recent initiatives in Montgomery County to conduct annual inspections of all rental units and adopt stricter penalties for code violations, and DC's loan program to eliminate safety and environmental hazards, are important local precedents.

Other anti-displacement tools that the region already has in place are strong tenants' rights policies, including regulations regarding condominium conversions, sales of rental properties, and rent control. Currently the District, Montgomery County, and Prince George's County are among the only jurisdictions in the country with laws that allow tenants or municipalities to purchase properties before landlords can offer them to outside buyers. In DC, the city pays nonprofits and legal advocates to advise tenants who want to purchase their properties and provides low-interest loans to help them make an offer. This program has had widespread success, saving approximately 7,500 affordable units in the District since its founding in 1978, including in some of the city's hottest neighborhoods.[13] However, in recent years, funding for the program has decreased while development pressures have increased, leading to a reduced number of tenant purchases.[14] DC's suite of tenant protections also includes rent control. However, it largely applies to units built before 1975, affects only landlords with more than four units and existing tenants, and has various loopholes that allow landlords to push up rents.[15] Stricter provisions for existing rent control and right-of-first-refusal regulations as well as additional funding for the latter are needed to slow the tide of displacement, particularly within the District.

On the regional front, MWCOG has little leverage to force local governments to adopt stricter rental laws, but many municipalities may be willing to sign on to a regional tenant's bill of rights. Adopted in DC and Montgomery County, these bills include provisions for ensuring home health and safety as well as combatting predatory rental practices that help advocacy groups hold municipalities accountable for adopting stronger tenant regulations.

For homeowners, tax relief and other forms of assistance designed to help residents stay in place need to be more aggressively adopted and funded. Tax relief policies generally benefit residents who have lived in their homes for a number of years by deferring property tax increases until they sell. Many jurisdictions in the region have such policies, but DC's policy is the most aggressive. Through the homestead deduction, it provides tax relief to residents who own their properties as a principal residence by limiting the amount of annual increase, with greater limitations for seniors and the disabled. The District also provides a refundable property tax credit to lower-income homeowners *and* renters. Other policies provide assistance for maintenance and repair costs that can cause elderly and low-income homeowners to sell their properties. In DC, such measures also need to be extended to families with multiple children, who find it increasingly difficult to remain in the city.

Capturing the Market in the Region's Most Valued Land

While the federal government provides local governments with critical affordable housing funding, these sources have been declining for decades and are insufficient. Municipalities have to come up with additional funds to meet demand, especially in expensive, high-growth regions like metropolitan Washington. A significant opportunity lies in capturing more property market value and better directing those funds into affordable housing near the region's most valued land, especially near transit.

Various municipalities, including the District, Montgomery County, Fairfax County, Arlington, and Alexandria have local housing trust funds, but they lack consistency in how and the extent to which they are capitalized. While some have dedicated funding sources, others rely largely on voluntary developer contributions. Some have invested heavily in their funds, as in the case of DC's $100 million investment in 2016, while others' investments have been more limited, as in the case of the City of Alexandria, which has collected only about $33 million over its fund's nearly thirty-year history.[16] Existing funds should require dedicated funding sources that take advantage of the region's growth, such as deed, recordation, and property tax revenues; they should be supplemented by, not reliant upon, voluntary contributions.

The region also needs non-municipal revenue sources not tied to local governments. In 2002, MWCOG was among the first US metropolitan areas to establish a regional housing trust fund. The Washington Area Housing Trust Fund (WAHTF) leverages corporate contributions to provide low-interest loans to affordable housing developers throughout the region. While that fund is largely defunct, in recent years Washington-area philanthropies, nonprofits, and businesses have established similar funds. Since 2014, the Greater Washington Housing Leaders Group, which is made up of over a dozen public and private sector leaders, has helped to push efforts like the DC Preservation Loan Fund, which leverages private capital to invest in the production and preservation of affordable housing in the Washington region. While attempting to revive its regional housing trust fund, MWCOG should also support the existing efforts of these regional foundations and nonprofits as a particularly effective funding source for its high-growth market.

In the use of both local and regional housing trust funds, priority needs to be given to the production and protection of affordable housing near transit. Currently, much of the region's highest-valued real estate is located near Metrorail lines, and in the coming decades, it is expected that the majority of new housing production will be near existing and new transit projects.[17] In DC and inner suburbs like Arlington and Silver Spring, the region has successfully used transit-oriented development (TOD) designations to create dense, mixed-use development. However, several municipalities do not require affordable housing within their TODs, and many non-Metrorail transit locations that face similar affordability challenges lack such policies. Within TOD sites, inclusionary zoning policies are needed that allow for both higher densities and a higher percentage of affordable housing units (up to 25 or 30 percent, as opposed to the 12 to 15 percent required by inclusionary zoning policies in much of the region). These sites should have standard policies regarding reduced parking minimums, waivers for historic preservation standards, and streamlined permitting processes to reduce the cost of affordable housing production. While inclusionary zoning has been a tough sell outside of the most progressive municipalities in the region, the protection of affordable housing near transit is a widely recognized regional goal. *Region Forward*, the region's 2010 vision plan produced by a coalition of local governments, includes the goal of having at least 80 percent of new or preserved affordable units located near critical transit nodes. Designated areas should include not only neighborhoods near Metrorail lines, but also other forms of transit, such as the Purple Line (the region's first light rail project), bus rapid transit routes, and streetcar lines.

Common standards for TOD sites should give attention to a range of housing needs, including workforce housing and housing for the region's most disadvantaged households. Priority for both rental and ownership opportunities in TOD sites should be given to residents seeking to live close to their work, not only to reduce transit times and costs, but also to increase the percentage in low-income residents downtown and in areas west of the city where most jobs are currently located. Given the severe shortage of units for the very-low-income residents of the region and the paucity of public housing units and rental vouchers, standards also need to include a percentage of units for those whose incomes fall below inclusionary zoning levels (i.e., 15 to 30 percent of AMI).

Encouraging Diverse and Dense Suburban Neighborhoods

While protecting existing affordable housing units and producing new housing near transit can significantly increase regional affordable housing, there are a number of suburban neighborhoods that fall outside of these areas. To promote more inclusion in these neighborhoods requires strategies focused on increasing the density and diversity of the existing housing stock, such as streamlined accessory dwelling unit (ADU) provisions, more mixed-use and higher density zoning policies near existing commercial and transit corridors, and strategies to reinvest in declining inner-ring suburban housing.

Many municipalities and counties, such as the District, Montgomery County, Arlington, and Fairfax County, have existing ADU policies that allow by-right small dwelling units on existing single-family lots. Such policies, however, contain different provisions across municipalities and are often too onerous to provide a reliable source of affordable housing units.[18] Existing policies need more standardized and streamlined provisions (such as for permitting requirements) and incentives for owners to take advantage of these provisions. The city of Santa Cruz, California, for example, waives development fees and offers low-cost construction loans for ADUs that are made available to low- and very-low-income households. They also subsidize ADU construction and education programs, offer expedited permitting, exempt ADU dwellings from certain parking requirements, and have modified setback requirements in single-family zones to encourage ADU construction.

Even with coordinated ADU policies and incentives in place, however, if they are not required by zoning, many suburban neighborhoods will likely continue to shirk their responsibility to contribute to the region's affordable housing challenges. *Region Forward*'s designation of Regional Activity Centers, areas currently targeted by local comprehensive plans for future employment and housing growth, provides a starting point for more aggressive zoning changes, including those that can make room for more mid-rise, multi-unit, and clustered housing in existing low-density suburban areas.[19] Montgomery County's Moderately Priced Dwelling Unit (MPDU) program, its inclusionary zoning program that has been in place since 1978, provides a model for mixing different unit sizes and housing densities in architecturally compatible ways.

It is also important to recognize that many inner suburbs facing decline already have a fairly dense supply of "missing middle" housing built in the post-war period.[20] Communities such as Langley Park in Prince George's County are struggling with rising costs associated with aging housing and infrastructure as well as increasing poverty rates, but often lack the policy tools and fiscal resources needed address these challenges.[21] In the 1990s, to revitalize its older suburbs, Baltimore County established a new county office that issued homeowner and business assistance loans, redeveloped town centers, and invested heavily in infrastructure.[22] Washington-area counties could establish similar revitalization programs that leverage their strong tax base and target communities most in need. When combined with strict code enforcement policies that hold developers accountable for maintaining high standards of housing, county governments can help to both stem the forces of inner-ring decline and invest in the revitalization of these communities.

Breaking through the East-West Divide with Regional Fair-Share Policies

One of the primary challenges of neighborhood equity and inclusion in the Washington, DC region is the stark difference between communities in its eastern and western sections. The lack of regional approach to tackling this divide leads to government inefficiencies, exacerbates income and racial inequality, and contributes to a lack of affordable housing.[23] However, the region has a history of working together to address housing issues and a platform upon which to build coordinated regional approaches to issues like homelessness and housing vouchers.

In March 2015, the District, Montgomery County, and Prince George's County announced plans to work together to end homelessness in the region. In doing so, government leaders committed to addressing issues of affordable housing, workforce development, economic development, and supportive services. While the details of this partnership are still being hammered out, it marks an important step towards a regional and multi-sectoral approach to homelessness. To be effective, this partnership should include more regional jurisdictions, set specific goals and targets, and identify funding sources for specific programs. Previous studies have, for instance, pointed to the need for more permanent supportive housing and rapid-rehousing programs, increased subsidized housing for extremely low-income residents, and job training for low-skilled and low-wage workers.[24] The partnership should also encourage municipalities to promote a more equitable distribution of homeless shelters and transitional housing within their jurisdictions. The District's recent efforts to distribute new homeless shelters in all wards of the city, though strongly resisted, shows what is possible with political will.

While regional fair share policies around subsidized housing are likely to face fierce opposition, there is an opportunity to make progress around the distribution and coordination of housing choice vouchers (HCVs). As Pendall's introductory essay in this volume notes, MWCOG has already begun conversations with regional stakeholders about conducting a regional Assessment of Fair Housing (AFH) that could be the basis of inter-jurisdictional cooperation on various housing policy issues, particularly HCVs. There are a range of issues that lead many voucher holders to concentrate in the region's most disadvantaged neighborhoods. These include the unequal distribution of housing vouchers, a lack of housing counseling, the willingness of landlords to accept vouchers, and limited affordable options in high-opportunity neighborhoods (i.e., those near jobs, high-performing schools, and transit).[25] Regional coordination around subsidized housing policies can address interregional mobility issues in various ways, such as by encouraging municipalities to adopt anti-source-of-income discrimination laws that prevent prospective landlords from considering a tenant's source of income. The District and several counties in Maryland have such laws, but many other municipalities and counties do not. Regional housing trust funds, DC Preservation Loan funds, or other regional sources could also be used to supplement federal vouchers to encourage residents to locate into more opportunity-rich neighborhoods.

CONCLUDING THOUGHTS

There are many challenges in implementing such an ambitious agenda for neighborhood racial and economic inclusion. Primary among them is stimulating the cooperation needed to make it happen, especially given the fragmented structure of municipal governance and land use authority. However, the Washington region is not as fragmented as many areas of the country, and many of the decisions related to housing policy are made at the county level. Further, the region has a strong track record and framework for collaboration. MWCOG convenes regional leaders on a monthly basis who have found common ground on plans for transportation, economic development, and the environment. Housing is always among the toughest issues to tackle regionally, but MWCOG already collects and shares affordable housing data and best practices, develops strategic partnerships among municipalities to promote affordability, and monitors the region's progress on creating and preserving affordable housing. Developing a housing plan and a more inclusive decision-making process could push housing issues forward on the regional front, while continuing to make progress in local communities.

A regional housing plan will help municipal leaders formulate shared goals and keep them on track to meeting them. An effective plan would contain specific local housing targets for production and preservation, with regional equity as a core planning principle. It would also specify regular monitoring and evaluation procedures and mechanisms to hold municipalities accountable for contributing to the goals. The *Region Forward* plan, which includes affordable housing goals, has already set the stage for such a plan. If completed, MWCOG would need greater authority to see that the plan's goals were met. In California, metropolitan planning organizations are required to create regional housing needs and allocation plans that are used to direct state housing funding. Similarly, MWCOG should be charged with distributing funds from its renewed regional housing trust or the DC Preservation Loan funds to meet plan goals.

To be effective, such a plan must also broaden the base of decision-making beyond local officials. Business leaders, housing advocates, nonprofit and for-profit developers, housing authorities, tenant organizations, and landlords all need to be at the planning table to generate buy-in and a willingness to work toward common goals. It also needs to be informed by the input of diverse local communities. Generating meaningful community engagement in regional plans is difficult, but can be effective when it relies on the efforts of organizations that have a foothold in the communities and can reach disadvantaged populations.[26] Outreach should aim to educate the public on issues of regional equity and affordability as well as to foster open dialogue about critical housing issues. Finally, planners and local policymakers need to be accountable for translating community feedback into plans and policies. A regional housing advisory committee made up of advocates and residents from across the region could advise planners on engaging diverse communities and ensure that their voices are reflected in the plan.

Such an ambitious agenda will not arise overnight. However, it is possible to start small and make steady progress. Building a broader table for coordinated regional planning by convening more diverse stakeholders around affordable housing issues, creating more common language around existing policies, and expanding existing regional collaborations, such as those around homelessness, are some potential areas to begin. In the longer term, these small steps can build support for larger regional actions. Battles over issues such as increasing densities in the region's suburbs, inclusionary zoning in TOD sites, and adoption of anti-source-of-income discrimination laws will take more time, the cooperation of multiple sectors, and lot of political will. Municipalities that have already shown a willingness to adopt affordable housing policies, such as the District and Montgomery County, need to provide leadership for these longer-term efforts. By working together to leverage new funding sources, create programmatic efficiencies, and adopt coordinated policies, they can demonstrate success and set the framework for broader regional cooperation.

The Washington, DC region currently has some of the most progressive policies in the nation for building more inclusive and diverse neighborhoods. Despite its complex and layered governance structures, it has managed to achieve an exceptional level of coordination on a number of issues, and many other regions around the US look to it as an example of what is possible. However, it cannot continue to claim leadership on these issues if political, business, and community leaders are not willing to invest in the regional infrastructure it has already built and also to look for new and creative ideas that will contribute to further progress.

Bibliography

Berube, Alan. 2012. "Where the Grads Are: Degree Attainment in Metro Areas." The Brookings Institution, May 31. http://www.brookings.edu/blogs/the-avenue/posts/2012/05/31-educational-attainment-berube

Blumenthal, Pamela, John McGinty, and Rolf Pendall. 2016. *Strategies for Increasing Housing Supply in High-Cost Cities: DC Case Study.* Washington, DC: Urban Institute.

Brookings Institution Center on Urban and Metropolitan Policy. 1999. *A Region Divided: The State of Growth in Greater Washington, DC.* Washington, DC: The Brookings Institution.

Chapman, Hilary. 2016. *Homelessness in Metropolitan Washington.* Washington, DC: The Metropolitan Washington Council of Governments.

City of Alexandria. 2016. *The City of Alexandria's Housing Trust Fund: From the 1980s to Today.* Alexandria, VA: City of Alexandria, Office of Housing, April.

Coalition for Nonprofit Housing and Economic Development. 2012. *A Decade of Progress: Investing in Lives and Neighborhood through the Housing Production Trust Fund.* Washington, DC: Coalition for Nonprofit Housing and Economic Development.

Finio, Nicholas, Willow Lung-Amam, Brandon Bedford, Gerrit Knaap, Casey Dawkins, and Eli Knaap. Forthcoming. *Towards an Equitable Region: Lessons from*

Baltimore's Sustainable Communities Initiative. Report to the Enterprise
Community Partners.

Florida, Richard. "Highest Levels of Overall Economic Segregation (All Metros)." 2015.
Toronto: Martin Prosperity Institute, University of Toronto. http://martinpros-
perity.org/content/highest-level-of-overall-economic-segregation-all-metros/

Gallaher, Carolyn. 2016. *The Politics of Staying Put: Condo Conversion and Tenant
Right-to-Buy in Washington, DC.* Philadelphia: Temple University Press.

Hanlon, Bernadette, John Rennie Short, and Thomas J. Vicino. 2010. *Cities and Suburbs:
New Metropolitan Realities in the US.* Oxford: Routledge.

Hendey, Leah, Peter A. Tatian, and Graham MacDonald. 2014. *Housing Security in
the Washington Region.* Washington, DC: Urban Institute and the Metropolitan
Washington Council of Governments.

Howell, Kathryn. 2014. *Accessing Opportunity: Housing Choice Vouchers and
Affordable Housing in the Washington, DC Region.* Arlington, VA: George Mason
University School of Public Policy, Center for Regional Analysis.

Hyra, Derek. 2014. "The Back-to-the-City Movement: Neighbourhood Redevelopment
and Processes of Political and Cultural Displacement." *Urban Studies* 52, no. 10:
1753–73.

Lovells, Hogan, Laura Biddle, Meghan Edwards-Ford, Joanna Huang, Deepika Ravi, Lisa
Strauss, and Mary Anne Sullivan. 2014. *Unfulfilled Promises: Affordable Housing
in Metropolitan Washington.* Washington, DC: Washington Lawyers' Committee
for Civil Rights and Urban Affairs.

Lung-Amam, Willow, Casey Dawkins, Zorayda Moreira, Gerrit-Jan Knaap, and Alonzo
Washington. 2017. *Preparing for the Purple Line: Affordable Housing Strategies
for Langley Park, Maryland.* College Park, MD: National Center for Smart
Growth Research and Education and CASA de Maryland.

Lung-Amam, Willow, Katrin B. Anacker, and Nicholas Finio. 2016. "Worlds Away in
Suburbia: The Changing Geography of High-Poverty Neighborhoods in the
Washington, DC Metro." Paper presented at the Association of American
Geographers, annual meeting, San Francisco, April.

Marchio, Nick, and Alan Berube. 2015. *Benchmarking Greater Washington's Global
Reach: The National Capital Region in the World Economy.* Washington, DC: The
Brookings Institution.

Parolek, Daniel. 2015. *Missing Middle Housing: Responding to the Demand for
Walkable Urban Living.* Berkeley: Opticos Design. http://missingmiddlehousing.
com/wp-content/uploads/2015/04/Missing-Middle-Housing-Responding-to-the-
Demand-for-Walkable-Urban-Living-by-Daniel-Parolek.pdf (accessed March 20,
2016)

Rivers, Wes. 2015. *Going, Going, Gone: DC's Vanishing Affordable Housing.*
Washington, DC: DC Fiscal Policy Institute.

Tatian, Peter. 2015. *A Preservation Strategy Will Help DC Meet Affordable Housing Needs.* Washington, DC: Urban Institute.

Vicino, Thomas J. 2008. "The Quest to Confront Suburban Decline: Political Realities and Lessons." *Urban Affairs Review* 43, no. 4: 553–81.

Washington DC Economic Partnership. 2016. *Washington, DC Development Report.* Washington DC: Washington DC Economic Partnership.

Wogan, J.B. 2015. "Why D.C.'s Affordable Housing Protections Are Losing a War with Economics." *Governing Magazine*, February.

Endnotes

1   Marchio and Berube (2015).

2   Berube (2012).

3   Unless otherwise noted, all demographic figures were taken from the U.S. Census, American Community Survey's 5-year averages for the Washington-Arlington-Alexandria, DC-VA-MD-WV Metro Area.

4   Florida (2015).

5   Brookings Institution (1999).

6   Blumenthal, McGinty, and Pendall (2016).

7   Rivers (2015).

8   Hendey, Tatian, and MacDonald (2014).

9   Blumenthal, McGinty, and Pendall (2016).

10 Hyra (2014); Lung-Amam, Anacker, and Finio (2016).

11 Rivers (2015).

12 Tatian (2015).

13 Coalition for Nonprofit Housing and Economic Development (2012); Gallaher (2016).

14 Wogan (2015).

15 Ibid.

16 City of Alexandria (2016).

17 Washington DC Economic Partnership (2016).

18 Blumenthal, McGinty, and Pendall (2016).

19 See, for instance, "missing middle" housing strategies in Parolek (2015).

20 Hanlon et al. (2010).

21 Lung-Amam et. al (2017).

22 Vicino (2008).

23 Lovells et al. (2014)

24 Chapman (2016).

25 Howell (2014).

26 Finio et al. (forthcoming).

Two Extremes of Residential Segregation: Chicago's Separate Worlds and Policy Strategies for Integration

MARISA NOVARA AND AMY KHARE
Metropolitan Planning Council

R adiating out from a city that for decades fought hand over fist to create and maintain near perfect segregation, the Chicago region faces contemporary challenges that make inclusion and equity an imperative, yet grapples with a history that has deeply entrenched its racial and economic separation. This history is coupled with present-day practices that reinforce its180-year history.

In this paper, we argue that a movement is needed to rethink strategies for desegregation at the region's two poles: concentrated poverty and concentrated wealth. We focus there not because the areas between the poles are unimportant, but because we recognize two factors: integration in these "middle" areas may be less challenging than at the extremes, and as income inequality has increased in recent years, more Chicagoans than ever before are either impoverished or affluent. We present policy recommendations to restructure Chicago's residential segregation and share our reflections along the way about the political realities of doing so.

OVERVIEW: CHICAGO'S ECONOMIC AND POLITICAL CONTEXT

While admired for its mounting influence in the global economy, the Chicago region is also known for its patterns of racial and economic segregation. The core of the Chicago metro area is dominated by the City of Chicago; with 2.7 million residents, it is by far the largest city in the state despite losing 1 million people since 1950. The city is often characterized through descriptions of its separate neighborhoods, such as the Gold Coast, Englewood, and Logan Square. Beyond the city, however, the surrounding suburbs range from very affluent to desperately poor. Increasingly, the divisions among

Acknowledgements: We would like to thank Rolf Pendall, Urban Institute, for his invitation to participate, as well as his keen insights about how to build regional collaboration towards an inclusive agenda. We would also like to thank Andres Villatoro, Metropolitan Planning Council, for his dedication to helping with the background research and preparation of the paper.

suburbs make intra-regional development and cross-jurisdictional political collaboration difficult, in part due to the heightening diversity among and the range of fiscal stability across suburbs. For example, the affluent North Shore contains predominantly white homeowners, while the South suburbs in Cook County and adjacent areas face rising levels of depopulation and disinvestment.

In the past several decades, intensifying income inequality has exacerbated the longstanding problem of residential segregation. While racial segregation has been a longstanding challenge and remains one to this day, Chicago also ranks in the top quarter of all metro areas with regards to economic segregation.[1] Chicago's white households are wealthier than the national average, while African American households have substantially less wealth than the national average.[2] These broad trends place Chicago in danger of becoming even more residentially segregated by race and class, as demonstrated by evidence that the number of concentrated low-income community areas is on the rise.[3]

Historically, the city's own urban redevelopment and housing policies contributed to the siting of African Americans in particular areas of the South and West sides, while also segmenting immigrants into neighborhoods best described as ethnic enclaves.[4] Chicago's development as a segregated city was largely dominated by powerful political processes, many of which reproduced barriers to housing mobility. As an example, housing and mortgage redlining policies kept African American residents confined to the city of Chicago's lower-income neighborhoods, while other policies encouraged white flight, highway expansions, and the growth of the suburbs.

These patterns of spatial segregation in the city of Chicago and later across the region have been politically controlled, since decisions by mayors, elected officials, zoning board officials, and others determined the opportunities for working-class households and minorities to relocate. State law leaves local governments a lot of discretion, which affluent communities have often used to exclude low-income people despite a state anti-NIMBY law modeled on Massachusetts' Chapter 40B. These spatial patterns are so woven into the fabric of the city that some observers question if and how the enduring configurations can ever truly be transformed.[5]

Chicago's class- and race-based urban development extends beyond its housing markets and into its government institutions. The city has long entertained a powerful mayoral coalition, aided in part by authority delegated to an overly large number of aldermen — fifty — whose allegiance to a central city government controlled by the mayor has been maintained over time. Aldermen enjoy a high level of political control over local zoning and resource allocation decisions within their wards, which in turn leads to a dearth of cross-city neighborhood development approaches that could aid in more comprehensive planning.[6]

Over the past two decades, the redevelopment of the central city generated profitable investment opportunities, while raising Chicago's global profile. The city of Chicago has moderate housing market demand overall, but demand is hot in some neighborhoods and very depressed, with severe population loss, in others. Select neighborhoods, such as the South and West Loop, were formerly commercial and light industrial, and are now attracting wealthy residential populations. Within this political context, former Mayor Daley and other city officials announced plans to demolish public housing buildings, while also initiating novel redevelopment strategies to create mixed-income communities. Federal HOPE VI funds were used to demolish iconic public housing structures such as the Near North Side's Cabrini-Green and the South Side's three-mile-long State Street Corridor. During this same period, other city neighborhoods were slated for redevelopment through the Local Initiatives Support Corporation (LISC) New Communities program aimed at comprehensive community revitalization. These and other changes laid the groundwork for transforming entire neighborhoods where people of different incomes and ethnic and racial backgrounds would co-habitate. Under Mayor Rahm Emanuel, the city continues its focus on economic development, attracting commercial ventures such as Google and the corporate headquarters relocation of formerly suburban McDonald's to redeveloped corridors.

During this same two-decade period, the entire Chicago region expanded its boundaries, stretching into the periphery of the neighboring states of Indiana and Wisconsin. New development on the edges of the urban bounds provided new opportunities for residential mobility, particularly for Latinos who moved into growing suburbs.

Most recently, the Chicago region has experienced growing levels of economic inequality. This marked increase in the number of extremely wealthy and extremely low-income populations has taken place during a period when middle-class populations have sharply declined in the city of Chicago. Racial shifts are afoot as well: census data show that in just ten years between 2000 and 2010, Chicago's population declined by nearly 200,000, of which 189,000 were African American. Furthermore, the 2008 economic crisis proved detrimental for local job opportunities, home prices, and home foreclosures, with disproportionately negative impacts on low-income communities of color.[7] The impact of the crisis can also be seen in diminishing city revenues as foreclosures reduced property tax payments, leading in turn to deeper shortages in the city's already pressed operating budget.[8]

In the city of Chicago, the socioeconomic characteristics of most low-income, primarily African American areas have changed very little over the past 30 to 40 years, but these areas have lost population, while formerly middle-income African American areas have become increasingly low-income. The net result is that Chicago now has a greater number of low-income African American areas than in the past, but these areas have a smaller total population. This change has occurred over the same time period as a dramatic loss in middle class population. The low-income African American West Side neighborhood of North Lawndale, for instance, saw its population decline from a high of 125,000 in 1960 to 36,000 in 2010, a decrease of 71 percent. More recently, the South Side neighborhood of Chatham, a quintessential African American middle-class area until the 1990s, has experienced a marked socioeconomic decline: from 2000 to 2010 alone, the median income dropped 19 percent and the unemployment rate rose 157 percent.[9]

For African Americans in Chicago, then, segregation has not much changed in recent decades, nor have its causes: government, structural, and individual racism, along with the deindustrialization that first led to disinvestment in these areas. And in African American areas, the socioeconomic changes that *have* taken place have often been for the worse. It is odd, then, that public discourse about housing in Chicago has recently focused on gentrification, so much so that it would seem to be around every corner. The reality says otherwise: a 2014 University of Illinois at Chicago Voorhees Center study of the forty-year span from 1970 to 2010 found that of 77 community areas, nine have gentrified while those in concentrated poverty have increased from 29 to 45.[10] The monoracial, low-income areas that have changed or are presently in the throes of gentrification are Latino. We talk about gentrification in Chicago much more than it is actually happening, especially where African Americans are concerned. Chicago neighborhoods that are more than 40 percent African American do not gentrify, a finding that reflects national trends.[11]

The city is facing century-old and current challenges that make inclusion and equity both imperative, but also incredibly difficult to address. It is within this context that we are working on a project to address Chicago's persistent racial and economic segregation through a cross-sector regional initiative called The Cost of Segregation, led by the Metropolitan Planning Council. In this paper, we argue that a movement is needed to rethink strategies for desegregation at the region's two poles: concentrated poverty and concentrated wealth. In growing areas of concentrated poverty, market-based strategies have long ceased to be effective, and in areas of concentrated affluence, efforts to induce the inclusion of affordable housing through regulatory measures have been met with resistance and even lawsuits. In both, new levels of political will and economic resources are necessary to achieve a less segregated and more equitable Chicago. As pragmatics committed to structural change, we also present initial policy recommendations that could restructure Chicago's persistent patterns of residential segregation. In exploring new policies for these two poles, we share our reflections about how to move the Chicago region decisively toward increased integration by race and income.

TACTICS FOR INCREASED INTEGRATION

In our work seeking policy ideas from around the country to advance racial and economic integration, we have noticed a clear trend in housing policy. Strong and gentrifying markets and more affluent areas capture abundant attention from policy-makers and others. When it comes to improving integration in strong markets, we have found no shortage of ideas. These range from improved Housing Choice Voucher porta-bility to innovative structures for hard units in opportunity areas, such as Chicago's own Regional Housing Initiative. HUD's recent emphasis on Affirmatively Furthering Fair Housing has furthered this trend, with many state housing authorities, including Illinois', adjusting their Qualified Allocation Plans to provide incentives to develop units in strong markets.

Likewise, we found that areas undergoing or under threat of gentrification are the beneficiaries of much attention, if not of commensurate policy interventions, concerning the protection of affordability. Media stories highlight the deleterious impacts of displacement. Citizens march and attend community meetings to draw attention to the changing dynamics within their neighborhoods, and elected officials publicly vow to protect affordability for their long-time constituents.

As professionals who have spent years in community development in many of Chicago's most disinvested neighborhoods, though, we are struck by how much deeper we had to probe to find comparable innovation, energy, and new ideas regarding cities' most impoverished neighborhoods. For the most part, as a field we seem to be doing the same things we've done for the past thirty years: We support community development corporations, which do the best they can to cobble together Low-Income Housing Tax Credit deals that are slow to come to fruition and not designed to house communities' lowest-income residents. And as scarce as the supply of affordable housing in these areas is, it is bountiful compared to the dearth of living-wage jobs. This is an unfortunate irony, especially given that the community develop-ment movement began with an intense focus on jobs and economic development.

We begin with this disinvested geography, and explore what factors might influence the desegregation of our most struggling neighborhoods, where housing markets and community renewal have been stagnant for decades.

INTEGRATION AND EQUITY IN AREAS OF DISINVESTMENT

Repairing a failed real estate market is extremely difficult. We focus first on the funda-mentals of market failure in disinvested areas; we then discuss strategies to address low property values and the challenges of building wealth or just breaking even in disinvested communities.

When property values are low, movement in the real estate market slows to a crawl and makes it less likely that traditional lending products will meet would-be buyers' needs.[12] A rash of foreclosures, as occurred in the wake of the Recession, leaves rock-bottom comparables on which to base appraised values. Many have argued further that, in a phenomenon known as appraisal redlining,[13] appraisers systematically undervalue property in low-income areas. As Squires documented, "The appraisal industry has had relatively little experience with, and simply does not know how to value property in, non-white communities."[14] The opposite problem occurred in the run-up to the Recession, when appraisers often inflated home values under pressure to appease lenders. In both cases, would-be homeowners of color in disinvested areas suffered the most. The combination of low real estate value along with poorly executed appraisals often results in a virtual standstill of market activity, as would-be investors and homeowners cannot get the credit they need to reinvest in the community.

We are interested in strategies to combat these challenges. To address the phenomenon known as the appraisal gap — in which the costs associated with rehabbing or constructing units are higher than the appraised value of the property itself — Chicago and Detroit have tried tactics to make up for this market failure and jumpstart reinvestment. In Detroit in 2014, of 3,500 single-family home sales, 87 percent were cash sales — a number that does not even include homes sold in foreclosure auction.[15] Conventional home loans are nearly impossible to come by due to the combined challenges of low land values and high rehab costs resulting from deferred maintenance. To combat this situation, the Detroit Home Mortgage Program allows qualified buyers to borrow against the replacement value of a home rather than the appraised value. This program addresses the appraisal gap by offering two mortgages: one for the appraised value of a home, and a second to cover the gap between the appraised value and the replacement value or the cost of renovations needed.

In Chicago, appraisal gap issues and lack of access to credit are less rampant overall than in Detroit, but they are just as severe where they do exist, mostly in African American and (to a lesser extent) Latino areas that have experienced an outmigration of middle-income homeowners. One strong sign of an appraisal gap in a given area is the amount of cash homebuying, which signals the collapse of a more traditional homebuyer market in favor of one dominated by investors. In the South Side neighborhood of Englewood, 87 percent of 2012 home purchases in one census tract were cash, compared to 23 percent citywide.[16] In 2009, values dropped so precipitously that nearly a quarter of sales in high-foreclosure areas were paid in cash for under

$20,000.[17] In Cook County in 2011, 90 percent of sales of bank-owned properties in high foreclosure areas were cash.[18]

Basing lending so heavily on property values led these areas to experience what Cook County Land Bank President Rob Rose calls a "self-fulfilling prophecy" in both the run-up and rundown of a housing bubble, as "irrationally exuberant" values build on themselves in a run-up and, when values disappear, collapse just as definitively. Several Chicago-based CDFIs with strong track records have designed alternative loan products that allow would-be investors and owners to borrow based not on property value but rather on ability to repay the loan. Products like these, which generally reach up to 140 percent of loan-to-value, work to establish value in areas that have experienced significant losses. (Such programs may sound uncomfortably close to the irresponsible lending practices that led to the Great Recession, but CDFIs' careful assessment of a borrower's ability to repay, which subprime mortgage lenders disregarded, is a crucial difference).

The City of Chicago recently announced the Chicago Neighborhood Rebuild Pilot Program, a $2 million pilot program for local contractors and developers to rehab vacant homes in disinvested areas. Partially intended as a jobs program for out-of-work young adults, it is also intended to increase homeownership and property values in areas where both are below the citywide average. The CDFI involved, Chicago Community Loan Fund, is able to reach 120 percent loan-to-value, and has recruited a loan loss reserve/first loss capital fund to provide the credit enhancement these markets demand.[19] While its current iteration is supported by one-time surplus funds from unclaimed property tax rebates, we recommend expanding it in similar markets across the city and suburban Cook County. Criteria for defining such similar markets could include percentage of foreclosures, or percent of mortgage activity compared to overall transactions. Traditional lenders could provide credit enhancement and count the loans in their Community Reinvestment Act portfolio.

A nascent proposal for a national Neighborhood Homes Tax Credit would provide a substantial boost to this framework. Modeled after the Low-Income Housing and New Markets Tax Credits, the Neighborhood Homes Tax Credit would focus on homeownership for disinvested areas suffering from appraisal gaps, with the credit bridging the financing gap between the cost of construction or rehabilitation and the sale price of the home. The proposal is not yet a bill, but has substantial support from groups such as NeighborWorks and the National Association of Affordable Housing Lenders. Notwithstanding valid criticism of over-reliance on tax credits versus directly allocating benefits, their use and proliferation is pragmatic, in contrast to an almost certainly doomed fight for direct allocations for investment in struggling areas. When President Trump threatens to "send in the Feds" to Chicago,[20] we wish it were actually a promise to do so with the kind of investment that would make the Neighborhood Homes Tax Credit unnecessary. Until then, we support its development and passage.

Revised lending criteria and improved appraisals would positively impact a large portion of the Chicago region's disinvested areas, making them more ripe for investment and, ultimately, more attractive for integration. Allowing appraisers to base their valuations on the cost and income approaches rather than the sales comparison approach is a key recommendation. This is far from the only need, however. Strategies warranting further exploration include: a comprehensive plan for the productive reuse of vacant land; home equity assurance; community and developer education on the value of dense, transit-oriented development to both connect to transit and leverage first-floor retail; and housing cooperatives and other shared equity options.

INTEGRATION AND EQUITY IN AREAS OF AFFLUENCE

Strong markets have their own set of unique challenges to increased integration as well. We are intrigued by efforts in other states to regulate their way to higher integration. Housing policymakers often cite Massachusetts' 40B, the Comprehensive Permit Act, which allows developers to override local zoning in areas where less than 10 percent of housing stock is affordable. Since it was enacted in 1969, studies show that 40B has accounted for 60 percent of all new affordable units in the state.[21]

This sounds like an ideal model, except for the political realities in Illinois. Our own attempt at a similar statewide law, the Affordable Housing Planning and Appeals Act (AHPAA) of 2004, was so gutted in negotiations for passage that it has no enforcement mechanism. In 2015, 68 Illinois municipalities fell short of meeting the 10 percent affordable housing goal, yet 40 of those municipalities, or nearly 60 percent, begged off the need to reach that goal because of their home rule status. Further, while more than 500 developments have been appealed in Massachusetts since 1970, in Illinois' 12-year AHPAA history, exactly zero developers have sued under the law. It turns out that developers in Illinois, at least, don't relish biting the hands of communities that they hope will feed them. A key difference from the Massachusetts law: if a community has under 10 percent affordability and rejects an affordable project, it immediately goes to court; in other words, it is not incumbent on the developer to sue.

A colleague at Massachusetts' Metropolitan Area Planning Council described 40B as an anti-home rule law in a very pro-home rule state, noting that the moment of its passage in the late 1960s is impossible to recreate. If we in Illinois did not manage passage of anything remotely comparable in the relatively shared chaotic aftermath of our own more recent Great Recession, is there any reason for hope here, where a stronger bill could reap substantial gains for affordability in the Chicago region?

It is possible that Massachusetts again provides a roadmap. As an alternative for communities chafing against 40B, the state more recently enacted two measures with incentives (rather than regulations) to provide affordable housing. We will focus on one of those, 40R, which provides financial incentives to communities that establish a smart growth zoning district (SGZD) requiring dense residential development of which at least 20 percent of must be affordable to those earning 80 percent of the area median income. Approved SGZDs receive a one-time incentive payment ranging from $10,000 to $600,000, depending on the number of units planned, along with a "density bonus payment" of $3,000 per housing unit once the building permit is issued, and the affordable units are as-of-right (read: no contentious public meetings need apply).

There are both empirical and politically practical reasons to like this approach. Lens and Monkkonen found that the higher the level of involvement of local government and citizens in permitting processes, the higher the segregation of all kinds and of segregated wealth in particular.[22] If the goal is more integrated communities, in other words, land use decisions cannot be concentrated solely in the hands of local actors.

From a political standpoint, while the State of Illinois is mired in budget gridlock, incentive payments created out of real estate transaction fees have some chance of passage, particularly if they were initially enacted in a smaller, more progressive geography than the state as a whole. Perhaps Cook County — the county in which the city of Chicago resides, and in which the current county president and multiple towns are notably progressive — could be a test case.

Yet, we're skeptical: as-of-right zoning is considered downright un-American in most of Illinois. This has also been true in Massachusetts. According to a 2004 report by the Metropolitan Area Planning Council, local officials were "critical or completely opposed to giving the state a degree of control over their zoning decisions" and felt that "the trade-off of giving up control to the state was not worth the money and possibly not worth any amount of money."[23]

Still, Illinois' attempt at a regulatory approach has been a dismal failure, and something incentive-based may be the only political possibility. Our experience with the City of Chicago's Affordable Requirements Ordinance (ARO) and Transit Oriented Development Ordinances has been that incremental change is possible and perhaps even preferable when it comes to changing the hearts and minds of developers and community members alike.[24] Importantly, the ARO is a requirement, but one that is mandated only when the developer needs a concession — city land, city money, or a zoning change — from the city. If local control is king, incremental but steady change may be our best hope.

On a final note specific to the City of Chicago: Chicago is one of only two cities with its own allocation of Low-Income Housing Tax Credits. At the state level, the Qualified Allocation Plan is based on a publicly reviewed and precise point system which recently underwent a change to include points for both "opportunity" and "revitalizing" areas. The city's QAP has always been an opaque instrument that, in contrast to the state's, has not been used to proactively set policy.

The result is that we've settled into a pattern in Chicago in which community development corporations and nonprofit developers produce subsidized housing, which is needed everywhere, in predominantly low-income communities on the South and West sides of the city. We err when we make these areas the predominant recipients of what should be city-wide and region-wide investments in affordable housing. Doing so not only further entrenches poverty and segregation, but also damages our overall economy. We are encouraged that the city's Department of Planning and Development recently released a draft QAP that, for the first time, sets the expectation for affordability throughout the city.

CONCLUSION

Chicago's current political and economic dynamics create conditions that make policy change both difficult and necessary. The latest findings from our Cost of Segregation study, in partnership with Urban Institute, demonstrate how residential segregation has negative effects on the social and economic outcomes of entire regions. Our findings show that while the Chicago region has decreased its economic, black-white, and Latino-white segregation by 10 to 11 percent between 1990 and 2010, such modest gains are far from sufficient. At our current pace, the region would not reach the median level of segregation of the nation's largest 100 regions until 2070. What then can we achieve within our lifetimes? If we can't reach the median by 2030, could we at least cut the distance in half through facilitated intervention in the most stubborn market types? Both growing income inequality in Chicago and the region's enduring spatial segregation require creative policy solutions, unprecedented levels of political courage and will, and the willingness to reallocate resources even in times of fiscal challenge for the city, region, and state.

In other times in history, we have seen massive shifts in political will and policy due to catastrophic national and worldwide events: the Great Depression, the Civil Rights Movement and social unrest of the 1960s, the Great Recession. Perhaps for Chicago, this time the impetus is much more local: murder rates not seen in 20 years, multiple police shootings of unarmed young African American men, and a mayor forced into a runoff election against a massively underfunded opponent combine to make the present moment ripe for boldness.

Bibliography

Acs, Gregory, Rolf Pendall, Mark Treskon, and Amy Khare. 2017. "The Cost of Segregation, National Trends and the Case of Chicago, 1990–2010." Washington, DC: Urban Institute.

Berkowitz, Karen. 2015. "Many Towns Snub State's Affordable Housing Mandate." *Chicago Tribune*, August 7.

Betancur, John, Karen Mossberger, and Yue Zhang. 2015. "Standing in Two Worlds: Neighborhood Policy, the Civic Arena, and Ward-Based Politics in Chicago." *Urban Neighborhoods in a New Era: Revitalization Politics in the Postindustrial City*, edited by Clarence Sone and Robert Stoker, 81–107. Chicago: University of Chicago Press.

Breymaier, Rob, Morgan Davis, and Patricia Fron. 2013. *Fair Housing and Equity Assessment: Metropolitan Chicago*. 2013. Chicago: Chicago Metropolitan Agency for Planning.

CFED (Corporation for Enterprise Development). 2017. "Racial Wealth Divide in Chicago." Washington, DC: Racial Wealth Divide Initiative, Corporation for Enterprise Development.

Chicago Defender Editorial Team. 2017. "Chicago Announces Pilot Program to Develop Vacant Homes." *Chicago Defender,* January, 10.

Chicago Rehab Network. 2013. "Chatham Community Area Fact Sheet." http://www. chicagorehab.org/resources/docs/fact_books/2015_ca_fact_sheets_extended/ crn_extended_community_area_fact_sheets_chatham.pdf.

Clark, Anna. 2015. "The Threat to Detroit's Rebound Isn't Crime or the Economy, It's the Mortgage Industry." *Next City,* December 7. https://nextcity.org/features/ view/detroit-bankruptcy-revival-crime-economy-mortgage-loans-redlininghttps:// nextcity.org/features/view/detroit-bankruptcy-revival-crime-economy-mortgage-loans-redlining (accessed March 22, 2017).

Ellen, Ingrid Gould, Keren Horn, and Katherine O'Regan. 2012. "Pathways to Integration: Examining Changes in the Prevalence of Racially Integrated Neighborhoods." *Cityscape* 14, no. 3: 33–53.

Hendrick, Rebecca, Martin Luby, and Jill Mason Terzakis. 2010. "The Great Recession's Impact on the City of Chicago." Chicago: Great Cities Institute.

Heudorfer, Bonnie, Chase Billingham, Barry Bluestone, and Lauren Nicoll. 2007. "The Greater Boston Housing Report Card 2006–2007: An Assessment of Progress on Housing in the Greater Boston Area." Boston: The Center for Urban and Regional Policy.

Hirsch, Arnold R. 2009. *Making the Second Ghetto: Race and Housing in Chicago 1940–1960*. Chicago: University of Chicago Press.

Hwang, Jackelyn, and Robert J. Sampson. 2014. "Divergent Pathways of Gentrification Racial Inequality and the Social Order of Renewal in Chicago Neighborhoods." *American Sociological Review* 79, no. 4: 726–51.

Hyra, Derek, and Jacob S. Rugh. 2016. "The US Great Recession: Exploring its Association with Black Neighborhood Rise, Decline and Recovery." *Urban Geography* 37, no. 5: 700–26.

Institute for Housing Studies at DePaul University. 2013. "Examining Cash Purchases of Residential Property in Cook County." Insititute for Housing Studies blog, August, 21. https://www.housingstudies.org/news/blog/examining-cash-purchases/ (accessed March 22, 2017).

Lens, Michael C., and Paavo Monkkonen. 2016. "Do Strict Land Use Regulations Make Metropolitan Areas More Segregated by Income?" *Journal of the American Planning Association* 82, no. 1: 6–21.

Louis, Errol T. 1997. "The Price is Wrong: Appraisal 'Redlining' Understate Millions in Community Assests." *Shelterforce: The Voice for Community Development*, May 1. http://shelterforce.org/1997/05/01/the-price-is-wrong/ (accessed July 13, 2017).

Massey, Douglas S., and Nancy A. Denton. 1993. *American Apartheid: Segregation and the Making of the Underclass.* Cambridge, MA: Harvard University Press.

Orfield, Gary, and Chungmei Lee. 2005. *Why Segregation Matters: Poverty and Educational Inequality.* Cambridge, MA: The Civil Rights Project, Harvard University.

Rollins, Darcy. 2006. "An Overview of Chapters 40R and 40S: Massachusetts' Newest Housing Policies." Policy Brief 06–1. Boston: New England Public Policy Center at the Federal Reserve Bank of Boston. https://core.ac.uk/download/pdf/6707059.pdf.

Sampson, Robert J. 2012. *Great American City: Chicago and the Enduring Neighborhood Effect.* University of Chicago Press.

Smith, Geoff, and Sarah Duda. "Cash or Credit: The Role of Cash Buyers in Cook County's Housing Market." 2012. Chicago: Institute for Housing Studies at DePaul University. https://www.housingstudies.org/media/filer/2012/06/05/researchreportfin.pdf.

Squires, Gregory D. 2014. "Appraisals: A Missing Link in Fair Housing/Fair Lending Debates." *Huffington Post*, July 22. http://www.huffingtonpost.com/gregory-d-squires/appraisals-a-missing link_b_5596879.html (accessed March 22, 2017).

Sternberg, Carolina, and Matthew Anderson. 2014. "Contestation and the Local Trajectories of Neoliberal Urban Governance in Chicago's Bronzeville and Pilsen." *Urban Studies* 51, no. 15: 3198–3214.

Voorhees Center for Neighborhood and Community Development. 2014. "The Socioeconomic Change of Chicago's Community Areas (1970–2010)." Chicago. https://docs.wixstatic.com/ugd/992726_a60305a8ecc34951a0f48e55f5366c5b.pdf.

Wagner, John, and Mark Berman. 2017. "Trump Threatens to 'Send in the Feds' to Address Chicago 'Carnage.'" *Washington Post*, January 25.

Williams, Sonya, George Galster, and Nandita Verma. 2013. "The Disparate Neighborhood Impacts of the Great Recession: Evidence from Chicago." *Urban Geography* 34, no. 6: 737–63.

Endnotes

1   Acs et al. (2017). Urban Institute used two indices to determine the trend and level of segregation in its 2017 study with the Metropolitan Planning Council. To analyze economic segregation, the study uses the Generalized Neighborhood Sorting Index (GNSI). The GNSI measures the extent to which people of similar incomes "clump" together within a given metropolitan region. To analyze racial segregation, the study measures both African American-white and Latino-white racial segregation using a spatial proximity (SP) index. This index explores the extent to which groups cluster together within a region.

2   CFED (2017).

3   Breymaier, Davis, and Fron (2013); Voorhees Center (2014).

4   Hirsch (2009); Massey and Denton (1993); Orfield and Lee (2005); Sampson (2012).

5   Sternberg and Anderson (2014).

6   Betancur, Mossberger, and Zhang (2015).

7   Hwang and Sampson (2014); Hyra and Rugh (2016); Williams, Galster, and Verma (2013).

8   Hendrick, Luby, and Terzakis (2010).

9   Chicago Rehab Network (2013).

10   Voorhees Center (2014).

11   On Chicago, see Hwang and Sampson (2014); on national trends, see Ellen, Horn, and O'Regan (2012).

12   We refer in this section to individual homebuyers in particular. For corporate investors, a bottomed-out real estate market is ideal due to low prices and high inventory in close proximity, and cash sales are not a barrier. While responsible investor ownership of formerly single family homes is certainly an improvement over buildings sitting vacant, community-based groups with which we work would prefer actual homeowners in single-family homes. We therefore refer to the barriers and needs of these individuals in this section.

13   Louis (1997).

14   Squires (2014).

15   Clark (2015).

16   Institute for Housing Studies at DePaul University (2013).

17   Smith and Duda (2012).

18   Smith and Duda (2012).

19   The Chicago Community Loan Fund's Neighborhood Investor Lending Program (NILP) lends 90 percent Loan to Cost and maxes out at 120 percent Loan to Value. Both features are non-conventional and allow more distressed properties to be financed. For example, if a property cost $30,000 to acquire and $70,000 to rehab and thus had a total development cost of $100,000, CCLF could make a loan of $90,000 as long as the appraisal was at least $75,000, resulting in 120 percent Loan to Value. The $15,000 gap in this scenario would stop most lenders from making this loan. CCLF's balance sheet and loan loss reserves that they have recruited for this purpose allow them to finance the deal, but if they had more at-risk capital on hand, they could finance properties with larger appraisal gaps. A 140 percent Loan to Value in this scenario would represent a property appraising at approximately $64,000 ($26,000 gap).

20   Wagner and Berman (2017).

21   Heudorfer et al. (2007).

22   Lens and Monkkonen (2016).

23   Metropolitan Area Planning Council report, quoted in Rollins (2006), 4.

24 Originally created in 2003, the City's Affordable Requirements Ordinance (ARO) was revised in 2015 to require that any residential development seeking city land, city financial assistance, or a zoning change provide 10 percent of its units as affordable to tenants making 60 percent of the Area Median Income. Twenty-five percent of the required affordable units must be built on site, and developers have the option to build the remaining units off-site (according to specified conditions) or to pay a "fee in lieu" for them. Some aldermen with strong markets require the full 10 percent of affordable units to be built on site, and one alderman requires as much as 21 percent. While much of the for-profit development community protested this change and one group even sued the City (the suit was dismissed), the City's Department of Planning and Development reports that development applications increased 36 percent in the year after the new rules went into effect as compared to the year before.

Originally passed in 2013, the Transit Oriented Development Ordinance was revised by the City of Chicago in 2015 to increase incentives for quality development near transit stations. The revised ordinance increased allowable parking reductions, density, and affordability, and expanded the applicable radius for these changes. To date, developers have taken advantage of this ordinance largely in strong markets. The Metropolitan Planning Council is working to raise awareness of the benefits of dense development near transit in weak markets as well, and has created an online calculator to assist the public with quantifying the benefits of increased tax base, local spending, transit riders, and affordability.

Can a Market-Oriented City Also Be Inclusive?

WILLIAM FULTON
Rice University

Once a traditional Southern city — at least in terms of its racial composition — Houston has emerged in the last 30-plus years as one of the most ethnically diverse cities in the United States. At the same time, however, Houston represents a challenge for inclusiveness that is both unique and important. It has a reputation as one of the most market-oriented cities in the nation for real estate development — and yet it nevertheless has a regulatory system, an abundance of land, and an uncoordinated set of financial incentives for economic development and real estate development, all of which combined create a sub-optimal situation for equitable development.

At a glance, Houston would appear to be a city of unparalleled opportunity for this diverse population, and in many ways, it is. The Houston metropolitan area has almost tripled in population since 1980, from 2.2 million to 6.3 million. It was the fastest-growing metro area in the United States in both 2014 and 2015, according to the US Census Bureau. Houston has moved far beyond the traditional white-black racial dynamic that once characterized the region. As Figure 1 shows, approximately 40 percent of the residents in Harris County, the region's core county, are Hispanic, a number that is expected to grow to 60 percent by 2050. Houston has one of the biggest South Asian populations in the United States — 118,000 Indian-Americans alone — much of which is located in suburban Fort Bend County, especially the affluent suburb of Sugar Land. Houston holds the largest Vietnamese population in the United States outside of California.[1] Adding to the diversity of the city, Houston accepts around 2,500 refugees annually, more than any other city in America.[2]

Houston also has a reputation as one of America's most affordable cities, at least for housing. Compared to cities on the coast such as New York, San Francisco, Los Angeles, and Washington, Houston is relatively affordable. According to Zillow, the median 2016 home value in metropolitan Houston was $310,000, compared to $610,000 in Los Angeles and $535,000 in Washington, D.C.[3] Price increases in Houston have been modest in recent years because of a slump in oil prices.

Figure 1: Population Projections of Harris County by Race/Ethnicity

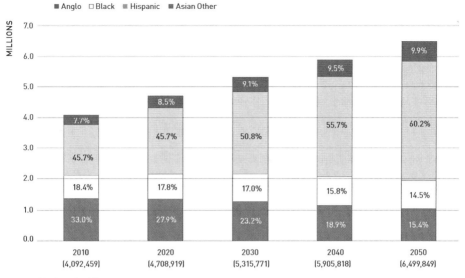

Source: Klineberg (2016).

There's no question that the Houston housing market, especially the suburban housing market, provides opportunity for people with good blue-collar and white-collar jobs. But the big picture masks growing inequality and disparity that is at least as bad as, and perhaps worse than, the national average.

Since 1980, Houston has seen a startling increase in the concentration of poverty, with almost 40 percent of all Census tracts in Harris County[4] now suffering from concentrated poverty, meaning 20 percent or more of the households in that tract are households in poverty.[5] Residents of Houston and Harris County also suffer from geographical disparities on almost every social and economic factor ranging from health to income. Some neighborhoods still feature income diversity, but most of these neighborhoods consist of moderate- and low-income residents of color. Affluent neighborhoods, especially affluent white neighborhoods, are increasingly segregated by income from the rest of the Houston region. In his new book, *The New Urban Crisis*, Richard Florida ranks metro Houston 7th nationally in his "segregation and inequality index" – trailing only New York and Los Angeles among large cities, and is ahead of San Francisco and Washington, D.C.[6] In this way, Houston is becoming less inclusive — that is, lower-income residents, including low-wage workers, are either being consigned to high-poverty neighborhoods or pushed to distant locations far from jobs.

Like many other cities, Houston also appears to be suffering from a displacement and gentrification problem, at least according to anecdotal evidence. Most of the Census tracts with increased concentration of poverty are not in central Houston, inside the

Figure 2: Median Household Income for Harris County by Zipcode, 2010–2014

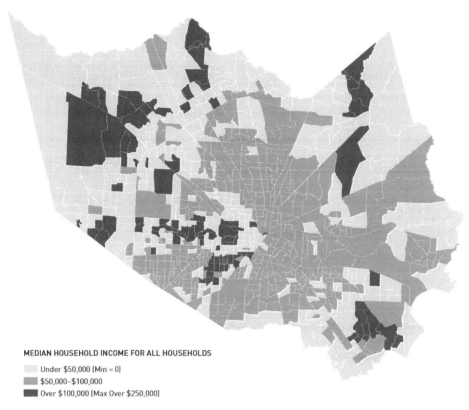

MEDIAN HOUSEHOLD INCOME FOR ALL HOUSEHOLDS

Under $50,000 (Min = 0)
$50,000–$100,000
Over $100,000 (Max Over $250,000)

Sources: O'Connell and Howell (2016).
American Community Survey (ACS) 5-year period estimates, 2010–2014.

I-610 Loop, but are rather in between the I-610 Loop and Beltway 8, meaning they are between six and fifteen miles away from downtown Houston.[7] Though suburban in built form, most of these neighborhoods are actually located inside the City of Houston's boundaries. For example, Gulfton, formerly a "young singles" apartment neighborhood just outside the I-610 Loop near tony Bellaire, became a "port of entry" neighborhood after the oil crash of the 1980s, with immigrants and refugees from all over the world now living there.

Meanwhile, the historically African-American neighborhoods around downtown Houston are rapidly gentrifying with luxury apartment buildings aimed at Millennials. In his book *The Great Inversion and the Future of the American City*, Alan Ehrenhalt tells the story of the Third and Fourth Wards, which are located immediately to the south and southwest of Downtown Houston, respectively.[8] The Fourth Ward was quickly gentrified, leading to resentment among the African-American community. As a

Figure 3: Concentrated Poverty for Harris County by Zipcode, 2006–2010

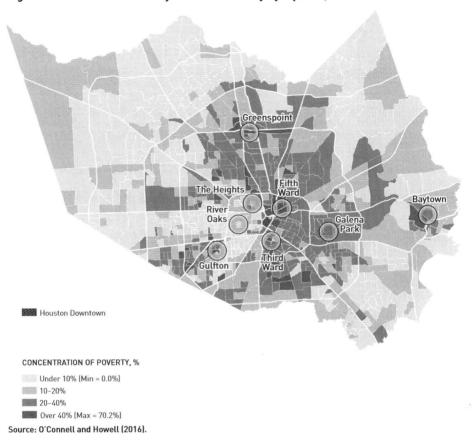

Houston Downtown

CONCENTRATION OF POVERTY, %

  Under 10% (Min = 0.0%)
  10–20%
  20–40%
  Over 40% (Max = 70.2%)

Source: O'Connell and Howell (2016).

result, political leaders in the Third Ward began using the local tax-increment financing district's funds to purchase land to block gentrifying development.

Displacement and gentrification in the Third Ward remains a risk, however. The neighborhood, whose residents have a median income of only $25,528, is situated in an ideal location, in between Downtown to the north and the affluent Museum District to the south and along Highway 288.[9] Demolition in the Third Ward has been rampant and wide-ranging.10 New construction has been concentrated along 288, where classic Houston "townhomes" (three-story attached and small-lot detached single-family units) are replacing the neighborhood's traditional housing stock. New townhome prices range from $350,000 to $450,000. (In the last 15 or so years, it has been common practice in older Houston neighborhoods to demolish one older single-family home and replace it with three to six townhomes.)

Figure 4: Single-Family and Other Demolition Activity in the Third Ward, 2005–2015

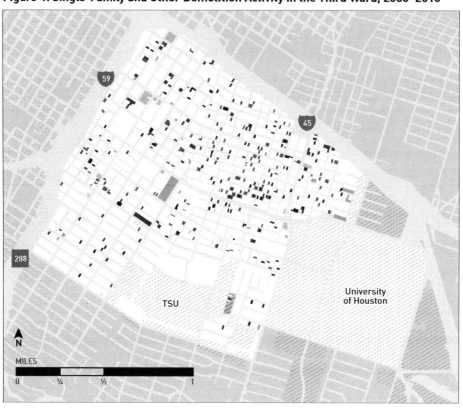

SINGLE FAMILY RESIDENTIAL DEMOLITIONS

▬ 2005–2008
▬ 2009–2012
▬ 2013–2015

OTHER DEMOLITIONS

▬ 2005–2008
▬ 2009–2012
▬ 2013–2015

▦ College / University

Source: Walker and Shelton (2016).
Map by Kelsey Walker. Institute for Urban Research.

So, at the same time that new townhomes and luxury apartments are being built in close-in neighborhoods, hundreds of thousands of families, many of which include low-wage workers, are living in older, substandard apartment buildings in inconvenient locations between the 610 Loop and Beltway 8 (see Figure 6.) These apartments are not formal, subsidized "affordable housing," but they provide an extremely important source of naturally occurring affordable housing for those on the wrong side of Houston's disparity divide.

Figure 5: Single-Family and Other Construction Activity in the Third Ward, 2005–2015

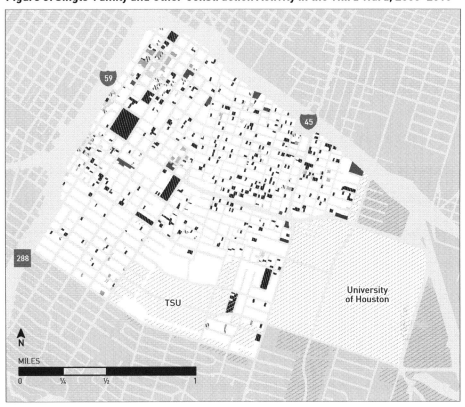

SINGLE FAMILY RESIDENTIAL CONSTRUCTION

▨ College / University

    2005–2008
    2009–2012
    2013–2015
    Building Permit Only

OTHER CONSTRUCTION

    2005–2008
    2009–2012
    2013–2015
    Building Permit Only

Source: Walker and Shelton (2016).
Map by Kelsey Walker. Institute for Urban Research.

HOUSTON'S UNIQUE CHALLENGES AND OPPORTUNITIES

Although its general pattern of disparity, displacement, and gentrification is typical of large American cities, Houston faces a unique set of challenges and opportunities in seeking to overcome spatial disparities associated with housing and transportation.

On the plus side, Houston has an abundance of land and, uniquely among large American cities, no use zoning — conditions which ought to present ample opportunities for both market-rate and subsidized affordable housing. Even neighborhoods in

Figure 6: Multifamily Buildings by Year of Construction

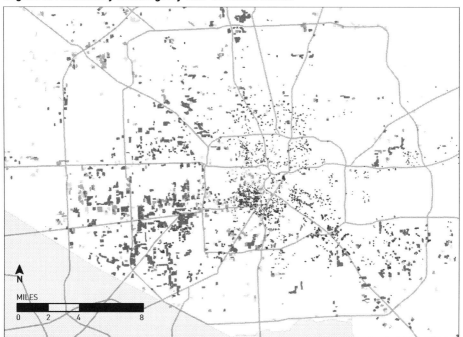

MULTIFAMILY RESIDENTIAL DWELLINGS WITH OVER 5 UNITS, YEAR BUILT

- 1900–1964
- 1965–1984
- 1985–2004
- 2005–2016

Source: Kinder Institute for Urban Research, Rice University.

the path of gentrification such as the Third Ward have large amounts of vacant land, though speculation has often driven up land prices. Other historically underserved neighborhoods, such as the historically African-American Fifth Ward and the historically Hispanic East End, also have ample land with lower prices.

But the general absence of strong government controls that exist in most other large cities, and the lack of use zoning specifically, also limit opportunities to use otherwise strong market forces to create affordable housing, both naturally and via subsidies.

The lack of use zoning means land that could be available for affordable housing is sold to the highest bidder irrespective of use. Land that might be reserved for housing in another city can be purchased by office or industrial developers. Land that might be reserved for high-density, multi-family, and mixed-use development in another city can be purchased by townhome developers to feed that portion of the market. And because there are both no use restrictions and few density restrictions, it is not possible to impose inclusionary zoning requirements that, in most other cities, yield either affordable housing units or funds to build affordable housing.

Partly for this reason, Houston also has a relatively weak community development infrastructure. Community development corporations (CDCs) often arise in cities with strong governmental land-use controls, in large part because those land-use controls provide opportunities to obtain both land and financing for affordable projects. Houston has some outstanding CDCs, including Avenue (which focuses on the Near North Side) and New Hope Housing (which builds housing citywide); these CDCs use low-income housing tax credits and other common mechanisms. In addition, the Houston office of the Local Initiative Support Corporation provides local leadership. Overall, however, the CDC ecosystem is spotty. Houston has a relatively small public housing infrastructure because the city sometimes rejected federal money for such purposes in the '60s and '70s.

At the same time, paradoxically, some land-use regulations in Houston are either onerous or used as zoning "workarounds" to prevent higher-density housing from being constructed in older neighborhoods.

For example, Houston may have no use zoning but, except for downtown, it has typi-cally suburban parking and setback requirements almost everywhere in the city. Most urban developments must go to the city planning commission to obtain a variance to build a truly urban project. (The city code contains some alternatives, including an optional transit-oriented development zone, but these are not frequently used.)

Similarly, in the absence of use zoning, several alternatives have been developed that are designed to prevent construction of urban housing types in many neighborhoods. Affluent neighborhoods in Houston have long been protected by restrictive deed covenants, some of which are enforced by the city (an unusual practice nationwide). In recent years, older close-in neighborhoods that are gentrifying have used the creation of an historic district as a way to prevent new dense development. Finally, neighborhoods in Houston have the option of seeking minimum lot-size ordinances, which effectively prevent the creation of townhome developments — or multi-family apartment developments.

The city does have a variety of tools at its disposal to create affordable housing, including state-sanctioned economic development subsidies and housing vouchers. However, these tools have not been used in a systematic way to produce affordable housing. In addition, Mayor Sylvester Turner, who was elected in 2015, recently ran afoul of the US Department of Housing and Urban Development by declining to use low-income housing tax credits for a project in a "high-opportunity" site near the

Galleria area. Indeed, not unlike Ben Carson, the new secretary of Housing and Urban Development, Turner has argued forcefully that children in underserved neighborhoods should not have to move to high-opportunity areas in order to find a path to success in life.

Turner, who grew up in the historically African-American Acres Homes neighborhood, recently told the *Houston Chronicle*: "I categorically reject the notion that in order for poor children — those who come from lower socioeconomic families — in order for them to participate in the American dream, that I have to move them from where they are and place them someplace else." Turner continued by asserting, "The answer is to invest in the communities where they are." Turner is currently investigating ways to use housing vouchers more effectively to create a better distribution of affordable opportunities throughout the city.[11] The mayor's role is especially important in Houston. The City Council adopts the budget and must approve many actions, but the Houston City Charter creates a very "strong mayor" system in which the mayor sets the agenda and has complete control over the executive departments.

A MORE INCLUSIVE MARKET-ORIENTED CITY

As was stated above, Houston is at once a market-oriented city and one whose regulatory system and financial incentives do not always align with the goal of inclusiveness. Within this seemingly contradictory set of conditions lies the opportunity to create a model for a more inclusive, market-oriented city. Specifically, four actions can help shape the market-oriented approach.

Align Economic Development Incentives with Inclusiveness Goals

As stated above, Houston actually does provide financial assistance to real estate developers in the form of so-called "380 agreements" — economic development agreements to provide financial assistance to developers. However, these incentives are not aligned with goals of inclusiveness.[12] The city rarely seeks, for example, affordable housing in return for economic development incentives. Aligning the city's own economic development incentives with inclusiveness goals would go a long way toward helping inclusiveness in Houston. In his Transition Team Report, Mayor Turner endorsed the idea of focusing the city's "investment resources," everything from housing assistance to public works projects, on underserved neighborhoods. This goal is contained in the city's 2015 general plan, which Mayor Turner has directed his staff to implement through its budget process. But the impact of "Plan Houston," as the general plan is called, is still in its infancy, and the city has not yet implemented a set of policies and strategies that delineate how it will concentrate resources in underserved neighborhoods. Mayor Turner is expected to provide detail in a new initiative he calls "Complete Communities."

Align Regulations with Inclusiveness Goals

Although Houston does not have use zoning, the city does have a wide variety of conventional development regulations — notably, parking and setback requirements — that drive up the cost of housing development and make the city less inclusive. The city should relax or adapt such regulations in specific locations where it hopes to encourage inclusive development. As the transit-oriented development (TOD) ordinance experience suggests, such regulatory relief must be carefully crafted if it is to be a preferable alternative to simple market-rate development that seeks variances from the planning commission.

Use Government and Institutional Landholdings Strategically To Pursue Inclusiveness Goals

Houston has an abundance of land even in close-in locations, though in many cases real estate speculation is driving up the cost of that land to the point where only high-end market-rate development is possible. However, especially in close-in locations, much of the land, especially vacant lots and parking lots, is owned by either government agencies such as Tax Increment Reinvestment Zones (TIRZ) or institutional entities such as churches. The city can move a long way toward inclusiveness by working with these entities to make at least some of this land available for affordable housing. Such an effort is already under way in the Third Ward, where a community land trust including some TIRZ and institutional land may be formed as a result of the joint efforts of neighborhood leaders and Houston philanthropies under the auspices of the Emancipation Economic Development Council.

Create a Broad and Comprehensive Approach to Inclusiveness Including Both Underserved and High-Opportunity Areas

Responding to concern about high-opportunity areas, the Turner administration is already considering a series of steps to encourage broader distribution of affordable housing, including more effective use of federal housing vouchers. Using this approach, *and* the steps outlined above, the city can create a comprehensive inclusiveness policy to encourage not only affordable housing in affluent areas but also mixed-income housing opportunities in historically underserved areas. Such a policy can take advantage of Houston's traditionally market-oriented approach combined with the public policy levers available to the city and related entities. Mayor Turner endorsed the idea of a comprehensive housing plan in his Transition Team Report.

CONCLUSION

At a time when income inequality is giving more market power to the affluent, it is no easy task to create greater inclusivity in a market-oriented city. Despite its "regulation lite" approach — or perhaps because of it — Houston appears to be among the most unequal large cities in the country. Making the city more inclusive will require both a comprehensive citywide approach and targeted efforts in underserved neighborhoods threatened by gentrification.

As mentioned above, the emerging effort in the Third Ward is likely to be a good testbed for some of these ideas. Located just south of Downtown Houston, the Third Ward is a culturally significant, historically African-American community — the location of the original Juneteenth celebration. Although its residents are still extremely poor, the Third Ward is facing gentrification now that land prices are going up and market-rate townhomes are being built.

It is likely that a comprehensive approach will help the Third Ward. The city will probably designate the Third Ward as one of its "Complete Communities" neighborhoods, thus concentrating city investment of all kinds there. As stated above, a community land trust might be created in order to assure that institutional and government-owned land is used for community benefit, including maintaining affordable housing, instead of private profit. And if any 380 agreements are executed in the Third Ward, they should carry the quid pro quo requiring developers to meet social as well as economic objectives.

At the same time, Houston will not become inclusive unless a comprehensive effort is undertaken to ensure that affordable housing is made available in high-opportunity areas near job centers. Mayor Turner's recent decision to kill an affordable housing project near the Galleria was a disappointment in this regard, but the city will go a long way toward inclusiveness by using vouchers and other resources to provide a greater range of housing opportunities in affluent neighborhoods.

Bibliography

City of Houston. 2013. "Median Household Income: City of Houston by Super Neighborhoods." http://www.houstontx.gov/planning/Demographics/docs_pdfs/SN/Median_Household_Income_by_SN.pdf (accessed February 16, 2017).

Ehrenhalt, Alan. 2012. *The Great Inversion and the Future of the American City.* New York: Alfred A. Knopf.

Elliott, Rebecca. 2017. "Turner, Feds Clash Over Affordable Housing Policies." *Houston Chronicle,* January 28.

Florida, Richard. 2017. *The New Urban Crisis: How Our Cities Are Increasing Inequality, Deepening Segregation, and Failing the Middle Class — and What We Can Do About It.* New York: Basic Books.

Klineberg, Stephen. 2016. "35 Years of the Kinder Houston Area Survey: Tracking Responses to a Changing America." Kinder Institute for Urban Research, Rice University.

O'Connell, Heather A., and Junia Howell. 2016. "Disparate City: Understanding Rising Levels of Concentrated Poverty and Affluence in Greater Houston." Kinder Institute for Urban Research, Rice University. https://kinder.rice.edu/uploadedFiles/Kinder_Institute_for_Urban_Research/Programs/Disparity/FINAL_DISPARATE_CITY.pdf (accessed February 16, 2017).

Sarnoff, Nancy. 2010. "Mayor Parker defends incentives to lure development." *Houston Chronicle*, September 13. http://www.chron.com/news/houston-texas/article/Mayor-Parker-defends-incentives-to-lure-1700527.php (accessed February 16, 2017).

U.S. Census Bureau. 2016. "ACS Community Survey." http://factfinder.census.gov (accessed February 16, 2017).

Walker, Kelsey A., and Kyle K. Shelton. 2016. "Houston in Flux: Understanding a Decade of Bayou City Development." Kinder Institute for Urban Research. https://kinder.rice.edu/uploadedFiles/Kinder_Institute_for_Urban_Research/Programs/DT-P/Houstoninflux.final.160524.pdf (accessed February 16, 2017).

World Refugee Day Houston. 2016. http://www.worldrefugeedayhouston.org (accessed February 16, 2017).

Endnotes

1   US Census Bureau (2016).

2   World Refugee Day Houston (2016).

3   Home values from Zillow.com: https://www.zillow.com/houston-tx/home-values, https://www.zillow.com/los-angeles-ca/home-values, and https://www.zillow.com/washington-dc/home-values (accessed February 16, 2017).

4   About half of the 4.5 million people who live in Harris County live in the City of Houston. Although the issues described in this paper are endemic to Harris County, we focus primarily on solutions in the City of Houston, in part because its governmental structure for housing issues is stronger than in the county.

5   O'Connell and Howell (2016).

6   Florida (2017).

7   The I-610 Loop is an area of almost 100 square miles inside Houston's first beltway, located between 6 and 8 miles from downtown Houston. The western half of this Loop, from University of Houston to the Uptown/Galleria area, includes most of the regionally significant locations and institutions in Houston, such as Houston's oldest neighborhoods (some very rich and some very poor), museums, sports arena, job centers, medical and educational institutions, and "crown jewel parks." Beltway 8 is the second beltway, located approximately 15 miles out, which includes mostly suburban residential areas developed between 1970 and 2000. See City of Houston (2013).

8   Ehrenhalt (2012).

9   City of Houston (2013).

10 Walker and Shelton (2016).

11 Elliott (2017).

12 Sarnoff (2010).

What Would It Take for the HUD Affirmatively Furthering Fair Housing (AFFH) Rule to Meaningfully Increase Inclusion?

Affirmatively Furthering Fair Housing: The Potential and the Challenges for Fulfilling the Promise of HUD's Final Rule

KATHERINE O'REGAN

New York University

The context for the Affirmatively Furthering Fair Housing final rule, issued by the Department of Housing and Urban Development (HUD) in July of 2015, begins more than fifty years ago in a highly racially segregated America experiencing urban civil unrest. HUD and its predecessors were among the large number of public and private actors that fostered and perpetuated that segregation. The Federal Housing Administration (FHA), created to revive the housing market and stimulate homeownership in the Great Depression, mirrored and even formalized the discriminatory practices that were widespread among private actors at the time.[1] Public housing was frequently segregated itself and sited so as to segregate large segments of the African American community in isolated areas.[2] Urban Renewal often targeted functioning minority communities, leading to displacement and further concentration in other areas.

Against this backdrop and one week after the assassination of Martin Luther King, Jr., Congress passed a long-debated Civil Rights bill on April 11, 1968. Title VIII of the legislation, known as the Fair Housing Act, expressly prohibits the kinds of discrimination that had evolved over the years to deny blacks equal access to housing. Given the historical role of HUD and other federal housing agencies in creating segregation, the Act requires more from such agencies than merely avoiding discrimination; they are to take steps through their programs to "affirmatively further" fair housing (AFFH). This obligation extends to those jurisdictions and entities funded by HUD.

While this AFFH obligation has existed for nearly fifty years, fair housing advocates and many others have criticized HUD for inaction on this portion of the Fair Housing Act. As laid out by Bostic and Acolin,[3] prior to the new rule, HUD had taken only limited steps to enforce the AFFH obligations through its grants programs. For example, internal and external reviews of the Analysis of Impediments (AI) process, the precursor to the current rule, found the approach greatly flawed.

HUD'S FINAL AFFH RULE

It is in this context, the existence of AFFH obligations for HUD grantees but the absence of a clear and effective process for achieving them, that HUD issued its AFFH final rule. In broadest strokes, the rule requires jurisdictions and grantees to conduct an Analysis of Fair Housing (AFH), assessing their fair housing issues and describing goals for affirmatively furthering fair housing. The content of the AFH is standardized through an on-line assessment tool, which contains a variety of mandatory categories of analyses and specific questions in each. The tool provides participants with associated data and maps on their jurisdiction and region. Those data and maps are also available to the public, and participants are required to enlist meaningful community participation in identifying fair housing issues and shaping goals. Those goals must then be linked to a program participant's Consolidated Plan and/or Public Housing Agency (PHA) plan. Unlike the AI, the AFH must be submitted to HUD, and HUD has 60 days to determine whether to accept it.

CURRENT STATE OF PLAY

The provision and use of data in a standardized assessment, combined with a process of public engagement and HUD final review, is a fundamentally different approach to AFFH that has been well received by many. It has also been loudly, and brutally, criticized. The Republican Party platform of 2016 referenced the rule as a threat to local control of zoning. Legislation has been entered into the House and Senate that would essentially erase the rule and anything like it, and also prohibit the use of federal dollars for the geospatial data.[4] HUD Secretary Ben Carson referred to the rule as "social engineering" prior to his nomination, although subsequent remarks suggest he has not finalized his views.[5]

KEY ISSUES AND CHALLENGES

This current state of affairs raises a set of key questions about what it would take for HUD's AFFH to meaningfully increase inclusion.

Achieving Long-run Success in Light of Near-term Threats

How can we help AFFH succeed in the long run if HUD is not supportive or is outright hostile right now?

Bostic and Acolin start us off by providing a clear and concise history and description of the rule. They note the critical role HUD could and should play in the near term. This would require HUD's investing not only in its own capacity to review and support AFHs, but also in the capacity of jurisdictions to conduct their AFH. Given federal budget discussions, no one expects HUD to do either. Yet there is minimal hand-wringing about the expected absence of HUD's near-term support in this set of papers. Collectively, the papers lay out a roadmap of what is needed from a much broader set of actors whose efforts can keep the AFFH rule headed towards long-term success. Lack of HUD efforts in the near term need not threaten the long-term success of AFFH.

The papers identify the largest immediate threat as the outright dismantling of the rule and the elimination of the associated online data. If the rule is dismantled, any future administration wishing to address the AFFH obligation would need to go through a full rule-making process, surmounting all of the obstacles that have slowed or stopped previous efforts.[6] This process would require sustained effort within HUD and cooperation across program offices that have historically held widely different views on AFFH, in addition to surmounting external political obstacles. In 1998, HUD did issue a Proposed AFFH Rule, to amend HUD regulations and establish AFFH performance standards. HUD received extensive public comments raising concerns about clarity and usefulness. HUD chose to not issue a final rule at that time. The most recent rule-making process raised no fewer concerns, and took most of the eight years of the Obama administration to get to completion. Even with the knowledge that the rule was a priority for the administration, there was considerable public skepticism that a final rule would be issued.

The long-run prospects of using the AFFH obligation in the Fair Housing Act as a lever for addressing segregation and fostering inclusion may not require HUD's active support in the near term, but does require that the architecture of the rule remain in place, even if temporarily dormant. If the rule remains intact but is not actively supported or enforced by HUD, there are still actors and jurisdictions who will move forward now. There could well be future leadership at HUD that will pick up where others left off. A question for broad supporters of the rule is: how do we ensure that the rule is not formally dismantled? Are there particular actions that should — or should *not* — be taken now so as to lower the likelihood that the current administration will undertake the effort of dismantling the rule?

It Takes a Village

Even under the best of circumstances, HUD alone cannot provide the needed resources and support for the creation and implementation of strong AFHs. How do we ensure robust participation by the broader set of actors needed for success?

Allen provides a clear list of what is needed at each stage of the AFH process for the rule to meet its full promise.[7] This list highlights the full arc of the AFH process, from initial analysis of data, to meaningful engagement of communities of color, through to designing and ultimately implementing effective strategies. Each of these stages can — and needs to be — supported by a range of actors who can add to local capacity. As he says, "the full promise of AFFH will not be realized without a 'ground game.'"[8] He specifically makes his call to action for the needed capacity to academics and foundations, rather than HUD. This goal creates a challenge, as those actors are dispersed, and there is not an obvious coordinating body for mobilizing local actors.

Data Alone Is Not Knowledge

This exercise is heavily dependent on analysis of HUD-provided data from national sources, as well as local data and knowledge. How do we ensure there is local capacity for the heavy analytical lift of a robust AFH?

The papers by Bostic and Acolin and by Allen both emphasize the powerful role of data in the new AFH process, and the critical role of local actors in leveraging those data. The data are meant to reduce the burden of the standardized assessment tool; to provide a minimum floor of analytics across jurisdictions; and, perhaps most importantly, to be publically available to empower members of those communities who might otherwise have little voice. Two conditions must be met for the data to play this role: that the national data are updated and made available in digestible form, and that jurisdictions have the capacity to analyze these (and local) data.

With regard to the first condition, there is certainly the risk that HUD will not continue to provide the data publicly. Even in the absence of legislative action to limit federal provision of such data, HUD could simply stop updating the existing data. HUD, however, does not have a unique advantage in translating what are primarily publicly available data into usable maps and tables. I would argue this first risk is fairly small as numerous others can — and will — step into this space. The second risk is the larger risk — that many jurisdictions and community members lack the capacity to analyze those data and combine them with local data. Such capacity is very uneven across jurisdictions, and with the likely retreat of HUD from providing assistance, even greater resources are needed for the data to have the empowering and equalizing effect originally intended. Allen in particular lays out extensive examples of fair housing cases where it was the capacity to analyze data appropriately that won the day. The distinction between data and effective analysis is not made often enough in understanding what it will take for AFFH to succeed. Jurisdictions need more than data: they and all interested parties need the capacity to make good use of the data.

Good Planning Versus Good Lawsuits

How do we manage the tension between AFFH's role as a planning tool and its role as an enforcement tool?

There is an inherent tension in the AFH process that connects to HUD's dual goals of supporting more effective planning and enforcing compliance with the Fair Housing Act. All three papers highlight these roles and potential tensions. Building on the stages of the AFH process laid out in Allen, Julian creates a very useful categorization of jurisdictions by their level of acceptance of the letter and spirit of the law, their capacity to analyze, and their capacity and willingness to ultimately implement strategies.[9] Those most willing and able are 1's; those who are outright hostile are 4's.

The distinction between willingness and capacity for the first stages of AFH and willingness and capacity to move from AFH to actual action is quite useful and made by both Julian and Allen. Different strategies are likely needed for jurisdictions lacking data capacity than for those unable to develop actionable plans to address issues that surface in their AFH. HUD's rule serves as a planning enhancement for jurisdictions lying on the spectrum from 1 to 3; its power is solely in enforcement for jurisdictions that are a 4. The stance HUD needs to take to partner well with jurisdictions in categories 1-3 is a different stance than jurisdictions in category 4. Such flexibility in approach may be necessary for success, but poses a challenge for HUD. Will HUD manage to navigate these dual roles? In the absence of HUD as enforcer, Allen and Julian both suggest non-HUD enforcement paths.

We Need a Bigger Boat

The geographic and sector scope of the problem – and solution, is larger than HUD's siloed planning requirements. Can we harness AFFH for larger, bolder solutions?

As pointed out in Bostic and Acolin, addressing residential segregation and the unevenness of opportunity across places requires a larger geographic scale than singular jurisdictions, and resources far beyond housing. Housing provides more than shelter, and it is the full complement of where one lives — the safety, the transit, the schools, that ultimately determines whether residents have full access to opportunity. The funding levers needed to adequately re-invest in distressed communities, a valid strategy within the 'balanced approach' endorsed by HUD, need to be tapped by having a broad engagement strategy across sectors and jurisdictions. While the HUD rule encourages collaboration on AFH submissions, there are limited incentives. What is the longer run path to supporting the type of regional AFHs needed for more impactful changes? Does this require a different or additional engagement strategy beyond Allen's suggestions?

CONCLUSION

The large number of advocates, policymakers, and communities concerned and frustrated by the persistence of racial segregation in the U.S. saw HUD's final rule as the architecture for truly — and finally — making progress. Recent political events have given pause as to the specific path forward, and perhaps reset expectations about what more might be required for HUD's rule to meaningfully increase inclusion. But these papers provide a rough preliminary roadmap, and some strategies for the broad group of stakeholders invested in creating a more equal society. The charge is clear: what it takes for HUD's rule to be impactful is not really about HUD. It takes us.

Bibliography

Allen, Michael. 2015. "HUD's New AFFH Rule: The Importance of the Ground Game." In *The Dream Revisited*, edited by Ingrid Ellen Gould and Justin Steil. September. http://furmancenter.org/research/iri/essay/huds-new-affh-rule-the-importance-of-the-ground-game.

———. 2017. "Speaking Truth to Power: Enhancing Community Engagement, Monitoring and Enforcement to Ensure Compliance with AFFH Requirements." This volume.

Bostic, Raphael, and Arthur Acolin. 2017. "The Potential for HUD's Affirmatively Furthering Fair Housing Rule to Meaningfully Increase Inclusion." This volume.

Carson, Ben. 2015. "Experimenting with Failed Socialism Again." *Washington Times*, July 23.

Goering, John M., ed. 2012. *Housing Desegregation and Federal Housing Policy*. Chapel Hill: University of North Carolina Press.

Julian, Elizabeth. 2017. "The Duty to Affirmatively Further Fair Housing: A Legal as well as Policy Imperative." This volume.

Endnotes

1 http://www.bostonfairhousing.org/timeline/1934-FHA.html.

2 For background, see Goering (2012).

3 Bostic and Acolin (2017).

4 "Local Zoning Decision Protection Act of 2017," H.R. 482 in the House and S. 103 in the Senate.

5 Carson (2015).

6 This assumes that the dismantling of the final rule is not done through legislative action that would prohibit future rulemaking.

7 Allen (2017).

8 Allen (2015).

9 Julian (2017).

The Potential for HUD's Affirmatively Furthering Fair Housing Rule to Meaningfully Increase Inclusion

RAPHAEL BOSTIC
Federal Reserve Bank of Atlanta

ARTHUR ACOLIN
University of Washington

The United States was founded on the rights to life, liberty, and the pursuit of happiness, yet its citizens have had unequal opportunities to enjoy these rights. Rather, as borne out by the experiences of previous generations as well as by empirical research, certain groups have been largely excluded from this promise of America.[1]

Opportunity is intimately linked with place. For individuals to have equal opportunity, they must have equal access to neighborhoods with a wide range of amenities that they can leverage to live out their preferences. Recent research provides striking evidence about what happens when this does not occur: children raised in lower-income, amenity-poor neighborhoods fare far worse in terms of wages in adulthood than children who grow up in more affluent areas.[2]

The structure of the US housing market does not grant equal access to housing opportunity for many reasons. Persistent barriers, including overt and subtle forms of discrimination, legal structures such as Jim Crow, and private and public institutional practices, have limited and continue to limit equal access.

The Fair Housing Act of 1968 was one of a series of laws enacted to address these barriers. The law established two mandates for the US Department of Housing and Urban Development (HUD): eliminate illegal discrimination in housing-related activities, and affirmatively further fair housing. Much energy has been devoted to executing the Act's prohibitions against discrimination based on race, color, national origin, religion, sex, familial status, or disability status.[3] This effort has resulted in the emergence of an ecosystem of public, nonprofit, and private institutions that conduct audits, litigate, and provide support to fight discriminatory behaviors. This ecosystem has produced significant changes in laws and practices.[4] Nonetheless, individuals belonging to protected classes continue to have unequal access to certain housing types and neighborhoods.[5]

The second mandate—affirmatively furthering fair housing (AFFH)—differs in important ways from the mandate to eliminate illegal discrimination. Instead of stopping behaviors that make access to housing unequal, the AFFH mandate seeks to promote behaviors that make access more equal. Historically, AFFH has been much harder to implement and enforce than anti-discrimination. Few, if any, organizations have AFFH as their primary mission, jurisdictional engagement and regulatory monitoring has been uneven, and the scope of the mandate has often not been well-defined.

In 2015, in part in response to that rocky history, HUD released a revised AFFH rule. The new regulatory approach changes the scope of the mandate in substantial ways, and provides incentives and tools to help communities act on it. In this chapter, we discuss the potential of the new rule to produce meaningful change and the things needed in the next five to ten years to maximize its effectiveness in producing true access to opportunity for all. We begin with a brief description of residential segregation in the US. In the second section, we discuss how the new AFFH rule differs from and improves upon its predecessor rule. Finally, we provide a series of "musts" that need to occur over the next five to ten years if the rule is to meaningfully increase inclusion.

RESIDENTIAL INCLUSION: AN ELUSIVE GOAL

The US remains characterized by high levels of segregation due, in part, to a long history of structural and individual discrimination based on personal characteristics such as race, ethnicity and disability.[6] Segregation is an embodiment of the barriers faced by certain groups to inclusion in general and to equal access to housing in particular. It was one of the main motivating factors driving the Civil Rights movement and remains a major barrier to equal access to opportunity.[7] Residential racial segregation, particularly against African Americans, peaked between the 1960s and 1970s. Though it declined substantially after that, leading Glaeser and Vigdor to controversially declare "the end of the segregated century,"[8] segregation by race and ethnicity remains high.[9] In addition, socioeconomic segregation has increased, resulting in a complex interaction of sorting by ethnicity and social class.[10]

Some have argued that individual preferences are an important contributor to the residential sorting and concentration of individuals by race, ethnicity, or other characteristics.[11] Indeed, there is a large literature on racial and ethnic enclaves and the benefits they afford that suggests that such preferences exist and are acted upon.[12] The question that remains, however, is how important this driver of sorting is relative to other factors that constrain choices. Research on this question suggests self-sorting is only a secondary factor.[13]

Segregation is only one manifestation of the barriers to access to opportunity faced by members of protected classes. A key driver of segregation, discrimination remains persistent in housing markets and influences the ability of minority families to rent housing units, purchase homes, and obtain mortgages. As reviewed by Oh and Yinger, the first audit studies that estimated the prevalence of discriminatory practices in housing markets found large levels of discrimination against black applicants.[14] Subsequent studies sought to identify explanatory mechanisms and also consider the extent of discrimination against other groups, including Hispanics, single-headed families with children, individuals with disabilities, same-sex couples, and housing voucher recipients.[15] The studies consistently find differences in treatment of members of protected classes by real estate agents, landlords, and mortgage lenders. These differences in treatment contribute to limits on equal access to opportunity.

The findings of these studies and others strongly suggest that effective progress towards truly inclusive communities will require purposeful attention. In short, the AFFH mandate remains as relevant as ever. We now turn to a brief history of AFFH to provide context for the 2015 revisions.

IMPLEMENTING AFFH THROUGH 2015

HUD took limited actions to implement the AFFH mandate in the years immediately following the adoption of the Fair Housing Act.[16] Under Secretary George Romney, HUD initially took an aggressive AFFH stance, and proposed using coercive measures to push state and local governments to implement changes to decrease segregation and increase inclusion by creating "stable, racially diverse neighborhoods."[17] However, these early actions were vigorously opposed by the White House and local governments, and HUD subsequently retreated.[18]

In the 1980s, HUD required Community Development Block Grant recipients for some of its programs to certify that they would affirmatively further fair housing. In 1992, the requirement to meet Fair Housing Review Criteria was expanded to all community planning and development programs managed by HUD, and in 1995, the certification criteria were combined into a Consolidated Plan that required local communities to perform an Analysis of Impediments (AI) and to identify actions to affirmatively further fair housing.[19] The AI components were further clarified in 1996 in the "Fair Housing Planning Guide," and included analyzing local barriers to housing access for members of protected classes as well as proposing actions to overcome these barriers.[20]

The AIs were expected to be updated every five years and communicated to HUD, and thus to spur actions that would promote inclusion. However, their impact was limited because HUD did not provide resources or incentives to conduct the AIs and did not effectively review them or monitor the implementation of proposed actions, limiting the accountability of grantees and creating little commitment to furthering fair housing.[21] A Government Accountability Office report found that among 441 AIs it surveyed in 2010, 29 percent were prepared before 2004 and 11 before 2000 despite HUD's guideline that they should be updated every five years.[22] In addition, reports pointed out that many actions proposed in AIs did not include timeframes for implementation.[23]

THE 2015 REVISED AFHH RULE

Up to 2015, the actions taken by HUD to implement the AFFH mandate largely failed to produce meaningful results. Housing advocacy groups and government agencies pointed to serious flaws in the approach to implementing AFFH through the AIs[24] and to the limits of piecemeal actions at the local level in response to court cases.[25] Spurred in part by the 2010 GAO report, HUD, under the Obama administration, embarked on a multi-year revision process that culminated with the announcement in 2015 of a new rule for implementing the AFFH mandate.[26]

The new rule's focus is to help local and state institutions covered by the rule actively work to increase access to opportunity for minorities and other underrepresented groups. Its defining feature is the Assessment of Fair Housing (AFH), which replaces the AI and provides a structure designed to focus jurisdictions on a relatively small set of explicit metrics for assessing success in furthering fair housing and providing access to opportunity. Like the AI, the AFH must be completed every five years. It contains six elements (see Table 1). The AFH is a roadmap designed to help local jurisdictions achieve the goals of the AFFH regulation. First and foremost, the AFFH is a community planning process intended to ensure that considerations of fair housing and equal access to opportunity inform each jurisdiction's consolidated plan. Hence, the jurisdiction's priorities and strategies are important results of the AFH process. Another critical element, discussed further below, is the democratizing of information on local housing and market conditions so that a broader range of stakeholders can participate in the process on equal footing.

The revised rule has several significant features that distinguish it from its predecessor. First, the rule explicitly defines a primary goal of fair housing as equal access to opportunity, and so returns to the origins of the Fair Housing Act, which was enacted in part because of the existence of disparities in access to opportunity. This emphasis clarifies the metrics for success, so that jurisdictions will have a better understanding of how HUD and others are assessing their investment decisions. Moreover, the metrics established provide clarity regarding the language of opportunity, and so jurisdictions

Table 1. The Elements of the Assessment of Fair Housing (AFH)

Element	Substance
Summary of fair housing issues and institutional capacity	Details whether there have been compliance and enforcement actions in the community during the period of analysis, as well as the allocation of resources devoted to enforcing fair housing laws and regulations.
Data Analysis	• Reports, using data provided by HUD via a geospatial data tool, on where the jurisdiction currently stands, and how it has evolved, along three "community performance metrics": • the persistence of segregated communities, particularly racially and ethnically concentrated areas of poverty that result in worse outcomes for their residents and impose costs on the overall community; • the existence of disparities in access to amenities that contribute to inequality of opportunity for people in protected groups; • acute shortfalls in meeting the housing needs of individuals belonging to protected classes, and the trajectory of these shortfalls (increasing, static, or decreasing).
Assessment of fair housing issues	Describes the local and other forces — such as historic patterns of discrimination, poor public schools, or exclusionary zoning — that underlie the persistence of segregation and disparities in access.
Identification of local fair housing priorities and goals	Develops goals and strategies for addressing the barriers to opportunity that are faced by the local jurisdiction, and metrics to assess progress, based on the results of the data analysis and assessment of fair housing issues.
Summary of efforts directed toward ensuring broad community participation	Reports on the procedures followed to ensure broad inclusion of the entire community, including efforts to get input from members of protected classes in the process of developing the AFH.
Review of progress since the submission of the previous AFH	To be completed in follow-up AFHs; explains and evaluates the progress made in achieving the goals and strategies adopted in previous AFHs, using the submitted metrics and a consideration of factors that affected the extent of success.

should be less unsure about whether proposed strategies fit into the AFFH framework. Significantly, the opportunity lens is agnostic about the question of whether it is better to promote equal access through mobility or community development vehicles; it leaves that decision to local communities. It is not agnostic, though, on whether strategies need to promote equal access itself.

Second, the new rule seeks to focus jurisdictions' attention on racially and ethnically concentrated areas of poverty. These areas are particularly debilitating for their residents. The combination of racial concentration and poverty concentration creates far higher levels of economic isolation and social chaos than does either racial or economic concentration alone. Therefore, people living in areas with both racial and poverty concentrations face barriers that are considerably more difficult to overcome.[27] Moreover, these are areas to which local governments often devote disproportionate amounts of police, emergency response, and other resources.[28] Thus, they are quite expensive to manage. Both facts suggest that "solving" these areas can produce increasing returns, making more resources available in the long run to address other local priorities. The new rule thus can potentially help focus localities on approaches to housing that will deliver higher returns on investment.

Third, depending on implementation (see below), the new rule could introduce a new mindset regarding the pursuit of fair housing at the local level. Few jurisdictions cherish the opportunity to engage in fair housing issues. In part, this is because their only experiences with fair housing involve threats of litigation or actual lawsuits. As a consequence, there is distressingly little proactive pursuit of fair housing strategies, even though evidence makes clear that more diverse communities are more productive and more resilient.[29] The new rule could potentially change this, as it envisions local governments engaging in the AFFH process with HUD as a partner rather than as an enforcer. If this partnership takes hold—a big if (see below)—and strategies bear fruit, then many more jurisdictions may start to view fair housing as something that can provide benefits, not just litigation-based costs. AFFH could be the "carrot" to the enforcement infrastructure's "stick."

Underlying this possibility is a hypothesis about whether jurisdictions will truly try to find feasible fair housing strategies.[30] There is broad consensus that, at the extremes, some jurisdictions will embrace the rule's processes with gusto and will have the capacity to produce high quality plans, while other jurisdictions will rebuff any and all efforts to engage in the process. Less certain is the behavior of the large number of jurisdictions between these extremes. In particular, it could be that a majority of those in the middle would like to pursue AFFH strategizing in good faith but have not yet done so mainly because they lack capacity and in-house expertise. These would correspond to Julian's jurisdictions in category 2, demonstrating an "acceptance of both the letter and spirit of the Rule, but a limited capacity to use the Tool and the Rule's requirements."[31] Alternatively, it could be that most in the middle have no interest in engaging in fair housing exercises and would shirk at the first opportunity, falling into Julian's category 3 of jurisdictions that show an "acceptance of the need to comply with the specific requirements of the Rule to get federal funds," but also demonstrate "a lack of understanding or willingness to develop a plan to actually address the problems."[32]

In an important way, the revised AFFH rule embraces the first view of the broad middle group of jurisdictions. Via the new rule, HUD provides local jurisdictions with a new geospatial data tool that can generate many of the reports and initial maps on which to base community engagement and dialogue. This new tool reduces the capacity demands placed on local jurisdictions and so makes it easier for them to complete the AFH. While there is some debate as to how much the tool reduces the administrative burden, early experiences will provide some insights in this regard.

Either way, the new tool is a strong signal of HUD's intent to work constructively with local communities. And it assumes they will take HUD up on this offer.

There are other important benefits to the tool. For example, it helps to level the playing field within communities across groups with varying levels of sophistication in analyzing data and planning. The publicly available data can empower local organizations to develop their own analyses based on alternative sets of priorities. The information in the maps and tables of the data tool can also be used by advocates and by the press to see that public officials do not forget, ignore, or overlook challenges faced by those in their communities whom the Fair Housing Act was enacted to protect.

The 2015 AFFH rule also addresses some of the previous flaws in the mandate's implementation. The new data tool is designed to lower the burden of producing the foundational AFFH report (i.e., the AI or AFH). The rule's guidance and partnership structure are intended to make it easier for local jurisdictions to develop feasible strategies for improving equal access to opportunity. It establishes a regime for HUD review of the AFH with deadlines that create a clear framework for accountability, thus limiting a jurisdiction's uncertainty regarding litigation risk.

WHAT CAN BE DONE GOING FORWARD TO ENSURE THE AFFH RULE'S IMPACT

The new AFFH rule was adopted in 2015.[33] A number of jurisdictions have started the process of developing their AFH or even submitted it to HUD. However, it will take time for it to produce effects, and the next few years will be crucial in determining its success. Actions by a set of public, nonprofit and private actors at the national and local levels will determine these outcomes. This section identifies a list of nine conditions that will impact the rule's success:

1. HUD must build and maintain an internal capacity so the agency can be a true partner. This rule works only if HUD can effectively provide leadership and guidance about it, and there are legitimate questions about whether HUD has the necessary capacity. HUD must conduct an assessment of its existing capacity to determine whether its current level of staffing and the the subject matter expertise of its staff members are sufficient to provide high quality consulting to jurisdictions about developing effective housing policies to address barriers to opportunity. Once this assessment is completed, HUD needs to then find resources to address any shortcomings identified. While the Office of Fair Housing and Equal Opportunity (FHEO) and its regional offices should be emphasized in this assessment, HUD should also examine the Offices of Community Planning and Development and Policy Development and Research, as they will also play critical roles. HUD must have this capacity if it is to be a true partner for jurisdictions as they go through the AFH and subsequent strategy implementation process.

2. HUD must build an infrastructure to help increase local capacity to engage in these issues. Resources must be allocated to build an infrastructure that will makes it easy for jurisdictions to fulfill their AFFH responsibilities. The vast majority of jurisdictions do not have the staff and capacity to conduct a thorough technical analysis to identify barriers and strategies to overcome them. They will need technical support and examples of best practices, which can be provided either directly by HUD or through HUD-supported third party providers with the topic expertise. An example of such a structure is the National Resource Network, a consortium of public and private organizations formed and financed by HUD as part of the Strong Cities, Strong Communities initiative.[34]

A first element of this infrastructure is the online mapping and data tool, a powerful resource that allows local government to quickly produce information that will facilitate meaningful conversations. We also view the regional training symposia offered by FHEO in the context of the anti-discrimination efforts as a model worthy of examination. We encourage HUD to think hard about what other types of resources might make them a strong partner to jurisdictions striving to fulfill the AFFH mandate.

3. In building strategies to address local access to opportunity challenges, all parties must affirm the principle of local primacy. One source of resistance to this regulation at the local level is a concern that HUD will mandate certain strategies. This concern arises out of a history of local plans and actions being challenged and some-times vetoed by the federal government. In some instances, these challenges are fully appropriate. Other challenges, however, have been perceived as driven by individual staff with specific views about best practices. The mistrust and resentment arising from this latter set of cases must be overcome if the new AFFH rule is to succeed.

Therefore, especially in the early years of the new rule, HUD officials should err on the side of permissiveness regarding locally proposed priorities strategies, provided there is some legitimate basis for them; they should do so even if these strategies differ from what individuals (or even a majority of staff) at HUD might prefer. This tension will likely arise in discussions about whether mobility strategies or redevelopment approaches are preferable for improving access to opportunity.[35]

Different approaches have been proposed with regards to ensuring compliance while respecting local jurisdictions' primacy. One enforcement strategy would define a set of components to the AFH that, if met by jurisdictions, would provide them a "safe harbor." This approach would have the benefit for jurisdictions of limiting litigation risks with regard to compliance with the FHA; a downside is that jurisdictions might revert to a "check the box" strategy to meet the "safe harbor" criteria rather than engaging in creative solutions. Another approach favors granting HUD officials discretion in determining what plans meet the rules requirements. While this approach would leave jurisdictions with a degree of uncertainty about what constitutes compliance, it would also provide them more incentive to develop new solutions to furthering access to opportunity. There are pros and cons to either approach; policymakers need to give substantial attention to how HUD plays its enforcement role, as this will affect how willing communities will be to engage in the process.

4. Local jurisdictions must make a good faith effort. In the deliberations that led to the development of the final rule, concerns were routinely raised about the potential response of bad actors to rule provisions. While these concerns are appropriate, the belief that prevailed ultimately was that the vast majority of jurisdictions would try to fulfill their responsibilities in good faith. This belief was born out of field-testing of the AFH with local government officials during its development. If it proves incorrect, then broad success will be difficult to achieve.

HUD must therefore consider the spirit in which an AFH is produced when assessing its details. The deference we recommended in the previous section should definitely be afforded to those jurisdictions whose AFH product emerges from a good faith effort that features an inclusive local process and a genuine willingness to improve access to fair housing and opportunity. But we do not believe such deference should be absolute. Indeed, HUD is not only a partner in the AFH process; as a regulator, it has a responsibility to ensure compliance. This tension between its roles as partner and as regulator, mentioned in other chapters of this volume,[36] is something that HUD will have to grapple with continuously.

5. All must think regionally and beyond housing provision. The renewed focus on opportunity included in the rule requires strategies broader than housing provision. Achieving the American ideal of equal opportunity requires more than a roof over one's head: it requires access to a home in neighborhoods with quality schools, access to jobs, investments in public services (e.g., safety, parks and recreation). But these elements of opportunity rarely respect jurisdiction boundaries. Rather, effectively reducing local barriers to opportunity often entails cooperation across jurisdictions.

The new rule encourages such cooperation by making it possible to produce regional AFHs. The advantages for jurisdictions of adopting a regional approach include the ability to share staff resources, consulting services, and elements of the public input process. The hope is that the reduced cost of producing a regional AFH will incentivize jurisdictions to develop an AFH and strategies that better align with the regional nature of opportunity. Such plans should be more impactful in achieving desired goals.

6. Local jurisdictions, foundations and nonprofit organizations must leverage data to empower those without voice during the planning process. The ability of information to change housing market practices has been demonstrated by the changes to the mortgage lending practices that arose from the availability of data through the Home Mortgage Disclosure Act (HMDA). In this case, consumer and community activists analyzed the HMDA data intensively and used patterns they found to raise issues and ultimately create opportunities for dialogue that generated change.

The HMDA experience could be a template for the promise of the AFFH data tool. But this will occur only if the fair housing counterparts to the consumer and community advocates in the HMDA case are engaged and working to identify patterns, raise issues, and drive change. All of the parties at the local level, including public sector players, can play this role. We believe the extent of HMDA-type engagement by local parties using the data tool will significantly determine the scope of the new rule's success in expanding equal opportunity.

7. Foundations and nonprofit and fair housing organizations must be monitors and partners for local governments during the AFH process and strategy implementation. Foundations and local nonprofit and fair housing organizations have long played an important role in advancing inclusion and fair housing objectives, and they will need to play a similar role under the new regulation. They can be a source of external discipline to help local jurisdictions engage in the process in good faith by ensuring that all segments of the community—particularly those who have historically not had a voice—have access to the data tool, know how to use the tool, are aware of public meetings, and are sufficiently organized to meaningfully engage in the process. Moreover, their experience in fighting discrimination will provide insight about strategies to further inclusion and increased opportunity for all.

In addition, these organizations can be important players in the AFFH implementation process in at least two ways. First, because these organizations have missions that align with the AFFH objectives, they could provide direct support in executing whatever strategy the jurisdiction has decided to pursue. Such support might include funding and operating mobility counseling programs, funding the acquisition of affordable housing in opportunity communities, and recruiting mission-driven property managers for that housing. Second, they can monitor jurisdictions' progress towards strategic goals, particularly in terms of ensuring that strategies are not prematurely abandoned or undermined. A useful model for this role has been given by the community groups involved in monitoring banking institution compliance with the Community Reinvestment Act

(CRA). Pressure from these groups pushed banks to take questions of equality in access to credit more seriously, resulting in the establishment of CRA agreements that have effectively increased access to credit in underserved communities.[37]

8. AFFH must survive political risk. For AFFH to thrive, it needs to retain resources and authorized legitimacy. There are two political risks in this regard. First, deficit concerns and beliefs that some domestic programs should have lower priority have led some policymakers to seek significant reductions in the funding for HUD. In the wake of the 2016 election, many of these policymakers are ascendant, raising questions as to the level of future funding for HUD. If there are steep cuts, HUD will not be able to make the investments in itself and in a supporting infrastructure required to make AFFH implementation effective. Here, foundations may have a critical role to play: they can support high-quality assistance to jurisdictions, presenting examples of best practices in assessing and overcoming barriers to fair housing so as to inspire creative strategic thinking.

Second, anti-discrimination policy generally, and fair housing policy specifically, have always been sensitive political topics, with some not believing that federal resources should be devoted to such policies. Indeed, in January 2017, early in the 115th Congress, the "Local Zoning Decisions Protection Act of 2017" was introduced as a bill in both the House and Senate.[38] If adopted, these bills would nullify the 2015 AFFH rule and the assessment tools developed by HUD and made available to jurisdictions to conduct the AFH. The bills would also prohibit federal funds from being "used to design, build, maintain, utilize, or provide access to a Federal database of geospatial information on community racial disparities or disparities in access to affordable housing." HUD would be charged with leading a consultation to replace the rule in order to respect the mandate of the FHA as upheld by the Supreme Court, but it could make recommendation for a replacement rule only if a consensus is reached between "the Secretary, the State officials, local government officials, and officials of public housing agencies consulted." If no consensus is found, the AFFH rule would be rescinded with no immediate replacement. Bills such as this have been proposed in the past without much traction. However, with the new political makeup of Congress, they may have a higher likelihood of being adopted.

These provisions would weaken the mandatory nature of AFFH. Combined with statements by HUD Secretary Ben Carson opposing the AFFH rule before he was nominated to head the agency, the introduction of the new bills creates substantial uncertainty with regard to future efforts at the federal level to implement the mandate given by HUD.[39] Even if the rule ultimately stays in place, it is possible that for the coming years, local initiatives by public officials, nonprofits, and foundations will be the main drivers of innovative practices to increase inclusion and access to opportunity.

For the AFFH rule to be successful, government, advocates, and citizens need to embrace the framework put forth by the rule and support actions to overcome the barriers to opportunity. Whether the rule remains in place and HUD allocates sufficient resources to its implementation in the coming years is currently in question. Even if the rule relies on local jurisdictions to develop the asseesment and identify and implement strategies, HUD needs to be a partner for them, providing consistent guidance and support. Without a commitment of resources by HUD, the impact of the rule is likely to be limited to a few high-capacity jurisdictions with the resources and local community of fair housing groups to develop and implement creative strategies to AFFH.

CONCLUSION

Almost fifty years after the adoption of the 1968 Fair Housing Act, the structural forces at work in the US housing market that led to residential segregation and disparities in opportunity are still operative. Much remains to be done to ensure that all families have access to neighborhoods with amenities that afford them the opportunity to pursue their dreams. HUD's 2015 Affirmatively Furthering Fair Housing rule is an important step towards increasing residential inclusion and meeting the mandate given to the department by the Fair Housing Act. However, the full impact of the rule will depend on HUD's commitment to the rule's philosophy and its devotion of resources to the implementation of the law. The rule's impace will also depend critically upon decisions by local governments, community organizations, and individuals to use the resources they have, through the rule and from other sources, to effectively remove barriers to fair housing in their communities.

Bibliography

Alesina, Alberto, and Eliana La Ferrara. 2005. "Ethnic Diversity and Economic Performance." *Journal of Economic Literature* 43, no. 3: 762–800.

Aranda, Claudia L. 2015. "Targeting Disability Discrimination: Findings and Reflections from the National Study on Housing Discrimination Against People Who Are Deaf and People Who Use Wheelchairs." *Cityscape* 17, no. 3: 103.

Bayer, Patrick, Fernando Ferreira, and Robert McMillan. 2007. "A Unified Framework for Measuring Preferences for Schools and Neighborhoods." *Journal of Political Economy* 115, no. 4: 588–638.

Bostic, Raphael, and Arthur Acolin. Forthcoming. "Affirmatively Furthering Fair Housing: The Mandate to End Segregation." In *The Fight for Fair Housing*, edited by Greg Squires. New York: Routledge.

Bostic, Raphael W., and Breck L. Robinson. 2003. "Do CRA Agreements Influence Lending Patterns?" *Real Estate Economics* 31, no. 1: 23–51.

Chetty, Raj, Nathaniel Hendren, Patrick Kline, and Emmanuel Saez. 2014. "Where Is the Land of Opportunity? The Geography of Intergenerational Mobility in the United States." *Quarterly Journal of Economics* 129, no. 4: 1553–1623.

Cutler, David M., Edward L. Glaeser, and Jacob L. Vigdor. 1999. "The Rise and Decline of the American Ghetto." *Journal of Political Economy* 107, no. 3: 455–506.

———. 2008. "When Are Ghettos Bad? Lessons from Immigrant Segregation in the United States." *Journal of Urban Economics* 63, no. 3: 759–74.

Edin, Per-Anders, Peter Fredriksson, and Olof Åslund. 2003. "Ethnic Enclaves and the Economic Success of Immigrants—Evidence from a Natural Experiment." *The Quarterly Journal of Economics* 118, no. 1: 329–57.

Fair Housing Act. 1968. Accessed September 1, 2016: https://www.justice.gov/crt/fair-housing-act-2

Friedman, Samantha. 2015. "Commentary: Housing Discrimination Research in the 21st Century." *Cityscape* 17, no. 3: 143–49.

Friedman, Samantha, Angela Reynolds, Susan Scovill, Florence R. Brassier, Ron Campbell, and McKenzie Ballou. 2013. "An Estimate of Housing Discrimination Against Same-sex Couples." HUD Office of Policy and Research. https://www.huduser.gov/portal/Publications/pdf/Hsg_Disc_against_SameSexCpls_v3.pdf

Galster, George C. 1999. "The Evolving Challenges of Fair Housing since 1968: Open Housing, Integration, and the Reduction of Ghettoization." *Cityscape* 4, no. 3 : 123–38.

———. 2002. "An Economic Efficiency Analysis of Deconcentrating Poverty Populations." *Journal of Housing Economics* 11, no. 4: 303–29.

GAO (Government Accountability Office). 2010. "Housing and Community Grants: HUD Needs to Enhance it Requirements and Oversight of Jurisdictions' Fair Housing Plans." http://www.gao.gov/new.items/d10905.pdf.

Glaeser, Edward, and Jacob Vigdor. 2012. "The End of the Segregated Century: Racial Separation in America's Neighborhoods, 1890–2010." Manhattan Institute for Policy Research.

Gobillon, Laurent, Harris Selod, and Yves Zenou. 2007. "The Mechanisms of Spatial Mismatch." *Urban Studies* 44, no. 12: 2401–27.

Goetz, Edward G. 2010. "Better Neighborhoods, Better Outcomes? Explaining Relocation Outcomes in HOPE VI." *Cityscape* 12, no. 1 : 5–31.

Greenberg, Zoe. 2017. "Advocates of Fair Housing Brace for a Tough Four Years." *New York Times*. January 27. https://www.nytimes.com/2017/01/27/realestate/advocates-of-fair-housing-brace-for-a-tough-four-years.html?_r=0

HUD (US Department of Housing and Urban Development). 1996. "Fair Housing Planning Guide." http://fhic.nfhta.org/media/710.

———. 2015a. *Affirmatively Furthering Fair Housing Rule Guidebook.* https://www.hudexchange.info/resources/documents/AFFH-Rule-Guidebook.pdf.

———. 2015b. "Affirmatively Furthering Fair Housing: Final Rule." https://www.huduser. gov/portal/sites/default/files/pdf/AFFH_Final_Rule.pdf.

———. 2017. National Ressource Network. http://www.nationalresourcenetwork.org/ en/home/who_we_are.

JCHS (Harvard Joint Center for Housing Studies). 2017. "Fostering Inclusion in American Neighborhoods." This volume.

Julian, Elizabeth. 2017. "The Duty to Affirmatively Further Fair Housing: A Legal as well as Policy Imperative." This volume.

Kain, John F. 1968. "Housing Segregation, Negro Employment, and Metropolitan Decentralization." *The Quarterly Journal of Economics* 82, no. 2: 175-97.

Krysan, Maria, and Reynolds Farley. 2002. "The Residential Preferences of Blacks: Do They Explain Persistent Segregation?" *Social Forces* 80, no. 3: 937-80.

Massey, Douglas S. 2015. "The Legacy of the 1968 Fair Housing Act." *Sociological Forum* 30, no. S1: 571-88.

Massey, Douglas S., and Nancy A. Denton. 1989. "Hypersegregation in US Metropolitan Areas: Black and Hispanic Segregation Along Five Dimensions." *Demography* 26, no. 3: 373-91.

———. 1993. *American Apartheid: Segregation and the Making of the Underclass.* Cambridge, MA: Harvard University Press.

Massey, Douglas S., Jonathan Rothwell, and Thurston Domina. 2009. "The Changing Bases of Segregation in the United States." *The Annals of the American Academy of Political and Social Science* 626, no. 1: 74-90.

Misra, Taniv. 2017. "Fair Housing Faces an Uncertain Fate." *The Atlantic City Lab,* February 3. http://www.citylab.com/housing/2017/02/ fair-housing-faces-an-uncertain-fate/515133/.

Oh, Sun Jung, and John Yinger. 2015. "What Have We Learned from Paired Testing in Housing Markets?" *Cityscape* 17, no. 3: 15-59.

Opportunity Agenda. 2010. "Reforming HUD's Regulations to Affirmatively Further Fair Housing." https://opportunityagenda.org/files/field_file/2010.03ReformingHUDR egulations.pdf.

Phillips, David C. 2017. "Landlords Avoid Tenants Who Pay with Vouchers." *Economics Letters* 151: 48-52.

Sampson, Robert J., Patrick Sharkey, and Stephen W. Raudenbush. 2008. "Durable Effects of Concentrated Disadvantage on Verbal Ability Among African-American Children." *Proceedings of the National Academy of Sciences* 105, no. 3: 845-52.

US Supreme Court. 2015. *Texas Department of Housing and Community Affairs v. Inclusive Communities Project,* Inc. https://www.supremecourt.gov/ opinions/14pdf/13-1371_m64o.pdf.

Endnotes

1   See, for example, Massey (2015).

2   Chetty et al. (2014).

3   Sex was added as a protected class through the 1974 Housing and Community Development Act. Familial situation and disabilities were added as part of the 1988 Fair Housing Amendments Act.

4   See for example US Supreme Court (2015), a case in which the court ruled that disparate impact forms of discrimination are covered by the Fair Housing Act.

5   Bostic and Acolin (forthcoming).

6   Ibid.

7   Massey and Denton (1993); Massey (2015).

8   Glaeser and Vigdor (2012).

9   JCHS (2017).

10 Massey, Rothwell, and Domina (2009).

11 For discussion of these arguments, see JCHS (2017).

12 Krysan and Farley (2002); Edin, Fredriksson, and Åslund (2003); Cutler, Glaeser, and Vigdor (2008).

13 Kain (1968); Cutler, Glaeser and Vigdor (1999); Bayer, Ferreira, and McMillan (2007); Gobillon, Selod, and Zenou (2007).

14 Oh and Yinger (2015).

15 Friedman et al. (2013); Aranda (2015); Friedman (2015); Oh and Yinger (2015); Phillips (2017).

16 Galster (1999); Bostic and Acolin (forthcoming).

17 Galster (1999), 123.

18 In some cases, HUD did more than retreat. Instead, the department supported local authorities that were sued for furthering segregation; see Massey (2015).

19 Bostic and Acolin (forthcoming).

20 HUD (1996).

21 GAO (2010); Opportunity Agenda (2010).

22 Opportunity Agenda (2010).

23 GAO (2010); Opportunity Agenda (2010).

24 GAO (2010); Opportunity Agenda (2010).

25 Massey (2015).

26 HUD (2015a); HUD (2015b).

27 Sampson, Sharkey, and Raudenbush (2008).

28 Galster (2002).

29 Alesina and La Ferrara (2005).

30 Julian (2017).

31 Ibid.

32 Ibid.

33 HUD (2015b).

34 HUD (2017).

35 Goetz (2010); Bostic and Acolin (forthcoming).

36 For example, Julian (2017).

37 Bostic and Robinson (2003).

38 H.R. 482; S. 103. For the text of the House bill, see https://www.congress.gov/bill/115th-congress/house-bill/482/text?q
    =%7B%22search%22%3A%5B%22Gosar%22%5D%7D&r=1.

39 Greenberg (2017); Misra (2017).

Speaking Truth to Power: Enhancing Community Engagement in the Assessment of Fair Housing Process

MICHAEL ALLEN[1]
Relman, Dane, and Colfax PLLC

> [The Fair Housing Act] imposes ... an obligation to do more than simply refrain from discriminating ...This broader goal [of truly open housing] ... reflects the desire to have HUD use its grant programs to assist in ending discrimination and segregation, to the point where the supply of genuinely open housing increases.

—Judge Stephen J. Breyer[2]

The recent presidential election, the advent of the Trump administration and the apparent ascendancy of hostile forces in Congress have temporarily unsettled the expectations of advocates and elected and appointed officials concerning the obligation of states, localities, and public housing authorities ("Recipients") to affirmatively further fair housing ("AFFH"). Although HUD's interpretation of a Recipient's obligation to analyze race-based and other impediments is "firmly rooted in the statutory and regulatory framework and consistent with the case law,"[3] the Trump administration and a number of Republican lawmakers have suggested they may seek to repeal AFFH regulations promulgated by the Obama administration, suspend recipients' obligations to comply, defund HUD's enforcement, or prohibit HUD from disseminating data related to segregation and discrimination.[4]

After eight years of HUD's heightened expectations that Recipients should identify and take steps to overcome fair housing impediments, and with each Recipient now "on the calendar" for producing a comprehensive Assessment of Fair Housing ("Assessment") and action plans to overcome fair housing barriers in the next five years, stakeholders are looking for some clarity about how to proceed in the short and medium terms.

As another paper in this symposium articulates,[5] AFFH is the law of the land and Recipients can and will be held to its obligations regardless of inaction by the Trump administration or attempts by Congress to weaken enforcement tools. But this much is clear: Five decades after it was adopted as part of the Fair Housing Act of 1968, the AFFH provision has never been self-executing, and entities seeking to implement and enforce it have had to tangle with powerful political and private market forces that favor segregation.

HUD's July 2015 AFFH regulation (the "Final Rule") provides both carrots and sticks to ensure robust community participation. On the one hand, HUD will offer technical assistance on techniques to encourage participation by groups that otherwise might not participate.[6] On the other, it warns that a Recipient that fails adequately to involve stakeholders is at risk of having its Assessment rejected as "substantially incomplete,"[7] which could lead to reduction or elimination of federal funding.

Overall, then, the Final Rule sets high expectations for "community engagement" and requires certain minimum procedural steps involving outreach, communications, and consultation,[8] but prescribes little about how a Recipient should encourage participation by people most directly affected by fair housing impediments.

The Final Rule sets the table for robust conversations about hard topics—like discrimination and segregation—that most communities have tried hard to avoid for decades. But it leaves to local discretion how to get the right stakeholders to the table for those conversations. While there is some evidence that this "federal nudge" may help communities to break free of some historical restraints and adopt new policies that address longstanding needs,[9] that kind of success does not take place in a vacuum. Rather, as this paper suggests, the full promise of AFFH can be achieved only in communities where there are concerted efforts by community groups, academics, and foundations to build capacity for: meaningful community participation by people of color and their advocates in the Assessment process and designation of actions to counteract segregation; robust local data collection and analysis; mobilization of political constituencies to implement those actions and, if all else fails, to enforce the AFFH obligations through litigation, administrative complaints and grassroots advocacy. In communities where these constituents come together to mobilize a strong "ground game,"[10] historically disadvantaged constituencies are likely to secure concrete commitments to address fair housing impediments, and organizing models can be tested and brought to bear on communities whose Assessments are due later in the process.

THE CENTRALITY OF COMMUNITY ENGAGEMENT

Nearly fifty years ago, Senators Edward Brooke (R-MA) and Walter Mondale (D-MN) understood that, to be fully successful, the Fair Housing Act needed an AFFH provision invoking Congressional power under the Constitution's Spending Clause in support of its twin goals of nondiscrimination and racial integration. Since then, Congress and HUD have added parallel AFFH provisions in the authorizing statutes for the Community Development Block Grant ("CDBG"), HOME Investment Partnership ("HOME"), and public housing programs.[11] As a condition of receiving that funding, federal law requires those entities to certify their compliance—and actually comply with[12]—a number of civil rights obligations, including the obligation to AFFH.

All of these programs—under which HUD distributed more than $38 billion in FY 2015[13]—have, for years, required Recipients to adopt citizen or resident participation plans. But, unless local advocates have insisted, few of these plans have resulted in full-throated community engagement. As a consequence, most such planning processes have been "top-down," with a handful of municipal experts serving up fully-formed plans for grassroots groups to review and digest during fairly short public comment periods.

Perhaps recognizing that Recipients' funding under the above-referenced programs actually "belongs to poor people with housing problems,"[14] the Final Rule and its associated guidance seek to reverse the approach: "The goal of community engagement in the development of the [Assessment] is to create a product that is informed by and supported by the entire community and establishes a standard for inclusive decision making." Going forward, HUD expects "meaningful community participation," and expects local governments to "employ communications means designed to reach the broadest audience." In other words, it is entirely fitting that the authentic voices of people intended to benefit from these programs be amplified in the Assessment process.

At the moment, the Final Rule's provisions on community engagement are something of a blank canvas. Every community will start with a different palate, and no finished product will look like any other. But folks in the housing justice movement have been organizing for a long time, and there are sophisticated training materials and countless examples of successful campaigns—six of which are summarized below—to inform groups around the country seeking to insert themselves into similar conversations that are part of an Assessment process.

There are also substantial reasons—beyond fear of enforcement and loss of funding—for Recipients to embrace and promote deep community engagement. Without grassroots partners, no top-down approach will be effective against the obligation that each Recipient take "meaningful actions, in addition to combating discrimination, that overcome patterns of segregation and foster inclusive communities free from barriers that restrict access to opportunity based on [race, national origin, and other] protected characteristics."[15] Nor, without honest conversations about discrimination and its antidotes, will any Recipient be able to "address significant disparities in housing needs and in access to opportunity, replacing segregated living patterns with truly integrated and balanced living patterns, transforming racially and ethnically concentrated areas of poverty into areas of opportunity, and fostering and maintaining compliance with civil rights and fair housing laws."[16]

POWER CONCEDES NOTHING WITHOUT A DEMAND: LOCAL AFFH ADVOCACY

Over the past decade—sometimes with governmental and philanthropic support and sometimes without—community-based organizations have developed AFFH advocacy strategies at the state or local level that may be worthy of emulation as we move into a period in which HUD's affirmative efforts are less robust. Each of the matters listed below provides an example of how an advocacy or grassroots group made room for itself at the community table and instigated conversations about discrimination and segregation.

Anti-Discrimination Center

After comparing Westchester County's Analyses of Impediments (AIs)—the precursor to the Analysis of Fair Housing Assessment ("Assessment") mandated by the Final Rule—and other submissions to HUD with data on discrimination and segregation, in late 2005, the Anti-Discrimination Center ("ADC") concluded that the County's certifications of compliance with its AFFH and related civil rights obligations were not truthful. When ADC sought an explanation for the discrepancies, the deputy planning commissioner revealed that the County routinely approved funding for municipal members of its funding consortium without respect to whether those members had exclusionary zoning provisions or otherwise resisted proposals to develop affordable housing within their borders.

ADC eventually brought suit under the federal False Claims Act, alleging that the County's AFFH certifications were knowingly false because the County had taken no steps to identify or overcome race-based impediments and that the County had steered funding for the development of affordable housing principally to racially-segregated and low-income neighborhoods. ADC's ability—through an expert demographer—to conduct data analysis and mapping of segregation and affordable housing units was critical to establishing the County's liability for violating its AFFH obligations.

The U.S. District Court in Manhattan granted summary judgment for ADC, holding that no reasonable jury could conclude that the County had conducted an appropriate analysis of race-based impediments as part of its 2000 and 2004 AIs.[17] The matter settled in August 2009, and the County was required, among other things, to ensure the development of 750 units of affordable housing in predominantly white areas, and to conduct a new AI and zoning analysis of each municipal member of the funding consortium. The County's progress (and lack thereof) in fulfilling its obligations is chronicled at http://www.antibiaslaw.com/westchester-case. Contact: Craig Gurian, craiggurian@antibiaslaw.com.

Texas Low Income Housing Information Service and Texas Appleseed

Following Hurricanes Dolly (July 2008) and Ike (September 2008), Congress appropriated several billion dollars in CDBG disaster recovery funding, roughly $3.1 billion of which was allocated to the State of Texas.[18] Texas Low Income Housing Information Service ("TxLIHIS") and Texas Appleseed are statewide advocacy organizations with long histories of fighting for housing equity and transparency in affordable housing programs administered by the State of Texas. In the mid-1990s, the groups got the state legislature to produce an annual report on low-income housing in Texas. For ten years prior to Hurricanes Dolly and Ike, that annual report provided detailed data on the current ethnic and racial composition for each multifamily housing development receiving any form of assistance from the State, along with the number of households in each development with children, with disabilities, and making use of housing choice vouchers.

Through analysis of this and other local data, the groups were able to establish that the recovery programs developed by the State of Texas would perpetuate racial segregation and limit housing choice. Among other things, their analysis showed that the state housing agency's limitation on rebuilding single-family homes on existing sites would require homeowners of color to return to neighborhoods that were disproportionately high in crime, racially segregated, and characterized by low employment and educational opportunity. Similarly, the programs the State proposed for rebuilding affordable multifamily housing emphasized rebuilding in segregated neighborhoods and permitted higher-opportunity neighborhoods to avoid new construction of affordable housing through enforcement of Low-Income Housing Tax Credit rules that grant homeowners associations and local politicians veto power over such proposals. TxLIHIS and Appleseed were also able to document the State's plan to distribute billions of dollars of disaster recovery funds to localities with discriminatory land use rules, deeply entrenched segregation, and documented hostility to racial integration.

On December 1, 2009, TxLIHIS and Appleseed filed an administrative complaint with HUD, alleging that the State's disaster recovery programs involving housing and community development violated the Fair Housing Act and the State's AFFH obligations, and asking HUD to suspend funding until the State came into compliance. During the next six months—during which TxLIHIS and Appleseed showed clear data mastery exceeding the capacity of the State—the parties negotiated a Conciliation Agreement, pursuant to which the State agreed to conduct a new AI and to commit hundreds of millions of dollars to rebuilding housing in a manner consistent with AFFH.[19] The Agreement also required each locality seeking federal funding to complete a Fair Housing Assessment Statement, identifying local fair housing impediments and making specific local commitments to actions intended to overcome those impediments. Contacts: John Henneberger, john@texashousing.org; Maddie Sloan, msloan@texasappleseed.net.

Greater New Orleans Fair Housing Action Center and Lawyers Committee for Civil Rights

Greater New Orleans Fair Housing Action Center ("GNOFHAC") is a private, full-service fair housing enforcement organization that found itself at the epicenter of fair housing issues after Hurricane Katrina hit the region in late August, 2005.[20] Building on its post-Katrina experience, at a January, 2011 conference held in a church basement,[21] GNOFHAC introduced the concept of a "People's AI," designed to engage community members in identifying, analyzing, and responding to segregation and other fair housing barriers that they experienced every day, but that had been omitted from the AI produced by the City of New Orleans. Published in December 2011 by GNOFHAC and the Lawyers' Committee for Civil Rights Under Law, "People's Analysis of Impediments (AI) to Fair Housing for New Orleans"[22] provides a roadmap for community groups to participate in fair housing planning efforts. Because of its insights into local conditions and its work on the "People's AI," GNOFHAC was selected as a contractor for the development of the Assessment for the City of New Orleans and the Housing Authority of New Orleans, which was the first Assessment pursuant to the Final Rule.[23] Contact: Cashauna Hill, chill@gnofairhousing.org.

Latino Action Fund, Fair Share Housing Center, and New Jersey State Conference, NAACP

After Superstorm Sandy hit New Jersey in October, 2012, Congress appropriated nearly $3 billion in CDBG funds to assist in recovery efforts. Three statewide advocacy groups—Latino Action Network, Fair Share Housing Center, and the New Jersey Conference of the NAACP—conducted community forums and undertook data collection and analysis to determine the extent to which the Christie administration's disaster recovery programs were serving low-income families of color, particularly those living in multifamily rental housing.

After determining that the State's initial action plan proposed to favor higher-income homeowners disproportionately to the harm they had suffered, and that the State was not meeting its requirements with respect to federal Limited English Proficiency ("LEP") regulations meant to ensure that non-English speakers would have an equal opportunity to benefit from the recovery programs, the advocacy groups filed an administrative complaint with HUD in April, 2013, alleging violations of Title VI of the Civil Rights Act of 1964 ("Title VI"), the Fair Housing Act, and the AFFH obligation. Those groups provided HUD both insight and sophisticated data analysis with respect to program beneficiaries, and their close monitoring of state agencies identified several thousand applicants who had lost the opportunity to participate because of LEP violations as well as several thousand applications that were erroneously denied by a private contractor.

The parties entered into a Conciliation Agreement[24] on May 30, 2014 that requires the State to target $240 million in additional funds to the communities hardest hit by the storm, with an emphasis on serving low-income renters, who are much more likely than homeowners to be people of color. The agreement also mandates immediate steps to address language barriers that had prevented many Sandy victims from participating in the recovery programs. The agreement governs the State's administration of nearly $2.8 billion in HUD disaster recovery funding, and requires the State to add supplemental funding of $215 million to its principal program to build replacement units for households displaced by the storm. It also establishes an additional $15 million for immediate help for renters who are still displaced from Sandy, which can be used for up to two years while replacement homes are being built, and $10 million for mobile home owners. Contacts: Kevin Walsh, kevinwalsh@fairsharehousing.org; Adam Gordon, adamgordon@fairsharehousing.org.

Metropolitan Interfaith Council on Affordable Housing

Until the mid-1990s, the Minneapolis-St. Paul ("Twin Cities") metroplex had one of the country's most sophisticated, pro-integration fair share affordable housing programs, under the supervision of the Metropolitan Council, a regional government entity that awarded money for transportation, parks, and regional infrastructure to suburbs that embraced affordable housing, and withheld if from those who did not. Concerned that state and local governments had abandoned their commitment to such programs, the Metropolitan Interfaith Council on Affordable Housing ("MICAH") worked closely with the Institute on Metropolitan Opportunity at the University of Minnesota Law School to develop local data on the funding and location of affordable housing over a two-decade period, documenting the rapid re-segregation of neighborhoods and public schools in the Twin Cities and inner-ring suburbs.

When grassroots advocacy with the affected municipalities yielded no change in housing policy, and when the Metropolitan Council issued new fair share guidance that would accelerate affordable housing obligations in lower-opportunity neighborhoods and slow it in high-opportunity neighborhoods, MICAH and other groups filed an administrative complaint with HUD in May, 2015, alleging the Cities of Minneapolis and St. Paul had violated Title VI, the Fair Housing Act, and the obligation to AFFH. One of MICAH's chief complaints was that the Regional AI on which the Twin Cities and eleven other jurisdictions based their entitlement to CDBG, HOME, and related funds did not address residential and school segregation, or the extent to which municipal housing and funding policies were perpetuating segregation. HUD brought the parties together for settlement talks, and they entered into a Conciliation Agreement on May 25, 2016.[25] The Cities and eleven suburban entitlement jurisdictions agreed to revise the Regional AI by June, 2017, using the analytical tools associated with HUD's Final Rule. The revised analysis will identify fair housing barriers within each jurisdiction and across the region, with a special focus on patterns of integration and segregation, racially or ethnically concentrated areas of poverty, disparities in access to opportunity, and disproportionate housing needs. MICAH and the other Complainants secured the right to participate on the Regional AI advisory committee, and to help conduct the community engagement process to ensure that key stakeholders participate in the process.[26] Press coverage of the agreement suggests that it will alter how affordable housing is approved and built in the region.[27] Contact: Sue Watlov Phillips, sue@micah.org.

Metropolitan Milwaukee Fair Housing Council

For nearly 50 years (and irrespective of income), the Milwaukee Metropolitan Statistical Area has been one of the most racially segregated regions in the country.[28] The Metropolitan Milwaukee Fair Housing Council ("MMFHC") began tracking the efforts of Waukesha County and several dozen members of its CDBG and HOME funding consortium in late 2007, and quickly compiled local demographic data and information concerning municipal land use restrictions on the development of afford-able, multifamily housing. More than three years of meetings with County officials yielded no commitments to revise the County's AIs or to identify shortcomings in oversight of the fair housing performance of consortium members.

In September 2011, MMFHC filed an administrative complaint with HUD, alleging violations of Title VI, the Fair Housing Act, and AFFH. Prolonged settlement discussions ensued, and the parties finally entered into a Conciliation Agreement with an effec-tive date of January 24, 2017.[29] Under the terms of the Agreement, the County will undertake a variety of activities with the aim of promoting integration and expanded fair housing choice. Among these, it will collaborate with the City and County of Milwaukee to produce an Assessment of Fair Housing report, which will identify public and private impediments to fair housing choice. On an annual basis, the County will provide to HUD an action plan that will describe actions to overcome those impediments. The County will also require each municipality which receives CDBG or HOME funds to create an annual Fair Housing Impact Statements that identifies the specific actions the municipality will take to address fair housing impediments, and report on annual progress in eliminating those impediments. The municipalities will also be required to identify actions that promote affordable housing for families, and the County will develop a land inventory that will identify parcels suitable for develop-ment of affordable, multifamily housing. This appears to be the first resolution of an AFFH complaint during the Trump administration, and may be some evidence of the

continued utility of HUD administrative complaints. Contact: Bill Tisdale, wrtisdale@
fairhousingwisconsin.com

THE PATH AHEAD

As outlined above, many of the most successful grassroots AFFH efforts have combined
some kind of enforcement action with sophisticated collection and analysis of local
data and the capacity to mobilize allies to participate in fair housing planning and to
demand that local elected and appointed officials adopt policies and actions to undo
segregation and address other fair housing barriers. That is to say that enforcement
without analysis and mobilization may be insufficient. But each effort described above
has resulted in collective knowledge that is available to other advocates—in the form
of written materials, settlement agreements, promising practices or simply contact
information for the principal actors.

Even during the latter stages of the Obama administration, HUD began signaling that it
would not be accepting new administrative complaints alleging only an AFFH violation,
and would instead consider such complaints under its other civil rights authorities
based on the Spending Clause, including Title VI, Section 109 of the Housing and
Community Development Act of 1974, and—in the context of disability—Section 504
of the Rehabilitation Act of 1973.[30] In fact, the successful resolution of complaints in
the Latino Action Fund, MICAH and MMFHC matters described above all explicitly
referenced Title VI and Section 109.

So, while the Trump administration (and its Congressional allies) may be signaling
hostility to AFFH concepts and complaints, it still has statutory and regulatory
mandates to receive, investigate, conciliate, and adjudicate complaints alleging violations of all the Spending Clause statutes and the Fair Housing Act. In other words, an
administrative enforcement route will remain available to enforce claims similar to
those described above. And, as another paper in this symposium makes clear,[31] parties
aggrieved by segregation and discrimination can seek direct judicial enforcement of
Title VI, the Fair Housing Act, and the U.S. Constitution in federal courts and may, under
some circumstances, use the False Claims Act to enforce AFFH obligations.

But as we look forward to what may be a period of HUD passivity (or hostility) toward
AFFH principles, we must focus our attention on building the capacity of local groups
to collect and analyze data about fair housing barriers; participate meaningfully in
the Assessment process; and mobilize allies to ensure transparency in the Assessment
process and commitment to actions that will undo segregation and expand fair
housing choice. Because there will be insufficient resources to ensure that every
community can secure the full promise of AFFH, advocates, academics, and funders
should purposefully identify several "laboratories of democracy" in which to support

grassroots organizations to achieve two objectives: (1) better fair housing outcomes for the individual community or region; and (2) model advocacy approaches that can be shared with other communities whose Assessments are further down the road. The criteria for selection should be discussed widely, but might prioritize cities of significant size and early Assessment deadlines, with pronounced patterns of segregation and sufficient advocacy infrastructure in place or available.[32]

The Primacy of Data

The uniform data sets that HUD will provide each Recipient, pursuant to the Final Rule, will often permit stakeholders to develop a high-level understanding of geographic disparities in access to community assets, areas of concentrated poverty, and areas of minority concentration. But, without more, such data will do little to help a Recipient or advocates understand how such conditions arose and what steps will be necessary to address them. The Final Rule requires Recipients to rely on "local data"[33] and "local knowledge"[34] as part of the Assessment process.[35] Because Recipients may lack the capacity or interest to fully collect and analyze such information, and because the Final Rule requires robust community participation, consultation, and coordination,[36] grassroots advocacy organizations can play a significant gap-filling role in the Assessment process by gathering and analyzing local data and local knowledge and preparing reports and recommendations based upon that material.

There are some strong models for building local capacity to conduct data analysis and mapping to support advocacy. For instance, TxLIHIS has documented how a number of Texas municipalities have perpetuated housing segregation, and its work has provided the basis for subsequent enforcement actions, media coverage, and legislative action.[37] Similarly, reports from Fair Share Housing Center have led to systemic reforms in post-Sandy recovery programs.[38] Other groups have relied on academic research centers for such capacity.[39] Either way, as we move forward on AFFH matters, foundations, state and local governments, and HUD must redouble their efforts to fund capacity-building for local groups to promote the inclusion into the Assessment process of source information to contextualize local fair housing conditions.

Enhancing Stakeholder Involvement and Mobilizing Political Support

In my experience, many grassroots advocacy groups are not fully informed about their localities' AI or Assessment processes, and so are not prepared to engage fully in shaping the outcomes of those processes. GNOFHAC's "People's AI" can serve as a desk reference for other grassroots groups. Other national groups have developed materials to demystify similar fair housing and funding distribution processes.[40]

If we expect grassroots groups to get fully engaged in local Assessment processes, national advocacy groups must prioritize materials and training programs that will help to build local capacity so that the first round of Assessments submitted—which are likely to be seen as models for later efforts—become part of the feedback loop. HUD has funded a number of national technical assistance consultants to support Recipients in completing the Assessment process but, despite recommendations going back a decade or more,[41] has made no comparable investment in the capacity of local stakeholder groups. The Ford Foundation and Open Society Foundation have provided multi-year funding support for Fair Share Housing Center, TxLIHIS and selected other state and local groups to engage in the AI or Assessment processes.[42] But in order to go to scale—even with respect to the "laboratories" mentioned above—the investment in such an effort must be substantially larger. The templates offered by GNOFHAC, Center for Community Change, and Technical Assistance Collaborative provide a solid start, but priority must be given to the development of a comprehensive guidebook and resource materials on the Assessment process, hands-on training for the most capable grassroots groups and coalitions in the target communities, and funding for ongoing technical assistance to help guide such groups through the process and to provide advice on how enforcement mechanisms, media coverage and community organizing strategies can be combined to secure better AFFH compliance.

Securing Protections at the State and Local Level

Finally, as progress on the national level may become more complicated, advocates must consider how legislation on the local and state levels can advance AFFH and other equity principles. For the past decade, ADC has helped to lead campaigns to broaden civil rights protections and to establish standards of proof that more effectively ensure positive civil rights outcomes. The passage of the Local Civil Rights Restoration Act expanded substantive protections against retaliation, extended protections to domestic partners, and increased penalties for violations. Just as importantly, the Restoration Act established canons of statutory construction that require New York City's Human Rights Law to be "construed liberally for the accomplishment of the uniquely broad and remedial purposes thereof, regardless of whether federal or [state laws] … have been so construed."[43]

Similarly, on February 15, 2017, California Assemblymember Miguel Santiago introduced Assembly Bill 686 ("AB 686") to establish that all government agencies have an AFFH obligation as a matter of state law.[44] Unlike the federal AFFH obligation, AB 686 would provide for a private cause of action to enforce the state AFFH provision. The content of that obligation would mirror the Final Rule in that all state and local agencies, regional transportation agencies and councils of government would be required to "tak[e] meaningful actions, in addition to combating discrimination, that overcome patterns of segregation, promote fair housing choice, and foster inclusive communities free from barriers that restrict access to opportunity-based characteristics protected by this part; and that transform racially and ethnically concentrated areas of poverty into areas of opportunity, while protecting existing residents from displacement."

We need to help model such local advocacy for groups in the targeted communities, so that AFFH principles do not erode during a time of national inattention or hostility.

CONCLUSION

In his opinion in *NAACP v. HUD*, then-Judge Breyer identified a useful metric that should be applied in every upcoming Assessment: whether the supply of "genuinely open housing" is increasing. I suggest that if the answer is not "yes," then a community has not satisfied its AFFH obligations and must redouble its efforts. But Breyer's metric ought also to apply to advocates, academics, and foundations. Until we sufficiently support local capacity to influence the Assessment process, we have not achieved the promise of AFFH. And we must redouble our efforts.

Bibliography

Allen, Michael. 2008. "Strong Enforcement is Required to Promote Integration." Testimony before National Commission on Fair Housing and Equal Opportunity. September 22. http://www.prrac.org/projects/fair_housing_commission/boston/allen.pdf.

———. 2015. "HUD's New AFFH Rule: The Importance of the Ground Game." In *The Dream Revisited*, edited by Ingrid Ellen Gould and Justin Steil. September. http://furmancenter.org/research/iri/essay/huds-new-affh-rule-the-importance-of-the-ground-game.

Blumgart, Jake. 2017. "Fair Housing Still Has a Chance under Trump." *Slate*, March 14. http://www.slate.com/articles/business/metropolis/2017/03/the_affirmatively_furthering_fair_housing_rule_is_still_working_under_trump.html.

Callaghan, Peter. 2016. "Settlement Could Alter How Affordable Housing Is Built Throughout Twin Cities metro." *MinnPost*, May 13. https://www.minnpost.com/politics-policy/2016/05/settlement-could-alter-how-affordable-housing-built-throughout-twin-cities-m.

Eligon, John, and Robert Gebloff. 2016. "Affluent and Black, and Still Trapped by Segregation." *New York Times*, August 20. https://www.nytimes.com/2016/08/21/us/milwaukee-segregation-wealthy-black-families.html?_r=0.

Fair Share Housing Center, Latino Action Network, and NAACP New Jersey State Conference. 2015. *The State of Sandy Recovery: Two and a Half Years Later, Over 15,000 Families Still Waiting to Rebuild*. February. http://fairsharehousing.org/images/uploads/State_of_Sandy_English_2015.pdf.

Gramlich, Ed. 1998. *HUD's Consolidated Plan: An Action Guide for Involving Low-Income Communities*. Washington, D.C.: Center for Community Change. https://web-beta.archive.org/web/20061016081939/http://www.communitychange.org:80/shared/publications/downloads/conplan.pdf.

Greater New Orleans Fair Housing Action Center and Lawyers' Committee for Civil Rights Under Law. 2011. "People's Analysis of Impediments for New Orleans." http://www.gnofairhousing.org/wp-content/uploads/2012/03/2011-12-20-Peoples-AI-FINAL.pdf.

Gurian, Craig. 2005. "A Return to Eyes on the Prize: Litigating Under the Restored New York City Human Rights Law." *Fordham Urban Law Journal* 33, no. 2: 100–176.

Housing Authority of New Orleans. 2016. "Assessment of Fair Housing Tool." http://www.nola.gov/community-development/documents/2016-updated-afh-plan-090516/afh-plan-090516-final/.

HUD (U.S. Department of Housing and Urban Development). 2013. "Memorandum: Compliance-Based Evaluations of a Recipient's Certifications that it has Affirmatively Furthered Fair Housing." March 5. On file with author.

Julian, Elizabeth. 2017. "The Duty to Affirmatively Further Fair Housing: A Legal as well as Policy Imperative." This volume.

Junge, Barbara. 1995. "Consolidated Plan Advocacy for Affordable Housing and Community Development." *Clearinghouse Review* 29, nos. 7–8. http://povertylaw.org/files/docs/article/chr_1995_november_december_junge.pdf

Livesley-O'Neill, Will. 2016. "How City Actions Perpetuate Houston's Housing Segregation and Violate Civil Rights." *Texas Housers*, December 16. https://texashousers.net/2016/12/16/how-city-actions-perpetuate-houstons-housing-segregation-and-violate-civil-rights/.

Metropolitan Milwaukee Fair Housing Council. 2017. "Fair Housing Council Settles Discrimination Complaint Against Waukesha County." *Urban Milwaukee,* February 3. http://urbanmilwaukee.com/pressrelease/fair-housing-council-settles-discrimination-complaint-against-waukesha-county/.

Minnesota Housing Partnership. 2017. "A New Approach to Fair Housing Community Engagement." July. http://www.mhponline.org/images/stories/docs/research/A-New-Approach-to-Fair-Housing-Community-Engagement.pdf.

National Low Income Housing Coalition. 2016. "From the Field: New Orleans Submits First Assessment of Fair Housing in the Nation." http://nlihc.org/article/field-new-orleans-submits-first-assessment-fair-housing-nation.

Public Advocates. 2017. "Asm. Member Santiago Introduces Legislation to Buck Trump Admin. on Fair Housing." http://www.publicadvocates.org/resources/news/assemblymember-miguel-santiago-introduces-legislation-to-buck-trump-administration-on-fair-housing/.

Technical Assistance Collaborative, Inc. 1999. *Piecing it All Together in Your Community: Learning to Use HUD's Consolidated Plan to Expand Housing*

Opportunities for People with Disabilities. http://www.tacinc.org/media/13210/
Piecing%20it%20All%20Together.pdf.

Walsh, Kevin. 2014. "Settlement Reached in Sandy Civil Rights Case." Fair Share
Housing Center Blog, May 30. http://fairsharehousing.org/blog/entry/
settlement-reached-in-sandy-civil-rights-case/.

Endnotes

1   Michael Allen is a partner in the civil rights firm Relman, Dane & Colfax, PLLC. He was co-counsel in the *Westchester*
    case and lead counsel in nearly a dozen other AFFH cases brought in federal courts or as HUD administrative
    complaints. Extensive AFFH enforcement and compliance materials are available at http://www.relmanlaw.com/affh/
    index.php.

2   *NAACP v. Secretary of Housing and Urban Development* 817 F.2d 149. 1st Cir (1987).

3   *U.S. ex rel. Anti-Discrimination Center v. Westchester County*, 495 F. Supp. 2d 375, 387 (S.D.N.Y. 2007).

4   H.R. 482 and S. 103 are identical bills providing, in relevant part, that the Final Rule and other HUD notices providing
    for an AFFH Assessment Tool "shall have no force or effect," and that "no Federal funds may be used to design, build,
    maintain, utilize, or provide access to a Federal database of geospatial information on community racial disparities or
    disparities in access to affordable housing." See Local Zoning Decisions Act of 2017, H.R. 482 and S. 103, 115th Cong.
    (2017).

5   Julian (2017).

6   Preamble to Final Rule, 80 Fed. Reg. 42272, 42295.

7   24 C.F.R. §§ 5.162, 91.500.

8   24 C.F.R. §5.158.

9   Blumgart (2017).

10 Allen (2015).

11 42 U.S.C. §§ 5304(b)(2), 12705(b)(15), 24 C.F.R. §903.7(o).

12 *Langlois v. Abington Housing Authority*, 234 F. Supp. 2d 33, 73, 75 (D.Mass. 2002).

13 HUD's final appropriations for Fiscal Year 2015 provide for approximately $4.5 billion in HUD block grant funding
    for State and local governments and $33.5 billion in public housing and rental assistance funding to public housing
    authorities and similar agencies.

14 Junge (1995).

15 24 C.F.R. §5.152.

16 Ibid.

17 *U.S. ex rel. Anti-Discrimination Center v. Westchester County*, 668 F. Supp. 2d 548, 563 (S.D.N.Y. 2009).

18 Texas General Land Office, "Recovery," http://www.glo.texas.gov/recovery/.

19 "Conciliation Agreement between Texas Low Income Housing Information Service, Texas Appleseed, and the State of
    Texas," May 25, 2010, http://www.relmanlaw.com/docs/Texas-AFFH-Final-Conciliation-Agreement-signed-by-HUD.pdf.

20 Greater New Orleans Fair Housing Action Center, "St. Bernard Parish," http://www.gnofairhousing.org/programs/
    enforcement/st-bernard-parish/; "Conciliation Agreement between U.S. Dep't of Hous. and Urban Dev., Greater New
    Orleans Fair Housing Action Center, and Jefferson Parish," June 24, 2013, http://www.relmanlaw.com/docs/GNOFHAC-
    2013.06.24-Executed-Conciliation-Agreement-Jefferson-Parish.pdf.

21 Greater New Orleans Fair Housing Action Center, "Fit for a King 2011," Flickr album, Jan. 14, 2011, https://www.flickr.
    com/photos/58782715@N08/sets/72157625898694712.

22 Greater New Orleans Fair Housing Action Center and Lawyers' Committee for Civil Rights Under Law (2011).

23 National Low Income Housing Coalition (2016); Housing Authority of New Orleans (2016).

24 Fair Share Housing Center, Latino Action Network, and NAACP New Jersey State Conference (2015).

25 "Voluntary Compliance Agreement between U.S. Dep't of Hous. and Urban Dev., The City of St. Paul, and the Metropolitan Interfaith Council on Affordable Housing," May 25, 2016, https://portal.hud.gov/hudportal/documents/huddoc?id=16vcasigned.pdf.

26 As this chapter was going to press, the Minnesota Housing Partnership published a report cataloguing many of the efforts to bring grassroots groups into the AI or Assessment Process. Minnesota Housing Partnership (2017).

27 Callaghan (2016).

28 Eligon and Gebloff (2016).

29 Metropolitan Milwaukee Fair Housing Council (2017).

30 HUD (2013), 4–5.

31 Julian (2017).

32 A review of such criteria might suggest the following jurisdictions (with Assessment due dates in parentheses) for consideration: Philadelphia (10/4/17; LA County (10/4/17; Dallas (1/4/18); Austin (1/4/19); New York City (4/6/19); Chicago (4/6/19); Milwaukee (4/6/19); St. Louis (4/6/19); Pittsburgh (4/6/19); Minneapolis/St. Paul (9/5/19); and Houston (10/5/19).

33 The Final Rule defines "local data" to include "metrics, statistics, and other quantified information, subject to a determination of statistical validity by HUD, relevant to the program participant's geographic areas of analysis, that can be found through a reasonable amount of search, are readily available at little or no cost, and are necessary for the completion of the [Assessment] using the Assessment Tool." 24 C.F.R. §5.152.

34 The Final Rule defines "local knowledge" to include "information to be provided by the program participant that relates to the participant's geographic areas of analysis and that is relevant to the program participant's [Assessment], is known or becomes known to the program participant, and is necessary for the completion of the [Assessment] using the Assessment Tool." 24 C.F.R. §5.152.

35 24 C.F.R. §§5.154(c), (d)(2).

36 24 C.F.R. §5.158.

37 See for example Livesley-O'Neill (2016).

38 Fair Share Housing Center, Latino Action Network, and NAACP New Jersey State Conference (2015).

39 Examples include the Institute for Metropolitan Opportunity (https://www.law.umn.edu/institute-metropolitan-opportunity), the Kirwan Institute for the Study of Race and Ethnicity (http://kirwaninstitute.osu.edu/), the Haas Institute for a Fair and Inclusive Society (http://haasinstitute.berkeley.edu/), and the Furman Center for Real Estate and Urban Policy (http://furmancenter.org/).

40 Gramlich (1998); Technical Assistance Collaborative, Inc. (1999).

41 Allen (2008), 4 (calling upon HUD to fund an organization to enhance the capacity of local organizations to review and analyze AIs and to "participate in the process of identifying fair housing impediments and appropriate actions to overcome them").

42 Ford Foundation, "Grants Database," https://www.fordfoundation.org/work/our-grants/grants-database/grants-all?page=9; Open Society Foundations, "U.S. Programs—Texas Low Income Housing Information Service," https://www.opensocietyfoundations.org/about/programs/us-programs/grantees/texas-low-income-housing-information-service.

43 Gurian (2005), 103, quoting from N.Y.C. Local Law no. 85 of 2005 (October 3, 2005).

44 For background materials on the proposed legislation, see Public Advocates (2017).

The Duty to Affirmatively Further Fair Housing: A Legal as well as Policy Imperative

ELIZABETH JULIAN
Inclusive Communities Project

"We make two general assertions: (1) that American cities and suburbs suffer from galloping segregation, a malady so widespread and so deeply imbedded in the national psyche that many Americans, Negroes as well as whites, have come to regard it as a natural condition; and (2) that the prime carrier of galloping segregation has been the Federal Government. First it built the ghettos; then it locked the gates; now it appears to be fumbling for the key. Nearly everything the Government touches turns to segregation, and the Government touches nearly everything."

— Senator Edward Brooke, 114 Cong. Rec. S2280 (1968),

The Fair Housing Act declares that it is "the policy of the United States to provide, within constitutional limitations, for fair housing throughout the United States."[1] In one of the first Fair Housing Act cases decided by the U.S. Supreme Court, the Court noted the words of the Act's co-sponsor, Senator Walter F. Mondale, that "the reach of the proposed law was to replace the ghettos 'by truly integrated and balanced living patterns."[2] The Second Circuit U.S. Court of Appeals declared the following year that, under Title VIII, "[a]ction must be taken to fulfill, as much as possible, the goal of open, integrated residential housing patterns and to prevent the increase of segregation, in ghettos, of racial groups whose lack of opportunities the Act was designed to combat."[3] The history and scope of residential segregation in the United States, and its relationship to the purposes of the Fair Housing Act, is cogently laid out in the Housing Scholars Amici Curiae brief, filed at the Supreme Court in the case upholding disparate impact under the Fair Housing Act (FHA).[4] Justice Kennedy's opinion affirmed the important role that the FHA must continue to play in avoiding the Kerner Commission's grim prophecy that "[o]ur Nation is moving toward two societies, one black, one white—separate and unequal," and the Court acknowledged the Fair Housing Act's continuing role in "moving the Nation toward a more integrated society."[5]

THE STATUTORY DUTY TO AFFIRMATIVELY FURTHER FAIR HOUSING

While the sections of the Act prohibiting discrimination are crucial to our efforts to ensure that bad actions are remedied and bad actors held accountable, the Fair Housing Act contains another equally important section requiring federal agencies to administer all federal housing and urban development programs in a manner to affirmatively further the purposes of the Fair Housing Act (AFFH). This mandate imposes an affirmative obligation on the federal government and recipients of funds it administers to take actions to undo historic patterns of segregation and other types of discrimination and afford access to opportunity long denied. It was of that challenge that Senator Brooke was speaking on the floor of the U.S. Senate almost fifty years ago.

This obligation has been repeatedly reinforced by Congress in HUD program statutes over the years by requiring that program participants certify, as a condition of receiving federal funds, that they will affirmatively further fair housing.[6]

Like the FHA, these statutes themselves do not define the precise scope of the affirmatively furthering obligation in specific programs. However, over the years courts have made clear that more is required than simply to not discriminate: some affirmative actions to further the goals of the FHA are required, and those actions by and large depend on the facts on the ground.[7]

Litigation

In spite of the fact that for much of the life of the Fair Housing Act, HUD has taken the position that compliance with the AFFH duty is not reviewable by courts, federal courts which have dealt with the issue have consistently disagreed.

Boston Chapter of NAACP

The seminal case involving the AFFH provision in the Act was brought in 1978 by the Boston Chapter of the NAACP. NAACP alleged that HUD's administration of housing and community development programs violated various civil rights statutes, including HUD's duty to affirmatively further the policies of the Fair Housing Act.[8] The federal district court found that Boston had a history of racial discrimination in housing, that Boston suffered from a shortage of low-income family housing, that a higher proportion of black than white families were renters, and a higher proportion of black than white renters were families with children; that Boston's neighborhoods were racially separate and that "at least in part as the result of the lack of safe, desegregated housing in white neighborhoods black families found it difficult to move out of black areas." The court also found that both city and federal officials were aware of these facts, that the city had not effectively enforced fair housing requirements, that neither the city nor HUD had complied with HUD regulations regarding the need to assess special needs of identifiable segments of the lower-income population, and that taken together the facts added up to a violation of HUD's duty to affirmatively further fair housing. In particular, the Court noted that HUD's failure to use its "immense leverage" over the programs at issue "to provide desegregated housing so that the housing stock was sufficiently large to give minority families a true choice of location in the context of Boston's history and practices, violated HUD's Title VIII obligations."

The First Circuit provided further clarification regarding the provision in an opinion written by then Judge, now Justice, Stephen Breyer, ruling that a court could review HUD's actions under the Administrative Procedure Act (APA) and decide whether they violated HUD's obligation to affirmatively further fair housing, separate and apart from whether HUD has engaged in discriminatory conduct or has funded discriminatory conduct with the purpose of furthering the grantee's discrimination.[9] The facts upon which liability was found in NAACP are instructive of the viability of actions to enforce the obligation to affirmatively further fair housing through the federal courts even in the absence of regulatory guidance from HUD. Given our country's history, it is not unlikely that a similar pattern of conduct might be found in many places.

Westchester

In 2007 and 2009, a federal court revisited the obligation of recipients of federal housing and community development funds to affirmatively further fair housing, this time in the context of a False Claims Act claim against Westchester County, New York brought by a New York-based civil rights organization. The judge in that case held that "a local government entity that certifies to the federal government that it will affirmatively further fair housing as a condition to its receipt of federal funds must consider the existence and impact of race discrimination on housing opportunities and choice in its jurisdiction."[10] She subsequently ruled that Westchester County had repeatedly falsely certified that it was affirmatively furthering fair housing, and that millions of federal dollars had been dispensed to Westchester County based on those false certifications.[11] HUD was not sued.

Regulation

As described in the papers by O'Regan and by Bostic and Acolin, since 1968 there have been two regulations promulgated by HUD related to HUD's statutory duty to affirmatively further fair housing in housing and community development programs. The first, in 1995, required recipients of HUD funds to prepare an Analysis of Impediments to Fair Housing (AI), develop an action plan for addressing those impediments, and maintain records related to the process. The AI regulation did not require submission to HUD, and there was no formal process for objecting to or complaining about the adequacy of the process or product. After the initial rollout of the regulation, political and resource limitations made the regulation honored mostly in the breech.[12] An attempt to enact a more robust regulation in 1998 failed.[13]

The second HUD AFFH regulation came in the wake of the Westchester case discussed above. The Westchester litigation's timing was fortuitous. It gave the incoming Obama administration an opportunity to take hold of the issue and in some ways make it its own. A settlement between the parties was brokered by HUD, and public pronouncements from the highest levels in the department declared that HUD was going to move forward with a more robust effort to comply with the statutory mandate as it pertained to recipients of federal funds administered by the department.

Over the next seven years, HUD engaged in an extensive process to develop an AFFH regulation that would provide more specificity about what it means to affirmatively further fair housing, and address the concerns raised by the Westchester litigation. Those concerns were generally articulated as follows: jurisdictions did not know what AFFH meant, did not know what compliance required, and did not have the resources and/or capacity to generate the information and data necessary to know what they needed to know to formulate a plan to affirmatively further fair housing. The listening tour undertaken by the HUD leadership was exhaustive, and resulted in a regulation that finally put meat on the bones of the AFFH statutory mandate. The Final Rule, promulgated in 2015, requires recipients of federal block grant funds administered by HUD to develop an Assessment of Fair Housing (AFH) (replacing the ineffective Analysis of Impediments to Fair Housing) and submit it to HUD for approval as a condition of receiving funds under the covered programs. The purpose of the AFH is to allow recipients of HUD funds to develop their own plan to address racial segregation and inequality in housing and community conditions in their local communities. The regulation and supporting material give jurisdictions a wealth of data and information about local circumstances, as well as very detailed guidance about how to put together an AFH that will both pass muster with HUD and actually effect change on the ground in the communities involved.

The Final Rule's limitations are most obvious in terms of the lack of an effective "stick" to go with the "carrots." The enforcement capacity of HUD in the context of the AFH Rule (as well other civil rights laws) is limited by the institutional structure of HUD, by the different and often conflicting interests of HUD's various constituencies reflected in their ability to exert influence both internally and externally through the political process, and, last but not least, by resource capacity. To most people, HUD's primary job is to funnel federal funds related to housing and community development to people, places, and institutions through a myriad of programs created by Congress. While all of those programs have civil rights-related requirements imposed by various civil rights laws, only the Office of Fair Housing and Equal Opportunity (FHEO) has direct responsibility for seeing that those laws are complied with and enforced. FHEO has historically been the least well-funded and most politically impotent of the "Big Four" program offices in HUD. For FHEO to "enforce" anything related to civil rights against a recipient of HUD funds requires FHEO to take on the powerful constituencies of the other program offices, be it mayors, governors, public housing authorities, affordable housing and community development nonprofit or for-profit institutions, or Congress itself. The record of HUD's failures to take on those constituencies is found in the decades of litigation against HUD for knowingly funding entities that have engaged in discrimination and perpetuation of segregation.[14] In addition, the statutory AFFH provision is not self-enforcing. There is no recognized private right of action for violation/non-compliance against recipients of HUD funds. While the regulation speaks to the consequences of failing to submit an approvable AFH, the Final Rule is essentially designed to give jurisdictions the tools they need to prepare an AFH that will pass muster. In that sense, it is focused more on process and data/information than on actual results on the ground. In the hands of jurisdictions acting with some degree of good faith and intent to both do what is required and further the goals of the FHA, there is the possibility of some progress, particularly over time. But it will depend in large part on the cooperation and support of HUD program offices that have not historically seen such progress as their responsibility, and their cooperation will certainly be impacted by the political environment in which the effort is being undertaken.

What Will "Compliance" with the AFFH Regulation Look Like?

It should be anticipated that the response of jurisdictions will be uneven, but will fall into 4 basic categories:

1 Full acceptance of both the letter and spirit of the AFH Rule and the demonstrated capacity to use the AFH Tool and the Rule's requirements to develop and implement a plan to effectively address the problems caused by segregation and exclusion in the community.

2 Acceptance of both the letter and spirit of the Rule, but a limited capacity to use the Tool and the Rule's requirements to develop and implement a plan to effectively address the problems that exist because of segregation and exclusion in the community.

3 Acceptance of the need to comply with the specific requirements of the Rule to get federal funds, but actions that demonstrate a lack of understanding or willingness to develop a plan to actually address the problems caused by segregation and exclusion in the community.

4 Resistance to the Rule, both in letter and spirit, as demonstrated by refusal to demonstrate compliance with the basic minimal requirements outlined in the Rule, and perhaps by an assertion that there are no problems caused by segregation and exclusion in the community in the face of clear evidence to the contrary.

Jurisdictions that fall into the first two categories are likely to benefit from HUD's involvement in a supportive and incremental way to get them to improve and achieve their long-term goals under the AFH. HUD should recognize and reward the high achievers, and offer technical assistance and other support to those in category 2 to encourage them to use the AFH process more effectively to achieve results over time. Those that fall into category 3 will benefit from the sort of "enforcement" of which HUD is realistically capable. That would involve the using the administrative steps outlined in the Rule to withhold approval of the AFH until necessary issues are appropriately addressed. At some point in the process, those in categories 2 and 3 may demonstrate that they really should be in category 4, but the process of getting there will be instructive for both HUD and the jurisdiction. And the role of the outside advocate will be crucial to that process playing out as it should.

It is the premise of this paper that, whatever the potential of the Rule and HUD to deal with those in categories 1–3, there are significant limitations on HUD's ability to effectively deal with jurisdictions in category 4. Those jurisdictions will have to be dealt with by an external, relatively independent, and well-resourced enforcement structure. It must be external for the reasons discussed above concerning the inherent tensions and conflicts between the different program offices and who they see as their primary constituents or clients. An external structure also helps ensure independence from relationships or perspectives that, in other contexts, might be valuable to the people involved in doing their jobs. And independence means that the enforcement structure must not be dependent upon funds that can be easily withdrawn in order to shut down or retaliate against an enforcement effort. For that reason, it is doubtful that private fair housing organizations will be up to that task, unless they are funded by non-governmental sources which support a real litigation capacity and ultimately are able to access the resources of an independent federal judiciary.

LESSONS FROM THE VOTING RIGHTS ACT

It is instructive to look, by analogy, to the Voting Rights Act of 1965, and the tools it provided for addressing the historic, official, systemic, institutional, and widespread effort to deny people the right to vote throughout the states of the Old Confederacy (and a few other places with specific circumstances). By the time the VRA passed, it was clear that overt resistance to extending the franchise of a fair and non-discriminatory basis was a creative and ever changing endeavor. It was not an individual harm, but a class based harm that would not be effectively addressed simply by providing retrospective remedy though traditional laws making such actions unlawful, which require a plaintiff challenging a practice as discriminatory to engage in lengthy and complicated litigation, involving issues of legal standards of proof, and evidence as well as what constituted appropriate relief even if they were successful. More often than not, once a practice was successful challenged the offending jurisdiction would simply enact a new discriminatory provision, which would require a new, drawn out challenge, and the new discriminatory policy would be in effect until a new ruling was obtained, often years later. The solution was a dramatic and ultimately incredibly effective provision in the VRA, knows as Section 5, which required that states and certain smaller jurisdictions that had such a history of denying African Americans the right to vote, submit any changes in voting policies, practices or procedures to a "pre-clearance" process before they could be implemented. The pre-clearance could be through an administrative process administered by the U.S. Department of Justice (where most issues were resolved), or through a declaratory judgment process through the federal courts. In effect, Congress shifted the burden of proof, so that jurisdictions that had a sordid history of voting discrimination had to prove that the new policy or procedure was NOT discriminatory before it could be implemented. This important enforcement provision changed the face of political participation and political representation in the South forever. By the time a conservative majority on the Supreme Court effectively struck down the provision in 2013 on the grounds that it was no longer justified,[15] the experience under Section 5 had provided ample evidence of the effectiveness of the "preclearance" approach.

The AFH process, while not nearly as stringent a provision as Section 5, does place a "speed bump" to jurisdictions continuing to take federal funds without any demonstrated compliance with the AFFH obligation. That speed bump requires jurisdictions to slow down and look at the legacy of segregation in their communities, and develop a plan to address that legacy. The result, if done right, should address unequal conditions in communities as a result of segregation, promote greater inclusion, choice and equal access to opportunity, and insure that the jurisdiction continues to receive federal funds for their housing and urban development activities. The Regulation has a "progressive discipline" approach built in that should insure that most jurisdictions will move into at least basic compliance rather than jeopardize their access to federal funds. In those hopefully rare instances where a jurisdiction demonstrates a resistance/hostility to the purposes of the FHA, and specifically the AFFH duty, the matter will require more adversarial intervention. That intervention could come from the Department of Justice, Civil Rights Division, which can act on a referral from HUD or based on other information about a jurisdiction's conduct. The Civil Rights Division, however, has prosecutorial discretion, and there is no guarantee that an unsympathetic or even hostile administration will undertake enforcement activity. For that reason, it is imperative that private litigants be prepared to bring cases that get the facts before a court when necessary.

Indeed, whatever the possibilities prior to November 2016, it is probably not realistic to assume that the Department of Justice, at least for the next few years, will be a helpful partner in insuring compliance with the duty to affirmatively further fair housing. On January 24, 2017 a bill was introduced in the Congress to invalidate the AFFH regulation promulgated by HUD, which is discussed in other papers. Advocates are preparing to employ all tools at their disposal to prevent Congress and the Executive Branch form undoing this important and long overdue effort by HUD to meet its obligation under the Fair Housing Act. Over the longer term, if the basic structure of the Regulation or something like it remains, the possibility of a real and effective progress toward the goals of fostering more inclusive communities of opportunity is real. But that progress will depend on enforcement efforts by outside advocates working in affected communities to complete the compliance/enforcement infrastructure of AFFH.

USING AFFH TO ENFORCE THE FAIR HOUSING ACT AND RELATED CIVIL RIGHTS LAWS

In the meantime, civil rights advocates should look for opportunities to combine the AFFH requirement with more direct statutory provisions in the FHA that prohibit discrimination. A jurisdiction which is resistant to meeting its obligation to AFFH is likely to have a history of segregation and discrimination that has never been effectively addressed. While the AFH Rule may be aimed at fostering worthwhile policy objectives of inclusion and equity for their own sake, it should be remembered that where jurisdiction has an unaddressed legacy of official segregation, the legal imperative to desegregate may also be in play.[16] While it may not be possible to directly sue a jurisdiction for failure to AFFH, the jurisdictions actions in responding to the regulatory requirement could certainly be current evidence of policies and practices that intend to and/or have the effect of singling out a racially identifiable group because of race for unequal treatment that makes housing unavailable and/or perpetuates segregation, actionable under the Fair Housing Act as well as Title VI of the 1964 Civil Rights act, and the 14th Amendment to the U.S. Constitution. While advocates may be able to effectively participate in the AFFH process and move a community toward greater understanding of the need for and ways to achieve more inclusiveness, in those instances where more adversarial advocacy is called for, the AFFH rule can provide an excellent road map. And of course, as the decades of case law make clear, HUD can itself be sued under the APA for its own failure to comply with the duty to affirmatively further fair housing.

AFFH BEYOND HUD

It is also important to remember that the HUD Rule, as important and sweeping as it is, only covers what is required of recipients of HUD's block grant funds. Section 3608 is much broader. It mandates not only that HUD shall administer all of its housing and community development programs in a manner that affirmatively furthers the policies of the FHA, it also mandates that "all executive departments and agencies shall administer their programs and activities related to housing and urban development (including any Federal agency having regulatory or supervisory authority over financial institutions) in a manner affirmatively to further" the purposes of the Act. Pending litigation in the Northern District of Texas against the U.S. Treasury Department and the Office of the Comptroller of the Currency involves a claim under the Administrative Procedure Act (APA) that those agencies have failed to meet their obligation to administer the LIHTC program in a manner that affirmatively furthers fair housing.[17] The Court's willingness to allow the AFFH claim to go forward against Treasury and OCC suggests possible fertile ground for private enforcement activity against other federal agencies administering housing and community development programs, particularly if the federal agency environment is not friendly to fair housing.

In addition to direct litigation against federal agencies under the APA, the False Claim Act cause of action upon which the Westchester County litigation was based, always a viable legal theory, may be get renewed traction. As earlier noted, there were some who saw the HUD push to promulgate a AFFH regulation to replace the AI process as a way to hit the "reset" button for local jurisdictions who had not, for a number of reasons, demonstrated a robust interest in compliance with the AFFH obligation. To the extent that the goal was to provide jurisdictions acting in good faith with clarity and cover, the new Rule could provide a path to pardon for past sins. If the Rule is either voided, or the agency otherwise fails to enforce it, then it is conceivable that jurisdictions whose certifications and AIs are the only thing standing between them and a False Claim finding could be challenged on the same grounds as Westchester County. Depending on how long the litigation is in the courts it is not inconceivable that a different administration might view the situation differently again at some point in the future. For that reason alone Jurisdictions who are subject to the HUD AFFH Rule may come to see the Rule as their "safe harbor" and not be all that excited to see it go.

CONCLUSION

All is not lost. The HUD regulation is an excellent road map for jurisdictions seeking to address the difficult and persistent challenges posed to community health and viability by a legacy of segregation, discrimination, and a culture of exclusion. While it will certainly depend on the local circumstances, it is possible that at least some recipients of HUD funds will see the wisdom of meeting their obligation to affirmatively further fair housing, and take to heart the Rule's information and guidance on how to do so, at least to some degree. Over the next five to ten years, with persistence, those communities could become more inclusive places of opportunity for everyone. Where there is intransigence, and there will no doubt be in places, then the legal tools will be available to civil rights advocates to address those situations. It will not necessarily be quick or easy, as the history of HUD's efforts to comply with its own obligations under the FHA demonstrate. But it will be worth the effort.

Bibliography

Allen, Michael. 2017. "Speaking Truth to Power: Enhancing Community Engagement in the Assessment of Fair Housing Process." This volume.

Bostic, Raphael, and Arthur Acolin. 2017. "The Potential for HUD's Affirmatively Furthering Fair Housing Rule to Meaningfully Increase Inclusion." This volume.

Brief for Housing Scholars as Amici Curiae, *Texas Department of Housing and Community Affairs et al. v. Inclusive Communities Project, Inc. et al..,* No. 13–1371. https://static1.squarespace.com/static/58b9e76e17bffc3590518d43/t/58bedb23c534a57a90fd2e88/1488902952222/Housing+Scholars.pdf.

Civil Rights Act of 1964, 42 U.S.C. 2000d; 24 C.F.R. Part 1.

Daniel & Beshara, P.C. Inclusive Communities Project v. U.S. Department of Treasury and Office of Comptroller of the Currency. https://www.danielbesharalawfirm.com/icp-v-treasury-and-occ/.

HUD. 2015. Final Rule: Affirmatively Furthering Fair Housing. https://www.huduser.gove/portal/sites/default/files/pdf/AFFH_FInal)Rule.pdf.

Novara, Marisa. 2017. "Organic Is for Apples: Why I've Had It with Leaving Desegregation to Chance." Metropolitan Planning Council Blog. March 6. http://www.metroplanning.org/news/7404/Organic-is-for-apples-Why-Ive-had-it-with-leaving-desegregation-to-chance? (accessed March 22, 2017).

O'Regan, Katherine M. 2017. "Affirmatively Furthering Fair Housing—the Potential and the Challenges for Fulfilling the Promise of HUD's Final Rule." This volume.

Voting Rights Act, 42 U.S.C. 1973(c).

Endnotes

1   Title VIII of the Civil Rights Act of 1968, 42 U.S.C. 3601.

2   *Trafficante v. Metro. Life Ins. Co.*, 409 U.S. 2005 (1972).

3   *Otero v. N.Y. City Hous. Auth.*, 484 F.2d 1122, 1134 (2d Cir. 1973).

4   Brief for Housing Scholars as Amici Curiae.

5   *Texas Department of Housing and Community Affairs v. Inclusive Communities Project*, 135 S.Ct. 2507 (2015).

6   HUD, "Final Rule," at 42274, fn.3.

7   HUD, "Final Rule,", at 42274.

8   *NAACP, Boston Chapter v. Harris,* 567 F. Supp.637 (D.Mass.1983).

9   *NAACP, Boston Chapter v. HUD,* 817 149 (1st Cir 1987).

10 *United States ex rel. Anti-Discrimination Center of Metro New York, Inc. v. Westchester Cnty.*, 495 F.Supp. 2d 375, 376 (2007).

11 *U.S. ex rel. Anti-Discrimination Center v. Westchester County,* 668 F.Supp. 2d 548, 563 (S.D.N.Y. 2009); *Shelby County v. Holder,* 570 U.S. 2 (2013).

12 Bostic and Acolin.

13 O'Regan.

14 *Hills v. Gautreaux*, 425 U.S. 284 (1976); *Young v. Pierce*, 685 F. Supp 986 (1988); *Walker v. HUD, 734 F.Supp. 1231 (N.D.Tex. 1989); Thompson v. HUD*, 348 F. Supp2d 398 (2004).

15 *Shelby County v. Holder*, 570 U.S.2 (2103).

16 Novara.

17 *ICP v. U.S. Dept. of Treasury and U.S. Comptroller of the Currency*, Northern District of Texas, CA No. 3:14-3013-D.

What Would It Take for Housing Subsidies to Overcome Affordability Barriers to Inclusion in All Neighborhoods?

Strategies for Maximizing the Benefits of Housing Subsidies

MARGERY AUSTIN TURNER
Urban Institute

WHERE WE LIVE REALLY MATTERS FOR PEOPLE'S WELL-BEING AND LONG-TERM LIFE CHANCES

Raj Chetty's recent findings extend a substantial body of research on the importance of place, establishing that where we live matters to our well-being and long-term life chances.[1] Compelling evidence shows that every year of exposure to a more opportunity-rich community improves a child's chances of economic success as an adult.[2] And children whose parents were able to escape from deeply poor neighborhoods (through the Moving to Opportunity experiment) achieved substantially better outcomes as young adults than those in a control group.[3] Life expectancies can differ by as much as twenty years between rich and poor neighborhoods within the same city.[4] And other recent research finds that living in a high-poverty neighborhood undermines some outcomes across generations.[5] High levels of residential segregation and poverty concentration block economic mobility and exacerbate inequality, undermining our nation's vitality and economic performance. These findings argue strongly that scarce housing subsidy resources should enable lower-income families to live in neighborhoods of their choice that offer a decent quality of life and access to opportunities for both parents and children.

Federal Housing Policies Have Often Undermined of Neighborhood Choice and Inclusion

For much of the 20th century, federal housing programs (aimed at assisting both low-income renters and aspiring homeowners) have intersected with exclusionary land use regulations and discriminatory market practices to block low-income families and people of color from communities that offer safety, good schools, a healthy environment, and homeownership opportunities. The historical record clearly demonstrates that our nation's stark patterns of racial segregation and poverty concentration were established through public policy, including the enforcement of restrictive covenants, local land use regulations, underwriting requirements for federally insured mortgage loans, federally funded urban renewal strategies, and siting and occupancy regulations for public housing.[6]

At its inception, federally subsidized rental housing (targeted to households at the bottom of the income ladder) was largely segregated by race as a matter of law. Beginning immediately after World War II, when thousands of public housing units were built to address the nation's housing shortage, housing developments built in black neighborhoods (and on isolated tracts of vacant land) were designated exclusively for occupancy by blacks, while separate developments were built in white neighborhoods for occupancy by whites.[7] Urban renewal projects of the 1950s and 60s further exacerbated racial segregation and the concentration of poverty. In cities across the country, the Urban Renewal program targeted "slum" neighborhoods for redevelopment and relocated the mostly low-income black residents to public housing in already segregated neighborhoods.[8] At the same time, the Federal Housing Administration's mortgage insurance program encouraged and enabled moderate- and middle-income white families to buy homes in predominantly white suburbs (from which minorities were largely excluded) and discouraged mortgage lending in racially mixed or minority neighborhoods.[9]

In 1968, the Fair Housing Act charged HUD to combat the longstanding patterns of housing discrimination and segregation that block free and fair access to housing and neighborhoods. Despite this mandate, the Department continued to acquiesce to local decisions about the siting and occupancy of public housing.[10] By the 1980s, most public housing residents were black and living in developments isolated from mainstream economic and social opportunities.[11] The racial and economic isolation of these communities was further exacerbated by tenant selection policies that targeted housing subsidies to those with the most severe housing needs.[12]

In the 1960s and '70s, Congress created new programs to subsidize the development of rental housing, making it affordable for low-income renters. Private (or nonprofit) entities rather than public housing agencies owned and managed the new generation of subsidized housing developments. Nonetheless, their locations were constrained by local zoning and land use regulations. HUD's site and neighborhood standards were intended to prevent the over-concentration of assisted housing in high-poverty and predominantly minority neighborhoods, and to expand affordable housing availability in non-poor neighborhoods. But these standards were not vigorously enforced and allowed for numerous exceptions.[13] As a result, most of the rental housing developed for low-income families was located in central cities, and often in the same lower-income neighborhoods as public housing.[14] Thus, the second generation of federally subsidized housing production — like the first — largely failed to offer low-income renters access to high-quality neighborhood environments, thereby reinforcing existing patterns of segregation and poverty concentration.[15]

Today's Federal Housing Subsidy Policies Fall Short of Their Potential to Promote Neighborhood Choice and Inclusion

In principle, the federal housing voucher program gives families at the bottom of the income ladder the ability to move to neighborhoods of their choice. However, the program has never realized its full potential to provide low-income families access to lower-poverty and less segregated communities. Housing vouchers have consistently been found to produce better locational outcomes than traditional public housing, but they perform better in this regard for recipients who live in suburban areas than for those in central cities, for white recipients than for African-Americans and Hispanics, and for the elderly than for non-elderly families and disabled people.[16]

The Low-Income Housing Tax Credit (LIHTC) plays a critical role today in supporting the production of rental housing affordable for households with low to moderate incomes. State policies shape the geographic distribution of LIHTC units, and for many years, most units reinforced existing patterns of economic segregation.[17] Recent evidence suggests that LIHTC has increasingly been used to develop affordable housing in suburban jurisdictions, potentially expanding opportunities for low- and moderate-income renters to find affordable housing in opportunity-rich communities.[18]

Although federal housing finance institutions no longer enforce redlining, they do little to reverse the legacy of segregation or encourage inclusion of low- and moderate-income homeowners in neighborhoods of opportunity. The federal government currently provides almost no direct subsidies for homeownership, although local housing authorities are authorized to allocate a portion of housing vouchers to very low-income homebuyers.[19] However, through the mortgage interest deduction, the federal tax code provides significant subsidies to homeowners, with the biggest subsidies going to the highest-income households.[20] As discussed further in Chris Herbert's essay on homeownership in this volume, the mortgage interest deduction helps perpetuate racial and economic segregation by raising house prices and exacerbating affordability barriers.

Too often, policies aimed at expanding access to opportunity-rich neighborhoods (i.e., fair housing policies) are pursued separately from housing subsidy policies. And tensions between these goals and their respective constituencies arise often — in decisions about whether to invest in the preservation of affordable housing located in distressed or marginal neighborhoods, about whether to help low-income families move to non-poor neighborhoods or prioritize the redevelopment of neighborhoods where they are currently concentrated, and about how much to spend per household or housing unit (since land, and therefore housing, is more expensive in high-opportunity neighborhoods, requiring higher subsidies).

Looking Ahead, Housing Subsidy Policies Can and Should Enable Low-Income Families to Live in Opportunity-Rich Communities while also Contributing to the Revitalization of Distressed Neighborhoods

But this vision cannot be achieved if investments in affordable housing development are allocated one project at a time, or if programs targeting the poorest renters and those serving moderate-income renters and homeowners operate in isolation. Often, conflicts between alternative uses for scarce housing subsidy resources stem from the fact that individual investments are assessed in isolation, rather than as part of a strategic portfolio of investments. To illustrate, when a policymaker has to decide whether the next available $1 million should be used to launch an assisted housing mobility program, preserve and rehabilitate affordable housing in a gentrifying neighborhood, or build mixed-income housing in a distressed community, one strategy does indeed have to win at the expense of the others. But a more deliberate citywide — or better still, regionwide — planning process allocating $5 million to promote housing affordability and inclusion might well decide that these three initiatives would be complementary and should all be funded.

To maximize the benefits of housing subsidies, policymakers should develop and pursue *portfolio strategies* that target different investments and interventions to different types of neighborhoods. This kind of portfolio strategy would ideally encompass both affordable rental housing and accessible homeownership and address the needs of households with incomes ranging from extremely low to moderate. Other papers in this volume focus on land use and regulatory issues, which would contribute to a portfolio strategy aimed at housing affordability and inclusion. The papers in this section focus on the role of housing subsidies.

Here I offer a set of basic principles about how housing subsidies should be deployed in four stylized types of neighborhoods: 1) severely distressed, 2) stable low-income, 3) emergent, and 4) opportunity-rich. To be clear, this typology is intended to highlight the value of a comprehensive approach that tailors interventions to the particular challenges and assets of different neighborhoods that make up a city or region. In reality, the borders between these four types are blurry and dynamic, requiring that local stakeholders make judgment calls about the likely trajectories of individual neighborhoods and about the most appropriate mix of investments.

In *severely distressed neighborhoods,* subsidized housing probably should not be further concentrated. Investments in these neighborhoods should focus instead on the most urgent problems facing residents — often safety, school quality, and access to jobs will top the list. Renovation or replacement of existing subsidized housing should be pursued only as part of a larger neighborhood revitalization effort. But, when launching a wholesale revitalization effort, planners should assume their efforts will ultimately succeed and plan for the preservation of affordable rentals and for-sale housing from the outset.

The argument against further concentrating new subsidized housing also applies in other, more *stable low-income neighborhoods*. Here, subsidized housing investments should focus on renovation and preservation of the affordable housing stock, including publicly and privately owned rental properties as well as owner-occupied housing. In some cases, subsidies to help low- and moderate-income households acquire and renovate vacant homes can expand affordable housing options while also contributing to neighborhood stability.

Preservation and expansion of affordable housing options should be the top priority in *emergent neighborhoods*. As amenities and opportunities expand in these neighborhoods and market pressures intensify, planners should protect the existing subsidized stock and add to it. They should also support the acquisition and preservation of existing unsubsidized housing — both multifamily and single-family — providing subsidies to individual households, property owners, and community partnerships to keep this stock affordable for a mix of households with incomes ranging from very low to moderate. Ideally, these efforts can get underway before market pressures have pushed land values and acquisition costs too high, so that a range of affordable housing options are effectively "built in" as the neighborhood revitalizes.

Finally, in *opportunity-rich neighborhoods,* housing subsidies should be deployed (along with other policy tools) to expand affordable housing options. The federal Housing Choice Voucher program can play an important role here, if local authorities use it to help recipients find, move into, and stay in housing located in communities that offer high-quality amenities and opportunities. In addition, public agencies can acquire existing properties and make them available for rental at below-market rents, target Low-Income Housing Tax Credits to expand the supply of affordable rentals in high-opportunity neighborhoods, and enable low- and moderate-income homebuyers to purchase in these communities.

The right mix of strategies will vary across metro areas, because the distribution of neighborhoods across these four types varies, along with the social and economic geography of the region as a whole. Prosperous metros with intense demand pressures and high housing costs have more emergent neighborhoods (relative to distressed and low-income) and higher housing costs in all types of neighborhoods than weaker market areas. Consequently, the need for preservation is more intense, and investments in distressed or stable low-income neighborhoods are more likely to spark revitalization (with its opportunities and challenges). In softer markets, on the other hand, acquiring or producing affordable housing in high-opportunity neighborhoods may be considerably less costly, and housing acquisition and renovation in stable low-income neighborhoods can significantly expand the availability of decent, affordable housing over the long term.

The design and execution of this kind of portfolio strategy is, of course, more easily said than done. The three papers that follow dig into some of the specifics, focusing in turn on 1) how to balance development of new housing with investments in low-income communities; 2) what it takes to expand subsidized rental housing in high-opportunity neighborhoods; and 3) how to restructure homeownership incentives and subsidies to promote inclusion.

Bibliography

Chetty, Raj, and Nathaniel Hendren. 2015. "The Impacts of Neighborhoods on Intergenerational Mobility: Childhood Exposure Effects and County-Level Estimates." Cambridge, MA: Harvard University.

Chetty, Raj, Nathaniel Hendren, and Lawrence F. Katz. 2015. *The Effects of Exposure to Better Neighborhoods on Children: New Evidence from the Moving to Opportunity Experiment.* Boston, MA: Harvard University and NBER.

Devine, Deborah J., Robert Gray, Lester Rubin, and Lydia Taghavi. 2003. *Housing Choice Voucher Location Patterns: Implications for Participant and Neighborhood Welfare.* Washington, D.C.: U.S. Department of Housing and Urban Development.

Ellen, Ingrid Gould, and Margery Austin Turner. 1997. "Does Neighborhood Matter? Assessing Recent Evidence." *Housing Policy Debate* 8, no. 4: 833–66.

Galvez, Martha M. 2010. "What Do We Know About Housing Choice Voucher Program Location Outcomes? A Review of Recent Literature." Washington, D.C.: The Urban Institute.

Hirsch, Anorld R. 2000. "Searching for a 'Sound Negro Policy': A Racial Agenda for the Housing Acts of 1949 and 1954." *Housing Policy Debate* 13, no. 2.

— — —. 2003. "Second Thoughts on the Second Ghetto." *Journal of Urban History* 29, no. 3: 298–309.

Mapping Life Expectancy. 2014. Virginia Commonwealth University Center on Society and Health. http://www.societyhealth.vcu.edu/work/the-projects/mapping-life-expectancy.html

Massey, Douglas A. and Nancy A. Denton. 1993. *American Apartheid: Segregation and the Making of the Underclass.* Cambridge, MA: Harvard University Press.

Massey, Douglas S., Len Albright, Rebecca Casciano, Elizabeth Derickson, and David N. Kinsey. 2013. *Climbing Mount Laurel: The Struggle for Affordable Housing and Social Mobility in an American Suburb.* Princeton: Princeton University Press.

McClure, Kirk. 2006. "The Low Income Housing Tax Credit Program Goes Mainstream and Moves to the Suburbs." *Housing Policy Debate* 17, no. 3.

McClure, Kirk, Alex F. Schwartz, and Lydia B. Taghavi. 2014. "Housing Choice Voucher Location Patterns a Decade Later." *Housing Policy Debate* 25, no. 2: 215–33. http://www.tandfonline.com/doi/full/10.1080/10511482.2014.921223#abstract.

Newman, Sandra J., and Ann B. Schnare. 1997. "'...And a suitable living environment': The Failure of Housing Programs to Deliver on Neighborhood Quality." *Housing Policy Debate* 8, no. 4: 703–41.

Polikoff, Alexander. 2006. *Waiting for Gautreaux: A Story of Segregation, Housing, and The Black Ghetto.* Evanston, IL: Northwestern University Press.

Popkin, S. J., V.E. Gwiasda, D.P. Rosenbaum, L.M. Olson, and L. F. Buron. 2000. *The Hidden War: Crime and the Tragedy of Public Housing in Chicago.* New Brunswick, NJ: Rutgers University Press.

Rohe, William, and Lance Freeman. 2001. "Assisted Housing and Residential Segregation — the Role of Race and Ethnicity in the Siting of Assisted Housing Developments." *Journal of the American Planning Association* 67, no. 3: 279–92.

Sharkey, Patrick. 2013. *Stuck in Place: Urban Neighborhoods and the End of Progress toward Racial Equality.* Chicago: University of Chicago Press.

Spence, Lewis H. 1993. "Rethinking the Social Role of Public Housing." *Housing Policy Debate* 4, no. 3: 355–72.

Tegeler, Philip. 2005. "The Persistence of Segregation in Government Housing Programs." In *The Geography of Opportunity: Race and Housing Choice in Metropolitan America*, edited by Xavier de Souza Briggs, 197–218. Washington, D.C.: The Brookings Institution.

Turner, Margery Austin, and Lynette A. Rawlings. 2005. *Overcoming Concentrated Poverty and Isolation: Ten Lessons for Policy and Practice.* Washington, DC: Urban Institute.

Turner, Margery Austin, and Lynette Rawlings. 2009. "Promoting Neighborhood Diversity: Benefits, Barriers, and Strategies." Washington DC: The Urban Institute.

Turner, Margery Austin, Eric Toder, Rolf Pendall, and Claudia Sharygin. 2013. *How Would Reforming the Mortgage Interest Deduction Affect the Housing Market?* Washington, D.C.: The Urban Institute.

Turner, Margery Austin, and Charlene Wilson. 1998. *Affirmatively Furthering Fair Housing: Neighborhood Outcomes for Tenant-Based Assistance in Six Metropolitan Areas.* Washington, D.C.: The Urban Institute.

Turnham, Jennifer, Naomi Michlin, Gretchen Locke, Michelle Wood, and Michael Baker. 2003. *Voucher Homeownership Program Assessment.* Washington, D.C.: U.S. Department of Housing and Urban Development.

Endnotes

1   This literature is discussed more fully in the introductory paper for this symposium. Also see Ellen and Turner (1997) and Turner and Rawlings (2009) for reviews of research on neighborhood effects.

2   Chetty and Hendren (2015).

3   Chetty, Hendren, and Katz (2015).

4   Mapping Life Expectancy (2014).

5   Sharkey (2013).

6   Massey and Denton (1993); Polikoff (2006).

7   Hirsch (2000).

8   Ibid.

9   Ibid.

10 Hirsch (2000); Hirsch (2003).

11 Hirsch (2003).

12 Spence (1993); Popkin et al. (2000).

13 Tegeler (2005).

14 Rohe and Freeman (2001).

15 Newman and Schnare (1997).

16 Turner and Wilson (1998); Devine et al. (2003); Galvez (2010); McClure, Schwartz, and Taghavi (2014).

17 Newman and Schnare (1997).

18 McClure (2006).

19 Turnham et al. (2003).

20 Turner et al. (2013).

Expanding the Toolbox: Promising Approaches for Increasing Geographic Choice

STEPHEN NORMAN AND SARAH OPPENHEIMER
King County Housing Authority

D espite growing evidence regarding the importance of neighborhood quality for child and family well-being, residents in federally subsidized housing continue to be concentrated in high-poverty areas. Presently less than 10 percent of the 1.7 million families with children that receive federally subsidized housing assistance reside in low-poverty neighborhoods (see Table 1).[1,2] This pattern reinforces historic patterns of racial and economic segregation and plays an important role in perpetuating intergenerational poverty.[3] Federal housing assistance programs designed to provide affordable, quality housing to extremely low-income individuals[4] offer a critical and unique opportunity to facilitate broader neighborhood options rather than reinforce racial and economic segregation.

This article speaks to how federal housing subsidies can be used, from a practitioner's perspective, to provide families with broader neighborhood choice. Informed by growing national evidence on the effects of neighborhood quality on life outcomes, King County Housing Authority (KCHA) has built concerted efforts to increase neighborhood options for its program participants. We first review *tenant-based mobility approaches* that have been a focus of national conversations to date, and around which KCHA has built several initiatives. We then discuss site-based affordability approaches, a group of less known but equally important strategies that have been implemented by KCHA to complement mobility approaches. Through a combination of these efforts, over 31 percent of KCHA's federally subsidized households with children currently reside in low-poverty areas (see Table 1).

We base this discussion on the premise that different markets require different approaches. A single strategy for expanding neighborhood options cannot be applied to all places. Rather, housing investment strategies — both tenant- and site-based — should be understood as a broad, varied, and growing set of tools that should be deployed based on local markets and conditions. This paper outlines the toolkit of options currently being used in King County, Washington, and identifies additional work that is called for

Table 1. Federally Subsidized Households with Children by Area Poverty Rate, KCHA and Nationally

Census Tract Poverty	Tenant-based Vouchers		Site-based Units		Public Housing		Total	
	KCHA	U.S.	KCHA (Project-based Vouchers)	U.S. (Project-based Rental Assistance)[a]	KCHA	U.S.	KCHA	U.S.
< 10%	30.3%	12.9%	55.1%	5.7%	24.1%	3.9%	31.2%	9.4%
10%–20%	38.4%	28.1%	26.2%	22.4%	41.8%	14.5%	38.0%	23.9%
≥ 20%	31.3%	59.0%	18.7%	71.9%	34.1%	81.6%	30.8%	66.7%
N	4,654	986,014	550	328,406	1,280	389,792	6,484	1,704,212

Sources: Federal statistics—Center for Budget and Policy Priorities (CBPP) analysis of 2014 HUD administrative data and the 2010–2014 American Community Survey published in Sard and Rice (2016), 26, Table A-1. KCHA statistics—KCHA 2016 administrative data.

as we refine our understanding of promising and sustainable strategies for expanding housing choice and neighborhood quality for low-income families.

Intersections Between Neighborhood Quality and Life Outcomes

Over the last decade, there has been growing evidence on the critical intersections between neighborhood quality and education, health, employment, and other domains.[6] For Public Housing Authorities (PHAs), this research has provided greater certainty that the investments necessary to provide access to high-quality neighborhoods can effectively shape children's later educational and economic success, and has re-energized conversations on both expanded geographic choice and place-based investments.

As much as the work by Chetty and colleagues has sparked renewed momentum in mobility conversations, their evidence also highlights the need for PHAs to redouble efforts to improve the neighborhoods where the majority of poor children already live. Policymakers, practitioners, and academics cannot assume a dichotomy between broadening geographic choice (the focus of the present paper) and investing in poor neighborhoods through place-based initiatives. Rather, a focus on *both* of these approaches is necessary.[7]

In determining the balance between mobility- and place-based initiatives, KCHA views the region's housing market and demographic patterns through a long-term lens — looking not just at current conditions but also at the likely evolution of markets and communities based upon population growth, sub-market economic trends, and other development factors. This approach yields three general neighborhood categories:

1 Neighborhoods already classified as high-opportunity (typically high-cost/low-poverty areas);

2 Neighborhoods expected to become opportunity areas through natural market processes and where displacement of existing low-income households will become an increasing issue;[8] and

3 Neighborhoods where historic disinvestment and long-standing patterns, or a new influx of the region's poor, have created high concentrations of poverty and low opportunity.

The mobility and site-based strategies discussed in this article are particularly appropriate for the first and second neighborhood types. KCHA has employed place-based strategies that are largely outside the scope of this paper to invest in the third neighborhood category.[9]

King County Housing Authority: A Regional Perspective on Broadening Housing Choice

KCHA serves the metropolitan area surrounding Seattle, a jurisdiction spanning 38 suburban cities and towns that reflect a wide diversity of neighborhood conditions and economic opportunities. The east side of the County's urban/suburban core includes Bellevue, Redmond, Kirkland, and other cities at the epicenter of recent technology booms. In contrast, cities in the south of the County have experienced acute and growing suburban poverty.[10] School statistics provide a telling marker of neighborhood differences: across the 19 school districts in King County, subsidized meal rates range from a low of 3 percent on Mercer Island to a high of 75 percent in Tukwila (see Fig. 1, Panel A).

King County is home to nearly 2.1 million residents.[11] With only 653,000 people living within the City of Seattle, the bulk of King County's population now resides in low-density suburban communities south and east of Seattle. Between 1990 and 2015, King County's population increased by 36 percent, compared to a national increase of 29 percent.[12]

Along with this rapid population growth, King County has experienced rapid economic expansion, especially during the recovery period from the Great Recession. By 2015, median annual household income had grown to $75,302,[13] an increase of over 41 percent since 2000; among peer counties, only New York experienced more rapid income growth during this period.[14] Such increases, while positive for the region, mask growing disparities, with a broadening gap between upper and lower income quintiles. These economic disparities align with racial and ethnic patterns in King County, wherein persons of color are overrepresented in lower-income communities, and indicate increasing concentrations of poor minorities, including refugee and emigrant populations, in South King County in particular.[15]

Economic prosperity, job creation, and population growth are presently driving significant rent growth in King County.[16] Between 2012 and 2016, the two-bedroom 40th percentile rent — the HUD Fair Market Rent (FMR) — in King County increased by 27 percent. Rent growth has held steady across both low- and high-cost markets in the region, and vacancy rates have dropped below 3 percent.[17] As a result, the number of shelter-burdened, unstably housed, and homeless households is rising significantly.[18]

Serving Vulnerable Families in Low-Poverty, High-Opportunity Areas

KCHA is the largest affordable housing provider for low-income families in the region. In 2016, KCHA supported 15,461 extremely low-income households through federal subsidy programs that included tenant-based vouchers (10,893), project-based vouchers (2,285), and public housing units (2,283).[19,20] Households receiving these federal housing subsidies represent a particularly vulnerable group. They include 14,742 children, over half of whom were residing in single-parent households. Median household income in 2016 was just $11,858 annually. Reflecting local admission preferences and dedicated supportive housing partnerships, over half of entering households in 2016 had experienced recent homelessness prior to program admittance.

KCHA has participated in the Moving to Work (MTW) program since 2003, and is currently one of only 39 PHAs in the country that benefit from the flexibility provided by this program.[21] The MTW program provides participating PHAs with their Housing Choice Voucher (HCV) and Public Housing funding as a block grant and allows the waiver of many of HUD's program rules in order to design approaches tailored to local market conditions.

Despite serving an extremely vulnerable population, KCHA has been relatively successful in supporting families in moving to and remaining in low-poverty, high opportunity communities. As noted in Table 1, the proportion of extremely low-income households with children living in low-poverty neighborhoods (31.2 percent) is more than three times the national figure. This difference is most pronounced for families in Public Housing where the proportion of KCHA residents in low-poverty areas is six times greater compared to national numbers. A significant proportion of all KCHA residents using PBVs also reside in low-poverty areas.

These results suggest that the strategies described below have been successful in supporting families in accessing and retaining housing in low-poverty markets. However, these numbers are also a reflection of King County's comparatively low regional poverty rate,[22] which has pushed KCHA to consider more than just poverty

Figure 1. King County Free and Reduced Meal (FARM) Rates and Opportunity Rankings
Panel A. King County School Districts FARM Rates (2016)

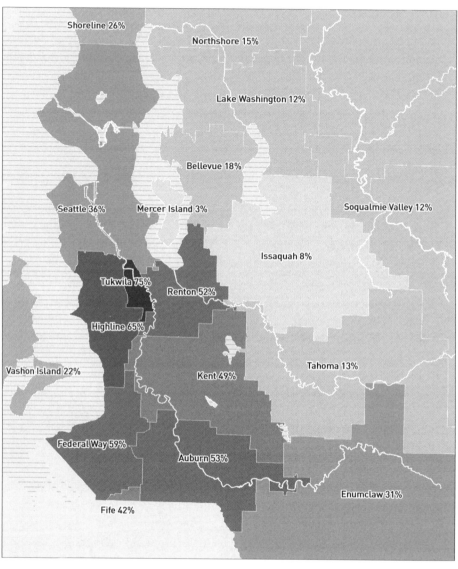

FREE AND REDUCED MEAL RATE, %

- 3–10%
- 10.1–20%
- 20.1–30%
- 30.1–40%
- 40.1–50%
- 50.1–60%
- 60.1–70%
- 70.1–80%
- 80.1–90%

Sources: FARM Rates — Office of Superintendent of Public Instruction (OSPI), Washington State Report Card (2016).
Kirwan rankings — Puget Sound Regional Council.

Figure 1. King County Free and Reduced Meal (FARM) Rates and Opportunity Rankings
Panel B. Kiwan Comprehensive Opportunity Rankings for King County census tracts.

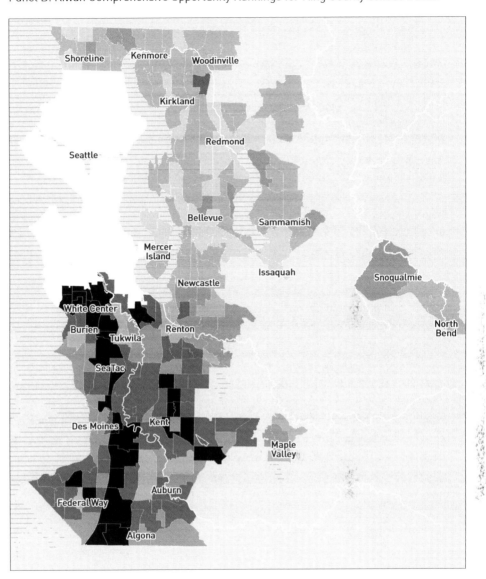

COMPREHENSIVE OPPORTUNITY INDEX

■ Very Low Opportunity
▓ Low Opportunity
▒ Moderate Opportunity
░ High Opportunity
□ Very High Opportunity

Sources: FARM Rates — Office of Superintendent of Public Instruction (OSPI), Washington State Report Card (2016).
Kirwan rankings — Puget Sound Regional Council.

in defining neighborhood quality. In 2010, KCHA collaborated with the Puget Sound Regional Council (PSRC) and the Kirwan Institute for the Study of Race and Ethnicity (Ohio State University) to rank census tract opportunity levels across five major categories: education; economic health; housing; transportation and mobility; and health and environment. Categorical opportunity rankings were then aggregated to create a comprehensive score of very low, low, moderate, high, and very high opportunity (see Figure 1, Panel B).[23] The PSRC/Kirwan measure provides a more nuanced classification of neighborhood quality than simple poverty rate, and in 2012, KCHA passed a Board Resolution embedding this neighborhood quality metric in all subsequent policy and siting discussions. Except as otherwise noted, all references to "opportunity neighborhoods" as used in this paper refer to the PSRC/Kirwan definition.

Table 2A provides the distribution of all KCHA households with children by opportunity-ranked neighborhoods. In 2016, 23.3 percent of federally subsidized households with children resided in high/very high-opportunity areas. KCHA's success to date and the growing body of research on the impacts of neighborhood quality have inspired its ambitious goal that by 2020, 30 percent of all federally assisted families with children will reside in high/very high-opportunity areas. Two philosophies underlie KCHA's approach to geographic choice. The first — building from prior research on the importance of long-term and persistent neighborhood exposure[24] — is that access to opportunity neighborhoods alone is not sufficient; rather, success hinges on families' being able to access *and* stay in such neighborhoods. The second is a belief that KCHA's policies should expand, not prescribe, families' choices, and in doing so, should not mandate opportunity moves. The agency believes that families are — especially when given adequate information and options — the best persons to make decisions about their housing. This belief again speaks to the necessary balance between investing in existing poor neighborhoods and providing access to high-opportunity settings.

CONSIDERING LOCAL MARKETS

Our experience in King County demonstrates that strategies for broadening geographic choice among federally subsidized families will vary by region and market based on numerous conditions. These include: current and trending demographic patterns; housing market characteristics; neighborhood characteristics and resources[25]; transportation infrastructure; employment opportunities; local and state regulatory frameworks regarding tenant rights and community development; and the nature and extent of housing and mobility resources available, including the capacity and flexibility of local PHAs. A careful assessment of local characteristics is necessary to determine which strategies are most likely to improve access to quality neighborhoods.

Table 2. KCHA Federally Subsidized Households with Children by Opportunity Ranking

A. All KCHA Federally Subsidized Households with Children				
Opportunity Ranking	Tenant-based Vouchers	Project-based Vouchers	Public Housing	Total
Very High	5.1%	26.5%	6.0%	6.8%
High	13.1%	46.8%	18.6%	16.5%
Moderate	16.5%	0.5%	14.6%	16.5%
Low	37.6%	18.2%	30.6%	34.8%
Very Low	25.7%	8.0%	30.2%	25.4%
N*	4,542	427	1,266	6,235

B. Tenant-based Voucher Households with Children			
	In KCHA units**	In private-market units	Total
Very High	20.2%	4.2%	5.1%
High	27.1%	12.2%	13.1%
Moderate	16.8%	18.6%	18.5%
Low	16.1%	39.0%	37.6%
Very Low	19.8%	26.0%	25.7%
N*	273	4,269	4,542

*Opportunity ranking N is less than for census tract poverty due to some census tracts being omitted that fall outside the urban growth area.
**KCHA units include KCHA workforce housing units where a tenant-based voucher holder has chosen to reside.
Source: KCHA 2016 administrative data.

Once these local characteristics have been examined, housing practitioners may consider two broad sets of approaches for increasing subsidized housing recipients' interest in, access to, and persistence in both existing and emerging opportunity neighborhoods: 1) *tenant-based mobility strategies* that focus on expanding residents' demand for and access to opportunity areas, and; 2) *site-based affordability strategies* that focus on increasing the supply of deeply-subsidized housing options in opportunity areas. We believe these two kinds of strategies are complementary, and that their effectiveness will depend on market and resident characteristics.

TOOLBOX A: TENANT-BASED MOBILITY STRATEGIES

The most widely documented approach for increasing neighborhood options is the use of tenant-based HCVs. Though these vouchers can be used in any rental unit in a region that falls within the specified FMR range, voucher-holders have generally persisted in moving to or remaining in high-poverty areas. This phenomenon has led to a rich and additive history of program and research strategies focused on supporting families with HCVs in moving to lower-poverty or otherwise defined 'opportunity' communities, including the Gautreaux lawsuit in Chicago in the 1970s, HUD's Moving to Opportunity (MTO) demonstration in the 1990s, and more recent initiatives in Baltimore, Dallas, Chicago, and other areas.[26] This work has spurred further mobility pilot programs implemented by PHAs throughout the country, each focused on increasing HCV families' access to opportunity neighborhoods.[27]

Informed by this growing knowledge-base, KCHA's tenant-based mobility strategies have focused on two complementary approaches to increase voucher-holders' knowledge of, interest in, and access to high-opportunity neighborhoods: small-area payment standards, and high-touch mobility counseling. As of 2016, 18 percent of KCHA's tenant-based HCV families with children lived in high/very high-opportunity areas (see Table 2A).

Small-Area Payment Standards

KCHA has long recognized the disparities in rental markets between east and south areas of the County. To account for this, in 2003, KCHA used its MTW authority to establish a two-tier payment standard that reflected rent differentials across the region, and to decouple payment standards from regional FMRs. These early actions served to increase the purchasing power of vouchers in more expensive Eastside markets.

In 2016, KCHA expanded on this initial policy shift by moving to a five-tier payment standard that further aligned with changing and varied housing sub-markets. Under the five-tier system, subsidy levels matched local market prices through a more finely-grained, zip-code-based approach that ensured that HCVs did not lead the market in lower-cost areas while providing adequate purchasing power to enable households to access or remain in high-cost/high-opportunity markets. Following this policy shift, the 2016 cost differential between the voucher payment standard for a two-bedroom apartment in the lowest and highest payment tiers was $740 per month or nearly $9,000 annually, and maximum permissible rents ranged from 84 percent to 132 percent of the HUD regional two-bedroom FMR.[28] This difference speaks to the tremendous variation in local housing markets in King County.

Preliminary results suggest that KCHA's small-area payment standards hold promise for both cost savings and expanded geographic choice. Conservative estimates suggest that the five-tier system saves KCHA over $750,000 annually as compared to the old two-tier system and upwards of $1 million annually as compared to a one-tier system.[29] These cost savings allow KCHA to issue more vouchers, serve more families, and ensure that they are more likely to access their preferred neighborhoods. Initial data on the impact of this policy change on housing location is encouraging: the percentage of all new voucher holders that moved to higher-cost/opportunity tiers increased by 22 percent between 2015 and 2016; for new voucher holders with children, the increase was an even more pronounced 79 percent.[30] Early evidence also indicates that KCHA's shift to small-area payment standards has reduced the growth in shelter burden, enabling existing tenant-based voucher holders to remain in higher-cost neighborhoods where rents are rapidly escalating. These preliminary but promising results suggest a possible alternative to the approach currently being explored by HUD.[31]

High-Touch Mobility Counseling

In 2013, KCHA funded a local community-based organization to provide high-intensity mobility counseling to existing HCV holders with elementary-aged children interested in moving from lower- to higher-opportunity schools.[32] The Community Choice Program (CCP) ran from 2013 to early 2017 and provided intensive housing counseling, housing search assistance, flexible financial assistance for pre- and post-move needs, and post-move counseling and services. This pilot program provided important evidence that housing search and moving assistance was a common need for many families with vouchers in King County, regardless of the preferred neighborhood; in higher-opportunity markets, these needs appeared to be even greater. Although families were encouraged to move to a subset of opportunity neighborhoods,[33] move decisions ultimately rested with families and no constraints were placed on where CCP participants' vouchers could be used.

Among CCP participants that had moved with housing assistance by the end of 2016, 60 percent had relocated to opportunity areas, and all of these families had subsequently remained in their housing (many for a year or longer). The CCP demonstration helped KCHA to identify effective service and financial assistance elements. Caseload sizes remained small to ensure counseling staff availability for one-on-one case management and housing search. Though this approach reflects best practice themes in the literature,[34] the cost, both in staffing and in the use of flexible financial assistance for pre- and post-move supports, all of which appear to have been key to program participation and successful moves, raises questions about the program model's long-term sustainability and scalability.

Additional Considerations from KCHA's Experience with Tenant-Based Mobility Strategies

While small-area payment standards and high-intensity mobility counseling appear to hold promise for broadening geographic choice, more needs to be learned about the effectiveness of these approaches — mobility counseling, search assistance, payment standard constructs, financial incentives — relative to one another and when implemented as complementary elements. To this end, KCHA is currently embarking on a revised tenant mobility strategy, Creating Moves to Opportunity (CMTO), in partnership with a dozen other PHAs and an interdisciplinary research team led by Raj Chetty and Nathan Hendren that will further test and refine approaches to mobility. The first demonstration for CMTO will take place in Seattle and King County and will test various tenant-centered strategies using a randomized trial design to evaluate the effectiveness and efficiency of various approaches.

Though the strategies noted above are promising, they have historically not been widely available to PHAs. KCHA was able to move to small-area payment standards only because of its MTW status.[35] Similarly, KCHA's MTW authority provided the financial flexibility necessary to fund high-intensity counseling and other non-traditional forms of client assistance. Agencies without MTW funding flexibility must rely on court settlements and external funding sources to support mobility efforts, a challenging model for long-term sustainability and one prone to service fragmentation. Federal reductions in funding for PHA administrative fees, currently at a 77 percent prorate, only exacerbate this picture.

The long-term success and sustainability of tenant-based mobility strategies hinge on the degree to which families are successful in both accessing and retaining housing in high-cost markets. Tenant-based mobility strategies are tied to market dynamics, and as market costs increase, so too will voucher program expenses. Initial program cost savings secured through a shift to more fine-grained payment standards will not, over time, offset increased per unit and program costs as programs scale up and larger numbers of HCV participants choose to live in higher-cost markets. This raises the difficult issue of balancing geographic choice objectives with the need to support as many households as possible during a time of rising homelessness and declining federal funding.

TOOLBOX B: SITE-BASED AFFORDABILITY STRATEGIES

Tenant-based mobility strategies are not the only — and over the long term, perhaps not the most effective — approach for expanding neighborhood access. For this reason, over the last decade, KCHA has evolved a set of *site-based affordability strategies* that provide access to housing in opportunity areas in the form of hard units.[36] KCHA sees this strategy as complementary to tenant-based mobility supports. KCHA has advanced four approaches to expanding access to quality neighborhoods through site-based interventions:

Strategy 1: Acquisition and preservation of subsidized workforce housing

Over the last 20 years, KCHA has developed or acquired and preserved an extensive portfolio of workforce housing.[37] KCHA currently owns or controls 4,868 units of housing not funded through traditional HUD programs[38]; 55 percent of these units are located in high/very high-opportunity neighborhoods. Of these 2,700 units, 28 percent house extremely low-income households through the use of either project-based (224) or tenant-based (529) HCVs; the remaining 72 percent serve families between 40 and 100 percent of AMI.

Targeted acquisitions are generally older, 100-plus-unit, class B multifamily developments, where KCHA typically holds initial rents to pre-acquisition levels and dramatically slows rent growth by basing increases on operating costs and not on market-driven demand. KCHA's controlled rents become more affordable compared to surrounding market rents over time, and project-based HCVs are layered in for a limited percentage of the units (typically 15–20 percent). This approach preserves long-term affordability for workforce housing in increasingly costly markets, provides mixed-income communities through project-based subsidies, and affords neighborhood access for extremely low-income households with tenant-based vouchers who would otherwise have difficulty securing landlord acceptance in these opportunity markets.[39]

Acquisitions are generally financed through private debt, with Low-Income Housing Tax Credit (LIHTC) partnerships utilized where significant rehabilitation or new construction is involved.[40]

Strategy 2: Purchase of smaller apartment complexes for conversion to public housing

Utilizing HOPE VI grants and MTW flexibility, KCHA has demolished obsolete public housing in high-poverty neighborhoods and renovated other complexes through conversion to project-based HCVs and LIHTC financing. These demolitions and conversions have placed the agency below its federal allocation ("Faircloth limit") of public housing subsidies. To redeploy these resources, KCHA is purchasing smaller apartment complexes (typically in the 30-unit range) in high-opportunity areas and re-activating banked public housing subsidies. To address the inability of public housing properties to support debt, KCHA is financing these acquisitions through the use of MTW working capital and through pooled multi-property refinancings where excess cash flow from the pool is covering the additional debt. KCHA's Property Management Department directly manages these properties once public housing subsidies are activated. Between historic siting patterns and new acquisitions, KCHA currently has 1,233 public housing units sited in high-opportunity neighborhoods. Significant reductions in public housing funding proposed for FFY 2018 would effectively end the use of this approach.

Strategy 3: Layering project-based HCV subsidies onto regional nonprofit development

A third site-based strategy matches project-based HCVs to a development pipeline of nonprofit-sponsored affordable housing in opportunity neighborhoods. KCHA currently serves 247 households across 17 properties that employ this approach. These projects are typically financed through a combination of LIHTCs and local soft funding sources.[41] Similar to Strategy 1, this approach layers deep rental subsidies on top of units typically priced at 60 percent of AMI in order to serve extremely low-income families. KCHA's MTW status has simplified the agency's ability to coordinate project-based voucher contracting with local government funding decisions by allowing KCHA to utilize its government partners' competitive project selection processes in lieu of HUD's separate project-basing procurement requirement for placing rent subsidies.

Strategy 4: Layering project-based HCV subsidies onto Inclusionary/Incentive Zoning and Multifamily Tax Exemption (MFTE) Programs

KCHA is also exploring ways to layer HCVs on affordable housing units being developed under a variety of inclusionary/incentive zoning and MFTE programs being offered by East King County cities. These programs typically set affordability targets at 60–80 percent of AMI and are inaccessible to extremely low-income families as well as lower-wage working families. KCHA is exploring the inclusion of mandatory or voluntary project-based HCV contracts for a percentage of these 60–80 percent AMI units. Rents would remain at the currently required affordability levels and KCHA would layer in rental subsidies to make units available to households at or below 30 percent of AMI.

Promising Evidence on the Effectiveness of Site-Based Affordability Strategies

Although site-based affordability strategies require further evaluation and research, preliminary indications suggest that KCHA's approach is effective.

Long-term cost containment. KCHA's site-based strategies seem to have mitigated the prohibitively high subsidy costs involved in supporting extremely low-income households' access and retention of housing in rapidly escalating, high-cost markets over time. Over time, both operating cost-based and AMI-indexed rents will lag significantly behind market rent levels, relieving the need for subsidy expenditures to escalate with the market in order to maintain household affordability. Figure 2 illustrates such cost containment, demonstrating the actual $528/month (over $6,000 per year) difference in 2016 between rents at the Newporter, a typical 120-unit KCHA workforce housing complex in the Newport neighborhood of Bellevue, and rents for comparable units in that neighborhood. Given current trends, site-based strategies provide cost-effective alternatives to tenant-based HCVs in high-cost markets.

Persistence in opportunity neighborhoods. Early evidence indicates that families in units provided through KCHA's site-based strategies exhibit housing stability for several years after move-in. Such outcomes have likely been positively affected by KCHA's use of its MTW authority to waive exit voucher requirements for project-based vouchers.

Figure 2. Private Market and KCHA Property Rent Trends in East King County, 1996–2016

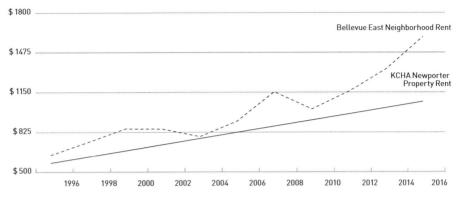

Sources: KCHA administrative data; Dupre and Scott Renal Market Trends reports.

Additional Considerations from KCHA's Experience with Site-Based Affordability Strategies

As with KCHA's tenant-based mobility strategies, the agency's MTW status helped support the flexibility necessary for implementing site-based affordability strategies by removing the limit on the number of vouchers the agency can project-base, by streamlining the project-basing process, and by waiving exit voucher requirements. Taking site-based strategies to scale also requires access to private capital. KCHA's credit enhancement arrangement with King County is an essential tool for property acquisition. Portfolio scale and the length of time KCHA has been pursuing these approaches have also been critical in providing seasoned properties with reduced debt and increased cash flow as well as the strong balance sheet necessary for access to capital markets. KCHA's decision to invest early in higher-poverty communities , before they transitioned (under Kirwan metrics) to opportunity areas, also allowed KCHA to get ahead of rising acquisition costs later in these neighborhoods' evolution.

One critique of site-based affordability strategies has been that they could lead to re-concentrations of poverty. KCHA's experience has been that this is not the case, as the agency carefully accounts for the number of deeply subsidized units in a given area and strategically positions sites when making acquisition decisions. In this vein, site-based approaches may be better positioned than tenant-based approaches to foster social networks among extremely low-income residents as well as connections between residents and community services.

CONCLUSION: FUTURE DIRECTIONS FOR PRACTICE, RESEARCH, AND FUNDING

KCHA's experiences provide one example of how extremely low-income residents' neighborhood options can be expanded in a large suburban region comprised of heterogeneous neighborhoods. Given King County's sub-market characteristics, the toolbox for expanding geographic choice mixes tenant-based mobility and site-based affordability strategies. Much remains to be learned about the ideal balance between these two approaches, and about what strategies and tools will work for PHAs in other regions.

Practitioner Flexibility and Practice-Based Learning

As noted at the outset, geographic choice among low-income families cannot be broadened through a one-size-fits-all approach but must be addressed through locally-driven innovation. For this reason, practitioners and researchers need to foster a more robust national conversation, including shared lessons from the field, on how to assess and respond strategically to regional conditions. Such conversations may be most necessary for formulating site-based affordability strategies, about which there has been relatively little dialogue.

Additionally, practice-based improvement in approaches to broaden families' geographic choice is contingent on expanded HUD support for program innovation. The MTW program, slated to expand by another 100 PHAs over the next five years, will be critical in encouraging continued innovation. As noted throughout this paper, the MTW program has played an important role in providing KCHA with the program and funding flexibility necessary to develop strategies that align with local needs and market challenges. Similar flexibility will be critically needed by incoming MTW agencies and more broadly by the industry in general.

Research on Both Tenant-Based and Site-Based Strategies

In addition to the development and dissemination of practice-based knowledge, there is a need for rigorous research on different mobility approaches.

With regard to tenant-based strategies, a number of research questions remain untouched. Within the realm of mobility counseling, matters including ideal dosage, service focus, and service timing require further study, and questions remain as to how mobility services should be implemented and scaled cost-effectively. Future research must also account for the relative effects of financial incentives, as compared to counseling or other service strategies, on housing access, retention, and costs. Differences in the effectiveness of tenant-based strategies for different population subgroups should be investigated, as should (if differences exist) ways of effectively targeting these subgroups. Finally, as neighborhood dosage is an essential underpinning to positive long-term outcomes, additional research is needed on strategies for connecting households to new neighborhoods and improving neighborhood persistence.

Similarly, there are myriad research directions for better understanding site-based affordability strategies. Expanding on positive preliminary evidence, additional research is needed on the experiences and outcomes of families living in site-based opportunity housing. While site-based strategies do inherently restrict residents' choices about both units and neighborhoods, there is a need to explore whether this has an adverse effect on tenant interest in site-based housing options, on their experiences during or following access to housing, and on longer-term life outcomes for children. Future research should also explore whether residents in site-based units are more likely to access and/or persist in high-opportunity communities as compared to tenant-based voucher holders in the same areas. Relatedly, future inquiry should explore the effects of site-based affordability strategies (as compared to tenant-based mobility approaches) on fostering social networks as well as connections to social services. Rigorous analyses are also needed on the costs of specific site-based strategies over time and in relation to tenant-based mobility approaches.

More generally, the mobility research to date has been largely hampered by the lack of a consistent and national metric for capturing opportunity. Such a metric is an important next step for this research, and will facilitate both effective geographic targeting and cross-site research and evaluation. Broader research should also incorporate more comprehensive and consistent benefit-cost approaches that consider longer-term cost savings of mobility approaches across multiple publicly funded systems as well as longer-term impacts upon the national economy that may be driven by improved life outcomes for low-income children.

Increased Resources for Housing Assistance

At their core, the strategies being used in King County and elsewhere require long-term federal resources to support extremely low-income families' access to (any) housing markets. As housing needs continue to grow, so does the call for federal resources. Declining support from HUD means not only that fewer families can be served, but that fewer families can be served in opportunity areas, impacting not only choice but also voucher-assisted households already residing in these higher-cost markets. This will have long-term effects on the ability of housing assistance to curb intergenerational poverty trends and to reverse racial and economic segregation. The reality is that *more* funds, not less, are needed in order to serve both the growing number of shelter-burdened and homeless families, and to do so in a way that expands geographic options and improves long-term life outcomes. Much as KCHA has taken the long view with its regional mobility work, a similar orientation is required at the national level to ensure that practitioners have the necessary resources and flexibility to innovate in response to local market conditions and, ultimately, to substantially change the playing field for low-income families served by federal housing assistance.

Bibliography

Andersson, Fredrik, John C. Haltiwanger, Mark J. Kiutzbach, Giordano E. Palloni, Henry O. Pollakowski, and Daniel H. Weinberg. 2016. "Childhood Housing and Adult Earnings: A Between-Siblings Analysis of Housing Vouchers and Public Housing." Working Paper 22721. National Bureau of Economic Research. October.

Briggs, Xavier de Souza, Susan J. Popkin, and John Goering. 2010. *Moving to Opportunity: The Story of an American Experiment to Fight Ghetto Poverty.* New York: Oxford University Press.

Chetty, Raj, Nathaniel Hendren, and Lawrence F. Katz. 2016. "The Effects of Exposure to Better Neighborhoods on Children: New Evidence from the Moving to Opportunity Experiment." *American Economic Review* 106, no. 4: 855–902.

Cunningham, Mary K., Molly Scott, Chris Narducci, Sam Hall, and Alexandra Stanczyk. 2010. "Improving Neighborhood Location Outcomes in the Housing Choice Voucher Program: A Scan of Mobility Assistance Programs." Washington, DC: Urban Institute.

Dupre and Scott. 2016. *Apartment Vacancy Report* 34, no 2 (September).

Galvez, Martha M., Jasmine Simington, and Mark Treskon. 2017. "Moving to Work and Neighborhood Opportunity: A Scan of Mobility Initiatives by Moving to Work Public Housing Authorities." Washington, DC: Urban Institute.

Kahn, Peter B. and Geoffrey B. Newton. 2013. "The Small Area FMR Demonstration." *Cityscape* 15, no. 1: 325–28.

King County, Office of Economic and Financial Analysis. 2015a. "Demographic Trends of King County." http://www.kingcounty.gov/independent/forecasting/bench-marks/Demographics.aspx (accessed March 24, 2017).

———. 2015b. "Household Income in King County." http://www.kingcounty.gov/inde-pendent/forecasting/benchmarks/Household%20Income.aspx (accessed March 24, 2017).

Kneebone, Elizabeth, and Alan Berube. 2013. *Confronting Suburban Poverty in America.* Washington, DC: Brookings Institution Press.

Mayo, Justin, and Lornet Turnbull. 2011. "Shifting Population Changes Face of South King County." *Seattle Times*, February 23.

Polikoff, Alexander. 2006. *Waiting for Gautreaux: A Story of Segregation, Housing, and the Black Ghetto.* Evanston, IL: Northwestern University Press.

PRRAC. 2015. "Housing Mobility Programs in the U.S." Poverty and Race Research Action Council.

Rosenberg, Mike. 2016. "Seattle Rents Now Growing Faster Than in Any Other U.S. City." *Seattle Times,* July 21.

Sard, Barbara, and Douglas Rice. 2016. "Realizing the Housing Voucher Program's Potential to Enable Families to Move to Better Neighborhoods." Washington, DC: Center on Budget and Policy Priorities.

Schwartz, Heather L. 2010. "Housing Policy is School Policy: Economically Integrative Housing Promotes Academic Success in Montgomery County, Maryland." New York: Century Foundation.

Schwartz, Heather L, Kata Mihaly, and Breann Gala. 2016. "Encouraging Residential Moves to Opportunity Neighborhood: An Experiment Testing Incentives Offered to Housing Voucher Recipients." *Housing Policy Debate* 2, no. 2: 230–60.

Sharkey, Patrick. 2013. *Stuck in Place: Urban Neighborhoods and the End of Progress Toward Racial Equality.* Chicago: University of Chicago Press.

Turnbull, Lornet. 2013. "Poverty Hits Home in Local Suburbs like S. King County." *Seattle Times,* May 19.

US Census Bureau. 2016. "Quick Facts, King County, Washington." https://www.census.gov/quickfacts/table/PST045216/53033,53 (accessed March 24, 2017).

Endnotes

1   Sard and Rice (2016).

2   Low-poverty neighborhoods are defined as those in which less than 10 percent of residents fall below the Federal Poverty Level (FPL). Federal housing subsidies include: 1) tenant-based Housing Choice Vouchers, 2) project-based Housing Choice Vouchers, and 3) public housing.

3   Sharkey (2013); Chetty, Hendren, and Katz (2016).

4   "Extremely low-income" is defined as having a gross household income less than 30 percent of Area Median Income (AMI).

5   National numbers are not available for the distribution of Project-based vouchers (PBVs). While PBVs and Project-based Rental Assistance are both site-based, given their programmatic differences, they should not be compared directly.

6   Chetty, Hendren, and Katz (2016) has given new momentum to this discussion.

7   Recent results from Andersson et al (2016) demonstrate benefits, including children's increased later earnings and lower incarceration rates, from subsidized housing occupancy even in higher poverty/lower opportunity neighborhoods.

8   In King County, this includes currently high-poverty communities along the expanding light rail corridor in South County.

9   One example is in White Center, an unincorporated pocket of King County south of Seattle that is one of the poorest and most diverse communities in the region, where KCHA has led a decade-long effort to redevelop over 130 acres of World War II-era public housing into mixed-income communities. This initiative has reduced the number of federally-subsidized units in White Center, shifting subsidies on a one-for-one replacement basis for use in site-based strategies in opportunity neighborhoods. The remaining deeply subsidized rental units are integrated with market-rate homeownership units and extensive new community facilities with a strong educational focus.

10 See Kneebone and Berube (2013); additional information from the authors that is specific to suburban King County can also be found at: http://confrontingsuburbanpoverty.org/the-communities/tukwila-seattle/.

11 US Census Bureau (2016).

12 King County, Office of Economic and Financial Analysis (2015a).

13 US Census Bureau (2016).

14 King County, Office of Economic and Financial Analysis (2015b).

15 Mayo and Turnbull (2011); Turnbull (2013); Kneebone and Berube (2013).

16 In 2016, a Zillow report indicated that rents in Seattle—up 9.7 percent from the previous year—were rising faster than in any other city in the country. See Rosenberg (2016).

17 Dupre and Scott (2016).

18 As evidence of this rise, in 2015, the County Executive and the Mayor of Seattle declared a state of emergency over homelessness.

19 This includes 3,078 tenant-based voucher households that have ported into King County from other areas. Approximately half of these households are from Seattle, reflecting the trends of gentrifying neighborhoods pushing low-income families out to lower-cost suburban areas. Port-in numbers are included in the statistics presented in this article.

20 In 2016 the agency also provided 4,868 units of workforce rental housing financed primarily through the Low-Income Housing Tax Credit (LIHTC) and bond programs.

21 There are currently over 3,800 Public Housing Agencies in the United States.

22 Sixty-three percent of census tracts in King County were classified as low-poverty in 2015 as compared to 39 percent of all census tracts nationally. Relatedly, only 1 percent of census tracts in King County exhibited concentrated poverty (i.e., poverty rates greater than 40 percent among residents) as compared to 5 percent of census tracts nationally. (Numbers based on ACS 2015 5-year estimates.)

23 More information about the PSRC/Kirwan opportunity mapping can be found at: http://www.psrc.org/growth/tod/growing-transit-communities-strategy/equity/opportunity-mapping/.

24 Schwartz (2010).

25 Including culturally appropriate amenities and support networks.

26 For detailed descriptions of these initiatives, see, for example, Polikoff (2006) and Briggs, Popkin, and Goering (2010).

27 Further description of such mobility (assistance) pilots can be found in Cunningham et al. (2010), PRRAC (2015), and Galvez, Simington, and Treskon (2017). A detailed summary of evidence on barriers faced by voucher holders in accessing opportunity areas, and on pilot mobility counseling and financial assistance programs in overcoming these barriers, can be found in Schwartz, Mihaly, and Gala (2016).

28 It is important to note that the shift to the five-tier system did not result in lower subsidy amounts for voucher holders in any tier. This was partly a result of KCHA holding payment standards flat in 2015 in anticipation of the policy shift to be made the following year; this outcome also reflected rising housing costs in all tiers in King County (including in the lowest tiers) and the corresponding market adjustments made by KCHA to reflect actual area housing costs. In limited cases, existing rent levels were grandfathered where payment standards in that submarket were reduced.

29 Preliminary projections suggest a range of possible cost savings, with these values being the most conservative. Additionally, it should be noted that projected cost savings will diminish as more families move to higher cost/opportunity markets.

30 For all new voucher holders, the percentage moving to high-cost/opportunity tiers rose from 16.6 percent in 2015 to 20.2 percent in 2016. Among new voucher holders with children, these percentages increased from 10.6 percent in 2015 to 19.0 percent in 2016.

31 Kahn and Newton (2013).

32 This work was informed by Schwartz (2010)'s study of academic performance among children in subsidized housing who moved to high-opportunity areas.

33 Opportunity areas for CCP were initially defined according to a small subset of areas near high performing schools that also had high Kirwan/PSRC area rankings; eventually and to balance out lack of housing supply in these narrowly-defined areas, the program's opportunity area definition was expanded to include all Kirwan-defined High and Very High Opportunity areas.

34 Cunningham et al. (2010).

35 When KCHA made these changes and without MTW flexibility, KCHA would have been required to apply a single regional payment standard or to participate in HUD's Small Area Fair Market Rents (SAFMR) demonstration. We believe this program involves an overly complex number of payment tiers. Dallas currently uses more than 65 payment standards based on over 300 zip codes (see http://www.dhadal.com/PDF/S8/2017%20PS%20HCV.pdf). See Kahn and Newton (2013) for the methodology used to determine payment tiers in HUD's Small Area Fair Market Rents (SAFMR) demonstration. Non-MTW PHAs may apply for an exception rent waiver to allow payment standards to exceed the regional FMRs; however, this approach is generally limited to 120 percent of the FMR and would not adequately capture the full range of sub-markets in many regions. It should also be noted that as of late 2017, HUD's

final rule on SAFMRs had been upheld and was in full effect thus allowing non-MTW PHAs to adopt SAFMRs in place of the metro area FMR or as the basis of exception payment standards.

36   We differentiate *site-based affordability strategies* from *project-based strategies* which typically refer to just one subsidy type (project-based HCVs) as well as from *place-based* or *place-conscious strategies* which typically describe PHAs' efforts to improve housing and broader neighborhood quality in higher poverty, lower opportunity neighborhoods.

37   Workforce housing generally targets residents earning 40 percent to 100 percent of AMI.

38   That is, not funded through the public housing, multi-family Section 8, or Section 202 programs.

39   As noted in Table 2B, 47.3 percent of tenant-based voucher households with children who choose to live in KCHA-owned units are located in high/very high-opportunity areas—a much higher percentage than reside in private-market units in such areas. The difference suggests the importance of PHA- or nonprofit-owned workforce housing in facilitating voucher holders' access to opportunity markets.

40   KCHA utilizes bank lines of credit to enable closings on new acquisitions within timeframes that are competitive with private-sector purchasers. KCHA's overall bankability is the product of a strong revenue-producing asset base of workforce housing, strengthened by a credit enhancement agreement with King County that confers the County's AAA credit rating on KCHA's debt instruments. The ability to periodically roll short-term debt into longer-termed pooled refinancings which include more seasoned properties with strong cash flow has enabled KCHA to achieve debt coverage requirements and reduce front-end equity gaps. KCHA's workforce housing portfolio is managed by outside third-party management companies under the supervision of an in-house Asset Management Department.

41   In King County, one such local source has been ARCH (A Regional Coalition for Housing), a consortium of East King County Cities that pool funding to assist with preserving and increasing the supply of housing for low– and moderate-income households in this high opportunity sub-region of the County. More information can be found at http://www.archhousing.org.

Expanding Access to Homeownership as a Means of Fostering Residential Integration and Inclusion

CHRISTOPHER HERBERT, SHANNON RIEGER, AND JONATHAN SPADER
Joint Center for Housing Studies of Harvard University

E fforts to enable greater integration of communities by socioeconomic status and race/ethnicity have to confront the issue of housing affordability. Cities, towns and neighborhoods that offer access to better public services, transportation networks, shopping, recreational opportunities, parks and other natural amenities have higher housing costs. Expanding access to these communities for those with lower incomes and wealth necessarily entails some means of bringing housing in these areas within their financial reach. While households' financial means are central to this issue, affordability intersects with race/ ethnicity in part because minorities are more likely to be financially constrained. But to the extent that these areas are also disproportionately home to majority-white populations, discrimination and other barriers to racial/ethnic integration must also be confronted along with affordability barriers.

Enabling greater integration also entails some means of fostering residential stability by maintaining affordability in the face of changing neighborhood conditions. This issue is perhaps most salient in the context of neighborhoods that are experiencing gentrification, where historically low-income communities are experiencing rising rents and house values, increasing the risk of displacement of existing residents and blocking access to newcomers with less means. More generally, increases in housing costs in middle- and upper-income communities may also contribute to increasing segregation by putting these areas further out of reach of households with more modest means.[1]

It is common to think of subsidized rental housing as the principal means of using public resources to expand access to higher-cost neighborhoods and to maintain affordability in areas of increasing demand. But for a host of reasons, policies that help to make homeownership more affordable and accessible should be included as part of a portfolio of approaches designed to achieve these goals.

For example, survey research consistently finds that homeownership remains an important aspiration of most renters, including large majorities of low- and moderate-income households and racial/ethnic minorities.[2] Moreover, because owner-occupied homes account for substantial majorities of the existing housing stock in low-poverty and majority-white neighborhoods, expanding access to homeownership offers the potential to foster integration and to increase access to opportunity for low-income households and households of color. There is also solid evidence that homeownership remains an important means of accruing wealth, which in turn can help expand access to higher-cost communities.[3] Owning a home is associated with greater residential stability, in part because it provides protection from rent inflation, which can help maintain integration in the face of rising housing costs. Finally, in communities where owner-occupied housing predominates, there may be less opposition to expanding affordable housing options for homeowners.

The goal of this paper is to identify means of structuring subsidies and other public interventions intended to expand access to homeownership with an eye towards fostering greater socioeconomic and racial/ethnic integration. While the policies presented here are largely designed to address financial and informational barriers to homeownership associated with lower incomes and wealth, given the disproportionate share of minorities among these households, efforts to make homeownership more attainable has the potential to foster greater racial/ethnic integration as well. Of course, efforts to eradicate discriminatory treatment, both explicit and implicit, in housing and mortgage markets are also of great importance. However, these efforts are not the main focus of this paper, but are covered extensively in other papers prepared for this symposium.

The first section of this paper describes the principal barriers to homeownership and key existing policies aimed at them and discusses what is known about the potential for these approaches to foster integrative moves. The next section presents a set of policy options to support homeownership that could be enacted over the next five to ten years with the effect of fostering greater racial/ethnic and economic integration on a meaningful scale. The paper concludes with some final thoughts on the rationale for the recommended policy approaches and the importance of simultaneous efforts to combat discrimination and expand the supply of affordable housing as complementary activities.

BARRIERS TO HOMEOWNERSHIP, THE PRINCIPAL EXISTING POLICIES TO ADDRESS THEM, AND THEIR SPATIAL IMPACTS

A review of the principal barriers to homeownership and existing policies designed to address them is a helpful starting point for the recommendations to follow. A key goal of this review is to evaluate existing policies' potential for fostering or discouraging greater economic and racial integration so as to envision changes to them that would enhance their integrative potential. This section is structured around three broad categories of barriers: the affordability of homeownership, access to credit, and informational deficits. In general, policies will be more likely to foster integration to the extent that they increase the relative purchasing power of low- and moderate-income households, expand knowledge of housing options to enable integrative moves, and alleviate displacement pressures from rising house prices.

Affordability

The most fundamental barrier to homeownership for low- and moderate-income households is not having sufficient income or wealth to qualify for a home mortgage. Herbert et al. (2005) conduct a comprehensive review of the literature assessing barriers to homeownership and come to the conclusion that a lack of savings to meet downpayment requirements and pay closing costs is by far the most significant financial barrier to buying a home. For this reason, policies providing downpayment assistance are consistently found to have the greatest potential for increasing home-ownership rates among low-income and minority households.[4] In addition, subsidies in the form of downpayment assistance have the potential not only to make it feasible for such households to buy a home, but also to increase purchasing power to bring lower-poverty neighborhoods more within their reach.

In practice, downpayment assistance is available through a variety of federal, state and local programs, although the overall scale of these efforts is relatively small.[5] There has been very little formal evaluation of downpayment assistance programs and so not much is known about the location choices of those assisted through these programs. One study of buyers assisted through the HOME program found that the pre- and post-purchase neighborhoods of participants were quite similar on most dimensions, including incomes, house prices, poverty rates, and racial composition, suggesting that the program had little effect — for better or worse — on the choice of neighborhood.[6] However, this result likely stems in part from the fact that the program targets fairly low-income households and generally provides relatively modest amounts of assistance.

In order to facilitate moves to higher-cost areas, downpayment assistance levels may need to be higher per household than is common in most existing programs, a policy consideration that points to several important tradeoffs. First, fewer households could be assisted for a given amount of funding. Second, to the extent that the assistance is in the form of a grant, the households assisted would be receiving a much larger windfall in being selected for the grant. Shared equity homeownership models, where the assistance is in one way or another recaptured upon sale of the home along with a share of the home's appreciation, can address these concerns.[7] Many shared equity models are also structured so that the subsidy is tied to a specific housing unit (often in support of new construction) and so have the potential for expanding the supply of affordable homeowner units in neighborhoods that might otherwise be out of reach of low- and moderate-income buyers.

The principal means of funding either shared equity purchases of existing homes or subsidizing the development of affordable homeownership units generally are the federal HOME Partnerships program, the Federal Home Loan Banks Affordable Housing Program (AHP), and locally-mandated inclusionary zoning (IZ) programs. However, each of these efforts is fairly small-scale.[8] In addition, relatively little is known about the neighborhood location of units supported by shared equity programs or development subsidies. One ongoing study of shared equity programs has preliminary findings that in some cases buyers do appear to gain access to higher-income neighborhoods, while in others there is little change in neighborhood conditions upon purchase.[9] With regard to IZ programs specifically, Schwartz et al. (2012) examined the location of IZ units in 11 programs and found that overall these homes were located in a broad range of neighborhoods, but were generally areas with low poverty.

While financial supports for downpayments or to lower purchase prices have the most potential for increasing homeownership attainment, by far the most widespread financial subsidy for homeownership is the mortgage interest deduction (MID), which effectively subsidizes mortgage payments through the federal tax code. However, as documented by analysis from the Joint Committee on Taxation (2017), low- and moderate-income households are both much less likely to claim the deduction and are likely to realize smaller tax savings if they do since the value of the credit increases with the amount of interest paid, the taxpayer's marginal tax rate, and the degree to which the total deductions exceed the standard deduction.

Given the low incidence and modest financial benefit accruing to households most likely to be on the cusp of being able to afford to buy a home, it is not surprising that the MID is consistently found to have little effect on overall homeownership rates.[10] This conclusion is also consistent with the results of studies that have simulated the impact of lower interest rates on the ability to qualify for a mortgage and found that even reductions of interest rates on the order of several percentage points have little impact on the likelihood of qualifying for a mortgage.[11]

But while the MID's net impact on the homeownership rate is small, several studies have found that the neutral impact at the national level reflects an average of increases in homeownership rates in some markets and decreases in others, with the variations reflecting differential impacts on local house prices. Hilber and Turner provide the most in-depth assessment of these inter-metropolitan impacts, finding that in markets where the housing supply is more restricted the MID inflates house prices and reduces overall homeownership rates for higher-income households (earning more than 120 percent of the area median income), while in less restricted markets there is little effect on home prices and so the tax subsidy does help to increase homeownership rates among higher-income households.

Importantly, this same study also finds no effect in any markets on homeownership among lower-income households (earning less than 80 percent of area median income). Regarding this finding the authors conclude: "We speculate that this is because the housing market within a city tends to be segmented by income and the MID provides a tax subsidy only to the relatively higher income households that itemize. Consequently, we expect that lower income housing will generally not experience house price changes due to changes in the subsidy." While not a focus of their study, one implication of the MID's effect of inflating house prices only at the upper end of the price distribution would be to contribute to income segregation by pushing higher-cost communities farther out of reach for lower- and moderate-income households.

Access to Credit

In addition to income and wealth constraints that make it harder to qualify for a mortgage, access to credit for low-income and minority renters can also be constrained by weaker credit histories, less stable employment histories, and higher debt levels that make it difficult to meet typical underwriting standards.[12] Based on several comprehensive reviews of the literature, discrimination in mortgage markets, while difficult to assess, also likely remains an important obstacle to purchasing a home for minorities by deterring applications and making it more difficult to be approved for a loan and more difficult to obtain favorable terms if approved.[13] Indeed, there is substantial evidence that in the years leading up to the housing bust, minorities were more likely to obtain high-priced subprime loans with risky and arguably predatory features even after controlling for the credit risk of applications.[14]

In general, greater difficulty in qualifying for mortgage credit would be expected to reduce homeownership rates for lower-income and minority households. To the extent that moves to homeownership may support greater integration, particularly for Hispanics and Asians, this barrier to homeownership would potentially contribute to higher levels of segregation.[15] In addition, to the extent that borrowers are steered to subprime or otherwise higher-priced credit and away from conventional conforming loans, these credit barriers may reduce the size of mortgages that could be obtained, limiting the location choice of borrowers to areas with lower housing costs.

The principal policy levers for expanding access to mortgage financing are various forms of duty-to-serve provisions aimed at low-income and minority consumers who apply to financial institutions, with the most important being the requirements for depository institutions under the Community Reinvestment Act (CRA) and for the government-sponsored enterprises (GSEs), Fannie Mae and Freddie Mac, as part of their regulatory oversight. While these duty-to-serve provisions have the potential to reach a broad swath of the market, there is only limited evidence of their efficacy in increasing access to credit among target populations and even less that they actually increase homeownership rates. In their review of existing evidence, Levitin and Ratcliffe (2014) conclude that the GSE and CRA rules have had modest but positive effects on overall credit flows to low- and moderate-income individuals and areas, with CRA tending to have somewhat larger impacts on lending volumes. In a review of the literature related to the GSE housing goals, Jaffee and Quigley (2012) conclude that to the extent the GSEs did expand credit flows to target groups, this expansion was achieved largely by replacing lending available through the Federal Housing Administration (FHA). However, as Levitin and Ratcliffe argue, the replacement of FHA lending with GSE-backed loans may provide benefits through lower borrowing costs.

In a review of fair housing concerns arising from regulation of the GSEs, Korman (2013) points out the tension inherent in the housing goals that on the one hand establish metrics aimed at expanding lending to low-income borrowers regardless of where they live and at the same time also set metrics aimed at expanding lending in low-income communities and in particular in areas with substantial minority populations. The locational aspects of these latter goals could have the effect of reinforcing the concentration of low-income households — and particularly minority households — in these areas. Of course, these spatial goals were included to remedy historical patterns of redlining which cut minority communities off from access to mainstream credit, and so are not without merit.

There has been very little empirical analysis of the extent to which duty-to-serve provisions increase lending to lower-income borrowers in higher-income neighborhoods or support access by minorities to predominantly white neighborhoods. Friedman and Squires (2005) is one of the few studies that examine whether CRA has been associated with expanded lending to minorities in predominantly white neighborhoods. These authors do find evidence of an increase in this lending in metropolitan areas where CRA lenders have higher market shares. In a comprehensive analysis of CRA's role in expanding access to credit, the Joint Center for Housing Studies (2002) also examined whether CRA lenders have higher volumes of lending to low-income borrowers in higher-income neighborhoods and found that there is a statistically significant effect, although the increase in lending is smaller than in neighborhoods targeted by the duty-to-serve provisions.

Information Deficits and Limitations on Housing Search

The process of becoming a homeowner is also impeded among low-income and minority households by a lack of information and knowledge about the homebuying process, including searching for a home, negotiating the purchase, and qualifying for a mortgage. In a 2003 national consumer survey, Fannie Mae found that blacks, Hispanics, and low-income households were more likely than all households to rate themselves as having below-average understanding of, and less confidence in their ability to complete key stages in, the homebuying process.[16] More recently, a similar Fannie Mae survey found that blacks, Hispanics, and low-income households had less understanding of the qualifications needed to obtain mortgage financing, which would potentially limit their attempts to pursue homeownership.[17] Ethnographic research on minorities and immigrants further supports these findings.[18]

Housing searches aiming to purchase homes in whiter or higher-cost neighborhoods may face greater constraints due both to discrimination and to differences in knowledge by race and socioeconomic status about housing options and the level of effort required for search. Specifically, integration may be affected by the degree to which there are racial or socioeconomic differences in how individuals search for homes to purchase, and in particular whether there are differences in the neighborhoods selected for home search. Importantly, Krysan (2008) finds that while a majority of blacks search for homes (including both for purchase and for rent) in neighborhoods where whites are in the majority, whites are very unlikely to search in areas where they account for less than 70 percent of the population. Thus, white search behavior may be more important for reinforcing patterns of racial segregation than search by African Americans. Meanwhile, Krysan and Bader (2009) examine how knowledge of different communities in the Chicago metropolitan area differs among whites, African Americans and Hispanics and by socioeconomic status, and how these differences influence where members of these groups search for housing. Overall, the findings of these studies point to the importance of affirmative efforts to promote integration by addressing shortfalls in the knowledge of different communities in a region both among racial and ethnic minorities and those of lower socioeconomic status.

Efforts to address the information gaps among potential homebuyers are among the broadest-reaching kinds of public supports for homeownership, with HUD-supported efforts serving several hundred thousand people a year. These services aim to improve homebuying choices by educating and counseling people about the homebuying and mortgage finance process, including whether to buy a home or not. Despite its widespread availability, homeownership education and counseling (HEC) has not been subject to much rigorous evaluation. Collins and O'Rourke (2011) review the available evidence on the efficacy of counseling, which finds some limited support counseling contributes to lower default rates. However, there is no available evidence about whether HEC has any effect on the attainment of homeownership.

In terms of the spatial implications of HEC, while standard curricula provide information about the housing search process, there does not appear to be any emphasis on how prospective buyers ought to select where to search for a home. Many of the organizations offering HEC are community-based organizations in lower-income communities and so may have a tendency to support home purchases in their service areas. Thus, while HEC may present an opportunity to help inform homebuyers about a broader range of communities in which to search, HEC efforts to date have not focused on this goal and so have probably had more limited integrative effects than they could.

OBSERVATIONS ON EXISTING EFFORTS TO SUPPORT HOMEOWNERSHIP AND THEIR CONTRIBUTION TO INTEGRATION

In considering the range of existing policies that provide support for homeownership, a few broad conclusions can be drawn. First, the principal barrier to homeownership for low- and moderate-income households is a lack of savings to meet downpayment and closing cost requirements. For that reason, policies that promote savings or provide upfront subsidies will have the greatest impact in bringing homeownership within reach. Expanding access to conventional mortgage financing also has an important role to play by directly addressing affordability concerns and also because of the association of subprime lending with higher degrees of segregation, particularly among African-Americans.

But in order for an expansion of homeownership to contribute to socioeconomic and racial/ethnic integration, prospective homebuyers have to be able to afford homes in higher-cost neighborhoods. To expand residential opportunities, the degree of financial support provided has to both be significant enough to open up the doors to these communities and well-targeted to lower-income households so as to increase the relative purchasing power of this group. A second broad conclusion is that beyond financial subsidies, there is also a need to better inform minority and low-income households about the homebuying process and specifically to expand the range of communities included in the housing search process by whites and minorities alike to create the possibility of more integrative moves.

A third broad conclusion is that while for the most part homeownership policies have not been constructed with an explicit focus on their impact on residential integration, there is no doubt that various homeownership supports have made a significant contribution to segregation over time, and so whether intended or not these policies often have a spatial dimension.[19] Certainly, further research is needed to better understand the effects of homeownership supports on socioeconomic and racial/ethnic integration. But this history points to the importance of understanding the spatial implications of homeownership supports and tailoring them to encourage integration and not reinforce existing patterns of segregation.

Indeed, given what is known, there are clear opportunities to tailor housing policies to be more likely to foster integration by increasing the relative purchasing power of lower-income households, by addressing information deficits that may constrain the search process of low-income and minority homebuyers, and by assuring access to safe and fairly priced mortgage products. The next section presents our recommendations in each of these areas.

WHAT WILL IT TAKE FOR HOMEOWNERSHIP POLICY TO MOVE THE NEEDLE ON INTEGRATION?

There are two critical considerations in framing homeownership policy options that could move the needle on residential integration: first, whether the policy would affect a large enough number of households to make a difference in residential patterns across the country; and second, whether the policy is fiscally feasible given the current political environment (meaning, the policy cannot require a large increase in public spending). Of course, there is also the question of whether, fiscal questions aside, the policy is otherwise likely to gain enough political support to be enacted. While difficult to handicap, the ideas presented below have been developed with an eye toward having at least the potential for bipartisan support.

The policy options outlined below are not new ideas, though in this paper they are newly filtered through the lens of how they would be expected to contribute to racial and economic integration. While not all of the policies have an explicit spatial dimension, to the extent that they increase the purchasing power of low- and moderate-income households relative to higher-income households, they arguably have the potential to foster integration by opening up a broader range of communities to lower-income buyers.

There are four categories of policies proposed below: changes in federal income tax policy related to the mortgage interest deduction and savings; increased support for housing counseling; broad policy considerations in maintaining or modifying duty-to-serve obligations affecting mortgage lending; and recommendations for better targeting and potentially expanding funding for downpayment assistance.

Potential Reforms to Federal Tax Policy

With the passage of the Tax Cuts and Jobs Act of 2017 (TCJA), the near-term opportunity for reform of tax policy may have passed, but to the extent that the opportunity for changes to the tax code may arise again, there are a number of changes that should be considered that would better support homeownership among low- and moderate-income households. Given its high cost and lack of impact on homeownership rates, particularly among low- and moderate-income households, the MID has been the subject of numerous proposals for reform from both the political right and left.[20] While the TCJA did not eliminate the MID, it did limit its value by reducing the limit on the size of mortgages eligible for the deduction from $1 million to $750,000, by doubling the size of the standard deduction (thus reducing the incentive to itemize), and by capping the deductibility of state and local taxes (again, reducing the likelihood that taxpayers will claim the MID).

Past proposed reforms of the MID fall into two broad categories: those that would modify the way in which mortgage interest payments are treated and those that would, to avoid encouraging the use of debt, replace the MID with a one-time tax credit tied to home purchase and not to mortgage interest payments.[21] Most reforms to the treatment of interest payments would convert the deduction into a credit so that the value to the homeowner is not a function of marginal tax rate. In fact, adopting a credit for mortgage interest payments would mitigate the effect of the TCJA since the ability to claim the credit would not depend on whether taxpayers itemize their deductions. These credits could be made refundable in order to reach households with limited federal tax obligations or, to limit the fiscal impact, could be used only to offset actual taxes owed. These various proposals establish a share of interest payments that would be eligible for the credit (typically around 15 percent) up to a specified cap (either a fixed national limit or a limit linked to area house prices). The tax credit could also be subject to a phase-out at higher income levels to reduce the cost to the federal government and to target the benefits at those most likely to have their decision to own hinge on this benefit, although these goals may also be achieved by simply capping the amount of tax credit.

The use of a tax credit (rather than a deduction) subject to a cap and limited to primary residences results in much greater targeting of these tax benefits to low- and moderate-income households and thus has much greater potential to actually increase homeownership rates. Green and Vandell (1999) simulate this type of change and estimate that the impact on homeownership rates among low-income and minority households would be substantial, on the order of 6–10 percentage points.

Other proposals call for creating a tax credit that would be claimed upon purchase of a home rather than an annual credit linked to mortgage interest payments in order to avoid encouraging the use of debt. These relatively large, one-time credits are typically targeted at first-time homebuyers, although some proposals include all home purchasers. Limiting the credit to first-time buyers and to just the year of purchase would greatly reduce the foregone tax revenues and would focus the credit on addressing the downpayment constraint that is the principal financial obstacle to homeownership. Gale, Gruber, and Stephens-Davidowitz (2007) propose these types of credits, with estimates that refundable credits of $3,000 for single filers and $6,000 for married filers could be offered at a cost to the federal government of about $16 billion. Harris, Steuerle, and Eng (2013) propose much larger credits of $12,000 for single filers and $18,000 for married filers. They do not provide explicit costs of such credits, but they would obviously cost on the order of 3–4 times the smaller proposal, or perhaps more if more households are able to attain homeownership as a result. Credits of this magnitude would obviously have a much greater impact on the price of homes that would be within reach of homebuyers and so have a potentially larger integrative effect.[22]

If the goal of changing the tax code is to better target tax expenditures to increase homeownership for low- and moderate-income households, a large, upfront credit for first-time buyers would arguably be most effective as this would directly address the principal barrier to owning and bring a broader range of communities within financial reach. This type of credit would have the additional benefit of not being tied to the amount of debt taken on and so would not encourage borrowing. But if other fiscal or political considerations make such a switch unlikely, a refundable credit for interest payments that is capped and phased out at higher income levels would allow for larger benefits directed to households who are on the cusp of being able to afford a home.

Of course, any reform of the MID would have to be thoughtfully phased in over time to avoid disruptions to the housing markets in places where it has inflated home prices. Rappaport (2016) estimates that removing the MID would lower prices by an average of 5 percent across 269 metropolitan areas, ranging from a low of 1 percent to a high of 9 percent. This range is not dissimilar from earlier estimates by Capozza, Green, and Hendershott (1996) that gave a range of declines from 2 to 13 percent across 63 market areas. However, with the recent changes introduced by the TCJA, the share of tax filers itemizing their deductions will decline sharply, in effect eliminating the MID in most areas of the country. As a result, any impact on house prices of changing the MID will already have taken effect and so the potential for further impacts on housing prices from changes in the tax code will be limited.

One concern with offering substantial tax credits to enable home purchase is that households' inability to save for a downpayment and closing costs may be a sign of lack of financial readiness for the demands of homeownership. For these reasons, another avenue to support homeownership which should be adopted are subsidies to encourage savings to buy a home. Saving incentives would achieve multiple goals, including encouraging thrift, fostering improved budgeting skills, and drawing on more of the homebuyer's own savings to build up a downpayment.[23] Enhancing personal savings would also expand the purchasing power of low- and moderate-income households and so further integrative goals.

Modifications to existing tax incentives for retirement savings could better encourage savings and provide a simple and efficient means for delivering subsidies to homebuyers, potentially without any increase in federal tax expenditures. The Joint Committee on Taxation estimates that in 2016 the value of expenditures for defined contribution plans and individual retirement accounts (IRAs) amounted to $113 billion. As with the MID, these benefits currently largely accrue to higher-income households in part because they are based on the marginal tax rate of the filer since the benefit accrues from shielding the income saved from taxation.[24] Restructuring the availability and distribution of tax benefits for qualified savings would have the potential to reach millions of households and potentially have a significant impact on homeownership opportunities.

One model for reforming savings incentives is the Universal Savers Credit (USC) proposed by the Center for American Progress.[25] The USC would provide for a refundable tax credit for contributions to qualified savings plans. The credit could be subject to a cap and also scaled by income to reduce the level of expenditure and make the benefit more progressive. CAP estimates that a 30-percent credit for qualified savings with annual caps similar to current limits on retirement savings could be revenue-neutral relative to current expenditures but would be much better targeted to low- and moderate-income filers. Under this approach, savers would essentially be given a 30-cent match for each dollar saved up to the cap. As with current tax benefits, the credit would apply to savings in 401k and 403b accounts as well as IRAs but would also apply to new accounts that can be expressly used for purposes other than retirement savings, including buying a home, educational expenses, or health care costs. The new accounts could also be rolled over into qualified retirement accounts if the saver decides to not pursue these other goals.[26] Such a credit would also have the virtue of promoting savings among lower-income households for purposes other than homeownership.

A package of changes that create a modest-sized first-time buyer credit coupled with an incentive for household savings might offer the most effective means of enabling homeownership and greatly expanding the purchasing power of low- and moderate-income households. Limiting the size of the first-time buyer credit would result in less revenue spent on those who would buy a home in the absence of a credit, while those who need additional cash to afford a home would be induced to acquire it over time through savings, helping to ensure that buyers are better prepared for homeownership.

Expand Support for Housing Education and Counseling

A substantial expansion of the availability of homeownership education and counseling (HEC) also has the potential to reach a significant number of households at a reasonable cost. While there is not yet convincing evidence that pre-purchase HEC increases homeownership rates, given survey findings that lower-income and minority households in particular lack accurate information about mortgage products and mortgage qualifications, there is also a compelling case that HEC could address a potentially important barrier to homeownership for these groups. In recognition of this value, the Bipartisan Policy Center (BPC) Housing Commission included an expansion of federal support for HEC among its recommendations to support homeownership.[27]

More broadly available HEC would potentially contribute to greater integration by increasing homeownership opportunities among racial and ethnic minorities and low- and moderate-income households more generally. However, as discussed above, to date HEC programs have not been designed with the explicit goal of supporting pro-integrative moves. Thus, in addition to expanding HEC availability, there is also a need to develop and test approaches to enhance HEC's ability to overcome geographical blind spots that may impede moves that would foster integration.[28] These pilots could explore the development of HEC curriculum and tools to help broaden homebuyers' knowledge of metropolitan regions where they are seeking to buy and help identify communities that would provide appealing opportunities to live but might not otherwise be on a homeseeker's search list.

As noted by the BPC, in order to expand access to high-quality counseling there is a need for investment in the infrastructure of the HEC industry. This infrastructure would include the technology and networks needed to enable clients to receive assistance that is more convenient, tailored to their needs, and at lower cost. This infrastructure would also include public campaigns to raise awareness of the value and availability of HEC. An expansion of counseling would also need to come with safeguards to ensure the consistency and quality of the services delivered.

In order to achieve these goals, a steady and reliable source of funding is needed to support investments in technology, delivery systems, outreach, and service provision. HUD has long been the principal source of funding for housing counseling, providing $42 million in funding in the most recent fiscal year.[29] While one option would be to expand the amount of funding raised though Congressional appropriations, in the current environment an increase in direct appropriations may be difficult. Another funding source that has been proposed is to require that a small portion of the mortgage servicing fee (perhaps 1–3 basis points) collected by loan servicers be directed to a government-controlled fund to support housing counseling.[30] Since the value of housing counseling is realized by both borrowers and the mortgage industry, there is a clear logic for tying the funding to mortgage payments. The revenue raised by such a fee could be distributed via a competitive grant process, much as current HUD funding is distributed to support direct service provision, but would also include allocations for investment in technology and systems, the development of curriculum and other instructional tools, and organizational operating costs.

Maintain an Emphasis on Access to Credit

Regulatory mandates for the mortgage market to take proactive steps to reach lower-income and minority homebuyers are another critically important means of supporting sustainable homeownership at a significant scale. While there is a lack of evidence that mandates under CRA and the GSE housing goals have increased home-ownership, there is a body of research indicating that these rules do improve access to safe and fairly priced mortgage products. Specifically, a number of studies have concluded that CRA is associated with expanded access to credit for lower-income households and neighborhoods and may also increase lending to lower-income and minority borrowers in higher- income neighborhoods. There is less evidence that the GSE housing goals have expanded access to credit, but a more convincing case that the goals have increased the GSEs' market share at the expense of FHA lending. Still, such a substitution of credit source would yield benefits for borrowers in the form of lower costs. Perhaps more importantly, expanding access to lending from conventional sources would also act as a bulwark against the expansion of the high-cost and risky subprime lending that came to dominate many low-income, minority communities during the early 2000s.

Given the role these regulations have played in expanding access to credit, it is important that such duty-to-serve mandates be preserved as part of the regulatory oversight of financial entities engaged in mortgage lending — a particularly salient point with regard to the ongoing debate about GSE reform. Levitin and Ratcliffe (2014) present a compelling case that such duty-to-serve requirements are justified by the public sector's role in backstopping these institutions and are warranted given the existing evidence that these rules have not unduly increased financial risk and have had a positive impact on lending to targeted populations.

But even taking the mandate for duty-to-serve provisions as given leaves open the question of how they can be structured to incentivize lending that supports integrative home purchases and does not unduly concentrate lending to low-income and minority homebuyer in communities where these households are already concentrated. One way to mediate against this unintended consequence would be to avoid goals that include both borrower and neighborhood incomes in a single measure, such as the low-income area goal for the GSEs, which is currently defined (at least in part) based on both the income of the borrower and the income and racial composition of the neighborhood. Such goals can have the unintended consequence of encouraging lending to low-income borrowers in low-income and high-minority neighborhoods. Certainly, goals that encourage lending to low-income and minority communities are important to support demand and investment in these communities. But establishing goals that encourage lending to low-income borrowers throughout market areas would better support integrative areas.

A full assessment of reforms of CRA and GSE lending mandates that would better serve the goals of integration is beyond the scope of the present paper. But as opportunities arise for reform, more thought should be given to how the mandates can be used to support lending to lower-income and minority households that expands their range of neighborhood choice. Given the complexity of balancing the goals of expanding lending to specific populations and to neighborhoods traditionally underserved by the finance system, qualitative assessments of efforts by financial institutions to ensure that their loan products and services serve low-income and minority borrowers throughout metropolitan areas may well be more appropriate than quantitative measures of lending activity. CRA has long included such a qualitative review, while recent enacted duties to serve for the GSEs have also adopted this approach.

Expand the Stock of Shared Equity Housing

The most direct way to assure access to homeownership opportunities for lower-income households in neighborhoods they could not otherwise afford is to provide upfront subsidies to reduce the cost of the housing. However, depending upon the income level targeted and the cost of housing in the area, the subsidy amount required can be large, easily in the tens of thousands of dollars or more in the highest-cost markets. To ensure that public funds used for this purpose work to create a permanent stock of affordable housing in these areas, there should be a strong emphasis on some form of shared equity homeownership rather than on grants or low-cost loans.

The HOME program is one of the most significant sources of downpayment assistance for homebuyers, but given program rules most of this funding does not require afford-ability periods beyond the 5 to 15 years required by statute. As Lubell (2014) notes, HUD could steer participating jurisdictions to adopt shared equity approaches either by mandating much longer affordability periods for high levels of subsidies, or it could simply encourage greater adoption of this practice by disseminating model shared equity program guidelines.

However, an expansion of shared equity homeownership programs would require a substantial increase in funding for subsidies. Given the current budgetary climate, a significant expansion of HOME funding is unlikely — in fact, further cuts to this program are much more likely. For this reason, shared equity models are unlikely to be an approach that will move the needle on integration in the foreseeable future. Nonetheless, there is still good reason to seek opportunities to expand the existing stock of these units through whatever federal funding is available and through inclusionary zoning programs that are becoming increasingly common. While these efforts may add units at the rate of only thousands a year and not hundreds of thousands, over an extended period of time they may still accumulate a meaningful number of homes.

However, in addition to a source of funding for subsidies, increasing the scale of shared equity programs will require additional sources of operating funding for stewards of these programs and, given the reluctance of lenders to accept resale provisions in shared equity arrangements, a source of financing for homebuyers. Thus, there are additional roles for policy in helping to create models for sustainable funding of these efforts and a source of mortgage financing.

CONCLUDING THOUGHTS

Any meaningful effort to foster greater socioeconomic and racial/ethnic integration has to consider means of creating entry paths into higher-opportunity communities through homeownership — not only because a significant portion of homes in these areas are owner-occupied but also because homeownership remains an important aspiration of the vast majority of Americans. Expanding opportunities to buy a home would also benefit low- and moderate-income neighborhoods by providing residents with greater protection against rising housing costs, enhancing residential stability for their benefit and the benefit of the community. Homeownership may also promote greater inclusiveness of low-income and minority residents in these communities by putting them on more equal footing with other homeowners in these areas.

Ultimately, the goal of the recommendations presented above is to expand the range of housing choices available to lower-income and minority families and individuals by expanding the financial resources and information at their disposal. The principal avenues recommended for achieving these goals is for changes to federal policies that have broad market implications through the tax code, the provision of widely accessible housing education and counseling, and regulation of mortgage lending. Just as these policies in the past have been instrumental in creating the conditions that produced segregation and urban decline, they are also potentially powerful tools to promote integration and neighborhood stabilization. In today's fiscal climate, reform of these policies is also likely the only way to direct meaningful amounts of financial resources to this issue given the magnitude of existing tax expenditures for homeowners and retirement savers.

Bibliography

Bipartisan Policy Center. 2013. *Housing America's Future: New Directions for National Policy.* Report of the Bipartisan Policy Center Housing Commission.

Bischoff, K., and S.F. Reardon. 2014. "Residential Segregation by Income, 1970–2009." *Diversity and Disparities: America Enters a New Century*, edited by John Logan, 208–33. New York: Russell Sage Foundation.

Bostic, R.W., P.S. Calem, and S.M. Wachter. 2005. "Hitting the Wall: Credit as an Impediment to Homeownership." In *Building Assets, Building Credit: Creating Wealth in Low-income Communities*, edited by Nicolas Retsinas and Eric Belsky, 155–172. Washington, D.C.: Brookings Institution Press; Cambridge, MA: Joint Center for Housing Studies of Harvard University.

Bourassa, S.C., and M. Yin. 2008. "Tax Deductions, Tax Credits and the Homeownership Rate of Young Urban Adults in the United States." *Urban Studies* 45, no. 5-6: 1141-61.

Breymaier, R., forthcoming. "The Social and Economic Value of Intentional Integration Programs in Oak Park, IL." Cambridge, MA: Joint Center for Housing Studies, Harvard University.

Calavita, N., and A. Mallach, eds. 2010. *Inclusionary Housing in International Perspective: Affordable Housing, Social Inclusion, and Land Value Recapture.* Cambridge, MA: Lincoln Institute of Land Policy.

Capozza, D.R., R.K. Green, and P.H. Hendershott. 1996. "Taxes, Mortgage Borrowing, and Residential Land Prices." In *Economic Effects of Fundamental Tax Reform*, edited by Henry Aaron and William Gale, 171-210. Washington, D.C.: Brookings Institution Press.

Collins, J.M., and C. O'Rourke. 2011. "Homeownership Education and Counseling: Do We Know What Works?" Washington, D.C.: Mortgage Bankers Association, Research Institute for Housing America.

Congressional Budget Office. 2016. "The Distribution of Household Income and Federal Taxes 2013." Washington, D.C. June.

Drew, R.B. and C. E. Herbert, 2011. "Postrecession drivers of preferences for homeownership." *Housing Policy Debate* 23, no. 4, 666-687.

Fannie Mae. 2003. "Fannie Mae National Housing Survey." Washington, D.C.: Fannie Mae.

— — —. 2015. *What Do Consumers Know About the Mortgage Qualification Criteria?* Washington, D.C.: Economic & Strategic Research Group, Fannie Mae. December.

Fischer, M.J. 2013. "Black and White Homebuyer, Homeowner, and Household Segregation in the United States, 1990-2010." *Social Science Research* 42, no. 6: 1726-36.

Friedman, S., and G.D. Squires. 2005. "Does the Community Reinvestment Act Help Minorities Access Traditionally Inaccessible Neighborhoods?" *Social Problems* 52, no. 2: 209–31.

Friedman, S., H.S. Tsao, and C. Chen. 2013. "Housing Tenure and Residential Segregation in Metropolitan America." *Demography* 50, no. 4: 1477–98.

Gale, W.G., J. Gruber, and S.I. Stephens-Davidowitz. 2007. "Encouraging Homeownership through the Tax Code." *Tax Notes*, June 18: 1171–89.

Glaeser, E.L., and J.M. Shapiro. 2003. "The Benefits of the Home Mortgage Interest Deduction." *Tax Policy and the Economy* 17: 37–82.

Green, R.K., and K.D. Vandell. 1999. "Giving Households Credit: How Changes in the US Tax Code Could Promote Homeownership." *Regional Science and Urban Economics* 29, no. 4: 419–44.

Grinstein-Weiss, M., G.A.N. Chowa, and A.M. Casalotti. 2010. "Individual Development Accounts for Housing Policy: Analysis of Individual and Program Characteristics." *Housing Studies* 25, no. 1: 63–82.

Grinstein-Weiss, M., M.W. Sherraden, W. Rohe, W.G. Gale, M. Schreiner, and C. Key. 2013. "Long-Term Follow-up of Individual Development Accounts: Evidence from the ADD Experiment." *American Economic Journal: Economic Policy* 5, no. 1: 122–45.

Harris, B.H., C.E. Steuerle, and A. Eng. 2013. "New Perspectives on Homeownership Tax Incentives." *Tax Notes* 141, no. 12: 1315–32.

Herbert, C.E., D.R. Haurin, S.S. Rosenthal, and M. Duda. 2005. "Homeownership Gaps among Low-income and Minority Borrowers and Neighborhoods." Washington, D.C.: U.S. Department of Housing and Urban Development. http://www. huduser. org/publications/HOMEOWN/HGapsAmongLInMBnN. html.

Herbert, C.E., D.T. McCue, and R. Sanchez-Moyano. 2014. "Is Homeownership Still an Effective Means of Building Wealth for Low-income and Minority Households." In *Homeownership Built to Last: Balancing Access, Affordability, and Risk after the Housing Crisis*, edited by Eric Belsky, Christopher Herbert, and Jennifer Molinsky, 50–98. Washington, D.C.: Brookings Institution Press.

Hilber, C.A., and T.M. Turner. 2014. The Mortgage Interest Deduction and Its Impact on Homeownership Decisions." *Review of Economics and Statistics* 96, no. 4: 618–37.

Immergluck, D. 2011. *Foreclosed: High-risk Lending, Deregulation, and the Undermining of America's Mortgage Market*. Ithaca, NY: Cornell University Press.

Jackson, K.T. 1985. *Crabgrass Frontier: The Suburbanization of the United States*. New York: Oxford University Press.

Jaffee, D., and J.M. Quigley. 2012. "The Future of the Government-Sponsored Enterprises: The Role for Government in the US Mortgage Market. In *Housing and the Financial Crisis,* edited by Edward Glaeser and Todd Sinai, 361–417. Chicago: University of Chicago Press.

Joint Center for Housing Studies of Harvard University. 2002. *The 25th Anniversary of the Community Reinvestment Act:Access to Capital in an Evolving Financial Services System.* Cambridge, MA: Joint Center for Housing Studies of Harvard University.

Joint Committee on Taxation. 2017. "Estimates of Federal Tax Expenditures for the Fiscal Years 2016-2020." Joint Committee on Taxation, the Congress of the United States. January 30.

Korman, H. 2013. "Furthering Fair Housing, the Housing Finance System, and the Government Sponsored Enterprises." In *Where Credit is Due: Bringing Equity to Credit and Housing After the Market Meltdown,* edited by Christy Rogers and john a. powell, 267–98. Lanham, MD: University Press of America.

Krysan, M. 2008. "Does Race Matter in the Search for Housing? An Exploratory Study of Search Strategies, Experiences, and Locations." *Social Science Research* 37, no. 2: 581–603.

Krysan, M., and M.D. Bader. 2009. "Racial Blind Spots: Black-White-Latino Differences in Community Knowledge." *Social Problems* 56, no. 4: 677–701.

Levin, Ezra. 2014. Upside Down: Homeownership Tax Programs. Center for Enterprise Development.

Levitin, A.J., and J. Ratcliffe. 2014. "Rethinking Duties to Serve in Housing Finance." In *Homeownership Built to Last: Balancing Access, Affordability, and Risk after the Housing Crisis,* edited by Eric Belsky, Christopher Herbert, and Jennifer Molinsky, 317–50. Washington, D.C.: Brookings Institution Press.

Listokin, D., E.K. Wyly, B. Schmitt, and I. Voicu. 2001. "The Potential and Limitations of Mortgage Innovation in Fostering Homeownership in the United States." *Housing Policy Debate* 12, no. 3: 465–513.

Logan, J.R., and B.J. Stults. 2011. "The Persistence of Segregation in the Metropolis: New Findings from the 2010 Census." Census brief prepared for Project US2010.

Lubell, J. 2014. "Filling the Void Between Homeownership and Rental Housing: A Case for Expanding the Use of Shared Equity Homeownership." In *Homeowners hip Built to Last: Balancing Access, Affordability, and Risk after the Housing Crisis,* edited by Eric Belsky, Christopher Herbert, and Jennifer Molinsky, 203–30. Washington, D.C.: Brookings Institution Press.

Massey, D.S., and N.A. Denton. 1993. *American Apartheid: Segregation and the Making of the Underclass.* Cambridge, MA: Harvard University Press.

Mills, G., W.G. Gale, R. Patterson, G.V. Engelhardt, M.D. Eriksen, and E. Apostolov. 2008. "Effects of Individual Development Accounts on Asset Purchases and Saving Behavior: Evidence from a Controlled Experiment." *Journal of Public Economics* 92, no. 5: 1509–30.

Rappaport, David. 2016. "Do Mortgage Subsidies Help or Hurt Borrowers?" Finance and Economics Discussion Series 2016-081. Washington, D.C.: Board of Governors of the Federal Reserve System.

Ratner, M.S. 1996. "Many Routes to Homeownership: A Four Site Ethnographic Study of Minority and Immigrant Experiences." *Housing Policy Debate* 7, no. 1: 103–45.

Reid, C.K. 2014. "To Buy or Not to Buy? Understanding Tenure Preferences and the Decisionmaking Processes of Lower-Income Households." In *Homeownership Built to Last: Balancing Access, Affordability, and Risk after the Housing Crisis*, edited by Eric Belsky, Christopher Herbert, and Jennifer Molinsky, 143–71. Washington, D.C.: Brookings Institution Press.

Ross, S.L., and J. Yinger. 2002. *The Color of Credit: Mortgage Discrimination, Research Methodology, and Fair-Lending Enforcement.* Cambridge, MA: The MIT Press.

Schwartz, H.L., L. Ecola, K.J. Leuschner, and A. Kofner. 2012. "Is Inclusionary Zoning Inclusionary? A Guide for Practitioners." Technical Report. RAND Corporation.

Spencer, G. 2013. "Integrating Housing Counseling into the Residential Marketplace: A Strategic Framework for Bolstering Homeownership, Lowering the Risk to the Housing Finance System, and Creating Sustainable Funding." Working Paper. Washington, D.C.: Homeownership Preservation Foundation.

Theodos, B., K. Temkin, R. Pitingolo, and D. Emam. 2015. "Homeownership for a New Era: Baseline Report on the Cornerstone Homeownership Innovation Program." Washington, D.C.: The Urban Institute.

Turnham, J., C. Herbert, S. Nolden, J. Feins, and J. Bonjorni. 2004. "Study of Homebuyer Activity through the HOME Investment Partnerships Program." Washington, D.C.: Department of Housing and Urban Development.

Turner et al 1999

Turner, M.A., F. Freiberg, E. Godfrey, C. Herbig, D.K. Levy, and R.R. Smith. 2002. *All Other Things Being Equal: A Paired Testing Study of Mortgage Lending Institutions.* Washington, D.C.: The Urban Institute.

Weller, C.E., and S. Ungar. 2013. "The Universal Savings Credit." Washington, D.C.: Center for American Progress. July 19.

Wilson, E., and R.R. Callis. 2013. "Who Could Afford to Buy a Home in 2009? Affordability of Buying a Home in the United States." Current Housing Reports. Washington, DC: US Census Bureau. May.

Endnotes

1   Bischoff and Reardon (2014); Logan and Stults (2011).

2   Drew and Herbert (2011).

3   Herbert, McCue, and Sanchez-Moyano (2014).

4   Wilson and Callis (2013); Listokin et al. (2001).

5   Herbert et al. (2005).

6   Turnham et al. (2004).

7   Lubell (2014).

8   Herbert et al. (2005); Calavita and Mallach (2010).

9   Theodos et al. (2015).

10 Capozza, Green, and Hendershott (1996); Green and Vandell (1999); Glaeser and Shapiro (2003); Bourassa and Yin (2008); Hilber and Turner (2014).

11 Wilson and Callis (2013); Listokin et al. (2001).

12 Bostic, Calem, and Wachter (2005).

13 Ross and Yinger (2002); Turner et al. (1999).

14 Immergluck (2011).

15 Based on data from the 2000 Decennial Census, Friedman, Tsao, and Chen (2013) find that Hispanic and Asian homeowners are less segregated than Hispanic and Asian renters from white households, even taking into account differences in incomes and other household and market measures. Among blacks, homeownership is not as strongly associated with declines in segregation. However, Fischer (2013) finds that black recent homebuyers were less segregated from whites than all black homeowners over much of the period 1992–2010, suggesting that transitions into homeownership were somewhat supportive of integration. However, the differences were not significant by the end of the period.

16 Fannie Mae (2003).

17 Fannie Mae (2015).

18 Ratner (1996); Reid (2014).

19 Jackson (1985); Massey and Denton (1993).

20 See Levin (2014) for a summary of proposals since 2005.

21 Levin (2014).

22 However, an important question is what effect the credit would have on home prices since increases in home prices due to the credit would offset any increase in affordability it provides. Gale, Gruber, and Stephens-Davidowitz (2007) state that if the credit is limited to first-time buyers the price effects would be small, but they do not attempt to empirically assess this claim. Based on the findings of other studies, the degree of price impacts would depend not only on the number of homebuyers claiming the credit but on the degree of housing supply elasticity across markets.

23 Individual Development Accounts (IDAs) offer one proven model for subsidizing savings and supporting transitions to homeownership, but the cost of bringing these efforts to a much larger scale would be significant. For assessments of the efficacy of IDA programs in helping participants to achieve and sustain homeownership, see Grinstein-Weiss, Chowa, and Casalotti (2010), Grinstein-Weiss et al. (2013), and Mills et al. (2008).

24 Congressional Budget Office (2016).

25 Weller and Unger (2013).

26 Current tax rules already allow the penalty-free withdrawals from individual retirement accounts for first-time home purchase up to $10,000 for individuals and $20,000 for married couples. The new account would relax these caps and expand the use of funds.

27 Bipartisan Policy Center (2013).

28 Breymaier (2017).

29 See https://portal.hud.gov/hudportal/HUD?src=/press/press_releases_media_advisories/2016/HUDNo_16-094.

30 Spencer (2013).

What Would It Take for Cities Experiencing Gentrification Pressures to Foster Inclusion Rather than Replacement?

Can Gentrification Be Inclusive?

INGRID GOULD ELLEN
New York University

Gentrification is not a popular word in US cities these days, especially in coastal cities experiencing rapidly rising rents. As more high-income, college-educated, and white households move to downtown areas, existing residents feel increasingly anxious that they will be pushed out of their homes and communities. Yet there is some hope in gentrification too; affluent white households are opting for diverse, city neighborhoods over high-income, racially homogenous suburbs in far greater numbers than they did in earlier decades. These higher-income households can help to shore up city tax bases and possibly spur economic and racial integration. But absent policy intervention, that integration may be only fleeting.

It is worth starting with a definition of gentrification, as the term means different things to different people. I will use the term here simply to describe relative increases in household income, education levels, and/or percentage of residents who are white in initially low-income, central city neighborhoods. In other words, a gentrifying neighborhood is an initially low-income city neighborhood that moves up the socio-economic ladder within its metropolitan area. Using variants of this basic definition, it is clear that gentrification is becoming more common in US cities. For example, the share of initially low-income, central city census tracts that saw large gains relative to the rest of the metropolitan area in their share of residents with college degrees rose from 25 percent during the 1990s to 35 percent during the 2000s. (A large gain is an increase in the ratio of the census tract value to that of the metropolitan area of more than 0.1. For example, a tract that sees the ratio of its college educated share to that of the metropolitan area rise from 0.6 to 0.8 would experience a large relative gain.) The share of low-income city tracts seeing a large gain in percentage of residents who are white relative to the rest of the metropolitan area rose from 7 percent in the 1990s to 18 percent during the 2000s.[1] Other recent studies also highlight the rising incomes and education levels of downtown neighborhoods during the 2000s.[2]

These gains in neighborhood socioeconomic status have been driven largely by the in-movement of higher-income college graduates. To be sure, most college-educated and higher-income households are continuing to choose to move to the suburbs. In 2010, 61 percent of college graduates and 68 percent of higher-income households (those with incomes above the median in their metro area) who had moved in the past year chose homes in the suburbs.[3]

But as compared to recent decades, a larger proportion of higher-status households are now opting for cities, and for low-income and majority-minority neighborhoods within those cities. While their choices enhance integration in the short-term, the concern is that higher-income and college-educated households are bidding up housing prices and rents and displacing existing residents. There is clear evidence that prices and rents are rising in the low-income neighborhoods that are attracting higher-income in-movers. Consider that between 2000 and 2014, initially low-income central city census tracts that experienced large relative gains in income experienced a 42 percent increase in rents on average. By contrast, the initially low-income, central city tracts that did not see large gains in income between 2000 and 2014 saw more modest rent increases of 17 percent.

There is less consensus among researchers that higher-income entry is pushing out existing households. In fact, most of the papers on the topic have found scant evidence that gentrification fuels displacement.[4] These null findings are something of a puzzle as well as a frustration to many practitioners who are certain that they are witnessing low- and moderate-income households being displaced in their communities.

So why the disconnect between research and practice? To some degree, it's explained by the fact that low-income households tend to live in unstable housing conditions, regardless of the neighborhood where they live. In 2014, over 70 percent of renters with incomes under $15,000 paid more than half of their income in rent,[5] and as Matthew Desmond's *Evicted* so powerfully shows, they experience enormous instability in the private market, even when there is no sign of gentrification.

It's also possible that the studies have simply failed to capture the phenomenon because of poor measures and/or inappropriate timing. One shortcoming of existing analyses is that they have typically used residential mobility rates to capture displacement. But mobility does not necessarily equal displacement; many residential moves are voluntary and take people to better neighborhoods and homes. Displacement connotes involuntary moves that may force households to settle for inferior homes and communities. A recent study, which was able to identify the destinations of movers in Philadelphia, finds that disadvantaged residents who live in neighborhoods that gentrify are no more likely to leave their homes than other disadvantaged residents, but when they leave, they are more likely to move to a lower-income neighborhood, suggesting that these moves are less likely to be affirmative choices.[6]

Another issue is that most of the existing papers on displacement focus not on the present but on the 1980s and 1990s. During these earlier decades, the gentrification that took place involved higher-income households moving into neighborhoods that had been decimated by population losses during the 1970s. Consider that the neighborhoods that gentrified between 1990 and 2010 in New York City had lost 26 percent of their population during the 1970s (while the population citywide shrunk by 10 percent). Thus, as higher-income and college-educated households moved into these neighborhoods in the 1990s, high vacancy rates meant that the neighborhoods could accommodate additional residents without directly displacing existing residents or even putting much upward pressure on prices and rents. As the population in central neighborhoods has continued to grow, housing markets have been growing tighter and thus the risk of displacement has likely become higher.

Finally, even if residents are not directly displaced, the rising rents mean that lower-income households, absent subsidies, will likely find it increasingly difficult to move in and remain in gentrifying neighborhoods over time. Research has yet to answer the question of whether gentrifying neighborhoods are able to remain stably integrated over time. In the long-run, do cities experiencing greater gentrification pressures end up with more economically or racially integrated neighborhoods?

While the answer to this question is unclear, it seems likely that policy interventions will be needed to cement integration, at least in some neighborhoods where gentrification pressures are particularly strong. Most policy discussions surrounding gentrification center on efforts to protect individual residents at risk of displacement through legal representation or tenant-based vouchers. Yet while these efforts can be critical in helping individual tenants, they will do little over the longer run to preserve economic diversity, which is shaped much more by the composition of people moving into a neighborhood than by the pattern of exits.

So what can policymakers and community organizations do to secure long-run economic diversity and help make gentrifying neighborhoods more inclusive, or more welcoming to households earning a range of incomes? There are no easy answers, but one relatively simple, if potentially expensive, response is to preserve the substantial stock of affordable housing that already exists in gentrifying areas. Consider the case of New York City, where 12 percent of housing units in gentrifying areas of the city are public housing units and roughly another quarter are privately-owned subsidized housing. If preserved over time, these units can assure some level of economic mixing, and potentially racial mixing too. Preserving public housing is the most straightforward measure, though many public housing units need substantial infusions of capital.

Extending the subsidy agreements of privately owned subsidized housing is more challenging, especially in hot markets where owners demand substantial subsidies. Policymakers will need to decide how much they value integration as they confront trade-offs between preserving fewer units in gentrifying areas and more units in persistently poor areas. In some cities, this trade-off is large, while in others it is fairly modest. Ideally, local officials should negotiate extensions before markets heat up, but getting ahead of the market isn't easy.

Local policymakers can also try to entice owners of market-rate rental housing in gentrifying areas to keep rents affordable for some share of their units through offering property tax breaks or other incentives like low-interest renovation loans. But again, such carrots can be costly. As for sticks, local governments may be able to use their powers of code enforcement to gain leverage over landlords whose buildings need repairs and demand that they keep rents affordable.

In addition to preserving existing affordable units, cities might try to acquire and build new subsidized housing in gentrifying areas. This can be expensive given higher land costs, but where possible, policy makers can take advantage of city-owned land and lock in affordability over the longer run through deed restrictions, land leases, or community land trusts. Finally, another possibility is to harness the market through either mandating or incentivizing owners to include low-rent units in their buildings. In hot markets, developers will often willingly trade affordability restrictions in some set of units in exchange for additional density.

Finally, building truly inclusive and integrated communities may require more than just housing investments. It may take special efforts to knit a community together and ensure that all residents are able to enjoy a neighborhood's amenities and resources. Local community organizations are perhaps best equipped to break down the social, and sometimes physical, barriers that sometimes separate public and other subsidized housing residents from their neighbors and ensure that all residents in a community have a voice and gain from any new opportunities.[7]

In sum, gentrification offers the promise of inclusivity. But left to its own devices, the market is unlikely to deliver on that promise. To ensure longer-run integration, local leaders in partnership with community-based organizations can work hard to preserve existing affordable housing (through investing in public housing, extending afford-ability restrictions on privately owned units, and seeking opportunities to incentivize private owners to keep units affordable over time). Second, they can take advantage of publicly owned land and other opportunities to acquire and create new subsidized housing in neighborhoods experiencing market pressures. Third, they can harness the market to deliver affordable units through tools like inclusionary zoning. Finally, they can work with local community groups to help low- and moderate- income residents make the most of any growing opportunities arising in gentrifying neighborhoods. Of course none of this is easy, and none of this is cheap. Some deals will simply be too expensive, but city and community leaders who wish to make gentrification more inclusive should be vigilant in searching for opportunities. And meanwhile, researchers should be on the lookout for opportunities to build our understanding of the costs and benefits of different strategies.

Bibliography

Baum-Snow, Nathaniel, and Daniel Hartley. 2015. "Gentrification and Changes in the Spatial Structure of Labor Demand." Working Paper.

Chetty, Raj, Nathaniel Hendren, and Lawrence F. Katz. 2016. "The Effects of Exposure to Better Neighborhoods on Children: New Evidence from the Moving to Opportunity Experiment." *American Economic Review* 106, no. 4: 855–902.

Couture, Victor, and Jessie Handbury. 2017. "Urban Revival in America, 2000 to 2010." Working Paper. https://bfi.uchicago.edu/sites/default/files/research/3_CoutureHandbury_UrbanRevival_Paper_Chicago.pdf

Dastrup, Samuel, and Ingrid Gould Ellen. 2016. "Linking Residents to Opportunity: Gentrification and Public Housing." *Cityscape* 18, no. 3: 87–107.

Desmond, Matthew. 2016. *Evicted: Poverty and Profit in the American City.* New York: Crown.

Ding, Lei, Jackelyn Hwang, and Eileen Divringi. 2016. "Gentrification and Residential Mobility in Philadelphia." *Regional Science and Urban Economics* 61: 38–51.

Edlund, Lena, Cecilia Machado, and Maria Micaela Sviatschi. 2015. "Bright Minds, Big Rent: Gentrification and the Rising Returns to Skill." Working Paper no. w21729. Cambridge, MA: National Bureau of Economic Research.

Ellen, Ingrid Gould, and Lei Ding. 2016. "Gentrification: Advancing Our Understanding of Gentrification." *Cityscape* 18, no. 3: 3–8.

Ellen, Ingrid Gould, Keren Mertens Horn, and Davin Reed. 2016. "Has Falling Crime Invited Gentrification?" Unpublished Manuscript.

Ellen, Ingrid Gould, and Katherine M. O'Regan. 2011. "How Low Income Neighborhoods Change: Entry, Exit, and Enhancement." *Regional Science and Urban Economics* 41, no. 2: 89–97.

Hartley, Daniel. 2013. "Gentrification and Financial Health." Federal Reserve Bank of Cleveland. https://www.clevelandfed.org/newsroom-and-events/publications/economic-trends/2013-economic-trends/et-20131106-gentrification-and-financial-health.aspx (accessed February 22, 2017)

Freeman, Lance. 2005. "Displacement or Succession? Residential Mobility in Gentrifying Neighborhoods." *Urban Affairs Review* 40, no. 4: 463–91.

Hwang, Jackelyn, and Jeffrey Lin. 2016. "What Have We Learned About the Causes of Recent Gentrification?" *Cityscape* 18, no. 3: 9–26.

JCHS (Joint Center for Housing Studies). 2015. "America's Rental Housing: Expanding Options for Diverse and Growing Demand." Cambridge, MA. http://www.jchs. harvard.edu/sites/jchs.harvard.edu/files/americas_rental_housing_2015_web.pdf.

McKinnish, Terra, Randall Walsh, and T. Kirk White. 2010. "Who Gentrifies Low-Income Neighborhoods?" *Journal of Urban Economics* 67, no. 2: 180–93.

Vigdor, Jacob L. 2002. "Does Gentrification Harm the Poor?" *Brookings-Wharton Papers on Urban Affairs*: 133–82.

Endnotes

1   Ellen and Ding (2016).

2   Hwang and Lin (2016); Baum-Snow and Hartley (2015); Couture and Handbury (2016); Edlund, Machado, and Sviatschi (2015).

3   Ellen, Horn, and Reed (2016).

4   Ellen and O'Regan (2011); Freeman (2005); McKinnish, Walsh, and White (2010); Vigdor (2002).

5   JCHS (2015).

6   Ding, Hwang, and Divringi (2016).

7   Dastrup and Ellen (2016).

We Live Here Too: Incorporating Residents' Voices in Mitigating the Negative Impacts of Gentrification

MALO ANDRE HUTSON
Columbia University

FACTORS CONTRIBUTING TO GENTRIFICATION AND RISK OF DISPLACEMENT

Residents living in neighborhoods within strong-market cities such as Boston, New York, Seattle, San Francisco, and Washington, DC, are experiencing significant neighborhood change commonly known as gentrification.[1] Neighborhood change is so rapid and intense in some historically middle-class neighborhoods that some label it "super-gentrification."[2] To mitigate the potentially negative effects of such changes, longstanding community residents must organize and make their voices heard; in turn, governments and developers should work to include such residents in the planning of urban revitalization project from the outset: such inclusion will ensure the best outcomes for both longstanding residents and the community as a whole.

Research suggests that many factors contribute to the current levels of gentrification, including inadequate housing supply, global capital investment, bifurcation of the labor market, and an ever shrinking middle class in strong-market cities.[3] After a more detailed look at these key factors, this paper will discuss ways in which residents, governments, and developers can work together to include residents' voices in shaping the projects and policies that create and control gentrification.

Inadequate Housing Supply

First, the housing supply in many strong-market cities has not kept up with the increasing demand, especially for middle-class households with children seeking quality housing. San Francisco, for example, has some of the highest housing costs in the United States. Low supply and high demand contribute significantly to San Francisco's affordable housing crisis. Statewide construction of market-rate and affordable housing has not kept up with housing demand since the 1970s. Currently the state is in the process of building roughly 100,000 to 140,000 units of housing per year, but in order to begin to address the high demand for housing, it is estimated that housing developers would need to build upwards of 230,000 units of housing annually.[4] Increasing the supply of market-rate and affordable housing is especially challenging in cities like San Francisco where land values are high, resistance to large-scale housing developments is fierce, environmental policies are stringent, and the cost of construction is higher compared to other places.[5] The California Legislative Analyst's Office (LAO) concluded that a major factor preventing the increase of dense housing supply in coastal cities is communities' resistance to new housing; this resistance can be strong, and residents often use local land use authorities to slow or stop housing from being built. This especially burdens less affluent individuals and households.

A second factor contributing to housing costs within many strong-market cities has been the level of global capital investment into the housing market, by investors from Canada, China, Russia, South Korea, and elsewhere. New York City, for example, attracts billions of dollars of global capital into its real estate market. Most of this investment is for "market-rate" luxury housing that is beyond the reach of everyday New Yorkers. Annually, roughly $8 billion is spent on luxury housing units (defined as costing more than $5 million) in New York City, more than triple the amount of a decade ago, and over half of those sales in 2014 were to shell companies hiding the identity of the buyer. Perhaps one of the best examples of this phenomenon is the Time Warner Center in Manhattan, where recent sale prices for condominiums have averaged over $15 million, and 64 percent of the condominiums are owned by shell companies.[6]

In 2014, Canadian investors put $3.4 billion into New York City real estate; they were followed by Chinese investors at $3.35 billion, a 43 percent increase over 2013.[7] Recently, Chinese-owned companies have spent billions purchasing New York City commercial and residential properties, even the historic Waldorf-Astoria Hotel for nearly $2 billion.[8] This investment appears to elevate real estate prices and attracts additional institutional investors (such as banks and private equity firms). The foreclosure crisis has also transferred ownership and wealth from working- and middle-class homeowners to large institutional investors.

Bifurcation of the Job Market and Shrinking of the Middle Class

Many strong-market cities experiencing neighborhood change also have local economies fueled by high-skilled labor, investment capital, and entrepreneurial activity.[9] These cities have witnessed significant job growth in information- and knowledge-based jobs in sectors such as biotechnology, engineering, medical research and services, software development, and pharmaceuticals, which require formal education and/or advanced skills.[10] As a result, high-skilled labor has migrated to these cities in search of economic and entrepreneurial opportunities. These same spaces are seeing a bifurcation in the labor market, with high paying, high-skilled jobs on one end and low-wage, lower-skilled jobs on the other end, leaving fewer of the jobs that have traditionally supported the middle class.

A shrinking middle-class contributes to neighborhood change. Nationally, middle-class wages have remained stagnant, making it hard for families and the less affluent to afford rising housing costs. In New York, for example, the income gap has widened and real wages have remained stagnant. Real wages have skyrocketed for those at the top of the income ladder (top 1 percent) and remained relatively flat for those at the bottom (lower 20 percent). According to a study from the City University of New York's (CUNY's) Graduate Center, between 1990 and 2010, median income for the top 1 percent of earners went from $452,415 to $716,625, an increase of nearly 34 percent; this group controlled roughly 54 percent of total household income.[11] For those with incomes in the lower 20 percent, however, the increase was slight ($13,140 to $14,168); this group's share of total household income fell from 3.3 percent to 3 percent. The CUNY study also found that a pronounced income gap by race and ethnicity. New York City's non-Hispanic white population was the wealthiest out of all major race/ethnic groups in the City, and "had the largest share of their households in high income-earning categories."[12] Forty-two percent of non-Hispanic white households earned more than $100,000 yearly, whereas only 30 percent of Asian, 23 percent of non-Hispanic black, and 19 percent of Latino households earned more than $100,000 in 2010.

Stagnant wages impact affordability for less affluent residents. Even though recent analysis suggests real wages for New Yorkers have inched up a bit,[13] 42 percent of New York City families (or 2.7 million people) still cannot afford basic family needs.[14] It is unlikely that the financial situations of New York City's most vulnerable populations will improve unless some aggressive policy changes are made.

Many of San Francisco's families are similarly situated. San Francisco has experienced a significant loss of middle-class, middle-skill, or middle-wage jobs. Manufacturing and blue-collar logistics jobs (i.e. shipping and receiving clerks; stock clerks; packagers and packers; industrial truck and tractor operators, etc.) do not pay a living wage or are disappearing. Firms in these lines of business once hired large numbers of employees and provided middle-class wages. For the small number of such firms who have remained in the city or within the region, wages have been stagnant or spiraled downward. Sectors which need technical-level (often community college) credentials are not paying middle-class wages as reliably as they once might have. Two good salaries are typically needed for a family to reach even the self-sufficiency wage for living in the city.[15]

Risk of Environmental Gentrification

More Americans are demanding sustainable development,[16] a widely accepted strategy considered critical to combating climate change.[17] Sustainable development includes transit-oriented development — the creation of compact, mixed-use, pedestrian-oriented communities located around public transit stations.[18] Transit-oriented development appeals to people who want to live, work, and play in the same urban area.

Sometimes, however, a local government's efforts to promote environmentally sustainable urban revitalization can lead to what scholars have called environmental gentrification.[19] The idea of environmental gentrification is not that all environmental activism causes gentrification, but rather that, in the absence of an explicit social justice framework, it can do so: state-sponsored sustainable urban development sometimes "appears as politically neutral planning that is consensual as well as ecologically and socially sensitive, [but] in practice it subordinates equity to profit-minded development."[20] Put another way, such sustainability initiatives fail to meet their goals of promoting the principles of sustainability while also providing adequate community benefits to residents across the socioeconomic strata.[21]

For example, planning to revitalize transit-rich, historically low-income neighborhoods to accommodate and attract high-density, market-rate, mixed-use development can indeed address blight, climate change, and improve the tax base; however, if the government fails to engage the community already living in the neighborhood early on in the process, or does so in a superficial or perfunctory way, outcomes for residents can be damaging and unjust. In such cases, without any conscious planning about how to keep pre-existing residents in place, large-scale developments and revitalization efforts can result in substantial demographic shifts.[22] Any planning approach without a social justice framework can contribute to reproducing inequalities, burdening low-wage earners and the least educated, especially immigrants and marginalized people of color.[23]

ADDRESSING THE CHALLENGE: ENSURING THAT LOCAL RESIDENTS' AND ADVOCATES' VOICES ARE REPRESENTED AND REFLECTED IN DECISIONS ABOUT THE FUTURE OF GENTRIFYING NEIGHBORHOODS

In the face of the affordable housing crisis, economic restructuring, increased cost of living, and growing income inequality, residents can feel powerless and voiceless in planning and land use decisions. Especially in less-affluent racially and ethnically diverse communities, community organizing and coalition building at the grassroots level are therefore more important than ever. Such organizing can help diverse resident populations better articulate their needs and vision around economic, social, and environmental justice, and it can help the increase the financial, social, and political capital necessary to bring about positive change.

Community organizing and coalition building can also help increase community engagement, resulting in greater community capacity and political power for those affected by government decisions. Such organizing is necessary to give communities proper influence over elected officials' decision-making processes around housing, economic development, and the environment, especially in the face of financial and other private interests that also influence the democractic process. Community organizing can correct the unequal balance of power that often exists between historically marginalized residents and elected officials and government staff.

Finally, community organizing and coalition building enables local residents to forge important partnerships within and across the public and private sectors, connecting government, nonprofits, and firms. Such partnerships can more effectively highlight points of agreement and contention, resulting in more realistic strategies and policies that have a greater chance of being implemented at the city level. Multi-sector coalition building can also help avoid costly and time-consuming litigation that can be harmful for all parties involved, especially the most vulnerable city residents.

Community Organizing and Coalition Building to Mitigate the Negative Effects of Gentrification

To ensure that their voices are represented in decisions about the future of gentrifying neighborhoods, it is important for local residents and their advocates to organize their own communities and to form broad-based multi-sector coalitions. Nationally, communities experiencing high housing costs, intense gentrification, and displacement have formed or are forming community coalitions focused on protecting their interests and transforming their communities into sustainable healthy communities (defined as economically strong, environmentally clean, and socially just communities).[24] These community coalitions are deploying new strategies, different from those used in the past, to fight against urban revitalization. They are not fighting to stop economic development and growth; rather, they are struggling to be a part of the new economic and social transformation taking place in their neighborhoods.[25] They want to be "at the table" as equal and valued partners during the planning and development process. As a result, these community coalitions are pushing for the implementation of creative, place-based community development strategies to require private developers to construct affordable housing, create quality jobs, and invest in community programs and public education.[26] In short, these community coalitions have focused on organizing their base, listening to community priorities, and building strong support from the ground up.

In Boston, for example, as development pressures and housing costs began to rise around the Longwood Medical and Academic Area, the Jamaica Plain Neighborhood Development Corporation and their partners were set on helping local residents gain access to affordable housing, but initially lacked a comprehensive strategy. After community meetings and outreach, the JPNDC-led coalition realized that quality jobs were also a high priority. The coalition then built a strong base of 28 organizations comprised of community residents and nonprofit organizations (educational and social service), enabling it to forge relationships with the major hospitals, the government, and the private sector to help provide low-income individuals (mostly women of color with children) access to better-quality jobs.[27]

It is critical for community coalitions to act locally because so many of the key land use decisions that shape housing and environmental policies are made at the state and local levels. It is also critical that community coalitions articulate their needs and demands using an explicit environmental and social justice framework. Such a framework is not necessarily anti-development, but instead promotes development that fosters healthy communities; based on principles of sustainability and the circular economy, it supports local economic and community development, as well as the creation of inclusive affordable housing that fosters racially/ethnically and socioeconomically integrated neighborhoods. For example, in Washington, DC, Organizing Neighborhood Equity DC (ONE DC) used an equitable development framework to create their "People's Plan," which emphasized the importance of a community's control over land use and of not displacing local residents, especially those with low to moderate incomes.[28] Similarly, in San Francisco, a community coalition, dissatisfied with the lack of community input into the city's planning process, developed and presented to the city *The People's Plan for Housing, Jobs, and Community*.[29] These similar efforts are examples of an effective way to clearly present community priorities that led to positive changes. In San Francisco, coalition building and community participation in the planning process has resulted in the city constructing or preserving 30,000 units of housing, passing a $310 million bond for affordable housing, and recently establishing the Housing Accelerator Fund of at least $100 million for affordable housing. This Housing Accelerator Fund will attract money from several sources, including gifts from foundations, loans from financial institutions, and donations from private philanthropy.

In addition to clearly articulating a vision and principles, using sophisticated communication strategies to get demands out to the media and into the public increases political influence. For example, several community coalitions are engaged in a number of actions such as writing letters to government officials describing their needs and demands, holding public protests to attract the media to their causes, and utilizing social media to garner national and international attention. In San Francisco, Calle 24 SF, the community coalition fighting for affordable housing and other important issues within the Mission District neighborhood, have held town hall meetings

and staged public protests, including a "town hall" meeting at City Hall that successfully shut down City Hall.

Once a coalition has increased its political voice and influence, building relationships
across sectors and institutions and around issues can also move an agenda forward.
Take for instance Calle 24 SF's ability to build relationships with the mayor and other
government officials and agencies: this community coalition's relationship with
government has enabled them to attract financial support for their cause as well as
enhance their social and political capital within City Hall. Ultimately, the mayor and
other city agencies helped support Calle 24 SF's efforts to develop a Latino Cultural
District and moved them closer to being designated a special use district. This designation increases residents' control over the land development process. Calle 24 SF's
relationships with public institutional actors, nonprofit organizations, and the private
sector will likely result in bigger wins down the road for neighborhood residents, the
city, and even the region, so long as these relationships are built on trust, transparency,
and respect.

Compromise When Appropriate

Community organizations must clearly articulate their needs and demands, but be
willing to compromise and collaborate to achieve their goals when appropriate.
Compromising has become more difficult in our current hyper-polarized political and
social environment, but it is often necessary for a community's goals to be realized. In
Brooklyn, some people have been critical of BrooklynSpeaks' settlement agreement
with the State, City, and private developers around the Atlantic Yards development
project (now known as the Pacific Park development), initially a 22-acre development
with the Barclays Center at its heart. Founded in 2006, BrooklynSpeaks is an initiative sponsored by civic associations, community-based organizations, and advocacy
groups. The initiative's primary mission is to advocate for transparency by state and
city government officials and to involve the public in the decision-making process.[30]
After years of litigation, disputes around eminent domain, and the Great Recession,
BrooklynSpeaks was successful in reaching a settlement agreement that prioritized
and sped up the construction of 2,250 affordable housing units promised to residents
along with several other key community benefits. More importantly, by reaching a
compromise, the community can help monitor the community benefit process and
evaluate the outcomes of the Atlantic Yards/Pacific Park development via a community
development corporation that was created to monitor the development and construction process.

The Role of Community Benefits Agreements in the Fight for Equitable Development

Another strategy local residents and their advocates are utilizing to preserve afford-able housing and mitigate displacement is the community benefits agreement (CBA). Following Gross (2008), I define a CBA as *a legally binding contract (or set of related contracts), setting forth a range of community benefits regarding a development project or projects, and resulting from substantial community involvement.*[31] CBAs were initially developed in the late 1990s to measure local benefits such as jobs and affordable housing provided by development projects and to understand the exposure and risk to neighboring communities[32]; now, they represent a community's effort "to change policy and bring some of the benefits of development to residents directly affected by large projects."[33] As the familiarity and use of CBAs increases, some argue that an effective CBA must (1) be structured around a single development project; (2) be a legally enforceable contract; (3) be broad-based and address a range of community interests; and (4) result from significant community involvement and engagement.[34]

For a CBA to meet these criteria, the process of negotiating it must be inclusive and accountable.[35] For a CBA to be inclusive, the process leading up to its development should include broad outreach to, and inclusion of, as many community residents as possible before any contract is approved. The main challenges with ensuring that a CBA meets a community's needs lie in defining clearly who the "community" is and in developing comprehensive mechanisms to ensure that all members have been included in the CBA process. Just as accountability in process is important, it is also critical that a CBA be legally binding and have adequate enforcement mechanisms.[36] Although CBAs are defined as private agreements between a community coalition and a developer, cities often play a role. A city may not be a party to the agreement but may still be involved in the CBA negotiations — either by sitting at the bargaining table or by withholding its discretionary zoning approval on a project unless a developer has entered into a CBA with the community coalition.[37]

The Staples Center development in Los Angeles provides an illustrative example of an effective CBA. The LA Live CBA for the Staples Center involved 21 community groups and five labor unions agreeing to support the development of the Staples Center, which was funded in part by public subsidies.[38] In exchange, the developers agreed to make reasonable efforts to provide affordable housing, to make 70 percent of the 5,500 permanent jobs generated by the development living wage jobs, and to imple-ment a first-source hiring program that targeted groups whose homes or jobs were displaced by the development, low-income individuals living within a three mile radius, and low-income individuals from the city's poorest census tracts.[39]

The LA Live CBA is considered to be the model of a comprehensive CBA. Ten years later, researchers found that the developer had met its affordable housing development obligations and worked closely with community partners "to establish an effective local hiring program, and helped fund a newly created land trust."[40] The researchers attributed the developer's compliance in part to the developer's need for continued support from the community coalition — the strong community organizing infrastructure that benefited negotiations, monitoring, and implementation.[41]

Many community coalitions and their leaders are also advocating for better ways to monitor and evaluate outcomes negotiated through CBAs. For example, community coalitions are advocating for the creation of independent third-party monitors, consisting of individuals from multiple sectors who evaluate and report on the progress of developers' efforts to honor the promises made in CBAs. Monitoring and coordinating job and housing programs can take substantial staff resources, over and above what may be available to a community organization; therefore, "studies of the implementation of CBAs suggest that funding for staff should be part of such agreements."[42]

Efforts to promote CBAs have required community coalitions to organize and educate local residents about the city planning process, specifically around issues related to housing, land use, economic development, and public contracting. The goal of these coalitions is to require public entities to incorporate many of the same ideas enumerated in CBAs into public policies and regulations that impact large contracts and projects funded by public subsidies.[43] Ultimately, this strategy has enabled communities to incorporate land use tools as a strategy to monitor and, if needed, to slow down development and mitigate the negative effects of gentrification and displacement.

CONCLUSION

To mitigate the negative effects of gentrification and displacement, less affluent urban residents will have to continue building their base from the ground up, strengthening their community coalitions, and lending their voices and political support to policies that benefit them. True, income inequality and other large external forces shaping the current development patterns within cities will not be solved simply through community organizing efforts. It is important that private philanthropy and foundations also support efforts to build community capacity and multi-sector coalitions. Such efforts will increase community engagement and community participation in the planning process. They will also encourage local governments to more meaningfully incorporate residents into the planning process, as they have in cities such as Boston, New York, San Francisco, and Los Angeles, and thus to prioritize equitable economic, environmental, and social justice outcomes. For the most vulnerable residents of our cities, it is crucial to be heard early and often in the planning of major development project. For governments and developers, too, it is much better to hear residents' voices early in the planning process rather than belatedly in protests and litigation, which at the end of the day hurt the city as a whole.

Bibliography

"About BrooklynSpeaks." *BrooklynSpeaks*, http://brooklynspeaks.net/about.

Beitel, Karl. 2013. *Local Protest, Global Movements: Capital, Community, and State in San Francisco*. Philadelphia: Temple University Press.

Bergad, Laird W. 2013. "Trends in Median Household Income among New York City Latinos in Comparative Perspective, 1990 – 2011." Latino Data Project Report 54, table 2, p. 10, at http://clacls.gc.cuny.edu/.

——— *The Concentration of Wealth in New York City: Changes in the Structure of Household Income by Race/Ethnic Groups and Latino Nationalities 1990 - 2010*. New York: Center for Latin American, Caribbean, and Latino Studies, CUNY Graduate Center. http://clacls.gc.cuny.edu/files/2014/01/Household-Income-Concentration-in-NYC-1990-2010.pdf.

Checker, Melissa. 2011. "Wiped Out by the 'Greenwave': Environmental Gentrification and the Paradoxical Politics of Urban Sustainability." *City & Society* 23, no. 2: 210–29.

Dooling, Sarah. 2009. "Ecological Gentrification: A Research Agenda Exploring Justice in the City." *International Journal of Urban and Regional Research* 33, no. 3: 621–39.

Dowling, T. J. 2000. "Reflections on Urban Sprawl, Smart Growth, and the Fifth Amendment." *University of Pennsylvania Law Review* 148, no. 3: 873–87.

Dulaney, C. 2015. "Waldorf Astoria Hotel Sale Completed." Wall Street Journal, February 11. http://www.wsj.com/articles/waldorf-astoria-hotel-sale-completed-1423705536.

Fiscal Policy Institute. 2015. "New York City's Recovery Finally Starts Generating Wage Gains." New York. http://fiscalpolicy.org/wp-content/uploads/2015/04/NYCs-recovery-generating-wage-gains.pdf.

Glass, Ruth. 1964. Introduction to *London: Aspects of Change,* by the Centre for Urban Studies, University College, London. London: MacGibbon & Kee. Reprinted in Ruth Glass, *Clichés of Urban Doom*, 133–58. New York: Blackwell.

Gross, Julian. 2008. "Community Benefits Agreements: Definitions, Values, and Legal Enforceability." *Journal of Affordable Housing and Community Development Law* 17: 35–58.

Gross, Julian, Greg LeRoy, and Madeline Janis-Aparicio. 2005. "Community Benefits Agreements: Making Development Accountable." Washington, DC: Good Jobs First.

Hammel, Daniel J., and Elvin K. Wyly. 1996. "A Model for Identifying Gentrified Areas with Census Data." *Urban Geography* 17, no. 3: 248–68.

Hutson, Malo. 2016. *The Urban Struggle for Economic, Environmental, and Social Justice: Deepening Their Roots.* London: Routledge Earthscan.

JCHS (Joint Center for Housing Studies of Harvard University). 2016. "State of the Nation's Housing 2016." http://www.jchs.harvard.edu/research/state_nations_ housing (accessed January 8, 2017).

Kneebone, Elizabeth, and Natalie Holmes. 2016. "US Concentrated Poverty in the wake of the Great Recession." March 31. Washington, DC: Brookings Institution. https:// www.brookings.edu/research/u-s-concentrated-poverty-in-the-wake-of-the-great-recession/ (accessed January 17, 2017).

Knox, Paul L., and Linda McCarthy. 2005. *Urbanization: An Introduction to Urban Geography.* 2nd ed. Upper Saddle River, NJ: Pearson Prenctice Hall.

Lees, Loretta. 2003. "Super-Gentrification: The Case of Brooklyn Heights, New York City." *Urban Studies* 40, no. 12: 2487–2509.

Marcello, David A. 2007. "Community Benefit Agreements: New Vehicle for Investment in America's Neighborhoods." *The Urban Lawyer* 39: 657–69.

Moore, Eli, and Marvin Nettles. 2010. "Advancing Health Through Community Benefits Agreements: Four Case Studies and Lessons for the Redevelopment of the Oakland Army Base." Oakland, CA: Pacific Institute.

Moretti, Enrico. 2012. *The New Geography of Jobs.* New York: Houghton Miffilin Harcourt.

Negron, Michael. 2013. "Limited Authority, Big Impact: Chicago's Sustainability Policies and How Cities Can Push an Agenda Amidst Federal and State Inaction." *Harvard Law & Policy Review* 7: 277–97.

Newman, Kathe, and Elvin K. Wyly. 2006. "The Right to Stay Put, Revisited: Gentrification and Resistance to Displacement in New York City." *Urban Studies* 43, no. 1: 23–57.

Nolon, John R. 2013. "Shifting Paradigms Transform Environmental and Land Use Law: The Emergence of the Law of Sustainable Development." *Fordham Environmental Law Review* 24: 242–74.

ONE DC (Organizing Neighborhood Equity DC). 2015. "The People's Platform Manifesto." Washington, DC. http://www.onedconline.org/peoplesplatform.

Owen, David. 2010. *Green Metropolis: Why Living Smaller, Living Closer, and Driving Less Are Keys to Sustainability.* New York: Penguin.

Pearce, Diana. 2014. *Overlooked and Undercounted: The Struggle to Make Ends Meet in New York City.* Prepared for the Women's Center for Education and Career Advancement with support from The United Way of New York City, The New York Community Trust, and City Harvest. Available at http://depts.washington.edu/ selfsuff/docs/NYCity2014.pdf.

Pearsall, Hamil. 2012. "Moving In or Moving Out? Resilience to Environmental Gentrification in New York City." *Local Environment: The International Journal of Justice and Sustainability* 17, no. 9: 1013–26.

Reconnecting America and the Center for Transit-Oriented Development. 2007. "Why Transit-Oriented Development and Why Now?" http://reconnectingamerica.org/ assets/Uploads/tod101full.pdf. (accessed June 10, 2015).

Rubin, Victor, Hutson, Malo, et al. 2015. "Building a City that Works for All Its Families: Guidance for the Implementation of Children and Families First Initiative." Report Prepared for San Francisco Board of Supervisor Norman Yee. April 15. (Report). http://www.dcyf.org/modules/showdocument.aspx?documentid=4357.

Saito, Leland, and Jonathan Troung. 2015. "The LA Live Community Benefits Agreement: Evaluating the Agreement Results and Shifting Political Power within the City." Urban Affairs Review 51, no. 2: 263–89.

Salkin, Patricia E., and Amy Lavine. 2008. "Understanding Community Benefits Agreements: Equitable Development, Social Justice and Other Considerations for Developers and Community Organizations." *Journal of Environmental Law & Policy* 26: 291–332.

Smith, Neil. 1996. *The New Urban Frontier: Gentrification and the Revanchist City.* New York: Routledge.

———. 2002. "New Globalism, New Urbanism: Gentrification as Global Urban Strategy." *Antipode* 34, no. 3: 427–50.

Solomont, E.B. 2015. "The Year of the Chinese Investor." *The Real Deal: New York Real Estate News,* March 1. http://therealdeal.com/issues_articles/ the-year-of-the-chinese-investor/.

Story, Louise and Stephanie Saul. 2015. "Stream of Foreign Wealth Flows to New York Real Estate." *New York Times,* February 7. http://www.nytimes.com/2015/02/08/ nyregion/stream-of-foreign-wealth-flows-to-time-warner-condos.html?_r=0.

Swyngedouw, Erik, and Nikolas Heynen. 2003. "Urban Political Ecology, Justice, and the Politics of Scale." *Antipode* 35, no. 5: 898–918.

Taylor, Mac. 2015. "California's High Housing Costs: Causes and Consequences." Sacramento: California Legislative Analyst Office. http://www.lao.ca.gov/ reports/2015/finance/housing-costs/housing-costs.pdf (accessed March 18, 2015).

Wolf-Powers, Laura. 2010. "Community Benefits Agreements and Local Government: A Review of Recent Evidence." *Journal of the American Planning Association* 76, no. 2: 1–19.

Endnotes

1   For the purposes of this paper I define gentrification as the process in which more affluent populations move into an area of less affluence, resulting in higher prices for goods, services, and housing. This process of neighborhood change may lead to involuntary or voluntary displacement. I use "neighborhood change" and "gentrification" interchangeably throughout the paper.

2   Lees (2003) defines super-gentrification as "the transformation of already gentrified, prosperous and solidly upper-middle-class neighborhoods into much more exclusive and expensive enclaves."

3   Hutson (2016); Moretti (2012).

4   Taylor (2015).

5   Ibid.

6   Story and Saul (2015).

7   Solomont (2015).

8   Dulaney (2015).

9   Moretti (2012).

10   Ibid.

11   Bergad (2014).

12   Bergad (2014), 16.The median income for non-Hispanic white households was $80,500, compared with $61,200 for Asians, $55,386 for non- Hispanic Blacks, and $42,840 for Latinos; see Bergad (2013), 10, table 2.

13   Fiscal Policy Institute (2015).

14   Pearce (2014).

15   Rubin, Hutson et al. (2015).

16   Dowling (2000); Owen (2010); Nolon (2013).

17   Negron (2013).

18   Reconnecting America (2007).

19   Checker (2011); Pearsall (2012).

20   Checker (2011), 212.

21   Dooling (2009); Pearsall (2012).

22   Glass (1964); Smith (1996); Newman and Wyly (2006); Hammel and Wyly (2006).

23   Smith (2002); Swyngedouw and Heynen (2003); Pearsall (2012).

24   Hutson (2016).

25   Ibid.

26   Ibid.

27   Ibid.

28   ONE DC (2015); Hutson (2016).

29   Beitel (2013).

30   BrooklynSpeaks (2015).

31   Gross (2008).

32   Wolf-Powers (2010); Moore and Nettles (2010); Salkin and Lavine (2008).

33   Saito and Truong (2014).

34   Gross (2008).

35   Gross (2008); Gross, LeRoy, and Janis-Aparicio (2005).

36   Moore and Nettles (2010); Gross (2008); Marcello (2007).

37   In California, some local governments enter directly with the developer into master development agreements, in which the developer agrees to provide a series of community benefits that may look similar to those found in a CBA.

38   Salkin and Lavine (2008).

39   Ibid.

40   Saito and Truong (2014).

41   Ibid.

42   Ibid.

43   Ibid.

Inclusion through Homeownership

COLVIN GRANNUM

Bedford Stuyvesant Restoration Corporation

n Bedford Stuyvesant and surrounding communities, we are witnessing the displacement of African American households, especially those who are working- and middle-class renters. This paper assigns households that earn between $40,000 and $100,000 to these broad income bands. Working- and middle-class households are in many ways the lifeblood of New York City, working jobs in the public sector, in nonprofit organizations, and in the lower middle ranks of the private sector. This paper argues for promoting homeownership for working- and middle-class New Yorkers, particularly African Americans, through preserving and stabilizing existing homeowners and increasing the number of new homeowners. Homeownership affords such households an opportunity to acquire an asset that is likely to appreciate as a neighborhood improves. Homeownership is a tangible means of fostering inclusion, especially in communities where home values are rising.

BACKGROUND: CURRENT CONDITIONS
Homeownership in New York City

Historically, homeownership rates in New York City have been well below the national average because most of the City's housing stock consists of rental units. Today, New York City's homeownership rate is essentially half the rate for the United States overall (31 percent versus 63 percent).[1]

New York City's current homeownership rate is essentially the same as in 2000, but less than at the peak in 2006. In 2014, the homeownership rate varied widely across racial and ethnic groups: white, 42 percent; Asian, 39 percent; black, 26 percent; and Hispanic, 15 percent. Today more than half of New York City homes are unaffordable to the majority of households. Low- and moderate-income households comprised 51 percent of New York City households in 2014 (35 percent and 16 percent respectively), yet only 9 percent of home sales in the City were affordable to these households (3 percent were affordable to low-income households and an additional 6 percent were affordable to moderate-income households).[2] In contrast, in previous decades a significant portion of the homes in New York were affordable to

Acknowledgements: Preparation of this paper was greatly assisted by the contributions of: Kevin Chavers, Chairperson, Bedford Stuyvesant Restoration Corporation; Yolande I. Nicholson, President, New York State Foreclosure Defense Bar; and Christie Peale, Executive director, Center for NYC Neighborhoods.

working- and middle-class homebuyers. In Brooklyn, homes such as those for workers at the Brooklyn Navy Yard were specifically developed for the working- and middle-class market.[3] In addition, as one racial or ethnic group migrated from a neighborhood, they were oftentimes replaced by homebuyers of comparable or lesser means: for example, white flight from Central Brooklyn enabled working- and middle-class African Americans to purchase homes.[4]

Racial Wealth Disparities

Historically, white households have controlled significantly more wealth than African American and Hispanic households.[5] The wealth gap has increased since the Great Recession and resulting foreclosure crisis. In 2007, white households had median wealth 10 times that of African American households and eight times that of Hispanic households.[6] After the Great Recession, the wealth gap increased. White households had median wealth 13 times that of African American households and 10 times that of Hispanic households.[7]

Real estate trends underway in New York City are exacerbating the racial wealth gap. Neighborhoods across the City, including Bedford Stuyvesant, are attracting affluent residents. Prior generations of African Americans and working- and middle-class households were able to gain a foothold through the purchase of homes in these so-called "less desirable" yet affordable neighborhoods. However, the number of affordable neighborhoods in New York City is rapidly declining. As a consequence, the opportunities for African American and working and middle-income families to purchase homes, and thereby participate in the increasing value of the real estate market, are greatly reduced. This, in turn, leads to growing wealth disparities along racial lines. The City is on the trajectory of having only a small percentage of working- and middle-class households, and an even smaller percentage of African American and Hispanic households, as homeowners. In the absence of homeownership, the vast majority of African American New Yorkers are not likely to own any assets of significant value, especially given the fact that home equity accounts for 92 percent of the personal wealth of African American homeowners.[8]

Bedford Stuyvesant and Neighboring Communities

While homeownership rates in New York City and Bedford Stuyvesant were largely unchanged between 2000 and 2014, there is every reason to believe that the homeownership rates for working- and middle-class households, particularly African Americans, are declining. Homeownership in Bedford Stuyvesant and neighboring Central Brooklyn communities is increasingly burdensome to existing working- and middle-class homeowners, and inaccessible to prospective working-class and moderate-income homebuyers. Some of the pressures impacting the local markets are presented below.

Home prices are rising as a result of increased competition for housing in Central Brooklyn. Overall, the City's population is growing.[9] Young professionals, technology and knowledge workers from across the globe are flocking to neighborhoods all over the City but especially to centrally located communities that are affordable relative to Manhattan or Downtown Brooklyn. Working- and middle-class families are not able to compete with the new arrivals either for rental housing or homeownership opportunities. Bedford Stuyvesant households with children under 18 years old declined from 45 percent to 28 percent between 2000 and 2014.[10] Between 2000 and 2012, the African American population in Bedford Stuyvesant, also known as Brooklyn Community Board No. 3, declined from 75 to 53 percent, and the white population increased from 2 to 21 percent.[11] During this same period, in Brooklyn Community Board No. 2, a neighboring community including Downtown Brooklyn, Fort Greene, and Clinton Hill, the African American population declined from 42 to 27 percent, and the white population increased from 31 to 45 percent.[12]

The current strength of New York's real estate market and economy is recognized internationally. Global investment is flooding the City, including Central Brooklyn neighborhoods like Bedford Stuyvesant.[13] Investors, domestic and foreign, are buying existing homes as well as developing homes for resale at increasingly higher prices.[14] Between the third quarter of 2014 and the second quarter of 2016, sale prices in Bedford Stuyvesant increased 33 percent.[15] During the same period, the sales volume in Bedford Stuyvesant was at least twice that of communities such as Boerum Hill, Brooklyn Heights, and Downtown Brooklyn, to name just a few.[16] These high levels stand in stark contrast to just a decade ago.

Underutilization of land is also placing pressure on the real estate market. Large contextual down-zonings of Bedford Stuyvesant in 2007 and 2009 reduced the densities and height limits on residential streets while targeting up-zoning to several transit-oriented commercial corridors. However, the increased floor area ratio authorized by the up-zoning is only recently showing signs of utilization through new construction. Utilization has been slowed by the high sales prices being sought by property owners. Within a quarter mile of Restoration Plaza, nearly 300 of the 1500 properties are under-built by 50 percent or more. Many of the properties in question are occupied, one-story retail buildings which could be developed into eight- to ten-story mixed-use properties. Both the contextual down-zonings and failure to leverage the up-zonings have contributed to rising real estate prices that hinder the development of affordable housing.

Another potential pressure on the Bedford Stuyvesant real estate market is that units are being removed from the residential rental market. These units previously had been available for rental by working- and middle-class households. For example, many affluent owners of two-, three-, and four-family homes are designating larger portions of properties for their own personal use. In addition, some three- and four-family properties are being reduced to one- and two-family properties.[17] Similarly, many property owners are designating residential units for Airbnb and other comparable types of short-term rentals.[18] Proponents of Airbnb argue that the short-term rental option assists many working- and middle-class homeowners in paying for the costs of owning a home in New York City.

Many factors are driving up the cost of owning a home in Bedford Stuyvesant and thereby pushing existing working- and middle-class homeowners to the limit. Escalating real estate taxes and water and sewer charges are driving up ownership costs.[19] Decisions to impose historic district designation on portions of Bedford Stuyvesant and other historically working- and middle-class communities also increase the cost of maintenance and repair given that only approved materials and contractors may be used to undertake work on certain portions of properties designated as historic.[20] Finally, African American homeowners continue to be the targets of predatory practices such as deed theft and sham foreclosure prevention scams.[21]

Displacement

As noted above, between 2000 and 2014, the African American population of Bedford Stuyvesant declined from 75 to 53 percent, the Hispanic population remained flat, and the white population increased from 2 to 21 percent.[22] Households earning less than $20,000 declined from 36 to 29 percent, and the percentage of households earning $40,000 to $100,000 remained flat.[23] Further along the income spectrum, the percentage of households earning between $100,000 and $250,000 increased from 11 to 16 percent. Households earning above $250,000 remained flat at 1 percent.

In Bedford Stuyvesant, working- and middle-class households arguably are as vulnerable to displacement as low-income residents because Bedford Stuyvesant has fewer rent-regulated residential units than many other neighborhoods in Brooklyn.[24] Moreover, 32 percent of Bedford Stuyvesant households, including working- and middle-class households, are severely rent-burdened in that they pay more than 50 percent of their income on rent.

SOLUTIONS

Preserving existing homeownership and creating new homeownership opportunities for working- and middle-class households, particularly African Americans, will foster inclusion rather than displacement in Bedford Stuyvesant and comparable communities experiencing gentrification. Homeownership for working- and middle-class households, particularly African Americans, in gentrifying neighborhoods has the potential to create racially integrated, mixed-income communities that generate inclusion through broad access to economic opportunity.

Preserve Homeownership

African American working- and middle-class homeowners have been under siege for more than a decade. As the targets of predatory lending practices, and having suffered the brunt of the effects of the Great Recession, they have experienced foreclosures at an alarming rate.[25] Concerted action is required by all levels of government and industry to protect existing African American and working- and middle-class homeowners.

Prevent Foreclosures

Foreclosure rates have been so high among African American working-class and middle-class households that some policymakers argue that African American households, in particular, should not aspire to homeownership. First-time African American homeowners saw their wealth decrease nearly 50 percent between 2005 and 2007, a time of strong appreciation for most homeowners.[26] However, giving up on African American homeownership is not the right answer. Instead, the public and private sectors should affirmatively implement a range of initiatives to preserve and protect working- and middle-class homeownership, especially for African Americans, to redress the well-established history of discriminatory policies and practices in housing against African Americans.

1. Rigorous Prosecution of Predatory Practices. Federal and state prosecutors should rigorously prosecute persons involved in fraudulent and predatory mortgage lending and title practices, especially those who target African Americans and other minorities. During the foreclosure crisis of 2008, ample proof surfaced that African Americans in particular were targeted for risky and high-cost mortgages.[27] African Americans in New York City lost in excess of $3 billion of equity as a result.[28] While the activities of some lenders, brokers, and other actors in the real estate market were clearly illegal and often criminal, such actors conducted their activities without fear of prosecution, and indeed, few were prosecuted. The public sector must create an atmosphere intolerant of practices that victimize homeowners. Fraud crimes of this sort create severe and far-reaching repercussions. Households saddled with predatory mortgages and under threat of foreclosure live in great stress and ultimately lose not only their homes but often also the only assets they own. Frequently, the homes lost to foreclosure have been owned by families for two or more generations yet are only now appreciating in value at rates comparable to those in integrated or predominantly white communities. The mortgage litigation settlements won against banks, like those obtained by the New York State Attorney General against HSBC, are a positive step forward. What is truly needed is an environment that discourages fraud and predatory behavior and punishes violators with the most severe sanctions allowed.

2. Establish Mission-Based Nonprofit Funds to Purchase Non-Performing HUD, Fannie Mae, and Freddie Mac Mortgages. Sales of non-performing federally insured and Government Sponsored Entity (GSE) mortgage notes are stripping African American homeowners of their homes and accelerating gentrification and displacement. Until recently, the non-performing notes were sold almost exclusively to private investors. In 2015, HUD modified the non-performing note sale program to make it easier for nonprofits to purchase notes. The note sales to private investors appear to promote real estate speculation rather than prioritize preservation of homeownership. This, in turn, undermines racial and economic inclusion and accelerates the displacement of working- and middle-class homeowners and tenants, most of whom are African American.

According to estimates projected by the New York State Foreclosure Defense Bar (NYSFDB), there are no less than 12,000 active residential foreclosures in Brooklyn. The foreclosure rate in Brooklyn is estimated at 8 percent, which exceeds the national average of 4 percent and the New York City average of 6 percent. Foreclosures in Brooklyn have been concentrated in African American communities. In high-foreclosure Brooklyn neighborhoods, the percentage of residential mortgage loans in foreclosure was as high as 21 percent as of December 2011.[29] A large percentage of the mortgages in the foreclosure process are insured by FHA and the GSEs, and a disproportionately large share of those mortgages are against homes owned by African Americans in gentrifying neighborhoods. The NYSFDB estimates that foreclosures will cause the loss of between $3 billion and $10 billion in family wealth in Brooklyn communities of color between 2016 and 2021.

Preservation of homeownership is a statutorily imposed element of the missions of HUD and the GSEs. NYSFDB argues that evidence exists that the full menu of HUD-approved loss mitigation measures are not offered to African American homeowners even when the homeowners qualify for them. This unfortunately tracks historical discriminatory practices such as "redlining" and the more recent practices of subprime lenders who steered African Americans and other minority homebuyers into subprime loans even when they qualified for conventional mortgages. NYSFDB has also uncovered evidence that African American homeowners are improperly being denied Home Affordable Modification Program (HAMP)-style loan modifications such as lower interest rates, extended terms, and principal reductions.

In sales to private investors, HUD and the GSEs frequently discount the defaulted mortgages by 40 to 60 percent. The apparent justification for such discounts is to afford investors the flexibility to offer loss mitigation options to the distressed homeowners. Instead, in practice, investors increase the obligations of the homeowners by adding fees to the full unpaid balance, not the discounted balance.

Several nonprofits are raising funds for the purpose of purchasing discounted mortgage notes from HUD and the GSEs. The nonprofits intend to prioritize home-ownership preservation and loss mitigation above earning a speculative return on sale of the foreclosed home. The benefit of the discounted notes would be shared with the distressed homeowners for the purpose of keeping them in their homes and preserving their equity. To create meaningful impact, HUD would need to enlarge the pool of non-performing notes allocated for purchase by nonprofits, and the GSEs should also create a pool for purchase by nonprofits.

Properly constructed and administered, mission-oriented nonprofit funds that purchase federally insured notes could attract a range of public and private sector investors, including government, socially responsible individual and corporate investors, pension funds, and philanthropies. Government agencies such as FHA and Treasury would do well to capitalize nonprofit funds of this sort given the importance to the economy of stabilizing homeownership. The proceeds of settlements with financial institutions for mortgage lending impropriety are also an appropriate source of capital, given the offenses against homeowners upon which the settlements are based.

At least two models for mission-based funds are currently in operation in the New York Metro area. New Jersey Community Capital (NJCC) has purchased HUD loans and is committed to keeping homeowners in their homes. NJCC offers loss mitigation options such as loan modifications including principal reduction; leases; leases with the option to purchase; and transfer of deed in lieu of foreclosure. NJCC has also sold properties to tenants in cases where the homeowner opts not to participate and cannot be located. NJCC has had success in raising funds from corporations such as MetLife and Prudential who are seeking a double bottom line. The second fund involves the Center for NYC Neighborhoods, the City of New York, Restored Homes, MHANY Management, Inc., and the National Community Stabilization Trust. This fund has purchased approximately 24 mortgages — a relatively small number — which are being restructured for the purpose of keeping homeowners in place.

3. Re-Examine All City Policies. All city policies should be examined to determine their effect on minority, working-, and middle-class homeownership, and policies should be implemented that will protect and preserve such homeownership. Some municipal policies disproportionately burden minority, working-, and middle-class homeownership. One example is New York City's annual tax lien sale. The tax lien sale law was enacted in 1996 to eliminate the City's roles in collecting real estate taxes on, taking title to, and maintaining properties that fell behind on paying real estate taxes. A study undertaken by the Coalition for Affordable Homes found that the tax lien sale disproportionately impacts communities of color.[30] The City is six times more likely to sell a lien in a majority-African American neighborhood as in a majority-white neighborhood, and twice as likely to sell a lien in a majority-Hispanic neighborhood. The lien sale process contributes to the displacement of long-time homeowners and their renters in communities that are already facing extensive market pressure and speculation. Nearly half of the one-to-three-family homes in the 2011 tax lien sale (42 percent) were sold within five years of the lien sale, compared to 13 percent of all one-to-three-family properties in Brooklyn.[31]

In January 2017, the City's tax lien sale law was renewed with minor revisions. Homeownership advocates, such as the Coalition for Affordable Homes, continue to press for legislative and administrative measures to preserve homeownership by avoiding tax lien sale foreclosures. Among other measures, advocates have proposed a "Preservation Trust" which could buy tax liens and service them with the intention of preserving affordability. Alternatively, the City itself, through HPD, the city's housing preservation and development agency, could create and administer such a program. Homeownership advocates also argue that HPD should exercise its discretion to proactively pull properties from the lien sale for the purpose of keeping current homeowners in place or transferring the properties to a community land trust designed to preserve long-term affordable homeownership.

Similarly, New York's processes for increasing real estate taxes and creating historic districts should be examined from the perspective of their impact on working- and middle-class homeownership. In New York City, tax increases in historically African American neighborhoods appear to be disproportionately larger than tax increases in mature predominantly white neighborhoods. Such tax increases likely track the increasing values driven by speculation and gentrification; however, when combined with stagnant wages, such increases place significant burdens on longstanding African American working- and middle-class homeowners in a community like Bedford Stuyvesant. Similarly, designating neighborhoods as architecturally signifi-cant historic districts raises the cost of home maintenance and repair to a level many working- and middle-class households cannot afford. The City must be mindful of the many cost variables impacting working- and middle-class homeownership and must craft policies that preserve rather than jeopardize homeownership for African Americans and other minorities.

Promote New Homeownership for African Americans

In addition to preserving homeownership for existing working- and middle-class homeowners in gentrifying communities, new homeownership opportunities should be created for prospective working- and middle-class homebuyers, especially African Americans. As noted above, recent housing market data reports that as of the second quarter of 2016, the average home price in Bedford Stuyvesant was just over $1 million, up from $756,000 in the third quarter of 2014.[32] Many homes sell for well in excess of $1.5 million, and those that sell for significantly less than $1 million are the subject of intense competition and typically require hundreds of thousands of dollars of rehabilitation.[33] In short, the homeownership market in Bedford Stuyvesant is increasingly inaccessible to working- and middle-class households. Without a public sector intervention, the community will become less economically and racially diverse. It is foreseeable that the percentage of working- and middle-class households in Bedford Stuyvesant will decline even more than the percentage of low-income households. This is because low-income households may seek refuge in public and other subsidized low-income housing, while working- and middle-class households cannot. This plausible scenario could make Bedford Stuyvesant not only less economically integrated but also more economically polarized. The presence of working- and middle-class residents has benefited Bedford Stuyvesant. Such residents often serve as the glue of the community through their involvement in the public school system and civic activities. The loss of working- and middle-class families diminishes the prospects for economic and social integration.

New government subsidized homeownership opportunities could be created based on a shared equity model that ensures permanent affordability of the subsidized units while providing for accumulation of equity by the homeowners. African American homeownership can also be boosted by widespread adoption of Individual Development Accounts to assist working- and middle-class households in gathering sufficient resources for the down payments needed to purchase homes.

1. Shared Equity Homeownership. Under shared equity homeownership, home price appreciation is shared between a homebuyer and a nonprofit program sponsor to achieve a balance between the individual's interest in building wealth and the societal interest in ensuring long-term affordability.[34] Shared equity homeownership allows working- and middle-class families to purchase homes at a below-market price. When the home is sold, the seller and program sponsor divide contractually agreed-upon shares of the profits. Under one shared equity model, the program sponsor's share of the profit is retained in the home as a subsidy for the next working- or middle-class buyer.[35]

Shared equity has proven to be less risky for the homeowner than traditional home-ownership. It affords the buyer the same housing stability as traditional homeownership as well as the opportunity to accumulate equity while also mitigating some of the risks of traditional homeownership.[36] Specifically, the below-market price acts as a buffer against equity loss in the event home values decline, reducing the chance of foreclosure. Under the shared equity model, the program sponsor monitors the well-being of the homebuyer to avoid foreclosure and mortgage delinquency and assists the homebuyer through challenging circumstances. For example, the program sponsor would actively counsel the homeowner to guard against predatory lenders or to pay real estate taxes.

A significant public investment in shared equity homeownership could create a stock of permanently affordable homes and keep the dream of working- and middle-class homeownership alive, in Bedford Stuyvesant and elsewhere. City-subsidized home-ownership programs that predated gentrification justifiably did not anticipate the massive and rapid escalation in home prices. The programs successfully revitalized many neighborhoods and rewarded fortunate purchasers of subsidized homes with increased equity because the subsidy was a forgivable loan. However, the programs did not contribute to long-term affordability.

The housing stock in Bedford Stuyvesant and neighboring communities is amenable to shared equity homeownership because the multi-level brownstones may be config-ured into three or four individual condominiums. Shared equity homeownership units may also be constructed in sections of the community zoned for mandatory or volun-tary inclusionary housing, and they may be mixed in with market-rate condominiums.

2. Down Payment Assistance: Many African American, working-, and middle-class households have limited success in saving for a down payment on a house. Compared to white households, African Americans and Hispanics have fewer resources available to them for down payments. In fact, white households are three times more likely to rely on family assistance for down payments than African American households, and nine out of every ten African American homeowners cover the entire down payment with their own savings. Family assistance also allows white homebuyers to make larger down payments, which tends to lower interest rates and lending costs.[37]

Individual Development Accounts (IDAs) are an initiative that could spur homeowner-ship especially when connected to shared equity. IDAs incentivize saving by matching the designated savings of individuals with modest means who wish to save towards the purchase of a lifelong asset, such as a home. Such savings are matched primarily by external sources, such as foundations, corporations, religious institutions, and government. IDA savings can be used for education and training, homeownership, and development of home-based and micro-enterprise businesses. IDA programs are offered as partnerships between sponsoring organizations (often nonprofits or state/local government agencies) and financial institutions. Although they are a relatively recent policy innovation, IDAs have a track record of success.

Sustainable funding is a major concern for IDA program sponsors. Both operating and matching funds are often difficult to secure. Federal state and local agencies and the private sector should fund IDAs at levels sufficient to incentivize tens of thousands of working-class and moderate-income households to become homeowners.

CONCLUSION

Homeownership for working- and middle-income households is a tangible means of reducing displacement and fostering inclusion in high-cost cities. Historically, however, homeownership has underperformed as an asset creation strategy for African Americans, primarily due to policies and practices that promote racial segregation in housing. In high-cost cities experiencing gentrification, current African American homeowners are facing mounting challenges such as real estate speculation, fraud, and increasing maintenance costs. In addition, an inadequate number of new homeownership opportunities are being created for working- and middle-income households. In high-cost cities, these trends may be reversed through public and private sector intervention in support of working- and middle-class homeownership.

Bibliography

Bayer, Patrick, Fernando Ferreira, and Stephen Ross. 2016. "What Drives Racial and Ethnic Differences in High Cost Mortgages? The Role of High Risk Lenders." Working Paper 22004. Cambridge, MA: National Bureau of Economic Research.

Center for New York City Neighborhoods. 2016. "The Impact of Property Flipping on Homeowners and Renters in Small Buildings." http://cnycn.org/wp-content/uploads/2016/04/CNYCN-NYC-Flipping-Analysis.pdf.

Clarke, Katherine. 2015. "Bubbling Up: Prices Have Gone Up So Much in Bed-Stuy that Investors Are Calling It a Day." *New York Daily News*, March 5.

Coalition for Affordable Homes. 2016. "Compounding Debt: Race, Affordability and NYC's Tax Lien Sale." http://cnycn.org/wp-content/uploads/2014/02/CAH-tax-lien-sale-report-final.pdf.

Davis, John Emmeus. 2006. "Shared Equity Homeownership: The Changing Landscape of Resale-Restricted, Owner-Occupied Housing." Montclair, NJ: National Housing Institute.

Durkin, Erin. 2017. "Most Airbnb Hosts in Black Neighborhoods Are White, Study Shows." *New York Daily News*, March 1.

Feng, Emily, and Alexandra Stevenson. 2016. "Small Investors Join China's Tycoons in Sending Money Abroad." *New York Times*, December 11.

Furman Center for Real Estate and Urban Policy. 2015. "State of New York City's Housing and Neighborhoods in 2015." New York University. http://www.nyc.gov/html/mancb3/downloads/resources/NYUFurmanCenter_SOCin2015_9JUNE2016.pdf.

———. 2016. "State of New York City's Housing and Neighborhoods in 2016." New York University. http://furmancenter.org/files/sotc/SOC_2016_Full.pdf.

Houghten, Tim. 2016. "New York Real Estate and Tax Trends in 2016." Property Tax Adjusters blob, January 28. Property Tax Adjusters, Ltd. http://www.ptaxny.com/new-york-real-estate-and-tax-trends-in-2016/.

Hymowitz, Kay. 2017. *The New Brooklyn: What It Take to Bring a City Back*. Lanham, MD: Rowman & Littlefield.

Kochhar, Rakesh, and Richard Fry. 2014. "Wealth Inequality Has Widened along Racial, Ethnic Lines since End of Great Recession." *Fact Tank: News in the Numbers*, December 12. Pew Research Center. http://www.pewresearch.org/fact-tank/2014/12/12/racial-wealth-gaps-great-recession/.

Kusisto, Laura. 2013. "City's Boom Spurs a Need for Housing." *Wall Street Journal*, June 10.

———. 2016. "Rising U.S. Rents Squeeze the Middle Class." *Wall Street Journal*, May 8.

Lubell, Jeffrey. 2013. "Filling the Void Between Homeownership and Rental Housing: A Case for Expanding the Use of Shared Equity Homeownership." Cambridge, MA: Joint Center for Housing Studies, Harvard University. http://www.jchs.harvard.edu/sites/jchs.harvard.edu/files/hbtl-03.pdf.

Newman, Sandra, and C. Scott Holupka. 2015. "Is Timing Everything? Race, Homeownership and Net Worth in the Tumultuous 2000s." *Real Estate Economics* 44, no. 2: 307–54.

Powell, Michael, and Janet Roberts. 2009. "Minorities Affected Most as New York Foreclosures Rise." *New York Times*, May 9.

REBNY (Real Estate Board of New York). 2016. "Bedford Stuyvesant Housing Market Survey 2016."

Rosenblum, Constance. 2014. "Argument Over a Brownstone Neighborhood: The Case For and Against a Bed-Stuy Historic District." *New York Times,* February 21.

Saul, Stephanie. 2015. "Real Estate Shell Companies Scheme to Defraud Owners out of Their Homes." *New York Times,* November 7.

Shapiro, Thomas, Tatjana Meschede, and Sam Osoro. 2014. "The Widening Racial Wealth Gap: Why Wealth Is Not Color Blind." In *The Assets Perspective: The Rise of Asset Building and its Impact on Social Policy*, edited by Reid Cramer and Trina R. Williams Shanks, 99–122. New York: Palgrave Macmillan.

Theodos, Brett, Kenneth Temkin, Rob Pitingolo, and Dina Emam. 2015. "Homeownership for a New Era: Baseline Report on the Cornerstone Homeownership Innovation Program." Washington, DC: Urban Institute. http://www.urban.org/sites/default/files/publication/49841/2000207-Homeownership-for-a-New-Era.pdf.

Tippett, Rebecca, Avis Jones-DeWeever, Maya Rockeymoore, Darrick Hamilton, and William Darity, Jr. 2014. "Beyond Broke: Why Closing the Racial Wealth Gap Is a Priority for National Economic Security." Washington, DC: Center for Global Policy Solutions.

Willis, Mark, Maxwell Austensen, Shannon Moriarty, Stephanie Rosoff, and Traci Sanders. 2016. "NYU Furman Center/Citi Report on Homeownership & Opportunity in

New York City." Furman Center for Real Estate and Urban Policy. http://furman-
center.org/files/NYUFurmanCenterCiti_HomeownershipOpportunityNYC_
AUG_2016.pdf

Wolff, Edward. 2004. "Changes in Household Wealth in the 1980s and 1990s in the U.S."
The Levy Economics Institute and New York University. Working Paper No. 409.

Endnotes

1   Willis et al. (2016).

2   Ibid.

3   Hymowitz (2017).

4   Ibid.

5   Wolff (2004).

6   Kochhar and Fry (2014).

7   Ibid.

8   Tippett et al. (2014).

9   Kusisto (2013).

10 Furman Center for Real Estate and Urban Policy (2015).

11 Ibid.

12 Ibid.

13 Feng and Stevenson (2016).

14 Ibid.

15 REBNY (2016).

16 Ibid.

17 Center for New York City Neighborhoods (2016)

18 Durkin (2017).

19 Houghten (2016).

20 Rosenblum (2014).

21 Saul (2015).

22 Furman Center for Real Estate and Urban Policy (2016).

23 Ibid.

24 Kusisto (2016).

25 Powell and Roberts (2009).

26 Newman and Holupka (2015).

27 Ibid.

28 Bayer, Ferriera, and Ross (2006).

29 Federal Reserve Bank of New York, *Regional Mortgage Briefs*, www.newyorkfed.org/ regionalmortgagebriefs/index.

30 Coalition for Affordable Homes (2016).

31 Ibid.

32 Bedford Stuyvesant Housing Market Survey, REBNY.

33 Clarke (2015).

34 Lubell (2013).

35 Theodos et al. (2015).

36 Davis (2006).

37 Shapiro, Meschede, and Osoro (2014).

What More Do We Need to Know about How to Prevent and Mitigate Displacement of Low- and Moderate-Income Households from Gentrifying Neighborhoods?

VICKI BEEN[1]
New York University

The extent to which gentrification results in the displacement of low- and moderate-income households from neighborhoods undergoing signifi- cant change is still the subject of study and debate among urban policy researchers.[2] Recent evidence suggests that, at least in areas outside low- vacancy "superstar cities"[3] with intense gentrification, renters who likely are the most vulnerable to displacement generally do not move away from gentrifying neighborhoods at higher rates than such households move from nongentrifying areas.[4] Elected officials, housing advocates, and the public, on the other hand, have no doubt that gentrification can and does cause displacement.[5]

There are a number of reasons the research findings on displacement may be less accu- rate or complete than reports from affected neighborhoods. First, there is considerable disagreement, especially early in the process, about which neighborhoods actually are gentrifying. Second, data tracking people's moves to and from neighborhoods is limited because of concerns about the confidentiality of tax, social service, and other governmental data files that follow individuals over time, and because private sources of linked data, such as credit reporting bureau files, are incomplete in a variety of ways (some households don't have credit files, for example). Third, even if residents of gentrifying neighborhoods may move no more often from gentrifying neighborhoods than similar households in other areas, they may move for different reasons. Residents of non-gentrifying neighborhoods may more often move voluntarily — seeking better neighborhoods or jobs, for example — while residents of gentrifying neighborhoods may more often move involuntarily, wanting to stay in the neighborhood but unable to afford it. Fourth, residents of gentrifying neighborhoods may be displaced earlier, or later, in the cycle of neighborhood change than researchers have typically studied.

Finally, residents of gentrifying neighborhoods in high-cost cities with low vacancy rates may experience different pressures to leave the neighborhood than such residents in the cities with less constrained housing markets that have been the subject of some displacement studies.

Further, few would dispute that households and advocates fear the rent increases associated with gentrification, in part because they worry that those increases may result in displacement.[6] Also, the most recent research shows that when vulnerable households do move from a gentrifying area, they are more likely to move to lower-income neighborhoods than similar households moving from non-gentrifying neighborhoods.[7] Even residents of gentrifying neighborhoods who have not been physically displaced may experience what feels to them as displacement — changes in the look, feel, or culture of the neighborhood, or a feeling of being unwelcomed by, or unconnected to, recent arrivals to the neighborhood — but remain in the neighborhood nevertheless.[8] The common belief that gentrification causes displacement, fear of rent increases regardless of whether they actually cause displacement, concern about those who do move from gentrifying areas, and the contested nature of what constitutes displacement all affect the public's perception of the desirability of new development and therefore make land use approvals all the more difficult. Local governments, land use and housing officials, and affordable housing providers and advocates accordingly are scrambling to find effective ways to counter concerns about displacement. The tools available for that task, however, have not been sufficiently tested to ensure that jurisdictions are deploying the best tool or combination of tools to address the particular issues their changing neighborhoods face.

This chapter will briefly summarize the strategies currently in the toolbox and outline a research agenda for filling gaps in our understanding about how effective those strategies are in various circumstances.

ANTI-DISPLACEMENT STRATEGIES

At a recent conference on gentrification and displacement, Jeff Lubell[9] provided a helpful typology of current tools local governments can use to achieve those goals:

1 *Preservation* of existing affordable rental units.

2 *Protection* of long-time residents who wish to stay in the neighborhood.

3 *Inclusion* to ensure that a share of new development is affordable.

4 *Revenue generation* that harnesses growth to expand financial resources for affordable housing.

5 *Incentives* for developers of affordable housing.

6 *Property acquisition* of sites for affordable housing.[10]

The Furman Center's report, "Gentrification Response," also explores a variety of strategies, categorized somewhat differently.[11] Others have suggested additional strategies ranging from rental assistance vouchers for current residents of gentrifying neighborhoods,[12] condominium conversion restrictions[13] and preservation of single-room occupancy hotels (SROs),[14] to minimum wage requirements and other income-boosting strategies.[15]

WHAT MORE DO WE NEED TO KNOW TO DETERMINE HOW WELL THOSE TOOLS WORK?

While various of those tools have been evaluated in general,[16] or in contexts other than neighborhood changes that may threaten displacement or fear of displacement, little research evaluates how well these strategies work specifically to prevent or miti-gate displacement. There are a number of reasons to worry about how effective these tools will be in addressing the concerns local governments may have about displace-ment and fears of displacement. First, gentrification and other neighborhood changes take many forms, in many different kinds of communities with different housing market conditions, so it is unlikely that any particular tool will be equally appropriate in all circumstances. Tools that have been effective in addressing other problems will not necessarily transfer successfully to the gentrification context.[17] Because the tools address different aspects of the threat of displacement, they may need to be used in specific combinations. Further, some tools come with high costs that should be avoided if less costly means can accomplish the goal.[18] Finally, some tools may have unintended consequences that make them inefficient or unfair. The discussion below outlines some of the potential issues with the various tools, and suggests what more we need to know in order to evaluate each tool's potential for preventing or mitigating displacement, and to fine-tune the tool to be most effective.

Preservation

Preservation of our affordable housing stock[19] is absolutely critical for many reasons, and may be necessary to preserve the economic diversity of neighborhoods undergoing change.[20] First, preservation is essential to prevent displacement of the households living in buildings that are reaching the end of affordability restrictions in changing neighborhoods. When such a building opts out of affordability restrictions, its residents may enjoy some protections (such as enhanced vouchers and protection through rent regulations), but some are likely to be displaced.[21]

Even the most robust preservation efforts, however, are unlikely to be a sufficient antidote to displacement pressures and fears. The Furman Center's analysis of subsi-dized properties in New York City, for example, found that as of 2011, of 234,000 units financed through affordability programs, 62,000 (or 27 percent) were no longer subject to the affordability restrictions of those programs, despite the City's robust preservation programs.[22] Similarly, large numbers of subsidized units across the nation have left affordability programs.[23] A fair number of the affordable housing projects eligible to exit affordability programs in the coming years are in the gentrifying neighborhoods,[24] and preserving those units will be particularly difficult and costly because of the significant gap between market and restricted rents when property values are increasing.[25]

Further, even if a jurisdiction can afford the cost and can convince owners to renew affordability restrictions, households fearing displacement pressures may consider preservation efforts irrelevant to them for various reasons. Families in need of public or subsidized affordable housing may feel that they are unlikely to receive it: turnover in affordable housing projects, at least in high-cost cities, is typically low,[26] and many projects have long wait lists for people hoping to move in as vacancies arise.[27] Furthermore, re-rentals (lease-up of units that have been vacated through tenant turnover) are not always distributed in a transparent process like a housing lottery. Finally, when residents of gentrifying areas are asked to weigh in on land use approvals that might ease housing pressures, local governments are often not yet able to provide assurance that owners whose affordability restrictions will expire in the coming years will agree to preservation offers.

Research on the following questions would help policymakers better shape preservation efforts in gentrifying neighborhoods:

What happens to the residents of subsidized or other affordable housing in gentrifying areas? Do buildings that remain affordable have lower turnover than they did prior to the gentrification, or compared to similar projects in non-gentrifying areas? When residents of affordable buildings in gentrifying neighborhoods leave, where do they go, and do their destinations differ from those of residents leaving similar subsidized buildings in non-gentrifying areas, or from those of residents leaving non-subsidized buildings in the gentrifying neighborhood?

What are the costs and benefits of gentrification for the residents of affordable housing in gentrifying neighborhoods? Do the residents of subsidized housing see income gains from greater economic opportunity in the neighborhood that may make it possible for them to pay more rent in their subsidized housing or to find and afford housing in non-subsidized buildings?[28] Do they enjoy more or better job opportunities, improved schools, better healthcare, increased transit options? Do children living in affordable housing in gentrifying neighborhoods achieve better educational, employment, or other outcomes than those in similar but non-gentrifying neighborhoods? How do the benefits and costs of gentrification for households compare,[29] and how do households assess costs such as changes in the culture or cohesiveness of the neighborhood,[30] loss of autonomy,[31] feelings of alienation,[32] conflicts over space,[33] or discrimination by newcomers?

Does the presence of subsidized or public housing in a neighborhood affect the existence or pace of gentrification? The government's investment in affordable housing in a neighborhood may help to stabilize it and moderate house price appreciation or depreciation.[34] Conversely, some argue that investments in affordable housing may spur gentrification.[35] Knowing more about whether either new construction of subsidized housing or the presence of subsidized housing reaching the end of its affordability restrictions affects the extent of gentrification in a neighborhood is critical to efforts to assess the value (or cost) of preserving affordable housing in different kinds of neighborhoods.

Are gentrifying neighborhoods with a significant share of subsidized or public housing more diverse than gentrifying neighborhoods with little such affordable housing? The preservation of existing affordable housing as a neighborhood gentrifies seems likely to protect the neighborhood from re-segregation by preserving economic and racial diversity. But the level of protection may differ if, for example, the residents of the affordable housing are of the same race or ethnicity as the people moving into neighborhood. It is also possible that turnover in the affordable housing could undermine its role in preserving diversity in the neighborhood. The effects, if any, of public housing may differ from the effects of subsidized privately owned housing, and may vary with differences in the incomes served by the various kinds of affordable housing. As a first step to addressing these issues, it would be helpful to analyze how the characteristics of households living in, applying for, or moving into subsidized and public housing units in gentrifying neighborhoods differ from the characteristics of residents of the neighborhood who are not in such housing, and then to study how characteristics of applicants and residents of affordable housing change as the neighborhood changes. There may also be some threshold of affordable housing necessary to prevent a neighborhood from becoming re-segregated by race, so researchers should examine how the demographic characteristics of changing neighborhoods vary with the neighborhoods' share of affordable housing.

What happens to market rate, but still affordable, housing when neighborhoods gentrify? Does the volume of sales of those buildings (often small buildings owned by landlords who are not professional property managers) change in gentrifying neighborhoods? Are the buyers of those buildings different from buyers in non-gentrifying areas or from buyers in the neighborhood before it began to gentrify? How much of the increased values of the homes in gentrifying areas are captured in sales by homeowners versus by investors?

Protection

The Furman Center and Lubell both suggest a variety of ways to protect current residents of gentrifying areas from displacement: restricting conversion of rentals to condominiums; giving current tenants the option to buy their buildings when they are offered for sale; regulating rents; imposing just-cause eviction protections; helping low- and moderate-income homeowners deal with increases in property taxes; giving preferences for subsidized housing or rental assistance vouchers to people at risk of displacement; and adopting shared equity ownership models (including community land trusts).[36] Other potential protections include legal services for tenants facing eviction in gentrifying areas,[37] vouchers or low-interest loans to give current residents of gentrifying communities the choice of staying or moving;[38] and changes in zoning and building codes to allow homeowners to use accessory dwelling units and other rental units to help pay for increased taxes and other costs (and to expand the rental housing stock).[39]

Assessing whether those strategies are likely to achieve the various goals of local governments must start with a better understanding of the problems we are attempting to solve. We know little about how gentrification increases costs for particular types of households, how people who face increasing housing costs manage to stay in place, or what happens to people who cannot stay in place. Research on the following issues would help local governments better focus their efforts:

To the extent that housing cost increases (or other pressures that may lead to displacement) are not evenly distributed across residents, what explains this uneven distribution? Tenants in rent-regulated apartments should see lower rent increases than those in unregulated apartments, and if they don't, the protections of rent stabilization may need to be re-examined.[40] Senior citizens may be protected in part[41] through special programs designed to help senior homeowners, such as Boston's Senior Home Repair Loan program,[42] or through rental assistance programs for seniors, such as New York City's Senior Citizen Rent Increase Exemption program.[43] Long-term renters may be protected from rent increases through their relationships with landlords, especially in smaller buildings.[44] On the other hand, members of racial and ethnic groups may be especially vulnerable to rent increases because of discrimination by landlords.[45] How long have households who face housing cost increases lived in the neighborhood? Were those people subject to discriminatory practices that made the neighborhood less desirable or, conversely, kept them there in the past when they might have preferred other areas?[46] Sorting out who is most at risk from displacement pressures will allow local governments to prioritize those households for assistance.

How do households facing increasing rent or housing cost burdens adjust their income or spending habits to pay those higher costs? Households may attempt to increase their income by working more hours or taking a different or an additional job, or by having more members in the household seek employment. They may also (or instead) attempt to pay rising housing costs by cutting back on other expenditures, reducing the size or quality of their housing, delaying the formation of new households, or expanding the size of the household (taking in relatives, friends, or borders, or using Airbnb and other services).[47] Knowing more about the strategies people use would help local governments target assistance more effectively.

What leads a household to move to a new neighborhood rather than stay in the neighborhood? Which households do move? For example, are the movers more likely to be families with children rather than single person households or seniors? Were those who leave considering moving even before the neighborhood changed, with the change merely serving as a final deciding factor? Do those tenants who move leave when their lease is up and the rent increase for renewal is steeper than usual? Or, do they leave because they are the subject of eviction actions? What percentage of those who leave receive "buy-out" payments from their landlord, and how much are those payments?

Where do those who leave go? Lei Ding and his colleagues concluded from their study of Philadelphia that households with higher credit scores have somewhat higher mobility in gentrifying neighborhoods than in non-gentrifying areas, and that they move to higher-quality neighborhoods.[48] While they find that disadvantaged residents of gentrifying areas move no more than such residents in other areas, their research shows that the most vulnerable residents who do move from gentrifying neighborhoods suffer downward mobility and move to neighborhoods with lower incomes than the gentrifying neighborhood.[49] We need to understand more about who moves where, and whether moves to more disadvantaged neighborhoods are driven simply by the availability of housing at lower rents in those neighborhoods, or are influenced by other factors such as discrimination on the basis of race, disability, or source of income; time pressures on finding a new home; search behavior of the displaced household; or the influence of informal networks.

What effect do moves associated with gentrification have on residential income and racial segregation? If, as Ding's research shows, gentrification results in middle-class residents moving to more homogenous middle-income areas, might we see the gentrifying areas become bimodal — home to the rich and to the poor (particularly if the neighborhood has a large stock of subsidized housing), but not to the middle class? Or might the areas to which those households move become solidly middle-and upper-class, with little room for lower-income families?[50] Similarly, Ding's troubling finding that "gentrification redistributes less advantaged residents into less advantaged neighborhoods"[51] may mean that we could see poorer neighborhoods become even more uniformly poor. All these questions depend in part upon better information about the race, ethnicity and income of those who stay, those who leave, and those who move into, areas undergoing change.[52]

To the extent those moving from a gentrifying or changing neighborhood receive buy-outs, relocation assistance, vouchers, or other subsidies to help them relocate, how do those payments/subsidies affect the characteristics of the housing and neighborhoods to which the recipients move? What might happen if such tools were conditioned upon (or their amounts vary depending upon) the household moving to a higher opportunity neighborhood? How could the value of buyouts be communicated to tenants in light of the choices they are likely to face in using that buyout to relocate? Is there a way to structure buyouts or relocation assistance to make them more protective -- should the buyouts be regulated, for example? Are movers staying within the jurisdiction, so that the jurisdiction can provide help with the move, or are they moving across jurisdictions, in which case a local government might want to work with the communities to which people are most likely to move to provide portable vouchers, for example?

How are homeowners in changing neighborhoods harmed and benefitted by gentrification? Are homeowners in gentrifying neighborhoods capturing the increasing value of their properties in sales prices, and if not, why not? Where do homeowners who have enjoyed increases in value move when they sell? To the extent that they are capturing the increases in value, do the disadvantages of moving nevertheless outweigh the increased sales price they received for the home? If homes are increasing in value, but owners' incomes do not allow them to pay for increases in costs, such as property taxes, are there financing tools that allow them to borrow against the increased value to pay current expenses? If so, what are the barriers to using those tools?

The answers to all those questions will help local governments better target tools to the particular needs of households living in areas undergoing gentrification. But it would be difficult to limit many of the protections to those neighborhoods, both because of the difficulty of identifying gentrification soon enough to implement programs in those areas alone, and because of the difficulty of predicting whether particular investments will result in gentrification. Further, even if our predictions about neighborhood change were found to be accurate enough to rely upon, some of the tools (such as community land trusts) have long lead times, so it might be inefficient to try to target them precisely rather than diversifying efforts across neighborhoods at risk of gentrification. Other tools (such as rules on rent regulation) have significant implementation costs, which might render it impractical to apply them only in changing areas.

Furthermore, many of the tools have not been validated in general, much less in the particular case of displacement pressures. The value of community land trusts, for example, depends upon the cost-effectiveness of the long-term stewardship of the property by the trust entity.[53] The effects of just-cause statutes, legal representation of tenants facing eviction, and other tenant protections on tenants' long term mobility and well-being have not been subject to sufficient study.[54]

Inclusion

Many analysts have suggested that one of the best ways of keeping gentrifying areas diverse is to ensure that a share of new construction be reserved for affordable housing through inclusionary zoning.[55] That makes intuitive sense, of course, but such programs could be fine-tuned in gentrifying areas with better information about questions such as the following:

What are neighborhood residents' perceptions of subsidized housing as an antidote to displacement? Many residents of neighborhoods in which new housing is proposed do not trust that the new affordable housing will be available to them. They express concerns that without a preference in the housing lottery for community members, the huge demand for affordable housing citywide will make their chances of winning the lottery too low. Some worry, rightly or wrongly, that other factors will keep them from securing the housing, even if they "win" the lottery: bad or no credit records, criminal justice involvement, eviction histories, and other factors may, in fact, prevent those vulnerable to displacement from qualifying for subsidized housing. Similarly, current residents may worry that the affordability levels are too high or too low for them to qualify. The mere availability of affordable housing, then, may have little effect on people's worries, or on their opposition to changes in the neighborhood. Additional policies may be required, such as preferences for local residents, public awareness campaigns about how to qualify for housing, and financial empowerment counseling to improve credit records and help households prepare for the application and qualification process.

In inclusionary housing provided to take the pressure off rising rents in gentrifying areas, what is the turnover, and what explains that turnover? It may be that factors other than rents are responsible for mobility from gentrifying neighborhoods: people may feel like the neighborhood no longer welcomes them, for example, or may see their support networks (doctors, childcare providers, social service agencies) move away as the neighborhood changes.[56] So, even those households who stay in the neighborhood for some period of time with the help of inclusionary housing may leave sooner than they otherwise would have. Studying the rates, and causes, of turnover from inclusionary housing as neighborhoods gentrify therefore would help policymakers craft better solutions to displacement pressures.

What kinds of affordable housing are most successful in gentrifying neighborhoods, and what is the cost/benefit ratio for that kind of housing? There may be differences in the turnover rate, tenant satisfaction, and tenant outcomes in inclusionary housing depending upon whether that housing is provided in the same building as the market-rate housing, or off-site within the same neighborhood. To design the most effective inclusionary program for gentrifying areas, any such differences need to be considered. For example, if the most successful but also most expensive housing is located in the same building as the market-rate housing, are the benefits worth the cost? Or, might those worried about displacement prefer more affordable housing, built off-site but in the neighborhood, to on-site affordable housing?

What incomes should be targeted in new housing built in gentrifying neighborhoods? While some advocates who fear displacement call for new housing to be targeted to the incomes of people currently in the neighborhood, it is not clear that that will lead to the most diverse neighborhoods over the long run. As noted above, we don't yet know enough about whether gentrifying areas resegregate — change from disproportionately high percentages of low-income and/or racial and ethnic minority residents to disproportionately wealthy and/or white residents. To prevent resegregation, is it preferable to direct affordable housing only to the lowest-income households, or to provide affordable housing to a range of very low-, low-, and moderate-income households? Is there some mix of incomes that slows or stops gentrification? Even if resegregation were found not to be a threat, what distribution of incomes in a mixed-income neighborhood results in the best outcomes for all income groups?

Revenue Generation and Incentives

Many of the questions raised above about the effectiveness and design of preservation, new construction, or tenant protection programs will inform discussions about how to generate revenue that can be used to finance those programs. In addition, answers to the following questions can help jurisdictions design the most efficient revenue mechanisms:

To the extent that fees, inclusionary housing requirements, tenant protections, or other anti-displacement tools impose costs on developers, do those costs merely delay gentrification in the neighborhood, or do they redirect the gentrification (or even just divert growth) to other neighborhoods or jurisdictions? If public policies simply delay or divert gentrification, then policymakers need to evaluate whether the benefits are worth the costs overall.[57] Courts and policymakers also may need to consider whether a jurisdiction seeking to prevent gentrification imposes costs upon neighboring jurisdictions that should be taken into account in the decision.[58]

Who bears the ultimate cost of fees and other revenue measures in jurisdictions that are trying to manage gentrification? Economic theory would predict that the owners of land will bear some of the costs of fees imposed upon land development or requirements such as inclusionary housing, as long as the supply of land is somewhat elastic. But further work needs to be done to understand the incidence of those costs in gentrifying neighborhoods,[59] especially those in so-called "superstar" cities.[60]

CONCLUSION

The need for anti-displacement tools is acute and immediate, but policymakers considering potential remedies should be mindful of how little we know either about the problem those tools are being called upon to resolve or about how effective the potential remedies are. Without a better understanding of how gentrification affects existing residents of the gentrifying neighborhood, other neighborhoods, and other jurisdictions, our tools for fighting displacement are fairly blunt instruments, and may have many unintended consequences. That is not to say that jurisdictions should ignore the tools available; doing nothing is not necessarily better than trying tools that ultimately fail or turn out to have costs that outweigh benefits. Decision-makers often must act on incomplete information. Rather, the point is that researchers could provide significant value to policymakers by helping to fill some of the gaps this chapter has identified.

As this review of the outstanding questions reveals, there is a need for both quantitative and qualitative research. Learning more about why people move away from gentrifying areas, for example, likely would best be answered through well-designed qualitative studies such as focus groups based upon thoughtful sampling strategies. Understanding how various tenant protections work likely will require both quantitative analysis of causes and effects and qualitative studies of why some tenants don't use particular protections.

Answers to all the questions outlined were needed years ago. Unfortunately, the questions will require years to answer. Because policymakers don't have the luxury of waiting for perfect information when communities are demanding solutions, it would be helpful for researchers to talk with local policymakers about which questions they would prioritize. Researchers, along with foundations and others who play coordinating roles, should then act on those priorities by developing a logical order for their research, by dividing responsibility to avoid duplicative efforts and allow research to build on emerging knowledge, and by designing an optimal means of sharing data and analysis. For local governments, the stakes are high, so the research community should do all it can to provide the information policymakers need efficiently and in the most concrete and policy-relevant form possible.

Bibliography

Barton, Michael, and Joseph Gibbons. 2017. "A Stop Too Far: How Does Public Transportation Concentration Influence Neighborhood Median Household Income?" *Urban Studies* 54, no. 2: 538–54.

Bay Area Regional Health Initiative. 2016. "Displacement Brief." http://www.gethealthysmc.org/sites/main/files/file-attachments/barhii-displacement-brief.pdf (accessed June 30, 2017).

Begley, Jaclene, Caitlyn Brazill, Vincent Reina, and Max Weselcouch. 2011. "State of New York City's Subsidized Housing: 2011." NYU Furman Center for Real Estate and Urban Policy. http://furmancenter.org/files/publications/SHIPReportFinal.pdf.

Cashin, Sheryll. 2004. *The Failures of Integration: How Race and Class Are Undermining the American Dream.* New York: Public Affairs.

Center for Community Progress. 2017a. "Preserving and Expanding the Neighborhood's Affordable Housing Stock." Washington, DC. http://www.communityprogress.net/read-more—preserving-and-expanding—pages-254.php (accessed June 30, 2017).

———. 2017b. "Preventing Involuntary Displacement of the Neighborhood's Low-Income Residents." http://www.communityprogress.net/preventing-involuntary-displacement-of-the-neighborhood-s-lower-income-residents-pages-243.php (accessed June 30, 2017).

Chen, Michelle. 2016. "Can Neighborhoods be Revitalized Without Gentrifying Them?" *The Nation,* April 11. https://www.thenation.com/article/trusting-baltimore-communities/.

City of Boston. 2017. "How to Apply for Senior Home Repair." https://www.boston.gov/departments/neighborhood-development/how-apply-senior-home-repair (accessed June 30, 2017).

City of New York. 2017. "Senior Citizen Rent Increase Exemption." http://www1.nyc.gov/nyc-resources/service/2424/senior-citizen-rent-increase-exemption-scrie (accessed June 30, 2017).

City of New York Office of the Mayor. 2015. "State of the City: Mayor de Blasio Puts Affordable Housing at Center of 2015 Agenda to Fight Inequality." February 3. http://www1.nyc.gov/office-of-the-mayor/news/088–15/state-the-city-mayor-de-blasio-puts-affordable-housing-center-2015-agenda-fight#/0.

Coscarelli, Joe. 2014. "Spike Lee's Amazing Rant Against Gentrification: 'We Been Here!'" *New York Magazine,* February 25. http://nymag.com/daily/intelligencer/2014/02/spike-lee-amazing-rant-against-gentrification.html.

Cox, Murray. 2017. "The Face of Airbnb, New York City: Airbnb as a Racial Gentrification Tool." *Inside Airbnb: Adding Data to the Debate.* http://insideairbnb.com/face-of-airbnb-nyc/ (accessed June 30, 2017).

Crispell, Mitchell. 2016. " How to Stop Displacement." Urban Displacement Project blog. February 17. http://www.urbandisplacement.org/blog/how-stop-displacement.

Dastrup, Samuel, and Ingrid Gould Ellen. 2016. "Linking Residents to Opportunity: Gentrification and Public Housing." *Cityscape* 18: 87–107.

Davis, John Emmeus, and Rick Jacobus. 2008. "The City-CLT Partnership: Municipal Support for Community Land Trusts." Cambridge, MA: Lincoln Institute of Land Policy. http://www.lincolninst.edu/sites/default/files/pubfiles/the-city-clt-partnership-full.pdf.

DC Preservation Network Preservation Strategy Working Group. 2014. "Maintaining Economic Diversity and Affordability: A Strategy for Preserving Affordable Rental Housing in the District of Columbia." https://dl.dropboxusercontent.com/u/95427853/DC%20Preservation%20Network/DCPN%20Preservation%20Strategy%20Paper%20FINAL.pdf (accessed June 30, 2017).

Dietz, Robert. 2015. "How Many People Have Benefitted from the Affordable Housing Credit?" *Eye on Housing*, November 16. http://eyeonhousing.org/2015/11/how-many-people-have-benefitted-from-the-affordable-housing-credit/.

Ding, Lei, Jackelyn Hwang, and Ellen Divringi. 2016. "Gentrification and Residential Mobility in Philadelphia." *Regional Science and Urban Economics* 61: 38–51.

Dubinsky, Zach. 2016. "Reality Check: Can B.C.'s New Foreign-Buyer Tax Cool Vancouver's Housing Market?" *CBC News*, July 27. http://www.cbc.ca/news/business/bc-foreign-homebuyer-tax-housing-market-toronto-1.3696511

Duggan, Paul. 2016a. "After a Decade of Gentrification, District Sees a Surge in Families Crushed by Rent." *Washington Post,* December 23.

———. 2016b. "Study: D.C. Gentrification Can Cause Pockets of Poverty to Grow, Especially East of the Anacostia River." *Washington Post*, November 23.

Ellen, Ingrid Gould, and Katherine O'Regan. 2011. "How Low Income Neighborhoods Change: Entry, Exit, and Enhancement." *Regional Science and Urban Economics* 41: 89–97.

Ellen, Ingrid Gould, and Mary Weselcouch. 2015. "High-Opportunity Neighborhoods in NYC are Losing Affordable Housing." NYU Furman Center for Real Estate and Urban Policy. http://furmancenter.org/thestoop/entry/report-new-york-city-losing-affordable-housing-stock-in-high-opportunity-ne.

Epstein, Richard A. 1989. "Rent Control Revisited: One Reply to Seven Critics." *Brooklyn Law Review* 54: 1281–1304.

Florida, Richard. 2015. "The Complicated Link Between Gentrification and Displacement." *CityLab*, September 8. http://www.citylab.com/housing/2015/09/the-complicated-link-between-gentrification-and-displacement/404161/.

Freeman, Lance. 2006. *There Goes the 'Hood: Views of Gentrification from the Ground Up*. Philadelphia: Temple University Press.

Freeman, Lance, and Jenny Schuetz. 2017. "Producing Affordable Housing in Rising Markets: What Works?" *Cityscape* 19, no. 1: 217–36.

French, Susan F. 2006. "Perpetual Trusts, Conservation Servitudes, and the Problem of the Future." *Cardozo Law Review* 27, no. 6: 2523–35.

Furman Center (NYU Furman Center for Real Estate and Urban Policy). 2009. "State of New York City's Housing and Neighborhoods 2008." http://furmancenter.org/files/sotc/State_of_the_City_2008.pdf.

Furman Center and Johns Hopkins (NYU Furman Center for Real Estate and Urban Policy and Johns Hopkins Institute for Policy Studies). 2013. "Maintenance and Investment in Small Rental Properties: Findings from New York City and Baltimore." http://www.urban.org/sites/default/files/publication/24251/412967-Maintenance-and-Investment-in-Small-Rental-Properties-Findings-from-New-York-City-and-Baltimore.PDF (accessed June 30, 2017).

Gainza, Xabier. 2017. "Culture-Led Neighbourhood Transformations Beyond the Revitalisation/Gentrification Dichotomy." *Urban Studies* 54, no. 4: 953–70.

Godsil, Rachel D. 2013. "The Gentrification Trigger: Autonomy, Mobility, and Affirmatively Furthering Fair Housing." *Brooklyn Law Review* 78, no. 2: 319–38.

Gorska, Karolina, and Mitchell Crispell. 2016. "Condominium Conversion Policy Brief." Urban Displacement Project, University of California–Berkeley. February. http://www.urbandisplacement.org/sites/default/files/images/urbandisplacementproject_condoconversionbrief_feb2016.pdf.

Gyourko, Joseph, Christopher Mayer, and Todd Sinai. 2013. "Superstar Cities." *American Economic Journal: Economic Policy* 5, no. 4: 167–99.

Herrine, Luke, Jessica Yager, and Nadia Mian. 2016. "Gentrification Response: A Summary of Strategies to Maintain Neighborhood Economic Diversity." NYU Furman Center for Real Estate and Urban Policy. http://furmancenter.org/files/NYUFurmanCenter_GentrificationResponse_26OCT2016.pdf.

HUD (US Department of Housing and Urban Development). 2013. "Preserving Affordable Rental Housing: A Snapshot of Growing Need, Current Threats and Innovative Solutions." *Evidence Matters* (Summer). http://www.huduser.org/portal/periodicals/em/summer13/highlight1.html (accessed June 30, 2017).

———. 2016. "Assisted Housing: National and Local Dataset." https://www.huduser.gov/portal/datasets/assthsg.html (accessed June 30, 2017).

Hughen, W. Keener, and Dustin C. Read. 2014. "Inclusionary Housing Policies, Stigma Effects and Strategic Production Decision." *Journal of Real Estate Finance and Economics* 48, no. 4: 589–610.

Hutson, Malo. 2016. *The Urban Struggle for Economic, Environmental, and Social Justice: Deepening Their Roots*. New York: Routledge.

Ihlanfeldt, Keith R., and Timothy M. Shaughnessy. 2004. "An Empirical Investigation of the Effects of Impact Fees on Housing and Land Markets." *Regional Science and Urban Economics* 34, no. 6: 639–61.

JCHS (Joint Center for Housing Studies of Harvard University). 2015. "America's Rental Housing: Expanding Options for Diverse and Growing Demand." Cambridge, MA. http://www.jchs.harvard.edu/sites/jchs.harvard.edu/files/americas_rental_housing_2015_web.pdf.

Kirkland, Elizabeth. 2008. "What's Race Got to Do With it? Looking for the Racial Dimensions of Gentrification." *Western Journal of Black Studies* 32, no. 2: 18–30.

Knafo, Saki. 2015. "Is Gentrification a Human-Rights Violation." *The Atlantic,* September 2. https://www.theatlantic.com/business/archive/2015/09/gentrification-brooklyn-human-rights-violation/402460/.

Korngold, Gerald. 2007a. "Resolving the Intergenerational Conflicts of Real Property Law: Preserving Free Markets and Personal Autonomy for Future Generations." *American University Law Review* 56, no. 6: 1525–82.

———. 2007b. "Solving the Contentious Issues of Private Conservation Easements: Promoting Flexibility for the Future and Engaging the Public Land Use Process." *Utah Law Review:* 1039.

Lens, Michael C., and Vincent Reina. 2016. "Preserving Neighborhood Opportunity: Where Federal Housing Subsidies Expire." *Housing Policy Debate* 26: 714–32.

Lubell, Jeffey. 2016. "Preserving and Expanding Affordability in Neighborhoods Experiencing Rising Rents and Property Values." *Cityscape* 18: 131–50.

Mahoney, Julia D. 2002. "Perpetual Restrictions on Land and the Problem of the Future." *Virginia Law Review* 88, no. 4: 739–87.

McKinnish, Terra, Randall Walsh, and T. Kirk White. 2010. "Who Gentrifies Low-income Neighborhoods?" *Journal of Urban Economics* 67, no. 2: 180–93.

McLaughlin, Nancy A. 2013. "Perpetual Conservation Easements in the 21st Century: What Have We Learned and Where Should We Go from Here?" (symposium introduction). *Utah Environmental Law Review* 33, no. 1: 1–39.

Metropolitan Area Planning Council. 2015. "Managing Neighborhood Change Toolkit: Anti-Displacement Literature Review." Boston. http://www.mapc.org/Anti-Displacement_Literature (accessed June 30, 2017).

Mock, Brentin. 2016. "In Search of Answers on Gentrification." *CityLab,* November 3. http://www.citylab.com/housing/2016/11/in-search-of-answers-on-gentrification/506267/.

National Low Income Housing Coalition. 2016. "The Long Wait for a Home." *Housing Spotlight* 6, no. 1. http://nlihc.org/sites/default/files/HousingSpotlight_6-1_int.pdf (accessed June 30, 2017).

NYCHA (New York City Housing Authority). 2017. "NYCHA 2017 Fact Sheet." https://www1.nyc.gov/assets/nycha/downloads/pdf/factsheet.pdf (accessed June 30, 2017).

Reina, Vincent, and Jaclyn Begley. 2014. "Will They Stay or Will They Go: Predicting Subsidized Housing Opt-Outs." *Journal of Housing Economics* 23 (March): 1–16.

Sanneh, Kelefa. 2016. "Is Gentrification Really a Problem?" *The New Yorker,* July 11 and 18. http://www.newyorker.com/magazine/2016/07/11/is-gentrification-really-a-problem.

Schwartz, Heather L., Raphael W. Bostic, Richard K. Green, Vincent J. Reina, Lois M. Davis, and Catherine H. Augustine. 2016. "Preservation of Affordable Rental Housing: Evaluation of the MacArthur Foundation's Window of Opportunity Initiative." Santa Monica, CA: Rand Corporation. https://www.macfound.org/media/files/Window_Of_Opportunity_Evaluation_2016.pdf (accessed June 30, 2017).

Schuetz, Jenny, Rachel Meltzer, and Vicki Been. 2011. "Silver Bullet or Trojan Horse: The Effects of Inclusionary Zoning on Local Housing Markets in the United States." *Urban Studies* 48, no. 2 (February): 297–329.

Seron, Carroll, Martin Frankel, Gregg Van Ryzin, and Jean Kovath. 2001. "The Impact of Legal Counsel on Outcomes for Poor Tenants in New York City's Housing Court: Results of a Randomized Experiment." *Law & Society Review* 35, no. 2: 419–34.

Siegesmund, Kristin A. 2000. "The Looming Subsidized Housing Crisis." *William Mitchell Law Review* 27, no. 2: 1123–42. http://open.mitchellhamline.edu/wmlr/vol27/iss2/35.

Super, David A. 2011. "The Rise and Fall of the Implied Warranty of Habitability." *California Law Review* 99, no. 2: 389–463.

Vigdor, Jacob. 2010. "Is Urban Decay Bad? Is Urban Revitalization Bad Too?" *Journal of Urban Economics* 68, no. 3 (November): 277–89.

Waters, Thomas J., and Victor Bach. 2016. "Making the Rent 2016: Tenant Conditions in New York City's Changing Neighborhoods." May. http://www.cssny.org/publications/entry/making-the-rent-2016 (accessed June 30, 2017).

Zheng, Siqi, and Mathew E. Kahn. 2013. "Does Government Investment in Local Public Goods Spur Gentrification? Evidence from Beijing." *Real Estate Economics* 41, no. 1: 1–28.

Endnotes

1   Boxer Family Professor of Law at New York University School of Law; Faculty Director, Furman Center for Real Estate and Urban Policy. I would like to thank Ingrid Gould Ellen, moderator of the panel on displacement, along with the organizers and other participants in the Harvard University Joint Center for Housing Studies' A Shared Future 2017 symposium, for their helpful comments. I am indebted to Alex Wilson (NYU Law '18), Daniel Raymer (NYU Law '19) and Lauren Richardson (NYU Law '19) for excellent research assistance.

2   For a recent review of the academic debate, see Ding, Hwang, and Divringi (2016); see also Florida (2015).

3   Gyourko, Mayer, and Sinai (2013).

4   Ding, Hwang, and Divringi (2016), 49.

5   For a taste of the public discussion, see Knafo (2015); Coscarelli (2014); Sanneh (2016).

6   For examples of expressions of that fear, see Duggan (2016a).

7   Ding, Hwang, and Divringi (2016).

8   See, for example, Freeman (2006); Godsil (2013); Hutson (2016).

9   Lubell is the director of Housing and Community Initiatives at Abt Associates, http://www.abtassociates.com/About-Us/Our-People/Associates/Jeffrey-Lubell.aspx#sthash.vjCtCVLk.dpuf

10 Lubell (2016), 132; see also Bay Area Regional Health Initiative (2016) on "the five 'P's' of housing stability": Protection; Preservation; Production; Participation; Placement. For a literature review regarding anti-displacement tools, see Metropolitan Area Planning Council (2015).

11 Herrine, Yager, and Mian (2016).

12 See Godsil (2013), 335–37, proposing a voucher that people in gentrifying areas could use to pay increases in rent or to move elsewhere if they wished.

13 Gorska and Crispell (2016). See also Crispell (2016).

14 See the Urban Displacement Project's map of tools in use, http://www.urbandisplacement.org/policy-tools-2 (accessed June 30, 2017).

15 Mock (2016).

16 See, for example, the literature evaluating inclusionary zoning, such as Freeman and Schuetz (2017); Schuetz, Meltzer, and Been (2011).

17 See for example Chen (2016) (noting the "uncharted waters" of translating the community land trust model to urban areas facing gentrification).

18 Rent regulation, for example, may impose high costs, concentrate those costs on a limited subset of property owners who are no more responsible for neighborhood change than many other beneficiaries, and provide incentives for people to use rental properties inefficiently. See for example Godsil (2013), 335; Epstein (1989), 1293–94.

19 As Lubell points out, preservation shouldn't be limited to extending the regulatory agreements of projects that received subsidies in the past, but should include attempts to bring so-called "naturally occurring affordable housing" into affordability regimes, as well as programs to preserve the viability of public housing; Lubell (2016), 135–36. See also Center for Community Progress (2017a).

20 See for example Schwartz et al. (2016); DC Preservation Network Preservation Strategy Working Group (2014); HUD (2013).

21 Begley et al. (2011).

22 Ibid., studying housing subsidized under the Low-Income Housing Tax Credit; HUD's project-based rental assistance, insurance or financing; and the state's Mitchell Lama financing program). Note that some of the units may have continued to be rent-regulated, or may have renewed affordability restrictions under a different program that the original source of financing.

23 See, for example, JCHS (2015), 33, summarizing research on loss of projects in various subsidized housing programs. See generally Siegesmund (2000), 1135.

24 Lens and Reina (2016); Ellen and Weselcouch (2015).

25 See Lens and Reina (2016), 714; Reina and Begley (2014).

26 For 2016, across all HUD programs nationwide, the percentage of tenants who had moved in the past year was 12 percent; HUD (2016).

27 New York City's public housing, for example, has a wait list of almost 260,000 families, and another 133,000 families are on the wait list for housing choice vouchers; NYCHA (2017). See also National Low Income Housing Coalition (2016).

28 Dastrup and Ellen (2016); Ellen and O'Regan (2011). See also McKinnish, Walsh, and White (2010) (finding income gains, which could be caused either by increasing incomes of stayers or by the changing composition of the neighborhood).

29 See Vigdor (2010).

30 Freeman (2006); Hutson (2016).

31 Godsil (2013), 322.

32 Dastrup and Ellen (2016), 105.

33 See for example Gainza (2017).

34 The Furman Center found a strong correlation between government investment in affordable housing in a neighborhood and the neighborhood's rates of depreciation in falling markets; investment in affordable housing was somewhat associated with larger increases in price appreciation in upturns. See Furman Center (2009), 17.

35 For discussion of the role that public investments in transit play in gentrification, see for example Barton and Gibbons (2017); Zheng and Khan (2013).

36 See Herrine, Yager and Mian (2016), 15; Lubell (2016), 136–38.

37 See for example City of New York Office of the Mayor (2015) (announcing $36 million to provide free legal services for tenants facing harassment, building neglect or eviction proceedings in neighborhoods being rezoned).

38 Godsil (2013), 335–37.

39 Center for Community Progress (2017b).

40 See Waters and Bach (2016), (explaining how the use of preferential rents might lead rent regulated tenants to see larger increases than market rate tenants).

41 Lei Ding and colleagues find low outward mobility from gentrifying areas by senior citizens. Ding, Hwang, and Divringi (2016), 33 n. 25.

42 See City of Boston (2017).

43 See City of New York (2017).

44 See Furman Center and Johns Hopkins (2013).

45 See for example Kirkland (2008).

46 See Godsil (2013), 324–29.

47 See Cox (2017).

48 Ding, Hwang, and Divringi (2016), 50.

49 Ibid.

50 See Cashin (2004).

51 Ding, Hwang, and Divringi (2016), 50.

52 That information is not available in the credit bureau files Ding and colleagues used, and the micro-level census files that might allow access to that information pose other methodological limits. But see McKinnish, Walsh, and White (2010) for some evidence about the demographic shifts in gentrifying neighborhoods.

53 See for example Davis and Jacobus (2008), 28–33. The experience with conservation land trusts is more robust than that for community land trusts, and has revealed a number of problems with the tool. See for example McLaughlin (2013), 31–37; Korngold (2007a); Korngold (2007b); French (2006), 2526; Mahoney (2002).

54 Existing studies include Seron et al. (2001); Super (2011).

55 For the most recent review of the literature about what we know, and don't know, about how well inclusionary housing programs work in appreciating markets, see Freeman and Schuetz (2017).

56 Freeman and Schuetz (2017), 163.

57 Measures to tax foreign investment or non-resident owners in order to control gentrification, for example, may cause those buyers to shift to similar jurisdictions that have not yet imposed such fees. See for example Dubinsky (2016).

58 See for example Associated Home Builders v. City of Livermore, 557 P.2d 473 (Cal. 1976) (en banc).

59 See for example Hughen and Read (2014); Ihlanfeldt and Shaughnessy (2004).

60 Gyourko, Mayer, and Sinai (2013).

What Would It Take to Foster Residential Outcomes that Support School Integration, and Vice Versa?

The Interdependence of Housing and School Segregation

ANURIMA BHARGAVA

Open Society Foundations

Housing and education in America have long been inextricably and intricately linked. First, due to the nation's history and widespread practice of assigning students to their neighborhood school, where housing is segregated, so are schools. Indeed, despite concerted efforts to desegregate schools in hundreds of jurisdictions across the country, school segregation has generally progressed in lockstep with residential segregation, and school and residential segregation have been mutually reinforcing.[1] Second, funding for schools is often tied to property taxes; consequently, the funding available for and quality of schooling is closely related to the value of the property within the residential area being served. Not surprisingly, racially segregated schools in areas of concentrated poverty have fewer resources, higher teacher turnover and a lower quality of education.[2] Third, residential insecurity and mobility have an adverse and often significant impact on student engagement and educational attainment. Recognizing how disruptive a lack of housing can be on a child's education, federal law provides an affirmative right for homeless or transitioning students to be able to enroll immediately in school.[3]

Below is a brief introduction to the links between housing and education, specifically desegregation and school diversity efforts; school financing and housing; and the impact of residential insecurity and mobility on educational attainment. This discussion serves as background and overview for the more extensive explorations of the relationship between housing and education contained in this volume.

SCHOOL AND RESIDENTIAL SEGREGATION

Through much of the twentieth century, residential segregation was legally enforced, and persisted through "violence, collective antiblack action, racially restrictive covenants, and discriminatory real estate practices."[4] Prior to the Supreme Court's landmark ruling in *Brown v. Board of Education*,[5] schools also played a role in maintaining residential segregation. To keep African-American families from moving into white neighborhoods, localities would "plac[e] the only schools that served African American children in designated African American neighborhoods and provid[e] no transportation for African American students who lived elsewhere."[6] Families were forced to reside in those designated neighborhoods to make sure their children could get an education. Even after *Brown*, the Supreme Court described the "profound reciprocal effect" of school assignment on residential segregation.[7]

After *Brown*, significant efforts were made to desegregate schools, within and across areas that remained residentially segregated. Hundreds of school districts were placed under court order to desegregate during the 1960s and 1970s, and remained under court order until the vestiges of segregation had been addressed to the extent practicable.[8] These cases resulted for some time in more desegregated schools throughout the United States. And in turn, the desegregation of schools played an important role in breaking down residential segregation: "School districts that employ robust desegregation programs also enjoy stable residential integration."[9] Indeed, when students learn and play together, they are more likely to live and work together.[10]

From the 1980s onwards, however, legal support and resources for school desegregation have waned. Hundreds of school districts have been released from court supervision, and as those and other school districts around the country returned to neighborhood school assignment, schools rapidly resegregated.[11] The peak of integration, then, came in the late 1980s and early 1990s, when school districts were still under desegregation orders.

For the most part, the resegregation of schools previously under court orders to desegregate, and the continuing segregation of schools in areas such as New York City and Atlanta, reflect persistent residential segregation along race and class lines. Largely because the neighborhoods where schools are located are so segregated, schools are now as about as segregated than they were in 1970.[12] Indeed, in 1970, the typical African American student attended a school in which 32 percent of the students were white. By 2010, this exposure had fallen to 29 percent.[13]

Court-Ordered Desegregation Cases

Nearly 200 school districts remain under court order to desegregate today. The school desegregation cases serve as a powerful means to ensure that educational inputs — from chemistry labs to athletic facilities to teachers — are equitable, and to address structural inequalities that persist in schools. In determining whether a school district has desegregated, courts will examine the following areas: student assignment (both across schools and within schools); faculty; staff; extracurricular activities; transportation; facilities; and the quality of education provided to students.[14] In addition, issues such as harassment, discipline, violence, and the school-to-prison pipeline — specifically when disproportionately impacting African American and Latinx students — have been addressed through the desegregation cases. And, while the vast majority of school desegregation cases have addressed *racial* segregation, the

United States Department of Justice, along with numerous civil rights organizations, have also addressed segregation of students with disabilities and the segregation of students due to language status.[15]

School districts under court order to desegregate have a set of tools and resources that can, and in some cases must, be used to address the impact of residential segregation on where students attend school. Perhaps the most important tool to address the impact of residential segregation is the drawing and/or monitoring of district and school attendance boundaries. School zoning, much like residential zoning, can dramatically change the racial composition of schools within a district, and school district lines can similarly impact the racial composition of schools within a particular region. Segregation across school district lines is far more difficult to tackle after the Supreme Court's decision in *Milliken v. Bradley*, which restricted school desegregation remedies to the school district under court order to desegregate.[16] In *Milliken*, the Supreme Court ruled that suburban schools could not be part of efforts to address pervasive segregation in Detroit public schools, because the suburban school districts had not been found to have engaged in the intentional segregation of students.

In cases where neighborhoods are both racially segregated and it is not geographically feasible to zone white and black neighborhoods to the same school, districts have used majority-to-minority (M-to-M) transfers, which allow, as one example, a white student who is in a disproportionately white school to transfer to a disproportionately black school. Other common tools to address school segregation that results from residential segregation are magnet schools (which provide offerings to draw students outside of their zoned school) or the pairing of schools (where schools serving different school zones are paired together and, as a result, all students at a certain grade level attend school in the same school building).

Voluntary School Diversity Efforts

A decade ago, on June 28, 2007, the United States Supreme Court issued its ruling in *Parents Involved in Community Schools v. Seattle School District* ("PICS"), the only Supreme Court case specifically addressing school segregation in more than twenty years.[17] The decision involved two cases, one out of Louisville, Kentucky, and the other from Seattle, Washington, challenging the voluntary efforts of those two communities to promote diversity and address racial isolation in their schools. More than fifty *amicus* (friend of the court) briefs were filed that underscored the importance of such diversity efforts in building strong and integrated communities, addressing violence, and promoting racial and economic opportunity and growth.

The Supreme Court, in a 5–4 decision penned by Chief Justice John Roberts, found both the Seattle and Louisville plans to be unconstitutional. Justice Anthony Kennedy concurred only in part in that judgment; his separate concurring opinion, together with that of the four dissenting justices, is otherwise controlling, and provides the roadmap for what tools schools could continue to use to promote diversity and address racial isolation in schools.[18] Justice Kennedy emphasized that while schools could continue to take account of the racial composition of a student's neighborhood in determining where and how that student was assigned to school, schools were only to take account of an individual student's race in the school assignment process as a last resort. As a result, voluntary efforts to promote diversity and address racial isolation in schools were left to rely upon the composition and racial segregation of neighborhoods as the primary, if not sole, factor in how students are assigned to school.

Put another way, after the PICS decision, residential segregation became an important factor in affirmative efforts to voluntarily address racial segregation in schools. While a school district could generally not assign a black student to a predominantly white school based on that student's race, it could allow for the assignment or transfer of students from a black neighborhood to that predominantly white school. Residential segregation became an engine for school integration.

If Chief Justice Roberts had wholly prevailed in PICS, the Court would have further curtailed school districts' ability to promote diversity and avoid racial isolation, leaving few (if not no) tools that could be used in such efforts. In his view, school districts could not voluntarily address the segregation of schools because, among other reasons, such segregation was the result not of government sponsored segregation, but rather of the private choices of residents about where to live.[19] So while Chief Justice Roberts recognized the relationship between residential segregation and school segregation, he would have left communities no path to address segregation on any front: schools are segregated because of where people live, and consequently, school districts should be prohibited from addressing (in Justice Roberts' view) or limited in how they address (in Justice Kennedy's controlling view) that segregation.

Justice Roberts' view that residential segregation results from private rather than governmental choices is belied by the evidence and briefing presented to the Court in PICS, which underscored the nation's long and deep history of government-sponsored and facilitated residential segregation.[20] Housing scholars directly laid out the reasons for the high level of segregation and distortion within the housing market in order to address the Court's suggestion in *Milliken* that those factors were "unknown and perhaps unknowable."[21] On the basis of a detailed analysis and review, the housing scholars clearly conveyed that "today's residential patterns are not the product of unfettered choice." Moreover, "for school districts to do nothing when faced with today's levels of residential segregation is effectively to choose school segregation."[22]

School "Choice" Programs

School desegregation efforts have long served as a platform for students to exercise choice in where they attend school. Magnet schools and transfer programs, for example, allowed, if not specifically encouraged, students to exercise choice and attend schools outside of their neighborhood. These desegregation "choice" programs have, like housing choice programs, been touted, with varying success, as means to address segregation and allow students to engage across neighborhood lines. Particularly given that such desegregation "choice" programs have often been implemented in schools serving residential areas without aligned housing choice programs, they can be the only way some students are exposed to peers from different neighborhoods.

In recent years, charter schools and voucher programs have been implemented by states and school districts under court order to desegregate. Those programs must comply with the desegregation orders in place. In several cases, charter and voucher programs have negatively impacted ongoing desegregation efforts.[23]

In states and school districts across the country, "choice" programs, such as charter schools and voucher programs, have been widely implemented outside of the school desegregation context. For the most part, such "choice" programs have not contributed to addressing school or residential segregation. Instead, studies have shown that charter and voucher programs have led to as much, if not more, racial segregation in schools.[24]

SCHOOL FINANCING AND SEGREGATION

Property values play an important role in school funding across the country. In general, the local and state revenues that support schools are correlated to the property values in the district where the school is located. For that reason, the higher the property values, the better resourced the school.[25] Residential segregation — that concentrates neighborhoods by race and by class — directs and is substantially reflected in how schools are financed and resourced.[26]

Nationally, high-poverty neighborhoods spend 15.6 percent less per student on schools than low-poverty neighborhoods.[27] That funding disparity, in addition to those monies that may be contributed through parent and school associations and other funding streams, accounts for a significant difference in the resources available to schools in areas of concentrated poverty. Moreover, given differences in wealth and income by race, schools are likely to be even less resourced in racially segregated areas of concentrated poverty.[28]

RESIDENTIAL MOBILITY AND EDUCATIONAL OPPORTUNITIES

Housing — and in particular residential mobility and insecurity — is intimately intertwined with whether students have an opportunity to be educated. The impact of residential mobility on educational engagement and attainment has been well documented. Residential mobility is negatively associated with student educational attainment and effectiveness, both in the short[29] and long term.[30] Particularly when resulting from eviction or other forced displacement, residential mobility is itself a form of violence and trauma that impacts how students are behaving and performing in school, and is associated with behavioral and socioemotional issues,[31] increased rates of violence,[32] student disengagement and dropout.

In *Evicted*, Matthew Desmond narrates the impact of residential mobility on the educational opportunities afforded to children, as families are pushed into segregated areas of concentrated poverty: "Eviction itself often explained why some families lived on safe streets and others on dangerous ones, why some children attended good schools and others failing ones. The trauma of being forced from your home, the blemish of an eviction record, and the taxing rush to locate a new place to live pushed evicted renters into more depressed and dangerous areas of the city."[33] Not only does eviction push families into areas where schools are segregated and of lower quality, but the cycles of eviction often also mean that a child does not spend more than a few weeks at any given school. Children quickly fall behind and have little or no sense of connection to school and to their peers.[34]

The impact of residential mobility and insecurity on a child's education is explicitly recognized in the law; indeed, homeless students are the only group of students that have an immediate right to enroll in school under federal law. The McKinney-Vento Homeless Assistance Act provides an affirmative right to homeless students to immediately enroll in school.[35] "Homeless student" is broadly defined to include students living temporarily with relatives, in trailers, or in many other forms of temporary shelter.[36] Homeless students have a right to stay in the school that they had been attending — with transportation provided — or to enroll in the school assigned to the area where they are temporarily residing; they cannot be segregated in separate schools or separate programs within a school, and must be educated within a regular education program, not at a shelter; and homeless students with disabilities and/or English Learners must be provided the educational services to which they are entitled at the school where they are enrolled.

When families have experienced residential insecurity, and in particular during times of crisis when families have been displaced, schools have provided a stable anchor and platform for students. The protections provided to homeless students are perhaps the clearest indication in the law of the importance of housing to educational access and engagement, and of the deep reciprocal relationship between housing and education that has long been recognized in efforts to address segregation.

CONCLUSION

We are living in a time of deep racial divides. Those divides are fueled and perpetuated by the ongoing segregation of our neighborhoods and our schools. As noted above, schools and neighborhoods are as, if not more, segregated than they have been in decades. Students who reside in neighboring areas are growing up in different worlds where they rarely encounter one another. Rather than preparing students for a future where they live and work together, schools that remain deeply segregated across the country contribute to the likelihood of misunderstanding and racial violence.

Segregation and residential mobility are forms of trauma that have a lasting impact on our democracy and the future of this nation. The trauma of living in a racially segregated area of concentrated poverty is endemic: "Especially for poor African American families — who live in neighborhoods with rates of violence and concentrated poverty so extreme that even the worst white neighborhoods bear little resemblance — living in degrading housing in dangerous neighborhoods sent a clear message about where the wider society thought they belonged."[37] Schools are an important anchor and catalyst for change and to break down the barriers of residential segregation. Indeed, efforts to address both school segregation and residential segregation and insecurity must be at the forefront of efforts to support healthy and thriving communities, promote democracy, and strengthen America's future.

Bibliography

Adam, Emma K., and P. Lindsay Chase-Lansdale. 2002. "Home Sweet Home(s): Parental Separations, Residential Moves, and Adjustment Problems in Low-Income Adolescent Girls." *Developmental Psychology* 38, no. 5: 792–805.

Astone, Nan Marie, and Sara S. McLanahan. 1994. "Family Structure, residential mobility and school dropout: A research note." *Demography* 31, no. 4: 575–94.

Desmond, Matthew. 2016. *Evicted: Poverty and Profit in the American City.* New York: Crown.

Frankenberg, Erica, and Genevieve Siegel-Hawley. 2013. "A Segregating Choice? An Overview of Charter School Policy, Enrollment Trends, and Segregation." In *Educational Delusions? Why Choice Can Deepen Inequality and How to Make Schools Fair,* edited by Gary Orfield & Erica Frankenberg, 119–144. Berkeley: University of California Press.

Hagan, John, Ross MacMillan, and Blair Wheaton. 1996. "New Kid in Town: Social Capital and the Life Course Effects of Family Migration on Children." *American Sociological Review* 61, no 3: 368–85.

Haveman, Robert, Barbara Wolfe, and James Spaulding. 1991. "Childhood Events and Circumstances Influencing High School Completion." *Demography* 28, no. 1: 133–57

Malkus, Nat. 2016. "Differences on Balance: National Comparisons of Charter and Traditional Public Schools." Washington, D.C.: American Enterprise Institute. https://www.aei.org/wp-content/uploads/2016/08/Differences-on-balance.pdf.

Massey, Douglas S., and Nancy A. Denton. 1993. *American Apartheid: Segregation and the Making of the Underclass.* Cambridge, MA: Harvard University Press.

NPR (National Public Radio). 2016. "Why America's Schools Have a Money Problem." April 16. http://www.npr.org/2016/04/18/474256366/why-americas-schools-have-a-money-problem

Oishi, Shigehiro. 2010. "The Psychology of Residential Mobility: Implications for the Self, Social Relationships and Well-Being." *Perspectives on Psychological Science* 5, no. 1: 5–21.

Oliver, Melvin, and Thomas M. Shapiro. 2006. *Black Wealth/White Wealth: A New Perspective on Racial Inequality.* 2nd ed. New York: Routledge.

Ong, Paul M., and Jordan Rickles. 2004. "The Continued Nexus Between School and Residential Segregation." *African American Law & Policy Report* 6: 178–93.

President's Commission on School Finance. 1972. *Schools, People, Money: The Need for Educational Reform.* Washington, D.C.

Pribesh, Shana, and Douglas B. Downey. 1999. "Why Are Residential and School Moves Associated with Poor School Performance?" *Demography* 36, no. 4: 521–34.

Reardon, Sean, Elena Grewal, Demetra Kalogrides, and Erica Greenberg. 2012. "Brown Fades: The End of Court-Ordered School Desegregation and the Resegregation of American Public Schools." *Journal of Policy Analysis Management* 31: 876–904.

Rothstein, Richard. 2017. *The Color of Law: A Forgotten History of How Our Government Segregated America.* New York: Liveright.

Sharkey, Patrick, and R. J. Sampson. 2010. "Destination Effects: Residential Mobility and Trajectories of Adolescent Violence in a Stratified Metropolis." *Criminology* 48, no. 3: 639–81.

Simpson, Gloria A., and Mary Glenn Fowler. 1994. "Geographic Mobility and Children's Emotional/Behavioral Adjustment and School Functioning." *Pediatrics* 93, no. 2: 303–309.

U.S. Department of Education. 2013. *For Each and Every Child: A Strategy for Education Equity and Excellence.* Washington, D.C. https://www2.ed.gov/about/bdscomm/list/eec/equity-excellence-commission-report.pdf.

Wells, Amy Stuart, and Robert L. Crain. 1994. "Perpetuation Theory and the Long-Term Effects of School Desegregation." *Review of Education Research* 64: 531–55.

Wood, David, Neal Halfon, Debra Scarlata, Paul Newachek, and Sharon Nessim. 1993. "Impact of Family Relocation on Children's Growth, Development, School Function, and Behavior." *JAMA* 270, no. 11: 1334–38.

Endnotes

1 Ong and Rickles (2004).

2 Brief of 553 Social Scientists, *Parents Involved in Community Schools v. Seattle School District,* 551 U.S. 701 (2007).

3 The McKinney-Vento Homeless Assistance Act of 1987 (Pub. L. 100-77, July 22, 1987, 101 Stat. 482, 42 U.S.C. § 11301 et seq.). The school provisions of the McKinney-Vento Act were amended in part and reauthorized by the No Child Left Behind Act of 2001.

4 Massey and Denton (1993), 42.

5 347 U.S. 483 (1954).

6 Rothstein (2017), 132.

7 *Keyes v. School District No. 1,* 413 U.S. 189, 202 (1973).

8 *Board of Education v. Dowell,* 498 U.S. 237 (1991).

9 Brief of Housing Scholars, *Parents Involved in Community Schools v. Seattle School District,* 26-29, http://www. prrac.org/pdf/HousingScholarsBrief.pdf; cited hereafter as Brief of Housing Scholars.

10 See, e.g., Wells and Crain (1994), 551-52.

11 Reardon et al. (2012).

12 Rothstein (2017), 179.

13 Ibid.

14 *Green v. County School Board of New Kent County,* 391 U.S. 430 (1968); *Freeman v. Pitts,* 503 U.S. 467 (1992).

15 The Justice Department filed a complaint against the State of Georgia for the unnecessary segregation of students with disabilities. United States of America v. State of Georgia, Complaint (Aug. 23, 2016) https://www.justice.gov/crt/file/887356/. A number of resolution agreements involving English Learner students contained provisions against the unnecessary segregation of EL students from non-EL students. See, e.g., Settlement between the United States of America and the Boston Public Schools, 16 (Apr. 19, 2012) (https://www.justice.gov/sites/default/files/crt/legacy/2012/04/25/bostonsuccessoragree.pdf;.

16 *Milliken v. Bradley,* 418 U.S. 717 (1974).

17 *Parents Involved in Community Schools v. Seattle School District,* 551 U.S. 701 (2007).

18 Ibid., 788.

19 Rothstein (2017), xiv.

20 Brief of Housing Scholars.

21 *Milliken v. Bradley,* 756 n.2.

22 Brief of Housing Scholars, 3.

23 Frankenberg and Siegel-Hawley (2013).

24 Ibid.; Malkus (2016).

25 President's Commission on School Finance (1972); U.S. Department of Education (2013).

26 NPR (2016).

27 National Center for Education Statistics, Education Finance Statistics Center Table A1, https://nces.ed.gov/edfin/Fy11_12_tables.asp (viewed August 12, 2017)

28 See Oliver and Shapiro (2006), detailing wealth disparities between Black and white communities.

29 Residential mobility has short-term negative associations with both children's and adolescents' school achievement and functioning. Pribesh and Downey (1999); Simpson and Fowler (1994); Wood et al. (1993).

30 The long-term relationship between mobility and educational attainment also appears to be negative. Several studies find that moving is associated with lower educational attainment by late adolescence. Astone and McLanahan (1994); Hagan, MacMillan, and Wheaton (1996); Haveman, Wolfe, and Spaulding (1991).

31 Adam and Chase-Lansdale (2002); Oishi (2010).

32 Sharkey and Sampson (2010).

33 Desmond (2016), 250.

34 "Jori tried to adjust to his new school. He was technically in eighth grade but so far behind that he might as well have been in seventh" (ibid., 287); "He and his brother would have to switch schools. Jori didn't care. He switched schools all the time. Between seventh and eighth grades, he had attended five different schools — when he went at all" (ibid., 283).

35 Sec. 722 E(3)(e)(ii) of the McKinney-Vento Act.

36 U.S. Department of Education, "Title VII-B of the McKinney Vento Homeless Assistance Act: Non-Regulatory Guidance" (2004), https://www2.ed.gov/programs/homeless/guidance.pdf.

37 Desmond (2016), 257.

Addressing the Patterns of Resegregation in Urban and Suburban Contexts: How to Stabilize Integrated Schools and Communities amid Metro Migrations

AMY STUART WELLS, LAUREN FOX,
DIANA CORDOVA-COBO, AND DOUGLAS READY
Columbia University

A large body of research has documented the *patterns, degree,* and *effects* of racial segregation.[1] We argue that what is missing from this literature is a more nuanced understanding of the *process* by which segregation is reproduced time and time again. People move. Constant migration and resettlement patterns occur within and between major metro areas. Amid this movement people too often end up segregated and then resegregated by race, ethnicity, social class, and religion.[2]

Our research examines the racial resegregation *process* — how and why segregation patterns repeat themselves when people move — and the role of housing and schools in that process. Through our mixed-methods study of the housing-school nexus in both suburban and urban contexts, we have learned that resegregation occurs in part because homebuyers' or renters' perceptions of the *reputations* of local communities and, by association, their public schools are affected by the race of the people who live there.

The central role played by the "reputations" of different places and schools in housing choices, as well as the relationship between race and these reputations, is something many homebuyers know intuitively but rarely admit. In reality, constructions of "good" and "bad" neighborhoods and schools are based only partly on "tangible factors" such as the physical characteristics of houses and school resources and outcome data. Indeed, "intangible factors," such as the word-of-mouth reputation and status of one community or school district versus another, strongly sway those with the most choices. The US Supreme Court's 1954 *Brown v. Board of Education* decision noted that both tangible and intangible factors matter in the field of education, and we argue that is still the case.

If intangible factors did not have such sway, neighborhood reputations, identities, and property values would not change as quickly as they often do when demographics change prior to tangible changes. For instance, within the rapid gentrification of New York City, the southern side of Harlem — a neighborhood that was seen as "bad" and avoided by many white New Yorkers only 10 years ago — is now one of the hottest real estate markets in the City, even as most of the housing stock has remained constant. What has changed in Southern Harlem is the race of its residents more than anything, which has influenced the area's reputation.

The space between easily measured "tangible" factors and the reality of how people choose neighborhoods and schools can be studied when researchers control for key tangible factors to examine *when and why* intangible factors such as reputations vary, and how these variations relate to race. In this chapter, therefore, we present findings from our research on the home buying and school choice process in one suburban county and several neighborhoods within a gentrifying city that exhibit high levels of mobility, demographic change, and racial and ethnic segregation.

In these moments of change, when members of a new racial/ethnic group begin moving into a formerly all-white suburb or a once all-black and/or Latino urban community, the correlation between tangible and intangible factors is often temporarily out of sync. That is, in the *suburban context,* the resources and tangible measures of a so-called "good" formerly all-white community and school system could remain high, while the "intangible" factors such as reputation decline with the percentage of white residents. In *urban gentrifying communities,* school reputations can change quickly as more white students enroll and white parents take charge of the PTA, quickly raising thousands of dollars. Other than the PTA coffers, tangible changes in these schools often lag behind. In both instances, *reputations and realities may be far apart*, but that does not stop families — particularly white families with the most housing and neighborhood options — from making choices based on what other people like them say and think,[3] thereby feeding into the process of resegregation.[4]

THE RATIONALE FOR ADDRESSING THE PROCESS OF RESEGREGATION AT THIS TIME

There are many important reasons why researchers and policymakers should focus on the process by which racial, ethnic, and socioeconomic status (SES) segregation recurs in housing and schools today. First of all, the *demographics* of the country are becoming increasingly racially/ethnically diverse as well as socioeconomically divided via income inequality.[5] These changes are even more dramatic among the school-age population where more than 50 percent of students in public schools are now members of one or more racial/ethnic "minority" groups and more than 50 percent are from low-income families.[6] Yet, at the same time, we know from research on both neighborhood and school segregation that more racial/ethnic diversity does not necessarily lead to more integration,[7] but it does make integration more possible, and makes the need to fight segregation more urgent.

Secondly, the *metro migration* patterns of the last 30 years have realigned the post-WWII, late-20th-century housing patterns of predominantly black and Latino cities versus predominantly white suburbs. As other chapters in this volume illustrate, growing numbers of middle- and working-class black, Latino and Asian families left cities for the suburbs, seeking the lifestyle whites had sought decades earlier — larger homes and good public schools. Meanwhile, a growing number more affluent whites are moving back into "gentrifying" urban centers.[8] These recent metro migration patterns have led to a "demographic inversion" of cities and their suburbs.[9] In theory, as both suburban and urban spaces become more racially and ethnically diverse, there are new opportunities to create, foster and sustain racially and socioeconomically integrated communities and schools.

And finally, amid these demographic changes and migration patterns, research indicates that *racial attitudes* are also changing, as a growing number of people of all racial and ethnic backgrounds in the US, particularly younger cohorts, are more likely to accept cultural differences and view diversity in communities and schools positively.[10][11] These attitudinal changes appear to be particularly common among whites who attended desegregated schools themselves[12] and Millennials (those aged 20–35), a racially diverse cohort that is much more likely to prefer living in racially diverse communities.[13]

Taken together, these three factors — demographic change, metro migration patterns, and changing racial attitudes — suggest the potential to increase the number of racially and ethnically diverse schools and communities. The research on residential patterns and school segregation trends, however, tells us a different story — about a process of fleeting or "pass through" diversity, in which communities become diverse on the forefront of suburban and urban change, followed by a process of resegregation as whites continue to flee changing suburbs and people of color are displaced from gentrifying cities.[14]

EVIDENCE THAT THE PROCESS OF RESEGREGATION CONTINUES IN NEIGHBORHOODS AND SCHOOLS

The factors noted above have definitely contributed to an early 21st-century metropolitan America with urban and suburban neighborhoods that are more racially mixed than they have been since the 1920s,[15] but also incredibly unstable and fragile,[16, 17] as low-income families of color are being displaced from gentrifying urban communities, and the pattern of white flight is recurring in suburbs with increasing numbers of residents of color.[18]

Indeed, recent migration patterns have produced "global" neighborhoods that sometimes mirror the racial composition of these diverse metropolitan areas as a whole.[19] But the instability of these communities is evident, particularly when blacks enter once all-white neighborhoods before Latinos and Asians are already living there,[20] suggesting that diversity is conditional and fragile.

In fact, another nascent area of research on diverse, mixed-income, and mixed-race neighborhoods highlights how, even when some level of diversity at the community level is achieved, the process of micro-segregation, or "intimate" or "symbolic" segregation, often develops within otherwise diverse spaces, making them less stable.[21] In fact, much of the research on housing and segregation patterns concludes that stabilizing demographically changing neighborhoods requires not just public policies, but also a new level of openness to change and a deeper understanding of what *integration* (as opposed to desegregation and assimilation) means, particularly for those with the most choices.[22]

Meanwhile, the research on school choice suggests a similar form of fragility situated in the difference between white parents' embrace of "diversity in the abstract" and the act of choosing diverse schools programs. Furthermore, recent research shows that even when parents consider diversity to be a benefit, they still tend to choose schools and special or "gifted" programs within schools that are racially homogenous.[23] The unfortunate reality is, therefore, that even when white parents say they prefer racially diverse schools, they often only want diversity at a symbolic level or on their own terms, making "diverse schools" easier to accomplish in theory than in practice.[24]

It is evident, therefore, that diverse communities *and* public schools are often fragile, unstable, unequal within, and in the process of resegregating. Thus, studying this *process* of resegregation is important to understanding how we might stop or reverse it as our nation becomes increasingly diverse. Below we provide a brief description of the research we conducted from 2009 to 2015 in the suburbs, and from 2015 to today in a city, to document this process of resegregation in both contexts.

OUR URBAN-SUBURBAN RESEARCH ON THE FRAGILITY OF DIVERSE COMMUNITIES AND SCHOOLS

To better understand the fragility of diversity in demographically changing suburban and urban communities, we conducted two studies, one of suburban Nassau County and the other of gentrifying neighborhoods of New York City. Our research in the suburbs coincided with the aftermath several federal policy initiatives encouraging moderate-income families to buy suburban homes and simultaneous efforts to foster enterprise zones and thus gentrification in the cities.[25] It was clear that the metro migration patterns described above were well underway and that the suburbs of rapidly gentrifying New York City were becoming increasingly black, Latino, and Asian. In this context, we focused on the relationship between housing choice, racial/ethnic segregation, and public school district boundary lines. We set out to examine how people made sense of "place"—especially the word-of-mouth reputations of school districts—when buying homes.

Our research was mixed-method and multi-stage and began with qualitative interviews and case studies of Nassau County school districts, followed by quantitative analysis of demographic patterns, academic outcomes, and property values across school district boundaries. Next, using our findings from the quantitative analysis as our guide, we conducted a survey of recent homebuyers and further qualitative interviews with educators, realtors, parents, and survey respondents about perceptions of neighborhood and school "quality."[26] This integrated mixed-methods design allowed us to study the relationship between people's understandings of the reputations (intangible measures) of communities and their public schools and the material inequalities (tangible factors) across those places. *What we learned from our suburban research is that the racial makeup of school districts matters a great deal in the construction of their reputations, even when tangible factors across districts with different demographics are similar. These different reputations, in turn, affect property values and eventually lead to inequality in tangible factors across school district boundaries. Through our approach, we were able to track this self-fulfilling prophecy of the process of racial resegregation as it occurred.*

Meanwhile, in New York City, in our more recent work in gentrifying communities on the other side of the urban-suburban divide, we are conducting collaborative research[27] with public schools caught in the whirlwind of demographic change that are trying to make racial/ethnic and socioeconomic diversity "work" for all students. Through our Public School Support Organization (PSSO) called The Public Good, we initially partnered with three public schools in gentrifying communities. In each of these schools, we conducted more than 75 in-depth interviews with parents, educators, and local stakeholders to understand their perception of changes occurring in these schools and their hopes for what meaningful integrated schools would look like. Our sampling technique assures that a wide range of perspectives is captured. We then engage the school staff and parents in a deep dialogue about our findings to unearth areas of difference, particularly points of contention across racial and ethnic lines.

RECONSTRUCTION OF NEIGHBORHOOD AND SCHOOLS REPUTATIONS: WHAT RACE HAS TO DO WITH IT

From these two related research projects, we have learned a great deal about the fragility of diverse urban and suburban neighborhoods and schools. In this section of the paper we provide a brief description of the framework we are using to help explain the role of "reputation" or the intangible factors of the housing-school nexus that lead to resegregation over time. In our efforts to understand this process, we turned to a little-known social theory, the Sociology of Reputation, which argues that "reputations" of places and institutions are socially constructed within and in the service of social stratification. Most notably, the reputations of communities and schools are not, as we often assume, based entirely or even primarily on objective criteria that would warrant a good reputation. *Rather, the "reputation" of a given institution or place relates fundamentally to the social status of the people associated with it. Thus, reputations of communities and schools can vary dramatically depending on who lives there and which students enroll, even when other measurable variables – e.g. the quality of the housing, the school test scores and resources – are the same.*

It is true that oftentimes, this strong correlation between high-status people and high-status institutions or neighborhoods is reinforced by profound differences in the "objective" or tangible factors between institutions or places. This is often the case because those most "objective" measures of the "quality" of places and institutions — e.g., "tangible" factors related to resources, academic outcomes, and property values — are measured in a way that privileges those institutions affiliated with the highest-status people.[28] But recent research, ours included, demonstrates that even when these tangible factors are controlled for, the differential status of people, based on race, ethnicity, and SES, strongly correlates with the status and thus the "reputation" of a place or institution.[29] In other words, no matter how phenomenal teachers in a school serving low-income students of color may be, these places are rarely, if ever, deemed highly reputable or "good."

Exclusions from neighborhoods and institutions have historically been "inescapable marks of inferior public standing in the United States."[30] For instance, people rejected by institutions such as elite country clubs and sororities are often lower status than those who were admitted. In other words, institutions and communities that are most selective or expensive and thus most difficult to access have the highest status and, in turn, confer the most status upon their members.[31] Scarcity of access makes something more desirable and valuable, even if tangible differences between two institutions are negligible. To learn more about the process of resegregation, therefore, the places we most need to study are those communities and school districts in which the relationship between tangible and intangible factors is out of sync as the racial/ethnic makeup of the student body is changing quickly. *In some schools that are in the first phases of these demographic transitions, the tangible factors, including funding, curricular offerings, teaching staff, and student outcomes, change very little initially. But as the skin color of the student population changes, becoming either less (suburbs) or more (gentrifying city) white, the intangible reputation of the district often declines or increases even absent tangible changes.* In these moments, suburban homebuyers and parents in gentrifying city neighborhoods make decisions about education often based primarily on the reputations of schools as constructed by their peers and social networks.[32]

THE COLOR OF PROPERTY VALUES

One obvious way to estimate the value of reputations of communities and school districts is through the price individuals and families are willing to pay to live in particular places. A central challenge in estimating the relationship between school socio-demographics and home prices is disentangling the effects of school characteristics from the effects of home quality (in terms of size and construction) and neighborhood quality (both physical and reputational characteristics). Much of the prior research on the link between school quality and home prices has relied on standard hedonic price models, which decompose home price into its constituent characteristics (e.g., age, number of bedrooms, bathrooms), and obtain estimates of the contributory value of each characteristic. This approach, however, typically fails to adequately control for neighborhood characteristics.[33]

In Nassau County, we addressed this concern by using a "boundary fixed-effect"[34] approach, starting with Geographic Information System (GIS) software to spatially identify homes in close proximity to school district boundaries. We then restricted our analyses to homes directly on either side of the same district boundary (within a 0.25 mile), with the assumption that they are comparable in terms of neighborhood characteristics, even as they are located in different school districts.

We then explored the extent to which home values and school district racial/ethnic composition are linked after accounting for such tangible differences in home, school district, and neighborhood characteristics. We found an association between school district racial/ethnic composition and home values, even after controlling for covariates related to school, neighborhood, and home characteristics. Specifically, we found that a 1-percent increase in Black/Hispanic enrollment is associated with a 0.3-percent decrease in home values ($p<.001$). *Put another way: given Nassau County's 2010 median home price of $415,000, if two homes are similar with respect to measurable home, community, and school district characteristics and unmeasurable neighborhood characteristics, but one is in a 30 percent black/Hispanic district* *while the other is in a 70 percent black/Hispanic district, their prices would differ by almost $50,000 (see Wells et.al, 2014 for a detailed discussion of these findings).*

COLORBLIND EXPLANATIONS FOR THE COLOR OF PROPERTY: SCHOOL DISTRICT REPUTATIONS

The findings above pointing to the relationship between racial demographics and property values across school district boundaries, even after controlling for the tangible variables most likely to affect the cost of a home, help us to see the gap between the material reality and the intangible construction of the reputation, status, and ultimately desirability of one community and school district over another. In this section, we present the findings from our survey of Nassau County homebuyers[35] to help us understand how people make meaning of the reputation or "desirability" of a community and school district and how that changes as the student population changes prior to measurable differences in the tangible factors. We compared data on tangible characteristics related to public schools in Nassau County — particularly standardized test scores and other student outcomes, student demographics, and per-pupil funding — across the 56 school districts and then compared these characteristics to survey responses on school district reputations.

Our survey of residents who bought homes in Nassau County between 2005 and 2010 was designed to elicit feedback on how people moving into (or within) the racially divided county made decisions about where to live. We wanted to know what was most important to them in making home buying choices amid Nassau County's multiple municipal and school district boundaries. Because we had the home addresses of all the survey respondents, we were able to analyze their responses broken down by the racial makeup of the school districts into which they moved. We learned from the survey, among other findings, that there are associations ($p<.001$) between the racial makeup of students in a respondent's local school district and the degree to which they were persuaded to move into their district by their perceptions of the public school reputations (i.e., how others talked about the quality of the local public schools). We found, for instance, that schools' reputation mattered more in the decision-making process for homebuyers who moved to districts with high propor-tions of white and/or Asian students than for those in districts serving predominantly black and/or Hispanic students (see Wells et.al, 2014). In other words, homebuyers in predominantly white and/or Asian districts put more emphasis on intangible character-istics related to *where* the house is located than do those in districts with more black and/or Latino students. These findings further our understanding of the sociology of reputation as it relates to racial distinctions in institutional reputations.[36]

STATUS OF SCHOOLS, STATUS OF STUDENTS: CHOOSING CLASSMATES WHEN CHOOSING NEIGHBORHOODS

As our analysis of property values and survey data suggest, the housing-school nexus is as much about intangible (reputational) factors as it is about tangible (material) factors. Furthermore, we see how the reputations of communities and their schools are co-determined by the social status of their members.[37] In the context of a racially stratified society, school status, in most instances, is inversely correlated with high proportions of "minorities," especially blacks.[38] Predominantly white and/or Asian schools regularly have much better reputations, whether the reputations are based on tangible measures of success or not.

The co-determined relationship between the reputation of a school and the status of the students and families associated with it no doubt affects school choices, with race as a central feature of how status is constructed. The research on school choice clearly demonstrates a negative correlation between white parents' perceptions of school quality or reputation and the percentage of students of color enrolled.[39] For instance, one study that focused on the effects of school racial composition and several nonracial school characteristics on white parents' school choices found that *the proportion of black students in a hypothetical school has a consistent and significant inverse association with the likelihood of white parents enrolling their children in that school, even after controlling for many school quality factors.*[40]

Given the power of race to influence white parents' perceptions of school reputations, we studied, through qualitative interviews, how parents understand school quality and how this affects the *process* of resegregation. Here we draw on the interview data from the suburban and urban phases of our research to emphasize two key points:

1 Parents with children in highly reputable, predominantly white schools sometimes question the validity of these reputations, which suggests they may not be warranted.

2 Many K-12 education policies perpetuate different school reputations by race.

These two themes look slightly different in the urban gentrifying versus the suburban context of increasing diversity because in the urban neighborhoods parents have access to more school choices — either public schools of choice, charter, or private schools — without having to move. In the suburbs, where housing choices and school choices are more tightly tied, parents are more aware of the housing-school nexus when they buy a home.

WHEN THE REPUTATION OF A PLACE PRECEDES IT

As we noted above, tangible distinctions across school districts with varied reputations are often real and meaningful, as schools serving low-income students of color are more likely to lack resources, attract fewer highly qualified teachers, and have less challenging curriculum.[41] *But our in-depth interview data also suggest that there are moments in which the respondents see the gaps between the reputations and reality, between the intangible and tangible.* But even in those moments, when respondents question their own certainty about the value of one district over another, they are quick to defend their choices, which ultimately rationalizes their movement away from those suburbs in which the demographics of the students are changing most rapidly.

Still, there is ample evidence in our data of the multiple ruptures within the strong relationship between tangible and intangible factors that make a place and school district what it is. The interviews revealed uncertainty and critique of most of the highly reputable school districts and urban schools, as respondents suggested that their reputations are exaggerated. Some respondents seem to think that some of the "hype" related to certain schools or districts had as much to do with the status of the families associated with these institutions as it did with the actual quality of the education within the schools. Strongly related to the survey responses, the interview data reveal that "recommendation, reputation, and word-of-mouth shared understandings" are key reasons why people with resources and choices move where they do. They frequently defend the reputation of their schools by noting one or more dimensions of the "quality" of people associated with them.

Interestingly enough, these respondents also voice dismay about the lack of racial and ethnic diversity in these high-status schools, noting that such diversity is more representative of the "real world." Still, status and reputation — especially as it corresponds to the status of the residents who live there — trumps "reality" in terms of their concerns about school quality or the downsides of racial/ethnic and socioeconomic homogeneity. In the end, what people *think* about a place is as important – sometimes more so — as what the place actually is.

For instance, a white, upper-middle-class parent who is one of the leaders of the district-wide PTA in an affluent, highly reputable suburban school district where she and her husband bought a home ten years earlier, exemplifies this theme. She questioned many aspects of the "quality" of the educational system in her district, but she did not question the fact that most people perceive the district to be very good and that those with the resources to live there will pay the hefty housing costs and the property taxes that come with it:

My husband grew up in the next town over, and I think he always felt like this was better. I don't know why. I just think its reputation precedes it. I think that many people believe that, and I think historically they look to what they've heard more so than anything else. I don't know how much research is actually out there that says this is so much better than that. I think it was really the … location.

This mother was not the only person in this high-priced school district who simultaneously wondered if the district was worth the hype — or the cost — and yet was happy to live in such a reputable, virtually all-white and affluent community and school district. In fact, we saw many instances in which people put a lot of time, energy and resources into being in the "right" school districts based on recommendation, reputation, and word-of-mouth shared understandings. Given the cost of living in these communities, it is amazing that reputation and reality are not better synchronized, but in fact, there were many, many instances in which respondents questioned the tangible price or the market "value" of the property and houses in a particular school district. Many respondents said they thought the prices people pay for certain houses are completely out of line with the tangible dimensions of their purchase. As the superintendent of one of the most highly ranked school districts (according to test scores, graduation rates, and college acceptances) noted, homebuyers assess school district quality based on the reputation, or "word on the street," even more than on the tangible data on schools or houses. The cost of a house in his district, he said, is highly inflated as a result:

> You move to [this district] for one reason. Very frankly you're not moving here because the house that you're paying $800,000 for is particularly pretty … it's not a particularly big house or pretty house. You're moving here to send your kids here to school… My guess is I would show you an $800,000 house that you would be unimpressed with. You'd say, 'My God for $800,000 I'm not buying that.

Similarly, in the urban, gentrifying context, we have interviewed white, affluent parents whose apartment buildings have been re-zoned for a predominantly black and Latino, low-income school. While most of these parents are opting out of putting their children in this school, seeking public schools of choice, charter, or private school options, they are making these choices somewhat defensively because they have heard that the new zoned school has much to offer, even if the test scores are not as high as they are in other schools with more white and affluent students. Additionally, they worry that these other highly reputable schools may not be as good as they are said to be.

One mother told us that there were many unspoken problems with the highly reputable school her son attends, which also has more white and affluent students than the newly zoned school. She talked about overcrowding, too many entitled children and parents, and some questionable teaching methods. This was an affluent parent who had researched the "new zone," mostly black and Latino school and was impressed with many aspects of the program, including the science curriculum, and the quality of the teachers. Furthermore, the new zone school is much closer to her apartment than the reputable school her son attends. She noted that even several months after her son started kindergarten at the other school, "we still today are not sure that we did the right thing. I have no idea. I'm hesitant. I cannot tell you it was the right thing to do."

In the end, she chose reputation above all else when deciding where to enroll her son in kindergarten, which resulted in him attending a more racially homogeneous but highly reputable school with higher test scores. In the final section of this paper, we discuss the ways in which the accountability system in K-12 education in the US perpetuates and legitimates such school choices despite some uncertainty on the part of parents.

K-12 EDUCATION POLICIES AND PRACTICES THAT PERPETUATE DIFFERENT SCHOOL REPUTATIONS BY RACE

At a recent meeting of white, affluent New York City parents of pre-school children now zoned for the "new zone" public elementary school (90 percent black and Latino) discussed above, one father shouted angrily that this school is a "disaster." When asked how he knew this, he said the "metrics," meaning the standardized test scores for English Language Arts and Math in grades 3–5, are "abysmal." When asked if he had ever visited the school or attended one of the many parent tours it offers, he said "no," adding that the data tell him everything.

The average test scores for the students in this school are indeed much lower than those of the predominantly white school that his child would have attended prior to the zoning change. But the school this father vehemently labeled a "disaster" is, based on our in-depth research on the programs and pedagogy, far from a disaster. As the mother quoted above notes, this "new zone" school has many laudable educational assets, including a strong science curriculum, a focus on the social and emotional development of children, a nurturing early childhood program, some excellent teachers, and a deep and meaningful connection to the African American community it had served for years. While this school may not be the best "fit" for every family in its new, broader attendance zone, to call it a "disaster" without ever stepping foot inside its doors seems more than unfair. Still, this irate parent's view of this school due to its standardized test scores alone is the "new normal" in public education. Parents base extremely important and life-changing decisions on the intersection between the "word of mouth" reputations of schools and the data that rationalizes these decisions. And we rarely question the veracity of those reputations or the narrow metrics that reinforce them.[42]

Within the sociology of reputation literature, researchers have studied the uses of data, especially the test scores of incoming students, in the ranking of higher education institutions in the popular press. This process has created status hierarchies based primarily on narrow measures that make schools hypersensitive to their positions. Research on the law schools' response to these rankings has shown they adjust their behavior to increase their ranking, which helps them attract "high-quality" (based on the same measures) students and faculty members. As a result, law schools have increased their spending on merit-based scholarships as they attempt to "buy" top students.[43] In turn, these desirable students, whose credentials augment the law school's ranking, are attracted to the highest-ranked schools.

In the K-12 educational context, we argue, the two most popular educational reforms of the last few decades — the standards/accountability movement and free-market school choice policies — have combined to create the same sort of cyclical process.[44] Since the 1990s, all states have implemented new standards and tests to hold schools accountable for student outcomes, and almost all have adopted one form of market-based school choice policy: either charter schools, open enrollment programs, vouchers, or tuition tax credit policies.[45] Federal laws and competitive programs have required, prodded, and/or supported these state accountability and school choice policies.[46]

While these policies have been promoted as colorblind and outcomes-based solutions to the racial achievement gap, we argue that their colorblindness — in fact, a blindness to what we know about the long history of the correlation between race, SES, and standardized test scores[47] — actually converts the long legacy of racial inequality and the racial biases of these tests into false evidence about educational quality. Thus, the increased reliance on such tests in education policy has reinforced negative percep-tions of public schools enrolling large numbers of black and Latino students.[48] But we also know, based on our analysis above in which test scores are controlled, that these perceptions of schools enrolling mostly students of color would most likely exist any way. The scores simply provided the "evidence" that racialized understandings of school quality are legitimate.

A school board member in a Nassau County school district, which had changed from 95 percent to less than 60 percent white in a short period of time, talked about the district leadership trying to preserve some of the non-test-related programs such as art and music — areas in which many students who do not have high test scores excel. But when so much emphasis is being placed on test scores and budgets are being cut,

Figure 1. The Housing-School Nexus and The Process of Resegregation

Intangible differences: perceptions of school quality based on implicit racial bias

Changing demand for and cost of housing

Racial segregation and concentration of wealth and poverty

Tangible differences in resources, including property tax revenues, across district boundaries

Accountability measures of "good" schools, like test scores, correlate with race and SES

Changing demographics in school districts as people with housing choices flee and property values decline

priorities need to be set. This creates a quandary for district leaders who understand education to be more multi-faceted. According to this Board member:

> If you're talking about the whole child and, you know, really kind of encouraging children to flourish in all aspects of their personality and educational opportunity, then arts is as important as academics. And you can't test those things ... tests are not the only thing that can determine ... the worth of a school district.

POLICY RECOMMENDATIONS TO ADDRESS THE SELF-FULFILLING PROPHECY OF RESEGREGATION

Policymakers and advocates who want to address racial inequality in American housing and schools must appreciate the iterative relationship between *intangible* and *tangible* factors in the housing-school nexus. One begets the other, in a cyclical process outlined in Figure 1, as neighborhood demographics change. This process eventually turns the biased perception that whiter schools are better and less-white schools are worse into a self-fulfilling prophecy.

Breaking this cycle at the point at which intangible perceptions of place have changed but tangible measures of housing and schools have not is critical to disrupting the housing-school nexus of racial segregation. *The following recommendations are a start:*

Policymakers should capitalize on changing racial attitudes in the US, particularly among the younger generations, to promote and stabilize diverse communities and public schools. Everything from student assignment policies to support and incentives for curriculum and teaching approaches that tap into the educational benefits of diversity in classrooms can and should be attempted.[49] Indeed, in the midst of changing demographics, Americans of all racial and ethnic groups are increasingly likely to be accepting of cultural differences and to view diversity in social situations as a positive characteristic.[50]

Policymakers must consider how current accountability policies in the field of education exacerbate segregation and inequality. Fair-housing advocates have increasingly prioritized the stabilization and sustainability of diverse communities; education policy and practice needs to follow suit. Successful diverse public schools help all students succeed by tapping into the gifts and talents that each student brings to the classroom while providing meaningful support services to students who lack some of the academic skills needed to keep up with their more privileged peers.[51] Such successful racially, ethnically, and socioeconomically diverse public schools help stabilize diverse communities and send important, inclusive messages about who belongs there. But unless we change the way we rank, measure, and evaluate racially and ethnically diverse public schools and districts, we will never solve the problem of separate and unequal public education.

Within racially diverse schools, educators and parents must push back against policies and rankings that focus primarily on standardized test scores to define "good" schools. Such narrow measures devalue schools that enroll more students from lower-income and recent-immigrant, non-English-speaking families. These diverse schools may have somewhat lower test scores but they better prepare children for culturally complex colleges and work environments. Such educational factors should be "valued" in the real estate market — on sites such as Trulia — and in societal definitions of "good" schools.

In diverse districts, local leaders and their constituents must embrace the new demographics of their communities and promote them as places forward-thinking people want to "be," not "flee," in both suburban and urban contexts. In suburban contexts, education officials need to work with realtors, developers, and local zoning boards to ensure that their residential population remains balanced and relatively stable in terms of racial identities, cultural backgrounds and income levels. Local infrastructure, including "downtown" areas, must be maintained, and moderate-income housing should be scattered to assure that no one part of town or neighborhood elementary school becomes seen as less "desirable."

Across the country, many changing suburbs like Ferguson, Missouri, are beginning to follow the lead of places like Oak Park, Illinois outside of Chicago; Shaker Heights, Ohio, which borders Cleveland; or Maplewood-South Orange near Newark, New Jersey. These communities, working with local realtors, set out several decades ago to assure that as blacks and Latinos moved in, white residents did not flee. Organizers knew that too much white flight too quickly would lead to a downward spiral of lower property values, tax revenue and local services. While these efforts have helped to stabilize the residential populations in these towns, there is still work to do in the local public schools as educators struggle to address within-school segregation and white flight to private schools.

Meanwhile, in urban, gentrifying areas, sustainable and affordable housing and school enrollment policies must support diversity in rapidly changing neighborhoods. As more white and affluent parents move in to the communities their grandparents fled after World War II, public policies must assure that low-income families of color that have lived in these communities for many years are able to find affordable housing and keep their children in local public schools. Such proactive policies sustain diverse neighborhoods and schools.

In both urban and suburban contexts, therefore, we must support efforts to sustain racially and ethnically diverse school districts *and* to stabilize their residential and student populations. We must value that diversity as an important factor in preparing children for the twenty-first century. The future of our increasingly diverse country requires policymakers and leaders, from DC to the state capitals to the local town councils and school boards, to take action.

Bibliography

Abrams, Samuel E. 2016. *Education and the Commercial Mindset.* Cambridge, MA: Harvard University Press.

Adair, Suzanne. 2005. "Challenging Public School Resegregation: The Use of Small-Scale Social Movements to Preserve the Promise of *Brown*." PhD diss., Pennsylvania State University.

Alba, Richard, and Victor Nee. 2003. *Remaking the American Mainstream: Assimilation and Contemporary America.* Cambridge, MA: Harvard University Press.

Berger, Erica. 2014. "Gentrification, Inc." *Fast Company*, August 7.

Billingham, Chase M., and Matthew O. Hunt. 2016. "School Racial Composition and Parental Choice: New Evidence on the Preferences of White Parents in the United States." *Sociology of Education* 89, no. 2: 99–117.

Bischoff, Kendra, and Sean F. Reardon. 2014. "Residential Segregation by Income, 1970–2009." In *Diversity and Disparities: America Enters a New Century*, edited by John Logan, 208–33. New York: The Russell Sage Foundation.

Black, Sandra E. 1999. "Do Better Schools Matter? Parental Valuation of Elementary Education." *The Quarterly Journal of Economics* 114, no. 2: 577–99.

Burdick-Will, Julia, Jens Ludwig, Stephen W. Raudenbush, Robert J. Sampson, Lisa Sanbonmatsu, and Patrick Sharkey. 2011. "Converging Evidence for Neighborhood Effects on Children's Test Scores: An Experimental, Quasi-Experimental, and Observational Comparison." In *Whither Opportunity?* edited by Greg J. Duncan and Richard J. Murnane, 255–276. New York: Russell Sage Foundation.

Caldeira, Teresa P. R. 2005. "Fortified Enclaves: The New Urban Segregation." In *Theorizing the City: The New Urban Anthropology Reader,* edited by Setha M. Low, 83–110. New Brunswick, NJ: Rutgers University Press.

Caplow, Theodore. 1964. *Principles of Organization.* Harcourt, Brace & World.

Chaskin, Robert, Amy Khare, and Mark Joseph. 2012. "Participation, Deliberation, and Decision Making: The Dynamics of Inclusion and Exclusion in Mixed-Income Developments." *Urban Affairs Review* 48, no. 6: 863–906.

Clotfelter, Charles T. 2001. "Are Whites Still Fleeing? Racial Patterns and Enrollment Shifts in Urban Public Schools, 1987–1996." *Journal of Policy Analysis and Management* 20, no. 2: 199–221.

Coates, Ta-Nehisi. 2011. "A Hard Look at Gentrification." *Atlantic Monthly* blog, July 21. https://www.theatlantic.com/national/archive/2011/07/a-hard-look-at-gentrification/242286/.

Cohn, D'Vera, and Andrea Caumont. 2016. "10 demographic trends that are shaping the U.S. and the world." *The Pew Research Center* Fact Tank, March 31. http://www.pewresearch.org/fact-tank/2016/03/31/10-demographic-trends-that-are-shaping-the-u-s-and-the-world/

Cose, Ellis. 2004." Beyond *Brown v. Board:* The Final Battle for Excellence in American Education." A Report to the Rockefeller Foundation, Survey Published in Newsweek Magazine.

Davidson, Mark. 2009. "Displacement, Space and Dwelling: Placing Gentrification Debate." *Ethics, Policy and Environment* 12, no. 2: 219–34.

Deener, Andrew. 2012. *Venice: A Contested Bohemia in Los Angeles.* Chicago: University of Chicago Press.

DeSena, Judith and Timothy Shortell. 2012. *The World in Brooklyn: Gentrification, Immigration and Ethnic Politics in a Global City.* New York: Lexington Books.

Education Week Research Center. 2014. "A New Majority in K-12." http://www.edweek. org/ew/section/multimedia/charts-a-new-majority-in-k-12.html (accessed August 19, 2014).

Ehrenhalt, Alan. 2012. *The Great Inversion and the Future of the American City.* New York: Vintage.

Ellen, Ingrid Gould, Keren Horn, and Katherine O'Regan. 2012. "Pathways to Integration: Examining Changes in the Prevalence of Racially Integrated Neighborhoods." *Cityscape* 14, no. 3: 33–53.

Engel, Kathleen C., and Patricia A. McCoy. 2008. "From Credit Denial to Predatory Lending: The Challenge of Sustaining Minority Homeownership." In *Segregation: The Rising Costs for America*, edited by James H. Carr and Nandinee Kutty, 81–124. New York: Routledge.

Freeman, Lance. 2011. *There Goes the 'Hood: Views of Gentrification from the Ground Up.* Philadelphia: Temple University Press.

Frey, William H. 2011. "Melting Pot Cities and Suburbs: Racial and Ethnic Change in Metro America in the 2000s." Brookings Institution, Metropolitan Policy Program.

Glaeser, Edward, and Jacob Vigdor. 2012. "The End of the Segregated Century: Racial Separation in America's Neighborhoods, 1890–2010." New York: Manhattan Institute for Policy Research.

Goldstein, Dana. 2014. *The Teacher Wars: A History of America's Most Embattled Profession.* New York: Anchor Books.

Gould, Stephen Jay. 1996. *The Mismeasure of Man.* New York: Norton.

Helms, Janet E. 1992. "Why Is There No Study of Cultural Equivalence in Standardized Cognitive Ability Testing?" *American Psychologist* 47, no. 9: 1083–1109.

Holme, Jennifer Jellison. 2002. "Buying Homes, Buying Schools: School Choice and the Social Construction of School Quality." *Harvard Educational Review* 72, no. 2: 177–206.

Hyra, Derek. 2015. "Greasing the Wheels of Social Integration: Housing and Beyond in Mixed-Income, Mixed-Race Neighborhoods." *Housing Policy Debate* 25, no. 4: 785–88.

Jencks, Christopher. 1998. "Racial Bias in Testing." In *The Black-White Test Score Gap*, edited by Christopher Jencks and Meredith Phillips, 55–85. Washington, D.C.: Brookings Institute Press.

Jencks, Christopher, and Meredith Phillips. 1998. *The Black-White Test Scope Gap: Why It Persists and What Can Be Done.* Washington, D.C.: Brookings Institute Press.

Jiménez, Tomás R., and Adam L. Horowitz. 2013. "When White Is Just Alright: How Immigrants Redefine Achievement and Reconfigure the Ethnoracial Hierarchy." *American Sociological Review* 78, no. 5: 849–71.

Johnson, Heather Beth, and Thomas Shapiro. 2003. "Good Neighborhoods, Good Schools: Race and the 'Good Choices' of White Families." In *White Out: The*

Continuing Significance of Race, edited by Ashley W. Doane and Eduardo Bonilla-Silva, 173–88. New York: Routledge.

Karsten, Sjoerd, Guuske Ledoux, Jaap Roeleveld, Charles Felix, and Dorothé Elshof. 2003. "School Choice and Ethnic Segregation." *Educational Policy* 17, no. 4: 452–77.

Krysan, Maria, and Sarah Moberg. 2016. "Trends in Racial Attitudes." University of Illinois: Institute of Government and Public Affairs. Retrieved from http://igpa.uillinois.edu/programs/racial-attitudes. August 25.

Lacireno- Paquet, Natalie, and Charleen Brantley. 2012. "Who Chooses Schools, and Why?" In *Exploring the School Choice Universe: Evidence and Recommendations*, edited by Gary Miron, Kevin Welner, Patricia H. Hinchey, and William J. Mathis. Charlotte, NC: Information Age Publishing.

Lees, Loretta, Tom Slater, and Elvin Wyly. 2013. *Gentrification.* New York: Routledge.

Leinberger, Christopher B. 2008. "The Next Slum?" *The Atlantic*, March.

Leonardo, Zeus, and W. Norton Grubb. 2013. *Education and Racism: A Primer on Issues and Dilemmas*. New York: Routledge.

Lewis Mumford Center. 2000. "Metropolitan Racial and Ethnic Change. Census 2000." SUNY-Albany.

Linn, Robert L. 2001. "Reporting School Quality in Standards-Based Accountability Systems." National Center for Research on Evaluation, Standards, and Student Testing.

Logan, John R., Elisabeta Minca, and Sinem Adar. 2012. "The Geography of Inequality: Why Separate Means Unequal in American Public Schools." *Sociology of Education* 85, no. 3: 287–301.

Logan, John R., and Charles Zhang. 2010. "Global Neighborhoods: New Pathways to Diversity and Separation." *American Journal of Sociology* 115, no. 4: 1069–1109.

Logan, John. R., and Wenquan Zhang. 2011. "Global Neighborhoods: New Evidence from Census 2010." US2010 Project. Russell Sage Foundation and Brown University. https://s4.ad.brown.edu/Projects/Diversity/Data/Report/globalfinal2.pdf

Louie, Josephine. 2005. "We Don't Feel Welcome Here: African Americans and Hispanics in Metro Boston." Cambridge, MA: The Civil Rights Project, Harvard University.

Lucy, William H., and David L. Phillips. 2003. "Suburbs: Patterns of Growth and Decline." In *Redefining Urban and Suburban America: Evidence from Census 2000*, edited by Bruce Katz and Robert E. Lang, 117–36. Washington, D.C.: Brookings Institution Press.

Massey, Douglas S., and Nancy A. Denton. 1993. *American Apartheid: Segregation and the Making of the Underclass*. Cambridge, MA: Harvard University Press.

Mele, Christopher. 2013a. "Neoliberalism, Race and the Redefining of Urban Redevelopment." *International Journal of Urban and Regional Research* 37, no. 2: 598–617.

——— . 2013b. "Race, Space, and Soft Exclusion." Panel on gentrification and race at the American Anthropological Association Annual Meeting, Chicago.

Mickelson, Roslyn Arlin. 2008. "Twenty-First Century Social Science on School Racial Diversity and Educational Outcomes." *Ohio State Law Journal* 69: 1173–1227.

Newman, Kathe, and Elvin K. Wyly. 2006. "The Right to Stay Put, Revisited: Gentrification and Resistance to Displacement in New York City." *Urban Studies* 43, no. 1: 23–57.

Orfield, Gary. 2011. "Schools More Separate: Consequences of a Decade of Resegregation." Cambridge, MA: The Civil Rights Project, Harvard University.

Orfield, Myron, and Thomas F. Luce. 2013. "America's Racially Diverse Suburbs: Opportunities and Challenges." *Housing Policy Debate* 23, no. 2: 395–430.

Penuel, William R., and Daniel J. Gallagher. 2017. *Creating Research-Practice Partnerships in Education.* Cambridge, MA: Harvard Education Press.

Pew Research Center. 2014. "Millennials in Adulthood: Detached from Institutions; Networked with Friends." Washington, DC.

powell, john. 2002. "An 'Integrated' Theory of Integrated Education." Paper presented at the conference on Resegregation of Southern Schools, Chapel Hill, NC.

Reardon, Sean F., and Ann Owens. 2014. "60 Years after *Brown*: Trends and Consequences of School Segregation." *Annual Review of Sociology* 40: 199–218.

Reardon, Seah. F., John. T. Yun, and Anna K. Chmielewski. 2012. "Suburbanization and School Segregation." In *Research on Schools, Neighborhoods, and Communities: Toward Civic Responsibility,* edited by William F. Tate IV, 85–102. Lanham, MD: Rowman & Littlefield.

Rhodes, Anna, and Siri Warkentien. 2017. "Unwrapping the Suburban 'Package Deal': Race, Class, and School Access." *American Educational Research Journal* 54, no. 1_suppl: 168S–189S.

Roda, Allison, and Amy Stuart Wells. 2012. "School Choice Policies and Racial Segregation: Where White Parents' Good Intentions, Anxiety, and Privilege Collide." *American Journal of Education* 119, no. 2: 261–93.

Rosenblum, Nancy. 1998. "Compelled Association: Public Standing, Self-Respect, and the Dynamic of Exclusion." In *Freedom of Association*, edited by Amy Gutmann, 75–108. Princeton: Princeton University Press

Rothstein, Richard. 2013. "Why Children from Lower Socioeconomics Classes, on Average, Have Lower Academic Achievement than Middle-Class Children." In *Closing the Opportunity Gap: What Americans Must Do to Give Every Child an Even Chance*, edited by P. Carter and K. Welner, 61–76. New York: Oxford University Press.

Sampson, Robert J., and Patrick Sharkey. 2008. "Neighborhood Selection and the Social Reproduction of Concentrated Racial Inequality." *Demography* 45, no. 1: 1–29.

Saporito, Salvatore J. 1998. "The Structural Consequences of Strategic Social Action: Increasing Racial Segregation and Socioeconomic Stratification through School Choice." PhD diss., Temple University.

Sauder, Michael. 2005. "Symbols and Contexts: An Interactionist Approach to the Study of Social Status." *Sociological Quarterly* 46, no. 2: 279-98.

Slater, Tom. 2009. "Missing Marcuse: On Gentrification and Displacement." *City* 13, no. 2-3: 292-311.

Stillman, Jennifer. 2011. "Tipping in: School Integration in Gentrifying Neighborhoods." PhD diss., Columbia University.

Strathdee, Rob. 2009. "Reputation in the Sociology of Education." *British Journal of Sociology of Education* 30, no. 1: 83-96.

Tach, Laura M. 2009. "More than Bricks and Mortar: Neighborhood Frames, Social Processes, and the Mixed Income Redevelopment of a Public Housing Project." *City & Community* 8, no. 3: 269-99.

———. 2014. "Diversity, Inequality, and Microsegregation: Dynamics of Inclusion and Exclusion in a Racially and Economically Diverse Community." *Cityscape* 16, no. 3: 13-45.

Wall, Patrick. 2017. "The Privilege of School Choice." *The Atlantic*, April 25.

Weininger, Elliot B., Annette Lareau, and Dalton Conley. 2015. "What Money Doesn't Buy: Class Resources and Children's Participation in Organized Extracurricular Activities." *Social Forces* 94, no. 2: 479-503.

Wells, Amy Stuart. 2014. "Seeing Past the 'Colorblind' Myth of Education Policy: Addressing Racial and Ethnic Inequality and Supporting Culturally Diverse Schools." Boulder, CO: National Education Policy Center.

———. 2015. "Diverse Housing, Diverse Schooling: How Policy Can Stabilize Racial Demographic Change in Cities and Suburbs." Boulder, CO: National Education Policy Center.

Wells, Amy Stuart, Lauren Fox, and Diana Cordova-Cobo. 2016. "How Racially Diverse Schools and Classrooms Can Benefit All Students." New York: The Century Foundation.

Wells, Amy Stuart, and Erica Frankenberg. 2007. "The Public Schools and the Challenge of the Supreme Court's Integration Decision." *Phi Delta Kappan* 89, no. 3: 178-88.

Wells, Amy Stuart, and Jennifer Jellison Holme. 2005. "No Accountability for Diversity: Standardized Tests and the Demise of Racially Mixed Schools." In *School Resegregation: Must the South Turn Back?*, edited by John Charles Boger and Gary Orfield, 187-211. Chapel Hill, NC: University of North Carolina Press.

Wells, Amy Stuart, Jennifer Jellison Holme, Anita Tijerina Revilla, and Awo Korantemaa Atanda. 2009. *Both Sides Now: The Story of School Desegregation's Graduates.* Berkeley, CA: University of California Press.

Wells, Amy Stuart, Douglas Ready, Lauren Fox, Miya Warner, Allison Roda, Tameka Spence, Elizabeth Williams, and Allen Wright. 2014. "Divided We Fall: The Story of Separate and Unequal Suburban Schools 60 Years after *Brown v. Board of Education.*" New York: Center for Understanding Race and Education, Teachers College.

Welner, Kevin Grant. 2008. *NeoVouchers: The Emergence of Tuition Tax Credits for Private Schooling.* Lanham, MD: Rowman & Littlefield.

Zukin, Sharon. 2010. "Gentrification as market and place." In *The Gentrification Debates: A Reader*, edited by Japonica Brown-Saracino, 37–44. New York: Routledge.

Endnotes

1   Burdick-Will et al. (2011); Logan, Minca, and Adar (2012); Massey and Denton (1993); Mickelson (2008); Reardon and Owens (2014); Sampson and Sharkey (2008); Wells and Frankenberg (2007).

2   Bischoff and Reardon (2014); M. Orfield and Luce (2013); Reardon, Yun, and Chmielewski (2012).

3   Holme (2002); Weininger, Lareau, and Conley (2015).

4   Wall (2017).

5   Cohn and Caumont (2016)

6   Education Week Research Center (2014).

7   M. Orfield and Luce (2013); Wells et. al. (2014)

8   Coates (2011); DeSena and Shortell (2012); Freeman (2011); Lees, Slater, and Wyly (2013); Zukin (2010).

9   Ehrenhalt (2012).

10   powell (2002); Adair (2005); G. Orfield (2011); Wells et al. (2009); Stillman (2011); Lacireno-Paquet and Brantley (2012).

11   Stillman (2011); Lacireno-Paquet and Brantley (2012).

12   Clotfelter (2001); Wells et al. (2009).

13   Pew Research Center (2014).

14   Wells et al. (2014).

15   Ellen, Horn, and O'Regan (2012); Glaeser and Vigdor (2012); Logan and Zhang (2011); M. Orfield and Luce (2013).

16   Hyra (2015); Logan and Zhang (2011); M. Orfield and Luce (2013); Wells et. al (2014).

17   Berger (2014); Logan and Zhang (2010).

18   DeSena and Shortell (2012); Wells et al. (2014); Zukin (2010).

19   Logan and Zhang (2011)

20   Logan and Zhang (2011)

21   Chaskin, Khare, and Joseph (2012); Deener (2012); Mele (2013b); Tach (2009); Tach (2014).

22   Caldeira (2005); M. Orfield and Luce (2013); Wells et al. (2009); Wells et al. (2014).

23   Lacireno-Paquet and Brantley (2012); Roda and Wells (2012).

24   Wells et al. (2009); Lacireno-Paquet (2012); Roda and Wells (2012).

25   Engel and McCoy (2008); Ehrenhalt (2012); Frey (2011).

26   Wells et al. (2014).

27 Penuel and Gallagher (2017).

28 Caplow (1964); Jencks and Phillips (1998); Jiménez and Horowitz (2013); Leonardo and Grubb (2013).

29 Caplow (1964); Saporito (1998); Strathdee (2009).

30 Rosenblum (1998), 83.

31 Caplow (1964).

32 Holme (2002); Rhodes and Warkentien (2017).

33 Black (1999).

34 Black (1999).

35 We had only mailing addresses for the properties bought and sold during this time period, thus we could administer the survey only by mail, with each mailing addressed to "resident." Our final response rate was 10 percent, with a total of nearly 500 surveys returned. While this response is not as high as we had hoped, it is acceptable for a mailed survey, and our findings for several important questions are statistically significant.

36 It is important to note that our demographic analysis of where respondents live shows no significant difference across school districts in whether the respondents have school-age and pre-school children, their self-ranking in terms of politics, or whether they rent or own their current residence.

37 Caplow (1964).

38 Wells (2014).

39 Johnson and Shapiro (2003); Karsten et al. (2003); Saporito (1998); Roda and Wells (2012).

40 Billingham and Hunt (2016).

41 Wells and Frankenberg (2007).

42 Jencks (1998); Jiménez and Horowitz (2013).

43 Sauder (2005).

44 Helms (1992); Linn (2001); Rothstein (2013); Wells and Holme (2005); Wells (2014).

45 Abrams (2016); Goldstein (2014); Welner (2008).

46 Leonardo and Grubb (2013); Wells (2014).

47 Gould (1996).

48 Wells (2014).

49 Adair (2005); powell (2002).

50 Alba and Nee (2003); Krysan and Moberg (2016).

51 Wells et al. (2016).

The Social and Economic Value of Intentional Integration Programs in Oak Park, IL

J. ROBERT BREYMAIER
Oak Park Regional Housing Center

Since 1972, the Oak Park Regional Housing Center has been committed to its mission of achieving meaningful and lasting racial diversity in Oak Park. The program has been recognized as a model of best practice within the community and across the nation. This model even has a name: "The Oak Park Strategy." Yet, despite the model's relatively high profile, its full value and impact are not fully understood. The promotion of racial diversity, and especially racial integration, has provided Oak Park with a structure that fosters economic and social benefits for the community.

The origins of the Housing Center are rooted in twin concerns affecting the Chicago region in the 1960s — open (i.e., non-discriminatory) housing and racial re-segregation. While still 99 percent white in the 1970 Census, Oak Parkers had become increasingly supportive of the open housing movement that included an eight-month campaign in Chicago in 1966. Meanwhile, they witnessed the rapid racial change and disinvestment that occurred on the west side of Chicago. They formulated a policy that, by embracing integration as a solution, would promote open housing while avoiding block-by-block resegregation.

The idea was the brainchild of the Housing Center's founder, Roberta Raymond. Raymond wrote her Master's thesis on racial change in Oak Park and surveyed other communities across the nation that had been facing similar issues. After analyzing programs from other communities, she formulated the model of working proactively to assist with housing searches in order to promote integration and avoid discrimination.

The strategy was successful and can be seen in hindsight as far ahead of its time. Raymond recognized that in the entrenched environment of segregation dominating American metropolitan areas, intentional action would be required to foster integration. This remains true into the present. Without such intentional action, white communities commonly segregate in one way or another. They tend to develop as exclusive communities with formal and informal barriers to people of color, especially African Americans, or they suffer from white flight and avoidance that results in concentrations of poverty and disinvestment.

Diversity is now a fundamental component of Oak Park's brand and value. Yet, the condition that gives diversity its strength — integration — is not guaranteed. Thus, investment in the Housing Center and the Oak Park Strategy is critical. Community leaders now accept as fact that the Housing Center's effort to sustain integration positively affects property values, social cohesion, and civic life. It is as much an issue of community culture as of public policy and programing.

THE HOUSING CENTER MODEL

In its earliest days, the Housing Center worked on integrating both the rental and ownership markets. Quickly, it became clear that rental integration was both more turbulent and more influential on housing patterns generally. Thus, the focus turned to the rental market. This was also due to Oak Park's significant rental stock. While firmly middle-class, the community was approximately half rental in the 1970s. Rental units still make up nearly 40 percent of all housing units in Oak Park. New rental high-rises are currently adding to that percentage.

Other important factors also encouraged the focus on rental housing. The rental market is more malleable than the ownership market. As prospective tenants are making a decision that involves only a one-year commitment, they are more likely to consider integration than first-time homebuyers who are making a 30-year commitment.[1] Rental turnover rates are also higher than ownership rates. Typical annual rental turnover across the nation is about 50 percent. In Oak Park, this rate is lower but still at least 30 percent. Thus, nearly one-third of all rental units will change tenants in a given year. This change can have either positive or negative outcomes. If intentional efforts are in place, they allow for relatively quick integration of a building and, more importantly, promote integration stability. However, if left to the market, turnover can result in rapid segregation.

The Housing Center can also have significant influence on housing providers (landlords) because it provides them with demand and services such as fair housing education, management advice, and technical assistance with marketing, tenant screening, and government relations that they would not otherwise enjoy. By providing services landlords need, the Housing Center can improve their commitment to integration and fair housing compliance.

As renters become homeowners, those with experiences renting in integrated settings are more likely to become homeowners in an integrated setting. While local data on this is hard to gather formally, homeowners in Oak Park regularly informally communicate at community meetings and other public arenas that they first came to Oak Park as renters through the Housing Center.[2]

In addition, the Housing Center learned quickly to collaborate with real estate agents in Oak Park. Real estate agents cooperate with the Housing Center on efforts to integrate neighborhoods by showing homebuyers properties throughout the community. While agents cannot promote integration as directly as the Housing Center, the community is small enough that they can reasonably show houses across the community to each of their clients, even when the client asks only to see one part of the community. This strategy has been successful for decades. Housing Center employees communicate with managing brokers and many agents annually to reinforce this effort. In essence, the Housing Center outsources this activity, leveraging hundreds of thousands of dollars in activity annually among well-meaning agents and brokers.

Segregation in a rental building also has a greater impact on neighborhood perception than in single-family dwellings. It is more visible than homeownership segregation, particularly in Oak Park where people typically enter single-family homes from alleys and garages but renters enter from the street or open parking lots. Residents perceive the segregation of rental buildings as an indicator of the racial makeup of a neighborhood. If a building appears segregated, it reinforces a perception of racial isolation in the surrounding area.

Promoting a Diverse Demand for Oak Park
In order to build a diverse community, Oak Park must have a diverse demand for its housing stock. This requires an approach that includes 1) promoting the assets and desirability of Oak Park, 2) promoting the open and inclusive nature of the community, and 3) marketing the community so as to ensure demand from all racial backgrounds.

This seemingly straightforward approach is in fact difficult, and requires sophistication and finesse. The Housing Center's advertising always focuses on the community, never on one building or apartment. The advertising message has to highlight the amenities of Oak Park without making the community appear exclusive, and it has to promote demand from groups that are under-represented or less likely to choose Oak Park. Because the Housing Center has continuously updated data from its registered clients, it always knows which groups are under-represented or searching for homes in Oak Park at a lower rate than expected. Its mission is to communicate a welcoming and inclusive community in Oak Park.

Figure 1: A Typical Housing Search without Housing Center Intervention.

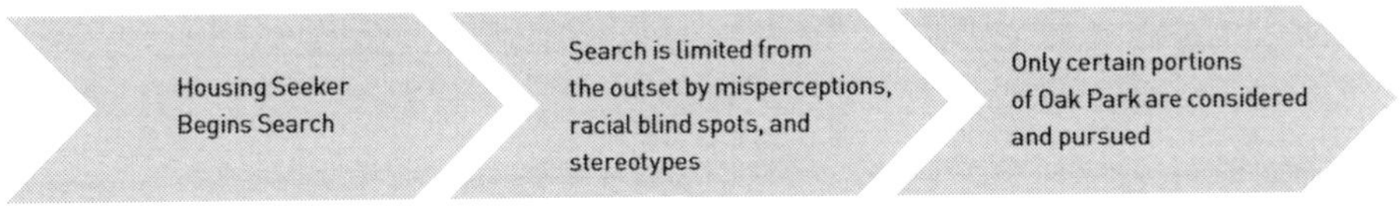

Housing Seeker Begins Search → Search is limited from the outset by misperceptions, racial blind spots, and stereotypes → Only certain portions of Oak Park are considered and pursued

Promoting Integration within Oak Park

Diversity of demand is only a first step in the Housing Center model. Once prospective renters choose to search for housing in Oak Park, they often have preconceived attitudes about where they want to live within the community. While many will state that they want to live in a diverse community, but also that they want to avoid certain parts of Oak Park. These attitudes correlate closely with racial demographic patterns within and surrounding Oak Park.

Oak Park is more integrated than other diverse suburbs. Moreover, almost all of the communities that surround Oak Park have clear predominant racial groups and high segregation levels. The Chicago regional residential pattern is also highly segregated.[3] These patterns, which influence attitudes about Oak Park neighborhoods, are outside local control and will continue for the foreseeable future. Thus, Oak Park must continue countering these forces to remain integrated.

When searching for an apartment, people get information from friends, family, and co-workers warning them about certain parts of Oak Park. Clients who use the Housing Center often tell staff that someone from Oak Park or former residents of Oak Park warned them to stay "west of Ridgeland," "off Austin Boulevard," or "as far west as possible." All of this online and social information, in addition to general implicit biases from societal cues,[4] is at play in the minds of rental seekers as they look for a place to live. Websites and social media also play a role in perpetuating false stereotypes about neighborhoods in Oak Park. The success of the Housing Center's model lies in its ability to correct for these misperceptions through conversation with prospective renters.

The actual conversations are far more important than any other part of the process. It is through direct, face-to-face conversation that the Housing Center addresses irrational fears, provides missing information, replaces myths and stereotypes with facts, and engages in gentle persuasion to consider new options. This results in a much different housing search than would occur without the Housing Center. The staff can answer questions about crime, school quality, neighborhood amenities, and even the general feel of neighborhoods. This combination of data and personal experience has a level of authenticity and sincerity that can overcome the much greater amount of misinformation available online and through social networks.

Figure 2: A Search by a Housing Center Client

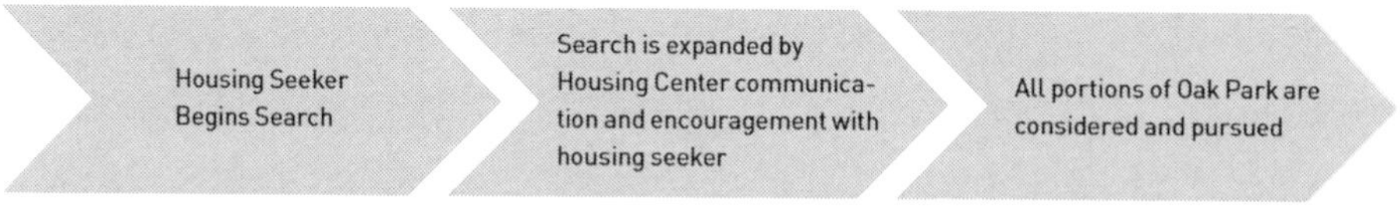

Housing Seeker Begins Search → Search is expanded by Housing Center communication and encouragement with housing seeker → All portions of Oak Park are considered and pursued

In a typical housing search without intervention from the Housing Center, the housing seeker begins with a limited set of options that are highly informed by racial and economic stereotypes. Often, non-African Americans avoid areas that they believe are within or near to predominantly African American areas. The search is limited in a way that will make integration nearly impossible.

A separate phenomenon occurs for African Americans. Despite the reputation and rhetoric of a welcoming community in Oak Park, prospective black residents enter with some hesitation about moving into areas perceived to be the whitest, as promises of equality are not always kept. Some begin by playing it safe, limiting their searches to eastern Oak Park to avoid possible isolation or harassment.

When the Housing Center intervenes in a search, the housing seeker is presented with additional options that they normally would have ignored or actively avoided. In the process, the cycle of segregation is disrupted with new information and personalized service to encourage consideration of an affirmative move — a move that will sustain or improve the integration of a building or block. This includes both active listening and gentle challenges to reduce the reluctance towards such a move.

Advisors do not simply provide listings. They converse with a client for about 40 minutes on average in their first meeting. In about a third of all cases, clients also revisit for a follow-up meeting with an advisor that normally will last about 20 minutes. Additional calls and emails are regularly exchanged between advisors and clients during the search for an apartment. Over the previous five years, the rate for affirmative moves by Housing Center clients is 68 percent, and improves to 80 percent when clients move to units in the Housing Center's listings from cooperating landlords.

In cases where 1) the Housing Center can suggest a unit that will result in an affirmative move, 2) it has keys to the unit, and 3) a client is interested in being shown the unit, the Housing Center will offer to have a guide show them units. Guides provide additional encouragement for an affirmative move and have further discussion with clients to overcome misperceptions about the community. Moves that result from guides showing apartments are extremely successful (94 percent) in promoting integration.

Table 1: Rental Moves and Affirmative Move Rates in Oak Park, IL

5-Year Total from 2010 - 2014	Moves by Housing Center Clients	Moves by Other Renters	Explanation
All Moves	4,612	6,687 [1]	Housing Center is responsible for 40% of moves to Oak Park.
Affirmative Rate	68%	25% [2]	Housing Center affirmative rate is 2.7 times better than the general affirmative rate. The general rate would result in rapid segregation.
Moves to Units Listed with Housing Center	2,798	2,090	Housing Center rents 57% of the units listed with us.
Affirmative Rate	80%	53%	Housing Center affirmative rate is 1.5 times better than the general affirmative rate. The general rate is just barely integrative.
Moves to Multi-Family Housing Incentives Program Listed Units	798	339	Housing Center is responsible for 70% of moves to Village-supported MFHIP buildings.
Affirmative Rate	94%	49%	Housing Center affirmative rate is 1.9 times better than the general affirmative rate. The general rate would result in segregation.

Notes: Grayed data is based on estimates.

[1] Estimate based on remaining 60 percent of market turnover minus a 2 percent vacancy rate.
[2] Estimate based on rate of integrated moves in the Chicago region using the Panel Study of Income Dynamics data and a 50 percent increase in that rate as an "Oak Park effect"

These services are unique to the Housing Center. Landlords do not offer them, primarily for two reasons. First, as owners and managers of housing, landlords do not have the same legal ability to engage in integration activity that the nonprofit and property-free Housing Center enjoys. Second, landlords are, as would be reasonably expected, profit-driven, not mission-driven. Their primary function is to rent out their units in a profitable manner, not to promote racial integration.

Another factor that makes it difficult for owners to market their units affirmatively is that, with a few exceptions, landlords in Oak Park do not own property in enough different areas of the village to encourage integration. Many landlords own three or fewer buildings. In nearly all of these cases, their buildings are located near each other. The supply available to each landlord does not allow for them to pursue wider integration efforts without help from the Housing Center.

Data shows the Housing Center's efficacy in producing residential integration in Oak Park. In moves where the Housing Center advises a client, the integration rate is significantly higher than when the Housing Center is not involved. Of 2,778 moves made by Housing Center clients to listed units from cooperating landlords within Oak Park, 2,224, or 80 percent, were affirmative. Of the 2,090 moves to units listed with the Housing Center but rented by non-clients, only 53 percent were affirmative. As shown in Table 1, this disparity is even greater for moves to units in the Multi-Family Housing Incentives Program (MFHIP), which are the most vulnerable to segregation.

It is also worth noting that even for the moves by "Other" renters on this graph, the Housing Center is exerting some influence through its technical assistance to the cooperating landlord listing the unit. The nonprofit Residence Corporation's buildings

Table 2: Changes in Population Shares for Oak Park, IL and Adjacent Communities: 2000 - 2013

Race/Ethnicity	Austin	Berwyn	Cicero	Elmwood Park	Forest Park	Oak Park	River Forest
White	-1%	-25%	-11%	-11%	-5%	-1%	-5%
Black	-4%	5%	2%	0%	2%	-1%	1%
Asian	0%	-1%	-1%	0%	1%	1%	3%
Latino	5%	22%	10%	10%	2%	1%	0%

Source: 2000 Census and 2013 American Community Survey

are also included in these numbers. If this graph included only for-profit private landlords, the affirmative rate for "Other" moves would fall below 50 percent.

Unique in the Area

Oak Park is unique in the region for its racial stability and integration. Neighboring communities are showing greater tendencies toward overall population shifts, as Table 2 demonstrates.

Berwyn, Cicero, and Elmwood Park are experiencing rapid racial changes in their populations. Forest Park and River Forest are experiencing changes at a slower rate. However, population losses are only in the white category. In Forest Park, these changes are resulting in a greater deviation from the regional average for population shares. In River Forest, recent changes could signal progress toward integration if future trends begin to include black and Latino populations at a greater rate. While already predominantly African American, Austin continues to lose white population but is now experiencing an increase in Latino population.

Only Oak Park is experiencing small, demographically stable changes. This stability is important for planning purposes and for community cohesion. Moreover, those changes are bringing Oak Park closer to regional population averages, indicating that people of all races are looking to Oak Park as a place to live. Indeed, with the exception of its relatively small share of Latinos, Oak Park is closer to regional averages for population shares than any of its neighbors (see Table 3). Oak Park's overall difference from the regional average is also the smallest. It is an amazing accomplishment given that prior to the Housing Center, Oak Park was 99 percent white and deviated wildly from the regional averages.

The segregation within surrounding communities also has an influence on decisions to move to Oak Park. Even as the Housing Center continues to promote integration within the community, segregation dominates most of western Cook County.

Table 3: Variance from Regional Population Shares for Oak Park, IL and Adjacent Communities: 2013

Race/ Ethnicity	Region	Percentage Point Difference between Region and Community						
		Austin	Berwyn	Cicero	Elmwood Park	Forest Park	Oak Park	River Forest
White	53%	-49%	-22%	-45%	20%	-7%	11%	28%
Black	17%	68%	-12%	-15%	-17%	15%	3%	-12%
Asian	6%	5%	-4%	-6%	-4%	2%	-1%	-1%
Latino	22%	-13%	38%	66%	-1%	-12%	-15%	-17%
Total Variance	N/A	135%	76%	131%	42%	35%	31%	58%

Source: 2013 Area Community Survey

THE VALUE OF THE HOUSING CENTER AND INTEGRATION

The intentional effort to sustain the integration of our diverse community is an investment with many social and economic benefits for Oak Park. It results in a more harmonious and a more prosperous community.

Typically, when a community sees a change in diversity, that change is accompanied by patterns of segregation. Examples of this are abundant in the Chicago region, including in nearby community areas and suburbs. Moreover, this trend has continued throughout history to the present day. In fact, segregation has been a historically consistent and fundamental form of perpetuating inequality in America, particularly since the Reconstruction era. During the Great Migration to Midwestern and Northeastern cities, segregation was heavily enforced by local, state, and federal government policies. As a result, 24 of the 30 most segregated cities and metropolitan regions in the nation are in the Midwest and Northeast. Chicagoland consistently ranks in the top five most segregated regions.[5]

Even in communities that at one time had integration efforts in place but later scaled them back or abandoned them, diversity has been accompanied by segregation. Shaker Heights, Ohio and University City, Missouri, both had integration programs predating even the Oak Park Strategy, but they dramatically scaled back these efforts; they have subsequently sustained diversity but experienced diminished integration.

Meanwhile, segregation often results in negative economic consequences, particularly in areas that have higher minority populations, but also for whole communities. The Voorhees Center at the University of Illinois at Chicago has mapped how incomes have declined in Chicago census tracts that have racially segregated to become predominantly minority tracts. They also demonstrated that the current income inequality divide is almost identical to the pattern of racial segregation in Chicago.[6]

Arguably, the negative effect on a whole community is more pronounced in suburban contexts where populations and geographical areas are smaller. Often, the negative consequences of segregation overtake a whole suburb, resulting in lower property values, lower tax revenue, and diminished services. The Chicago Metropolitan Agency for Planning has mapped regional opportunity. This geospatial index includes access to employment, good schools, and other important quality-of-life factors. It also includes the fiscal capacity of each municipality. There is an extremely close correlation between communities of color, constrained fiscal capacity, and a lack of opportunity.[7] Thus, racial integration strategies in diverse communities are more than social justice programs: they promote economic prosperity as well.

Many of the Chicago region's majority-black south suburban communities formed a collaboration called Diversity, Inc. to promote diverse and integrated communities. All of these communities continue to provide housing for middle-class or working-class households. However, they suffer economically, probably due to perceptions of majority-black communities that are influenced by implicit biases, racial blind spots, and stereotypes.

Two phenomena particularly detrimental to majority-black communities, depressed home values and retail redlining, are pronounced in these poor south-side neighborhoods. If segregation were to occur within Oak Park, it is reasonable to expect that areas with greater African American populations would lose value and be less desirable for retail development. This is a consistent outcome of segregation. The structural forces of racism result in negatively skewed home values in neighborhoods of color.

Table 4 shows that even though the southern suburbs of Flossmoor and Olympia Fields have higher median incomes than Oak Park, their median home values are lower. In the case of Flossmoor, the difference is astonishing. While median income is $22,000 higher, median home value is $102,000 lower. Homewood and Matteson have slightly lower incomes, but the corresponding home values are about half those in Oak Park. These lower property values reduce property tax revenues and strain the fiscal capacity of these communities to provide high quality services and comfortable lifestyles.

Arguably, Oak Park is more conveniently located than Flossmoor. The west-side suburb of LaGrange has a location more comparable to Flossmoor's: both towns have commuter rail access and a similar commute time into downtown Chicago. The two communities have nearly identical median incomes, and both are similarly residential, with about the same owner-to-renter ratio. The only significant difference is race: Flossmoor is 41 percent white, while LaGrange is 82 percent white. The difference in home values is striking. Median home values in LaGrange are $437,600, while

Table 4: Median Income and Median Home Value for Oak Park, IL and Comparable Municipalities in Chicago's South Suburbs

Community	Median Income	Median Home Value
Flossmoor	$100,941	$256,500
Olympia Fields	$85,917	$246,500
Oak Park	$78,802	$358,800
Homewood	$70,121	$180,100
Matteson	$70,000	$167,500

Source: 2010 Census

in Flossmoor they are $256,500. Race appears to be a significant influence on the differing home values in the two communities.

Retail redlining also harms majority-black communities. They lose retail opportunities due to the perceptions associated with the racial makeup of the communities. William Bellinger and Jue Wang found that African American communities are systematically underserved by retail, even though Latino and low-income communities are not.[8] Direct discussion with south suburban municipal officials concurs with this research. They struggle consistently to attract new businesses to their communities despite the fact that they have middle-class populations.

To most Oak Parkers' minds, an equally unappealing change would be a community that segregated toward an exclusivity that significantly reduced populations of people of color. While research does not indicate that this would typically result in economic losses, Oak Park would certainly suffer socially. Diversity is a core value of Oak Park. Failure to sustain a diverse and integrated community would be a loss to the identity and sense of place in Oak Park. In essence, the integrated diversity of the community is its brand. A loss of diversity and integration would likely cause some instability as more progressive-minded homeowners reconsidered their commitment to living in the community.

Through intentional efforts to sustain integration, Oak Park has built diversity into a competitive advantage. Those searching for a predominantly white community with a quality of life similar to Oak Park have hundreds of choices in the Chicago region. What brings them to Oak Park is a unique quality of diversity with prosperity. This diversity also sustains other parts of Oak Park life that residents value. It enhances arts and cultural life and fosters a civic mindedness and generosity among residents. The diversity of Oak Park sets it apart from other communities in the region and often puts it in a positive media spotlight that markets the community nationally.

With its integration strategy, Oak Park has created an environment where diversity and prosperity coexist. It is unlike communities where diversity broadens without an integration strategy. The following graph shows the uncommon nature of Oak Park by charting the change in white population percentages and the change in the equalized assessed value of real estate in the community standardized to 2010 dollars. As Oak Park lost white population, property value increased in real dollars. This return on investment for homeowners and property investors has run counter to the conventional wisdom that diversity brings disinvestment and instability.

HOUSING AND SCHOOLS

One final factor regarding integration in Oak Park is the connection between housing and schools. The Oak Park Strategy has also included efforts to promote school integration. At the high school level, the community has always had only one campus. While the high school has approximately 4,000 students, this single campus ensures that all children attend the same high school and that attendance boundaries will not affect neighborhood choice.

The elementary and middle schools required greater intervention. The community once had ten K-8 schools that all served as neighborhood schools. This did encourage segregation to some degree, as school reputations influenced neighborhood choice. It became clear that some elementary districts were experiencing a degree of white avoidance in the late 1970s.

To overcome this issue, two of the elementary schools were converted to middle schools. The boundaries of the remaining eight elementary districts were redrawn with integration in mind. This system dramatically reduced the influence of schools on housing choices. All of the new boundaries included at least modest integration. Over time, the boundaries have been adjusted as needed. Today, seven of the eight districts are similar in their diversity patterns. Only one continues to have lower than normal percentages of African American and Latino students.

The two middle schools were also set up to promote integration. Each receives students from four elementary schools. One receives from the northeastern and southwestern schools. The other receives from the southeastern and northwestern schools. This checkerboard pattern corrects for small segregation patterns that might occur at the elementary level.

School board policies over the past ten years have also accounted for the effects of historic and geographic momentum. The four schools on the eastern side of Oak Park receive slightly more resources than those on the western side of the community to ensure that they remain both aesthetically and academically desirable for new

Figure 4: White Population Share and Standardized Property Value based on the Equalized Assessed Value in Oak Park (2010 $)

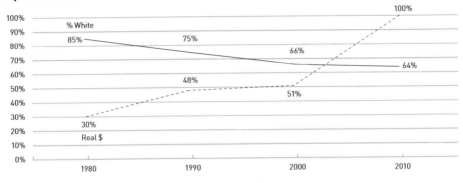

Sources: US Census 1980–2010 and Oak Park Township Assessors Office

residents. While there is no significant difference in school performance across the eight elementary schools, the lasting effects of past disparities remain an influence. This state of affairs is among the factors that the Housing Center has to discuss with clients as they consider where to move in Oak Park. As with other factors, a combination of data and personal experience allows Housing Center staff to improve understanding about school quality and eliminate schools as a factor in the housing choice process.

Finally, the schools play a role in educating the community regarding its integration strategy. In collaboration with the Housing Center, presentations about how Oak Park works intentionally to promote diversity and integration ensure that the next generation will understand the effort required to sustain the community's core values.

CONCLUSION

The Oak Park Strategy serves Oak Park both economically and socially. The Housing Center ensures strong and stable property values and provides a foundation for community harmony that makes diversity an important community asset. Its mission to achieve meaningful and lasting racial diversity in the community is critical to the public brand and core values of Oak Park.

Because the housing market is always in motion, the work of the Housing Center constantly remains relevant. Thousands of moves into and within Oak Park occur annually. Each one of these moves can result in either integration or segregation. As the data show, the Housing Center is critical to ensuring positive outcomes of these moves.

This sustained success of the Housing Center and the Oak Park Strategy has provided a replicable model for other communities. It has transformed Oak Park from a 99 percent white community to a community that reflects the diversity of its metropolitan region. Moreover, as diversity broadened and integration improved, the community also enjoyed greater prosperity and an increased commitment to social harmony. Today, it exhibits many of the qualities that fair housing and racial justice advocates hope to achieve elsewhere.

The community's focus on integrating its housing also ensures an integrated school system. Oak Park can maintain a neighborhood school system because of the integration in its housing market. This residential integration also has an effect on integration in social networks, park utilization, business ownership, and community participation.

Perhaps the most succinct justification for Oak Park Strategy comes from Dr. King. While in the Midwest, he plainly stated, "For as long as there is residential segregation, there will be de facto segregation in every area of life."[9] Oak Park has shown that the converse is also true. For as long as integration has been promoted in the housing market, integration has improved in every area of life within Oak Park.

Bibliography

Bellinger, William, and Jue Wang. 2011. "Poverty, Place, or Race: Causes of the Retail Gap in Smaller US Cities." *Review of Black Political Economics* 38: 253–70.

Breymaier, Rob, Morgan Davis, and Patricia Fron. 2013. "Fair Housing and Equity Assessment: Metropolitan Chicago." Chicago Metropolitan Agency for Planning and Chicago Area Fair Housing Alliance. Available at http://www.cmap.illinois. gov/livability/housing/fair-housing.

Friedman, Samantha, Hui-shien Tsao, and Chang Chen. 2013. "Housing Tenure and Residential Segregation in Metropolitan America." *Demography* 50, no. 4: 1477–98.

Nolan, Lauren. 2015. "A Deepening Divide: Income Inequality Grows Spatially in Chicago." The Voorhees Center for Neighborhood and Community Improvement Blog. March 11. https://voorheescenter.wordpress. com/2015/03/11/a-deepening-divide-income-inequality-grows-spatially-in-chicago/.

Hipp, John R. 2012. "Segregation Through the Lens of Housing Unit Transition: What Roles Do the Prior Residents, the Local Micro-Neighborhood, and the Broader Neighborhood Play?" Demography 49: 1285–1306.

Krysan, Maria and Michael D. M. Bader. 2009. "Racial Blind Spots: Black-White-Latino Differences in Community Knowledge." Social Problems 56, no. 4: 677–701

Krysan, Maria, Mick P. Couper, Reynolds Farley, and Tyrone A. Forman. 2009. "Does Race Matter in Neighborhood Preferences? Results from a Video Experiment." American Journal of Sociology 115, no. 2: 527–559

Rosenbaum, Emily and Grigoris Argeros. 2005. "Holding the Line: Housing Turnover and the Persistence of Racial/Ethnic Segregation in New York City." Journal of Urban Affairs 27, no. 3: 261–281.

Charles, Camille Zubrinsky. 2000. "Neighborhood Racial-Composition Preferences: Evidence from a Multiethnic Metropolis." Social Problems 47, no. 3: 379–407

Quillian. Lincoln. 2002. "Why Is Black-White Residential Segregation So Persistent? Evidence on Three Theories From Migration Data." Social Science Quarterly 31: 197–229.

Endnotes

1   Black-white segregation is lower for renters than for homeowners; see Friedman, Tsao, and Chen (2013).

2   See the Oak Park Regional Housing Center's Facebook Page for videos of residents talking about their moves.

3   Breymaier, Davis, and Fron (2013).

4   Hipp (2012). Krysan and Bader (2009). Krysan, Couper, and Farley (2009). Rosenbaum and Argeros (2005). Charles (2000). Quillian (2002)

5   The Chicago region is the 5th most segregated. 3 adjacent regions are 1st (Gary, IN), 3rd (Milwaukee, WI), and 74th (Rockford, IL) according to CensusScope http://www.censusscope.org/us/rank_dissimilarity_white_black.html.

6   Nolan (2015).

7   See Breymaier, Davis, and Fron (2013), 46, Map 10: "Regional Areas of Opportunity."

8   Bellinger and Wang (2011).

9   A transcript of King's speech at Western Michigan University, December 18, 1963, is available at http://wmich.edu/sites/default/files/attachments/MLK.pdf.

Disrupting the Reciprocal Relationship Between Housing and School Segregation

PHILIP TEGELER AND MICHAEL HILTON[1]
Poverty & Race Research Action Council

n spite of their deep and obvious connections, housing and school policy have evolved separately, with little attention to their mutually reinforcing impacts. In civil rights law, the US Supreme Court initially recognized the "reciprocal relationship" between housing and school segregation in a sophisticated 1973 opinion in the Denver schools case,[2] only to retreat to a stance of willful ignorance a year later in the Detroit schools case,[3] describing the causes of school segregation as "unknown and perhaps unknowable."[4] In Congress, committees with jurisdiction over housing and education are completely separate, mirrored by separate federal agencies that have had virtually no policy interaction until very recently. This same pattern of policy separation is repeated at the state and local level, with separate legislative committees and separate executive departments, so that finally at the local community level it is rare for a school board to have any contact with the local housing department, zoning board, or public housing authority.

This willful disconnect between housing and school policy does not, of course, mean that housing and school policy are not connected. Historically, they have worked together to maintain racial hierarchy and separation and to protect the privileges of the dominant groups in our society, which partly explains why their obvious connections have been submerged. But by acknowledging these mechanisms of separation, and working to disrupt them, we can continue to make incremental progress toward a more inclusive and integrated society.

This chapter will examine what we know about current laws, policies, and practices that mutually reinforce housing and school segregation, and present some examples of how housing and school policy can work together to disrupt the cycle.

EDUCATION POLICIES THAT INFLUENCE HOUSING SEGREGATION

The racial and economic makeup of public schools can have a profound intergenerational effect on residential segregation or integration by affecting students' academic outcomes and career prospects, their interracial attitudes, and their desire to live and work in integrated settings as adults.[5] These are the deeper ways in which education policy influences housing patterns. But we are also concerned here with the ways in which current educational policies, structures, and decisions influence residential housing patterns and families' decisions about where to raise their families. By examining the influence of educational policies that support residential segregation, particularly the boundary-drawing that is so prevalent in American education, we can begin to develop policies to disrupt these patterns.

School district boundaries and school assignment policies are key drivers of school segregation,[6] but they are also the education policies that have the greatest impact on residential segregation. In the Jim Crow South, residential segregation was not necessary to preserve white access to higher-quality, better-resourced schools. But after court-ordered desegregation in both the South and North, school boundary lines took on much greater importance in sorting families by race and class, becoming a key factor in family residential choices and a priority for white policymakers seeking to preserve the segregated status quo.

Some of the key elements of school boundary-drawing that influence residential segregation include: school district boundaries that are co-terminous with local land use jurisdiction boundaries; state policies that prohibit or discourage school enrollment across school district lines; school attendance zones that are closely tied to demographically identifiable neighborhood boundaries; uncontrolled school choice policies (charters, vouchers, and open enrollment); school siting decisions that do not take into account patterns of residential racial and economic segregation; resource allocation among schools; school rating systems and parental perceptions of school quality; and student transportation policies.

School District Boundaries and Local Land Use Jurisdiction Boundaries

Wide variations in perceived school quality are a major driver of racial and economic segregation across school districts, particularly in highly fragmented metropolitan areas.[7] The disproportionate presence of higher-income students in a school district naturally leads to higher test scores.[8] In turn, reports of these scores increase demand among higher-income families for housing in the district, and thus the cost of housing.[9] This type of district-shopping and sorting by family income, informed by one-dimensional school ratings,[10] is a primary driver of income segregation in US metro areas.[11] The underrepresentation of African American and Latino families in the upper income quintiles guarantees that this increasing trend of income segregation for families with children will also include significant racial segregation. In fact, regions with high levels of school district fragmentation tend to have significantly higher rates of racial segregation between districts.[12] The existence of racially identifiable schools may also influence white parents and more affluent parents to make residential moves to less diverse neighborhoods and schools — based on either racial fears or implicit assumptions about school quality based on racial composition.[13] Real estate brokers and real estate marketing practices can exacerbate this tendency by focusing on school test scores and public perceptions of school quality. The greater the racial and economic disparities across school districts in a region, the greater the fluctuation in housing value and neighborhood racial instability will be, as higher-income and higher-wealth families with children rapidly bid up the price of housing in the "highest-performing" districts.[14]

Likewise, in highly fragmented metropolitan regions with multiple school districts serving the same housing market, state policies that prevent cross-district enrollment can further encourage district-shopping among homebuyers, exacerbating residential segregation by income and race.[15] A good example of these policies can be found in Connecticut, prior to the 1996 *Sheff v. O'Neill* state Supreme Court decision, where (with limited exceptions) school districts had been required by law to be coterminous with town boundaries, and students were required by law to attend public schools in the district where they resided. These state policies were found in *Sheff* to be the immediate cause of unconstitutional segregation in the greater Hartford region.[16]

The phenomenon of shared municipal authority over land use and school assignment (which is common in the Northeast and Midwest) can exacerbate these patterns of segregation and school sorting, as school districts' local zoning boards practice exclusionary zoning to prevent the entry of lower-income students into affordable housing in the district, thus ensuring a higher tax base, higher test scores, and a well-resourced school system for local students.

School District Secession and Residential Segregation

A related problem arises in emerging efforts by local communities to secede from larger county-wide school districts, particularly in the South. Ironically, many county-wide districts in the South were originally created to prevent African American political control of urban schools,[17] yet the presence of consolidated regional districts later permitted the courts to assert jurisdiction over an entire region in school desegregation cases, in contrast to the courts' withdrawal from regional jurisdiction in fragmented Northern regions like Detroit.[18] In response to increasing diversity and continuing efforts to maintain school integration, some white communities have petitioned for separation from larger county districts, in the name of "local control" and "neighborhood schools."[19] When a predominantly white, upper-middle-class community breaks off from a racially and economically diverse county school district, it is reasonable to expect some degree of middle-class and white exodus from the county school district.[20] In recent years a number of school districts in the South have seen predominantly well-off and white suburban school districts seceding from county school systems,[21] with notable examples in Memphis, Tennessee,[22] and Baton Rouge, Louisiana.[23]

School Attendance Zones and School Assignment Policies That Are Closely Tied to Demographically Identifiable Neighborhood Boundaries

Like school district boundaries, school attendance zone boundaries can have a powerful impact on residential segregation patterns. Inclusion of a diverse neighborhood *within* the zone of a perceived high-performing school can stabilize housing prices and residential turnover in a neighborhood. Conversely, the carving out of diverse neighborhoods from predominantly white school zones can accelerate neighborhood racial transition and loss of housing values.[24]

Uncontrolled School Choice

Well-planned and well-executed systems of school choice can be useful tools in efforts to decouple residential segregation and school segregation. However, unfettered choice systems have the propensity to do significant harm to students, lowering overall academic outcomes and exacerbating existing patterns of school segregation. The promise of school choice as a driver of racial and socioeconomic integration, therefore, depends on strategically designed systems rather than on free-market choice.

Research indicates uncontrolled choice policies that permit the free exodus of middle-class and higher-income families from the regular public school system have been shown to have a segregative impact on public schools, leaving behind lower-income students of color and other less advantaged families.[25] Charter schools, which are some of the most commonly employed schools of choice, have been shown to increase segregation by race, socioeconomic status, and language ability if implemented without thoughtful systems put in place to prevent such outcomes.[26] Likewise, research on existing school voucher programs, both in the United States and abroad, has shown that such programs not only result in higher levels of school segregation, but also tend to harm academic achievement in participating students.[27]

Additionally, research indicates that open enrollment schemes, which allow students to enroll in schools located in neighboring districts, have a net segregative effect if enacted without supports (in particular, transportation support across district lines). Minnesota's history with open enrollment laws provides a particularly illustrative example. The state has operated under open enrollment laws since the 1990–91 school year, and while the statutory scheme requires receiving districts to provide transportation once students are inside district lines, there are no requirements for districts to move students across district boundaries. The absence of free student transportation exacerbates the "creaming" effect of uncontrolled school choice policies, as children without good transportation options are routinely left behind in increasingly poverty-concentrated schools.[28]

School Siting Decisions That Do Not Take into Account Patterns of Residential Racial and Economic Segregation

As Justice Powell noted 44 years ago in *Keyes*, the siting or expansion of schools or the drawing of school attendance zones with an intent to segregate is unconstitutional. But how do we assess the decision today to site a new "neighborhood" school in a highly segregated neighborhood? While neighborhood schools are politically popular, especially at the elementary level, and contribute to policy values like walkability and community cohesion, they can also exacerbate racial and economic disparities. In the twenty-first century, it is increasingly difficult to hide the racial impacts of school siting and attendance zone boundary drawing decisions, and the lines between intentional, foreseeable, and "unintentional" segregative school decisions are becoming blurred.[29] Perhaps through creative siting decisions and school assignment policies, it may be possible to combine the values of "neighborhood" schools and school integration. In 2007, Justice Kennedy, speaking for five members of the Court, noted that the siting of schools or drawing of school attendance zones *with the intent to integrate* is a constitutional means of achieving the government's compelling interest in school diversity.[30] Justice Kennedy's concurrence is a pointed invitation to analyze the segregation impacts of any new school siting decision.

Resource Allocation Among Districts

Reliance on local property tax revenue to fund public schools leads not just to inequity between rich and poor districts but also inexorably to racial and economic segregation across districts.[31] As higher-income homebuyers leave "lower-performing" districts, the local tax base declines at the same time as the district struggles with greater levels of need. A few miles away, higher-performing districts have every incentive to keep higher-need students out of the district, driving housing prices up and keeping tax revenue high, to better fund schools with very low levels of poverty and student need.[32] This is the classic example of what sociologists have called "opportunity hoarding"— in this context, the ability of wealthier towns to maintain high housing prices, commensurately high tax bases and well-resourced schools, and creating costly externalities in nearby cities and towns that have disproportionate shares of poor families — and it is a key structural driver of segregation.

School Rating Systems and Parent Perceptions of Quality

Primitive school ranking systems based solely on average test scores primarily reflect the demographics and parental education levels of a school's student population, and do not measure a school's overall academic quality or its value as a diverse learning environment. Ranking of systems based on overall test scores deters higher-income families from purchasing in "lower-ranked" school zones, depressing housing values and tax base and exacerbating racial transition and neighborhood segregation.

Amy Stuart Wells has also documented the impact of peer networks on housing and school choices.[33] This word-of-mouth rating system, usually among same-race networks, is often influenced by implicit assumptions about school quality based on schools' racial makeup.[34]

Housing, Tax, and Land Use Policies That Influence School Segregation

In metropolitan areas where school attendance is strictly defined by neighborhood or otherwise narrowly drawn school district boundaries, decisions about housing cost and density, the location of multifamily rental housing, and the distribution of government-assisted housing subsidies will impact patterns of school enrollment based on race and income.

Exclusionary zoning, particularly policies that exclude low-cost homes, and multifamily rental housing for families, have the most significant impact on school composition. Because of the disproportionate representation of African Americans and Latinos among low and moderate income families, it is no secret who is being excluded from these suburban communities. Indeed, some exclusionary zoning is explicitly designed as "fiscal zoning," to reduce the financial impact of additional children on local schools. The racial impacts of exclusionary zoning policies have frequently been the target of civil rights lawsuits,[35] and the fiscal impacts of exclusionary zoning reinforce opportunity hoarding. The greater the reliance on local property taxes to fund local education, the greater these disparities become. And these disparities are exacerbated by the federal mortgage interest tax deduction, which favors higher-income homeowners and, in effect, subsidizes schools in higher-income, less diverse districts.[36]

Federal housing programs exacerbate segregated metropolitan school patterns by effectively "steering" low-income families with children into lower-performing, higher-poverty schools.[37] Some of the federal housing policies that perpetuate and increase school segregation include the absence of civil rights guidance in the federal Low-Income Housing Tax Credit program,[38] the low range of allowable rents in the Section 8 Housing Choice Voucher program,[39] and the intentionally segregated siting of traditional public housing developments. There have also been instances where housing siting decisions have been made specifically to prevent greater school integration in white communities.[40] The segregated patterns that characterize these federal programs are enhanced by the exaggerated deference that the federal government pays to local government decisions about participation in government housing programs.[41]

As noted earlier, real estate marketing practices that promote housing sales based on local school achievement scores (which are primarily reflective of student demographics) reinforce segregation by bidding up housing prices for these "higher-performing" districts and schools.[42]

Private market discrimination against African American and Latino families continues to play a role in access to communities with high-performing schools,[43] as do private choices by families about where to live — although those choices are severely constrained by a racially distorted housing market, and by lack of knowledge and information about less segregated housing choices that may exist.[44]

POLICY CHOICES THAT CAN POTENTIALLY DISRUPT THE HOUSING AND SCHOOL SEGREGATION CYCLE

While housing and school segregation are currently linked in a mutually reinforcing cycle, there are a number of policy options which, if pursued in earnest, could do much to dissolve the relationship and move toward greater degrees of integration on both fronts.

Student Assignment Policies that Promote Residential Integration

The best way to ensure residential stability and integration within a diverse school district is to minimize the presence of racially identifiable schools, or schools with high levels of poverty. If renters or homebuyers understand that wherever they live within the district, there will be relatively similar levels of need, racial integration, and equitable funding, there will be less "shopping" for particular school assignment zones, and housing demand will be distributed more evenly across the district. This type of stability can be created through student assignment policies that explicitly take race and socioeconomic patterns into account, consistent with constitutional guidelines.[45]

Districts can also promote intra-district stability through the use of magnet schools, controlled choice plans, and flexible boundaries for student assignment. State racial imbalance laws can also play a valuable role in ensuring that diverse districts do not become internally segregated. Massachusetts' racial imbalance law considers schools with more than 50 percent nonwhite students as racially imbalanced, while schools with 30–50 percent nonwhite students are racially balanced, and schools with less than 30 percent nonwhite students are racially isolated.[46] Similarly, under Connecticut's racial imbalance law, schools are considered imbalanced if they have minority student enrollment that varies more than 25 percentage points from the district average.[47] A recent decision by a suburban school district in Fairfield County, Connecticut to take more transfer students from a nearby urban district in order to achieve compliance with the state racial imbalance law illustrates the positive real world impact of these statutory schemes.[48]

At the very least, districts should avoid school zone boundary changes that increase racial or economic segregation. Although a broader use of Title VI is unlikely under the current federal administration, the increasingly prospective application of Title VI racial impact analysis during the Obama administration suggests that in the future, racial impacts of school boundary decisions could be required before such changes are permitted.[49] A similar approach was used recently in Minneapolis, under the aegis of the state's school integration guidelines.[50]

Disrupting the Effects of School District Boundaries on Residential Segregation

Just as sharp variations in racial and economic composition of schools *within* a district affect housing segregation, so too does residential racial and economic segregation *across* districts drive school segregation. The key to disrupting this pattern is to decouple residential location from school district attendance, making school district lines more porous. The presence of a predictable regional school integration plan, in contrast, tends to promote stability in residential racial patterns over time.[51] The two-way school integration plan in Hartford, with its mix of regional magnet schools and city-to-suburb transfers, is a good example of this type of system, though it has been in operation only for about fifteen years and does not yet reach a majority of city children. Real estate marketing in areas with stable school integration plans also tend to rely less on local school quality as a "selling point" for homebuyers.[52]

Preventing School District Secession in Larger County Districts

Since local school district boundaries are defined and created by state law, most states have procedures in place that govern creation of new districts or changes to district boundaries. However, only a handful of states specifically address the racial and economic segregation impacts of school district secession.[53] A 2013 case in Pennsylvania demonstrates how more broadly worded state statutes can be adapted to take into account the impacts of segregation. In that case, parents from the predominantly white neighborhood of Porter Township petitioned to transfer from the racially and economically diverse East Stroudsburg district to the predominantly white Wallenpaupeck district. The East Stroudsburg district appealed to the state department of education, successfully arguing that the petition did not have "educational merit," because it would increase segregation in the East Stroudsburg district and deprive students in predominantly white Porter Township of the benefits of diversity.[54.]

A similar type of challenge to school district secession can be raised in the context of Title VI, through a racial impact complaint to the federal Department of Education. A recent school district secession fight in Jefferson County, Alabama, illustrates the difficulties associated with focusing on the unitary status analysis rather than Title VI's protections from discrimination based on race. In this instance, the ruling judge recognized race as a motivating factor for the creation of a new school district in the predominantly white and comparably wealthy suburb of Gardendale; however, due to the complicated nature of unitary status litigation, the U.S. District Court judge ruled that the suburb would be given the opportunity to run a separate school system so long as they remained in compliance with Jefferson County's ongoing court-ordered desegregation efforts.[55]

School Financing Systems That Promote Integrated Schools and Housing

Equitable school financing systems that reduce reliance on local property taxes, spread the cost of education fairly, compensate for decades of neglect, and allocate per pupil spending based on student need will also eliminate a key driver of segregation. But in developing more equitable financing systems, it is important to avoid financial incentives that "reward" high-poverty schools with enhanced funding — districts need a counter-incentive that rewards reduction of poverty concentration in individual schools.

School Rating Systems That Promote Diversity and Accurately Reflect School Quality

School rating systems used by realtors and online marketing platforms like Zillow should highlight the value of student diversity, year-to-year growth, school climate, and personal parent reviews, rather than simply relying on overall test scores.[56] More nuanced rating systems that emphasize these more important factors, along with overall test scores, would encourage more families with choices to consider purchasing housing in more diverse school districts and would maintain housing prices and residential stability over time.[57] Realtors can also play an important role in this process. For example, an innovative program in Pasadena recently brought local realtors into the Pasadena schools to dispel some of the stereotypes associated with an increasingly diverse student body — and it appears that realtors are now projecting a much more realistic and positive view of the city schools to potential homebuyers.[58]

Housing Policies that Promote School Diversity

Where school assignment is closely tied to residential location, housing policies have an obvious and direct impact on school composition. Housing policies designed to give low-income children of color access to low-poverty, high-performing schools will have the most direct impact on school integration.[59] These policies include: affordable housing siting policies for the Low-Income Housing Tax Credit and other programs that take into account school composition and performance[60]; housing voucher policies that target high-performing, low-poverty schools[61]; mortgage assistance programs that promote school integration[62]; state zoning laws that prioritize school integration; elimination of tax incentives that reward purchase of homes in high-income school districts[63]; and real estate marketing practices that emphasize the value of school integration.[64]

DEVELOPING A HOUSING POLICY-SCHOOLS POLICY DIALOGUE

Concerted efforts at every level of government are needed to overcome the stark separation between housing and school policies (and policymakers). Community activists can sometimes lead these efforts, but for permanent collaborations to flourish, permanent policy intersections need to be created within programs and planning processes.

At the federal level, housing and school policy were merged early in the Obama administration by a formal connection between the Choice Neighborhoods program (a HUD public housing redevelopment program) and the Promise Neighborhoods program (a Department of Education small-scale variant on Geoffrey Canada's "Harlem Children's Zone"). This collaboration focused on the important goals of improving resources, conditions, and outcomes for children within the context of a segregated system; unfortunately, it did not address segregation itself, the underlying racial isolation and poverty concentration of these neighborhoods and schools. It took longer for the Obama administration to connect HUD's housing integration goals with the Department of Education's school diversity priorities — this step finally occurred at a national conference in June 2016, with the release of a joint guidance letter from the Secretaries of Housing, Education, and Transportation calling on state housing, education, and transportation agencies to work together to promote integration.[65] The guidance letter included a series of concrete recommendations for state agencies, reflecting suggestions from advocates.[66]

HUD has also formally recognized, in its 2015 "Affirmatively Furthering Fair Housing" planning rule,[67] that access to quality educational opportunity is an important aspect of fair housing. In its "Assessment of Fair Housing" tool to be used by all jurisdictions receiving significant HUD funding, HUD acknowledges that "the geographic relationship of proficient schools to housing, and the policies that govern attendance, are important components of fair housing choice," and further that "the quality of schools is often a major factor in deciding where to live, and school quality is also a key component of economic mobility." It therefore requires its grantees, in assessing fair housing, to consider the following factors and policies:

> Relevant factors to consider include "whether proficient schools are clustered in a portion of the jurisdiction or region, the range of housing opportunities close to proficient schools, and whether the jurisdiction has policies that enable students to attend a school of choice regardless of place of residence. Policies to consider include, but are not limited to: inter-district transfer programs, limits on how many students from other areas a particular school will accept, and enrollment lotteries that do not provide access for the majority of children.[68]

At the local level, one positive example of housing and education policy collaboration began in Richmond, Virginia in 2015, with a series of meetings organized by the Poverty & Race Research Action Council, Housing Virginia, and faculty at Virginia Commonwealth University. The meetings were designed initially to bring together all the key policy stakeholders at the regional level — city and suburban school board members, a former city superintendent, directors of the city and regional housing authorities and the city housing department, nonprofit advocacy leaders, and key representatives from the state education and housing departments. The meetings worked out a series of planning documents with goals, obstacles, and strategies for collaboration. This collaboration has continued as efforts have moved forward to develop regional magnet schools for the Richmond area,[69] and Housing Virginia is developing a toolkit for other regions of the state on how to bring together housing and school officials for joint planning exercises.[70]

CONCLUSION

In spite of their deep connections, housing and school policies continue to follow separate trajectories, with little coordination.[71] The lack of coordination begins at the federal level, with its separate congressional committees, executive agencies, and legal frameworks, and is mirrored at the state and local level — an overall "absence of formal governance structures to sustain coordination across housing and education sectors."[72] Although the Obama administration took initial steps to undo this separation, given the abrupt change in direction at the federal level, supporters of coordinated housing and school integration policy will need to focus on state and local advocacy and innovation for the foreseeable future.

Bibliography

Abdulkadiro lu, Atila, Parag Pathak, and Christopher Walters. Forthcoming. "Free to Choose: Can School Choice Reduce Student Achievement?" *American Economic Journal: Applied Economics.*

Ayscue, Jennifer, and Gary Orfield. 2014. "School Lines Stratify Educational Opportunity by Race and Poverty." *Race and Social Problems* 7, no. 1: 5-20.

Bifulco, Robert, and Helen F. Ladd. 2007. «School Choice, Racial Segregation, and Test-Score Gaps: Evidence from North Carolina›s Charter School Program." *Journal of Policy Analysis and Management* 26, no. 1: 31-56.

Bischoff, Kendra. 2008. "School District Fragmentation and Racial Residential Segregation: How Do Boundaries Matter?" *Urban Affairs Review* 44, no. 2: 182-217.

Breymaier, Rob. Forthcoming. "The Benefits of Intentional Integration for Oak Park, IL." Cambridge, MA: Joint Center for Housing Studies of Harvard University.

CollegeBoard. 2016. *2016 College-Bound Seniors: Total Group Profile Report.*

Cramer, Philissa. 2017. "Memphis's New Municipal Districts Reflect a Broader Trend: School District Secessions." *Chalkbeat,* May 12.

DeLuca, Stefanie, and Peter Rosenblatt. 2017. "Walking Away from *The Wire:* Housing Mobility and Neighborhood Opportunity in Baltimore." *Housing Policy Debate* 27, no. 4: 519–46.

Eaton, Susan. 2014. "How a 'New Secessionist' Movement Is Threatening to Worsen School Segregation and Widen Inequalities." *The Nation,* May 15.

EdBuild. 2016. *Fault Lines: America's Most Segregated School District Borders.* Jersey City, NJ. http://viz.edbuild.org/maps/2016/fault-lines/.

———. 2017. *Fractured: The Breakdown of America's School Districts.* Jersey City, NJ. https://edbuild.org/content/fractured.

Ellen, Ingrid Gould, and Keren Mertens Horn. 2012. *Do Federally Assisted Households Have Access to High Performing Public Schools?* Washington, DC: Poverty Race and Research Action Council.

Fischel, William A. 2009. *The Homevoter Hypothesis.* Cambridge, MA: Harvard University Press.

Fischer, Will, and Barbara Sard. 2017. "Chart Book: Federal Housing Spending Is Poorly Matched to Need." Washington, DC: Center on Budget and Policy Priorities. March 8. https://www.cbpp.org/sites/default/files/atoms/files/12-18-13hous.pdf.

Frankenberg, Erica. 2005. "The Impact of School Segregation on Residential Housing Patterns: Mobile, Alabama, and Charlotte, North Carolina." In *School Resegregation: Must the South Turn Back?* edited by John Charles Boger and Gary Orfield, 164–86. Chapel Hill, NC: University of North Carolina Press.

———. 2009. "Splintering School Districts: Understanding the Link between Segregation and Fragmentation." *Law & Social Inquiry* 34, no. 4: 869–909.

Frankenberg, Erica, Liliana Garces, and Megan Hopkins, eds. 2016. *School Integration Matters: Research-Based Strategies to Advance Equity.* New York: Teachers College Press.

Frankenberg, Erica, Genevieve Siegel-Hawley, and Jia Wang. 2010. *Choice without Equity: Charter School Segregation and the Need for Civil Rights Standards.* Los Angeles: Civil Rights Project/Proyecto Derechos Civiles at UCLA.

Guzman-Lopez, Adolfo. 2017. "Pasadena Schools Turn Realtors into Allies." Southern California Public Radio (KPCC), April 25. http://www.scpr.org/news/2017/04/25/70900/pasadena-schools-turn-realtors-into-allies/.

Hirsch, Arnold. 2005. *The Last and Most Difficult Barrier: Segregation and Federal Housing Policy in the Eisenhower Administration, 1953–1960.* Washington, DC: Poverty & Race Research Action Council.

Holme, Jennifer Jellison. 2002. "Buying Homes, Buying Schools: School Choice and the Social Construction of School Quality." *Harvard Educational Review* 72, no. 2: 177–206.

Housing Virginia. Forthcoming. *Community Conversations:Aligning Local Housing and Schools Policy for Successful Schools in Strong Neighborhoods.* Richmond,VA.

Institute on Metropolitan Opportunity. 2012. *Open Enrollment and Racial Segregation in the Twin Cities: 2000-2010.* Minneapolis: University of Minnesota Law School.

Institute on Race & Poverty. 2006. *Minority Suburbanization, Stable Integration, and Economic Opportunity in Fifteen Metropolitan Regions.* Minneapolis.

Krysan, Maria. 2008. "Confronting Racial 'Blind Spots.'" *Poverty & Race* 17, no. 5: 8-9.

Lerner, Michele. 2015. "School Quality Has a Mighty Influence on Neighborhood Choice, Home Values." *Washington Post,* September 3.

Mathis, William J., and Kevin Welner. 2016. *Do Choice Policies Segregate Schools?* Boulder, CO: National Education Policy Center.

McKoy, Deborah, and Jeffrey M. Vincent. 2008. "Housing and Education: The Inextricable Link." In *Segregation: The Rising Costs for America,* edited by James H. Carr and Nandinee K. Kutty, 125-150. New York: Routledge.

Mickelson, Roslyn Arlin. 2011. *The Reciprocal Relationship Between Housing and School Integration.* Research Brief no. 7. Washington, DC: National Coalition on School Diversity. http://www.school-diversity.org/pdf/ DiversityResearchBriefNo7.pdf.

Mickelson, Roslyn Arlin, Stephen Samuel Smith, and Amy Hawn Nelson, eds. 2015. *Yesterday, Today, and Tomorrow: School Desegregation and Resegregation in Charlotte.* Cambridge, MA: Harvard Education Press.

National Advisory Commission on Civil Disorders. 1968. *Report of the National Advisory Commission on Civil Disorders.* Washington, DC.

Newkirk, Margaret. 2014. "Baton Rouge's Rich Want New Town to Keep Poor Pupils Out." *Bloomberg,* February 6.

Oppenheimer, Sarah. 2015. *Building Opportunity II:A Fair Housing Assessment of State Low-Income Housing Tax Credit Plans.* Washington, DC: Poverty & Race Research Action Council.

Orfield, Gary. 2001. "Metropolitan School Desegregation: Impacts on Metropolitan Society." In *In Pursuit of a Dream Deferred: Linking Housing and Education Policy,* edited by john a. powell, Gavin Kearney, and Vina Kay. New York: Peter Lang.

Orfield, Gary, John Kucsera, and Genevieve Siegel-Hawley. 2012. *E Pluribus... Separation: Deepening Double Segregation for More Students.* Los Angeles: Civil Rights Project/Proyecto Derechos Civiles at UCLA.

Orfield, Myron, and Thomas Luce. 2009. *Region: Planning the Future of the Twin Cities.* Minneapolis: University of Minnesota Press.

———. 2013. "America's Racially Diverse Suburbs: Opportunities and Challenges." *Housing Policy Debate* 23, no. 2: 395-430.

Owens, Ann. 2016. "Inequality in Children's Contexts: Income Segregation of Households with and without Children." *American Sociological Review* 81, no. 3: 549–74.

———. 2017. "Racial Residential Segregation of School-Age Children and Adults: The Role of Schooling as a Segregating Force." *Russell Sage Foundation Journal of the Social Sciences* 3, no. 2: 63–80.

Owens, Ann, Sean F. Reardon, and Christopher Jencks. 2016. "Income Segregation between Schools and School Districts." *American Educational Research Journal* 53, no. 4: 1159–97.

Pearce, Diana. 1980. *Breaking Down Barriers: New Evidence on the Impact of Metropolitan School Desegregation on Housing Patterns.* Washington, DC: National Institute of Education.

Potter, Halley. 2017. *Do Private School Vouchers Pose a Threat to Integration?* Washington, DC: The Century Foundation.

Roisman, Florence Wagman. 2007. "Affirmatively Furthering Fair Housing in Regional Housing Markets: The Baltimore Public Housing Desegregation Litigation." *Wake Forest Law Review* 42, no. 2: 333–92.

Rothstein, Richard. 2014. "The Racial Achievement Gap, Segregated Schools, and Segregated Neighborhoods – A Constitutional Insult." *Race and Social Problems* 6, no. 4.

Siegel-Hawley, Genevieve. 2016. *When the Fences Come Down: Twenty-First-Century Lessons from Metropolitan School Desegregation.* Chapel Hill, NC: University of North Carolina Press.

Siegel-Hawley, Genevieve, Tom Shields, Brian Koziol, John Moeser, and Taylor Holdren. Forthcoming. *Becoming Stronger Together: Confronting School and Housing Segregation in the Richmond Area.* Virginia Commonwealth University and University of Richmond.

Suarez, Christopher. 2015. "Democratic School Desegregation: Lessons from Election Law." *Pennsylvania State Law Review* 119, no. 3: 747–800.

Tegeler, Philip. 1994. "Housing Segregation and Local Discretion." *Journal of Law and Policy* 3, no. 1: 209–36.

———. 2016. "Predicting School Diversity Impacts of State and Local Education Policy: The Role of Title VI." In *School Integration Matters: Research-Based Strategies to Advance Equity*, edited by Erica Frankenberg, Liliana M. Garces, and Megan Hopkins, 145–55. New York: Teachers College Press.

Tegeler, Philip, Megan Haberle, and Ebony Gayles. 2013. "Affirmatively Furthering Fair Housing at HUD: A First Term Report Card." *Journal of Affordable Housing & Community Development Law* 22, no. 1: 27–60.

Tegeler, Philip, Henry Korman, Jason Reece, and Megan Haberle. 2011. *Opportunity and Location in Federally Subsidized Housing Programs: A New Look at*

HUD's Site & Neighborhood Standard as Applied to the Low-Income Housing Tax Credit. Washington, DC: Poverty & Race Research Action Council.

Tegeler, Philip, and Genevieve Siegel-Hawley. 2015. *Linking Housing and School Integration Policy: What Federal, State and Local Governments Can Do.* Issue Brief No. 5. Washington, DC: National Coalition on School Diversity.

Turner, Margery Austin, Susan J. Popkin, and Lynette Rawlings. 2009. *Public Housing and the Legacy of Segregation.* Washington, DC: Urban Institute.

University of Richmond School of Professional and Continuing Studies, HOME, and Virginia Commonwealth University School of Education, *Confronting School and Housing Segregation in the Richmond Region: can we learn and live together?* (Univ. of Richmond, Virginia Commonwealth Univ., August 2017), available at http://school-diversity.org/pdf/Richmond_Housing-Schools_Report_2017. pdf.

US Commission on Civil Rights. *Report on Racial Isolation in the Public Schools.* Washington, DC: US Government Printing Office, 1967.

US Department of Housing and Urban Development. 2012. *Housing Discrimination against Racial and Ethnic Minorities 2012.* Washington, DC: HUD Office of Policy Development and Research.

———. 2015. "Affirmatively Furthering Fair Housing: Final Rule." 80 Fed. Reg. 42272. July 16.

———. 2016. *Breaking Down Barriers: Housing, Neighborhoods, and Schools of Opportunity.* Washington, DC: Office of Policy Development and Research.

———. 2017. "Assessment of Fair Housing Tool for Local Governments." January 13. https://www.hudexchange.info/resources/documents/Assessment-of-Fair-Housing-Tool-for-Local-Governments-2017-01.pdf.

US Departments of Education, Housing and Urban Development, and Transportation. 2016. "Joint Letter on Interagency Cooperation on Affirmatively Furthering Fair Housing." Washington, DC. http://www.prrac.org/pdf/Joint_Letter_on_Diverse_Schools_and_Communities_AFFH.pdf.

US Departments of Housing and Urban Development, Education, and Transportation. 2016. "Joint Letter on Coordinating State Housing, Education, and Transportation Policy to Promote Racial and Economic Integration." June 3. Available at http://www.prrac.org/pdf/Joint_Letter_on_Diverse_Schools_and_Communities_AFFH.pdf.

US Departments of Justice and Education. 2011. "Guidance on the Voluntary Use of Race to Achieve Diversity and Avoid Racial Isolation in Elementary and Secondary Schools." Washington, DC. https://www2.ed.gov/about/offices/list/ocr/docs/guidance-ese-201111.pdf.

Valenzuela, Juan Pablo, Cristian Bellei, and Danae de los Ríos. 2013. "Socioeconomic School Segregation in a Market-Oriented Educational System. The Case of Chile." *Journal of Education Policy* 29, no. 2: 217–41.

Weiss, Laura. 2017. "Timeline Set for School District's Racial Imbalance Plan." *Fairfield Citizen*, April 13.

Wells, Amy Stuart. 2015. *Diverse Housing, Diverse Schooling: How Policy Can Stabilize Racial Demographic Change in Cities and Suburbs*. Boulder, CO: National Education Policy Center.

Wells, Amy Stuart, and Robert L. Crain. 1994. "Perpetuation Theory and the Long-Term Effects of School Desegregation." *Review of Educational Research* 64, no. 4:531–55.

Wilson, Erika. 2016. "The New School Segregation." *Cornell Law Review* 102: 139–210.

Endnotes

1   Philip Tegeler is the Executive Director of the Poverty & Race Research Action Council; Michael Hilton worked as a Policy Counsel at PRRAC and also helped to staff the National Coalition on School Diversity. The authors are grateful for the contributions of Gina Chirichigno to this chapter, and for helpful comments from Megan Haberle and research assistance from Pooja Patel.

2   *Keyes v. School District No. 1, Denver, Colorado* 413 US 189 (1973) was an early challenge to segregative school boundary-drawing outside the context of Southern *de jure* school segregation policy. By drawing school attendance lines to mirror neighborhood patterns of racial segregation, school officials were held liable under *Brown* even without an express racial separation law or policy.

3   *Milliken v. Bradley* 418 US 717 (1974) involved a challenge to stark school segregation in Detroit and the Detroit region. A sharply divided Court held that a school integration remedy could not be extended to suburban school districts without a separate showing of a constitutional violation in each district.

4   "It is this essential fact of a predominantly Negro school population in Detroit — caused by unknown and perhaps unknowable factors such as in-migration, birth rates, economic changes, or cumulative acts of private racial fears — that accounts for the 'growing core of Negro schools,' a 'core' that has grown to include virtually the entire city" (*Milliken v. Bradley*, opinion of Justice Stewart).

5   Mickelson (2011); Wells and Crain (1994).

6   Siegel-Hawley (2016).

7   Ayscue and Orfield (2014); Owens (2016).

8   Average math and reading scores on standardized assessment tests have a linear relationship to family income. See CollegeBoard (2016).

9   Owens (2017).

10   Wells (2015); Lerner (2015).

11   Owens (2017).

12   Bischoff (2008).

13   Wells (2015); Frankenberg (2005); Holme (2002).

14   Owens (2017).

15   Frankenberg (2009).

16   *Sheff v. O'Neill* 238 Conn. 1 (1996).

17   Fischel (2009); Suarez (2015); Wilson (2016).

18   Wilson (2016).

19   Eaton (2014). The education research group EdBuild also recently published a comprehensive survey and critique of school secession policies across the country; EdBuild (2017).

20   Frankenberg (2005).

21 Eaton (2014); EdBuild (2017).

22 Cramer (2017).

23 Newkirk (2014).

24 M. Orfield and Luce (2013).

25 Mathis and Welner (2016); Potter (2017).

26 Frankenberg, Siegel-Hawley, and Wang (2010); Bifulco and Ladd (2007).

27 Valenzuela et al. (2013); Abdulkadiro lu, Pathak, and Walters (2015).

28 Institute on Metropolitan Opportunity (2012).

29 Tegeler (2016).

30 *Parents Involved in Community Schools v. Seattle School District No. 1*, 551 US 701 (2007).

31 Owens, Reardon, and Jencks (2016)

32 EdBuild (2016).

33 Wells (2015).

34 Ibid.

35 See discussion in *Texas Department of Housing and Community Affairs v. Inclusive Communities Project, Inc.,* 576 US ___ (2015).

36 The average combined federal subsidy from the mortgage interest deduction and property tax deduction to homeowners with over $200,000 in combined family income is over $6000 per year; Fischer and Sard (2017).

37 Ellen and Horn (2012).

38 G. Orfield (2001); Roisman (2007).

39 Tegeler, Haberle, and Gayles (2013).

40 Hirsch (2005).

41 Tegeler (1994).

42 Siegel-Hawley (2016); Wells (2015).

43 US Department of Housing and Urban Development (2012).

44 Krysan (2008).

45 US Departments of Justice and Education (2011); *Parents Involved in Community Schools v. Seattle School District No. 1*, 551 US 701 (2007).

46 Racial Imbalance Act, Mass. Gen. Laws Ann. ch. 71, § 37D.

47 Conn. Gen. Stat. § 10-226b (2010).

48 Weiss (2017).

49 Tegeler (2016).

50 M. Orfield and Luce (2009).

51 Brief of Housing Scholars as *Amici Curiae* (2006), *Parents Involved in Community Schools v. Seattle School District No. 1*, 551 US 701 (2007), available at www.prrac.org/pdf/HousingScholarsBrief.pdf. See also Pearce (1980); Frankenberg (2005); Institute on Race & Poverty (2006).

52 G. Orfield (2001).

53 EdBuild (2017).

54 Commwealth of Pennsylvania, State Board of Education, "Report And Recommendation Of The Special Committee On The Porter Township Initiative," In Re Application of the Porter Township Initiative Independent School District for Transfer from the East Stroudsburg Area School District to the Wallenpaupack Area School District, available at http://www.stateboard.education.pa.gov/Documents/Current%20Initiatives/Applications%20and%20Petitions/Porter%20Township%20Opinion%20FINAL.pdf

55 *Stout v. Gardendale Board of Education*, Memorandum Opinion and Order, N.D of Alabama (2017) (the case is on appeal as of publication date)

56   Wells (2015); Siegel-Hawley (2016).

57   US Department of Housing and Urban Development (2016); Wells (2015).

58   Guzman-Lopez (2017).

59   US Department of Housing and Urban Development (2016).

60   Oppenheimer (2015); Tegeler et al. (2011); G. Orfield, Kucsera, and Siegel-Hawley (2012).

61   DeLuca and Rosenblatt (2017).

62   US Department of Housing and Urban Development (2016).

63   See for example Fischer and Sard (2017).

64   Breymaier (forthcoming).

65   US Departments of Housing and Urban Development, Education, and Transportation (2016).

66   Tegeler and Siegel-Hawley (2015)

67   US Department of Housing and Urban Development (2015).

68   US Department of Housing and Urban Development (2017), Appendix C, 12.

69   *Confronting School and Housing Segregation in the Richmond Region: can we learn and live together?* (Univ. of Richmond, Virginia Commonwealth Univ., August 2017), available at http://school-diversity.org/pdf/Richmond_Housing-Schools_Report_2017.pdf.

70   Housing Virginia (forthcoming).

71   Tegeler and Siegel-Hawley (2015).

72   McKoy and Vincent (2008), 145.

Contributors

Xavier de Souza Briggs
Ford Foundation

Sheryll Cashin
Georgetown University

Nancy McArdle
diversitydatakids.org

Dolores Acevedo-Garcia
Brandeis University

Jennifer Hochschild and Shanna Weitz
Harvard University

Justin Steil and Reed Jordan
Massachusetts Institute of Technology

Ralph McLaughlin
Veritas Urbis Economics

Cheryl Young
Trulia

Tarry Hum
City University of New York

Maria Krysan
University of Illinois at Chicago

Kyle Crowder
University of Washington

Rolf Pendall
Urban Institute

Willow Lung-Amam
University of Maryland

Marisa Novara and Amy Khare
Metropolitan Planning Council

William Fulton
Rice University

Katherine O'Regan
New York University

Raphael Bostic
Federal Reserve Bank of Atlanta

Arthur Acolin
University of Washington

Michael Allen
Relman, Dane, & Colfax

Elizabeth Julian
Inclusive Communities Project

Margery Austin Turner
Urban Institute

Stephen Norman and
Sarah Oppenheimer
King County Housing Authority

Ingrid Gould Ellen
New York University

Malo Hutson
Columbia University

Colvin Grannum
*Bedford Stuyvesant Restoration
Corporation*

Vicki Been
New York University

Anurima Bhargava
Open Society Foundations

Amy Stuart Wells, Lauren Fox, Diana
Cordova-Cobo, and Douglas Ready
Columbia University

J. Robert Breymaier
Oak Park Regional Housing Center

Philip Tegeler and Michael Hilton
Poverty & Race Research Action Council

Made in the USA
Middletown, DE
11 September 2021